The Poetry of Cinema
by John Madden

Disney Business, Disney Films, Disney Lands
Daniel Cerruti

Feminism and Shakespeare
by B.D. Barnacle

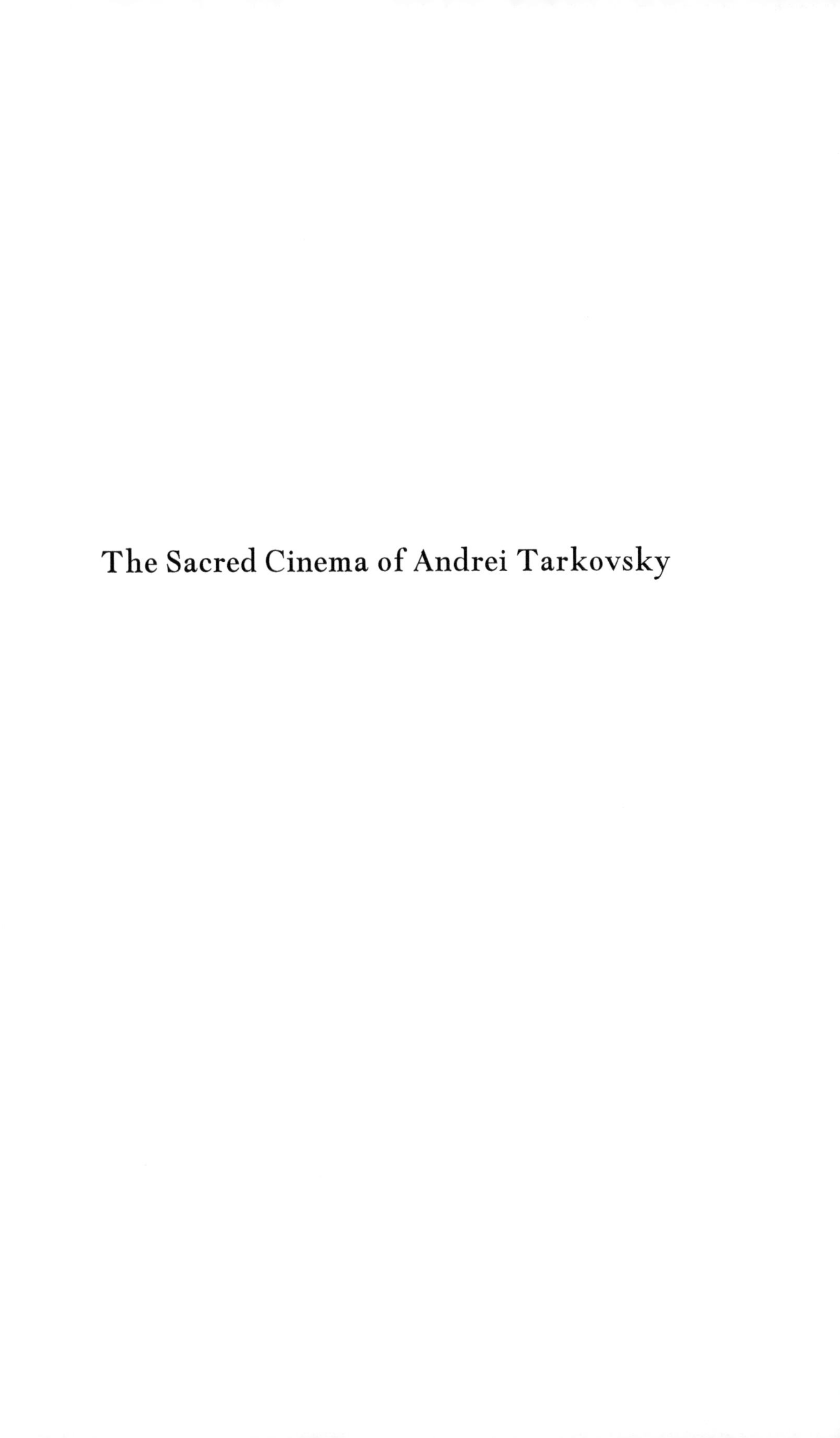

The Sacred Cinema of Andrei Tarkovsky

The Sacred Cinema of
Andrei Tarkovsky

Jeremy Mark Robinson

CRESCENT MOON

CRESCENT MOON PUBLISHING

P.O. Box 393

Maidstone

Kent, ME14 5XU

United Kingdom

First published 2006.
© Jeremy Mark Robinson 2006.

Printed and bound in Great Britain.
Set in Goudy Modern, 9 on 14pt, Gill Sans and Helvetica.
Designed by Radiance Graphics.

British Library Cataloguing in Publication data

The Sacred Cinema of Andrei Tarkovsky
    1. Tarkovskii, Andrei Arsenevich, 1932-1986
    – Criticism and interpretation
    1. Title
    791.4'3'0233'092

ISBN 1-86171-028-3 (Pbk)
ISBN 978-186171-028-4 (Pbk)
ISBN 1-86171-096-8 (Hbk)
ISBN 978-186171-096-3 (Hbk)

CONTENTS

CONTENTS LIST

The poetics of cinema; cinema as poetry; Tarkovsky's theory of 'poetic cinema'; Tarkovsky and the history of poetry; haiku.

Types of religious cinema; filming the divine; sci-fi, fantasy and horror cinema; also, a section on the European religious art film (Pasolini, Buñuel, Bergman, Dreyer, etc), and a section on Pasolini's The Gospel According to St Matthew; *Tarkovsky and Bergman; Tarkovsky and Dreyer.*

A survey of religious cinema, from the early days of cinema to the present day, including discussions of historical and Biblical epics, 'sword-and-sandal' films, and so on, including Ben-Hur, Cleopatra, *and* The Last Temptation of Christ.

Acknowledgements

Thanks to: Danny Rivers, Nick Shaddick, Mark Tompkins, Tony Maestri, Chris Fassnidge, Cath Richmond, Ruth Herbert, Artificial Eye, British Film Institute Library, University College for the Creative Arts Library, Kent County Library, West Kent College Library.

Acknowledgements to authors quoted and their publishers: British Film Institute. Faber & Faber. Indiana University Press. Oxford University Press. Seagull Books, Calcutta. Prentice-Hall. Penguin. Thames & Hudson. *Iskusstvo kino. Sight and Sound. Positif.* McGraw-Hill. Russian Cinema Council. Routledge.

Picture credits:
Museum of Modern Art Film Stills Archive. Films Incorporated. Jerry Ohlinger's Movie Material Store. Evgeny Tsimbal. National Film Archive, London. Swedish Film Institute. Artificial Eye. Contemporary Films.

Abbreviations

ST = *Sculpting in Time,* by Andrei Tarkovsky

D = *Time Within Time: The Diaries 1970-1986* by Andrei Tarkovsky

CS = *Collected Screenplays,* by Andrei Tarkovsky

JP = *The Films of Andrei Tarkovsky* by Vida T. Johnson and Graham Petrie

For Danny

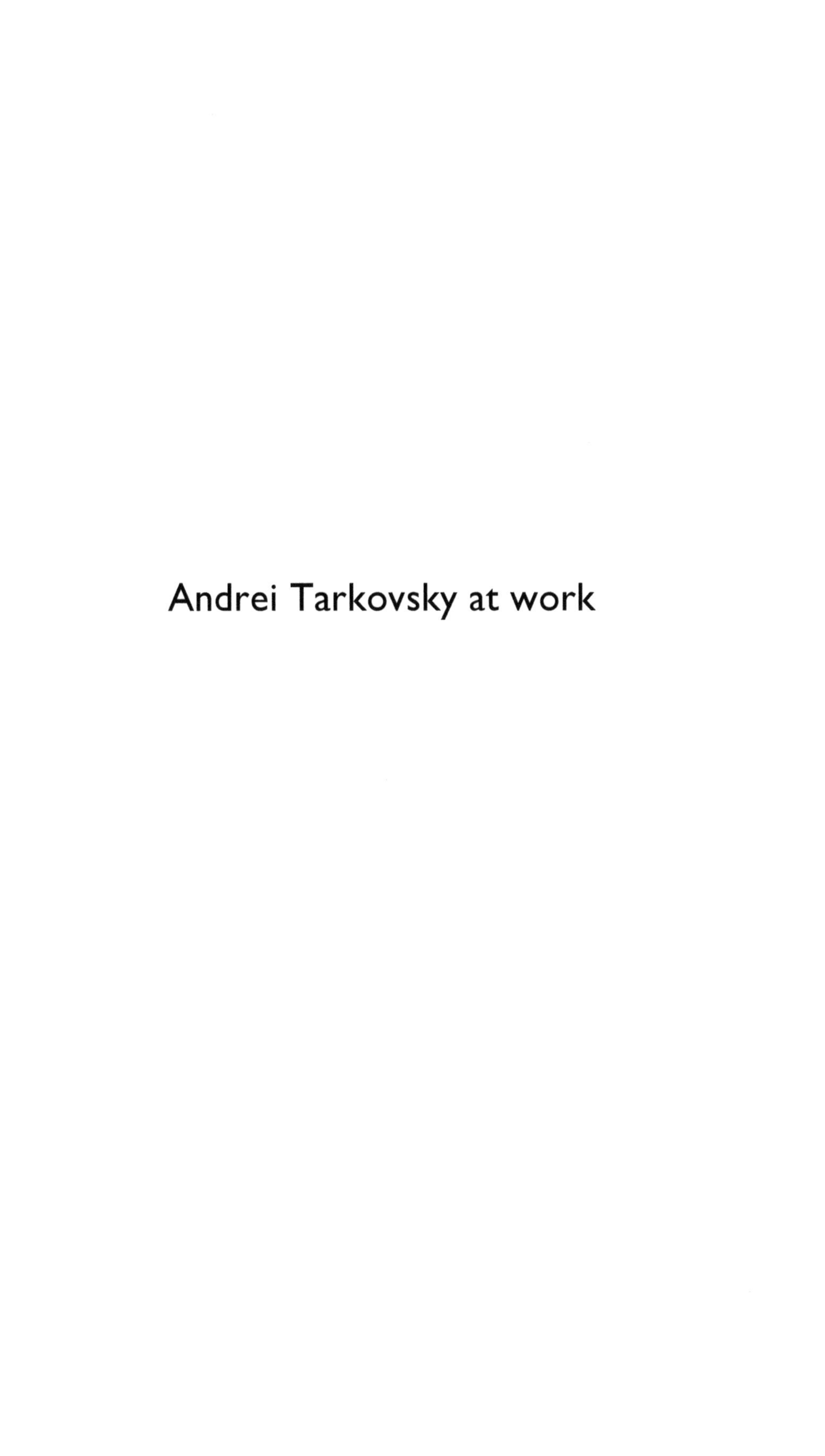

Andrei Tarkovsky at work

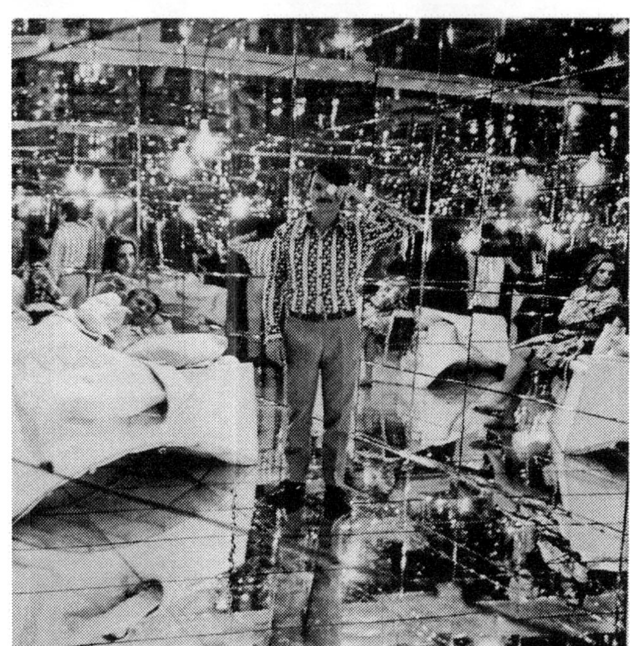

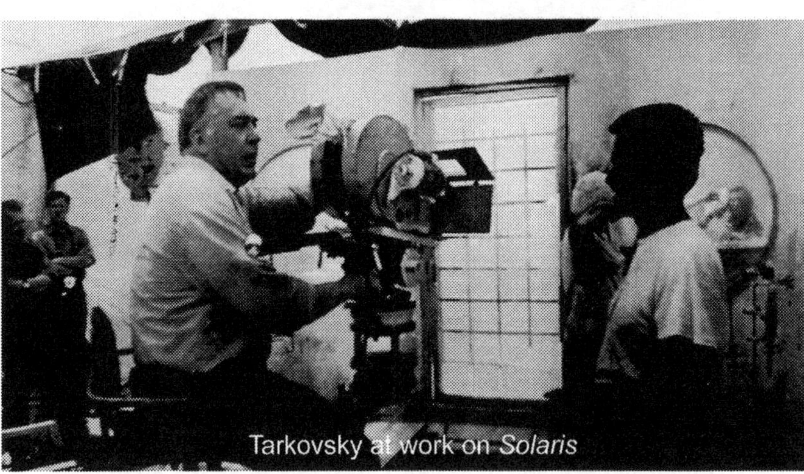

Tarkovsky at work on *Solaris*

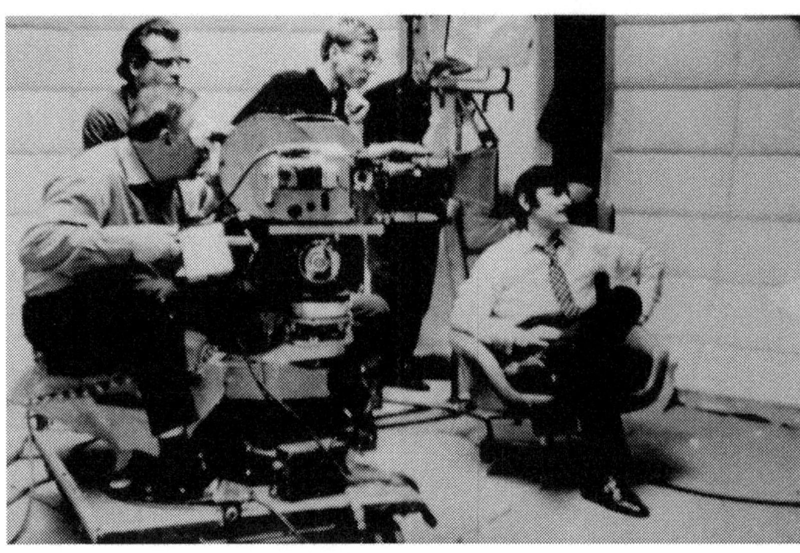

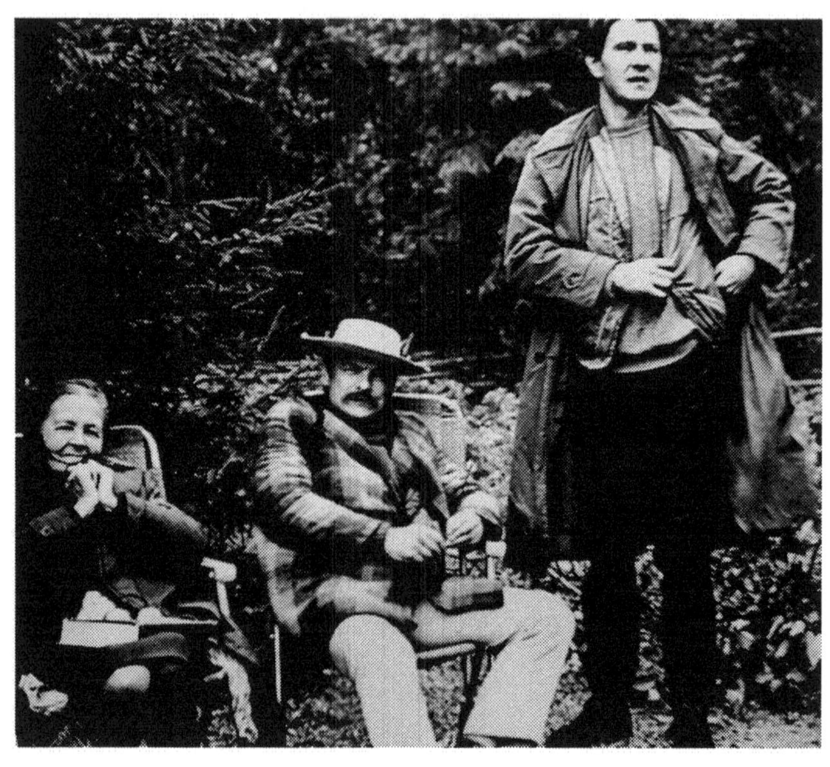

Tarkovsky at work: shooting *Mirror* (his mother's on the left).

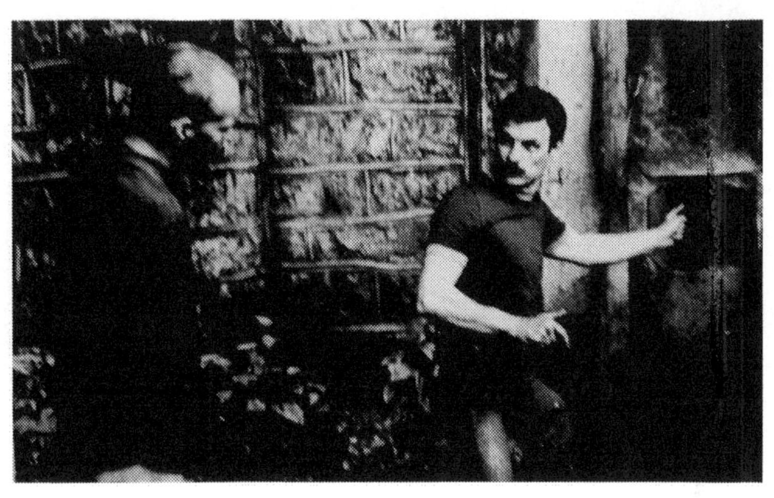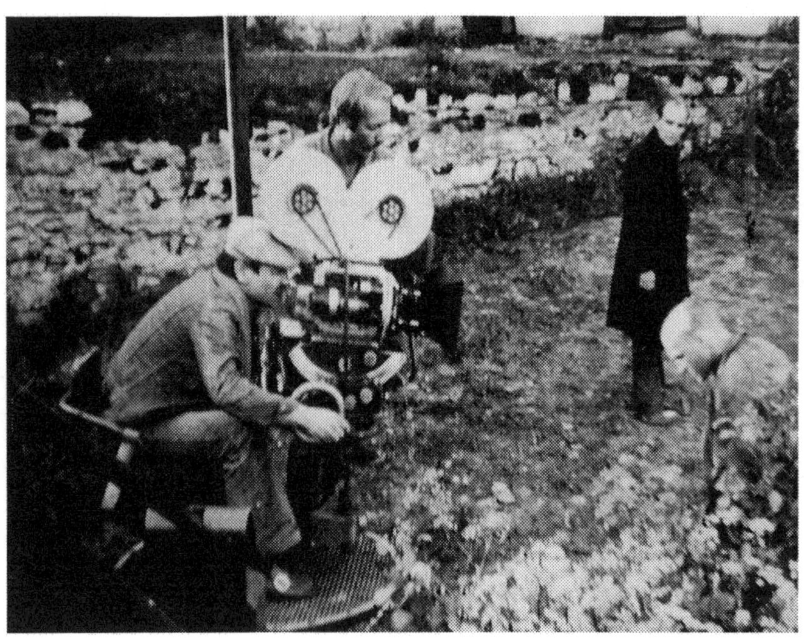

Tarkovsky at work on *Stalker*.

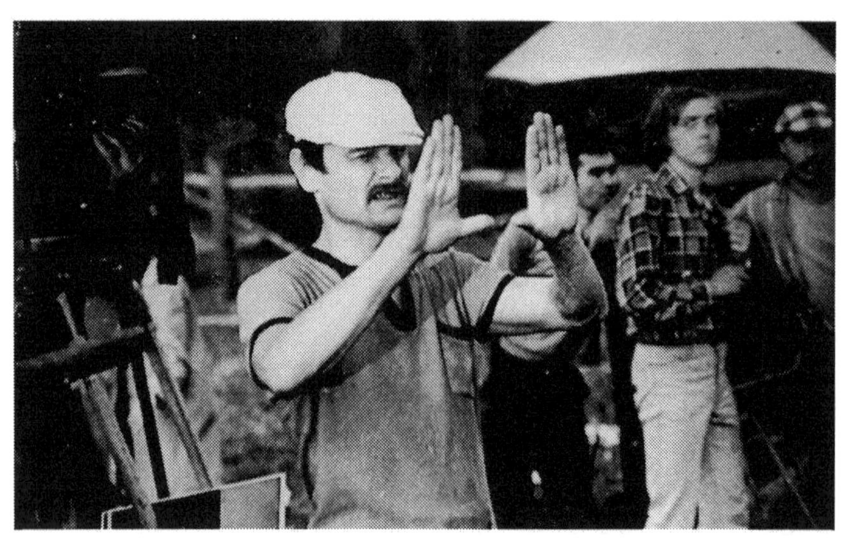

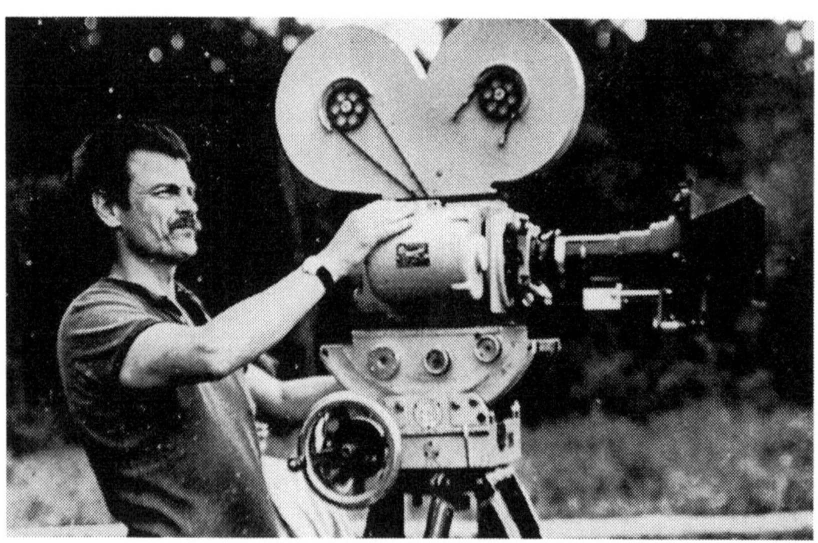

Tarkovsky at work on *Stalker*

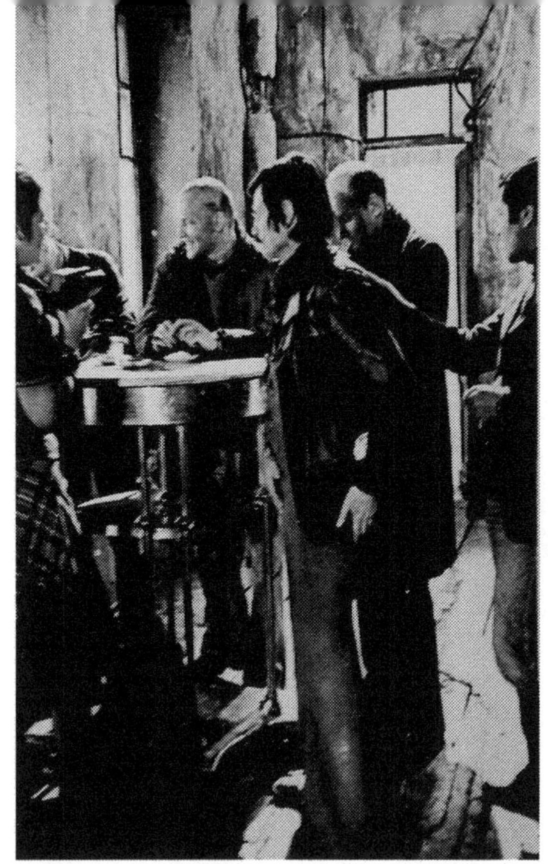

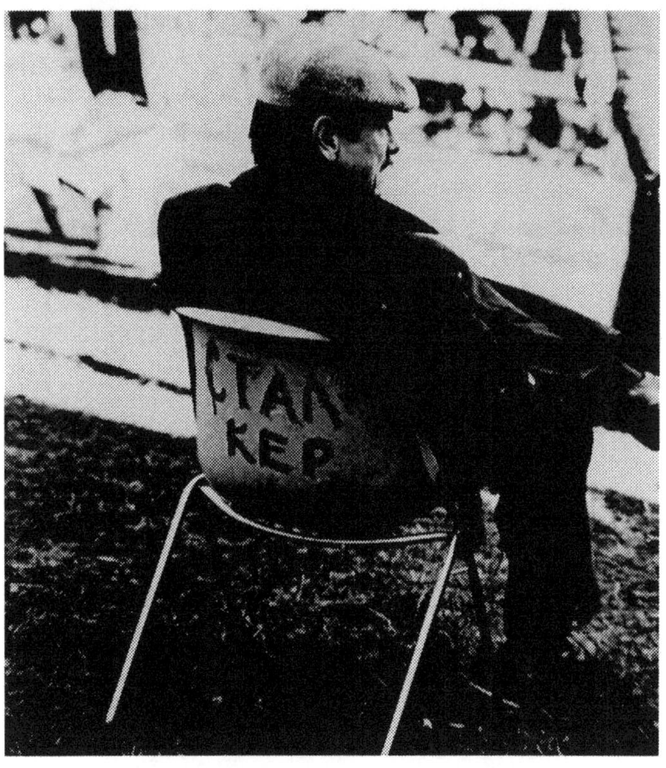

Tarkovsky at work: filming *Stalker*.

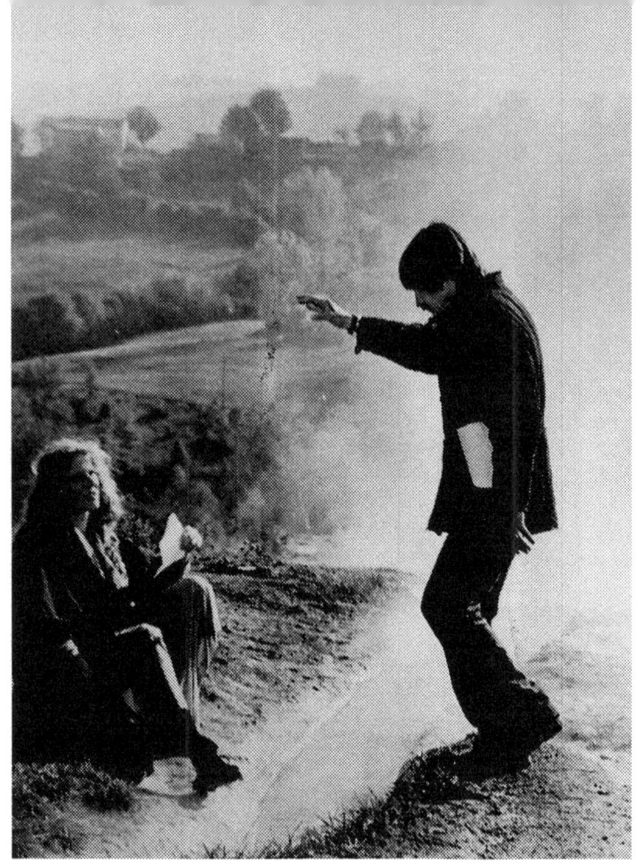

Tarkovsky in Italy: with actress Domiziana Giordano and writer
Tonino Guerra

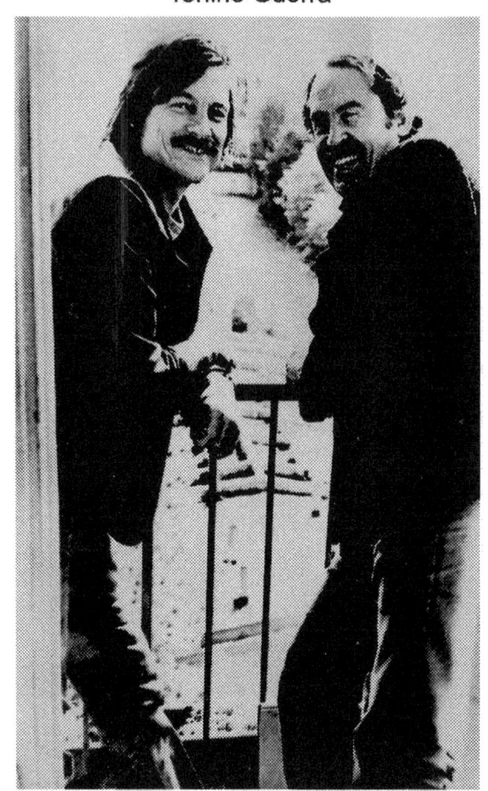

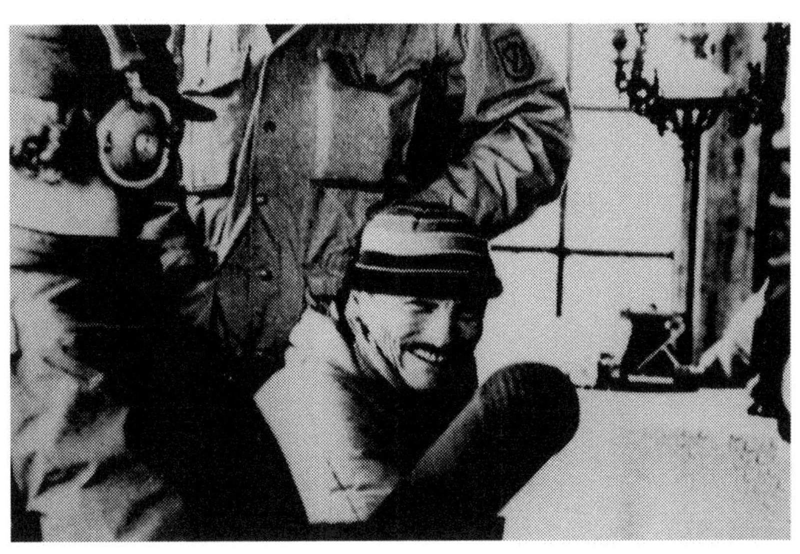

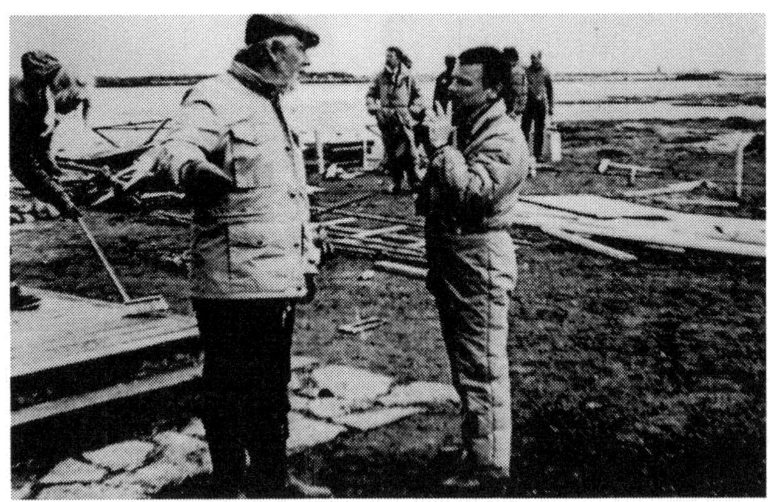

Tarkovsky at work on *The Sacrifice*

0

Introduction

0 : 1   LIFE

Andrei Tarkovsky (1932-1986) is one of the most fascinating of filmmakers. He is supremely romantic, an old-fashioned, traditional artist – at home in the company of Leonardo da Vinci, Pieter Brueghel, Aleksandr Pushkin, Fyodor Dostoievsky, Byzantine icon painters and Romantics such as Johann Wolfgang von Goethe. Tarkovsky is a magician, no question, but argues for demystification (even while his films celebrate mystery). He speaks endlessly of the 'truth', of 'spirit', of 'faith'. He talks in Christian, Platonic, Neoplatonic, Romantic, metaphysical and religious terms. He is a purist, always aiming for the essence of things. His films are full of magical events, dreams, memory sequences, multiple viewpoints, multiple time-scales and bizarre occurrences. He is a marvellous filmmaker, a creator of miracles, a 'maker', a poet (the Greek word *poeitas* means 'maker').

Few contemporary filmmakers have even a millionth of the mystery and depth of Tarkovsky's art. Tarkovsky has an extraordinary feeling for sensuous experiences. *The Sacrifice* is surely one of the most voluptuous films ever made. It has a præternatural feeling for surfaces, for texture and light and space. And yet, although Tarkovsky is a master of the presentation of surfaces – all that glass and water and polished wood and metal – his images also contain such depth. It is a depth only attained by directors such as Robert Bresson, Pier Paolo Pasolini and Werner Herzog. Tarkovsky has a deeply subtle sense of space. Contemporary Hollywood directors can create spaces very quickly and dynamically in films – with their over-determined, self-conscious use of the camera, point-of-view, motion and editing. But Hollywood's filmic spaces can appear as mainly superficial gloss, and the characters are too often cardboard cut-outs. Tarkovsky's cinema, meanwhile, achieves a sense of depth on every level: the visual, temporal, symbolic, kinetic, personal, social, narrative and spiritual.

Critic Herbert Marshall located Tarkovsky's films as part of a number which appeared in the Soviet Union following Sergei Paradjanov: Tengiz Abuladze's *Prayer*, L. Osyka's *The Stone Cross*, Georgi Shengelaia's *Pirosmani*, Ivan Drach and Iuri Ilenko's *On the Eve of Ivan Kupala*, and Paradjanov's *The Colour of Pomegranates*. These 'New Wave' films were seen as 'difficult', poetic, abstract, painterly, drawing on folk and fairy tales, religion, history and poetics.

> In these films every shot represents a self-contained part of the total composition; every shot is a painting in itself; every shot, even if it has an inner movement, freezes in its graphic expressiveness. At the same time speech and commentary also disappear.[1]

The Soviet New Wave, said film critic Mikhail Bleinman in *O Kino* (*On Cinema*), 'returns cinematography to the source of its natural quality of spectacle… It returns not only beauty to the screen but poetry and painting' (1973, 527). Soviet critics such as Bleinman and T. Ivanov noted how important painting was for the 'diffi-cult', poetic films, especially those of Sergei Paradjanov (such as *The Colour of Pomegranates* and *Shadows of Our Forgotten Ancestors*). This also applies to Andrei Tarkovsky's films. In an essay, "With *Perestroika*, Without Tarkovsky", Peter Shepotinnik, a *Iskusstvo kino* editor, wrote:

> At the moment, not all is well with our film geniuses. We are still living with the gradually fading light following Tarkovsky's death. Until recently his unique presence set the standard of spirituality (a purely Russian notion!) toward which all our directors tended, for they had before their eyes an example of supreme craftsmanship, philosophic profundity and artistic obsession.[2]

Andrei Tarkovsky studied film at VGIK (the All-Union State Cinema Institute, formerly GTK and GIK), founded in 1919 by Vladimir Gardin, Lev Kuleshov and others. Many of the great names of Soviet cinema studied or taught at VGIK, including: Sergei Bondarchuk, Nikolai Batalov, Alexander Dovzhenko, Mikhail Romm (one of Tarkovsky's teachers), Sergei Yutkevich, Marlen Khutsiev, Sergei Eisenstein, Vsevolod Pudovkin and Grigori Kotzintsev. At film school (VGIK), Tarkovsky saw many films as part of his course: *Citizen Kane, The Little Foxes*, Jean Renoir, Jean Vigo, John Ford, the Italian Neorealists, Andrzej Wajda and Andrzej Munk. When Tarkovsky was offering advice to young filmmakers about which filmmakers to study, he suggested five masters: Dovzhenko, Buñuel, Bergman, Antonioni and Dreyer (D, 361). At film school, students should watch lots of films, Tarkovsky recommended, and should also read lots of books (and not just the set texts).

At VGIK Tarkovsky made a short TV film (*Segodnya uvol'neniya ne budget/ There Will Be No Leave Today* [1959]) and his graduation diploma piece, *The Steamroller and the Violin* (1961). (Maya Turovskaya reckoned that Mikhail Romm was a significant influence on Tarkovsky's career, and many of his contemporaries too: Romm helped his students, lent them money, and defended their films against the authorities. Romm was 'the most lively and adaptable of the older generation of filmmakers' Turovskaya said [21]).

Tarkovsky sometimes discussed fellow Russian filmmakers who had gone to Hollywood. Though wary, he must have been tempted. After all, one of Tarkovsky's important collaborators, Andrei Mikhalkov-Konchalovsky, went to Hollywood and made some terrific movies: *Runaway Train* is a film any filmmaker would have been proud to have produced, and *The Odyssey* is a superb reinvention of Homer.

Konchalovsky (born in Moscow in 1937) was also at VGIK, under Mikhail Romm, graduating in 1965, four years after Tarkovsky. Konchalovsky's older brother, Nikita Mikhalkov, was a director; his father was a writer; Konchalovsky's films included adaptions of classic authors (Anton Chekov's *Uncle Vanya*, 1971, Ivan Turgenev's *A Nest of Gentlefolk*, 1969); the epic *Siberiad* (1979); Konchalovsky's Western (American) films included *Maria's Lovers* (1984), about a Russian soldier returning to Pennsylvania after the Second World War, with John Savage, Robert Mitchum and Keith Carradine as the men surrounding Nastassja Kinski, *Runaway Train* (1985) scripted by Akira Kurosawa, with Jon Voight, Eric Roberts and Rebecca De Mornay, a lean, mean and superlative Existential action drama about prisoners on the run in Alaska (it's one of the very best American action-adventure films), *Duet For One* (1986), with Julie Andrews, Alan Bates and Max von Sydow, about a violinist coping with multiple sclerosis, *Shy People* (1987), with Jill Clayburgh, Barbara Hershey and Martha Plimpton, a melodrama set in Louisiana, *Homer and Eddie* (1989), and *Tango and Cash* (1989), with Kurt Russell and Sylvester Stallone as buddy cops in Los Angeles in a Hollywood action-adventure movie. 1991's *The Inner Circle*, an Italian-Russian co-production, was a disappointing view of Thirties Stalinist Soviet life, starring Tom Hulce and Bob Hoskins.

One would not have imagined that Tarkovsky's friend and collaborator, who worked with him on *Ivan's Childhood* and *Andrei Roublyov*, would have gone on to make mediocre (but solid) Hollywood fare such as *Tango and Cash*, working with Hollywood stars such as Sylvester Stallone (best known as Rambo), Tom Hulce, Jack Palance and Kurt Russell (but the lure of Hollywood is immense). It was unlikely (at the time) that Tarkovsky would take such a route, and while Mikhail-Konchalovsky was making his first American films (*Maria's Lovers* and *Runaway Train*), Tarkovsky was still in Europe, making a slow, elegiac and intense chamber piece about religious faith and sacrifice, in Swedish, with (relatively) little known actors.

Tarkovsky was born in Zavrazhye, near Yuryevets, on the River Volga. His early life was spent in the country, when his parents moved out of Moscow (but the Tarkovskys moved back to the city fairly soon). Tarkovsky would later poeticize his early life near Yuryevets in *Mirror*, but he spent far less time there than in Moscow. During WW2, the family moved into the countryside around Yuryevets while Arseny Tarkovsky fought in the war. Vida Johnson and Graham Petrie call the 'major trauma' of Tarkovsky's youth the break-up of the family and Tarkovsky's father being absent (JP, 18).

In his youth, Tarkovsky worked in the far east of Russia, in the Turukhansky region and the Kureika river, making sketches and conducting research for a scientific institute. The year he spent exploring the *taiga* in Turukhansky was an important time for Tarkovsky. A lesser-known fact about Tarkovsky's career is that he worked in the mid-Sixties at the All-Soviet radio station. He directed a radio play based on a William Faulkner short story.

Tarkovsky's mother worked at the First State Publishing House in Moscow as an editor (some of that life finds its way into *Mirror*). Maria Ivanovna was a major force in inspiring Tarkovsky to become an artist; she was also 'a very strict disciplinarian' (JP, 19). Tarkovsky said that his mother 'obviously had a very strong influence on me — influence is not even the right word — simply the whole world is for me connected with my mother'.

Tarkovsky's first wife, Irma Rauch, had been his class mate at VGIK; they wed in 1957. Tarkovsky's first son, Arseny, was born in 1962. (Commentators have noted how Tarkovsky junior followed his father in leaving his first wife and child.) As echoed in *Mirror*, Tarkovsky grew up surrounded by women. Tarkovsky found the emotional environment oppressive as well as inspiring.

Tarkovsky married Larissa Pavlovna Yegorkina, his second wife, in 1970 (they had met and romanced during the shooting of *Andrei Roublyov*). They had a son, Andrei (born in 1970). Larissa worked on Tarkovsky's films on set (she was assistant director on *Mirror*, for instance). Since Tarkovsky's death in 1986, Larissa was increasingly the guardian of Tarkovsky's flame. She helped to edit Tarkovsky's diaries, which were published in 1991 as *Time Within Time* (*Martylog* in Germany). Much of Tarkovsky's private life was excised from the diaries, as well as his personal comments on his contemporaries and friends. By most accounts, Larissa Tarkovskaya was a formidable personality, and was keen to shape the Tarkovsky cult as it grew after the director's demise. Larissa in particular fell out with Tarkovsky's sister Marina (and she often fought with Tarkovsky too). Tarkovsky didn't know he had cancer while he was shooting *The Sacrifice*; he was diagnosed in December, 1985, when the film had already been shot.

After *Nostalghia*, Tarkovsky wasn't granted permission to continue to work outside Russia, and in 1984 he announced his decision to stay in the West. His wife, Larissa, had been allowed to join him in Europe, but not his son Andrei. While he lived in the West, Tarkovsky attended film festivals (such as Telluride), directed operas (*Boris Godunov*), and gave lectures.

Too old to be a hippy, really (he was 28 at the start of the Sixties), Tarkovsky's films do exhibit some of the traits of hippy culture. An obvious one is the exaltation of the natural world, and the urge to escape the city for nature. Like J.R.R. Tolkien and Thomas Hardy, Tarkovsky is a bit of a tree-hugger (people embrace trees in his films: Masha in *Ivan's Childhood*, Alexander in *The Sacrifice*, and trees play a significant role in every Tarkovsky film).

Lesser-known aspects of Tarkovsky's personality include his bisexuality, and his sadomasochism. (Few critics have approached Tarkovsky's films from a gay, lesbian or queer perspective. The sexuality in his films appears to be resolutely heterosexual (but open displays of homoeroticism are still rare in Russian cinema – and society). Though if one wanted to approach Tarkovsky's *œuvre* using gay and queer theory, it would be easy (consider the brotherhoods in *Andrei Roublyov* o r *Stalker*, for instance, the groups of men travelling together. The Stalker, for example, seems to have a more significant relationship with the Writer and the Professor than his own wife and daughter). Layla Garrett remarked that Tarkovsky 'was a very complex, difficult man'.

There's a disturbing element of the lecherous old man and voyeur in Tarkovsky's cinema, too. The eroticized red-haired girl with the chapped lip in *Mirror*, for instance, is a teenage object of sexual desire for both the middle-aged military instructor and the middle-aged narrator (and she was played by Tarkovsky's own step-daughter). Then there's the young woman Martha in *The Sacrifice*, seen naked in Alexander's dreams (with hints of incestuous desires); and Alex sleeps with a much younger woman. G. Petrie and V. Johnson see the lovemaking between Alex and the 'witch' as 'devoid of all eroticism' (JP, 249). True, it does seem somewhat chaste, and it is meant to be a spiritual union, a life-affirming act. But it is also presented specifically as lovemaking. In his diaries, Tarkovsky contemplated a film about an old man and a young woman. While art movies of the 1960s and 1970s regularly featured gorgeous young women in relationships with far older men, some of those films now take on a creepy, dubious edge (*Last Tango In Paris*, Woody Allen's *Manhattan*, *The Story of O*, and anything by Walerian Borowczyk are obvious examples that come to mind).

There's already a wealth of of information about Andrei Tarkovsky. Documentaries on Tarkovsky include *Andrei Tarkovsky Directs Nostalghia*, a.k.a. *Un Poeta nel Cinema* (Donatella Baglivo, 1983, CIAK, Italy), *Moscow Elegy* (Alexander Sokurov, 1987, USSR), *Directed By Tarkovsky* (Michal Leszcylowski, 1988, Sweden), and *In Remembrance of Things Past: The Exile and Death of Andrei Tarkovsky* (Ebbo Demant, 1987, Germany).

Chris Marker directed a 55 minute documentary on Tarkovsky, entitled *One Day in the Life of Andrei Arsenevich* in 2000. Donatella Baglivo also produced *Il cinema è un mosaico fatto di tempo* (*Cinema Is A Mosaic Made Up Of Time*) for CIAK (Italy) in 1984, and *Andrey Tarkovsky: A Poet in the Cinema* (1984).

Then there's a Russian documentary on *Andrei Roublyov* (*Andrei Rublov: How it Came into Being*, 2000), including interviews with many of the cast and crew. A BBC *Arena* programme about Tarkovsky (*Tarkovsky's Cinema*, 1987). A Channel Four documentary on *The Sacrifice* (*Behind the Scenes on The Sacrifice*, Jeremy Isaacs, 1987). *Stalker's Dreams* (1998, Evgenii Tsymbal) was a Russian documentary about actor Alexander Kaidanovsky. *After Tarkovsky* (2003) was a Russian documentary made by Peter Shepotinnik, and included interviews with people who had worked with Tarkovsky. A Japanese documentary, *Tarkovsky: A Journey to His Beginning*, appeared in 1996. *The Recall* (1996) was a 25 minute documentary made by Tarkovsky's son.

Other documentaries and films which discuss Tarkovsky include: a documentary on Tarkovsky's father: *Arseny Tarkovsky: Eternal Presence* (Viatcheslav Amirkhanian, 2004, Russia). *Student Andrei Tarkovsky* (Galina Leontieva, 2003). *Remembering Andrei Tarkovsky* (1987, Moscow). *At the shooting of the film Andrei Rublov* (1965, USSR). *The Three Andreis* (Dina Musatova, 1966, USSR). *Group of Friends* (M. Lakhovetsky, 1988, USSR). *Paradjanov: The Last Spring* (2004) has a section on Sergei Paradjanov and Andrei Tarkovsky. *The Reflected Time* (1998, Eugene Borzo, Russia). *Screenshot: 1: Lighting* (Kerstin Eriksdotter, 1988, Sweden), which featured Sven Nykvist shooting *The Sacrifice*. Tarkovsky had appeared in a Dutch TV documentary on Bresson (*The Road To Bresson*, 1984).

There is a Friends of the Andrei Tarkovsky Institute, which produces a newsletter. A book of Tarkovsky's polaroids (*Instant Light*) which also toured as an exhibition. A concert tour, *Imaginary Offering* (2005), inspired by Tarkovsky's films. A play of *Solaris* was directed by Martin Wuttke in 2004. There were 'Tarkovsky committees' campaigning on Tarkovsky's behalf in Iceland, Italy, France and England.

Tarkovsky and computer games? Yes. The video game *Stalker: Oblivion Lost* (designed by Ukranian Sergiy Grygorovych) was based on Tarkovsky's *Stalker*, as well as the Strugatskys' book *Roadside Picnic*, and the Chernobyl disaster. Erland Josephson wrote a play about shooting *The Sacrifice, A Night in the Swedish Summer*, which was staged in Sweden in 2002.

Tarkovsky's version of the opera *Boris Gudunov* was revived three times in London by 1994; it was part of the repertory of the Kirov Theater in St Petersburg, and was performed by Vienna Opera in 1991.[1] A stage play of Tarkovsky's script *Hoffmanniana* was performed in Paris in 2003. A radio programme, *Andrei Tarkovski ou le son de la terre*, was co-produced by the Tarkovsky Institute and Atelier création radiophonique.

There is a Museum of Tarkovsky, opened in 1996, situated 500 kilometres from Moscow, in Yuryevets (it was Tarkovsky's mother's home during WW2). There are also various websites on the internet devoted to various aspects of Tarkovsky's *œuvre*, some with links to other sites, such as *2001: A Space Odyssey* and sci-fi films. Some websites do come and go all too rapidly. For years the Tarkovsky site at www.skywalking.com was excellent. Probably the best site for research material is: www.nostalghia.com.

There is also a Czech site (www.nostalgia.cz), a Hungarian site (www.tarkovszkj.hu), a Korean site (www.nostalgiya.com) and a Spanish site (www.andreitarkovski.org). Pages can be found in many of the cinema websites (such as at Senses of Cinema: www.sensesofcinema.com). There are also websites dedicated to Sergei Paradjanov: www.parajanov.com.

Manufacturers and distributors of Tarkovsky's film on DVD and video include the Russian Cinema Council (Ruscico), Kino Video, Artificial Eye, Fox Lober, Criterion, Image Entertainment, and Facets Video. Home DVD and video distribution have brought new problems in Tarkovsky studies – with the quality of prints, of transfers, of audio quality, of soundtracks, and 'restoration'. Issues such as the director's 'intentions', 'director's cuts', and sound remixes are confronted yet again.

Sculpting In Time (1986 and 1989) is the major prose work Tarkovsky produced. It contains his thoughts on a wide variety of subjects, and is referred to throughout this study. Tarkovsky collaborated with Olga Surkova on the book *Sculpting In Time*. She was a fellow student at VGIK, and had worked on *Andrei Roublyov*. *Sculpting In Time* started out as a series of interviews between Surkova and Tarkovsky, but when it was eventually published in the West, Surkova's contribution was largely cut out. Thus, *Sculpting In Time* is not wholly Tarkovsky's work, though it looks that way (Surkova doesn't share a credit on the cover or title page, and isn't mentioned on the copyright page of the revised British edition from Faber & Faber).

The *Diaries* and the screenplays Tarkovsky wrote are further secondary sources for this book. (Perhaps the book Tarkovsky fans and critics would most like to see is an edition of his letters. A book of annotated scripts, storyboards and notes on production would also be nice).

In criticism, most of the work on Andrei Tarkovsky has appeared in essays and articles, published in the expected film studies arenas (*Cahiers du Cinéma*, *Positif*, *Iskusstvo kino*, *Journal of Religion and Film*, *American Film*, etc). Special numbers of journals have also been dedicated to Tarkovsky, as well collections of essays. Full-length studies have appeared by Maya Turovskaya, Mark Le Fanu, F. Borin, Tatyana Elmanovits, Balint Anrdás Kovács and Akos Szilágyi, V.I. Mikhalkovich, M. Zak, Peter Green, Vida T. Johnson and Graham Petrie (Johnson's and Petrie's *The Films of Andrei Tarkovsky* is undoubtedly the best of the bunch in Tarkovsky studies that's available in the West). But the primary texts employed in this study are the films.

The seven features are available on video and DVD in the West, though you may have to hunt around a bit to find them, even in big stores. Tarkovsky seems to have a dedicated but relatively small following. One can't imagine his films being consumed in large quantities in the home entertainment sector like mainstream films coming out of Hong Kong, Bollywood, Paris, Rome or Hollywood. On the plus side, it's not difficult obtaining the collected works on home entertainment formats: there are only seven features and two shorts to buy (*The Steamroller and the Violin* and *There Will Be No Leave Today*). The documentary by Michal Leszczylowski about the making of *The Sacrifice* is a must-have, as is the documentary Tarkovsky made in Italy, *Tempo di Viaggio*. (Some other documentaries are also available, including one on the making of *Nostalghia*). But there are no different editions or 'director's cuts' of the films to collect (though the different versions of *Andrei Roublyov* would be great to have, though it's highly unlikely they'll appear, given Tarkovsky's relatively small sales). Some of the DVDs and videos of Tarkovsky's films come with documentaries, some specially shot (valuable interviews with, for instance, Tarkovsky's cameramen, Vadim Yusov and A. Knyazhinsky, production designer R. Safiullin, composer Vyacheslav Ovchinnikov, or actors E. Zharikov and Natalia Bondarchuk).

In global cinema terms, Tarkovsky's films are a difficult sell. They have none of the selling points or marketability of entertainment cinema: no stars (and few well-known actors), no recognizable source material, and they're not in English (or French, or German, or Spanish, or Chinese, or Japanese, but the more 'difficult' languages, Russian and Swedish). They're known as 'difficult', long, tedious and pretentious (Tarkovsky recognized that poetic cinema could turn into pretentious-ness; it was a pitfall he was conscious of (though plenty of viewers and critics have felt that Tarkovsky's films are pretentious).)

Even among passionate film students and fans, Tarkovsky's films are not to everyone's taste. Many viewers don't seem to 'get' Tarkovsky; his films aren't as approachable as, say a Jackie Chan or Jet Li martial arts flick, or a Hollywood actioner. Tarkovsky is popular among some filmmakers and critics — he's a 'filmmaker's filmmaker' in that respect. But it's hard to imagine Tarkovsky's films increasing the size of their audience, despite the development since his death of the newer home entertainment formats like DVD, or the increase in the number of cinema screens globally.

Herb Slocomb, from Miami, reviewed *Andrei Roublyov* on the internet (in 2002) as 'one of the worst best movies ever made':

> slow moving, ponderous, little character development, with chaotic plot detours to what little plot there is, and the final payoff after 3 hours of this is that you get the "reward" of viewing some static images of Russian orthodox icon art.

Stuart Hancock's account of the first time he saw a Tarkovsky film reads like something out of a Woody Allen film:

> I will never forget the first time I saw *Andrei Rublev*. A friend had told me about a Tarkovsky retrospective at the Film Forum, which at the time was just off Varick Street in lower Manhattan. I had never heard of Tarkovsky, and when I arrived at the theater, I was surprised to find hundreds of Soho types lined up around the block, all dressed in black, smoking Egyptian cigarettes and looking like extras from a Fellini film. It was then that my friend informed me, 'The movie is in black and white, is three-and-a-half hours long, and in Russian with

subtitles.' I entered the theater expecting the worst... Thirty minutes into the film, I was hopelessly lost. (1986)

Another obstacle is that Andrei Tarkovsky doesn't offer an easy way in for audiences. There isn't one Tarkovsky film one could recommend as being representative and easy to watch. The obvious choice would be *Mirror* (being 106 minutes long and not one of the two-and-a-half-hour-plus films). But *Mirror* has a complex structure, three time zones, and the same actors playing characters in different historical periods. Maybe *Ivan's Childhood* or *The Sacrifice* would be good starting-points (*Ivan's Childhood* has a strong through-line and a character that's easy to identify with; *The Sacrifice*, while Tarkovsky's most accomplished work in many respects, is probably too dense, too intense and too downbeat to recommend as the First Tarkovsky Film). Not *Solaris* (probably too slow for some contemporary audiences – like the remake, which was wrongly marketed as a sci-fi flick when it's really a psychodrama about marital breakdown). Perhaps *Andrei Roublyov*, although a masterpiece in every possible respect, is too complicated, too long, and too obscure (and it's a period piece in black-and-white about a painter little-known in the West). Maybe if *Andrei Roublyov* had Kirk Douglas, Charlton Heston or Yul Brenner in it audiences might find it amenable. *Stalker* was the first Tarkovsky film for many Tarkovsky fans and, in a way, it might just be the one to put forward (if only it was half the length for the impatient folk!).[2]

But it's just not the same as considering a film director like, say, Orson Welles. With Welles, you just say: look at *Citizen Kane* and *The Magnificent Ambersons* and the genius should be fairly clear. Even a filmmaker like Werner Herzog, who can be as obscure and 'difficult' as Tarkovsky, has approachable films: Dracula remakes (*Nosferatu*), megalomaniacs in the Amazon (*Fitzcarraldo*), crazy Klaus Kinski chewing the scenery (*Aguirre: Wrath of God*), and dwarves running riot in *Even Dwarves Started Small* (1969), which even Bart Simpson, with the attention span of an average TV viewer, might find amusing.

But Herzog can be wilfully obtuse too: *Heart of Glass* (1976) is a truly strange film: set in rural Germany in perhaps the 18th century, the actors were hyptnozied (by Herzog himself) before shooting, resulting in bizarre, s-l-o-w, somnambulistic performances. Dreamy and mystery, yes, but far more eccentric than any of Tarkovsky's films. Indeed, every film viewer can probably remember films far weirder or more unwatchable than a Tarkovsky film. (Personally, I find plenty of stuff in cinema and TV that's excruciatingly difficult to watch. I'd rather watch a three hour Tarkovsky film than even five minutes of a Ken Loach, Mike Leigh, James Cameron or Guy Ritchie film).

0 : 3   THIS BOOK

This present study concentrates on Tarkovsky's seven feature films, with a more detailed reading of *Mirror*, *Nostalghia* and *The Sacrifice*, which illuminate Tark-ovsky's art. This book does not discuss Soviet/ Russian cinema, nor Tarkovsky's relation to Russian filmmakers. Dziga Vertov, Lev Kuleshov, Sergei Eisenstein, Vsevolod Pudovkin, Boris Barnet, Mikhail Kalatozov, Sergei Paradjanov, Alexander Dovzhenko, Sergei Bondarchuk and Andrei Mikhalkov-Konchalovsky are not the focus of this book. There will be too few references to Russian history, culture or life for some critics. The effect of Russian culture on Tarkovsky's life and art has been dealt with in other books (for example, V. Johnson & G. Petrie, 1994; M. Turovskaya, 1989; M. Le Fanu, 1987). Tarkovsky's life is not analyzed via a reading of his films.

The scene by scene analyses of Tarkovsky's films here are not discussions of every single scene in each of the films. Rather, scenes have been grouped together into sequences in some of the chapters. When film critics (and fans) talk about particularly scenes, they often mean sequences or groups of scenes. Tarkovsky's films contain so many lengthy shots, and he only made even feature films, it wouldn't take up too much space to list every shot in every Tarkovsky film.

Vida Johnson and Graham Petrie have reminded readers that it's easy to misinterpret Tarkovsky's films, to miss what's going on in the films, or recall them incorrectly (JP, xiv). Tarkovsky's films do demand careful readings – their ambiguity and complexity can confuse viewers, and some film critics have invented events and images that do not occur in Tarkovsky's films.

This study uses a post-*auteur* theory approach, a development of *la politique des auteurs* of Alexandre Astruc and François Truffaut. The *auteur* critical methodology is out of date and limited in its possibilities, but it is useful in analyzing Tarkovsky and his cinematic output. His films are also considered as cultural artifacts, financial, ideological or historical objects. Tarkovsky's films are placed within the 'art cinema' tradition here – that is, a (mainly European) tradition (of Ingmar Bergman, Luis Buñuel, Werner Herzog, Federico Fellini and Robert Bresson) rather than a Russian or Soviet film tradition. It is with the (European) art cinema tradition that Tarkovsky identified himself (throughout, for example, his major written text, *Sculpting in Time*).

Some of the hallmarks of European art cinema – most of which can apply to Tarkovsky's films – are: (1) Open forms, (2) Ambiguity, (3) Expressionism, (4) Non-linearity, (5) Psychology, (6) Digressions, (7) Subjectivity and (8) Revision of genre. All through the *Diaries* and *Sculpting in Time*, Tarkovsky mentions a group of filmmakers he admires, and they are all art cinema *auteurs*: Ingmar Bergman, Robert Bresson, Federico Fellini, Alexander Dovzhenko, Akira Kurosawa, Luis Buñuel, Kenji Mizoguchi and Michelangelo Antonioni.[1] This is the central group in the Tarkovsky pantheon of cinematic gods. Other directors Tarkovsky admired included Jean Cocteau, Charlie Chaplin, Jean Vigo, John Ford, Jean Renoir and nearly every filmmaker's favourite, Orson Welles. Tarkovsky was impressed by Andrzej Wajda, Andrzej Munk, and the Polish school, which he had seen at film school in the Fifties. Tarkovsky said that *Ashes and Diamonds* had been a revelation.

These were the filmmakers who didn't work in any particular genre. As Tarkovsky put it in *Sculpting in Time*: 'Bresson is Bresson. He is a genre in himself'. These directors were one-offs, as Tarkovsky remarked of Chaplin: 'he is Chaplin, pure and simple; a unique phenomenon, never to be repeated' (*Sculpting In Time*; hereafter as ST, 150). Bresson amazed Tarkovsky: he was 'serious, profound, noble', 'his concentration was extraordinary', all of his films were high art (ST, 189).

> When I am working, it helps me a lot to think of Bresson [Tarkovsky confessed]. Only the thought of Bresson! I don't remember any of his works concretely. I remember only his supremely ascetic manner. His simplicity. His clarity. The thought of Bresson helps me to concentrate on the central idea of the film.

Bresson was perhaps the only filmmaker whose finished films corresponded closely with the script, Tarkovsky maintained (ST, 94). For Tarkovsky, 'in the poetry of film, Bresson, more than anyone else, has united theory and practice in his work with a singleness of purpose, consistently and uniformly' (95). I think you could also add Bergman and Kurosawa.

Tarkovsky admired Federico Fellini's *8 1/2*, and *Casanova*, and the *Toby Dammit* section of *Spirits of the Dead*. It wasn't the story of *Casanova* Tarkovsky appreciated so much as the formal qualities. *Casanova* is an eccentric, sometimes wilfully obscure movie, with a highly stylized performance from Donald Sutherland, but for Tarkovsky 'the formal aspect is of an extremely high level, its plasticity is incredibly profound'. However, Tarkovsky was dismissive of Fellini's *Roma*, which was shown at Cannes in 1973. Tarkovsky remarked at Cannes that *Roma* pandered too much to the audience. The inner rhythm of a film, which Tarkovsky regarded as vital, was rejected in *Roma* in favour of a commercial product. As Tarkovsky put it, 'the editorial rhythm is so slick that one feels offended on behalf of Fellini'.

Most of the filmmakers Tarkovsky admired were European, or from the Far East (and Japan in particular). Few American directors were regularly cited by Tarkovsky, and hardly ever an American director working after Orson Welles. None of the 'movie brats' or filmmakers of the 'New Hollywood' were mentioned (Martin Scorsese, Peter Bogdanovitch, Francis Coppola, Brian de Palma, John Carpenter, Steven Spielberg, George Lucas *et al*. Spielberg was noted once or twice by Tarkovsky).

Note the omission of Sergei Eisenstein, perhaps the most influential Soviet filmmaker of the 20th century, from Tarkovsky's favourites. Tarkovsky disliked the intellectual flavour of Eisenstein's films, but, whether he was aware of it or not, Tarkovsky used some of Eisenstein's ideas (such as Eisenstein's 'dynamization of space', and theory of montage). Eisenstein's historical epics, *Alexander Nevsky* and *Ivan the Terrible*, inevitably influenced Tarkovsky's films, in particular *Andrei Roublyov*, which covers similar late mediæval periods in Russian history. Personally, I'm with Tarkovsky on Eisenstein: his films are extraordinary on many levels (formally, socially, politically), and are classics of world cinema, but they're not films to return to many times. (And the ideological aspect of Eisenstein's cinema – its alignment with Stalin and the Soviet regime – is problematic. Tarkovsky's cinema is also compromised by its links with the Russian authorities, but nowhere near as much as Eisenstein's films).

A questionnaire published in Tarkovsky's *Diaries* lists Pushkin, Dostoievsky,

Mann and Maupassant among writers; Bresson among directors; Bach among composers; and 'dawn, summer, mist' as his favourite landscape (D, 89). There's also an answer to 'what is a woman's driving-force?' which feminists won't like at all: 'submission, humiliation in the name of love'.

If, as some critics have suggested, that Tarkovsky didn't really like the sci-fi genre, he spent a significant part of his film career on sci-fi projects: two feature films (and *The Sacrifice*, with its nuclear war scenario, has affinities with sci-fi). The musician Eduard Artemiev remembered that Tarkovsky had a box of sci-fi books at his home.

As genre films, Tarkovsky's are some of the most accomplished in cinema. As science fiction films, *Stalker* and *Solaris* have no superiors, and very few peers. Only the greatest sci-fi films can match them: *Metropolis, King Kong, Close Encounters of the Third Kind* and *2001: A Space Odyssey*. Tarkovsky happily and method-ically rewrote the rules of sci-fi genre: *Stalker* and *Solaris* are definitely not routine genre outings. They don't have the monsters, the aliens, the visual effects, the space battles, the laser guns, the stunts and action set-pieces of regular science fiction movies. No one could deny that *Andrei Roublyov* is one of the greatest historical films to explore the Middle Ages, up there with *The Seventh Seal, El Cid, The Navigator* and Pier Paolo Pasolini's 'Life' trilogy. If you judge *Andrei Roublyov* in terms of historical accuracy, epic spectacle, serious themes, or cinematic poetry, it comes out at the top.

Finally, in the religious film genre, *The Sacrifice* and *Nostalghia* are among the finest in cinema, the equals of the best of Bergman, Buñuel, Bresson and Dreyer. (In a way, it was partly the *timing* of the release of Tarkovsky's religious films that has made them appear as anomalies: had *The Sacrifice* and *Nostalghia* been released during the 1950s and 1960s, they'd be regarded as instant classics, and placed beside the great religious films of the era: *The Seventh Seal, Viridiana, Diary of a Country Priest* and *The Gospel According To Matthew*. But by the time of the 1980s, with the 'Hollywood Renaissance' of the 1970s and the European New Wave over, films like *The Sacrifice* and *Nostalghia* seemed out of step with the drift of contemporary cinema.)

No particular school of film criticism is used in this study (although some of the methodologies of semiology, (post)structuralism, feminism and psychoanalysis are employed, with a view to exploring the deep structure of Tarkovsky's films). Some post-Jungian, post-Lacanian, post-Kristevan psychology is used to explore Tark-ovsky's recurrent motifs. Michel Foucault dreamt of 'a kind of criticism that would not try to judge, but to bring an *œuvre*, a book, a sentence, an idea to life... I'd like a criticism of scintillating leaps of the imagination' (326).

'The cinema does not just present images, it surrounds them with a world' wrote Gilles Deleuze in 1985.[2] In an interview in *Directed By Andrei Tarkovsky*, shot during *The Sacrifice*, Tarkovsky said there were two kinds of filmmaker: those who try to imitate their world, and those who create a world. The latter kind, Tarkovsky said, are poets. As examples, Tarkovsky cited 'Bresson above all', and also Mizoguchi, Buñuel, Kurosawa and Bergman. It's clear that Tarkovsky identifies himself with the filmmaker-as-poet. Ivor Montagu called Tarkovsky a *'realist poet in images'*, who digs underneath the narrative structure of his films to layer it with 'overtones and undertones, hints, symbols suggestive of and reflecting on the theme' (1973, 92).

In some ways, Andrei Tarkovsky is one of the last of the *auteurs*, the last of those filmmakers who were formed in (and by) the Sixties, like Michelangelo Antonioni, Jean-Luc Godard, Bernardo Bertolucci and Rainer Werner Fassbinder, who made large-scale personal films, films full of big ideas and passions, in the art cinema tradition. Tarkovsky lamented the passing of the 'greats': on June 6, 1980 he wrote in his diary (while in Italy):

> In the evening I watched Cocteau's *The Return of Orpheus* [*Le Testament d'Orphée*, 1960, France], on television.
> Where have all the great ones gone?
> Where are Rossellini, Cocteau, Renoir, Vigo? The great — who are poor in spirit? Where has poetry gone? Money, money, money and fear... Fellini is afraid, Antonioni is afraid... the only one who is afraid of nothing is Bresson. (D, 256)

Feminist Camille Paglia would agreed with Tarkovsky in lamenting the decline in cinema since the New Wave days: '[o]n the whole, film has fallen off in artistic quality from the high point of European art film in the late fifties and sixties'.[3] Krysztof Kieslowski, a filmmaker with many affinities with Tarkovsky, said that all the great film personalities and films were in the past, were dead or retired (1993, 33). For some critics, cinema is dying if not dead. How so? Tarkovsky asked 'where as the cinema greats?' Where is the great cinema being made in the years since the 1980s?

Raúl Ruiz believed that cinema wasn't in its death throes — it had already gasped its last (107). For Gilles Deleuze, cinema in the mid-Eighties was dying from its 'quantative mediocrity' which Deleuze related to the demands of late capitalism and its over-production, and also to the degeneration of cinema into 'state propaganda and manipulation, into a kind of fascism which brought together Hitler and Hollywood, Hollywood and Hitler' (1989, 164). Godard would say cinema's been dying for decades, and many agree that cinema was declining with the end of the silent era. Meanwhile, Mr *Godfather* (Francis Coppola), is ever-optimistic and reckons that cinema is still in its infancy, and will develop beyond anything that can be imagined at the moment. Technologically, maybe, but the humanists and left-liberals cling to the notion that cinema must have something 'to say', that it should 'deal with' social issues, that it can be an 'artistic statement'.

The question of feminism is pivotal to this reading of Tarkovsky's cinema. Can art, can cinema, be 'feminist'? No, if one agrees with the French feminist Hélène Cixous that it is impossible to create a truly 'feminine' text.[4] As Laura Mulvey has shown, the look in cinema is distinctly patriarchal.[5] The whole of cinema, its plots, characters, themes and images are thoroughly patriarchal, produced and consumed in a patriarchal context. Creating 'feminine' or 'feminist' cinema, in opposition to masculinist cinema, is fraught with problems. Can there be a 'women's cinema' when the texts, discourses, history, production modes, ideologies and images are so ruthlessly patriarchal and embedded in the masculinist view of life? It is not simply a case of having women writing and producing their own films because, as Luce Irigaray and Hélène Cixous have shown, texts are patriarchally contextualized. The sexuality of cinematic textuality is predominantly male or masculine. Tarkovsky's art, as will be apparent, does not engage with radical feminist politics, and is disappointingly mundane, ultimately, in its portrayal of women on screen.

My first encounter with Tarkovsky's art was seeing *Mirror*, when it was broadcast on British television in 1982. I was struck by the image of the trees blowing in the wind at night. This is intensely poetic – about as deeply poetic as cinema ever gets. It is one of the starting points for the film, for the childhood scenes. It is scene four: the boy is in bed; night noises are heard – a bird; cut to some trees and bushes: the camera tracks slowly, laterally, to the left; a breeze rustles the trees; cut back to the boy; he leans up in the bed and says 'Papa'. The yearning in this sequence is immense. It's so simple: just a shot of a boy in a bed and some trees. Yet Tarkovsky's sacred cinema manages to imbue it with such richness, such power, such mystery. One is not sure exactly how he does it. The elements appear mundane, viewed individually. One can recognize the language, the signs and symbols, and so on, but none of this knowledge explains the mystery. Tarkovsky's art transcends ordinary cinematic approaches.

Few filmmaker's works are so sparse, so economical, yet so rich and subtle (one thinks of Ingmar Bergman, Yasujiro Ozu, Robert Bresson). Tarkovsky's films contain many elements the hungry devotee demand from a film: (1) intensely sensuous images; (2) great acting; (3) subtlety; (4) religious and mythic themes and allusions; (5) poetic treatment and subject matter; (6) use of classical and folk music; (7) singular (natural) sounds; (8) magic and mystery; (9) clarity *and* complexity; (10) multiple layers; (11) multiple viewpoints; (12) eidetic details; (13) acknowledgement of the past (personal, historical and cultural); (14) use of the history of art and painting; (15) use of symbols; (16) nonlinear narration; (17) a deep sense of the family, of childhood and parents; and (18) an extraordinary sense of space, design, props and colour.[6]

But Andrei Tarkovsky's cinema is also in another realm from Western European (British, Italian, Spanish, French and German) cinema. It has perhaps more affinities with what used to be called East European cinema. In Tarkovsky's art, the European art film is fused with the majesty, tragedy and infinity of Eastern European and Russian culture (why is that phrase *Mother Russia* so potent, even if ideologically, politically and culturally suspect?). Tarkovsky's sacred cinema is suggestive; he shows things, but not completely; Tarkovsky is didactic, but not analytical or comprehensive (sometimes he's wilfully intellectually antiintellectual); his cinema shows the viewer events, but doesn't give them only one interpretation. One sees things, but mystery is still there. In Hollywood/ international (dominant) entertainment cinema, with its stolid camerawork, incessant swelling music underlining every gesture, routine dialogue, bynumbers plots, rampant materialism, promilitaristic ideology, and immovable (monoscopic) viewpoints, the viewer always knows exactly where they are. There is no room to manœuvre, no ambiguity. In Tarkovsky's cinema, one can move about, because his films are *spacious*.

Andrei Tarkovsky's images excite enormously: an angel under clear running water; a room full of rain; a glass bottle; a Leonardo da Vinci or Piero della Francesca painting; a house on fire (the *whole house*, not just the roof or a window, as in conventional films, but the *whole structure*). These images can be seen as rapturous and radiant. An image from a Tarkovsky film is easily identified as a Tarkovsky image, although the production crew, the script, the setting, and the actors are different. As an example of Tarkovsky's stunning imagery, take the birds flying out of the Madonna's body at the beginning of *Nostalghia*, for example. Many other filmmakers have excelled at slowly and carefully establishing a seemingly ordinary scene and having something bizarre happen in the middle of it to stun the viewer. Tarkovsky achieves cinematic wonder without all the techno-logical wizardry mainstream cinema can muster. And there are still many more and more surprises with every viewing of a Tarkovsky film.

Ingmar Bergman was reported to have seen *Andrei Roublyov* ten times (D, 248). Tarkovsky was one of Bergman's favourites: the Swede saw *Andrei Roublyov* at Svensk Filmindustri in 1971, in a print without subtitles. It made a big impression on Bergman. Bergman said that he had spent his 'entire life knocking at the door leading to the space where he moves with such obvious naturalness'.[7] Of Tark-ovsky, Bergman said he was 'the greatest, the one who invented a new language'.[8]

PART ONE

THE ARTIST

ONE

The Poetry of Cinema

I : I   THE RELIGION OF CINEMA

Certain *auteurs* – Ingmar Bergman, Rainer Werner Fassbinder, Alfred Hitchcock, Orson Welles, Akira Kurosawa, Jean-Luc Godard – often instil hallowed awe and unswerving devotion among film buffs. There are writer's writers (Francesco Petrarch, André Gide, James Joyce) and poet's poets (Arthur Rimbaud, Robert Graves, John Keats, Friedrich Hölderlin). Similarly, there are filmmaker's film-makers: Orson Welles is one of the most oft-cited ones, like Frank Capra, Claude Chabrol, Roberto Rossellini and Alfred Hitchcock (the darling of the *Cahiers du Cinéma* crowd of the French New Wave). These are the kind of filmmakers that constitute the core of the religion of cinema. They are the saints and martyrs, the theologians and philosophers, the priests and mystics of the cult of cinema.

To extend the analogy: D.W. Griffith is like an Old Testament patriarch – Moses or Abraham, perhaps. Georges Méliès, Thomas Alva Edison, Edwin S. Porter and the Lumière brothers are regarded as the founding Fathers, Old Testaments kings, the writers of the gospels of cinema, looked upon with respect and indulgence, and lost in the mists of time. G.W. Pabst, Erich von Stroheim, King Vidor, Raoul Walsh, Cecil B. DeMille, John Ford, Ernst Lubitsch, Jean Renoir, Walt Disney,

Josef von Sternberg and Fritz Lang form the Golden Days, the Middle Ages of film. *Avant garde* and abstract filmmakers are like the Gnostics and heretics — sects and subsects growing underneath the mainstream religion of cinema (Dziga Vertov, Luis Buñuel, Michael Snow, Maya Deren, Stan Brakhage). Leni Riefensthal, Walerian Borowczyk, Kenneth Anger and Russ Meyer are extraordinary one-offs. With Orson Welles, Alfred Hitchcock, Kenji Mizoguchi, Akira Kurosawa, Ingmar Bergman, Roberto Rossellini, Anthony Mann, Robert Siodmark and Billy Wilder, one reaches film's Renaissance era, where the God of the cinema is still believed in but cynicism is rife. The *nouvelle vague* and Neo-realist filmmakers are like the scientists, psycho-analysts and artists who destroyed the traditions and conventions of pre-20th century history. They are the Freuds, Marxes, Nietzsches, Einsteins and Darwins who ushered in the modern era. Jean-Luc Godard is a Freudian psychoanalyst, a gangster genius who questions the religion of cinema right down to its powerbase. Rainer Werner Fassbinder is a post-Marxist heretic, exposing the hypocrisies of urban civilization. Alain Resnais is cinema's metaphysician. Pier Paolo Pasolini reinvents cinema as mythic realism. Werner Herzog is a latterday mediæval vision-ary, difficult, wayward, ambitious. Federico Fellini is the *ciné*-cult's clown, indulg-ed *and* despised. In this pageant of cinema, Andrei Tarkovsky fits in as a late mystic and martyr, born in the wrong age, on the wrong side of the Renaissance. He was at first tolerated, like Walerian Borowcyzk or Werner Herzog, as an erratic and obscure modern age mystic. Now Tarkovsky is joining the ranks of the glorified: he has been canonized and beatified as a latter-day saint of film passion.

1 : 2 EMOTION AND SPECTACLE: VISCERAL CINEMA

In Jean-Luc Godard's wonderful film *Pierrot le fou* (1965, France), director Sam Fuller defines cinema in 'one word... Emotion'. Emotion (feeling, desire, affect) is important to the success of most artforms — whether painting, music, dance or drama. The American painter Adolph Gottlieb noted: '[p]aint quality is meaningless if it does not express quality of feeling'.[1] Cinema is emotional. Or in post-Freudian, Lacanian terms, cinema is pure desire. Or, to put it another way, at its best cinema works on a number of levels, of which the emotional is perhaps the most powerful. It is this gut-response that Hollywood cinema exploits, from D.W. Griffith to Steven Spielberg. Movies are marketed as 'experiences', like the theme park or heritage centre; in theme parks history is presented as a fairground attraction, complete with hidden voices, slides, models, lighting effects, moving dummies, animatronics, computers, video monitors and 'hands on' machines and toys. In terms of a sensory experience, the modern museum or heritage centre is far more sophisticated and varied than the cinema. In postmodern, post-everything philosophy, the search for meaning has been replaced by experience; no authorship, just effect. Not 'what does it mean?' or 'who's the author?' but 'what does it feel like?' or 'does it feel good?' A cinema of spectacle, visceral thrill, sensory overload.

Art's effect is emotional, Tarkovsky always said. It works first on a person's emotions, not their intellect, their mind, their thoughts (ST, 165). A film is an 'emotional reality', Tarkovsky claimed, and the audiences perceives it as a *second reality*' (ST, 176). The audience of a film, for Tarkovsky, always thinks of the events being depicted on the screen as something real, something truly there; whereas a painting, say, was always taken as an *image* of reality', a construct (ST, 178).

Since the Fifties and its battle with television (by using colour, widescreen, 3-D and stereo sound) cinema has built itself up as a major provider of visceral experiences (that's one view of entertainment history; another has the Hollywood studios not 'fighting' TV at all, but hungrily and efficiently incorporating it and exploiting it as another market for distribution and product). Films such as *2,001: A Space Odyssey, Cleopatra, Jurassic Park* and *Apocalypse Now* were intended from the outset to be (consumed as) giant spectacles that overwhelmed the viewer (Stanley Kubrick and Francis Ford Coppola have spoken of this ambition). But the same can be said of much earlier products, such as D.W. Griffith's *Intolerance* and Fritz Lang's *Metropolis*, films from cinema's infant years.

Spectacle in the cinema is nothing new. Cinema traded on spectacle from the beginning, when the vaudeville, funfair, circus and theatrical experience became absorbed in the cinematic experience. Here the cinematic sublime, as in Romantic visions of William Wordsworth, Caspar David Friedrich or Johann Wolfgang von Goethe, is of the epic scale, where the human scale view is blown up to gargantuan proportions. When applied to religious subjects, this over-inflated, pompous style often fails as spiritual cinema (in the films of Cecil B. DeMille, King Vidor and

George Stevens).

The most successful religious filmmakers – Ingmar Bergman, Robert Bresson, Luis Buñuel and Pier Paolo Pasolini – have made smaller scale films which are charact-erized by intense, lyrical moments. Tarkovsky is of the Robert Bresson School of Sacred Cinema – quiet, introspective, controlled (why shout when you can whisper just as effectively?). Yet both Tarkovsky's and Bresson's films are highly emotional, and as manipulative as DeMille or Spielberg (but all art is manipulation: great art is just better at hiding how much it's manipulating the audience).

Art critic Christopher Hussey defined seven aspects of the sublime (in painting), derived from Edmund Burke's *Philosophical Enquiry Into the Origin of Our Ideas of the Sublime and Beautiful* (1757): (1) obscurity (physical and intellectual); (2) power; (3) privations (such as darkness, solitude, silence); (4) vastness (vertical or horizontal); (5) infinity; (6) succession; and (7) uniformity (the last two suggest limitless progression).[2] ('Society seeks stability, the artist – infinity' said Tarkovsky [ST, 192]). These tenets of the sublime in art can be applied to cinema – to films such as *2,001: A Space Odyssey*, *Citizen Kane*, *Contact* and *Apocalypse Now* (as well as Tarkovsky's films), films which consciously encourage notions such as obscurity, darkness, vastness and infinity.

In its grander moments it's easy to see how Tarkovsky's cinema echoes the gestures of High Romanticism – its Blakean, Wordsworthian, Goethean, Turnerian gestures. The marks of late 18th / early 19th century European Romanticism include: exalting nature; going to extremes; the cult of solitude; the pre-dominance of subjectivity; rebellion; the artist as outsider; infinity; the sublime, and so on. Edmund Burke wrote:

> The passion caused by the great and sublime in *nature*, when those causes operate most powerfully, is astonishment: and astonishment is that state of the soul in which all its motions are suspended, with some degree of horror'.[3]

(Among film critics, Scott Bukatman has written most lucidly of awe, wonder, spectacle, sight and the sublime in modern cinema.)

Andrei Tarkovsky and his cinema embodies so many of the marks of High Romantic culture: (1) the cult of the artist as sacred creator (something Tarkovsky and most of the Romantics believed in); (2) the sovereignity of the artist; (3) the holy aloneness of the artist (the artist as outsider, marginal, apart, different); (4) the artist as rebel and romantic rebellion (the artist or individual versus the mob or establishment, such as Percy Bysshe Shelley, or Mary Shelley's Dr Frankenstein; one recalls Tarkovsky's long-running disputations with the Soviet authorities); (5) the Romantics' awe of the natural world (Friedrich Hölderlin's beloved Swiss Alps or William Worthsworth's Lake District); (6) going to extremes; (7) nostalgia and romanticizing the past (a recurring passion for Tarkovsky); (8) a love of the exotic, the far-off, the Oriental; (9) wildernesses, deserts, oceans, forests, mountains; (10) beauty; heightened sensuality; (11) synæsthesia and magical correspondences (à la Charles Baudelaire); (12) magic and the occult (as in Novalis or Goethe); (13) shamanism and religion; (14) mythology and history; (15) intensity; (16) horror and the Gothic (Romanticism has many links with Gothic literature, and there's a strong Gothic strain in Tarkovsky's cinema – not least in his *Hoffmanniana* script); (16) the urge towards the infinite and the eternal; (17) the visionary, spectacular and sublime; and (18) barely disguised spiritual longing and mysticism.

Tarkovsky's debt to or links with Romantic culture are no surprise, really, because the Romantic definition of the artist pretty much describes the modern artist. Tarkovsky and Tarkovsky's cinema would disagree, however, with post-modern and contemporary artists who exalt playfulness; irony, coolness and distance; surface not depth; objectivity not subjectivity; and the death of the author.

I : 3   THE POETICS OF CINEMA

In all these ways the ordinary commercial cinema maintains something at least of the fullness of the primal myth, blending, in various permutations, fact, drama, the 'Surreal', dream, magic and the supernatural powers of their play. Perhaps we too readily assume the mass media's lack of, and antagonism towards, poetry...

Raymond Durgnat[1]

Cinema poeticizes reality and the real. The filmmaker may not intend poetry, but, as in Eisensteinian montage, the effect, as far as the viewer is concerned, can be poetic. The images, the colours, the textures, the manipulation of time, the multiple viewpoints, the metaphors and connections made – all these can be made poetic. Certainly the films of Charlie Chaplin, Milos Forman, Atom Egoyam, Ermanno Olmi, Douglas Sirk and Li Shaohong, six very different filmmakers, contain moments of intense poetry. When the subject is bleak, such as poverty-stricken childhood (as in Bill Douglas's trilogy), or cannibalism (as in Jean-Luc Godard's *Weekend* [1967, France] or in Marco Ferreri's *Blow Out* [*La Grande Boufe*, 1973, Italy]), the results can still be very poetic. If lyricism is in the perception of the beholder, then any (and every) film can be poetic. Often it is the films that strive self-consciously to be lyrical that fail: the mythopœic experience can be elusive.

Like poetry, cinema is full of rhymes, of dissonances, assonances, cross-references, plots and sub-plots. Like poetry, cinema uses images, motifs, metaphors, allusions, allegories, repetitions, fables, refrains, subjective viewpoints, lyricism and so on. Many filmmakers, like most poets, have their own vocabulary, full of their own words (or shots), their own phrases (or camera movements, lighting styles) and their own quotes (or *hommages*, as the French New Wave filmmakers called them). A platitude of the academy is that writers have to establish their own 'voice', that the most successful artists have personal vision. Each of cinema's *auteurs* has her/ his own 'voice' – Tarkovsky has his long water-filled takes; Bergman has his ensemble playing, Expressionist camera and alienated winterscapes; Eisenstein has his montage, and so on.

In a 1964 essay, Tarkovsky said he wanted cinema to fuse the subjective and the objective, to be both facts and feelings, to have its own poetic logic, to have its own form, separate from literature or theatre, and to express the 'poetic concreteness' of dreams. Poetry, Tarkovsky asserted in *Sculpting In Time* (21), is 'an awareness of the world, a particular way of relating to reality. So poetry becomes a philosophy to guide a man throughout his life'. For Tarkovsky, poetic thinking (intuitive, subjective, associative) may be closer to life, and to thought itself, than the narrative logic of traditional drama (and cinema), which was the only model used for expressing dramatic conflict. It was cinema's task, Tarkovsky reckoned, to convey some of the impressions, the associations, the memories and subjective states of life (ST, 23).

Jean Cocteau, whom Tarkovsky admired, wrote that poetry has the ability to reveal things to people as if they're seeing them for the first time: '[i]n a flash we *see* a dog, a cab, a house for the first time. What is special, mad, ridiculous, beautiful in them is overwhelming… That is the role of poetry. It unveils, in the full meaning of the term'.[2] Cocteau is the classic case of the poet who became a filmmaker, the *ciné-poet*, and the subject of his films, Orpheus, is one of the icons of the whole history of poetry, like Sappho or Taleissin.

T.S. Eliot's *The Wasteland* is regarded by some critics as the first 'cinematic poem', with its collage of images cut up from the detritus of post-war culture (but Arthur Rimbaud's incredible *Illuminations*, which is far superior to Eliot's *ciné-poem*, precedes it by fifty years). Eliot's massively over-praised poem influenced Federico Fellini's *Satyricon* (1969, Italy), and Eliot was Michelangelo Antonioni's favourite poet. Both cinema and poetry foreground form, and probably the closest cinema comes to poetry is in its ability to present the spectator with a cluster of images which create poetic magic. True poetry, said British poet Robert Graves, should make the hair stand up on the back of one's neck. Graves spoke in *The White Goddess* of poetry in terms of its ability to sing praises to the Goddess:

> Sometimes, in reading a poem, the hairs will bristle at an apparently unpeopled and eventless scene described in it, if the elements bespeak her unseen presence clearly enough: for example, when owls hoot, the moon rides like a ship through scudding cloud, trees sway slowly together above a rushing waterfall, and a distant barking of dogs is heard; or when a peal of bells in frosty weather suddenly announces the birth of the New Year. (25)

These are the sort of poetic moments cinema can conjure up (a shot of trees rustling in the wind at night, from Tarkovsky's *Mirror*, or the snow falling at the end of *Nostalghia*). Tarkovsky made such suddenly thrilling evocations one of his specialities. The Tarkovsky shock moment was a set-piece that often revelled in the self-conscious fakery of cinema. But it is the images that do the talking, that stay in the mind, that creep in under the mundane architecture of dialogue, characters, action and plot.

Pier Paolo Pasolini's 'cinema di poesia', as expounded in his "Cinema of Poetry" essay, corresponded to an ideal, primitive, raw cinema which existed underneath cinema. It was a cinema of a pre-symbolic, pre-lingual realm, a cinema of poetry before signification and language, a realm between reason and unreason, the objective and subjective, the real and the ideal. It was an ideal, not a reality, however: even in his own films the cinema of poetry remained a theoretical ideal.[3]

In March, 1961, Michelangelo Antonioni said: 'I think its important for cinema to turn toward... ways of expression that are absolutely free, as free as painting which has reached abstraction; perhaps cinema will even construct poetry, a cinematic poem in rhyme'.[4] In an interview in *Cahiers du Cinéma* (October, 1965), Godard remarked: '[i]n my opinion the cinema should be more poetic – and poetic in a broader sense, while poetry itself should be more opened out'.[5] Tarkovsky would agree with such sentiments. But by 1961 cinema had long been poetic. Classics of poetic cinema (to cite some of the obvious examples) include: Kenneth Anger's *Fireworks* (1947, USA), Maya Deren's *Meshes of the Afternoon* (1943, USA), Jean Cocteau's *Orphée* films, *The Man With a Movie Camera* (Dziga Vertov, 1929, Russia), *Sunrise* (F.W. Murnau, 1927, USA) and *Un Chien Andalou* (Luis Buñuel, 1929, France). One might also cite the works of James Broughton, Stan Brakhage, Alejandro Jodorowsky, Walerian Borowczyk, Michael Snow, George Landow, Malcolm Le Grice, and much of abstract, formal film.

Andrei Tarkovsky's religious cinema goes beyond the poetic cinema of Alexander Dovzhenko and Lev Kuleshov: Tarkovsky says, repeatedly (in *Sculpting in Time*) how he hates the manipulative and artificial effects of Eisensteinian montage cinema ('I am radically opposed to the way Eisenstein used the frame to codify intellectual formulæ... Eisenstein makes thought into a despot' are two typical Tarkovskyan criticisms of Eisenstein [ST, 183]). Yet Tarkovsky employs poetic montage many times – in *Mirror*, for example, which is (really) one long poetic montage. There are sequences of montage in Tarkovsky's poetic cinema as manipulative (or overly 'intellectual') as anything in Eisenstein or Vertov, or in Russian 'poetic cinema', abstract and formal film, and American 1940s *avant garde* cinema.

Tarkovsky is not a filmmaker who employs movie references in his films. Indeed, he studiously avoids any shot or sequence that looks like the work of another filmmaker.[6] Some filmmakers load many allusions to the history of cinema into their films. Jean-Luc Godard is always discussing cinema in his films, either through his characters, his voiceovers, his *mise-en-scène*, or his quotations. Some filmmakers delight in producing *hommages* to films or filmmakers (Woody Allen to Ingmar Bergman, for instance, or Francis Coppola to Orson Welles or Akira Kurosawa, or Peter Bogdanovitch to John Ford), while others can't resist spoofing movies (Mel Brooks, Jim Abrahams, the Marx Brothers). Some movie franchises are built almost entirely on references to movies and popular culture: *Shrek, Scary Movie, Scream, Indiana Jones, Star Wars*, and don't seem have any 'centre' or 'substance' if you take away the quotes, allusions and jokes.

Tarkovsky's films are the polar opposite of that kind of playful, multi-allusive postmodernity. Tarkovsky's films *never* wink at the audience. Tarkovsky really means it, *maaan*. A movie is never 'just a movie' for Tarkovsky, as it is for so many filmmakers. *Just* a film! The idea is absurd in the Tarkovsky universe. And Tarkovsky's films haven't yet entered popular culture in the West like, say, the figure of Death in Ingmar Bergman's *The Seventh Seal*, who crops up in *Monty Python*, *The Simpsons* and *Bill & Ted* movies.

I : 4   ANDREI TARKOVSKY AS POET

For Andrei Tarkovsky, poetic cinema is subjective, intuitive, non-rational, non-literary. It begins and ends with an individual's perception (ST, 20). For Tarkovsky, ever the Renaissance philosopher, the individual is the measure of everything. Thus, Tarkovsky rejects logic, classical drama, cause-and-effect and simplistic notions of narration. Tarkovsky exalts dream-logic (what Elisabeth Sewell in *The Orphic Voice* called 'post-logic'), poetic associations, non-linearity, and the primacy of the individual response. 'Poetic cinema' is the best term for his kind of cinema. He defines it thus:

> I find poetic links, the logic of poetry in cinema, extraordinarily pleasing. They seem to me perfectly appropriate to the potential of cinema as the most truthful and poetic of art forms. (ST, 18)

Tarkovsky's concept of poetic cinema is the same as his concept of art: he exalts the spiritual, the search for 'truth', subjectivity and so on. Tarkovsky forces cinema to become increasingly dreamlike. Tarkovsky blurs the boundaries of dream and actuality. As Robert Bresson put it: '[y]our film must resemble what you see on shutting your eyes' (50). For Ingmar Bergman, Tarkovsky was the master of dream films: 'Tarkovsky is the greatest of them all. He moves with such naturalness in the room of dreams... All my life I have hammered on the doors of the rooms in which he moves so naturally'.[1]

For Barthelemy Amengual, Tarkovsky's cinema is like Byzantine icons: 'the icon transposes the spiritual into physical space; Tarkovsky transposes it into physical time'.[2] In his magisterial book on Yasujiro Ozu, David Bordwell suggested that like that of Bresson and Dreyer [one could also include Tarkovsky], evokes the ineffable as a by-product of remarkably constrained and exact choices. The point is not what it means but what it *does*: train us in nuance, suggest new possibilities for ordering experience, and – not least – invite us to contemplate the possibilities of the film medium when it is no longer subordinated to story construction. (140)

That approach helps with Tarkovsky's cinema: if one considers what it *does* not what it *means*: instead of trying to decipher the rain, smoke, horses and other Tarkovsky motifs and symbols, turning them into categories of written or verbal language, but accept them as experiences or effects. That is, of course, the overriding project of one strain of contemporary cultural theory which reckons that questions like 'what does it mean?' are no longer valid. More to the point is: 'what does it feel like?' and: 'what is its effect?' And Tarkovsky's films work elegantly on both these levels, on the levels of meaning and doing (and on other levels too).

Tarkovsky speaks of cinema in terms of poetry and music. Like music, he says, cinema needs no mediating language: it deals with reality (ST, 176-7). 'I classify cinema and music among the *immediate* artforms since they need no mediating language' (ST, 176). Any passage taken at random from *Sculpting in Time* gives a clear sense of Tarkovsky's notions of art: '[a]rt is born and takes hold wherever there is a timeless and insatiable longing for the spiritual' (ST, 38). Tarkovsky saw himself within Alexandre Astruc's *camera-stylo/ auteur* theory tradition. Tark-ovsky is a *ciné*-poet *par excellence*, a filmmaker who takes Vertov's *kino-glaz* ('cinema-eye') and theory of *kino-pravda* ('cinema-truth') to the point of mysticism. Tarkovsky's cinema is more mystical than most, in the true sense of the word. Not 'mystical' because it is strange, unreal, poetic or even religious, in the traditional sense, but 'mystical' because his cinema constantly strives, like authentic mysticism, for something wholly other, for the numinous, the divine, the beyond.

Authentic mysticism lies at the heart of religion (such as Sufic mysticism within Islam). In the same way, the mystical cinema of Carl Dreyer, Ingmar Bergman, Yasujiro Ozu and Tarkovsky lies at the centre of world cinema. The advances that people such as Bergman, Ozu and Tarkovsky have made are not in the mundane realm of visual effects, box office receipts or synergetic distribution, but in explorations of the human condition. For Andrei Tarkovsky, art, religion, cinema and poetry are all part of the same thing: a mysticism of cinema. 'Pictures must be miraculous' said the tragic painter Mark Rothko,[3] and Tarkovsky's images aim to be similarly thaumaturgic. The cinematic (or poetic) and the sacred are (or should be) equivalent for Tarkovsky. As Georges Bataille put it: 'all that is sacred is poetic and all that is poetic is sacred'.[4] Tarkovsky's mode of cinema is to construct the conditions in which an exploration of the sacred can occur. The long take, the slow tracking shot, bleached-out colour, Bach music — these are mechanisms by which Tarkovsky's cinema can evoke the numinous. As in all mysticism, the search for the sacred in Tarkovsky's cinema is a process doomed to failure: the would-be mystic can only carry on dauntlessly, trying to find the transcendent in the immanent, trying to nurture such delicate notions (or illusions) as hope and faith. Pier Paolo Pasolini said (*pace Accattone*, his first film) that he was trying to use 'a *technique of sacredness* that profoundly affected settings and characters'. Pasolini emphasized sacrality and frontality: '[h]ence, religion'. Pasolini remarked '[t]here is nothing more technically sacred than a slow pan'.[5] 'My vision of the world is in essence epico-religious' said Pasolini (ibid.). There are no technical problems in cinema, Tarkovsky stated, 'once you know exactly what to say' (ST, II0).

I : 5   ANDREI TARKOVSKY AND THE HISTORY OF POETRY

In his films Andrei Tarkovsky quoted Alexander Pushkin, Fyodor Tyutchev, William Shakespeare and, above all, his father, Arseny Tarkovsky (not to be confused with Aleksandr Tvardovsky, 1910-71). Ironically, the general public in Russia knew about Tarkovsky and his films before Tarkovsky senior and his poetry (so that Arseny Tarkovsky was known as the father of Tarkovsky the film director, not the other way around).[1]

Arseny Tarkovsky (who died in 1989), was a poet who remained unpublished during Tarkovsky's childhood. Today, Tarkovsky senior is regarded as a significant poet, though definitely not to be classed among the greats like, say, Pushkin, Blok or Yvetushenko. Tarkovsky's poetry is essentially lyrical — poetry in the classical sense: impressionistic experiences of the world. It does not have a self-conscious ideological or political agenda, for instance. But it was hugely important for his son's films:

when Andrei Tarkovsky quotes from a poet, it is from Arseny Tarkovsky more than any other (though he does quote from Pushkin and Tyuchev. Pushkin is one of Tarkovsky's poetry gods: Pushkin's poem 'The Prophet' was one of Tarkovsky's key poetic inspirations). A school friend (Yuri Kochevrin) recalled that Tarkovsky carried a book of Tarkovsky senior's poetry with him all the time (JP, 19).

Tarkovsky's father's poetry influenced much of Tarkovsky's cinema. It's easy to spot the influence of the conservative, classical, musical and metaphysical style of Tarkovsky senior in his son's films. Tarkovsky not only incorporated his father's poetry into the background and tone of his films, he also included them in the soundtrack and dialogue, most prominently in *Mirror* and *Nostalghia*. The first poem in *Zerkalo* (read by his father) is probably the best, most moving Arseny Tarkovsky poem appearing in a Tarkovsky film: 'First Meeting' (published in 1962):

> Every moment that we were together
> Was a celebration, like Epiphany,
> In all the world the two of us alone,
> You were bolder, lighter than a bird-wing,
> Heady as vertigo you ran downstairs
> Two steps at a time, and led me
> Through damp lilac, into your domain
> On the other side, beyond the mirror. (ST, 101)

The film goes on to trace the life led 'beyond the mirror'. After his father Arseny, Alexander Pushkin is Tarkovsky's main poetic influence (or most often cited). In poems such as 'Autumn', Pushkin created the dream of a mythical, snowbound Russia:

> O mournful season! How enchanting to the eye! Your beauty with its message of farewell delights me: I love nature's sumptuous fading, the woods clothed in purple and gold, the noise of the wind and the fresh breeze in the tree-tops, the skies covered with rolling mist, the infrequent sun-ray, the first frost, and the distant threat of hoary winter.[2]

This is the mist-soaked Russia Tarkovsky portrays in *Andrei Roublyov*, *Mirror* and *Nostalghia*. In *Mirror* the boy quotes Pushkin's letter of October 19, 1836 to Piotr Chadayev on the founding of Russia (ST, 195). Tarkovsky's poetic cinema is part of the Russian poetic tradition, and Pushkin is the spirit and apotheosis of Russian poetry. Tarkovsky worked in that Russian lyrical tradition, which runs from Pushkin and Fyodor Tyutchev through Alexander Blok, Anna Akhmatova, Boris Pasternak, Osip Mandelstam and Sergei Esenin, to Arseny Tarkovsky and Yevgeny Yvetushenko. Tyutchev is a passionate poet whom Tarkovsky appears to have liked enough to quote him directly in a film (*Stalker*). In his poem 'Silentium', Tyutchev wrote:

> Be silent, hide yourself, and conceal your feelings and your dreams. Let them rise and set in the depths of your soul, silently, like stars in the night, contemplate them with admiration, and be silent. (ib., 132)

One can see similarities between Tarkovsky's art and the cosmological visions of Dante in his *Divina Commedia*; with Shakespeare's tragic humanism; with the religious fervour of the British Metaphysical poets (John, Donne, George Herbert, Richard Crashaw and Henry Vaughan); with the nature-loving pantheism of Romantics such as Novalis, Hölderlin, Goethe and Wordsworth; with the music-ality and linguistic philosophies of the French Symbolists (Paul Verlaine, Stephane Mallarmé, Paul Valéry and Stefan George); and with modern European poets such as St-John Perse, Paul Celan and Georg Trakl.

One of the key works of literature that Tarkovsky quotes from in his films is the *Bible*. After the *Bible*, William Shakespeare, Alexander Pushkin and Fyodor Dost-oievsky are favourites. *Don Quixote* is referenced in *Solaris*; Fyodor Tyuchev in *Stalker*; Anton Chekhov, Dante Alighieri (the *Inferno*), Dostoievsky (*The Devils*), Arseny Tarkovsky and Pushkin in *Mirror*. In his book on cinema, *Sculpting In Time*, Tarkovsky frequently refers to literary figures: apart from the ones cited above are Boris Pasternak, Osip Mandelstham, Nikolai Gogol, Ivan Bunin, Herzen, Alexander Blok, Vyacheslav Ivanov and Nikolai Gumilyov among Russian writers and poets, and Hermann Hesse, G.W.F. Hegel, Paul Valéry, Ernest Hemingway, Emile Zola, Gustave Flaubert, Johann Wolfgang von Goethe, Dante Alighieri, Thomas Mann, Franz Kafka, and Marcel Proust among international writers.

Among modern poets, Tarkovsky's cinema has affinities with the poetry of Rainer Maria Rilke. Rilke's mystical lyricism, with its sense of exile and nostalgia for Russia, its ascetic quietism, its *Kunst-ding* (Existential 'thingness' or thing-in-itself), its exaltation of the peasant, its cultural sophistication and its talk of a philosophic Angel is very much in tune with Tarkovsky's sensibilities. 'Every angel is terrifying' said Rilke in his famous sequence of poems, the *Duino Elegies*.[3] The Rilkean Angel is spiritual, erotic, transcendent, difficult, opaque – all qualities which Tarkovsky's

poetic cinema enshrines. Rilke is one of a long line of mystical poets, who include
Jalal al-Din Rumi, Nur al-Din 'Abd al-Rahman Jami, St John of the Cross, Thomas
Traherne, William Blake and St-John Perse. Rilke's *Book of Hours* poems, based on
the mediæval *Book of Hours* (the illuminated prayer book, often dedicated to the
Virgin Mary), are the equivalents in written poesie of Tarkovsky's cinematic poetry
(for example, 'I am, O Anxious One' from the *Book of Hours*, or 'Evening' from the
Book of Pictures). Rilke's poem 'Before Summer Rain', from his important volume
New Poems (1908), seems particularly close to Tarkovsky's art:

> Auf einmal ist aus allem Grün im Park
> man weiß nicht was, ein Etwas, fortgenommen;
> man fühlt ihn näher an die Fenster kommen
> und schwigsam sein. Inständing nur und stark
>
> ertört aus dem Gehölz der Regenpfeifer,
> man denkt an einem Hieronymus:
> so sehr steigt irgend Einsamkeit und Eifer
> aus dieser einen Stimme, die der Guß
>
> erhören wird. Des Sales Wände sind
> mit ihren Bildern von uns fortgetreten,
> als dürfen sie nicht høren was wir sagen.
>
> Es spiegeln die verblichenen Tapeten
> das ungewisse Licht von Nachtmittagen,
> in denen man sich fürchtete als Kind.

(Suddenly, from all the green around you, something – you don't know what –
has disappeared; you feel it creeping closer to the window, in total silence. From
the nearby wood you hear the urgent whistling of a plover, reminding you of
someone's Saint Jerome: so much solitude and passion come from that one voice,
whose fierce request the downpour will grant. The walls, with the ancient
portraits, glide away from us, cautiously, as though they weren't supposed to
hear what we are saying. And reflected on the faded tapestries now: the chill,
uncertain sunlight of those long childhood hours when you were so afraid.)[4]

This sense of landscape, nostalgia, yearning, loss, relationships, history, suffering
and religion, all focussed through an intense lyricism, appears in Tarkovsky's poetic
films, which come from a similar sensibility, an emotional core which aims at transformation.

Andrei Tarkovsky used Japanese *haiku* to illustrate his arguments on cinema three times in *Sculpting in Time*. *Haiku* explains his notions of poetic cinema: '[w]hat attracts me in haikku is its observation of life – pure, subtle, one with its subject; a kind of distillation' (ST, 66). The seventeen-syllable *haiku* lyric, like the Greek epigram, is life compressed, an emblematic, economical distillation of life. *Haiku* poetry suggests enormous vistas with a minimum of means:

> Wind in the trees,
> fallen leaves
> gathering in the east. (by Yosa Buson)

> Journey's end –
> still alive
> this autumn evening. (by Matsuo Basho)[1]

Haiku poetry targets a space that is simultaneously commonplace and strange (like Tarkovsky's films). While the socio-cultural context of Yosa Buson's and Matsuo Basho's poetry (Japan in the 17th century) is quite different from that of Tarkovsky's cinema (Russia and Europe in the late 20th century), there are moments when the two poetries chime. Tarkovsky's films evoke a sense of mystery; they sometimes have the enigmatic quality of *haiku*. If one has to think about them too much, one has missed the point, as in Zen philosophy (Tarkovsky argued for a similar total acceptance of his images, without them needing to be analyzed). *Haiku* can so suddenly and completely evoke an atmosphere, a dream, a memory, an experience.

Matsuo Basho (d. 1694) is the acknowledged master of Japanese *haiku*, where the (Buddhist) philosophic theory of 'less is more' is magnificently demonstrated. For Tarkovsky (who quoted Basho in his journal), *haiku* moves closer to the essence of things. What Tarkovsky likes about *haiku* poetry is its anti-intellectual, anti-dramatic stance: '[t]he image as a precise observation of life takes us straight back to Japanese poetry' (ST, 106). The *haiku* poem hangs there in space, like the Chinese ink landscapes and mountainscapes which depict emptiness with a few brush-strokes. *Haiku* imagery is like the Japanese tree at the end of *The Sacrifice* – motionless, serene, impenetrable, life-giving. In fact, that image of the tree against the sun-dazzled ocean is straight out of *haiku* and Chinese landscape painting.

Tarkovsky makes sure the viewer notices this, for Alex draws attention to it in his dialogue at the beginning of the film. The next stage from this observation is to construct a *haiku* to go with the image at the end of *The Sacrifice*:

Boy under a tree
He speaks his very first words —
The sun is dazzling

I : 7   SERGIO PARADJANOV AND ANDREI TARKOVSKY

There are many affinities between Sergio Paradjanov and Andrei Tarkovsky. They knew each other, and admired each other's films. And they both influenced each other artistically. Sergio Paradjanov's most well-known film is *The Colour of Pomegranates* (1969, a.k.a. *Sayat Nova*), made for Armenfilm. It was an extra-ordinary exploration of poetic imagery; not just one of the great Russian films, *The Colour of Pomegranates* is one of the greatest films. The life and poetry of the 18th century Armenian poet Sayat Nova (Harutyun Sahakyan, known as the 'King of Song') was but the starting-point for Paradjanov's dense, allusive, highly lyrical and mystical film.

Tarkovsky greatly admired Sergei Paradjanov, and corresponded with him. He tried (with the critic Victor Shklovsky) to persuade the authorities to cease their persecution of Paradjanov in 1974 (when Paradjanov was on trial for homosexual acts). Tarkovsky wrote a letter with Shklovsky to V.V. Scherbitsky, First Secret-ary of the General Committee of Ukraine, protesting about Paradjanov's situation (D, 93-94). There are few people in the world would could replace Paradjanov artistically, Tarkovsky and Shklovsky wrote. (Tarkovsky also cited Georgian director Otar Ioseliani as an influence; in his lectures, he recommended students had a look at all of Ioseliani's films, as well as Paradjanov's.)

Sergio Paradjanov's talent for image-making was absolutely breathtaking. Very few filmmakers achieve his level of a magical facility with images. *The Colour of Pomegranates* employed a *tableaux* format, with episodes from the poet's life mounted as if they were illustrations from a mediæval illuminated book. The *tableaux* structure gave the scenes in *The Colour of Pomegranates* a flat, frontal, static and theatrical quality. Paradjanov also intercut the *tableaux* with symbols, still-life set-ups, and religious paintings. The soundtrack used Armenian folk and religious music, combined with single sounds magnified (water running was prominent). The camera was nearly always locked off, on a tripod, with medium and long shots predominating. Paradjanov used Eisensteinian montage, and New Wave jump cuts. The acting was full of hieratic gestures, and balletic movements; the actors often faced the camera, square-on, and looked into it.

The result was a hypnotic blend of image, colour, symbol and sound, at times startlingly beautiful: pomegranates staining white cloth; rows of *Bibles* and mediæval manuscripts drying on a church rooftop, pages flapping in the wind; horses prancing in procession; the ritual sacrifice of a goat; angels; old women stripping carcasses; a church full of sheep surrounding a coffin; rows of monks eating pomegranates; dyed wool dripping onto large metal platters.

The Colour of Pomegranates is one of the great colour films; in its control and deployment of colour, it rivals any of the great colour films (by some of the famous practitioners of colour in European-US cinema: Mickey Powell, Vincente Minnelli, Stanley Kubrick and Bernardo Bertolucci), and perhaps surpasses them. The costumes are particularly striking, shot with a heightened, fetishistic awareness of texture, fabric, and radiant hues. The surfaces of cloth — braid, cotton — combine with images of weaving, and dyeing fabric. Red was a recurring colour: dyed wool, pomegranate juice, monks pressing grapes, red dresses, and the blood of sacrifice and saints.

Philip Brophy wrote:

Richness of sound, image and gesture is so potent in *The Colour of Pomegranates* that a strange synæsthetic giddiness overtakes the film. Everything is tactile, edible, fragrant, sensual, arousing... Spices, plaster, goldleaf, blood, sand, feathers, silk, sweat, ash, steam, fruit, brass, metal, wax, dye, alabaster, tiles — a universe of decorative paraphernalia and ritual accoutrements are displayed in ethnographic gravure; museographic without being necrophiliac; natural while being ritual. (72)

Religious ritual — archaic, peasant, agricultural, Catholic and Eastern Orthodox — suffuses *The Colour of Pomegranates*. The impress of ancient cultures, age-old customs, a life of the soil. Much of the imagery and action in *The Colour of Pomegranates* was derived from Armenian culture, rendering it somewhat obscure to Western audiences. But when the whole enterprise is handled with such extraordinary skill and imagination, it didn't matter if the finer points of the cultural world (the gestures, the fabrics, the looks, the symbols) couldn't be decoded fully. *The Colour of Pomegranates* was not a documentary, and was as far away from the tired old tropes of realism and naturalism as was possible in live-action filmmaking. Even for a Russian (or Armenian) audience, *The Colour of Pomegranates* could have seemed very strange and hermetic. Paradjanov was not going to take the audience by the hand and lead them safely through the film. This was not simple A to B plotting, or conventional dramaturgy, or 'classical' cinema. That was apparent even from one or two frames.

The Colour of Pomegranates is one of those films that creates a whole world of its own, far, far away from any other film ('I am trying to create my own world on the screen' Tarkovsky commented [ST, 213]). It's not only a film quite unlike others, it has no ambition to be like other films. The desires of conventional cinema are not present: those goals of providing an audience a clear path through the film, or having an action beat every few minutes, or easily identified heroes and villains, or sympathetic characters, or easy resolutions and closure. Rather, *The Colour of Pomegranates* seemed to float in its own world, according to laws and codes it created for itself. It's a film, also, that requires a different set of critical criteria; you simply can't judge *The Colour of Pomegranates* the same way you can *Casablanca* or *Tootsie*.

Sergio Paradjanov's life was a tragedy, an outrage of world cinema – the imprisonment between 1973 and 1978, on trumped-up charges, and a further spell in prison (until 1982). So that, by the time of his death in 1990, Paradjanov had only made three further films (*The Legend of the Suram Fortress* [1985], *Ashik Kerib* [1988] and *The Gentle One* [1990]). Tarkovsky had contributed to the campaign to have Paradjanov released.

Born in Tbilisi, Georgia, in 1924, Paradjanov studied, like Tarkovsky, at VGIK. Before his first success, *Shadows of Our Forgotten Ancestors* (1965), he had made a few 'justified failures' (as he put it). The affinities between Sergio Paradjanov and Andrei Tarkovsky in their art are many: the emphasis on religion (archaic, divine, mystical); on imagery drawn from poetry; on a poetic approach to cinema; on the visual and the musical (without relying on dialogue); on the widespread use of symbols; on the sensuousness of images; and on the necessary and irreducible *mystery* of cinema.

The rain running down the walls in *Mirror*, for example, may have been influenced by the many shots in *The Colour of Pomegranates* of water cascading and flowing (Paradjanov also mixed the *sound* of water high on the soundtrack in *The Colour of Pomegranates*, which is one Tarkovsky's key motifs). Also, the use of still-life shots (books, fruit, candles); hieratic gestures from performers; long takes; horses; angels; poetry read in voiceover; use of folk music; a lack of local sound; the screen full of floating material (wool and feathers in *The Colour of Pomegranates*; dandelion seeds in *Andrei Rublyov*, snow in *Nostalghia*).

As well as water on the walls (water dripping down a stone wall, and over a statue of the Madonna and Child), other Paradjanov motifs include the books, the poet as a boy among books laid out to dry, the frontal space, red dye (few other filmmakers have employed the colour red so successfully), chickens, arcance gestures from mediæval culture, lace as masks, monks, whitewashed interiors, and spinning cherub in a frame.

The Shadows of Our Forgotten Ancestors (1964) was the film that brought Sergio Paradjanov to the attention of the critics. It is a completely extraordinary film. Finding the right words the viewer soon comes to grief: 'rhapsodic', 'romantic', 'poetic', 'lyrical', 'magical', 'spiritual'. Yes, all of these, and many more. *The Shadows of Our Forgotten Ancestors* is a truly visionary film, a masterwork from a director who is a total natural, who can make spectacular images with effortless ease and gracefulness. Paradjanov does seem to be born to conjuring marvellous images, a Paracelsus or Cornelius Agrippa of the cinema. And his mastery of the cinematic medium is not confined to the visuals, though these are incredible enough, but also to the soundtrack, to Paradjanov's choice of folk songs, heart-rendingly plangent music, use of rapid dialogue, and intricate layering of natural and found sounds. This is truly amazing stuff, that makes most films look extremely dull and lifeless.

One of the hallmarks of *The Shadows of Our Forgotten Ancestors* is the use of the crane or boom (Iuri Ilenko was DP). Rarely has it been employed to such exhilarating effect. One thinks of masters of the crane shot – Welles, Hitchcock, Griffith – but in Paradjanov's cinema there a new wildness of expressivity, a willingness for risk-taking.

There are moments in *The Shadows of Our Forgotten Ancestors* that are unbelievably good, that literally take the breath away. Even after seeing thousands of films, it is still possible for a viewer to be astonished by a cinematic artist. One occurs right at the beginning, in the third or fourth shot: a young boy (the hero) is walking in the Russian woods in deep snow, while his father chops down a tree. His father yells to him to get out of the way, and pushes him aside, sacrificing himself for his child. But at the moment when the tree falls, Paradjanov cuts to a God's-eye-view shot, from high up in the trees tops, looking down at the father and the son: the camera careens wildly down on top of the father. It's a very memorable take on the orphanning of the hero in fairy tales and folk tales. (Some critics have related the use of the crane here to Tarkovsky's in *Ivan's Childhood*; Tarkovsky's film was important in the Soviet 'thaw' in moving film towards a more 'poetic' form of cinema. But Paradjanov uses the boom far wilder than Tarkovsky).

Another moments that leaps out at the viewer in *The Shadows of Our Forgotten Ancestors* is where a character is attacked by an axe. Again, Paradjanov employs another subjective point-of-view shot at this crisis, with blood pouring down in front of the camera lens. That effect has been used before (in the horror genre, for example). But then, out of nowhere, Paradjanov suddenly cuts to a shot of horses leaping over the camera, which is on the ground, and the shot is *tinted red*. This montage has an eidetic, indelible power – it's as unexpected as it is poetic. Paradjanov continues to use a red tint over images, often fading up closing image of each chapter in *The Shadows of Our Forgotten Ancestors*.

There are so many stunning images and sequences in *The Shadows of Our Forgotten Ancestors*, it would take a long time to consider them all. A couple of others suggest themselves: a bunch of wooden rafts roped together passing underneath the camera which has craned out over a river. Mist drifts in the twilight. Men with torches are aboard, searching the river for the drowned heroine. The hero lies prone on the raft in anguish. As the raft floats past the camera, there is a tree planted on the end of the raft.

Religious rituals and processions. Masks. Candles. Icons. Crucifixes. A crowded orthodox church. A funeral wake that turns into a wild dance. A spiritual realm that is both Christian and pagan, both Orthodox and highly superstitious.

And the costumes! *The Shadows of Our Forgotten Ancestors*, like some of Paradjanov's other films, have the most exquisite sense of colour, texture, weave and form.

And not forgetting the rivers and streams. The snowfields. The forests. Mountains. As a film of the natural world, *The Shadows of Our Forgotten Ancestors* is unbeatable. Paradjanov has one of the most acute senses of location and place in cinema.

TWO

Religion and Cinema

*Well, we're grasping for two things at once. Partly for communion with others —
that's the deepest instinct in us. And partly, we're seeking security. By constant
communion with others we hope we shall be able to accept the horrible fact of our
total solitude. We're always reaching out for new projects, new structures, new
systems in order to abolish — partly or wholly — our insight into our own
loneliness. If it weren't so, religious systems would never arise.*

Ingmar Bergman[1]

2 : 1   SACRED CINEMA

Cinema is a secular medium. As Will Rockett put it: '[t]he popular cinema may often
seem a rather pedestrian art form in which to seek the transcendent' (14). Another
view is that cinema is an artform like any other (an artform, but also a technology, a
mechanism, a cultural product, a network). Cinema's origins, however, were not, as
with music, dance and painting, in religious art. All art was originally religious (or
shamanic), made for religious purposes, as Weston La Barre noted (1972). Cinema
grew out of the optical toys of the 19th century, technologically — the zeotropes and
thaumatropes (and photography). Early cinema was presented as a marvel, a

fairground oddity, an alternative entertainment to music hall, vaudeville and theatre. The origins of cinema were thoroughly secular. Werner Herzog said: '[m]ovies come from the country fair and circus, not from art and academism'.[1] In his novel *The Lost Girl* (1920), D.H. Lawrence talked about the 'dithering eye-ache of a film' (110), adding: '[t]he film is only pictures, like pictures in the *Daily Mirror*. Pictures don't have any life except in the people who watch them' (144).

Cinema is only pictures – the flicker of still frames on a bit of canvas. Yet one picture after another begins to tell a story, and this is where cinema scores, again and again. *Cinema tells stories* (but in a very particular way). This is one important reason why cinema and television have become the dominant artforms: because they tell people what is happening in the world. Narrative is fundamental to cinema's enduring impact, as with literature, poetry and fiction. This is precisely what myth does (or did): myth tells a sacred story; a myth tells a sacred narrative.[2] Cinema picks up on that storytelling tradition, which was originally oral, pre-dating technologies such as writing or recording. Finding out what is happening in the world is (deemed) essential. In this sense, all the media are mythological: they mythicize reality, turning everything into stories. At one level, all cinema is sacred, because it depicts life being lived. Simply being alive, as Mircea Eliade noted, was a sacred act:

> In the most archaic phases of culture, *to live as a human being* was in itself *a religious act*, since eating, sexual activity, and labour all had a sacramental value. Experience of the sacred is inherent in man's mode of being in the world. (1984, 154)

Cinema will usually work well with religious subject matter that has already been turned into stories – the *Bible*, from *Genesis* to *Revelations*, is the obvious example. But also the lives of the saints, the *Apocrypha*, Jacobus de Voraigne's massively influential *The Golden Legend* (c. 1275), the *Rig Veda*, the *Mahabharata* (which is a popular soap opera in India) and so on. Most of the subjects in the *Bible* had been made into narrative images before cinema arrived: there have been countless paintings, mediæval illuminations, statues and sculptures based on Biblical material. A cinema based on such narratives seems bound to be more or less understandable to a culture founded on Judæo-Christian religion.

It is the abstract concepts that are more difficult to film: the divinity of Christ or a saint; faith; right living; concupiscence; enlightenment. Religion trades in abstractions. Cinema's task is like that of painting: how to visualize inner states of (divine) being. Cinema, like painting, looks at the human animal from the outside. 'How can one render the inside?' asked Jean-Luc Godard. His answer was typical: '[p]recisely by staying prudently outside'.[3] The novel can jump inside a mind and rattle off twenty different states of being, from fear to ecstasy, in a couple of pages. Cinema can't get inside people's minds as easily as this. What T.S. Eliot called 'objective correlatives' have to be found. Cinema can be tremendously emotional – it has a host of techniques to exaggerate states of mind, such as expressive music on top of rapidly cut images. Or the perfectly composed close-up. But while the Hollywood strings are sawing away, cinema must produce visuals to go with such stirring sounds.

Music plus images – this is a pure state for cinema, and making films to music has satisfied filmmakers from D.W. Griffith and Walt Disney to the latest pop promo directors. But religion begins and ends with people. God is not available for interview. Only the insane and unstable claim to have his telephone number. If one can't study God, then one has to start with people. This is the commonsensical approach of psychologist of religions Weston La Barre:

> There is no mystery about religion. The genuine mysteries lie in what religion *purports to be about*: the mystery of life and the mystery of the universe. But religion itself is the beliefs, behaviours, and feelings of people. (1972, 1)

So most religious films are about the way people behave and feel spiritually. Religion doesn't need God, as Charles Baudelaire noted: '[e]ven though God did not exist, Religion would be none the less holy and divine' (3). People need religion and God, but God needs neither religion nor people. But, with or without God, religion is still a rich area to study and film. As Andrei Tarkovsky put it: '[r]eligion is still the one area set aside by man to define what is powerful' (D, 11). For Tarkovsky, artistic talent comes from God, and creative expression involves sacrifice, not ego and self-expression. Tarkovsky wondered if art could be the ultimate in being, the height of human consciousness.

The Hollywood entertainment film is a story or idea that must be acted out. Dramatization is the key with its emphasis on action, conflict, development, beginnings and endings. But the narrative film is not the only solution. A film like Dziga Vertov's vortiginous and vertiginous *The Man With a Movie Camera* (1928, Russia) is an exhilarating whirlwind of images that could be a religious experience for some – as could Maya Deren's *A Study in Choreography* (1945, USA).

Whether it is abstract, *avant garde*, Surrealist, expressionist or Hollywood enter-tainment narrative, the religious film has to deal with basic problems, such as: how to portray spiritual experiences? In painting, there is always a tension between what the image tries to represent and the art object itself. The painting *is* and *is not* the sacred. For the faithful, a picture of the Blessed Virgin Mary is not an image of the Madonna, but the Madonna herself, right there. In mediæval icon paintings, divinity is indicated by the use of haloes and the gold leaf ground – the deities float in an abstract gold glow. Cinema has (or appears to have) a greater degree of so-called 'realism' than painting. As with photography, the spectator seems to see 'real' people on the cinema screen. Paintings might be more accurate psychologically and physiologically, but cinema depicts people moving and talking. Cinema is a simul-acrum of 'real life'.

Films can be wonderful, expressive vehicles for symbols, motifs, faces, atmos-pheres, presences and absences – all of which can tell the spiritual story. Cinema in particular can generate atmospheres very quickly (in its sensory shorthand: 'L.S. of a blasted heath; twilight; sound of wind blowing'). This is suited to conveying spiritual states – cinema can show the protagonist, then the situation, then how the protagonist reacts to the situation, and so on (the conventional shot/counter-shot method). Cinema develops in time, in a way which sculpture and painting do not. This is Andrei Tarkovsky's way – to let a scene or shot unfold itself slowly, over time. Another way is to choose a symbol – such as fire, a circle, or a snake – and let the viewer use the symbol as a springboard to the sacred.

Like all art, cinema has the ability to use the mechanisms of art to reach the sacred, the numinous, the Divine Ground, the Transcendent, the One, Allah, God, Brahma, the Logos, whatever one wants to call it. Like art, cinema is able to mobilize symbols, colours, shapes, presences, worlds, music, time, gestures and meanings. People call cinema the artform of the contemporary epoch because it is able to use elements of every artform, and it communicates so well the experience of being in the modern era, in the so-called 'modern world'. Pier Paolo Pasolini said: 'I avoid fiction in my films. I do nothing to console, nothing to embellish reality, nothing to sell the goods'.[4] Mainstream Hollywood cinema does the opposite: it fictionalizes, it tries to console (with a wet kiss from a Disney rabbit), it is all embellishment and ornamentation.

Mysticism revolves around the passion for ecstasy and a horror of the void. One cannot know one without the other. The road to ecstasy and the experience of the void presupposes a will to make a soul a tabula rasa, *a striving towards psychological blankness. Once it has totally rejected the world, the soul is ripe for a long-term and fecund* emptiness... Ecstasy is plenitude in a void, a *full* void. *It is an overwhelming frisson which convulses nothingness, an invasion of* being *in absolute emptiness.*

E.M. Cioran (64)

There are many unsuccessful religious films, and few successful ones. The problem with the dialogue-rich narrative religious film is that speech smothers the mystery. Andrei Tarkovsky and Robert Bresson, for instance, are sparing with dialogue. Many say that the DeMille/ Vidor/ Griffith/ Hollywood epic style of religious film is trashy and utterly profane. Mystery is not allowed to breathe. But, as Peter Wollen reminds viewers, the idea that cinema can show the spectator the truth is a bogus one. The 'truth' is elsewhere:

> The cinema cannot show the truth, or reveal it, because truth is not out there in the real world, waiting to be photographed. What the cinema can do is produce meanings and meanings can only be plotted, not in relation to some abstract yardstick or criteria of truth, but in relation to other meanings.[1]

Many of the best religious films are ones that use the Buddhist ethic of 'less is more' (adopted by Minimal artists in the West from the 1960s onwards). 'Expression through compression' said Robert Bresson (86). Andrei Tarkovsky, Bresson, Yasujiro Ozu, Theo Angelopoulos and Ingmar Bergman produced austere films – films with lots of space, both visual and aural. Ozu has actors leave a room – while the camera lingers on the empty space, as in *Floating Weeds* (*Ukigusa*, 1959, Japan) for example. In the cinema of Ozu and Bresson, in particular, there is a sense of emptiness, the *mu* of Zen Buddhism. The object of Zen is 'seeing into one's own self-nature' by 'seeing into nothingness', said eighth century Buddhist Hui-Neng.[2] The concept of nothingness is also found in Christianity and Judaism (in the mediæval mystical text *The Cloud of Unknowing*, in Jan Ruysbroeck's mysticism, in Meister Eckhart's notion of 'from nothingness to nothingness' and in the black stage of the process of the 'Great Work' of Renaissance alchemy, for example). The

problem is, how to portray it? The New York painter Barnett Newman wrote:
'[e]mptiness is not that easy. The point is to produce it with paint'.[3] To show
nothingness in film one could have a blank screen, but viewers are restless. Such
literalism would not be enough. The US painter Ad Reinhardt attempted to make a
series of black abstract paintings throughout the Sixties. Reinhardt wanted, like so
many other artists (such as Gustave Flaubert, André Gide, Samuel Beckett and
Stendhal) to take out of the artwork all that was unnecessary. Stendhal's advice for
people who wished to write was: first, have something good to say, then say it
clearly and simply.[4] (How few writers and filmmakers stick to this principle.) Flaubert and Gide dreamt of a novel in which all the waste has been chucked out.
Beckett showed, in books such as *The Unnameable* and *Texts For Nothing*, one way
of doing it.

Night, blackness, creation (and the Creation), fecundity, wombs, chaos, madness
and mysticism are all bound up together in Western symbolism. Each of Ad Reinhardt's many versions of the *Abstract Painting, Black* tried to do away with
everything. As the Buddhist *Heart Sutra* put it:

> ...no body, no mind, no shape, no colour, no sound, no smell, no taste, no touch,
> no concept; no visible world...[5]

Reinhardt's solution was to produce five-foot square black paintings which would
be 'pure abstract, non-objective, timeless, spaceless, changeless, relationless, dis-
interested'.[6]

Ad Reinhardt failed: his paintings have contexts (a museum), physicality (canvas,
stretchers, textures), forms (a cruciform shape), colours (different sorts of black
pigment, ivory black, zinc black, or lamp black), and so on. The utterly formless is
beyond human production – it is as much a linguistic problem (the 'not-this-not-
that' of Oriental philosophy) as an æsthetic one. Reinhardt thought he was 'making
the last paintings anyone can make'.[7] They were not the 'last paintings' by any
means – millions have been painted since then, since Reinhardt's death in 1967. As
Reinhardt's contemporary, Jasper Johns, put it: '[a] lot of people have said that
painting is dead, but people continue to work'.[8]

It is the same with cinema, which does not end, has not ended yet, despite so
many predictions of its demise. There are many films which can be regarded as end-
points of cinema: *Last Tango in Paris*, *Weekend*, *Citizen Kane* and so on. Each of

these films marks the end of an era (modernism and the New Wave, postmodernism and the sound film). Ad Reinhardt's *Abstract Paintings, Black* seem to be the last abstract paintings, as if formal, painterly abstraction could go no further than black-on-black. But cinema is in fact a young artform (relative to forms such as painting, dance and music), and has a long way to go (Tarkovsky believed this). Indeed, cinema is just beginning – Ingmar Bergman thought Tarkovsky had invented a new form of cinema.

2 : 3   THE PHILOSOPHY OF BEING

Religious films are not end-points, but beginnings. Mystical cinema is about becoming, travelling, transcendence. It partakes of the *nunc fluens*, the 'now-streaming' of Eastern philosophy (to use Alan Watts' phrase).[1] Cinema is part of a flow. It is, like water, flow itself, an unending process of change and motion (Tarkovsky fills his films with flowing water). Mystical cinema, to be successful, must be aware of its being as well as its becoming. The film image exists in the present, as it's being projected. Everything else is memory – memory of an image, an event, a sequence (a memory of an Elsewhere, a Never There). The tension in the viewing experience of cinema is between the static frame or screen, which seems to contain and freeze the image, and the constant flow of images, over time (ignoring for the moment 10,000 other factors). The two are reconciled in the viewer and her/his sense of Western time, narration and ontological expectations. Cinema satisfies the need for large doses of time and experience, it seems (people go to the cinema for time, for time lost, said Tarkovsky in *Sculpting in Time*, in a Proustian/ Bergsonian mood). Tarkovsky said in an interview that 'what people are looking for in cinema is a continuation of their lives, not a repetition'.

Cinema operates at this intersection of the timeless (the sacred) and the temporally-bound (the secular). So one way of producing mystical cinema is by creating the 'timeless moments' of mysticism (one of the key definitions of mysticism is its access to timelessness, and ability to suggest a sense of the timeless). Cinema has this great ability to give the spectator moments, to take a moment and expand it — with montage, slow motion, camerawork, music, manipulation of space. The present moment in cinema can be spooled out endlessly. The European art film tracking shot, for instance, stretches time and perception, continually modifying it. Tracking along a building endlessly extends the experience of the building, and of space. Or think of Michael Snow's forty-minute zoom in *Wavelength* (1967). The timeless moment of cinema and other artforms partakes of Martin Heidegger's notion of 'presencing': 'presencing, presence speaks of the present... Being means presencing'.[1]

2 : 5   INVESTIGATING THE TRANSCENDENT

For the viewer, too, transcendence is possible: the mere act of watching a film can be a transcendent activity. As Nikolai Berdyaev (who has similarities of thought with Tarkovsky) said: '[a]n act of cognition is an act of transcendence' (39f). But the viewer has to remember that though the cinematic image has tremendous presence and power, it marks, like an art object, 'the point of intersection merely'.[1] The intersection is between the viewer and the divine, between subject and object, between self and Other. A film is the materialization of the artist's relation with the meaningful. In art, as in religion, *relationship* is just as important as status, role, subject, object. The good religious film, whether *The Passion of Joan of Arc* (Carl Dreyer, 1928, France) or *Winter Light* (Ingmar Bergman, 1962, Sweden) or *Viridiana* (Luis Buñuel, 1961, Spain) tries to portray a relationship with the divine, as well as the nature of both parties (the seeker and the Sought, the priest and God, the lover and the Beloved). It is the disposition, the stance, the attitude in life-philosophy that is crucial. One can't interrogate God, but one can investigate one's self and one's relation with God.

'The *moment* in which light comes *is* God' wrote C.G. Jung (1967, 298). Goethe's dying words were reportedly 'more light!' Many filmmakers have explored this moment. Light flooding the screen, the moment of enlightenment – such a moment occurs at the end of *The Sacrifice* and *Solaris*. The original Indo-European word for God, *diew*, means 'shining one' (see chapter six, 'Symbols and Motifs'). Light appearing out of darkness, the moment of revelation of divinity, occurs in a secular way every time a film is projected or a television set or computer is turned on. The mysticism of light appears in Christianity, Hinduism, Buddhism and Siddhism. There is the 'Light Verse' in the *Qu'ran*, and the Clear Light of the Void in Tibetan Buddhism, while Siddhism speaks of worshipping the 'dazzling, blazing, brilliant white light shining everywhere'.[1]

Steven Spielberg used suddenly appearing brilliant lights in many films, such as *Close Encounters of the Third Kind* (1977, USA), *Jurassic Park* (1993) and *A.I.* (2001), in a manner that required no explication. He called it his 'God-light' (it became, since *Close Encounters*, a common device in Hollywood cinema to suggest wonder and the numinous). The best religious filmmakers have usually controlled their lighting carefully, recognizing that light is one of their most expressive tools – think of that dark, sombre and utterly authoritarian Cross at the end of Robert Bresson's *Diary of a Country Priest* (1950, France), or Ingmar Bergman's stylized backlighting (in *Hour of the Wolf* [1968, Sweden]). It is the same with religious painters, who have carefully controlled the lighting in their depictions of the divine: Giotto, Piero della Francesca, Leonardo da Vinci, Mathias Grünewald, Rembrandt van Rijn and Marc Chagall. Cinema is, physically, coloured shadows, light passing through tinted still images flickering through veils and lenses. A number of painters have specialized in layering paint to attain special lighting effects: Jan van Eyck, Leonardo da Vinci, J.M.W. Turner and Mark Rothko. In cinema, many filmmakers layer light and colour, in order to achieve pictorial and ontological depth. Light lies at the heart of cinema's revelations.

The epiphany is the æsthetic shock or radiance felt on beholding an art work, according to James Joyce. Joseph Campbell wrote:

> when a fortunate rhythm has been struck by the artist, you experience a radiance. You are held in æsthetic arrest. That is the epiphany. And that is what might in religious terms be thought of as the all-informing Christ principle coming through.[1]

Whether the shot is of horror or beauty, the aim of religious filmmakers, from D.W. Griffith and Carl Dreyer to Andrei Tarkovsky, is this radiance, this æsthetic intensity. Werner Herzog wanted the viewer to simply see the image there before her/ him, with no analysis, no critical language being employed. Tarkovsky too desired such a total response, but the response must not stop at the image. One mustn't get fixed on the image, concrete and beautiful though it might be. One must, rather, look beyond it, to the spiritual truths, the divine, the miraculous and the magical in the beyond. The epiphany is important, and radiance must be experienced, but it is what the image *points towards* that is really important. Joseph Campbell has a term for this getting stuck on the image itself: the 'mask' of God, which he takes from Emile Durkheim:

> He [Durkheim] said that the whole problem of life is to become "transparent to transcendence": so that you realize that you are yourself a manifestation of this. That you live the myth. That you live the divine life within you. Yourself as a vehicle....[2]

'The symbol itself must be transparent to transcendence' Campbell says elsewhere (1989, 25). In art one looks through the symbol or image to the transcendent Beyond. The eternal problem is how to depict the divine, the One, to suggest it. Visually, Christianity, Eastern or Western, is heavily anthropomorphic: but Christ, Mary and God are manifestations of the divine. They are the 'masks of God'. In cinema, the film image has such presence, such apparent 'realism', that it's difficult to get beyond it. But in the religious film, one must get beyond this image, one must find what Paul Shrader called a 'transcendental style' (1972).

Andrei Tarkovsky attempted to create one kind of a sense of transparency by using glass, mirrors, surfaces, water and translucent forms. Tarkovsky's film image is in the process of melting away. It is so static yet so mobile. The flowing water dissolves the colours, washes out the actualities and the outlines. No hard-edged artist he, Tarkovsky's tendency is to make his image blur and deliquesce, to melt at the edges like the paintings of Mark Rothko or the watercolours of Emil Nolde. Filmically, the problem is to fix the signifieds and signifiers, the polysemy of the image: in Roland Barthes' words 'in the cinema itself, traumatic images are bound up with an uncertainty (an anxiety) concerning the meaning of objects or attitudes'.[3]

2 : 8   THE MODERN RELIGIOUS FILM

Pier Paolo Pasolini's *The Gospel According to Matthew* is only one kind of religious film (but it's probably the best), one that is faithful to the texts of Western religion.[1] (Of Pasolini's film of Christ, Tarkovsky remarked 'I like the picture. I like it precisely because its director did not succumb to the temptation of interpreting the *Bible*'.) More common is the religious film set in the modern, urban age in which people deal with spiritual issues or seek the spiritual dimension: this occurs in the films of Ingmar Bergman, Werner Herzog, Luis Buñuel, Paul Shrader, Robert Bresson and Andrei Tarkovsky. In Werner Herzog's *The Enigma of Kaspar Hauser* (1974, Germany) the search is for identity, in an existential sense, in an age of anxiety; this is also the quest of the cinema of Robert Bresson, Paul Shrader, Louis Malle, Alain Tanner, Wim Wenders, Luchino Visconti and Michelangelo Antonioni (in *The Passenger* [1975, Italy] for example).

Some modern religious films try to show how empty of religious feeling the world is: they explore the lack of religion (of God, of the transcendent, the mysterious) in contemporary society: Robert Bresson's *Mouchette* (1967, France) is particularly savage, as are Ingmar Bergman's *The Virgin Spring* (1959, Sweden) and *Shame* (1968, Sweden). Other films delineating a spiritual wasteland include: Roberto Rossellini's *Rome, Open City* (1945, Italy), *The Exterminating Angel* (Luis Buñuel, 1962, Mexico), *The Devil, Probably* (Bresson, 1977, France), *Salò* (Pasolini, 1975, Italy), *Hiroshima Mon Amour* (Alain Resnais, 1959, France) and *Stroszek* (Werner Herzog, 1977, Germany). In films such as Federico Fellini's *Otto e Mezzo* (1963,

Italy), which many filmmakers admire, the quest is of a personal, autobiographical and artistic nature (as in Tarkovsky's *Mirror*). Tarkovsky's films were part of a number in Russia in the 1960s and 1970s that looked at art and artists, such as Peter Illyich Tchaikovsky, Anton Chekhov, Sayat-Nova (Harutyun Sahakyan), Niko Pirosmani, and Vazha-Pshavela (Luka P. Razikashvili).

2 : 9 HORROR, FANTASY AND SCIENCE FICTION CINEMA

Transcendence can occur in a secular field, such as in the horror genre, with its 'cinema of cruelty' (Will Rockett's term). Here the transcendence is downwards, down through the depths of the soul, such as in *Rosemary's Baby* (Roman Polanski, 1968, USA), *The Shining* (Stanley Kubrick, 1980, GB/ USA) and *Nosferatu* (F.W. Murnau, 1922, Germany). The descent is mythic, spiritual, Orphic: into the underworld, where chaos overturns order, excess displaces harmony, and where violence, extreme actions and intensification are the norm. In science fiction films, such as *2,001: A Space Odyssey*, the transcendence is (unusually) evolutionary. It has already been noted that the gangster or thriller film may offer a transcendence and catharsis in the manner of Classic Greek tragedy (in *Angels With Dirty Faces*, *The Godfather*, Martin Scorsese's cinema, or Charles Laughton's *The Night of the Hunter* [1955, USA]). The films of Jean Cocteau and Kenneth Anger show how religiosity can be mixed with (Crowleyan) magick, poetry, mythology and gay culture (in Anger's *Scorpio Rising* 1963, USA, or Cocteau's *Orphée*, for example).

A religious film might occur if a mystical approach to cinema is employed, as in the works of Yasujiro Ozu, Michelangelo Antonioni, Theo Angelopoulos, Raúl Ruiz, Robert Bresson and Kenji Mizoguchi. In their films, the *style* can be religious, though the subjects may be quite mundane. But this also is rare. There are many failures in religious filmmaking. *Close Encounters of the Third Kind* (Steven Spielberg, 1977, USA) and other films such as *Cocoon* (Ron Howard, 1985, USA), *Contact* (Robert Zemeckis, 1997, USA) and *Altered States* (Ken Russell, 1980, USA) have tried to make quasi-religious pronouncements about other-worldly things, with somewhat unsatisfactory results.

Films of the supernatural or paranormal sometimes attempt statements on matters connected to religious subjects. Some of the films are endearing in their moral simplicity and surface innocence: *The Wicker Man* (Robin Hardy, 1973, GB), *Dead of Night* (Dearden/ Cavalcanti/ Hamer/ Crichton, 1945, GB), *Dr Jeckyll and My Hyde* (Victor Fleming, 1941, USA) or *Frankenstein* (James Whale, 1931. USA). The Universal *Dracula* and *Frankenstein* films of the Bela Lugosi/ Boris Karloff period are now rightly regarded as classics, as is F.W. Murnau's unsurpassed *Nosferatu*, or the 1933 *King Kong*. These are films with a primal power that remains potent after seventy, eighty, ninety years. It tends to be the unexpected exceptions to the horror genre, as with other genre movies, that stand out: films in the horror/ suspense/ supernatural genre, such as David Lynch's blackly comic *Eraserhead*, Hitch's mother-loving *Psycho*, the Todd Browning Thirties oddity *Freaks*, cult classic *The Wicker Man*, Charles Laughton's menacing one-off *The Night of the Hunter*, and Jacques Tourneur's magnificent *Night of the Demon*, seem to come out of nowhere, arriving all of a piece. These are self-contained narratives, sometimes extraordinary one-offs (*The Night of the Hunter*), or bizarre early works (*Eraserhead*), or the work of filmmakers who have spent years at their craft (*Psycho, Freaks, Night of the Demon*).

Anthony Shaffer's *The Wicker Man* was an oddity that combined Hammer horror-type camp and sex with a grinning, peculiarly British kind of occultism. *The Wicker Man* was filled with textbook pagan behaviour, the kind that can be gleaned in two minutes from riffling the pages of a paperback occult guide or one of the many underground magazines in the paranormal field available in Britain. There were ritual sacrifices, May Pole dances, fertility rites, corn dollies, frogs being used to cure sore throats, women leaping over a fire, and so on. As with many post-Production Code horror films, sex was mixed with the supernatural. Britt Ekland (and her body double) was shown writhing around nude, singing, rubbing herself on the walls and thumping the wall next to Edward Woodward, desperately trying to repress his sexuality in the bedroom. Christopher Lee acted the aristocratic Scottish island laird in purple flares and hippy prances.

The camp menace of *The Wicker Man* derived from the combination of the ordinary and the bizarre: Woodward's policeman was portrayed so upright, repressed, Protestant and decent, it made the antics of the villagers on the Scottish island appear all the more sexed-up and eccentric (a clever move, because the diversions of the islanders were pretty tame, compared with, say, a Russ Meyer or

John Waters film). Woodward dressed up as the Fool in the May Day procession, a bizarre way of a cop going undercover. Unusually in the genre, in a film which raised certain expectations, Woodward's character was killed at the end – burnt alive in a wicker giant while screaming 'the Lord is my shepherd' hoarsely at the pagan villagers, who blithely ignored him, singing 'summer is acomin' in', with Christopher Lee chanting 'death to you will be rebirth to our crops'. 'The sun sinks slowly in the west, yet again, and the credits being to roll on one of the strangest films ever made on these shores' wrote Ken Russell (1993, 147). Whether it was meant as a black comedy, a morality play, social commentary or a straight-faced horror film, *The Wicker Man* remains more bizarre than anything Ken Russell, Derek Jarman, Peter Greenaway or other British off-the-wall directors have produced.

Many horror and fantasy films veer into pornography, stupidity, over-indulgence, sexism, special effects, stereotyping, misogynism and banality (for example, *Dracula* [Terence Fisher, 1966, GB], *The Thing* [John Carpenter, 1982, USA], *Incubus* [John Hough, 1982, Canada], *Alien vs. Predator* (Paul S. Anderson, 2005, USA) and *The Entity* [Sidney Furie, 1983, USA]). *The Exorcist* (William Friedkin, 1973, USA) was thought to be a masterpiece of the horror genre. But in fact it merely reinforced the *status quo* of Western religious duality, the tired old battle between good and evil. *The Exorcist* showed that the Devil was sexy (nothing new there – it has been a standard theme in Western history since Biblical times) and re-hashed worn-out beliefs. The post-*Exorcist* films were even worse: *The Omen* series in particular dredged the dregs of religious subject matter. At the end of *The Omen III: The Final Conflict* (Graham Baker, 1981) a giant Christ-like figure appeared as the triumph of good Christian values over the much more exciting world of the Devil.

Since the revival in horror filmmaking of the 1970s, through the 'video nasties' of the 1980s, and the 'postmodern' teen horror flicks of the 1990s, film directors have raided topics such as witchcraft (*Salem's Lot*, *Charmed*, *The Craft*, *Practical Magic*), ghosts (*The Sixth Sense*, *Always*, *Ghost*, *The Others*), angels (*Michael*, *City of Angels*, *Dogma*), demons (*Spawn*), vampires (*Buffy*, *Bram Stoker's Dracula*, *The Little Vampire*, *Interview With the Vampire*, *Van Helsing*), sub-humans or mutants (*The Fly*, *Basket Case*), zombies (*Day of the Dead*), monsters (*The Relic*, *Jurassic Park*, *Arachnaphobia*, *Godzilla*, *Harry Potter*), werewolves (*An American Werewolf in London*, *The Howling*, *Wolf*), devilish aliens (*Critters*, *Gremlins*, *Species*, *Men In Black*, the *Alien* series), poltergeists (*Poltergeist*), crazy technology (*Videodrome, Christine*), killer dolls (*Magic, Child's Play*), killer robots (*The Terminator, Virus, I, Robot*), and endless stalk 'n' slash psychokillers and maniacs (*Candyman, The Hitcher*, the *Friday the 13th, Nightmare on Elm Street*, Hannibal Lecter, *Scream, Scary Movie, I Know What You Did Last Summer, Urban Legend* and *Hallowe'en* films). The Devil himself has had a minor resurgence in contemporary Hollywood: *The Devil's Advocate*, and Arny going up against Satan in *End of Days*, or in superhero flicks *Spawn* and *Constantine*.

Tarkovsky clearly loathed exploitation films, the low-budget zombie, flesh-eating, vampire, ghoul, slasher and monster films that flourished from the 1960s onwards and became infamous in their 'video nasty' incarnation. However, in a humorous essay on "The State of the Art Film", Anne Billson complained that lengthy, pretentious art films were much more difficult to sit through than tacky exploitation flicks: 'movies with exploding heads or stomach-bursting aliens or disco-thrashing Arnies were more artistically satisfying than pseudy foreign stuff in which nothing happened'. Tarkovsky's films are obviously in the latter category: Billson offered some marks of the typical art film: it must have subtitles; hardly any action; be pretentious; be gloomy; be needlessly long; have interchangeable charact-ers; be smutty; use lots of water (Tarkovsky certainly scores here); have irritating characters; and be heavy on style.[1]

One reactionary, rightwing view of the post-1970s horror films is that, like people with their hearts ripped out (as in David Lynch's *Dune*, 1984, USA) or their brains sucked out (like the zombies in *The Night of the Living Dead*, George Romero, 1968, USA), horror films have had their insides torn out. There's nothing left in them: they are empty, corpses with no souls. *Scanners, Nightmare on Elm Street, Dracula, Fright Night, Amityville Horror* – what these films show is that there is a fascination not only with the horror genre, with visceral/ spectacle cinema, with danger, and so on, but also with stories that subvert Christianity and the establishment. The search in these horror films is not for spiritual enlightenment but for visceral excitement. The religious dimension is not the point. For the rightwing establishment and moral guardians (such as religious fundamentalists and critics like Michael Medved in America), the post-1970s horror films are a threat to the stability of society; they can corrupt people, including children, they can create copycat behaviour, they lower moral standards, and so on. In this reactionary, right-wing view, horror films threaten societal order, exposing the primitive, instinctual drives underneath late capitalist society, undermining the family unit, marriage, education, the church and morality.

The horror filmmaker chooses an area such as Christianity to set a film in, because the iconography (for a Western film audience) is so familiar. Then they play Hell with it. The Devil (or some substitute – a psychopath, mutant, vampire, werewolf or whatever) is the best kind of (anti)hero there is: Satan or his stand-in is the Trickster God, always upsetting things, like a naughty adolescent (libido, id) gone wild, doing all the things the viewer dreams of doing but never quite has the guts to do. Look, it's Satan/ Dracula/ Frankenstein/ Freddy/ whoever doing really bad things! As in the gangster genre, the real hero in horror films is the baddie. The evil one can transgress more thresholds than the goodie, and spectators love that. In the cinema anything can happen: films can be the wish-fulfilments of nations. 'Ah!' people sigh, 'if *only* life were like the movies!' But life can be like a Hollywood movie, if one fancies cruising around in an opentop stretch limo, ripping people's heads off, having multi-orgasmic sex with the current most expensive starlet, gunning down aliens or gooks, stealing stacks of bucks and getting high on heroin. Life *is* like that, isn't it?

A Tarkovsky or Bresson or Ozu or Bergman film is naturally going to be a hateful prospect to an audience that buys into Hollywood entertainment cinema. Imagine it: a two-and-a-half hour film in a foreign language, with subtitles fer Chrissakes, with no cars, no money, no murders, no gangbangs, no guns, no cops, no psychopaths, no sex, no swearing, no drugs, no rock 'n' roll, no rapes, no spaceships, no machines blowing up, no laughs, no special effects and an ending of quiet ambiguity!

Another view of horror and fantasy films is that they simply reflect contemporary culture. They do not create violence or a slide in moral standards, but reflect back what is going on. In this liberal, quasi-left-wing view, a society gets the films it deserves (or needs). Hollywood is thus only doing what it should do. In some feminists' views, horror films express society's ambiguous relationship with issues such as race, gender, identity and the body.

If films are a culture's dreams, then one of the Westerner's dreams is of maximum materialism and consumption, out-and-out capitalism, living in the fast lane with a three-second attention span. The religious aspect is practically buried, snowed under mounds of dollars and cocaine (in countless gangster or heist films, such as *Casino* or *Scarface*). The Grail, the prize, the thing sought for in thousands of modern (Hollywood) films, is typically a suitcase full of money or drugs or some gizmo (it also might be having a great body, having a glamorous partner, having a sleek car or a large house). Contemporary cinema is full of people desperate to get hold of their prize. A suitcase full of money, the answer to all life's problems (what else could the Holy Grail be in a late capitalist society but money?).

Religious filmmakers such as Andrei Tarkovsky, Theo Angelopoulos or Robert Bresson are right at the other end of the philosophical scale. In the old days it was God not Mammon (in the *Bible*), but contemporary religious filmmakers are not at all sure about God. They fill their films not with money and drugs and killings and designer bodies, but with empty spaces, silences, inner restlessnesses, isolation, spiritual anguishes, and few characters. This is one aspect that characterizes the modern religious film: the small number of people. Whether it's *The Diary of a Country Priest* (Robert Bresson, 1950, France), Ingmar Bergman's *Hour of the Wolf* (1968, Sweden) or Tarkovsky's *Nostalghia*, the emphasis is on one person, maybe two or three, seldom more. Occasionally there is an American film centred on one or two people in a vast emptiness, but it is rare (*Badlands*, Terence Malick, 1974, USA, for example).

Although Andrei Tarkovsky's cinema uses many Christian symbols – the bread and wine in *Nostalghia* for instance, or *The Ghent Altarpiece* in *Stalker* – his religious films are set in the modern world. There are cars, cities and technology in his cinema, but his filmic spaces are not fixed to particular social environments. (There are cities in Tarkovsky's *œuvre*, despite his reputation as a film director fond of depicting natural landscapes or villages: Vladimir in *Andrei Roublyov*, Tokyo in *Solaris*, Rome in *Nostalghia*, and Moscow in *Mirror* and *The Steamroller and the Violin* (the latter film is also a *hommage* to contemporary Moscow).)

Like Jesus in *The Gospel According to Matthew*, Tarkovsky's protagonists go into the wilderness – the psychological wilderness, away from culture, into nature. Tarkovsky did film a crucifixion – the crucifixion in the snow in *Andrei Roublyov*.

Had the opportunity presented itself, had he lived longer, Tarkovsky would possibly have leapt at the chance of making a Biblical film, with Old or New Testament costumes and settings. In some ways, the film that Tarkovsky did not live to make that one would like to see most was *The Temptation of St Anthony*. Even if the film had a modern setting, it would have been impressive. If it had been made in the epic style of *Andrei Roublyov*, *The Temptation of St Anthony* could have been spectacular.

2 : 11   HYSTERIA AND MYSTICISM:
ANDREI TARKOVSKY AND INGMAR BERGMAN

Ingmar Bergman aimed for the tragic dimension of Shakespeare and the Classic Greek dramatists. His films occasionally attain Shakespearean grandeur – in the depth of their feeling, in the brilliant ensemble acting and direction, in the recurrent symbolism, in the anguish of lack and desire. Andrei Tarkovsky greatly admired Ingmar Bergman. In *Sculpting in Time* he uses Bergman's films to illustrate his ideas about cinema (scenes from *Winter Light* and *Through a Glass Darkly* to discuss sound, for example); he said he had seen *Persona* 'a great many times, and on each occasion it has given me something new' [ST, 166]). Bergman greatly admired Tarkovsky's work, and *Andrei Roublyov* in particular. 'Tarkovsky is the greatest of them all. He moves with such naturalness in the room of dream', Bergman wrote in his autobiography, *The Magic Lantern.*

There wasn't 'symbolism' in Ingmar Bergman's films, Tarkovsky maintained, but 'an almost biological naturalism' (ST, 149). Bergman was simply trying to get at the 'spiritual truth about human life that is important to him'. 'The fewer symbols the better! Symbolism is a sign of decadence' Tarkovsky averred. Tarkovsky wrote with emotion of a moment in Bergman's *The Virgin Spring* when it snows, the flakes landing on the young woman who lies dying (ST, 213). A 'stunning' shot, Tarkovsky called it, which went beyond meaning or symbolism.

For Jean-Luc Godard (writing in 1958), Ingmar Bergman was the last great Romantic, in the tradition of Beethoven or Balzac. This excerpt from a *Cahiers du*

Cinéma article by Godard could be about Tarkovsky:

> The cinema is not a craft. It is an art. It does not mean teamwork. One is always
> alone; on the set as before the blank page. And for Bergman, to be alone means to
> ask questions. And to make films means to answer them. Nothing could be more
> classically romantic.[1]

There are many correspondences between the films of Andrei Tarkovsky and
Ingmar Bergman. Take Bergman's *Through a Glass Darkly* (1961) and Tarkovsky's *The Sacrifice*. *Through a Glass Darkly* featured many of the usual Bergman
collaborators: cinematography by Sven Nykvist, music by Erik Nordgren, produced
by Allan Ekelund for Svensk Filmindustri, with Harriet Andersson, Gunnar
Björnstrand and the Bergman stalwart, Max von Sydow. It was, as usual, written
and directed by Bergman, and was premiered at Röda Kvarn and Fontänen on
October 16, 1961 (around this time, Tarkovsky was shooting his first film, *Ivan's
Childhood*).

The plot of *Through a Glass Darkly* seems relatively simple at first: four people
gather at a house by the sea: Martin (Max von Sydow), a doctor; David (Gunnar
Björnstrand), a writer and widower; his daughter, Karin (Harriet Andersson), a
young woman, married to Martin, who has been treated for schizophrenia; and her
brother Minus (Lars Passgard). A number of seemingly disconnected and minor
events occur: while David and Martin deal with the fishing nets, Karin and Minus
fetch milk (and Minus confesses that he struggles with erotic desires); the brother
and sister put on a little play for the David (helped by Martin). David, staying at the
island for a month to finish off his novel before going to Yugoslavia, has his own
demons.

More serious events happen at night, when Karin, unable to sleep (wakened by a
bird), wanders into the attic and experiences her schizophrenic split world. When
David and Martin leave the island for a while, on a fishing trip, Karin tells Minus
about her two worlds, taking him up to the attic. Minus doesn't know what to do
when he sees her acting increasingly oddly, but Karin seems back to normal when he
returns to the room (a brilliant touch in Bergman's staging: Minus watches Karin
anxiously as she tells him of her innermost feelings, and hearing voices behind the
wallpaper; she sits on the floor, and Minus leaves the room; he hesitates, comes back
and she's standing at the door as if nothing's happened). Later, Karin is found by
Minus in a shipwreck on the shore; they make love. Martin and David return,

Minus tells them about Karin's state, and Martin asks for a helicopter to take her to hospital. Karin goes to the attic again, to commune with her other world. She is taken away by the helicopter.

The bare bones of the story do not make *Through a Glass Darkly* much clearer. In fact the film is concerned primarily, like so much of Tarkovsky's cinema, with religious themes: Karin is seen by the medical establishment (represented by Martin) as schizophrenic (just as Tarkovsky's 'mad men' are misunderstood); but she thinks she is in touch with another world – with the Ultimate Other, in fact (i.e., God: he's the person they're waiting for, he's going to come through the door). As Ingmar Bergman put it in his workbook of March, 1960: '[a] god speaks to her. She is humble and submissive toward this god whom she worships'.[2]

Karin has some of the traits of what convention would regard as mental instability: acute hearing, for instance (noted as a product of her medical treatment in the film) and weather-sensitivity (she can sense the rain coming long before it does). Actually, acute sensitivity to the weather is not so uncommon. Peter Redgrove and Penny Shuttle reckon that 30% of people are weather-sensitive to the point of illness.[3]

What Ingmar Bergman is portraying is a kind of spiritual possession (one recalls Tarkovsky's characters: Domenico, the Stalker, and Boriska). Buried under the seemingly 'ordinary' events of the first half of *Through a Glass Darkly* is a deep and sometimes desperate spiritual feeling. 'A god descends into a human being and settles in her' writes Bergman (1994, 252). This is an extraordinary act then, yet *Through a Glass Darkly* is shot 'realistically' (heightened European Art Film Expressionism might be a better term). At first, the god is an inner voice, Bergman says, pleading, sometimes threatening. Gradually the god's presence becomes stronger inside Karin, and the woman becomes completely devoted to him (she turns away from Martin and his sexual advances; he becomes increasingly sexually frus-trated). When she has surrendered utterly to the god, he accomplishes his tasks through her then leaves her burned out.

The wallpaper in the attic signifies the border between the two worlds, of 'normality', domesticity, human passions. On the other side, is the god and his strange world – menacing, beseeching, repulsive, fascinating. *Through a Glass Darkly* is an exploration of the ways in which the spiritual world can infuse (and take over) a person. From the outside, it seems as if Karin is going mad. She is seen listening to the walls in the attic (the film was originally entitled *The Wallpaper*).

She confesses that she finds it difficult to keep moving between the two worlds (suggesting that for her crossing thresholds is as problematic as being in each of the worlds. One aspect of Karin's condition isn't noted in the film: the relation between her unstable state and 'women's' issues such as menstruation).

Ingmar Bergman's use of camera and staging meant that both viewpoints – Karin's intense innerness and David and Martin's detached objectivity – were given equal weight (and not forgetting Minu's confusion and sexual anxiety). The film does not side with any of the four people, nor with the medical establishment against individual spirituality. Bergman wrote that the film 'was a desperate attempt to present a simple philosophy: God is love and love is God. A person surrounded by Love is also surrounded by God' (1994, 248).

Critics saw *Through a Glass Darkly* as Ingmar Bergman becoming increasingly disillusioned with his Lutheran religious upbringing. In *Images* Bergman does say the film seems to represent an end to 'earlier attitudes' (1994, 243). Bergman's biographers point out that Bergman had a severely religious father, a 'severe, distant, often wrathful Lutheran minister, a real Old Testament God of a father, and [Bergman] absorbed his chill upbringing into his marrow.[4]

Bergman is not so keen on seeing *Through a Glass Darkly* as part of a trilogy with *Winter Light* and *The Silence*. Rather, Bergman asserts, *Through a Glass Darkly* is connected thematically with his marriage to Käbi Laretei (the film carries a dedication to his wife right after the opening credits, offering a surprising personal tone to proceedings).

In terms of acting, *Through a Glass Darkly* is a chamber piece, deliberately constructed in terms of chamber music.[5] The acting is powerful, as usual in Bergman's cinema. Max von Sydow is an intense screen presence (though Bergman felt he hadn't given Sydow enough lee-room as an actor). Bergman felt he had messed up Björkstrand's character, the novelist David, putting too much of his autobiography into the part, making it 'a dreadful stew' (1994, 254). But David doesn't come across like that: he's a troubled artist figure, and the autobiographical elements don't upset then narrative. For the part of Minus, Bergman chose a young actor, Lars Passgard, fresh out of drama school, who, Bergman thought, had been too inexperienced to make the character work successfully. (I don't think so: looking at *Through a Glass Darkly* again, Passgard is terrific).

It was Harriet Andersson's presence, however, which made *Through a Glass Darkly* so strong dramatically (she rightly received top billing). Andersson was absolutely brilliant at playing the introspective Karin. Bergman rightly called Andersson's acting 'miraculous', with a 'sonorous musicality', 'a clear tone and a touch of genius' (1994, 256). Andersson transforms the film, helping to turn it into something great. Andersson is in fact playing a character very rarely attempted by the cinema – or any artform: the spiritually possessed woman, the mystic. 'What I wanted, most deeply,' wrote Bergman in 1994, 'was to depict a case of religious hysteria or, if you will, a schizophrenic individual with heavily religious tendencies' (1994, 252).

Making the one who experiences God female alters the effect of the film: the masculine response to the numinous one knows about: the feminine experience of it is much less well-known (note that most of Tarkovsky's religious or visionary figures are male, and are usually older than Karin's character). There have been, though, many female mystics through the ages, who have contributed lyrically and significantly to the tradition of mysticism: such as Catherine of Genoa, St Teresa of Avila and Hildegaard of Bingen. These female mystics wrote poetically and lucidly about their passionate spiritual experiences. Some of the most ecstatic writing in history has been by women mystics.

For feminists, 'woman' is, like the poet (or artist), a shaman, a witch, a magician, moving beyond the symbolic/ œdipal/ patriarchal order; 'the female is the initiatrix' wrote Alex Comfort (96). This is a continuing theme in the writings of Julia Kristeva. In "The True-Real" ("Le vréel") she writes:

> We know… how logic and ontology have inscribed the question of *truth* within *judgement* (or sentence structure) and *being*, dismissing as *madness, mysticism or poetry* any attempt to articulate that impossible element which henceforth can only be designated by the Lacanian category of the *real*. After the flowering of mysticism, classical rationality, first by embracing Folly with Erasmus, and then by excluding it with Descartes, attempted to enunciate the real as truth by setting limits on Madness; modernity, on the other hand, opens up this enclosure in a search for other forms capable of transforming or rehabilitating the statues of *truth*. (1986, 217)

Feminists such as Luce Irigaray and Julia Kristeva have been concerned with the notion of 'woman' as 'outsider', of the otherness and outsideness of women in a patriarchal regime. The feminine, remarked Luce Irigaray, 'had to be deciphered as forbidden'.[6] Kristeva and Irigaray, among other French feminists, have spoken of something in 'women' or the 'feminine' that is 'unrepresentable', beyond art, beyond male culture. 'Woman' is always negative, always outside the symbolic realm; 'woman' 'isn't this (can't be defined), it isn't yet that (isn't yet here)'.[7]

Much of Tarkovsky's cinema pivots around the fear and desire of the mother, the symbolic other. The father is often absent from the screen, but is present as an ordering law in the voiceovers or poetry. Tarkovsky further conflates the Freudian-Lacanian œdipal scenario by using the poems of his actual father.

Hélène Cixous wrote in "The Laugh of the Medusa" of women as outsiders or witches, living in the unconscious or the wilderness, who must return 'from afar, from always: from "without", from the heath where witches are kept alive; from below, from "beyond" culture'.[8]

Irigaray depicts 'woman' as philosophy's 'other', so she is interested in those women who have been 'outsiders' in history – the hysteric, the witch, the mediæval mystic, those people who 'stand outside' culture, using the techniques of ecstasy (or 'ex-stase', as Irigaray spells it; *ex-tase*, from the Greek, meaning 'standing outside'). Tarkovsky's cinema is peopled by a few female outsiders: the 'pagan' woman or witch in *Andrei Roublyov*; the Stalker's daughter; the 'witch' in *The Sacrifice*. Both Irigaray and Kristeva spoke of the special creative positionality of the mediæval women mystics, who occupied the maternal liminal place of the mother, where the object of devotion became less fixed, more open, less dogmatic, more 'feminine'. The female mystic may be able to stand outside of (patriarchal) scopic representation, by being ecstatic. The ecstatic experience of mysticism appears to escape (masculine) specularization, its voyeurism and rationality.[9]

For Kristeva, Christianity offered a limited number of ways in which women can participate in the 'symbolic Christian order': for women who are not virgins or nuns, who have orgasms and give birth

> her only means of gaining access to the symbolic paternal order is by engaging in an endless struggle between the orgasmic maternal body and the symbolic prohibition – a struggle that will take the form of guilt and mortification, and culminate in masochistic *jouissance*. For a woman who has not easily repressed her relationship with her mother, participation in the symbolic paternal order as Christianity defines it can only be masochistic. (1987, 147)

Two of the classic ways in which women have been allowed to participate in Christianity is the '*ecstatic* and the *melancholy*' (ib.). According to Elizabeth Grosz, women can disavow their own castration (*contra* Freud) through hysteria – women phallicizing part of their bodies; the 'masculine complex' – women taking the phallus as their love object, and narcissism – women turning their bodies into the phallus.[10]

In Ingmar Bergman's film *Through a Glass Darkly* there is an exploration of such a female outsider figure. The wallpaper in the attic functions as the border of a sacred zone in which Karin might 'stand outside' ('ex-stase') the profane, everyday world. In *Through a Glass Darkly* one sees a woman exploring the limits of her world, in silent sequences where Karin is shown leaning against the wall, and later undergoing a paroxysm (which appears close to orgasmic pleasure or masturbation).

Karin is held in check by those who would guard her against herself – the patriarchal world of David and Martin. Karin's inner world is forbidden by the men, it is unknown, mysterious, and to them potentially harmful. Bergman adds an element of eroticism to the spiritual struggle: Andersson's 'miraculous' playing of the part generates a sexual tension in the film between the characters (between Karin and all of the male characters: there's the sexual frustration between Karin and Martin, the incestuous eroticism between Karin and Martin, and Karin playing the loving daughter to David: she sits on his lap, and is tucked up in his bed like a child when she's unable to sleep). And Andersson has never been more attractive on screen – except perhaps in the equally astonishing *Summer With Monika*.

The god who 'descends into her', Bergman explained, also descends into her brother Minus (that fascinating remark alters a conventional reading of the film, which would see Karin as the only mentally unstable character. Actually, as in other Bergman films, all of the characters are unstable in some way or other. They all have their demons to cope with).

As Minus begins to act oddly, the brother and sister are drawn to each other. In scenes such as in the shipwreck an incestuous bond is depicted between brother and sister. (The erotic connection between Minus and Karin was suggested a no. of times prior to this scene: (1) when Minus railed at Karin for appearing near him half-naked, and he didn't know what to do with the erotic desires she inspired; 2) when Karin embraces Minus and kisses him, in a fashion a little too close and friendly for siblings; and (3) when Karin snatches up a pornographic magazine Minus is reading, when he's supposed to be studying Latin, and they discuss the women in it).

That Minus and Karin make love is unmistakable: both Minus and Karin confirm it afterwards in their dialogue and acts (note how they tell their father David, not Martin). Bergman also employs a classic trope at the moment they (rather aggressively) embrace: he cuts to heavy rainfall, a clichéd sexual motif (as the rain stops, afterwards, Bergman holds on a long shot of the two young people on the floor of the tilting boat; the sun comes out; the framing, the sun and the rain stopping recalls the climax of *Stalker*.)

Through a Glass Darkly is filmed in dark, sombre black-and-white, at times incredibly beautiful and luminous (Sven Nykvist's cinematography was never better). Sequences such as Minus and Karin fetching the milk beside the sea or in the wrecked ship are as haunting as cinema ever gets. The *mise-en-scène* is masterfully controlled: the isolated house, the stony beach, the wooden jetty, the fishing nets, the garden, the attic. Bergman's use of twilights is particularly expressive in *Through a Glass Darkly* – as if at times the film were shot through a dark glass (the long twilights and half-lights of Sweden have never been exploited more poetically in a film). The soundscape, too, is haunting: foghorns of passing ships; heavy rain; distant birdsong; Harriet Andersson's screams; and the helicopter, when it comes, is a terrifying, loud mechanical sound.

There are spectacular moments in *Through a Glass Darkly*, too – in the climactic sequence when the helicopter descends as a spider-like shadow through the window, for example. Karin regards the god inside the wall as a spider towards the end of the film, as her descent into 'insanity' deepens (the door opens – all by itself, as in a Tarkovsky film – but a spider, not God, comes forth). The use of the helicopter as a spider-god at this point might have misfired badly, but Bergman pulls it off (by, for a start, not dwelling on it, by using the motif very briefly: there are two shots only of the helicopter, if memory serves: its presence is all the more powerful for being invoked through sound effects). The 'meaning' of scenes such fetching the milk is not clear: something to do with the lost maternal realm, perhaps, the bond between brother and sister in childhood, for milk often stands in for the lost mother (think of the use of milk in Tarkovsky's *Mirror*, which is later shattered by the roaring jets overhead in *The Sacrifice*).

There are numerous correspondences between *Through a Glass Darkly* and *The Sacrifice*: (I) both are chamber pieces; (2) both are set in isolated Swedish houses beside the sea; (3) both have scenes set on the shore; (4) both occur in a contemporary setting; (5) both are performed in Swedish; (6) both films are investigations into ontology and religion; (7) both are directed by filmmakers in the European art film tradition; (8) both films centre on an artist (writer and actor respectively) re-assessing their lives and their art; (9) both films hint (or depict) at incest (Minus and Karin in *Through a Glass Darkly*; Martha and the father-surrogate, Victor, in *The Sacrifice*); (10) both films use Johann Sebastian Bach's music; (11) in both films two men drug hysterical woman (the reaction of patriarchal figures is to control feminine wildness with tranquilizers); (12) both films have problematic relations between fathers and sons; (13) in both films fathers toy with suicide; (14) both films are shot by the same cinematographer, Sven Nykvist, in locations near each other; (15) there are further similarities of mood, time-scale, isolation, despair, symbolism, realism, other-worldliness, violence and passion.

Both *Through a Glass Darkly* and *The Sacrifice* end with a son affirming his relation with his father, and both affirmations pivot around language: 'Daddy talked to me' says the amazed Minus, with a sunset out of the doomed Romantic painter Caspar David Friedrich behind him; 'in the beginning was the Word; why is that, Papa?' asks Little Man at the end of *The Sacrifice*. In both endings the father gives the blessing of lingual expression to the son (the 'Name of the Father'). Both films close with the main character being taken away by the medical authorities. Both *Through a Glass Darkly* and *The Sacrifice* end on a note of optimism, and rebirth. Both final images are of the sun/ son shining onto the sea.

For some critics, the extraordinary epilogue of *Through a Glass Darkly* seems to be tacked on the end: the film should finish with Karin being taken away by the helicopter. But Minus's line, 'Daddy spoke to me!', is a marvellous articulation of œdipal tension and the entry into the symbolic realm, the Law of the Father. Bergman admitted that this line 'was written out of my need to be didactic' (1994, 243), and has regarded the epilogue as disappointing (again, I think he's being too hard on himself). In a way, then, in *The Sacrifice* Tarkovsky 'does' Bergman, films a sequel to Bergman, moving into distinctly Bergmanesque territory, with Bergman-esque themes, images, landscapes, and motifs, and filmed using key Bergman collaborators.

The correspondences between Andrei Tarkovsky and Ingmar Bergman can be applied to other films – to *The Virgin Spring*, or *Shame*, for instance. In *The Silence* (1963) Anna and Ester, two sisters, share an embrace (and suggested lesbian desire) beside a window and sitting on a bed which recalls the women in *Nostalghia* during Andrei's dream; much of *The Silence* is shot from a ten year-old boy's point-of-view, via low angle tracking shots, which recall the use of children in Tarkovsky's cinema – particularly *Mirror*, *Nostalghia* and *The Sacrifice*.

Bergman went further than Tarkovsky into investigating issues of gender, sexuality, women and women's mysteries. Bergman was an atheist; Tarkovsky was a believer. Both exalted the classics, and especially Shakespeare. Both directed theatrical performances of Shakespeare (though Bergman worked far more extensively in the theatre than Tarkovsky, and Bergman was by far the more prolific, in film, writing and theatre). Both have been fêted as great (European) art cinema *auteurs*. Both wrote as well as directed. Both were ambiguous in their final statements, but Tarkovsky ended up being the more hopeful for humanity. Bergman was the greater dramatist, the better organizer of actors and ensembles, while Tarkovsky's visual sense was as sharp, precise, and incisive as Bergman's. Both artists disliked analyzing their films, and sidestepped questions about their philosophies and intentions. But Tarkovsky, in *Sculpting in Time*, made statements about cinema and life Bergman would never make.

Tarkovsky's friend and collaborator, Andrei Konchalovsky, reckoned that in his later films Tarkovsky too obviously tried to emulate Ingmar Bergman, but lacked Bergman's genius with scriptwriting, with literary concepts, and with complex psychological characterization. It might be significant that Bergman and Tarkovsky chose not to meet when Tarkovsky was in Sweden shooting *The Sacrifice*.

2 : 12   ANDREI TARKOVSKY AND CARL THEODORE DREYER

There are obvious comparisons to be made between the cinema of Andrei Tarkovsky and Carl Theodore Dreyer – particularly Dreyer's *Ordet* and *The Sacrifice* and *Nostalghia*: the lengthy takes; the slowly drifting camera; the sparse sets; the use of offscreen sound; the chamber piece/ ensemble acting; the sense of the miraculous; and the Christian symbolism. Also, like Tarkovsky, Dreyer planned many films that never got made. After *The Passion of Joan of Arc* (1928), one of the great religious films, Dreyer only made four features: *Vampyr* (1932), *Day of Wrath* (1943), *Ordet* (1954) and *Gertrud* (1964), each one an undisputed masterpiece. The achievement of Dreyer, as with Tarkovsky, becomes greater, in a way, for having made so few films. One can see Dreyer's influence not only in the cinema of Tarkovsky, but also in Jean-Luc Godard, Ingmar Bergman, Andy Warhol, Robert

Bresson, Paul Shrader and William Friedkin.

Carl Dreyer's *Ordet* (1954) is an intense religious drama, based on the play by Kaj Munk. There are many affinities with *The Sacrifice*. *Ordet* is set in an austere rural Scandinavian *milieu*, familiar from the cinema of Ingmar Bergman. A chamber piece, *Ordet* is built around a lyrical depiction of the family: Borgen the aging, bearded patriarch and head of the family; the earnest, stalwart elder son Mikkel; his wife, the kindly Inger; their two children; Anders, the lovelorn youth; plus other figures, such as Karen the maid, the pastor, the doctor, and the rival family, headed by Peter Petersen, with their more ascetic type of Christianity. The most unusual character in *Ordet*, however, is Johannes, a mentally unstable youth who thinks he is Jesus Christ.

There are five plotlines, each concerning a member of the Borgen family; there are three main locations: the Borgen house, Petersen's house, and outdoors (featuring the road, the hearse, and the wagon). Most of the action takes place in the large family room at Borgensgaard, just like a stage set, with the kitchen and bedrooms leading off it. Characters come and go, or sit at the table in silence. They talk in fragments. The camera pans back and forth across this space, following actors, and sometimes not following them, stopping at various points: the sickroom, the telephone, the table, the door, the chest, the yarn chair, the window, and Anders' room.

Johannes wanders in and out from time to time, looking blankly into the distance, and mouthing Christian tenets or quotations from the *Bible* (like the 'holy fools' in Tarkovsky's cinema, such as the Stalker, who quotes from the *Bible* in the central section of *Stalker*, or Domenico in *Nostalghia*). The background explanation is that Johannes was studying theology, encouraged by his father, but was derailed by books (Johannes' fate recalls that of the German Romantic poet Friedrich Hölderlin, who underwent spiritual and psychological crises in his youth after writing some of the most sublime poetry in world literature. Hölderlin's tragedy left him insane for the rest of his life. It's as if Hölderlin was too sensitive, too refined, or lived in too rarefied a spiritual atmosphere to survive in this world).

The crisis in *Ordet* comes when Inger is about to give birth; this is a lengthy and painful sequence, with the (mainly male) characters pacing about behind Inger's prostrate form; her face is not shown much — instead, her gasps of pain are heard. Dreyer said he cut two-thirds of the Munk's play's dialogue, and extended the length of the play from a hundred minutes, when it was adapted by Mollander in 1943, to 129 minutes.

Like the films of Andrei Tarkovsky and Ingmar Bergman, Carl Dreyer's *Ordet* is soaked in Christian themes and symbols. *Ordet*, which literally means 'The Word', is partly about the power of language to transform life (echoing the prologue of *Mirror*). Johannes resurrects Inger with the (holy) word; he tells Inger's daughter Maren that her mother will arise when he says the name of the Lord. In a film of few words, when dialogue is spoken it resonates deeply. The climax is very moving, as all the characters in the film gather around the open coffin of Inger; Johannes, who has disappeared, inevitably returns. Then comes the resurrection, the longed-for miracle, an extraordinary moment, where Inger revives, moves her hands, then sits up, embraced by Mikkel. It is the child, Maren, who has the requisite amount of faith, the pure belief in Johannes, that he can bring Inger back to life. The moment is an epiphany, very simply done, but very emotional. Inger clasps Mikkel to her. The last images of *Ordet* are of the couple's faces pressed against each other, with Inger speaking of 'life... life'. One of Tarkovsky's father's memorable poems is entitled 'Life, Life', the opening stanza of which runs:

I don't believe in omens or fear
Forebodings. I flee from neither slander
Nor from poison. Death does not exist.
Everyone's immortal. Everything is too.
No point in fearing death at seventeen,
Or seventy. There's only here and now, and light;
Neither death, nor darkness, exists.
We're all already on the seashore;
I'm one of those who'll be hauling in the nets
When a shoal of immortality swims by. (in 1999)

Before this, the sub-plots of *Ordet* are tied up: Anders is granted permission to marry Anne, Mikkel regains his faith, and Borgen and Petersen are reconciled. In the last moments, Anders goes to the clock of the wall and moves the hands, as time is symbolically restarted.

The sound in *Ordet* consists of selective noises, many of them offscreen, as in Tarkovsky's cinema: the sound of the wind outside; the loud bleats of sheep or grunts of pigs; the agonized gasps and sighs of Inger, whenever the door to her room is opened; the loud ticking of the clocks, which are stopped when Inger dies. The black-and-white camerawork (by Henning Bendtsen) is lyrical and distanced: medium shots are favoured, with the camera tracking laterally and slowly, as in Tarkovsky's films. There are some beautiful compositions – the grassy dunes, for example, with the line of washing flapping in the wind and the cloudy sky behind. There are many long takes (about 114 shots in a 126 minute film, a comparable statistic with Tarkovsky's later films; contemporary movies have ten or twenty times that amount). Consequently, the viewer is given much time to study the actors and their ascetic surroundings. The average shot length is one-and-a-half minutes, with the longest shot at seven minutes (very unusual for the time *Ordet* was made, but still rare when Tarkovsky was making films from the 1960s and 1980s). *Ordet* is a film of near-empty spaces, both visually and aurally. The dialogue carries extra weight for being so sparse.

THREE

Andrei Tarkovsky and the Religious Film

Comparing Andrei Tarkovsky's films with other religious films is an illuminating exercise. His films turn out to be quite different from the usual kind of religious cinema. Films of the Christian story, based on the *New Testament*, have generally taken a pious, slavish tack, being as faithful and reverential to the *Gospels* as possible, whether in D.W. Griffith's *Intolerance*, or Cecil B. DeMille's *King of Kings* (1927).

Movies featuring Christ include *From the Manger to the Cross* (1912), *Civilisation* (1916), *Intolerance* (1916), *King of Kings* (1927), *Golgotha* (a.k.a *Ecce Homo*, 1935), *Day of Triumph* (1954), *Kings of Kings* (1961), *The Greatest Story Ever Told* (1965), *The Gospel According to Matthew* (1964), *The Milky Way* (1969), *Godspell* (1973), *Jesus Christ Superstar* (1973), *Jesus of Nazareth* (1977), *The Jesus Film* (1979), *The Day Christ Died* (1980), *Jesus of Montreal* (1989), *The Last Temptation of Christ* (1988), *The Garden of Eden* (1998) and *The Passion of the Christ* (2004). Jesus and his influence is featured in many films, including *Ben-Hur* (1959), *The Last Days of Pompeii* (1935), *Barabbas* (1961), *The Wandering Jew* (1933), *The Robe* (1953), *Quo Vadis?* (1951), *Life of Brian*

(1979) and *Bad Lieutenant* (1992).[1]

There have been many Christs in Hollywood's history: Robert Henderson-Bland, Robert le Vigan, George Fisher, H.B. Warner, Robert Wilson, Howard Gaye, Jeffrey Hunter, Max von Sydow, Chris Sarandon, Brian Deacon, Bernard Verley, Robert Powell, Ted Neely, Victor Garber, Willem Dafoe and Jim Caviezel. Except in films by idiosyncratic artists such as Luis Buñuel or Kenneth Anger, Christ is pretty much as he appears in the *Gospels* (no mainstream Hollywood films have been as critical of Christ and Christianity as those of Buñuel or Anger).

Choosing the right actor to play Christ was crucial: note that in *The Greatest Story Ever Told* (1965), *Jesus of Nazareth* (1977), *The Jesus Film* (1979), *The Passion of the Christ* (2004) and *Jesus of Montreal* (1989), European actors were chosen (von Sydow, Caviezel and Powell, and French-Canadian Lothaire Bluteau in the latter film). Jeffrey Hunter (in *King of Kings* [1961]) was derided as being a teen pin-up Jesus. When American actors were chosen, it was often not one of the major stars (as with Dafoe). One would not expect, in the 1950s and 1960s, Gary Cooper or Clark Gable being cast as Jesus. The dramatic device of not showing Christ was occasionally deployed; *Ben-Hur* (1959) offered the most famous example, with actors (principally Chuck Heston) seen reacting to him. Director William Wyler said he wanted 'not the face or the person at any time, but rather show the effect on other people'.[2]

Every actor playing Jesus had to contend with a thousand and a half years of religious art depicting the Saviour. Much of this sacred art was the pinnacle of achievement in Western art and was widely known (such as Leonardo da Vinci, Masaccio, Botticelli, Michelangelo, Rembrandt and Rubens). The actor playing Christ had to suggest both the humanity and the divinity of the man, and why he had launched a powerful two thousand year-old religion. Generally, most Hollywood films assumed that Jesus was divine. Jon Solomon outlined some of the problems of portraying Christ:

> He must be a believable human, yet he must reveal his divine spirit; he must stand above humans and never sway from his purpose, yet he must fall victim to human misunderstanding and have his brief moments of emotional doubt and physical pain. He must be able to soothe and heal the meek and suffering, yet he must be capable of terrifying an entire religious establishment and of single-handedly overturning the market inside the Jerusalem temple. He must boldly walk across the water, yet meekly be whipped and spat on by his adversaries. He must know that he is the Son of Man, yet he must be able to plead, "My God, why has thou

forsaken me?" (2001, 178)

How to portray Christ's divinity was also a huge challenge for actors and filmmakers. Most actors tended to hold back and speak quietly, letting the huge cultural
capital that had accumulated around Christianity do the talking (it's not so much
the lead role as all those around Jesus that really count in terms of portraying his
divinity). For the Hollywood entertainment film, Jesus must be played by a star (or
at least a very good actor); using a total unknown, with no acting experience, as Pier
Paolo Pasolini did, is not an option (Pasolini's casting was an immense gamble, which
paid off – although Enrique Irazoqui was voiced by another actor). The star must
have the right kind of appeal, looks, aura and identity, and must be associated with
the right sort of films in the audience's mind. An actor linked with playing vicious
villains, for example, would probably not be used.

Another problem is that Jesus is not a typical leading man – no action hero, with
no romantic interest, no sexual relations, no vices and few flaws.[3] A passive pacifist,
Jesus tends to react to people around him, his energy's directed inwards. Consequently, many Christ films tend to concentrate more on other characters, such as
Judas, Barabbas, Pilate, Peter or Mary Magdalene (there have been one or two rare
attempts, notably by Pasolini and Scorsese, to make Jesus more dynamic). When
Tarkovsky depicted Christ, in *Andrei Roublyov*, he made no attempt at evoking the
son of God's divine status. Rather, Tarkovsky's Jesus was very much in the earthy
mold of Pasolini: a man carrying a Cross, walking in snow (and eating snow). Just a
man, not saintly, not a god.

Films of the *Gospels* have to adhere to certain formal constraints, to having
events and people portrayed in a conventional way. For example, the Crucifixion has
to be staged largely according to traditions; the casting has to conform with
traditional views; as does the kind of performance, the vocabulary, idioms and
language used, the use of music, and so on. Renaissance art and Victorian illustration
determine much of the visual representation of the Christ story in films. In Britain,
for instance, the presentation of Jesus on film was banned from the time of the
BBFC's formation in 1912 to after World War 2.

The miracles of Christ offer a challenge to the filmmaker, and how s/he thinks
the story of Jesus ought to be portrayed. Are they going to be 'naturalistic'? Or done
with special effects? Or camera trickery? How the miracles are handled by a
filmmaker in a way shows how they view the whole Christian story. Martin

Scorsese and Pier Paolo Pasolini, for example, thought carefully about how to portray the miracles. Scorsese showed four, with two of them playfully portrayed.[4] The one aspect of the *Gospels* that cannot be fudged is the Resurrection, for this demonstrates Christ's divinity. The Resurrection was the most controversial aspect of *The Last Temptation of Christ* (1988), while *The Passion of the Christ* (2004) focussed obsessively on the flagellation and torture of Jesus to a pathologically explicit degree.

Discussing Christ isn't out of place at all in relation to Tarkovsky's cinema. Even when his films don't depict or refer to or discuss Christ directly, they are dealing with messianic and Christological issues. In his diaries, Tarkovsky railed against the corruption and barbarity of the modern world, and reckoned that only a 'genius who will formulate a new moral ideal' could save the world (D, 16), someone who could protest and bring about a new heresy to topple 'our wretched, barbaric world'. And religious, moral protest does occur in Tarkovsky's films – in the figures of the Stalker, Domenico, and Alexander in the later films, for instance. They are definitely not messiahs, but they are preaching a moral protest about saving the world.

The Hollywood Biblical epic movie in the early days of cinema included D.W. Griffiths' *Intolerance* and Cecil B. DeMille's films of the 1920s and 1930s. DeMille's *Samson and Delilah* (1949) revived the Biblical epic: subsequent Biblical and historical epics included *Quo Vadis, The Robe, Ben Hur, Spartacus, The Fall of the Roman Empire, David and Bathsheba, The Ten Commandments, Lawrence of Arabia, Doctor Zhivago, Cleopatra, Land of the Pharaohs, El Cid* and *Ivanhoe*. Cecil B. DeMille's extravagant remake of his own *The Ten Commandments* cost $13 million and used 25,000 extras. Some of the historical blockbusters showcased the new widescreen and sound technologies of the 1950s (such as *The Robe, Ben-Hur, Spartacus* and *The Fall of the Roman Empire*). The disaster of *Cleopatra* signalled the end of the Biblical/ historical epic film. *Cleopatra* had gone through many scriptwriters and various directors, but no amount of money spent on its lavish sets, or actors, or directors and writers, could save it. Darryl and Richard Zanuck were brought in to rescue Fox after its $40 million flop, which they did with *The Sound of Music*. Subsequent big budget musicals which tried to emulate *The Sound of Music*'s success, flopped, however (*Star!, Hello, Dolly!* and *Dr Doolittle*). Tark-ovsky was dismissive (and patronizing) about films like *Cleopatra*: 'that's a commercial spectacle intended to impress the imagination of simple people'. Cinema for Tarkovsky was high art, not entertainment.

Ancient world epics were among the first genres of cinema: films with Classical, ancient or mythological themes were being produced in the early 1900s, only a few years after cinema's invention. One reason is that ancient subjects were very much in the air – Shakespeare, the *Bible*, and best-selling novels such as *Quo Vadis?*, *The Last Days of Pompeii* and *Ben-Hur*.

The first wave of Biblical/ Roman/ ancient film epics began with the films of D.W. Griffith (particularly *Intolerance*, 1916, with Lillian Gish, Robert Harron and Mae Marsh), *Noah's Ark* (Michael Curtiz, 1929), with Dolores Costello, George O'Brien and Noah Berry Sr., the early Italian epics, and the films of Cecil B. DeMille (such as *The Ten Commandments*, [1923], *The King of Kings* [1927], and *The Sign of the Cross* [1932]). The Italian 'super-spectacles' included *Nero* (1909), *The Virgin of Babylon* (1910), *Hero and Leander* (1910), *The Slave of Carthage* (1910), *The Queen of Nineveh* (1911), *Spartacus* (1913), *The Martyr of Pompeii*, 1909), *Sardanapalus, King of Assyria* (1910), *Oedipus Rex* (1910), *The Odyssey* (1911), *Brutus* (1910), *Agrippina* (1910), *Marcantonio e Cleopatra* (1913), *Caius Julius Caesar* (1914), *Catilina* (1910), *Giulio Cesare* (1909), *The Fall of Troy* (1911), *Rameses, King of Egypt* (1912), *Christus* (1915), *One Vestale Virgin* (1909), *Attila* (1916), *The Triumph of the Emperor* (1914), *David* (1923) and *Salambo* (1914). Three of the most celebrated epics of the Italian Golden Age were *The Last Days of Pompeii* (1911), *Cabiria* (1914) and *Quo Vadis* (1912); the key directors included Arturo Ambrosio, Luigi Maggi, Ernesto Pasquali, Giuseppe De Liguoro, Enrico Guazzoni, Mario Caserini and Giovanni Pastrone. The gigantic production *Cabiria* featured Hannibal crossing the Alps, the sack of Carthage, and the Roman fleet burning at Syracuse. It was shot in North Africa, Sicily and Rome.

The second wave or 'golden age' of Hollywood's Biblical epics began with DeMille's *Samson and Delilah* (1949), with Victor Mature and Hedy Lamarr, *Quo Vadis?* (Mervyn LeRoy, 1951), with Peter Ustinov, Deborah Kerr and Robert Taylor, and *The Robe* (Henry Koster, 1953), with Victor Mature, Jean Simmons and Richard Burton. *Samson and Delilah* was the film that really kick-started the revival. The renascence of the ancient epic continued with *The Ten Commandments* (1956), Cecil B. DeMille's massive, mega-budget remake of his earlier film, with Charlton Heston (as Moses), Edward G. Robinson, Yul Brynner, Vincent Price and Anne Baxter, *Sins of Jezebel* (1953), *David and Bathsheba* (1951), *Sodom and Gomorrah* (Robert Aldrich, 1962), with Stewart Granger, Stanley Baker and

Anouk Aimée, *Esther and the King* (1960), *Hannibal* (1960), *Ben-Hur* (William Wyler, 1959), with Chuck Heston, Stephen Boyd, Jack Hawkins, Hugh Griffith and Haya Hareet, *Jesus of Nazareth* (Franco Zeffirelli, 1977), with Robert Powell and an 'all-star cast', *Barabbas* (Richard Fleischer, 1961), with Anthony Quinn, Vittorio Gassman, Silvana Mangano, Jack Palance and Ernest Borgnine, *The Greatest Story Ever Told* (George Stevens, 1965), with Max Von Sydow, Carroll Baker, Jose Ferrer, Charlton Heston, Telly Savalas and Sidney Poitier, *Serpent of the Nile* (1953), *Slaves of Babylon* (1953), *Spartacus* (Stanley Kubrick, 1960), with Kirk Douglas, Tony Curtis, Peter Ustinov, Laurence Olivier, Charles Laughton, and Jean Simmons, *Moses* (Gianfranco De Bosio, 1975), a British/Italian TV co-production with Burt Lancaster and Anthony Quayle, and *Cleopatra* (Joseph L. Mankiewicz, 1963), with Liz Taylor, Richard Burton, Roddy McDowall and Rex Harrison.

After the mid-1960s, few Biblical epic films were made. Italy also produced ancient world epics, directed by people such as Sergeo Leone, Mario Bara, Pietro Francisci, Vittorio Cottagari and Sergio Corbucci. Movies such as John Huston's *The Bible* (1966) and George Stevens' *The Greatest Story Ever Told* (1965) were the last of the big budget, all-star cast Hollywood Biblical extravaganzas, until the 1980s and films such as *King David* (Bruce Beresford, 1985), with Richard Gere, Edward Woodward, Denis Quilley and Alice Krige, *The Last Temptation of Christ* (Martin Scorsese, 1988), with Willem Dafoe, Barbara Hershey, Harvey Keitel, Harry Dean Stanton and David Bowie, and *The Passion of the Christ* (2004), Mel Gibson's violent, visceral exploration of the last hours in Jesus's life.[9]

From the beginning, Biblical/Roman/ancient world films were important box office draws: according to Joel Finler, the rentals for the early *Ben-Hur* were $4.5 million, $2.5 million for *The Ten Commandments*, and $1.5 million for *The King of Kings*, placing them 4th, 11th and 27th in the box office for 1914-31.[5] During the 'second wave' of Hollywood Roman/Biblical/ancient world epics, pictures such as *Samson and Delilah* and *Spartacus* were the number one box office draw (*Samson and Delilah*, in 1950, grossing $9 million, and *Spartacus* in 1960). *David and Bathsheba* (Henry King, 1952) was the most successful film of 1951; *Quo Vadis?* made $11 million and was the top film in 1952; *The Robe* grossed $17 million in 1953; DeMille's *The Ten Commandments*, which cost $13.5 million, made $43 million in 1956; *Ben-Hur* took even more. In the 1950s, Biblical and ancient world films took three out of the four top places in rentals: *Ben-Hur* was in first place, *The*

Ten Commandments was second and *The Robe* was fourth.

In the early 1960s, with production costs rising, Biblical/ Roman epics were still being made, but with diminishing returns. Four of the five top films of 1963 were epics (*Cleopatra, Lawrence of Arabia, How the West Was Won* and *The Longest Day*), but they were secular subjects. Films such as *The Bible, The Fall of the Roman Empire, Cleopatra* and *The Greatest Story Ever Told* were financial disasters, taking years to recoup their costs (if at all). *The Greatest Story Ever Told*, for example, cost $20 million but took $6.9 million.

The visual reference point for the Biblical and ancient era epic was the Italian Renaissance; not just in the depictions of the Crucifixion or the Madonna and Child, but in the depiction of the whole ancient world. Of course, modern American cinema is overtly secular (is any industry more secular?), while the Renaissance produced mainly religious art. Both artforms enshrine the artist; both cultures were awash with money; 'the aristocratic humanist, proto-capitalist culture of the Italian Ren-aissance and the populist, individualist-capitalist culture of 20th century America are like in their confident accommodation of religion and capitalist (proto-capitalist) ideologies' commented P. Babington and P. Evans.[6]

Babington and Evans define three main types of Biblical, sword-and-sandal epic: (1) Old Testament films; (2) films concerning Jesus; and (3) Roman/ Christian films (1993, 4). Old Testament films are quite different from New Testament ones: the New Testament is dominated by the figure of Christ, and consists of four *Gospels*, set in one small country (Palestine), and a few miracles. The Old Testament, by con-trast, has patriarchs, heroes, battles, exoduses, and miracles, in countries including Egypt, Syria, Beersheba and Mesopotamia.

In the Biblical, Roman or historical dramas, Claudette Colbert as Cleopatra lang-uished in asses' milk; Rita Hayworth as Salomé danced before Charles Laughton; Kirk Douglas sailed the Mediterranean as Ulysses or fought in the arena as Spartacus; James Robertson Justice built pyramids for Jack Hawkins' pharaoh; Peter Ustinov giggled as Nero; and Charlton Heston intoned mightily in beard and sandals as Moses, Ben-Hur and Noah.

Typical venues of the historical epic were the Circus Maximus, the Roman Forum, the gladiatorial arena, the Pyramids, the Avenue of Sphinxes, the Norman castle, Sherwood Forest, the Temple of Solomon, Golgotha, the enormous battle-field, and any number of palaces and state rooms. Biblical/ Roman/ ancient epics often began with a solemn prologue, with a voiceover explaining the historical situation (typically voiced by theatrical actors such as Laurence Olivier, Richard Burton or Orson Welles). In the Roman epics, the favoured time period was from the death of Jesus to around 64 A.D., when the first Christians were persecuted. Though the Roman films were not centred in the *Bible* or scripture, Christianity was often referred to, sometimes with Christ appearing in an indirect fashion (as in *Ben-Hur, Barabbas* [1961] and *Salome* [William Dieterle, 1953]), sometimes with a Roman turning to the new religion (as in *The Robe*). Aspects of the Old Testament epic included: the orgy; various ceremonies; extravagant costumes, jewels, furnishings and sets; spectacular architecture; battle scenes; epic, cosmic scenes and acts of God, such as the parting of the Red Sea, the burning bush or various miracles; slavery; sexuality; violence; images of pomp, royalty and empire.

The Biblical/ Roman epics of the 1950s were associated with the introduction of various widescreen technologies. 20th Century Fox's *The Robe* was the first CinemaScope film, and this became part of the film's publicity. By 1957, the CinemaScope process dominated the widescreen market, with 17,644 out of 20,971 screens in the US and Canada converted to it.[7] Note that when Tarkovsky came to make his historical epic, it was made in widescreen (Tarkovsky's only other scope film was *Solaris*). Each widescreen film was treated like a special big budget project. Epic movies advertized their budgets and production values: they were big screen productions portraying large-scale events. In short, 'conspicuous capitalism'.[8]

(Two of Tarkovsky's films were widescreen: *Andrei Roublyov* and *Solaris* – apparently imposed by the studio. Shooting *Andrei Roublyov* in scope can be related directly to the cycle of historical epics of the late 1950s and early 1960s. Tarkovsky was apparently not fond of the widescreen format, and it was the studio who ordered it for his two widescreen films, *Andrei Roublyov* and *Solaris*. Tarkovsky actually preferred the aspect ratio 1.37:1 (the format for *Stalker*, among others). It's a misconception that every filmmaker automatically likes to shoot in widescreen, if possible. Three of the most important American directors of recent years – Steven Spielberg, Woody Allen and Stanley Kubrick – often preferred to shoot in standard 35mm aspect ratios (*Barry Lyndon*, for instance, was shot in the unusual format of 1.66:1).)

Another aspect of the ancient world blockbusters (and the costume and heritage film in general) was their length: *The Ten Commandments* was 3 hours 39 minutes; *Ben-Hur* was 3 hours 37 mins; and *Spartacus* was 3 hrs 16 mins. Tarkovsky followed that penchant for two-and-a-half-hour-plus films from *Andrei Roublyov* onwards (only *Mirror* comes in under two hours).

Roman or 'Hollywood-on-the-Tiber' films include: *Julius Caesar* (Joseph L. Mankiewicz, 1953), a version of Shakespeare's play with John Gielgud, James Mason and Marlon Brando, *The Fall of the Roman Empire* (Anthony Mann, 1964), with Sophia Loren, Stephen Boyd, James Mason, Christopher Plummer, Alec Guinness and Anthony Quayle, *The Robe* (Henry Koster, 1953), *Jupiter's Darling* (George Sidney, 1955), *Coriolanus* (Giorgio Ferroni, 1965), *Brennus, Enemy of Rome* (1960), *The Centurion* (1962), *Goliath and the Rebel Slave Girl* (1963), *The Giants of Rome* (1963), *The Viking Queen* (Don Chaffey, 1967), *A Sword for the Empire* (1965), *Gladiator of Rome* (1962), *Sword of the Conqueror* (Carlo Campogalliani, 1961), *Demetrius and the Gladiators* (Delmer Davies, 1954), with Victor Mature, Susan Hayward, Michael Rennie and Ernest Borgnine, *Quo Vadis?* (Mervyn LeRoy, 1951), *Spartacus* (1960), *The Last Days of Pompeii* (Ernest B. Schoedsack, 1935), with Preston Foster, Basil Rathbone and Alan Hate, *Ben-Hur* (William Wyler, 1959) and *The Sign of the Pagan* (Douglas Sirk, 1954), with Jeff Chandler, Jack Palance and Jeff Morrow.

Films with a predominantly Greek narrative include: *The Colossus of Rhodes* (Sergeo Leone, 1960), *Androcles and the Lion* (1952), *Helen of Troy* (1955), *Atlantis, the Lost Continent* (1961), *Alexander the Great* (Robert Rossen, 1956), *Hercules* (Pietro Francici, 1957), *The 300 Spartans* (Rudolph Maté, 1962), *Jason and the Argonauts* (Don Chaffey, 1963), *The Clash of the Titans* (Desmond Davis, 1981). Late additions to the Greek epic genre included *Troy* (Wolfgang Petersen, 2004), and *Alexander the Great* (Oliver Stone, 2004).

Movies with an ancient Egyptian slant include: *The Land of the Pharaohs* (Howard Hawks, 1955), *Caesar and Cleopatra* (Gabriel Pascal, 1945), from George Bernard Shaw's play, and the film that signalled the beginning of the end of the 1950s-60s spate of sandal epics, *Cleopatra* (1963). Hollywood preferred to film ancient Rome and Egypt and the Biblical lands far more than ancient Greece. It's surprising, perhaps, that Hollywood did not attempt more versions of Homer, the epic writer to top all epic writers. *Ulysses* (Mario Camerini, 1957), starring Kirk Douglas and Sylvana Mangano, was a vastly shortened version of Homer; the Cyclops, Circe, Nausicaa, and the sirens were in, but the Lotus-Eaters, Laestrygones, Calypso, Scylla and Charybdis were left out. The reason for making a film such as *One Million Years BC* (Don Chaffey, 1966) seems to have been exclusively for the purpose of seeing Raquel Welch in an animal skin bikini. The Ray

Harryhausen dinosaurs had serious competition from Welch's pneumatic figure.

The Italian 1957 *Hercules*, starring Steve Reeves, was so successful it inaugurated a series of Italian 'muscle-men' sword-and-sandal epics, some 180 films (*Hercules* cost $120,000, and made $18 million; its budget was less than 1% of that of Hollywood's *Ben-Hur* or *The Ten Commandments*, and less than any of Tarkovsky's films, yet it made somewhere between 1/8th and 1/3rd as much).[10]

Cleopatra's story produced three well-known films (there are others, of course): Cecil B. DeMille's disappointing 1934 epic with Claudette Colbert, Gabriel Pascal's version of George Bernard Shaw's play *Caesar and Cleopatra*, and the 1963 20th Century Fox blockbuster, with Liz Taylor, Richard Burton and Rex Harrison. The 1963 *Cleopatra* contained enormous spectacle: the battles at Actium, Pharsalia, Philippi, and Alexandria, the Egyptian fleet burning at Alexandria, Cleopatra's barge, and the arrival of Cleopatra in Rome, riding atop a gigantic Sphinx, presenting Caesar's son to the cheering Roman hordes. The film was one of those mega-budget films plagued by production problems, including going over schedule, over budget, and going through a number of scriptwriters and directors. As Aubrey Solomon wrote in his financial history of the studio, 20th Century Fox, *Cleopatra* 'took almost four years to make, two directors, two producers, three production heads, two company presidents, and countless writers', and nearly brought down a studio (1988, 140).

Cleopatra's entry into Rome was probably the most elaborate and expensive pageant put on screen: there were tubae players on white horses, racing chariots, slaves throwing red ribbons, oxen, zebras and elephants, 15-foot sistra, men carrying white ostrich-feather fans, winged women, a pyramid float, 300 slaves in 6 rows pulling a porphyry float, carrying the queen and her son, surrounded by 4,500 Italian extras, against a backdrop of a Roman square and an Arch of Constantine.[11]

Hollywood concentrated on a small portion of Roman history – roughly, the first centuries before and after the birth of Christ. It was the Rome of mad emperors (Nero and Caligula), romance, adultery and betrayal (Julius Caesar, Cleopatra and Mark Antony) and plenty of wars and invasions. The emperors were often portrayed as effete, sexually perverted, morally corrupt, childish, over-the-top, tyrannical, superficial, haunted, sinister, cynical and tempermanetal. On the one hand, the Roman world embodied social order, political sophistication, philosophical debate, learning, military discipline and modern luxuries; on the other hand, it was decadent and debauched, based on slavery, fascism, tyranny, given over to gluttony, people lazing around in bathhouses, and orgies. Nascent Christianity offered a feminization of Roman masculine toughness,[12] and an 'authentic', monotheic spirituality compared to Roman plural 'paganism'.

Other Hollywood (or Hollywood-style) historical epic films include the post-Dark Age, mediæval, chivalrous, films: *Ivanhoe* (Richard Thorpe, 1952), *The Adventures of Quentin Durward* (Richard Thorpe, 1955), *Pathfinder* (Nils Gaup, 1987), *The War Lord* (Franklin Schaffner, 1965), *Alfred the Great* (Clive Donner, 1969), *A Touch of Zen* (King Hu, 1969), *Anchoress* (Chris Newby, 1993), *The Navigator* (Vincent Ward, 1988), *The Conqueror* (Dick Powell, 1956), *The Black Knight* (Tay Garnett, 1954), *Siege of the Saxons* (1964), *El Cid* (Anthony Mann, 1961), *The Vikings* (Richard Fleischer, 1958), *The Long Ships* (Jack Cardiff, 1964), *Taras Bulba* (J. Lee Thompson, 1962), *Saladin* (Youssef Chahine, 1963), *Ran* (Akira Kurosawa, 1985), *Galileo* (Joseph Losey, 1974), *The Name of the Rose* (Jean-Jacques Annaud, 1986), *The Lion in Winter* (Anthony Harvey, 1968), *The Lord of the Rings* (Peter Jackson, 2001-03), and *Braveheart* (Mel Gibson, 1995).

King Arthur and Arthurian legend is another sub-genre: *The Knights of the Round Table* (Richard Thorpe, 1953), *Excalibur* (John Boorman, 1981), *Lancelot du Lac* (Robert Bresson, 1974), *Lancelot and Guinevere* (Cornel Wilde, 1962), *The Sword in the Stone* (Wolfgang Reitherman, 1963), *Gawain and the Green Knight* (Stephen Weeks, 1973), *First Knight* (Jerry Zucker, 1995), *A Knight's Tale* (Brian Hegeland, 2001), *King Arthur* (Anton Fuqua, 2004) and *Camelot* (Joshua Logan, 1967). As are the films about Richard the Lionheart and the Crusades (Franklin Schaffner's *Lionheart* [1988] and *Kingdom of Heaven* [2005] were late arrivals).

Other Middle Ages sub-genres include films about Joan of Arc (such as Carl Dreyer's *The Passion of Joan of Arc* [1928], Robert Bresson's *The Trial of Joan of Arc* [1962], and Luc Besson's *Joan of Arc* [1999]); films about saints (such as *Francesco* and *Augustine of Hippo*); films about nuns and monks (*The Devils*); and not forgetting the many Robin Hood movies. Pirate and swashbuckler films are another genre of the costume epic (for example, Louis Hayward in *Fortunes of Captain Blood* [1950] and *Captain Pirate* [1952], or John Derek in *Rogues of Sherwood Forest* [1950], or Tyron Power in *Captain From Castile* [1947], *Prince of Foxes* [1949] and *The Black Rose* [1950], or Tony Curtis in *Son of Ali Baba* [1952], *The Black Shield of Falworth* [1954], *The Purple Mask* [1955] and *The Prince Who Was a Thief* [1951], or Stewart Granger in *Scaramouche* [1952], *Moonfleet* [1955] and *Lo Spadaccino di Siena* [1962]). The Napoleonic era also spawned its own historical genre, which inevitably featured vast battle scenes.[13]

There is also a tradition in the art film of historical films (which Tarkovsky is a part of): Roberto Rossellini's *Francesco* (1950), *Acts of the Apostles* (1969), *Socrates* (1970) and *Augustine of Hippo* (1972), Ken Russell's *The Devils* (1971), Derek Jarman's *Sebastiane* (1976), Ingmar Bergman's *The Virgin Spring* (1959) and *The Seventh Seal* (1957), Luis Magni's *Scipio* (1971), Michael Cacoyannis's *Electra* (1962) and *The Trojan Women* (1971), the films of Robert Bresson (*The Trial of Joan of Arc* [1962] and *Lancelot du Lac* [1974]), Carl Dreyer's films (*The Passion of Joan of Arc* [1928] and *Ordet* [1954]), the films of Luis Buñuel (*Simon of the Desert* [1965] and *Nazarin* [1958]), Akira Kurosawa's films (*Throne of Blood* [1957], *Ran* [1985], *Rashomon* [1951], *Kagemusha* [1980], *The Hidden Fortress* [1958] and *The Seven Samurai* [1954]), and the films of Pier Paolo Pasolini (*The Decameron* [1970], *Medea* [1970], *Oedipus Rex* [1967], *The Canterbury Tales* [1971], *Arabian Nights* [1974], *Theorem* [1968] and *The Gospel According to Matthew* [1965]).

The European art film produced some Biblical and Roman films, though not on the same scale as the Hollywood epics. They often concentrated on saints (St Augustine, St Francis, Joan of Arc, Tarkovsky's proposed St Anthony), rather than Christ himself. Only one or two European directors tried the Christian story itself (Pier Paolo Pasolini being the most obvious – and most successful – example). Italian cinema had a long tradition of making Biblical epics, and directors such as Fellini, Pasolini, Zeffirelli and Rossellini continued it. Rossellini made two films about saints: *Augustine of Hippo* was made for TV in 1972, while *Francesco* (co-written with Fellini), about St Francis and the first Franciscans, was made in 1950. Fellini made his own idiosyncratic, indulgent and over-the-top Roman epic, based on Petronius's *Satyricon*, Nero's cynical poet (who appeared in the 1951 *Quo Vadis*), the work Lawrence Durrell called the 'first European novel'. Fellini's 1969 film (also known as *Fellini-Satyricon*) was a 1st century A.D. romp, a film of excess, featuring sex, debauchery, castration, bisexuality and impotence.

One of Tarkovsky's favourite directors, Luis Buñuel, produced films which tended to explore Christian themes and ideas in more contemporary settings. In *Simón del Desierto* (1965), for example, Simon Stylites is taken from the ancient world to modern-day New York City (*Simon of the Desert* is a truly strange film: the lead character, the saint, spends most of the film on top of a pillar); in *Nazarin* (1958), a priest tries to follow Christ's teachings; in 1961's *Viridiana*, made in

Spain, a nun (Silvia Piñal), tries to help a poor community. *Viridiana* features Buñuel's dark parody of the Last Supper, performed by beggars to Handel's *Messiah*. The Italian director most committed to putting the ancient world in screen was probably Pasolini (his *Gospel According to Matthew* is discussed below); certainly Pasolini made more ancient world films than other Italian directors (and more historical films too).

The Biblical epic films were the Hollywood industry at its excessive, trashiest worst (or best, depending on one's taste) – suddenly the Holy Land looks like California, Italy, the former Yugoslavia or Spain (which is where many of the epics were shot), with expensive sets, and even more expensive stars immaculaterly made-up, dressed and coiffured for the camera to drool over them in soft-focus widescreen close-up. Hollywood's ancient world epics paraded their production budgets on the screen: big stars, big stories, big themes, big set-pieces, big costumes and big sets. A culture of excess and conspicuous consumption, reflecting the aggressive materialism and consumer capitalism of the late 1950s and throughout the 1960s (and Hollywood's own excesses inside the dream factory). The amount of money spent on the screen, the amount of talent required to recreate the ancient worlds, became the subjects of the epic film (M. Wood, 1974). The moments of chaos and destruction were Hollywood's 'ritual expression of a lack of need', symbolizing the 'spectacular waste of American life' (ib.). There were moments of ridicule, too: while Charlton Heston, Jack Hawkins, Stanley Baker, Yul Brynner, Sophia Loren, Jean Simmons and Stephen Boyd (Roman and Biblical epic regulars) were passable or brilliant, there were some silly casting decisions. For example, portly comic actor Robert Morley as a Chinese emperor in *Genghis Khan*; Stewart Granger as Lot in *Sodom and Gomorrah*; Gina Lollobrigida as the Queen of Sheba (*Solomon and Sheba*); and of course the Duke (John Wayne) as a Roman centurion in *The Greatest Story Ever Told* (this latter film has some of most notorious uses of cameos and stars – a common way of using talent from the Sixties onwards).

Costume dramas are full of idiotic dialogue: '[w]ar, War! That's all you think about, Dick Plantagenet!' says Richard the Lionheart's spouse. Some of the performances were outsize and eccentric, in keeping with the epic scale of the subjects: Hugh Griffith as Sheikh Ilderim, the Arabic horse lord in *Ben-Hur*, all eye-popping enthusiasm; or Yul Brynner's Asian warlord in *Taras Bulba*. Some actors were always cast as the bad guys, like Frank Thring. Some performers were always good: Charlton Heston, Yul Brynner, Sophia Loren, Jack Hawkins and Jean

Simmons. An actor such as Heston made historical heroes and leaders a speciality: Heston was Moses in *The Ten Commandments* (a brave decision by DeMille, as Heston was then relatively unknown, and young), El Cid, Abraham Lincoln and of course Ben-Hur. Those sorts of monumental, heroic roles are actually difficult to cast: there are few stars who can carry such roles (then or now).

Nicholas Ray's *King of Kings* was produced by Samuel Bronston and scripted by Philip Yordan, the team that had made *El Cid*. Bronston also made *55 Days at Peking* (1963) and *Circus World* (1964), which he financed by pre-selling distribution rights, a strategy used later for 'ultra high' budget films such as *Terminator 2*. Some of the films were made in Spain because the business investors had money tied up there; many ancient world epics were made in Europe because the Hollywood studios had frozen money tied up there; because labour was cheap; and due to beneficial tax rates (A. Lloyd, 234). The narration for *King of Kings* was written by Ray Bradbury and spoken by Orson Welles. The music was by Miklos Rozsa; it used some 300 sets, 20,000 extras and an $8m budget. It was shot, like so many films of the time, in Spain.

The first half-an-hour of *King of Kings* dwelt on the Romans and Barabbas's lackeys riding around the Spanish hills on horseback – it was a first century A.D. Spaghetti Western: the opening scene concerns the Romans marching into Jerusalem and taking over the Temple (the Roman general rides into the Temple on a horse, then rents the veil of the Temple with his sword before proceeding into the holy of holies). A battle takes up the first act, when the Romans are ambushed by Barabbas's rebels in a rocky valley, turning the Christ film into a cowboy action-adventure. Critics reacted against the use of 'blood and gore' in the battle scenes in the story of the 'Prince of Peace' (within a couple of minutes a row of high priests standing in front of the Temple have been speared to death). The drama of the *Gospels* themselves should have been enough on its own, critics said.[14] The scriptural scenes were counterpointed with the political battles between the Romans and the Jews (and narrated by one of the favourite solemn voices of the time, Orson Welles).

Long before Martin Scorsese's *The Last Temptation of Christ* or Mel Gibson's *The Passion of the Christ*, Nicholas Ray had introduced earthy, realistic and sometimes brutal scenes into the story of Christ. Herod was shown passing rows of crosses on a carriage. The corpses were seen being thrown into open graves. Later, scenes showing Jesus entering Jerusalem were intercut with the Romans overcoming

Barabbas's army. One of the set-pieces in *Kings of Kings* was the Sermon on the Mount sequence. Ray included some of the sayings from the *Gospel of St John* as well as some of the parables. With 81 camera set-ups, and a 160 foot track for a long dolly shot laid on a 58° mountain slope, the scenes understandably took twenty-one days to film.[15]

King of Kings, like *The Last Temptation of Christ*, explored the links between power and morality, violence and non-violence. Jeffrey Hunter bravely attempted a quiet, passive Christ, a performance offset by Harry Giordano's strident, politicized Barabbas, though Robert Ryan's not wild or obsessed enough as John the Baptist. Hunter was regarded as too lightweight an actor to play Jesus. He was described in the press as a teen magazine actor, a pin-up. *King of Kings* was thus dubbed *I Was a Teenage Jesus* (however, Hunter was terrific in films like *The Searchers*).[16] Some of his line readings were unconvincing, though. Siobhan McKenna was a suitably meek, loving Virgin Mary, and Frank Thring was a sleazy, lusty, cowardly and indecisive Herod Antipas (a performance that seemed to derive form the kind of characters Peter Ustinov played); during the feast scene he can barely keep his hands off his step-daighter Salomé. Brigid Bazlen, huge eyes thick with kohl, was a flimsy Salomé.

After *Jesus of Nazareth*, there were other big budget Biblical films, but very few: among them, *Masada*, *The Last Temptation of Christ*, *Moses*, *Anno Domini* (from Anthony Burgess's book *The Kingdom of Wickedness*), and *King David*. The latter (Bruce Beresford, 1985, US) which was a notable flop, with Richard Gere's feeble performance as the loinclothed hero. *King David* cost nearly $30 million and took only $5 at the box office. After the mid-1970s, Biblical and sandal-and-sword epics were viewed as an anachronism – they were also very expensive (*King David* and *Masada*). *The Clash of the Titans* (Desmond Davis, 1981, GB) was a last gasp of Ray Harryhausen's stop-motion legends, notable for its array of Harryhausen monsters.

Some post-1970s historical epic films were critically (if not financially) successful: *The Last Emperor* (Bernardo Bertolucci, 1987, China/ Italy), *The Name of the Rose* (J.-J. Arnnaud, 1986, Germany/ Italy/ France) and *Pathfinder* (Nils Gaup, 1987, Norway). Certainly costs account for the decline of the Biblical epic; other reasons might include increasing secularization, a turning away from religion (not for many people in the US, though); the movement towards the TV series; the 'infantil-ization' of cinema in the late 1970s Lucas-Spielberg era; the corresponding increase in the young, 15-24 age range of the audience; the movement from religious subjects to the quasi-religiosity of sci-fi and fantasy films (such as *Close Encounters of the Third Kind, E.T., Star Wars, Superman, Dune, Mad Max II, Waterworld*), the latter four being modern messiah/saviour movies, or towards the supernatural and horror genres (*Poltergeist, Alien, Ghost, Ghostbusters*). B. Babington and P. Evans suggest another reason: the increasing liberalization of society: before the 'permissive' era of the 1960s, Biblical epics had allowed an expression of displays of sexuality (such as in the Roman orgy) which the Production Code would not have permitted in other genres; but as Western cinema became increasingly explicit in the post-1960s era, Biblical epics no longer had this monopoly; further, if Biblical epics were explicit, they would incur the wrath of the religious fundamentalists (as *The Last Tempt-ation of Christ* had done). And if they weren't explicit, audiences could say they'd seen it all before (B. Babington, 8).

After *Jesus of Nazaraeth* and its antidote, *Monty Python's Life of Brian*, there was no going back. But Martin Scorsese tried to do so in his *The Last Temptation of Christ* (1988). This was easily the most controversial picture of recent years, if the many demonstrations, letters, petitions and debates are any indication of a film's disruptive nature (although Mel Gibson's *The Passion of the Christ* revived controversy yet again). *The Last Temptation of Christ* shows (in a dream sequence) Christ having sex with the Magdalene. Parts of the film are terrific; it is filmed in Scorsese's typical style (mobile camera, idiosyncratic use of music, grim realism, over-the-top acting, every cinematic trick is here). There is much pain and energy in the movie, but Scorsese bungles the key point of the film, the post-Crucifixion dream sequence, which boils down to the temptations of sex. Children and domesticity are only mentioned in passing. D.H. Lawrence's novella *The Escaped Cock* (1927) is a more authentic and powerful depiction of a resurrected, sexual Christ.

In animation, the ancient epic was revived in the 1990s with Disney's *Hercules* (1997) and *Atlantis* (2001), and DreamWorks' *The Prince of Egypt* (1998). The huge success at the box office (and the Oscars) of David Franzoni's *Gladiator* (Ridley Scott, 2000) inaugurated another cycle of ancient world epics in contemporary Hollywood. Rival biographies of Alexander the Great (from Oliver Stone and Baz Luhrmann), and *Troy* (Wolfgang Petersen, 2004). Films such as *The Lord of the Rings* (2001-03), *King Arthur* (2004, also written by Franzoni), *The Last Samurai* (2003), *The Patriot* (2000), *Kingdom of Heaven* (2005) and *Crouching Tiger, Hidden Dragon* (2000) were also part of renewed interest in big budget historical films.

The Hollywood religious cinema focussed on action and melodrama, on simplified characters who embody the paths of good and evil. The moral choices are relatively unambiguous. Love is often a force of salvation, not sex or lust, and the protagonists must choose accordingly. In Biblical epics, the hero's quest is often to return to the righteous path, to the ethics of love and social responsibility. In the end, good triumphs over evil, though sometimes at the cost of the hero's life (as with Samson). The films about Christ depict the ultimate triumph, over death. The melodramatic form of the religious films ensured that evil could never win out, although some of the suspense came from good possibly failing. The religious spectacular movies sometimes contrasted the rural and the urban worlds. The city (such as Rome or Jerusalem) was decadent, materialistic, lustful, violent. The rural world embodied honesty, the family, community, living close to nature.

Fiction films, and particularly religious films, tend to have the conflict between good and evil, the divine and the demonic, at their centre. The fear of evil makes the overthrow of evil all the more poignant (and recognizable). Similarly, the presence of the divine shows that the demonic has not prevailed. 'The joyous process of deliverance and the alternating moods of contraction and expansion so essential to religion are clearly dependent upon sustaining the tension between the demonic and the divine' wrote Will Rockett (10). Whatever else narrative films do, they always maintain a tension between various states, characters, desires, issues and spaces. Happiness or repose is not news, is not drama: cinema (and most narrative media) thrives on the journey from disorder to resolution. As Williams James noted in *The Varieties of Religious Experience*, the 'most completest religions' appear 'to be those in which the pessimistic elements are best developed'.[17] Christianity and Buddhism were the religions that James cited, religions of deliverance.

Spiritual transcendence is not a particularly sexy subject for movies. In the cinema of Bresson, Ozu, Bergman or Dreyer – and Tarkovsky – minute changes in consciousness or seemingly trivial events on the path to sacred transcendence does not necessarily entrance movie audiences. The laborious and slow journey toward enlightenment makes for a reserved, quiet kind of cinema, or at least one that tends to be without explosions, gun battles, spaceships, car chases or CG monsters (unless it's by Scorese or Spielberg).

FOUR

The Film Image

4 : 1   CAMERAWORK

Andrei Tarkovsky's film image is incredibly beautiful. His film image is apparently
so simple and so concrete: the faded stone, the water, the wood and trees. Real
beauty in the texture, the light, the form, concrete and plastic. Such presence, such
simplicity – the simplest of elements, yet so *sensuous*. Not like the remoteness or
abstraction of J.S. Bach's music at all, but sensuous, like Franz von Liszt or Ottorino
Respighi. Graham Petrie spoke of Tarkovsky's films' 'intense moral seriousness'.
Tarkovsky used the poetry of dreams in cinema to 'speak directly to the receptive
viewer by means of images whose beauty and suggestive power resonate with a
forcefulness unmatched by almost any other filmmaker' (1996, 647). The sense of
the beautiful is something Tarkovsky emphasized time and again in *Sculpting In
Time* (38, 40, 42, *passim*). 'Truth' and the 'absolute' were central elements in
Tarkovsky's poetics, but the insistence on the apprehension of beauty should never
be forgotten (it's a much more problematic issue deciding what is beauty and the
beautiful – a vast area in theology and philosophy, and beyond the scope of this
book).

   Tarkovsky is a modernist in his use of the camera (in the sense of the relation of

the camera to the narration, to the themes, to the image, to the artist wielding it):
the camera tracks through the printing works in *Mirror* as if through a maze –
down corridors, around machines, following people. This labyrinthine motion
recalls the camera of Rainer Werner Fassbinder's *Despair* (1977, West Germany),
Bernardo Bertolucci's *The Spider's Stratagem* (1970, Italy) and Jean-Luc Godard's
Breathless (1960, France). It's the familiar dollying camera of modernist, New
Wave cinema, the elaborate post-Wellesian camera moves which draw attention to
themselves. Bertolucci spoke of the 'unmotivated camera', where the camera moves
independently of the dramatic action:

> The camera has a dialectical relationship to the actors and is not merely recording
> the event, but is an invisible participant with its own soul. Sometimes the camera
> even enters into competition with the actor – while the actor moves, the camera
> moves independently. (1976b, 8)

Andrei Tarkovsky's camera often drifts on its own, as an independent participant
in the film. Commenting on the action, reframing it, reworking the blocking of the
actors against the background. Creating the film as it comments upon it. Tarkovsky's framing is often of the decentred, centrifugal kind (D. Cook, 796).

Tarkovsky uses crane or boom shots, but not in the style of Hollywood Westerns,
or the vertiginous manner of D.W. Griffith, Alfred Hitchcock or Orson Welles
(classic self-conscious filmmakers). In *Andrei Roublyov* there are epic-style crane
shots to capture the crowd scenes, as well as the ecstasy of the opening flying
sequence. But more typical is the slow crane shot in *The Sacrifice*, up the tree, at the
end of the film. This very obviously represents spiritual rebirth, psychological
renewal. It is a shot with a precise narrative function, and fits in exactly with the
structure of the film. The way Janet Leigh describes Alfred Hitchcock's cinematic
technique while making *Psycho* could apply to many filmmakers (though not
necessarily a favourite style with actors or crew): there was *no* collaboration, *no*
discussion. Hitch knew exactly what he wanted: 'his camera was absolute', in every
scene, Leigh remarked, and there was no way someone on set could suggest doing it
differently. 'Hitchcock's camera was the most important thing in his mind'.[1] This
sense of visual precision could apply to Orson Welles, Bernardo Bertolucci and
Andrei Tarkovsky, and other *auteurs* who were precious and precise with their
cameras.

Andrei Tarkovsky's hero Robert Bresson said that one of the film director's tasks was to find not just the *right* way of doing a shot, but the *only* way of doing it. One can see in their films *auteurs* such as Tarkovsky, Welles, Hitchcock and Bergman looking for the single best way of making a shot. It is a kind of artistic asceticism and purism, an inability to compromise. Tarkovsky was certainly an adherent of such an approach.

Tarkovsky sometimes operated the camera on parts of his films, but he didn't (couldn't) do everything: there were always camera operators, grips, assistants, sparks, gaffers and, of course, cinematographers. Tarkovsky said he regarded his DPs as the co-authors of his films (ST, 135). While we're discussing photography, the DPs and camera operators should be mentioned: Vadim Yusov (who shot all Tarkovsky's films through to *Solaris*), Georgy Rerberg, A. Nikolayev and I. Shtanko (*Mirror*), Alexander Knyazhinsky, N. Fudim, S. Naugolnikh, G. Verk-hovsky, L. Kazmin and T. Maslennikova (*Stalker*; Rerberg also shot the first version of *Stalker*), Giuseppe Lanci and Giuseppe De Crisanti (*Nostalghia*), Sven Nykvist, Lasse Karlsson and Dan Myhrman (*The Sacrifice*).

4 : 2 ANDREI TARKOVSKY AND MICHELANGELO ANTONIONI

Andrei Tarkovsky's use of the camera recalls Michelangelo Antonioni's: both use precise, static camera as well as slow tracking shots; both have a lightness of touch, so different from the heavy, machine-like camera of Alfred Hitchcock, or the self-consciously dynamic camera of Brian de Palma, Ridley Scott, Nic Roeg or John Carpenter, or the even more self-aware camera of Jean-Luc Godard.

Tarkovsky's *Nostalghia* in particular is bound to have similarities with Anton-ioni's work: Tonino Guerra, who co-wrote *Nostalghia*, worked on many of Anton-ioni's films, including *L'Eclisse* (1962, Italy), *Il Deserto Rosso* (1964, Italy), *Blow-Up* (1967, GB), *Zabriskie Point* (1969, Italy), *Il Mistero Di Oberwald* (1980, Italy) and *Identification of a Woman* (1982, Italy). The latter features a Tarkovskyan scene, where two characters lose each other in some fog (this also occurred in Antonioni's earlier *Red Desert*). *Nostalghia* was shot in Italy, in a number of locations, and Tarkovsky met Antonioni a few times before production began. As *Identification of a Woman* and *Nostalghia* were going into production, Tarkovsky and Antonioni argued because they both wanted to use the same DP and art director (D, 253ff).

Nostalghia also recalls Antonioni's *The Passenger* (1975, Italy). In this film, spaces are explored in a similar manner, whether they be Barcelona, the Spanish mountains or the North African desert. There is the same lucidity and transparency in Antonioni's film image, as there is in Tarkovsky's; both directors explore the long take, letting time fill up the frame. Both directors use the sequence shot to rearrange space, as at the end of *The Passenger*, when the camera travels past Jack Nicholson lying on the bed (apparently dead) and through the window, or in the memory sequences in *Nostalghia*.

In Antonioni's 1967 movie *Blow-Up* the camera frames the bushes blowing in the wind where the murder takes place. One imagines that a Tarkovsky thriller would be similar: focusing not on blood and gore, knives and guns, but on mysterious things such as a bush blowing in the wind, and would be, similarly, an exploration of existential identity (though with a spiritual dimension). A Tarkovsky thriller would be *The Big Sleep* meets Fyodor Dostoievsky, but without any of the witty, sexy Raymond Chandler dialogue, and a hero the opposite of Philip Marlowe and Humphrey Bogart. A Tarkovsky thriller or crime film would be fraught with Existential anguish, and hardly anything would happen in it. It certainly wouldn't satisfy fans of cool, tough detectives with quirks, savage murders, betrayals, mystery plots to be solved, tense run-ins with the DA and chief of police, face-offs with arch-villains in disused warehouses, or the sleazy mean streets of Los Angeles.

Other links between Antonioni's and Tarkovsky's cinema includes their Existentialist, post-Nietzschean philosophy; their grounding in mid-20th century European culture; their explorations of personal and national cultural identify; and the themes of estrangement and exile, and the double. Both *Nostalghia* and *The Passenger* concern a middle-aged man in exile, wandering in a country at once familiar and hostile. Both Gorchakov and Locke are accompanied on their travels by a woman who is potentially a lover, and are shadowed by a double.

Andrei Tarkovsky's typical movement of the camera is the slow tracking shot, often crabwise (i.e., parallel to the subject). Tarkovsky uses tracking shots that last longer than, say, Jean-Luc Godard's famous traffic jam shot in *Weekend* (1967, France), or Orson Welles' crane shot in *Touch of Evil* (1957, USA), or the brothel sequence in Max Ophüls' *Le Plaisir* (1952, France). Tarkovsky's tracking shots, like Theo Angelopoulos's, are some of the longest in cinema (in time if not in space). Each one could be regarded as a short film in themselves. Bernardo Bertolucci said precisely this: 'I want each take to be a film in itself'.[1] The candle-carrying scene in *Nostalghia*, for instance, is conceived as a complete sequence, in three acts, with a beginning (he lights the candle), tension (will he make it across the pool?), high and low points (he gets quite far – but the candle goes out and he has to go back) and an ending (he sets the candle, alight, down on the far side). Music fades in. He dies.

The tracking shot requires a careful orchestration of movement, timing, blocking, props, practical effects, lighting, dialogue and sound – it is a carefully controlled, very artificial cinematographic technique. Tarkovsky's enhances the artificiality – and unreality – of tracking shots sometimes, by building in actions or beats which draw attention to time expanding within the frame.

4 : 4   DISTANCE AND VIEWPOINT

As for the distance between camera and subject, Andrei Tarkovsky uses many long shots. He favours a cool objectivity, even though at times he can be highly contrived and self-conscious in his choice of angles, compositions and distance. He does not go in for Expressionist close-ups, like Carl-Theodor Dreyer, Charlie Chaplin, Ingmar Bergman or Orson Welles. He often uses cutaways and inserts – shots of objects, photographed lovingly in close-up. He often shoots people from slightly above – in *The Sacrifice* the camera tracks in and bears down upon the kneeling, praying figure of Alexander (as it does in *Stalker*, when the three men rest by the pool).

In a number of films the camera, in close-up, cranes down the body of a figure, emphasizing the stature, vulnerability and physiology of the person. *Behold the Man*, this kind of shot could be saying, as it travels over the landscape of the body (as at the beginning of *Nostalghia*), much as sculptor's gaze might, or a painter turning the body into a landscape, or a series of forms.

Sometimes a bird's-eye view is deployed, as of Kelvin in bed in *Solaris*, or the artisans in the wood before they are blinded in *Andrei Roublyov*. One sort of tracking shot – looking down on a tiny portion of a landscape – seems exclusive to Andrei Tarkovsky. It is used to great effect to illustrate (or to embody) the Stalker's dream: the camera tracks in close-up over a series of objects under some water. The same shot is used in *The Sacrifice*, across a snowbound chunk of earth, and in *Nostalghia*, over the model landscape at Domenico's home.

These high angle viewpoints are some of the most unreal in cinema – the world is rarely experienced by people in everyday life in this way. It is like flying slowly and gently over the Earth – an image from a flying dream. Alfred Hitchcock asserted that the chase is best suited to film (or cinema was the best at depicting a chase: 'the chase seems to me the final expression of the motion picture medium,' Hitch remarked in 1950; 'it's the time factor in movement that makes the chase').[1] In the same way, flying is well suited to cinema – and vice versa; cinema is well suited to depicting flight. Form and content fuse seamlessly.

4 : 5   SLOW MOTION

Andrei Tarkovsky's use of slow motion is not like Sam Peckinpah's, or as it is used in horror films – to stretch out moments of blood, guts and extreme violence, producing a cinema that is existentially visceral (eviscerating). But Tarkovsky does have a slow motion death: it's in *Andrei Roublyov*, as Roublyov's assistant Foma is pierced by an arrow and falls into the river. The ancestor of Tarkovsky's use of slow motion is Akira Kurosawa's cinema, and Foma's demise is a definite *hommage* to Kurosawa, and to the peerless *The Seven Samurai* in particular. The way that Tarkovsky cuts together slow motion, in his montages of dreams or heightened moments, is also inspired by the *sensei* of Japanese cinema. (As well as Peckinpah and

Tarkovsky, Kurosawa's influence is acknowledged by John Woo, John Milius, George Lucas and Paul Verhoeven, among many others).

Tarkovsky's slow motion is softly poetic, stemming from his lyrical view of life. There is a great deal of slow motion in Tarkovsky's cinema – mostly of the gentle kind, where actions are filmed in slight slow motion. In *Mirror* objects fall to the ground, people walk or run, fires flicker and the mother turns to stare into the camera in slow motion. The result is to alter perception, to re-organize reality, and take the film into another world. Often slow motion means an experience of the past, as in *Nostalghia*. But in *Mirror* slow motion is used to re-write, and re-present, many aspects of life. It does not, as it does in mainstream cinema, extend, elastically, some violent moment (a car crash, a bullet wound); rather, it poeticizes everyday reality. It is a lyrical device. (Slight slow motion has become far more common in Hollywood cinema, as well as TV advertizing, although the influence there comes from the speed ramping available on computers and in digital editing, and cameras which can switch film speeds within the same shot. Martin Scorsese is a particular fan of the in-camera technique).

No realist he, Tarkovsky is not a fantasist either. He used slow motion to imbue screen moments with the lucidity, the magnitude and the utter rightness of a dream. One of the most extraordinary and deeply poetic uses of slow motion occurs in Jean-Luc Godard's *Sauve qui peut la vie* (*Slow Motion*, 1980, France). A woman riding a bike is freeze-framed, and caught in very slow slow motion, to the sound of classical piano music. The effect is like projecting a film at a very slow speed (a technique used in Derek Jarman's *The Angelic Conversation*, 1985, GB). Films such as *The Matrix*, *GoodFellas* and *Casino* have employed freeze frames within shots, and speed ramping, familiar to audiences. Where slow motion might once have been employed by only a few film directors, with many more traditional directors too conventional to go near it, it's commonplace nowadays.

Andrei Tarkovsky's use of alternating colour and black-and-white is essentially no different from that of *The Wizard of Oz* (Victor Fleming, 1939, USA). Changing from colour to black-and-white (as in *Mirror* and *Nostalghia*) indicates a movement from one world, one mental state, one perception, to another. Sometimes Tarkovsky uses black-and-white to portray the past (in *Mirror* and *Nostalghia*), whereas in *Nostalghia* sepia-and-white images are part of Domenico's past and Gorchakov's Russian dreams. In a 1966 interview, Tarkovsky said he preferred black-and-white films over colour films, because black-and-white seemed closer, he asserted, to how perception works in real life, how colour isn't really noticed in real life, but colour films artificially attract attention to themselves (D, 356). Although the world is in colour, Tarkovsky reckoned that black-and-white film somehow came closer to the psychology of art (ST, 139).

Tarkovsky's restrained use of colour produced colours that were naturalistic, muted, often optically washed-out. For the desaturated look of *The Sacrifice*, Sven Nykvist employed a photographic technique which combined colour and a black-and-white dupes, made from a colour negative. An optical printer is used to blend them together until the right mix is achieved. About fifty of the night shots in *The Sacrifice* were treated optically to give them the right 'magical, mystical' effect. Nykvist said that he found out about the technique from John Huston's *Moby Dick* (which had been shot by Ossie Morris and Freddie Francis). Tarkovsky preferred to 'neutralize' the colour in a film, to make it subservient to the drama or expression. Tarkovsky was particularly suspicious of films that featured bold colours which fought against the expressivity of the image (ST, 138).

The near-monochrome look has become popular with filmmakers in the Nineties (particularly those who aren't allowed by studios to use total black-and-white — chiefly because executives think it puts audiences off — but who can have something approximating it instead). Steven Spielberg and Janusz Kaminski used it in *Minority Report, Saving Private Ryan, Seven,* and *Amistad*; Tim Burton employed it in *Batman* (shot by Roger Pratt) and *Sleepy Hollow* (shot by Emmanuel Lubezki); and it was the speciality of DP Darius Khondji (*Seven, Alien 4, City of Lost Children*). The bleach bypass process was combined with treated filters and lenses. Probably the most famous usage in modern cinema occurred in *The Godfather* films, shot by the 'prince of darkness', Gordon Willis (who provided the same look for Woody Allen's Bergmanesque *Interiors*).

Tarkovsky also liked, along with so many filmmakers, to shoot at the magic hour (some of the great magic hour movies include *The Black Stallion*; one of the very best is *Days of Heaven* [Terence Malick, 1978, USA], shot by Nestor Almendros and Haskell Wexler). On *The Sacrifice*, the dawn light meant shooting at two in the morning (in May in Gotland). Tarkovsky sometimes set-dressed the natural world to achieve particular effects (such as spray painting vegetation in *Stalker*, spraying trees with water in *The Sacrifice* to make them look darker, or, for *Mirror*, painting leaves gold).

There isn't a particular scheme to the use of black-and-white, sepia and colour in *Mirror*: while other films might employ colour for dreams and black-and-white for 'reality' (as in the most famous case, *The Wizard of Oz*), *Mirror* doesn't abide by a strict pattern. While Tarkovsky was fairly unusual in employing combinations of colour, near-monochrome and true black-and-white in nearly all of his films from *Andrei Roublyov* onwards, some filmmakers went further: Krzysztof Kieslowski comes to mind, with his love of complex filters and colouration (for the 1988 film *A Short Film About Killing*, Kieslowski's cinematographer, Slavoj Idziak suggested they try using filters on the camera to attain a particular look. Idziak had some 600 filters specially manufactured for *A Short Film About Killing* – many green, some sepia, some for two-shots, some for close-ups, some for long shots, some for skies. As a result, there is no film that looks quite like *A Short Film About Killing*. Idziak later took his unique filtration to Hollywood, using it on *Gattaca* [1997], *Men With Guns* [1997] and *Black Hawk Down* [2001]).

Sometimes it seems as if the different hues of black-and-white film stock in Tarkovsky's films (as in *Mirror* or *Stalker*) was deliberate, and sometimes it appears rather arbitrary, not part of a premeditated pattern (and simply the result of how the film stock was processed at the labs).

Tarkovsky often treats the colours in post-production (collaborating with his DP and the laboratories). The colours of *Nostalghia* are deliberately held-back, beaten-out, pale. *Nostalghia* uses black-and-white, sepia-and-white, muted colour, and full colour.

Tarkovsky's use of colour is, in general, very restrained, tending towards browns, greys, whites, blacks, greens and blues, usually in desaturated hues or a *chiaroscuro* style. Tarkovsky did not go for the excessive colour artificiality of, say, Vincente Minnelli in his MGM musicals, or Jacques Demy in *The Umbrellas of Cherbourg*

(1964). The move into full colour was inevitable for Tarkovsky in the commercial world of feature filmmaking. Fewer filmmakers are allowed to use straight black-and-white than ever before (even for prestigious or art films). Tarkovsky compromised by employing selective black-and-white sequences inside colour films, and for combining muted colours with black-and-white and sepia.

In *Stalker*, the Zone is a vividly green and abundant place in a post-industrial, post-apocayptic world of greys, blacks and browns. The summery, green growths of the Zone contrast boldly with the black-and-white world that surrounds it. The Zone, though a dangerous and perhaps radiated space, is in fact more alive than the rest of the world.

Tarkovsky's unusual in one key respect, however: while many filmmakers employ transformations between colour to black-and-white from time to time, or just the once, for Tarkovsky it's a recurring technique, employed up to and including his last film.

As for his lighting, Tarvosky favours natural light effects, hence his interiors are often very dim (the houses in *Mirror* and *The Sacrifice*). One reason that *Solaris* looks so odd in the Tarkovsky pantheon is all that bright, shadowless lighting. In *Nostalghia* and *Stalker*, and especially in *The Sacrifice*, characters lurk in deep shadows, as if in the dark recesses of Leonardo's *sfumato* lighting. Not as extreme as *film noir*, Tarkovsky's lighting is nevertheless full of dark zones. The exteriors too feature diffuse light, as if filmed under thin cloud cover. Tarkovsky's Italy is a mist-ridden pastoral landscape – every scene seems to have been filmed at dawn or in the magic hour.

The later films in particular are filled with a soft light, a glow which is emphasized by the candles, bonfires and domestic lamps. These are a feature of every film. The soft lighting brings out the texture of stone and wood, while the back-lighting makes rain shine (so many classic Tarkovsky images are stylishly back-lit, emphasizing the translucency and fluidity of water).

Andrei Tarkovsky has an unparalleled sense of surfaces in cinema – of wooden, tiled or stone floors; of the texture of hair, cloth and tree trunks; of the reflections on water; and of the untouchable presence of fire. The Tarkovskyan wall must rank as one of his major motifs. Look at the walls in *Mirror*, *Andrei Roublyov* or *Stalker*. They are battered, weathered, pitted, with peeling paint and plaster. The camera tracks along a cracked wall or bank of earth at the beginning of *Ivan's Childhood*. In *Mirror*, the walls fall apart on camera. (Irma Rausch, Tarkovsky's first wife, recalled that Tarkovsky used to point out particularly interesting old, textured walls when they were walking around Moscow [JP, 230]. You know you're with someone unusual when, of the things to notice, they notice old walls).

The last four Tarkovsky films in particular have an extraordinary sense of surface. One thinks again of Michelangelo Antonioni, but Tarkovsky goes beyond him. There is the table top in *Mirror*, with the drying condensation mark on it. There are the battered walls of Domenico's house, the polished wooden floor of *The Sacrifice*, and so on. The bare, weather-beaten walls recall Leonardo da Vinci, who used to look at walls in a Zen-like meditation, and see fantastic things in them. When he painted *The Last Supper* in S. Maria delle Grazie, Milan, in 1497, it was reported by Matteo Bandello that Leonardo sat for hours staring at his painting, not doing anything:

> ...from sunrise to dusk he never laid aside his brushes and went on painting, forgetting about food and drink. Then it so happened that he did not touch his brushes for two, three or even four days running, and yet he would often sit for one or two hours at a stretch examining his work only; he would look at his figures and think and appraise them.[1]

This is nothing unusual, though – many artists do this. The viewer is encouraged to sit and contemplate Tarkovsky's films in the same way. Tarkovsky's decayed walls are also similar in feel to the oil and wax textures of Jasper Johns and Robert Ryman, or Jean Dubuffet's mixed media canvases. Leonardo experimented with oil instead of fresco on *The Last Supper*, but his tests proved fatal, and 'the painting was already a wreck in his own lifetime'.[2] The fate of Leonardo's Milan painting offers an interesting parallel with Tarkovsky's career in films.

The emphasis on texture, glass, surface, mirrors, rain, back-lighting, *chiaroscuro* and *sfumato* light make Tarkovsky's film image very painterly. Although he admired the Early Renaissance painters, such as Fra Angelico and Sandro Botticelli, his film image looks more like Rembrandt van Rijn or Diego Velasquez. The end of *Solaris*, for example, when the father lays his hands on the shoulders of his kneeling son, exactly mirrors Rembrandt's *The Return of the Prodigal Son* (c. 1669, Hermitage Museum, St Petersburg). There are other directors who enjoy filming surfaces and the psychology behind them, who like exploring the ontology of frames, glass and mirrors: Borowczyk, Kubrick, Fassbinder, Bresson, Antonioni and Cocteau.

4 : 8   DECAY AND TRASH

Andrei Tarkovsky's floors and landscapes are full of trash, bits and pieces of junk, old machines, newspapers, chunks of wood, soggy cardboard, and all sorts of objects. His images look lived in, and old – not ancient, but severely humanized. Roublyov, Ivan, Domenico and the Stalker live in dilapidated places. The landscape of *The Sacrifice* looks post-Apocalyptic even before the bombers approach. The spaceship in *Solaris* is littered with defunct technology, a sci-fi 'look' not found in *2,001: A Space Odyssey* but in *Alien* (Ridley Scott, 1979, GB), the *Mad Max* films (George Miller, 1979-1985, Australia) and other post-*Star Wars* post-punk post-holocaust films. For Tarkovsky the world is a messy place, and although his films are spiritual investigations, they are set in sometimes filthy worlds. This is part of Tarkovsky's filmic 'realism'. The real world *is* chaotic (but people are a lot messier than nature, with their vast, industrial pollution).

Films that try to present the world as a clinically clean place usually tend to look artificial. This kind of artificiality Tarkovsky hates, being a searcher for 'the truth'. In this sense, his wet, dark, dirty images seem truer than most of film and television. There is a conflict between the worlds of shit and spirit in Tarkovsky's sacred cinema, as there is in Samuel Beckett's fiction. But as writers such as Arthur Rimbaud, D.H. Lawrence, Georges Bataille, Samuel Beckett and John Cowper

Powys show, the anal/ fæcal realm and the spiritual/ ecstatic realm are not so far apart, especially when treated by an imaginative mind that can transform things alchemically.[1]

4 : 9   ANDREI TARKOVSKY AND PHOTOGRAPHY

Among photographers, Andrei Tarkovsky's poetic vision recalls that of Josef Sudek, Josef Koudelka, André Kertész, Minor White and Edward Weston, some of the greatest modernist photographers. Tarkovsky's film image, with its acute evocation of texture, is like the still-life photographs of Weston – the flowers and shells that Weston photographed with four hour exposure times at f-256 apertures. The quiet, meditative, East European landscapes of Josef Sudek – of forest floors, for instance – are the equivalent of Tarkovsky's landscapes – particularly the trees in *Solaris* and *Andrei Roublyov*.

Tarkovsky photographs a landscape in a similar way to poetic photographers such as Eugéne Atget, Paul Strand, Ansel Adams, Alfred Stieglitz, Edward Steichen, André Kertész, Thomas Joshua Cooper and Edward Weston – who used long exposures, large depth of field, classic framing on pin-sharp large-format cameras, in order to let the essence of the landscape fill the frame. Photographers such as Thomas Joshua Cooper and Edward Weston use very long exposure times, as does Tarkovsky, whose single takes run up to nine or more minutes. Indeed, if he could have done so, Tarkovsky might have produced films many hours long – days even. As it was, he kept pushing his running time way beyond Hitchcock's bladder-rule of two hours for a film.

Josef Sudek made many timeless photographs of his studio in Prague – of apples, leaves, papers, statues, flowers and masks. The studio looks exactly like the interiors of *Nostalghia* or *Mirror*. Domenico's rain-soaked room in *Nostalghia* looks just like Sudek's studio. Like Tarkovsky, Sudek loved glass – bits of broken glass, or windows, or drinking glasses. Sudek's photographs of windows speckled with condensation or frosted over are the still equivalents of Tarkovsky's meditative style. The softly breathing curtain of the boy's bedroom in *The Sacrifice* crops up in the photographs of Sudek and Minor White. Veils upon veils, like the room of veils, curtains and hangings in *Mirror* – the wonderland of the transformed house which the boy enters and communes with family ghosts (*auteurs* like Federico Fellini, Martin Scorsese and Bernardo Bertolucci have employed veils, curtains, lace and frosted glass in many films. Tarkovsky uses curtains as Fellini did – to evoke the family, maternal home of the past). Josef Koudelka photographed a very Tarkovskyan image: an angel on a bicycle – a boy dressed up, on the way to some nativity play or procession (taken in Czechoslovakia, 1968).

FIVE

The Mysteries of Space and Time

So, montage is conflict… Conflict within the shot is potential montage, in the development of its intensity shattering the quadrilateral cage of the shot and exploding its conflict into montage impulses between the montage pieces. As, in a zigzag mimicry, the mise-en-scène splashes out into a spatial zigzag with the same shattering.

Sergei Eisenstein[1]

5 : 1   MYTHIC TIME

There are many kinds of time: cosmic, seasonal, evolutionary, historical, prehistoric, social, political, personal and atomic. Film, and literature, tends to deal with individual, psychological time. There are few films that work in cosmic time, for instance (although Stanley Kubrick's *2,001: A Space Odyssey* does feature a two million year jump cut). Time is a strange thing in cinema – perhaps the most mysterious thing about cinema. It resembles 'real time' but is always compressed, cut up, manipulated, expanded, mediated, abstracted. As most commentators have noted, the time element is what distinguishes cinema from other artforms. Although theatre, television and live performances take place within time, cinema has its own rigorously controlled temporal dimension.

Sergei Eisenstein created a theory of dialectics of montage and the manipulation of time. Montage, for Eisenstein, could be rhythmic, tonal, emotional, and so on. He spoke of '*dynamization in space* – an impression of spatial dynamics' and '*emotional dynamization*' (G. Mast, 82). Art critic Erwin Panofsky wrote of '*dynamization of space*' and 'spatialization of time' (ib., 154).

5 : 2   TIMELESS TIME

Cinema came into being as a means of recording the very movement of reality: factual, specific, within time and unique; of reproducing again and again the moment, instant by instant, in its fluid mutability. This is what determines the medium of cinema.

Andrei Tarkovsky, *Sculpting in Time* (94)

Andrei Tarkovsky was opposed to the manipulation of Sergei Eisenstein's *gestalt* theory of dialectical montage. But, like Eisenstein, Tarkovsky understood the possibilities of seeing everything at once. Not shot after shot, or sequences bound by linear time, but an all-at-once experience, a totality. This is what the Abstract Expressionist painters were trying to achieve. Barnett Newman wrote: 'I was concerned constantly in doing a painting that would move in its totality as you see it. You look at it and you see it'.[1] In a similar manner, Tarkovsky spoke of doing a film in a continuous shot. It is a dream of filmic intensity, a dream of cinema as revelation, where one sees (or rather, *feels*) everything at once. This is cinema moving towards Zen Buddhist *satori* or enlightenment, where there is an all-over experience, the James Joycean epiphany, the prime æsthetic experience. There's the object, and one sees it, all at once. It is a dream of every artist: instant and complete communication, inducing instant and complete understanding in the viewer. Tarkovsky wrote in *Sculpting in Time*:

I think that what a person normally goes to the cinema for is time: for time lost or spent, or not yet had. He goes there for living experience; for cinema, like no other art, widens, enhances and concentrates a person's experience – and not only enhances it but makes it longer, significantly longer. (ST, 63)

Tarkovsky's claims for cinema could also be made by music, painting and other artforms. This is cinema as Time Refound, Paradise Regained, life enhanced, the sacred re-affirmed. It is the return to the mythic centre of mysticism – of Taoism and modern mystics such as Thomas Merton. The mythic centre is found again, and the initiate can escape from what Mircea Eliade called the 'terror of history':

The "terror of history", for me, is the feeling experienced by a man who is no longer religious, who therefore has no hope of finding any ultimate meaning in the drama of history, and who must undergo the crimes of history without grasping the meaning of them. (1984, 128)

This, surely, is the state of Existential anguish the Tarkovskyan anti-hero finds her/ herself enduring: doomed or born into an areligious, ahistorical, apoetic, amusical world. So the Tarkoskian protagonist tries to re-instate the sacred, the divine, the poetic.

One way of doing this is to re-affirm the timeless. Cinema operates (not only at the point of theatrical projection) in the present moment. When the past is shown – in flashbacks, for instance – it is as if it is happening *now*. As with television news or soap opera, cinema inhabits an Eternal Now. And this can be mystical, for the present moment is the gateway to the timeless, to the Divine Being, as Aldous Huxley said (in *The Perennial Philosophy*). (The passageway cannot really be at any other time). True mysticism aims to make the mystical happen now, a sentiment shared by Zen Buddhist and Taoist mystics, as well as Occidental mystics such as Meister Eckhardt. Modern poets such as Rainer Maria Rilke, St-John Perse, Paul Eluard and T.S. Eliot have said similar things of time and timelessness.

Cinema has the potential to depict the mystical, because it can reveal the timeless moment, the perpetual present. Even if it can't depict the divine, it can at least offer up the eternal. It doesn't need to use slow motion or emotional music to do this: it does it automatically. Light speaks of the divine, and in its constant manipulation of light, cinema moves towards the religious. Combining with music, camera, setting and *mise-en-scène* can add to this mystical dimension.

But these are components of film language. The content too needs to be suitable for the construction of a sacred cinema. The film full of gangsters, money, sex, violence and city life may work against all the religious language or techniques one cares to employ. However, there might be scope for the themes of revenge, guilt, retribution and tragedy that are found in some gangster and crime films (such as those of the Italian-American filmmakerss – *The Godfather* (Francis Coppola, 1972, USA, or *Taxi Driver* (Martin Scorsese, 1975, USA). If one combines the language and imagery of the religious film (the light, symbols, music, *mise-en-scène*) with religious subject matter, as Bergman, Mizoguchi, Bresson and Tarkovsky have done, then one gets closest to sacred cinema.

Another recurring concern of Tarkovsky's films is war and conflict – from the Second World War in *Mirror* and *Ivan's Childhood*, to the Tartar raids in *Andrei Roublyov*, and global nuclear catastrophe in *The Sacrifice*. Those large, social concerns belie the received view that Tarkovsky's cinema only concentrates on subjective, poetic states. Tarkovsky's films are definitely not social and political commentaries like, say, Oliver Stone's explorations of contemporary America, or Jean-Luc Godard's Maoist-Marxist period. But they are concerned with the relation between the artist and her/ his social context, the artist's place within history, and wider, historical events such as the Second World War, or the formation of early modern Russia.

As to time periods and history, Tarkovsky, like most filmmakers, had his favourite periods: *Nostalghia*, *The Sacrifice*, *Mirror* and *Stalker* take place in the present (*Stalker* may be in the near future). *Mirror* and *Ivan's Childhood* go back to the Second World War (and both contain flashbacks to an idyllic childhood prior to the war). Alone among Tarkovsky's films, *Solaris* is set in the future. *Andrei Roublyov* goes back in time the furthest in the Tarkovsky canon: to the early 1400s, with a flashback to the Crucifixion (although it's shot as if it were contemporary with the rest of the film, not A.D. 33).

Having said that, the present day of Tarkovsky's films is not the straightforward one of most other films. *Stalker*, for example, could be set in any time since the 1940s to the present. The visual references in *Stalker* are vague enough for it to be 1979, when the film was released, or 1949. Or it maybe some time in the future.

Along with the life-affirming Eternal Now of cinema, there is also the inescapable dimension of mortality and death. Cinema is filmed death, in one sense. Jean-Luc Godard noted this: the actors one films will one day be dead, and so many of the people on that shimmering screen are long gone. Expanding this argument further, one can say that people are decaying as one watches them; that time is running out, literally, on the screen; that a film is a collection of dead moments, of once-but-never-been moments; that watching a film is a necrophilic experience; that a film is a graveyard. (But that's just the same as in life: everybody one knows – has known, will know – is dead, or dying, or will die).

It is no surprise that death is one of the main subjects of cinema. So many films contain people dying: there are so many deathbed scenes, shootings, axings, stabbings. Cinema is largely a cinema of death. It's easy to see why cinema is full of death – there is the historical angle (modern times have been full of mass death, brutalities in vast quantities), the philosophical slant (death lies at the heart of Western metaphysics and theology), the psychological aspect (identification with the victim, on every level), the visceral (death is exciting, dramatically and visually), and the mysterious element (death is ever mysterious: one can show, in a film, someone there, and the next moment they've slipped away; the mystery is endless, and is present in every film, from early cinema through the silent classics to the latest films).

There are deaths in Andrei Tarkovsky's films: slow motion deaths, heroic deaths, brutal murders and pathetic suicides. Death is bound to feature prominently in a filmmaker so bound up with eschatology. As with the Existentialist philosophers, death for Tarkovsky is the ultimate barrier, the absolute test. The main characters in *Stalker, Andrei Roublyov, Nostalghia* and *The Sacrifice* all come close to death. Tarkovsky doesn't go as far as German mediæval painting or the Mexican 'Day of the Dead' festival, and have skeletons wielding scythes as Death prancing about, but death is a strong presence in his cinema, and his characters are often peering over the abyss of their own unconscious, looking at the black depths of the soul below.

Since earliest days, time has been bound up with death. 'Time, which in progressing destroys the world' say the Hindu religious texts, the *Upanishads*. Andrei Tarkovsky doesn't explore the metaphysics of killing and eating, of mortality and decay, in the vivid, ironic manner of Luis Buñuel or Peter Greenaway.

His way is gentle, slow. Yet there is the same insistence on embracing one's own mortality, the connections between death and life that one finds in most of Occidental art, from Homer to V.S. Naipaul. Tarkovsky veers between the European *avant garde* ethic of sex = death, as espoused by the Marquis de Sade, Charles Baudelaire, Sigmund Freud and Georges Bataille, and the ever-hopeful contemporary theologies of Thomas Merton, William Johnston, Karl Barthes and Bernard Lonergan. Like most artists, Tarkovsky hovers between the Western stances of fear and desire, black despair and white hope. The stance is lucidly summed up by Joseph Campbell:

> The conquest of death is the recovery of life's joy. One can experience an uncon-ditional affirmation of life only when one has accepted death, not as contrary to life, but as an aspect of life. Life in its becoming is always shedding death, and on the point of death. The conquest of fear yields the courage of life. (1988a, 152)

5 : 4   TIME IN ANDREI TARKOVSKY'S CINEMA

Some of Andrei Tarkovsky's contemporaries have excelled in the realms of editing. Few filmmakers are as clinically precise as Stanley Kubrick, whose Bible was Vsevolod Pudovkin's book *Film Technique* (1926). Kubrick's *Dr Strangelove* (1963, GB) and *The Killing* (1956, USA) use parallel action and cross-cutting in a complex and powerful way. Kubrick's narrator gives the impression of having a God-like overview of a whole film, and all the layers in it. Similarly, Francis Coppola is a master of montage, as the endings of *The Godfather* (1972, USA), *The Cotton Club* (1984, USA) and *The Godfather III* (1990) demonstrate.

Andrei Tarkovsky, meanwhile, does not place this overview in his films. He rarely uses cross-cutting or parallel action (the basis of cinema as a chase). He says you have to show one thing after another; there's no other way (ST, 70). And that's what he does that at the climax of *Nostalghia*, where many another editor would have intercut the two climactic events. Tarkovsky doesn't even like reaction shots; he dubs them redundant in *Sculpting In Time* (70). His basic technique is to fill each shot with emotion and time, to achieve his effects with long takes, with the long sequence shot, rather than with the dialectics of Eisensteinian montage.

Tarkovsky was very much involved with the technical aspects of filmmaking, with preparing a shot, but when he came to shoot it, he preferred one or two takes. That meant a lot of effort went into preparation, rather than, as with perfectionists like Stanley Kubrick or Jackie Chan, repeating the same actions time after time (Tarkovsky was similarly a perfectionist, but not to the point of endless retakes). Sometimes, Tarkovsky might spend two days setting up a difficult shot, and shoot it on the third day. DP on *Stalker*, Alexander Knyazhinsky, explained that once the shot had been set up and rehearsed, it was shot as planned, without deviating from it. (Sometimes, Tarkovsky did inject spontaneity into a shot – such as throwing geese in front of the camera on *Andrei Roublyov* without telling anyone). (On *Stalker*, of course, two days could easily be set aside for camera rehearsals, if the shot ended up being a six minute take that made it into the final cut. An average Hollywood production shoots about 5/8ths of a page of script a day).

The low no. of takes also meant editing was usually a lot easier (except on *Mirror*), because there wasn't thousands of feet of takes of each scene to wade through (the *Lord of the Rings* movies [2001-03], for instance, shot over five million feet of 35mm film). Even though the editing of a Tarkovsky film often meant simply selecting the order for the scenes, there were still numerous ways the films could be cut (partly because Tarkovsky's films tended towards poetic, subjective or dream states of mind, which do not act in a linear or logical fashion). There was little waste, too, on a Tarkovsky film: most of what was shot appeared in the final cut. Tarkovsky rarely shot scenes that didn't make it into the release print. (On *Solaris*, two scenes didn't make it into the finished film: one in a mirrored room (a tiny fragment was left), and a night scene set on Earth).

In *Sculpting In Time*, Tarkovsky stated that for him editing was 'ultimately no more than the ideal variant of the assembly of the shots, necessarily contained within the material that has been put onto the roll of film' (ST, 116). A lot of film editors (and directors) would disagree with this. But Tarkovsky reckoned that the editing process was essentially one of finding the intrinsic pattern that already existed in the filmed material (the footage having been shot with the editing style in mind [119]). So that editing was 'simply a question of recognising and following this pattern while joining and cutting' (116). Thus, editing for Tarkovsky didn't mean creating new ideas and themes from the material (as in montage editing), but finding the ones that were already there in the footage.

Many film editors would say exactly the opposite: that a lot of editing is about discovering ideas, motifs and themes that weren't necessarily in the material as it was conceived or as it was shot. Plenty of editors, for instance, create new scenes or connections between scenes and characters via editing. But Tarkovsky resisted montage editing – at least in theory (in *Mirror*, for instance, there are clearly a series of montages in the dreams, memories and flashbacks which were largely constructed during post-production). So Tarkovsky would resist obvious places where parallel action could occur, as in the twin climaxes of *Nostalghia*, which many another editor would have intertwined them.

Sergei Eisenstein will speak of the ''psychological' vibrations of each piece',[1] and the result is that ABC = x (the whole is greater than the sum of the parts). In Tarkovsky's cinema, montage is mostly dropped in favour of the sequence shot. Thus, A = x. Tarkovsky's cinema goes for the 'mise-en-shot' rather than montage. He is like Bernardo Bertolucci in this respect. Both filmmakers like to capture as much as possible in one master shot, instead of a storyboarded assembly style (like the films of Brian de Palma or Martin Scorsese). While Bertolucci's camera will be craning and dollying about all over the place, Tarkovsky's camera stays still, or gently drifts sideways. This is how Michelangelo Antonioni's camera moves: of the famous seven-minute take at the end of *The Passenger*, Antonioni wrote:

> the undulating, just perceptible movements of the camera… I was trying uncon-
> sciously to find the same movement our imagination makes when it tries to give
> birth to an image.[2]

Pier Paolo Pasolini spoke of the 'infinite shot-sequence', which would be capable of reproducing reality exactly. Cinema, for Pasolini, was 'the writing of reality with reality', but the actuality of film undercut the ideal of cinema. 'Film rewrote cinema, brought the ideal down to earth'.[3]

Like Bernardo Bertolucci, Tarkovsky regards editing with suspicion. Bertolucci saw editing as an Imperialist mechanism, which flattens out all poetic gestures that were so lovingly created during shooting by the director:

> I move the camera as if I was gesturing with it. But imperialism is an enemy of
> these "gestures", of the assembling of the daily rushes into an ensemble of gest-
> ures. The moment of imperialism is the editing of the film.[4]

Tarkovsky realized that editing was still an imposition the material, and a coercion of the audience. So the viewer either goes along with the director's manipulation of rhythm and time, or they don't.

Many *auteurs* have carefully controlled the editing of their films (Welles, Chaplin, Hitchcock). Tarkovsky was clearly closely involved in editing each of his films. His editor on *The Sacrifice*, Michal Leszcylowski, said: 'I knew nothing would go wrong professionally, that I would be working with a genius'.[5] Nevertheless, it was not all Tarkovsky commanding and Leszcylowski obeying: Leszcylowski showed Tarkovsky that he could take out a few seconds from the celebrated climactic single take of the burning house, to cover up a moment where the action was delayed. Henri Colpi was supervising editor. (If Tarkovsky had made *The Sacrifice* in the age of CGI, that shot could have been cleaned up easily – actors could have been erased or replaced, or performed dangerous fire stunts, more smoke or fire could have been added, the sky could have been darkened, or clouds added, practical effects could have been retimed, and so on. It's just as likely, though, that a filmmaker like Tarkovsky might have insisted on shooting as much of the scene as practically as possible. Besides, the budget of two or three million bucks of *The Sacrifice* wouldn't have run to digital visual effects).

Time and rhythm were vital to film for Tarkovsky. As Tarkovsky put it, one could imagine a film without actors, music, settings or even editing, but not without a 'sense of time passing through the shot' (ST, 113). Rhythm wasn't editing, though: it wasn't the length of the shots that determined rhythm, but the 'pressure of time' that ran through the shots (ST, 117). The sense of time for Tarkovsky was a feeling that what you saw on screen was not limited to the visuals alone, but was 'a pointer to something stretching beyond frame and to infinity' (ibid.).

Time and rhythm were one of a director's signatures, Tarkovsky said – intuitive, a response to a director's 'innate awareness of life' (120). So editing became 'the ultimate embodiment of his philosophy of life'. It was thus easy to identify the editing styles of the great directors – Bergman, Kurosawa, Bresson, Antonioni – Tarkovsky reckoned, because their 'perception of time, as expressed in the rhythm of [their] films, is always the same' (121).

A very important person in Tarkovsky's cinema is editor Lyudmilla Feiginova, who edited all of Tarkovsky's Russian films (she started out as assistant editor on *Ivan's Childhood*). The editor is often a collaborator overlooked by critics, who are more likely to discuss composers, DPs, producers, production designers, visual effects designers or even stunt co-ordinators, before they get to editors (if they tackle technical stuff at all).

But Feiginova is hugely significant in Tarkovsky's cinema in being a major force in developing Tarkovsky's distinctive editing style. Critics of Tarkovsky's films routinely cite the visuals, but rarely the editing. The rhythm and pace of Tarkovsky's films, though, is as central as the *mise-en-scène* or the sound. Feiginova, for example, said it was her idea to use the scene with the stutterer as the prologue to *Mirror*. That particular film went through some twenty versions before the final one was chanced upon (Feiginova and Tarkovsky employed a common method of laying out the film – listing the scenes on cards and shuffling them about).

5 : 5   SCULPTING IN TIME

The image becomes authentically cinematic when (among other things) not only does it live within time, but time also lives within it, even within each separate frame.

Andrei Tarkovsky, *Sculpting in Time* (68)

Notable examples of the long take occur in the films of Alfred Hitchcock, Orson Welles, Kenji Mizoguchi, Bernardo Bertolucci, Carl Theodor Dreyer, Miklós Jancso and Jean Renoir, as well as many *avant garde* filmmakers (Michael Snow's *Wavelength*, for instance, was founded on an endless zoom). The entire shooting style of Andy Warhol and Theo Angelopoulos was built around the long take. The 'sequence shot' is known as the *plan-séquence*: instead of a series of shots, the filmmaker constructs the action so that it can be captured in one take. The long take often employs the mobile frame, via craning, tracking, tilting, panning and zooming, added to complex blocking of actors and props (and, in the celebrated long takes of Hitch and Welles, sliding set walls, repositioned lamps, and large crews manning huge cameras on cranes that lumbered around the studio).

Andrei Konchalovsky remembered Tarkovsky discussing long takes, saying that a shot that was slightly longer could be boring, but a longer one created a new interest. If a shot was even longer, 'a special intensity of attention' could be generated.[1]

For Tarkovsky, the rhythm of a film came from within a shot, sculpting within the time of the shot, rather than being imposed from outside by editing. Hence Tarkovsky's cinematic technique of long takes, allowing time to fill up the shot. Although the sequence shots were much longer in the later films, Tarkovsky was experimenting with long takes from his first film onwards (in *Ivan's Childhood*, for instance, there are lengthy sequence shots which cover dialogue and action: when Galtsev talks with the doctor in the bunker, for example, the camera tracks back and forth, following the characters, without cutting. And in *Andrei Roublyov* there are many lengthy takes).

Tarkovsky's extended takes are not always complex tracking shots, like the finale of *The Sacrifice* or the candle-carrying in *Nostalghia*; they often involve one actor talking to camera or another character, while the camera slowly zooms or tracks in.

The no. of shots in *Nostalghia* is about the same as in *The Sacrifice*: 115-120, giving an average shot length of about a minute (a very high amount). In *The Sacrifice*, it's even higher: an average of one minute twenty-five seconds. Shots of 2, 3, 4 or more minutes are common in Tarkovsky's last three films. In *Nostalghia*, long takes include Gorchakov's 'dream' in the hotel room, Eugenia berating Gorchakov, and the candle-carrying scene. In *The Sacrifice*, sequence shots include Otto telling Alex to visit Maria (7 mins 12 secs), the house burning, and the opening scene (which's 9 mins and 26 seconds, according to Graham Petrie and Vida Johnson – it's shorter on DVD and video, perhaps due to the way film is transferred – it's irritating the way films are sped up, when they don't have to be). In *Stalker*, the long takes include the telephone room (6m 50s), the Writer's speech in the room of sand dunes, the Stalker's wife's monologue, and the final shot.

Sometimes a single take can stand in for a whole scene, a minor dramatic episode, with a beginning, development and ending. Critic André Bazin wrote of the possibilities of the long take. Bazin compared Jean Renoir's use of the long take in the search for realism with Sergei Eisenstein's short shots. However, Eisenstein had contemplated using one single take for a scene in *Crime and Punishment*.[2]

Tarkovsky's sequence shots aren't quite as long as Andy Warhol's 35-minute take in *Blue Movie* (1968, USA). A dream of many filmmakers is to make a film in just one take. Bertolucci remarked: 'I would like to make a film of one long take'.[3] Hitchcock got close to it most famously in *Rope* (1948, USA) (though his approach was a little stagey and literary). Bertolucci added: 'I want to do as many long takes within a single film as possible' (ib.). Tarkovsky moves towards this ethic, especially in his last three features, each of which is based on the long take. Carl Theodor Dreyer said: '[y]es, I believe very much in long takes. You gain on all levels' (ib., 115).

The long take negates montage. 'Editing is the basic creative force' wrote Vsevolod Pudovkin in *Film Technique* (J. Leyda, 371). US *avant garde* filmmaker Stan Brakhage reacted against the intellectualism of Eisensteinian montage. His rebellion is like the ego against the superego of Freudian psychoanalysis:

> I have been too dependent on just that kind of creativity which tends to be very intellectual, like the term implies: editor. An editor is very censorial, a censor who moves in there and tries to tidy thing up.[4]

But Tarkovsky's long takes must contain tension. The tension can be suspense, waiting for something to happen. But more usually, the tension must be spiritual. The long take must illustrate, express or be the embodiment of some spiritual state. In the long sequence shot where Gorchakov carries the candle over the pool at Bagno Vignoni in *Nostalghia*, the tension, dramatically, is whether he'll make it without the candle blowing out. But this shot works on other levels; its placement within the structure of the film makes it a spiritual test and apotheosis. It is Gorchakov's baptism by fire, his Calvary and his martyrdom in *Nostalghia*.

More typical is when Tarkovsky unbalances the ordinariness of a shot by having something extraordinary happening within it: a door creaks open, a bottle falls off a table. Suddenly, the shot is charged with emotion and expectation. Time must breathe within the shot for Tarkovsky. Hence his use of bizarre occurrences, which kick the shot into suspense, into the unknown. The implication is that anything *might* happen. Tarkovsky displaces normality and lets uncertainty rush in. Strange-ness is just around the corner. This unexpectedness, this new, Zen-like wakefulness of living, is best summed up by Lawrence Durrell, who says that the most unexpect-ed things are what is happening in the next room.

Andrei Tarkovsky's cinema actualizes the strangeness of living. The strangeness is here, all around people, but they become immune to it. One of the artist's tasks is therefore to refresh body and soul, so that the incredible beauty and strangeness of life is once again experienced. In poetry the movement is towards the Blakean (and Coleridgean) direct contact with the world stemming from the cleansing of the senses. D.H. Lawrence spoke of the touch of tenderness, the pure touch, which reactivates hidden/ latent/ unconscious feelings. It is this touch, this new relation, that counts, that reactivates livingness. As Lawrence says: '[b]lossoming means the establishing of a pure, *new* relationship with all the cosmos. This is the state of heaven'.[5]

I remember the Cornish poet Peter Redgrove telling me that strangeness was everywhere, at the centre of life, to the point where people take it for granted, and overlook it.[6] All the wonder of living is *already* everywhere. Many mystics say this – Meister Eckhart, Jalal al-din Rumi, Hui-Neng and Chuang-tzu. 'Leap into the boundless and make it your home,' says the great Chuang-tzu, perfectly describing the Kirkegaardian risk and dare of the artistic act of creation.[7] People are dead, says Domenico in *Nostalghia*, so must have their faith reawakened. The way into the wonder for the artist is via the creative process; but for Tarkovsky's protagonists, the way is through a spiritual transformation.

To achieve life breathing through the frame, Tarkovsky films motion: grass, trees, clothes blowing in the breeze and (so often) running water. The soundtrack emphasizes motion: dripping, creaking, rustling, the noises of nature on the move, a world that never keeps still. Even when Tarkovsky's frame seems to be static, the soundtrack evokes motion. Robert Bresson wrote: '[t]o TRANSLATE the invisible wind by the water it sculpts in passing' (67). This is precisely what Tarkovsky tries to do: to depict the invisible by showing what it touches and moves. The invisible in Tarkovsky's philosophic cinema is the spiritual, the divine, the unknown and unknowable. So he depicts a group of trees and then has the wind rustle the leaves.

Andrei Tarkovsky spoke of editing in terms of rhythm, necessity, sense and unity (ST, 113-121). Each shot must be filled with time, like a glass bottle being filled up (gently but surely) by a stream of water. The aim of editing is unity – to make an organic whole out of all the parts. 'Editing brings together shots which are already filled with time, and organises the unified, living structure inherent in the film' Tarkovsky stated (ST, 114). This recalls Eisensteinian montage again. Each shot has its own 'time-pressure' (ib., 121) and these must be connected carefully.

Editing for Tarkovsky is a musical process of harmonizing and counterpointing, of refrains and codas. Editing is highly personal, the stamp of a creative personality. What Tarkovsky dislikes is the imposition of a foreign structure on the material. It should all be one – the planning, shooting, editing and post-production. Tarkovsky edited his films as they were being shot, so that he could rearrange what was still to be shot, and react to material already shot. When he moved to the Western system, he said he had to wait until all of *Nostalghia* was filmed before he could start editing. (Actually, quite a few filmmakers edit as they go along, having their editors start cutting the film as soon as it's been shot).

Gilles Deleuze was critical of Tarkovsky's insistence on time flowing with a shot, and Tarkovsky's opposition to montage, which he saw as higher up the cinematic hierarchy. Deleuze pointed out that 'montage itself works and lives in time' (1989, 42).

Andrei Tarkovsky's films are open structures. They could be edited in a number of ways. Tarkovsky proves this himself, when he admits the production team got into a terrible mess over *Mirror*, which was edited into 'some twenty or more variants' (ST, 116). Indeed, *Mirror* could be re-edited *ad infinitum*. Sections could be added, subtracted, re-shuffled. Tarkovsky spoke of working very hard at editing *Zerkalo*: the twenty edited versions were not just subtly different, but were 'major alterations in the actual structure, in the order of the episodes' (ST, 116). When they tried 'one last, desperate rearrangement', the film started to gel. Understandably, it took the director a long time to believe that *Mirror* was working at last. 'For a long time I still couldn't believe the miracle' (ST, 116).

One could re-edit the dreams in *The Sacrifice* or *Nostalghia* again and again. Like Jean-Luc Godard's cinema, Tarkovsky's cinema can be seen as postmodernist: one could fold all sorts of material into his films, and, providing it was shot by Tarkovsky, the result would probably be unified (just add the sound of running water).

Having said this, Tarkovsky's films are basically narratively linear: they progress (or decay) from one situation to another. Sometimes the order of events can be re-arranged (in *Nostalghia*, for instance), but his films are linear (except for *Mirror*). Works such as *Stalker* and *The Sacrifice* move towards definite endings. Even if the endings are open and ambiguous, they still have many elements of narrative and cinematic closure. (The end of *Nostalghia*, though ambiguous, is a spectacular finale to the film).

Within his narrative structures, Tarkovsky organizes his sequences meticulously. He thinks in terms of sequences – of dreams, of strange happenings (a family goes outside to watch a neighbour's house burning), of rituals, of memories. This is the standard Tarkovskyan way of making cinema. The set-piece, the elaborate sequence, the best (or most arrogant) of which are done in one shot (Alex's crucifixion by fire in *The Sacrifice* being the most obvious example). Each sequence in Tarkovsky's cinema is joined to the next one (sometimes with linking images or refrains, like the fires in *Mirror*). Sometimes he intercuts a shot from an earlier (dream) sequence into a later sequence, but his basic technique is the long master take expanded to the point of mysticism.

5 : 6   THE SACRALIZATION OF SPACE

Andrei Tarkovsky's sacred cinema has a Renaissance sense of space, in which the individual's subjectivity is paramount. Tarkovsky's cinematic perception recalls Leonardo da Vinci's Vitrivius figure, which embodied the Renaissance view of the individual as the centre of the cosmos. Like most *ciné*-poets, Tarkovsky tries to maintain a continuity of space. But filmic space is not and never was the space of painting. In cinema there is what art historian Erwin Panofsky called a 'dynam-ization of space' (G. Mast, 154), and what Eisenstein called 'an impression of spatial dynamics' (ib., 82). In Tarkovsky's cinema, the tendency is not a dynamicization or temporalization but a *sacralization* of space. That is, the sense of space in Tarkovsky's poetic films tends towards the sacred. The spaces in his films aim to be landscapes of the soul. The outer world, with its water, glass and run-down appear-ance, is designed to reflect inner states – of 'soul' and 'truth'. Titus Burckhardt, in his book *Sacred Art in East and West*, said that '"physical space" is always the objectivization of "spiritual space"' (47). In cinema, space has a temporal dimension – '[d]istance is time' said the artist Paul Klee.[1]

In Andrei Tarkovsky's cinema, space has a mystical dimension. As with the Renaissance painter Piero della Francesca, there is a movement in Tarkovsky's cinema towards spatial mysticism and abstraction. Tarkovsky tracks his camera into walls and surfaces. His films are full of veils, like Bernardo Bertolucci's – layers upon layers of glass, water, wind, shawls, smoke, fog and curtains. As the camera dollies in, it encloses a claustrophic, ever more abstract space. Tarkovsky's camera drifting into empty, modernist spaces has affinities with the filmic spaces of Godard, Bertolucci and Antonioni. This abstraction in Tarkovsky's cinema has a mystical dimension. From Kasimir Malevich and Wassily Kandinsky to Brice Marden and Frank Stella, abstraction has had a mystical edge. Kandinsky and Robert Motherwell spoke of abstract art as a mysticism. Yet, conversely, for Kandinsky and the sculptor Constantin Brancusi, abstraction was realism. 'Abstraction = Realism', asserted Kandinsky.[1] Kandinsky described the journey of abstraction thus: '[t]he sequence is emotion (in the artist) –› the sensed –› the art work –› the sensed –› emotion (in the observer).'[2]

Speaking about his decision to use 3-D – not false-front – sets on *Throne of Blood*, Akira Kurosawa said he wanted to achieve a sense of realism. 'After all, the real life of any film lies just in its being as true as possible to appearances' (D. Richie, 122f), a view that can apply to Tarkovsky (if possible, Tarkovsky would opt for three dimensional sets. And Steven Spielberg, in the age of CGI, still preferred to build real sets).

Georges Matthieu described the problem like this: '[f]rom the Ideal to the real, from the real to the abstract, from the abstract one moves to the possible'.[3] Whether non-objective or representational, the aim is for what Titus Burckhardt called 'spiritual realism' (150). It is impossible to authentically depict the divine: so religious art is automatically abstract as well as aiming to be spiritually realistic. Realism yes, but not naturalism. Although Tarkovsky's films depict the natural world, it is a psychological realism that Tarkovsky was aiming for (his films are definitely not 'naturalistic'). In Edmund Husserl's phenomenological terminology, the 'self-appearance' of the world is a kind of total objectivity, an 'itself there'.[4]

Cinema can never show the world exactly as it is, as 'itself there', as what Jean-Paul Sartre called a 'given'. Cinema always deals in images. Its sense of presence is largely manufactured; it's illusion (everything is a cheat). It is merely coloured shadows on a screen, T.S. Eliot's 'heap of broken images' in Plato's shadowy cave. Tarkovsky, like Ingmar Bergman, goes for psycho-spiritual truths. Realizing that cinema is a heap of coloured images, which best make sense when mediated through individual experience, Tarkovsky makes psychological cinema. The movement towards syntactic abstraction is countered by a concentration on semantic realism.

Tarkovsky's cinema (like most cinema) is representational and figurative, but it is non-objective in the sense of being very subjective, and has its moments of abstraction. Tarkovsky's art moves towards sacrality, mystery and interiorization. Cinema as religious contemplation of the sacred.

Tarkovsky might have profited by looking at Islamic art, with its intricate arabesques which intertwine so beautifully and speak of the unity of Allah. In Islamic non-representational art, mystery is retained and unity is glorified. The equivalent in cinema might be purely formal or abstract film, a field Tarkovsky didn't explore, but he suggested glimpses of it. Imagine *Nostalghia* without Gorch-akov or Eugenia or Domenico in it. It would be a series of gentle tracking shots into and along walls, over puddles and streams, and through empty hotel rooms. It would be a new, more abstract Tarkovskyan cinema, more difficult and more boring maybe, but perhaps also more mystical.

SIX

Symbols and Motifs

Of late I have frequently found myself addressing audiences, and I have noticed that whenever I declare that there are no symbols or metaphors in my films, those present express incredulity. They persist in asking again and again, for instance, what rain signifies in my films; why does it figure in film after film; and why the repeated images of wind, fire, water? I really don't know how to deal with such questions.

Andrei Tarkovsky (*Sculpting in Time*, 212)

6 : 1   ON SYMBOLISM

No other filmmaker uses rain, water, fire or flight in the same, idiosyncratic, hypnotic and profound way as Andrei Tarkovsky. The way these motifs or symbols are used is distinctly Tarkovskyan, setting him apart from other filmmakers. Yet Tarkovsky denies that these elements are 'symbols' – he dislikes symbols, metaphors, parables and phantasies. He acknowledges the power of dreams, the occurrence of miracles, the movement of inanimate objects and the existence of God, but he denies symbols and metaphors. Yet he so deliberately and self-consciously places fire or water in his filmic spaces. Often these 'motifs' appear on cue, timed to make the biggest impact – such as the rain falling at the end of *Stalker*, after the men have stopped fighting. The rain here, at this point in the film, is the re-affirmation of nature and the natural forces of life. It washes away the delusions of the three seekers, re-aligning their expectations. The rainfall through the smashed roof of the building next to the Room in the Zone makes the water glitter, and it sounds refreshing and calming.

Krzysztof Kieslowski said he didn't film in terms of metaphors, but if viewers wanted to see things in terms of metaphors, that was fine with him. The important thing was to move the audience in some way, to have an effect on them, 'to make people experience something. It doesn't matter if they experience if intellectually or emotionally' (1993, 193). If Kieslowski filmed milk, he said, it was just milk. It didn't symbolize anything more. Very rarely, in cinema, it would mean something more, a miracle. 'Welles achieved that miracle once. Only one director in the world has managed to achieve that miracle in the last few years and that's Tarkovsky. Bergman achieved this miracle a few times. Fellini achieved it a few times' (1993, 195).

Certainly Andrei Tarkovsky's motifs act on the symbolic level, as well as the concrete and the dramatic. The motifs play a part in the dramatic narrative of the film, but they also work on the symbolic, spiritual, social and ideological levels. Asked if there was any symbolism in *Mirror*, Tarkovsky replied: '[n]o! The images themselves are like symbols, but unlike accepted symbols they cannot be deciphered. The image is like a clot of life, and even the author may not be able to work out what it means, let alone the audience' (D, 369). But symbols are not meant to be 'deciphered'. Part of their power is that they go beyond rationalization. Tarkovsky is digging himself into a hermeneutic hole by claiming there is no symbolism in his films. There is, masses of it.[1]

Tarkovsky's intention is to be concrete and realistic, to portray rain as it is because it is part of people's lives, he said in *Sculpting in Time* (212), adding:

> I am therefore puzzled when I am told that people cannot simply enjoy watching nature, when it is lovingly reproduced on the screen, but have to look for some hidden meaning. (ib., 212)

One can simply enjoy seeing rain or fire on the screen. But the rain is *reproduced on the screen*, as Tarkovsky says: it isn't there of its own accord. It is manufactured firstly, then represented on a screen. Rain is *created* – with hoses, rigs, rain towers, pumps, fire engines. Tarkovsky's rain is as contrived and artificial as the tackiest Hollywood B-movie studio painted backdrop. Tarkovsky's rain has a materiality which is simultaneously sublime and pretentious, both sensual and synthetic, authentic and obsessive.

Probably the director prior to Andrei Tarkovsky who made rain one of his chief motifs was Akira Kurosawa (rain appears in most of his films). Kurosawa's use of is clearly the precursor of Tarkovsky's: *Throne of Blood*, *Rashomon* and *The Seven Samurai* come to mind as great rain movies. The *sensei* commented: 'I love all of Tarkovsky's films. I love his personality and all his works. Every cut from his films is a marvelous image in itself'.

Tarkovsky wanted the spectator to surrender to the cinematic experience, and the experience is of a world created by an *auteur* (ST, 213). Tarkovsky tried to create life itself – as he saw it, that is. It is a personal view, which exalts the unconscious, the intuitive, and is profoundly anti-scientific, anti-political, and anti-rational. Tarkovsky said he grew annoyed by viewers asking what the Zone was in *Stalker*: '[t]he Zone *doesn't symbolize anything, anymore than anything does in my films*: the zone is a zone, it's life' (ST, 200; my italics).

What the Zone definitely was, was a zone. That is, a space divided off from the rest of the world. The Zone was clearly a sacred space in amongst profane space. According to Mircea Eliade, marking out a space in the world is equivalent to creating a sacred space, a mythic centre. Before magicians begin their rituals they sometimes draw a nine-foot magic circle, which becomes a temporary sacred site. The Zone in *Stalker* is clearly of a similar religious nature: it is a goal of the three protagonists for a start, and the Room within the Zone is the end of their quest. Further, the Zone is regarded with religious awe by the Stalker (and Tarkovsky carefully delineates the spaces of the Zone, which are poetically evoked, as well remaining ultimately ambiguous).

A filmmaker – or any artist – doesn't have to justify every (or any) æsthetic component of their artwork. Many of the things in movies are there simply because *they look good* (rain, smoke and mist, for instance, look good when shot on celluloid – especially with backlighting). But, critically, film images, once they've left the filmmaker's control and entered the public domain, become everyone's property, and thus can be decoded in all sorts of ways, using the critical methodologies of third wave feminism, or Kristevan semiology, or French *auteur* theory, or post-Lacanian psychoanalysis, or post-colonial politics, or post-Maoist Marxism or whatever. The filmmaker makes the film, but, once made, it becomes the audience's (and the critic's). The spectator possesses the images (and they possess the spectator).

With Tarkovsky's poetic cinema, one is sure the motifs are there for a purpose, and have a special value, symbolic or concrete or spiritual or otherwise, as may be, for the director. Of *Mirror* Tarkovsky wrote that 'there is no hidden, coded meaning in the film, nothing beyond the desire to tell the truth' (ST, 133). Yet this is the film with more Tarkovskyan motifs than any other: rain, water, fire, painting, birds, wind and flying.

Ingmar Bergman too disliked the critical analysis of the motifs in his films. He said '[h]ere we have an unbridgeable gulf – at least between me and the people who write commentaries on my films. I can't correspond with such people.' He added:

> I think I can explain it chiefly like this. For me, a film can never be something theoretical. What I've been trying to tell you all the time is that behind each production there has lain a practical, tangible reality. (1986, 246)

In *Sculpting in Time*, Tarkovsky rather lamely tried to explain the contrived ending of *Nostalghia* (213-6), saying that he hoped it was 'free of vulgar symbolism' (216). Well, it is *full* of vulgar symbolism, but it is no less astounding for that. But vulgar or eclectic, the symbolic dimension cannot be denied. Indeed, Tarkovsky displays his lack of knowledge of symbolism, because the really powerful and authentic symbol is the one that is both concrete and spiritual, the one that exists naturally and plastically, while also being highly mystical. Think of the snake, circle, moon, egg or mirror. The mirror motif, one of the most appropriate symbols for cinema itself, is at home in most contexts. Yet the mirror has multiple layers of symbolism (explored so well by filmmakers such as Rainer Werner Fassbinder, or Jean Cocteau in the *Orpheus* films).

Tarkovsky said he always thought of himself as a poet rather than a filmmaker (ST, 221). The best way to think of Andrei Tarkovsky's motifs or emblems is poetically. He uses them as a poet uses images, as pieces of intuitive magic that occur quite logically. A tree, a candle, a lake – these are special effects made special by the gaze of the camera. Really, there is nothing unusual about them. They are distinctly non-urban. Tarkovsky rarely discusses the technological city in his films. It is inferred from the outside (in *The Sacrifice* and *Mirror*). When the city is filmed, as in *Solaris*, it is as a nightmarish, surreal place, full of strange noises. The establishing shot of Rome, centred on St Peter's Church, in *Nostalghia*, for instance, is accompanied by the whine of a jet.

6 : 2   RAIN

Rain enriches a landscape with its sound, as John Hull, a writer who went blind later in life, has noted. Rain, Hull remarked, has 'a way of bringing out the contours in everything; it throws a coloured blanket over previously invisible things'.[1] Rain has a similar effect in cinema which, though it's ultimately constructed from sounds and images, can activate those sense memories of common occurrences like rain or wind. So the *sound* of rain in film, as much as the *sight* of it on screen, expands the cinematic world.

The one emblem that Andrei Tarkovsky probably uses more than any other is rain. Traditionally, rain symbolizes beautitude, purification, fecundity, revelation, divinity, blessing (J. Cooper, 136). Clearly, rain doesn't 'mean' all these things in Tarkovsky's metaphysical cinema. Yet it is no coincidence that rain presides over much of the childhood *dacha* scenes in *Mirror* (and *Nostalghia*). In *Mirror*, the ruler of the narrator's childhood is his mother. She is deified, shot in a number of glorifying poses and lighting designs which exalt her as a Goddess. In *Mirror*'s opening image, she sits on the fence, presiding over that huge field of buckwheat, and the trees of the Ignatievo forest behind her (lyrically evoked in Andrei's father's poetry). She is an agricultural Goddess, an Earth Mother. So it's only natural that it rains here, for as Aeschlyus says: '[t]he rain, falling from the sky, impregnates the earth, so that she gives birth to plants and grain for man and beast' (in ib., 136).

The first mysterious event in *Mirror*, the house on fire, is framed by the rain dripping from the roof. Later, the mother washes her hair and the room rains; she runs to work through the rain; and at the printing works the water runs out on her in the shower. In this and other films, rain is a purifying and regenerating element, often associated with childhood, parents and sexuality. In *Solaris*, at the end, rain pours into the father's house, and the self-absorbed patriarch doesn't notice it. In *Stalker*, masculinist/ patriarchal science (the nuclear bomb) is broken up ritually,

and thrown into the feminine pool of regeneration; then comes that lengthy rainfall;
each protagonist muses on their life and future. In *Andrei Roublyov* and *Ivan's
Childhood*, rain seems not to have so much of a symbolic purpose, even though it
begins and ends on cue, as it does at the beginning of *Solaris*, when the father steps
inside the house to avoid a shower. However, it is raining during Ivan's third
dream, on the apple truck (rain heightened the dream's significance). And in *Andrei
Roublyov*, rain appears at many keys moments: the rain shower with the three
monks at the beginning; the flashback Roublyov has; when Boriska finds the right
kind of clay; and running down the paintings and the horses in the rain in the
epilogue.

6 : 3   WATER

Rain is part of Andrei Tarkovsky's mythology of water. When Tarkovsky's rain
slides down the screen it is a personal signature, one of the director's recurring
cinematographic devices. Yet the hermeneutics of water in Tarkovsky's cinema is
much deeper. Water is the source and grave of all life. J.C. Cooper remarked that
'[w]ater is the liquid counterpart of light' (188), which is an interesting point for a
filmmaker. Cinema is constructed, materially, from reflected light, and certainly
water is very filmic – it looks good. Like D.H. Lawrence in his novels *Sons and
Lovers* and *The Rainbow*, Andrei Tarkovsky sets many of his scenes beside water –
there are many rivers, for instance. Tarkovsky loves rivers, loves flowing water.
Scenes often take place *in* rivers (the boy swimming in *Mirror*, the 'pagan' woman
swimming in *Andrei Roublyov*, Gorchakov walking through the stream in *Nostalghia*). Tarkovsky said he preferred rivers and streams to the sea. The ocean was
too big (and monotonous) for him.

Contemplating water is often a way back into the past – Kelvin stares at the river
in *Solaris*, and the Stalker's dream features a long travelling shot over objects in a
flooded building, which are like a tapestry of the lost bits and pieces of history.
There are oceans too, in particular the calm sea next to Alex's house in *The Sacrifice*,
and the ocean of the unconscious itself in *Solaris*, which spins slowly like a galaxy,

and contrasts so vividly with the placid lake of Kelvin's home.

Objects are often sunk under water – the angel and the flooded church in *Nost-alghia*, the flooded forest in *Ivan's Childhood*. No doubt, if he had the facilities and budget, Tarkovsky might have shot a flood in action – sweeping into houses, drenching precious artifacts, the waves rushing down cobbled streets. A flood would have made a useful counterpoint to the burning houses of *Mirror* and *The Sacrifice*.

There are many puddles and pools in Tarkovsky's cinema – the pool in the Room in *Stalker*, the puddle in front of the *dacha* in *Nostalghia*, and the numerous puddles that surround Alex's house in *The Sacrifice*, as if it is partially an island (which seems to appear from nowhere). The muddy pools that surround the painter and the bell-maker at the end of *Andrei Roublyov*, and the pools the balloonist flies over. In *Stalker*, the Stalker lies down on a tiny island, surrounded by shallow water. The pools look as if there's been a heavy rainfall in between scenes ('there are so many damn puddles, you can't avoid them', the Wrtiter complains to Stalker in the script of *Stalker* [CS, 383]). Rain stops and starts unnaturally in Tarkovsky's films, and, if it isn't actually raining, it looks as if it has just rained.

These half-soaked landscapes (or half-dry waterscapes) reflect the in-between-worlds nature of the Tarkovskyan protagonist's predicament. These pools obscure reality and also invigorate it. Water runs down roads and – much stranger – down walls. *Mirror* features a whole room of wet walls. The mother (as wife here) has just washed her hair – she stands back and flails her arms mysteriously. Suddenly the room is full of rain and the ceiling starts caving in. Clearly this dream-rain refers to some powers or influences Maria has – powers over her husband, and over her son, who is the implied voyeur (like the viewer) of this bizarre scene (the scene portrays the estranged and erotic relationship between the mother and father). The woman, shaman-like, conjures up this psychic rainfall. In the corner of the room a flame flickers. Fire and water are similarly pointed up in the scene a few minutes earlier, when the neighbour's house burns.

Fire and water can represent (in traditional symbolism) the mythic figures of the Sky Father and the Earth Mother (J. Cooper, 188). In both scenes, water is in the foreground, fire in the background (the father is more distant, emotionally, and is absent for much of the film). Fire is male, but water (female) puts out fire. The mother clearly associates herself with water – she goes to the well and drinks water, leans on the well, and watches the fire. When she's seen in the doorway later on, rain falls in the window behind her; it's raining when she visits the doctor's wife;

water flows down the wall behind her when she kills the cockerel; when she's an old woman, she walks along a road with puddles.

Water on fire – the powerful symbolism is reversed in *Nostalghia*, when Gorchakov carries the candle over the drained pool. This is a patriarchal ending to the film, in which the two male protagonists both perform rituals of life and death. The woman, Eugenia, has been displaced and decentred. At the end of *Nostalghia*, in her final appearance, she is only an observer of Domenico's suicide, not an active participant (Gorchakov had rejected her sexual advances earlier).

Andei Tarkovsky's most water-drenched film is *Nostalghia*. Domenico's house is a water-logged building – there's a piece of polythene stretched above his bed, collecting water (wouldn't it make sense for him to move the bed?); it rains continually, even though it's sunny outside; there is the model of the Italian countryside, with a river running through it; Gorchakov wades through a stream to the submerged church; there are the Baths themselves; it rains outside the hotel window; in the Russian dream there is a river and a pool; it snows at the end, and so on.

Nostalghia is one of the wettest of all films. Not just visually, but in the soundtrack too. One doesn't see but one often hears water in Tarkovsky's films: sounds recorded in all sorts of contexts: dripping water in a birch forest; running water in a disused warehouse; water running through reeds in a river, and so on. Water noises for every occasion, a vast library of natural sounds.

The Taoist philosophers said 'the sound of water says what I think.' Clearly for Tarkovsky the sound of water has a meditative, sacral value. Water often has a ritual dimension in Tarkovsky's works – associated with the Christian rites of baptism and purification. Purification by water occurs in *Solaris* and *The Sacrifice*, when hands are ritually washed (in both cases by mother/ Mary Magdalene surrogates). Then there are the wells in *Stalker*, *Ivan's Childhood* and *Mirror*.

Whereas in many contemporary filmmakers blood features prominently (as bodies are cut or blown up – in the cinemas of Hong Kong and Hollywood), in Tarkovsky's *œuvre* there is an emphasis on *milk*. The cat in *Mirror* laps at milk; and later on, milk drips on the floor at the doctor's house. A bottle of milk lies on the ground beside the policeman as Domenico's wife bends down to embrace his feet after she is released from her imprisonment in *Nostalghia*. In *Andrei Roublyov*, milk seeps into the stream after the stone masons are blinded (here it might be a stand-in for blood – partly because of censorship, but also because red blood wouldn't show up in dark water in black-and-white). Milk also appears in *Stalker* (in the glass on the table at the end, and the dog licks milk), and in *Solaris.*

Milk is clearly a motif of childhood and innocence (recalling the Orphic formula: *like a kid I have fallen into milk*, and the cauldron of the Celtic Goddess Ceridd-wen).[1] Milk also speaks of suckling, mother-child bonding, domesticity and sexuality. In *The Sacrifice*, during the first airstrike, a large bottle of milk, seemingly straight out of *Mirror*, smashes spectacularly, needing no explication as a dramatic moment. The maternal realm is shattered by the Law of the Father, embodied by the over-flying bombers. The spilt milk marks the end of living within the mother-world, the end of calm and nurturance, the end of living within maternal *jouissance.*

Water is a manifestation of the essence of life. Rain, a tree, a river — these are the so simple and so ordinary natural phenomena that populate Andrei Tarkovsky's films. Yet he also manages to imbue them with a sense of immediacy, presence and mystery. It is as if one has never seen rain before. The effect of this presence is something like the found objects of American artists Robert Rauschenberg and Jasper Johns, the stones of land artist Richard Long, or the readymades of Marcel Duchamp. Objects are placed in an art gallery and one re-appraises them. Similarly, Tarkovsky says *here, look at water for a while, isn't it beautiful?* Water fills the film with time, as light fills the frame with space.

6 : 4   FIRE

Like water (but unlike air) fire is very filmic. Like water, it moves, it flows and flickers, it speaks of time flowing within cinema's looking glass. And it is supremely magical, and religious. As Weston La Barre explained, the word for God, *diew* (later *deus*), root of the names <u>Ze</u>us, <u>Ju</u>piter, and <u>Di</u>ana, originally meant 'the shining one':

> It can refer to the sun (or moon), the sky, the divine planets, lightning, Soma, light, life and fire, as simply manifestations of the same phenomenon: the divine light [wrote La Barre]. It is the male mystery: the life-soul. (*Muelos*, 80)

Fire, light, seed, semen, Soma, phallus and gold – all these are part of the same mystery.[1] For ancient Greek philosophers like Heraclitus, all was a flux of fire; with Empodecles the four elements (each of which Tarkovsky explores in his films), were established. Fire, in traditional Western symbolism, represents transformation, purification, renewal, energy, passion, transcendence, and so on. Many Christian mystics (such as Catherine of Genoa, Mechthilde of Magdeburg, Richard of St Victor and Jan van Ruysbroeck) spoke of their ecstatic experiences as like being burned. The fire of love is one of the most common tropes in Christian mysticism. Blood, fire, heart, love and passion are all connected in Christian symbolism.

Tarkovsky uses fire in an alchemical fashion: he burns it on screen in the hope of alchemically forging another element – preferably the Philosopher's Stone or a magical child, if not some cinematic gold. In *Mirror*, fire – in a field or in a grate – is the image that connects past and present, that binds space and time. The image of a hand warming itself functions like the dog in *Nostalghia*, it jogs the memory and induces the flight from the present into the past. In a number of films Tarkovsky explored how fire eats away at reality, replacing it with a blackened mass. There are the burning houses; the burning book (in *Nostalghia*); Kelvin burns his papers (the bonfire appears later in *Solaris* in the childhood sequence). François Truffaut had heaps of books burning in *Fahrenheit 451* (1966, France), where the message is of ideological violence. But Tarkovsky adds a personal dimension: the book Gorchakov burns is a collection of Tarkovsky's father's poems. Such an image cannot fail to have distinct personal resonance for Tarkovsky. Perhaps here, as he burns a book of Russian poetry, Gorchakov severs his links with the past, and gives up the possibility of returning to his life in Russia as it used to be.

There is an explicit religious dimension to the burning bush in *Mirror* – the narrator and his wife discuss the Biblical source of the burning bush. During this conversation the camera lingers on the narrator's wife: this is significant, because the episode of God talking to Moses through a burning bush (*Exodus*, 3:2) relates to the sacred virginity of the Virgin Mary. The mother in *Mirror* is again likened to the Virgin Mary (as are the mother and Eugenia in *Nostalghia*). Like the burning bush, Mary remained intact (J. Metford, 56). It is another example of the Goddess symbolism in the film. The relevant extract from the *Bible* runs thus:

And the angel of the Lord appeared unto him [Moses] in a flame of fire out of the midst of a bush; and he looked, and, behold, the bush burned with fire, and the bush was not consumed. (*Exodus*, 2:3)

There is religious continuity here, over five thousand years: Moses sees God in the burning bush, and the camera tracks to the window of a flat in modern Moscow, and outside is a burning bush.

In *Andrei Roublyov,* there is the astonishing imagery of the 'pagan' festival – the naked people flitting through the trees carrying torches. Later, fire will be used in an utterly secular gesture as the Tartars invade Vladimir. But the final use of fire is overtly alchemical: the bell-casting (and later the segue from the bonfire in black-white-and-white to Roublyov's paintings in colour). In Tarkovsky's cinema, fire and water are two great principles, both active, both necessary. The hot, dry soul is best, said Heraclitus, but the cold, wet dimension is also needed for life. Thus Tarkovsky often has fire and water in the same shot (in *Nostalghia* there is the Baths and the candle; and the burning book with the sun-dappled water behind it).

Tarkovsky's last two films both end with extraordinary fire rituals. Both rituals involve the destruction of a whole world – a human body and a house. Domenico's crucifixion by fire is a tremendously powerful act, a ritual suicide staged for maximum ideological shock. The music goes wrong, the tied-up dog barks, the people stand and stare, mutely – but this adds to the futility of the act. Domenico is consumed by fire, the symbol of Buddha, Zeus, Hermes, Shiva, Kali, Mazda and deities everywhere; yet, tragically, nobody reacts. Everyone is dumb. The police wearily climb the steps – to them it's merely another psychotic, another charred body to clear up, more forms to fill in.

The location is important: it is the Capitoline Hill, the ancient spiritual and political centre of the Eternal City. This is the capital of two dead empires: the Roman Empire and Catholicism. Rome condemned Christ to death. The madness of the Emperors, the pomposity of the Popes and Catholicism, the strident monument-alism of the architecture, the decadence of the city – all these and a million more associations with Rome are hinted at. Rome is a massive historical centre – there's nowhere else to compare with it as a history-making city (Jerusalem? Byzantium? Athens perhaps?). Tarkovsky chose Rome for its religious associations: the establishing shot of Rome centres on St Peter's Church not, for instance, the Roman Forum, Spanish Steps, the Colosseum, Vittorio Emanuele Monument or the Pantheon. That opening shot says 'Rome', like Big Ben says 'London' or the Eiffel Tower says 'Paris'. But the emphasis on St Peter's Church underlines the religious aspect – of dead religion, loss of spirituality, and martyrdom, all of which are part of Domenico's self-immolation. The flame leaves the body at death, and one sees very clearly the transference of power: Domenico dies, and Gorchakov, at that very moment, lights the candle, which is, on one level, Domenico's soul, but on the highest level, the candle and its carrying ritual represents hope for the future, for the rebirth of life. To light a candle is a tiny act, in the cosmic scheme of things. Yet Tarkovsky gives the gesture a cosmological and spiritual grandeur due to the structure and nature of the film. Suddenly the candle stands for all kinds of rebirth.

6 : 5   SNOW

Snow is part of Andrei Tarkovsky's water symbolism and is also, of course, a part of Russia's landscape. Snow appears in most of the films, as a naturalistic setting (in *Andrei Roublyov*), or as a psychological background (the dream sequence in *The Sacrifice*), or as an event of sudden beauty (in *Ivan's Childhood*), or as the landscape of childhood (in *Solaris*), or as the final, climactic addition to Gorchakov's Russian/Italian dream in *Nostalghia*. The snow falling so silently and beautifully here is (partly) a reference to Ingmar Bergman.

In *Solaris* Kelvin and Hari contemplate one of Pieter Brueghel's paintings of peasants at play in the snow (*Hunters in the Snow*, 1565, Kunsthistorisches Museum, Vienna). The camera pans around the many details of the painting, to the stately sounds of Johann Sebastian Bach. This is a long sequence: at the end of it, there is an insert of a boy and a swing in the snow. This is from Kelvin's father's home movie. Later, Kelvin replays this film, in which his mother appears. The viewpoints multiply as in a hall of mirrors (though in a gentle way, utterly different from the famous climax of Orson Welles' *The Lady From Shanghai*).

A similar Brueghel-inspired image (like Brueghel's snowscape) occurs in *Mirror* — anonymous people are dotted about the snowscape with a similar meticulous sense of *mise-en-scène* that informs *Last Year at Marienbad* (Alain Resnais, 1961, France). Tarkovsky condemns setting up scenes taken from paintings, yet here are two examples. It could be that here he is saying no more than 'I remember childhood Winters as if they were from a Brueghel painting.'

With most filmmakers, blowing wind could not be counted as a 'symbol' or 'motif'. Yet a wind machine is usually necessary for an Andrei Tarkovsky production. In *The Sacrifice*, for instance, there is an (imagined?) atomic blast wave that blows away some snow and old doors. There are two gusts of wind at the beginning of *Mirror*, which at first are simply mysterious, simply *there*. But the prologue of *Mirror* features a stutterer being 'cured'; and, after the wind has gone, the mother turns away and the poetry begins. Here the narrative proper begins: and it is the Creative Word through air which has set it in motion: from the stuttering youth, through the title sequence, to the wind in the field to the spoken words of the poetry, the gusts of the creative spirit blow through the film.

Wind and air is the spirit, the *pneuma*, the breath of life, associated with procreation (in Aristotle), orgasm and the soul. Wind or breath is part of the same holy male mystery of fire. One recalls that in *Mirror* fire suggests the father or the narrator (the son of the present) remembering, and that rain and water relates to the mother (or feminine principle). This fits; the pieces of Tarkovsky's jigsaw start to lock together, because wind and air fans and feeds fire. Indeed, the five-year-old boy thinks immediately of his father when he hears the rustling bushes outside his bedroom. Tarkovsky comes back to this shot a few times: by day or night, sometimes in slow motion, sometimes in black-and-white, one sees the trees and bushes next to the house blowing in the breeze. This is an image of otherness – the primal otherness of the natural world. But it also evokes the father, and what he brings with him – the otherness of the outside world, in a realm of exile, marginalized. He exists in the outer spaces, like Cathy's ghosts in *Wuthering Heights*.

If the air is not full of drifting snow or driving rain in an Andrei Tarkovsky film, it might be full of seeds which float dreamily by (in *Andrei Roublyov*). These images of snow or seeds falling or hair blowing or reeds streaming out under water, give a sense of weightlessness, a lightness of touch rarely matched in cinema. Again, time flows by, life flows by, everything is in motion, everything is changing.

Flying is transcendence, release, escape, transformation. In film it is simulated by a helicopter, a crane, a dolly, a blue screen, visual effects or a Steadicam shot (as in Stanley Kubrick's *The Shining* [1980, USA] or *Birdy* [Alan Parker, 1984, USA] for example). The crane shot itself has sexual undertones, as Bernardo Bertolucci explained:

> Well, a dolly shot is an erection pure and simple. They are deep breaths that give you the impression of flying through the air. When we dream about flying we are also responding to a very precise erotic drive. (1987, 197)

Géza Róheim put it thus: the 'flying dream is an erection dream... the flying dream is the nucleus of shamanism' (154). The archaic shaman 'flies' to other worlds, s/he climbs up the World Tree, and so on. Film is a waking dream, in some ways, which re-writes reality. The image of flight, central to shamanism (and shamanism is the origin of all religion) seems well suited to religious cinema, and to cinema in general. The dream of flying is one of the oldest dreams, and cinema is well-equipped to portray it. Certainly since early cinema (Georges Méliès' *Le Voyage dans la lune* [1902, France] for example) flight has always been a prime cinematic image.

In Andrei Tarkovsky's poetic cinema, flight is largely sexual. People float above their beds, dreamily spinning in post-orgasmic trances. In *Solaris* there is a gratuitous weightlessness sequence. Equally gratuitous, though far more spectacular, is the opening of *Andrei Roublyov*, with the flying machine which looks like something out of Leonardo da Vinci's sketches of fabulous machines (Leonardo is supposed to have 'invented' the helicopter). Flight is part of Tarkovsky's belief in the miraculous. It is something that simply occurs. It is rather like the Grail: if one doesn't believe in it, one doesn't see it. The emphasis on flight, which is scientifically 'impossible' in the way Tarkovsky imagines it, recalls Tertullian the Christian theologian again: one believes *because it is absurd.*

Although Tarkovsky is known for using motifs like birds, and flight, and levitation, and the natural elements, like water and earth, the sky is contemplated far less than expected in his cinema. In Steven Spielberg's films, characters are often looking up at the sky, spaceships zoom out of the clouds, or the camera lingers on starscapes, or giant moons, but Andrei Tarkovsky concentrates on the earth, on pools or rivers, on churches and *dachas*. Tarkovsky's cinema rooted in the soil and water.

6 : 8   BIRDS

The bird is a shamanistic animal *par excellence*, associated with transcendence, soul and flight to other worlds. Birds flutter out of the Madonna's womb in *Nostalghia*; after this sequence, a feather flutters down beside Gorchakov. An angel walks in front of the *dacha*. Gorchakov has, like the Stalker, a feather-like streak of white in his hair. He is a 'marked man', one of the 'touched' – half-angelic. Later, before Gorchakov gives his long monologue, there's an angel under water. There is a bird in his Russian wife's bedroom.

The ancestors of the angel in Western religion is again the shaman, who danced like birds and donned costumes of feathers (the American Indian feathered headdress is a late example of the bird-shaman's regalia). Birds and women are again connected in *Mirror*: the mother kills the cockerel; a bird breaks the pane of glass in the *dacha*; a bird flaps beside the floating woman. Most oddly of all, a bird lands on Asafyev's head, a miraculous shot. A bird represents the soul very clearly in the narrator's grandiose setting free of the tiny bird (a sparrow) that he's been holding on his death bed. *Andrei Roublyov* contains geese, birds flying in front of the aerial camera in the Tartar raid, and when Boriska looks up at the tree when he's searching for the place to cast the bell.

There are horses in most of Andrei Tarkovsky's films. For him, as for most artists, they are noble and magnificent animals. Tarkovsky makes references to artists' depictions of horses: Michelangelo Buonaroti's equestrian statue in Rome (in *Nostalghia*); and Leonardo da Vinci's horses in the *Adoration of the Magi* and other works (in *The Sacrifice*). In *Andrei Roublyov*, the battle scenes recall Leonardo's wildly mobile orchestrations of people and horses. But horses are also pure strangeness, as in D.H. Lawrence's *St Mawr*, as well as being the prime totem animal of so many Hollywood Westerns and historical epics. A horse walks into the Cathedral after the battle in *Andrei Roublyov*, and the effect is bizarre: a horse inside a church. Yet Roublyov hardly turns his head to look (he's in shock after the raid). *Andrei Roublyov* closes with a vision of horses in the rain: it is an image of nature in harmony, with its fecund water, like the end of *Stalker*. A horse strays from the rain-soaked ending of *Andrei Roublyov* into the beginning of Tarkovsky's next film, *Solaris*. It walks about, strange and independent, like an alien presence, a premonition of the otherness Kelvin will experience later on in deep space. The same Russian horse appears in the credit sequence of *Nostalghia*. Like the *dacha* and the dog, the horse seems to be an icon of Russia for Tarkovsky. He films the horse as D.H. Lawrence wrote about it: as an animal of power and *mystique* which people cannot resist or analyze.

The Tarkovskyan dog appears in every Tarkovsky film, apart from the 1962 feature (Tarkovsky had dogs as pets). Dogs are most prominent in *Nostalghia*: both Gorchakov and Domenico have dogs (it may be the same animal). Gorchakov's Russian dog, seen in his memories or dreams of Russia, appears in the Italian hotel, padding into the bedroom as if it's the most ordinary thing in the world. The dogs in *Nostalghia* appear at key moments: in Gorchakov's central dream in the hotel, in the final scene, and at Domenico's death in Rome. It is the dog, not the people watching, that cries out when Domenico burns himself to death. The dog is ironically the most 'human' voice present. Dogs appear in the home movies and dreams in *Solaris*. The barking of dogs is one of Tarkovsky's favourite off-screen sounds. Critics have also likened the dogs in Tarkovsky's films to Anubis, the ancient Egyptian god, and the dog in *Don Juan* by Carlos Casteneda. Cats also appear in Tarkovsky's cinema – notably in *Mirror*, before the burning house scene, when the two children play with a cat, pouring salt onto its head.

No object seems more suited to cinema than the mirror (as image, theme, motif, philosophy, etc). Andrei Tarkovsky is by no means the only filmmaker to be obsessed by mirrors: consider Jean Cocteau's *Orpheus* films, where characters step backwards into mirrors on their way to the Underworld, or the moment in *2,001: A Space Odyssey*, where astronaut Bowman contemplates himself in horror after travelling through the Stargate. The mirror is the perfect object for embodying modernism, whether it is used in Egon Schiele's stylized self-portraits, André Gide's self-reflexive *mise-en-âbyme* fiction, or the films of Ingmar Bergman, Rainer Maria Fassbinder, Orson Welles, and the Marx Brothers. In *Mirror* the mirror functions as an interface between past and present — this is made clear when, after the raining room sequence, the mother looks at herself in the mirror, then she's seen as an old woman: she wipes the mirror. The film subsequently travels, as the first poem says, 'beyond the mirror'.

Cameras can look into mirrors and one can't tell which is the reflection and which is the 'reality'. Cameras love mirrors, and make love with mirrors. Virtual, cyborg, real, dream, imaginary or contrived reality — all these blur in cinema. Only when the camera pulls back from a mirror can one see which side is which. Hundreds of filmmakers have exploited this kind of manipulation. The mirror is the perfect device for Jean-Luc Godard's postmodern explorations, where scenes are acted into mirrors (as in *Vivre Sa Vie*, 1962, France). At the beginning of *Peggy Sue Got Married* (Francis Coppola, 1986, USA), the godfather has a double mimic the motions of the lead actress (Kathleen Turner) making herself up in a dressing table mirror, echoing the best mirror gag in movie history — when Harpo skillfully imitates Groucho's every movement in *Duck Soup* (Leo McCarey, 1933, USA).

In *Nostalghia*, Gorchakov stares into a mirror on a wardrobe in the street and finds his *doppelgänger*, Domenico, staring back at him (it was a scene that came from the days of *Mirror*). This is a common motif of identification. At the end of the film, as the camera slowly zooms out from the house and Gorchakov, the first indication the audience has that he is not back in Russia is from the reflection of the arches of the Cathedral in the pool in front of him. This sense of unease is exacerbated even further: the camera is set up so that where the reflection of the Russian house should be, in the pool, one sees the Cathedral: this reflection accentuates the unreality of Gorchakov's state of mind, and the ambiguity of his nostalgic achievement. Cinema is automatically nostalgic, Tarkovsky reckoned, due to its ability to replay the same scenes again and again (ST, 140).

In *Solaris*, the mirrors are of a different order: there are the circular windows that look out onto the vortex of the Ocean; and the video screens which reflect back a different kind of image. In *The Sacrifice*, Alex is filmed in mirrors, and the *Adoration of the Magi* reproduction in Little Man's room is shot under glass so it acts as a mirror. Meanwhile, the floor of the main room downstairs is so highly polished it acts as a mirror. Often in Tarkovsky's films, characters stare at themselves in mirrors, in fascination, sometimes in vanity (adjusting their appearance), but also in fear, as if they're seeing something truly other. In *Hoffmanniana*, the mirror is the familiar seeing device of fairy tales: Hoffmann sees himself creeping down a corridor carrying a candle (CS, 348).

Stuart Hancock noted that:

Mirrors abound in [Tarkovsky's] films, and often his characters speak to one another's mirror image rather than to each other. In carefully staged scenes, characters stare off in different directions, aiming their words into thin air, even though those words work into each other's hearts like daggers. (1996)

In film after film, Tarkovsky's camera dwells on reflections in water, and often water and glass together. There are glass jars and bottles scattered on the floor of Domenico's house; and a large jar or bottle features in the childhood sequences of *Mirror*. In *The Sacrifice* glasses tremble and the jar of milk smashes. In *Solaris* the chandelier rattles. At the end of *Stalker* the glasses which at the beginning trembled as the train trundled by, skid along a table. Fish swim in a glass bowl, itself afloat, in the Stalker's dream.

Glass objects – in the form of bottles, cups, mirrors, vases, or jugs – are part of Tarkovsky's large props bag of still-life artefacts, which he sets up on table tops, or chairs, or window sills: eggs, books, plants, candles, lamps, curtains, lace and bed sheets.

Glass is often associated with death (in European fairy tales and Celtic mythology), the double or twin, as well as Buddhist transparency, self-awareness, celestial power, purity, perfection, the light of God and the self-luminous. Water and glass possess magic for Tarkovsky. He makes glass appear like some strange element, some new addiction to the Periodic Table of physics. The glass containers in his films look like the precious phials, crucibles and vessels of some mediæval alchemist or magus – snatched from the laboratories of Paracelsus or Cornelius Agrippa, say. The mirrors and glasses are filters, veils, barriers, walls enclosing secret worlds beyond reach. One can't quite cross the threshold of the mirror in Tarkovsky's cinema, as one can in Jean Cocteau's *Orpheus* films.

SEVEN

The Worlds of Andrei Tarkovsky

7 : 1   TARKOVSKY'S WORLDS

Andrei Tarkovsky's worlds are unlike those of any other filmmaker. As soon as one starts watching an Andrei Tarkovsky film one enters his worlds, and they are quite different from the worlds of, say, Shuji Terayama, Howard Hawks or Alexander Kluge. Stanley Kubrick might be associated with some bland five-star hotel foyer (out of *The Shining*) or the even blander space stations in *2001: A Space Odyssey*; Jean-Luc Godard's world is the cafés and boulevards of the Left Bank; Rainer Werner Fassbinder cruises Berlin's cosmopolitan streets; and Pier Paolo Pasolini inhabits a Southern Italian scrubland. And the world of Steven Spielberg would be a suburban housing estate in middle America (as in *E. T.*, 1982, USA or *Close Encounters of the Third Kind*, 1978, USA or *Sugarland Express*, 1974, USA). Tarkovsky's worlds are trash-strewn landscapes quite at home as the background to a painting by Pieter Brueghel the Elder or Leonardo da Vinci. Tarkovsky's world is more like that of Luis Buñuel, or Pier Palo Pasolini in his Middle Ages trilogy, or Werner Herzog in his *The Enigma of Kasper Hauser* (1974, West Germany). Pasolini's and Herzog's scruffy, ramshackle, earthy mediæval worlds have parallels with Tarkovsky's timeless worlds. 'My heart is very close to the late Middle Ages' said Herzog.[1] Tarkovsky's heart is happy in the late Middle Ages and Early Renaissance. He is not, like Max Ophüls or Stanley Kubrick, a Baroque artist — nor is he a Neo-Classicist, like Alain Resnais or Peter Greenaway. Tarkovsky always includes a lot of grit and sweat in his filmic worlds: they always look believable, in the sense that people are seen to be standing in mud or snow or water (rather than on a smooth studio floor), they are often dirty, shabby, weary, right in the thick of things. Sam Goldwyn had famously responded to a reviewer who complained that the slums in his films looked too nice, without any real dirt: 'they should do, they cost us so much!'

7 : 2   MISE-EN-SCÈNE

For Andrei Tarkovsky, *mise-en-scène* must be realistic, concrete, plastic, actual. Rain must look like real rain, not the spray from a fire engine and rig that's been hired for the day's shoot. *Mise-en-scène* must be true to life, he says. 'By its very nature cinema must expose reality, not cloud it' (ST, 72). But the 'truth' is subjective, psychological, and comes from the actors and the essence of a scene (ST, 74). Part of Tarkovsky yearns for a *mise-en-scène* that is transcendent and universal, dealing in essences — rather like the sculptures of Constantin Brancusi. But the other part of him aims for a *mise-en-scène* that is lodged in the real, messy, unpredictable world, and is restrained, not didactic. One of the central tensions in Tarkovsky's poetic cinema is precisely this: between the symbolic, Neoplatonic, religious, iconographic yearning, and the realist, plastic, immanent necessity. For Tarkovsky, *mise-en-scène* should not simply illustrate some meaning in a scene, should not be schematic, clichéd (that would be too simplistic), but should 'startle us with the authenticity of the actions and the beauty and depths of the artistic images' (ST, 25).

Poetic cinema ought to be emotional, intuitive, intense, Tarkovsky asserted. In Tarkovsky's poetic cinema, two worlds are in conflict: the inner and the outer, the individual and the social, the spiritual and the materialistic, the past and the present, the dream and the 'reality', the human and the natural. The struggle continues up to the end (and beyond the finale) of the films; in some, the personal and psychological aspect wins out (as in *Nostalghia*); in others, characters accept that they have to enter the social, material realm of the present again (*Andrei Roublyov*).

7 : 3   THE HOUSE

The primary Tarkovskyan environment is the house of childhood, the Russian *dacha*, which appears in most of Tarkovsky's films, but most fully realized in *Mirror*. This house is explored endlessly by the roving camera, which tracks around the rooms and picks out *that* particular table from memory and *this* magical window with its view over the buckwheat field and *those* bushes outside and the forest beyond. Ingmar Bergman is similarly obsessed with childhood:

> I'm deeply fixated on my childhood. Some impressions are extremely vivid, light, smell, and all. There are moments when I can wander through my childhood's landscape, through rooms long ago, remember how they were furnished, where the pictures hung on the walls, the way the light fell (1986, 84).

In *Nostalghia* the *dacha* is longed for: it is the symbol for Gorchakov of Russia, of the homeland and the heartland. He yearns for it so much he transplants it into the Italian cathedral where he ends up. *Nostalghia*, after all, takes as its plot the displacement of exiles and travellers from their heartlands. And in *Mirror*, significantly, the first newsreel images shown are of the Spanish civil war refugees, who are similarly displaced. Like the house in *Mirror*, it is shot in *Nostalghia* from the front, showing the porch and the people moving around outside it. Behind it are the trees of the Russian forest. In *Solaris* the house plays a similar role, the house of the father: Kelvin returns just as much to the house, with its lake and surrounding fields, as to the father and the family. The childhood home is a place of magic and ritual, where objects have a life of their own, where the Summers are resplendent, where children play endlessly (and often in slow motion) in the fields and trees.

In *The Sacrifice* the whole house is burnt to the ground: this is an act of œdipal violence, a Promethean rebellion against society, culture and the ghosts of patriarchy, to transcend the law of the father – as well as being a last, desperate attempt at transcendence (to kill the ego, to transcend the self, in the language of psychoanalysis). In *Nostalghia*, the wooden house is placed miraculously (but at great cost) inside the cathedral (partially placating the personal and œdipal ghosts). But in *The Sacrifice*, the homeland is decimated in a calculated way (though using a magical agent, fire). Both films indicate that the homeland (or the relation to the ancestors, earlier generations, the family forebears) is dead. And if it's not quite dead, then it should be burnt to cinders. Why? Because every past illusion and delusion and hope once clung onto must be shattered. In each film Tarkovsky's protagonists realize that the idea of the homeland is an illusion, a false hope, a desire that can never be repaid (most of his protagonists are wanderers).

Houses that are returning to the nature are another recurring motif, dwellings that once contained families and childhoods which are now crumbling into ruin, overgrown. The opposite of the Russian house is the degenerate, dilapidated apartment or warehouse. Alexander and the Stalker live in places that look like disused warehouses. They are not workers' cottages or houses, but post-industrial wastelands. These settings are places which are not functioning as they used to any more, and the people who dwell in them cling on to existence by their fingernails. The inhabitants of the Tarkovskyan wastelands always seem to be on the edge, holding on for dear life.

7 : 4   THE BED

Strange to think of the bed as a major setting in Andrei Tarkovsky's cinema – he is not a maker of pornography, for example, where actors are dragged over to beds that suddenly appear at every opportunity. The bed is a major site of familial emotions in Tarkovsky's cinema: the relations of blood and incest are at their strongest here. Whole families sleep in beds (*Stalker*), young boys witness the primal scene in beds (*Mirror*), and couples float in sexual reveries (*The Sacrifice* and *Mirror*). The bed is also the platform for dreams, and thus for someone like Tarkovsky who loves dreams, who notes down dreams copiously (in the *Diaries*) and who films dreams, the bed is bound to assume great importance. Beds appear as part of the childhood wonderland in Federico Fellini's cinema (in *Amarcord*, 1974, Italy) and, satirically, in *City of Women* (1980, Italy; in this film a row of men in a huge bed masturbate in front of giant images of screen goddesses).

Ingmar Bergman wrote that '[n]o other art medium – neither painting nor poetry – can communicate the specific quality of the dream as well as film can' (1986, 44). That unreal flicker of images in dreams, piling on top of each other, as well as their strangeness, can be rendered poignantly in films. But Bergman is wrong about painting and poetry. There are many paintings with dream-like qualities – think of the pictures of Tarkovsky's beloved Leonardo da Vinci, or Nicholas Poussin, Gustave Moreau, Odilon Redon, Marc Chagall and Arnold Böcklin, or poems by Arthur Rimbaud, H.D., Friedrich Hölderlin, Dante and Fyodor Tyutchev. Poetry, indeed, has its origins in the dream language of the shaman, the dancing sorcerer who is the original religionist/ priest/ artist/ poet.

Generally, Tarkovsky sticks to straightforward dream or memory sequences: it is assumed that Gorchakov's dreams in *Nostalghia*, for instance, are what he is really dreaming about (the dreams are not simply Gorchakov's memories, though: the viewer isn't asked to assume that the *dacha*, the trees, the pool, the dog and the groups of women in Gorchakov's dreams are what his life in Russia is *really* like). Tarkovsky always investigates the past, how memories of happier times haunt the protagonist (like Ivan's dreams of his mother). He does not use flashforwards, for instance, of what the future might be like for the characters (in *Nostalghia*, though, Gorchakov has a vision of Eugenia and his wife, the embodiments (the spirits, the *anima*) of Italy and Russia, embracing). And Tarkovsky does not (usually) insert flash cuts to confuse the audience: his memory and dream sequences are usually clearly signposted as such (in *The Sacrifice* and *Nostalghia*, though, the segues between 'reality' and dreams are more ambiguous). In *Mirror*, it is more complex, because some of the dreams or memory sequences are not wholly from the narrator's (Alexei's) point-of-view. The flashback to Maria's ominous experience in the printing works, for instance, is not something the narrator had direct access to.

What Tarkovsky doesn't do is follow Hollywood's penchant for narrative strategies such as: 'oh, it was all only a dream', or the virtual and alternate realities of films such as *The Matrix* (1999) or *Twelve Monkeys* (1995). Tarkovsky's films don't withhold vital information until the end of the film: like the revelation that Bruce Willis is a ghost in *The Sixth Sense* (1999), or the ghosts-within-ghosts in *The*

Others (2001), or that the 19th century community in *The Village* (2004) really exists in the present.

To suggest a move into a dream world, Tarkovsky employs pretty much all of the classic cinematic devices: mysterious music, heightened sound effects, losing local sound, electronically treated sounds, black-and-white, altered film stock, unusual or subjective camera movements, discontinuties of space and time, doubling of characters within the same space, impossible or unrealistic combinations of props, sets or actors, and so on.

7 : 5 FOREST OF TREES, FOREST OF SYMBOLS

The forest in symbolism and mythology is the realm of testing and initiation, the feminine zone of the natural world, secrets, death and transformation. In Andrei Tarkovsky's magical cinema it is the realm of dreams, of childhood and fairy tales, of the Baudelairean 'forest of symbols'. The 'dark forest' is a key environment of fairy tales, as it is of horror and Gothic films. It is the place of initiation and trial. It lies on the edge of the familiar, everyday world of the fairy tale. It is where the protagonist gets lost, meets strange creatures, undergoes transformations and spells. It is, typically, one of the first places the protagonist enters on the journey outwards from the home, in *Snow White*, *Little Red Riding Hood* or *Hansel and Gretel* for example, and, earlier, it is the opening scenario of Dante's *Divine Comedy*:

> In the middle of life's path
> I found myself in a dark forest
> where the straight way was lost... (*Inferno*, I: 1-3)

In the *Divine Comedy*, the forest is not only allegorical, but theological.[1] Dante's *selva oscura* or dark forest is associated, as in fairy tales and horror films, with (Christian) sin, alienation from God and error. The poet-pilgrim in the *selva oscura* is cut off from God, the 'straight way' is lost, and the task of the *Divine Comedy* is to reach the Divine Light. Fairy tales have similar (though secular) goals. At the end of *Little Red Riding Hood*, in the Grimm version, the protagonist learns the moral lesson of straying from the straight and narrow path: '[n]ever again will you stray from the path by yourself and go into the forest when your mother has forbidden it'.[2] The forest is a zone of otherness, strangeness, enchantment and the unknown. In (Jungian) psychological terms, it is the unconscious, or confusion, a realm of instability, a *regressus ad uterum*, a place of re-creation and re-birth, where the hero/ ego/ soul is tested and initiated. The enchanted or dark forest is a place of wild things, such as dragons in caves, or witches in their gloomy houses; it is also a place of death (and dragons, witches, caves and darkness are linked with death or the 'dark side' of life). The dark forest also has a 'feminine'/ uterine/ womb association, for it is the place of re-birth. The places in fairy tales linked with the dark forest (caves, marshes, deserts, wells, seas, underworlds) are also 'feminine'/ birth spaces. Entering the dark forest is essentially the 'descent and return' process of mythology (Orpheus, Jesus, Theseus, Persephone, Isis and others descended into the Underworld or Hell and returned changed and/ or reborn). The descent is towards the foundation of life, to the secret heart of nature. The initiate (whether Orpheus, Hansel, Little Red Riding Hood or Persephone) has to overcome fear and doubt, and learn courage and resourcefulness. Often a monster has to be encountered and sometimes slain (Theseus and the Minotaur, Perseus and St George against the dragon, Marduk and the monster Tiamat, Zeus and the Titans, Jack and the giant). The Grimm brothers, in their *Children's and Household Tales*, expressed some of the Germanic love of forests, which is fuelled by awe and mysticism. There are clichés that abound about the Germanic and (Russian) mystification of forests as places of ritual and magic, sites of notions of community, race and origins. However, these clichés about the dark forest do form much of the background of fairy tales, in Jacob and Wilhelm Grimms' books especially, and also in Russian culture.

In *Ivan's Childhood* there is the flooded forest; in *Andrei Roublyov* there is a birch grove which also featured in *Ivan's Childhood* (M. Turoskaya, 33). In *Mirror* and *Solaris* the camera lingers on trees, their forms and textures; in *The Sacrifice* the camera tracks around trees, and there is of course the 'Japanese' bo tree which is climbed by the camera on a crane, shaman-like, at the end of the film. This latter tree is clearly a cosmic 'Moon-Tree' or 'World Tree' of mythology and shamanism, linking two worlds, heaven and earth, the sacred and profane realms. It is the *axis mundi*, standing at the world centre. The boy sits under the Tree of Enlightenment just like the Buddha. The camera climbs up the tree like the shaman who attains magical powers and flies to other worlds. In Qabbalism the top of the Tree of Life is

Kether, the Crown, the One, the Tenth *Sephiroth*. In *kundalini* yoga serpent-power climbs up the *chakras* of the body to the top, the brain, the pineal gland, the third eye. Tarkovsky's Tree of Life is also Christian (Russian Orthodox): it is both the Cross, and the Tree from which Adam and Eve picked the forbidden fruit: it is the symbol prime of the Fall and Redemption (the Cross is also linked in symbolism to the maternal realm – the man dies on the body of the mother). Salvation and redemption and the re-instatement of primal unity are Alexander's aims in the film.

One origin of Tarkovsky's cinematic trees is probably those of his childhood home in the Ignatievo forest, the subject of his father's Arseny's poem:

> Embers of last leaves, a dense self-immolation,
> Ascend into the sky, and in your path
> The entire forest lives in just such irritation
> As you and I have lived for this year past.
>
> The road is mirrored in your tearful eyes
> Like bushes in a flooded field at dusk,
> You mustn't fuss and threaten, leave it be,
> Don't jar the stillness of the Volga woodland. (ST, 161)

Poet Sergey Esenin (d. 1925) wrote in a similar manner of Russia's '[d]ear birch woods'.[3] In a typically soulful lyric, Esenin wrote:

> O ploughed fields, ploughed fields,
> the sadness of provincial Russia;
> on my heart is yesterday,
> and inside my heart Russia shines,
>
> Like birds, the miles whistle
> from under my horse's hooves.
> And the sun sprinkles its rain
> in handfuls over me. (ib., 392-3)

This poem, like so many Oriental *haiku*, is practically a verbal parallel of Tarkovsky's poetic images.

The ruined church in *Ivan's Childhood*, the cathedral in *Andrei Roublyov*, the ruined cathedral in *Nostalghia*; these are settings which require no explication. The cathedral in *Andrei Roublyov* is a major setting in that film. It's seen with the white walls, before it's been painted; after the battle the icons and paintings are glimpsed behind the war-weary characters; the people take refuge in the cathedral – the Tartars ride into it, the most powerful image of the secular realm invading the sacred in all of Tarkovsky's cinema. In *Nostalghia*, the ruined church is clearly a symbol of the dying (or dead) religion of Christianity (and the bankruptcy of all religions in the thoroughly secular world Gorchakov inhabits). But, as Gorchakov walks through it, a dialogue between God, no less, and St Catherine (or their earthly representatives), is overheard. This (incredible) dialogue, ironic though it is, shows that belief and faith is still valued in Tarkovsky's cinema. The churches, the external manifestations of Christian faith, may be falling apart, but the inner spiritual search continues (think of the Stalker). Indeed, it is so powerful, it eats away at people, killing their bodies as well as their souls (as happens to Domenico).

In 1978, Tarkovsky wrote that it was necessary 'to love. And to believe. Faith is knowledge with the help of love' (D, 168). If churches don't appear in *Stalker*, *The Sacrifice* and *Mirror*, images from churches – icons and paintings – do, emphasizing that for Tarkovsky the æsthetic dimensions of religion have a value beyond their poetic beauty. The emphasis on religion and spirituality throughout Tarkovsky's cinema suggests that though his cinema has a modernist, New Wave outer shell, inside it is very traditional and pre-modern. Tarkovsky argued for spirituality not materiality, for inner freedoms rather than external freedoms, addressing moral, not material problems.

An old overcoat is the basic requirement for the male Tarkovskyan anti-hero, preferably grey or black, knee-length, and very shabby. An old woolly sweater, again dark (blue or black), is also required. In this outfit the Tarkovskyan protagonist could wander around Kafka's Prague, Bohemian Paris, *fin-de-siècle* Vienna or Stalinist or Dostoievskyan Moscow without bothering anybody, and without being bothered. The costume is classless, ageless, characterless. It is Outsider gear, but not restricted to any particular time or place. The costume could've wandered out of any classic novel from the past 150 years; it's a familiar outfit from the fiction of Knut Hamsun, André Gide, Jean-Paul Sartre, Albert Camus, Fyodor Dostoievsky or Charles Dickens. It is not flamboyant, doesn't draw attention to itself, and wants to blend in with the background. It's the costume of Northern Europe and Russia, a cold climate, where it's always Autumn or Winter, where there's barely enough wood to light the stove.

For women, Tarkovsky favours white cotton dresses and dark shawls, for the Russian/ homeland sequences (as in *Mirror* and *Nostalghia*). This costume seems based on his mother, women of the olde worlde, relating to the mythologies of Mother Russia. Again, it is timeless, a look that could be at home in the Middle Ages as well as the 20th century. The other sort of costume for women occurs in *Nostalghia* and *The Sacrifice*, the so-called 'modern woman', in long, floaty dresses, veils, shawls and scarves. The look ties in with the long, eroticized hair Tarkovsky favoured, and the Virgin Mary faces (women like Russian ikons). Eugenia, in particular, is very fashion-conscious – the effect is like Italian *Vogue* meets British *Home and Garden*. Again, dark, autumnal colours prevail, and, as with the mother in *The Sacrifice*, the assertion is of independence. (*Nostalghia* was partly filmed in Milan, so the link to the fashion world is fitting. Costumes on *Nostalghia* were designed by Lina Nerli Taviani and Annamode 68).

Tarkovsky dresses women as if they have wandered out of some imaginary Pre-Raphaelite painting entitled '*Redemption*'. Hair is worn long in most of Tarkovsky's female characters. Long hair is an object of fetishism, as in *Mirror* o r *Andrei Roublyov* (the fool). When it is worn loose it is a display of sexuality: the witch in *The Sacrifice* has very long hair, which she lets down and twines about Alexander on her bed – a stereotypical representation of the woman as sexual spider or serpent, weaving webs of lust around the victim. She is like an Edvard Munch *Madonna* or one of Gustave Moreau's *femme fatales*. The daughter too, who slips about naked, has long hair, while Adelaide is austere, repressed, piling her hair up.

Tarkovsky's costumes tend towards muted, dark colouration and soft fabrics. No pastels or primaries for Tarkovsky. Nothing like the bright reds, pinks, purples, greens, yellows and blues in Sergei Paradjanov's films, for instance, or the saturated hues of contemporary Hollywood cinema.

7 : 8   LANGUAGE

Pictures, visual images, are far better able to achieve that end [to pose questions and demonstrate problems that go to the very heart of our lives] than any words, particularly now, when the word has lost all mystery and magic and speech has become mere chatter, empty of meaning, as Alexander observes.

Andrei Tarkovsky, *Sculpting in Time* (228-9)

Language may not be a motif or a symbol, but it is certainly one of Andrei Tarkovsky's prime considerations. The Word is set against the Image. It can easily be seen from Tarkovsky's films, which feature little dialogue but extraordinary imagery, the means of expression Tarkovsky prefers. The ability to speak is creative, one of the primary marks of being human – linking back to the Creative Word of God (and the artist). Tarkovsky uses verbal expression – the revelation of it – to begin *Mirror*. In many films there are mute people (in *Solaris*, *Andrei Roublyov*, *Stalker*, *The Sacrifice*); there are stutterers; there are the 'holy fools', who speak the unspeakable; there are the many extracts of poetry, spoken in voice-over or by the characters; in *Nostalghia* there is a discussion on translation (poetry is what is lost in translation, said Robert Frost). Here, Tarkovsky investigates how much cultural exchange there can be between two nations, and how deep it can be. Pushkin and Tolstoy are set against Dante and Petrarch (the poetic deities of Russia vs. those of Italy). If poetry or soul cannot be translated, then Gorchakov must have left his soul in Russia.

But surely much of religion (if not soul or spirit) is translatable? Otherwise, what about the *Bible*, which has been translated from Hebrew and Greek into Latin and English and countless other languages? After all, Christianity is not 'native' to Russia, yet Tarkovsky (apparently) believes in the Judæo-Christian God, a deity from 2,000, 3,000 or 4,000 years ago, created in another culture, another place, another time. The problem of language and translations is vast and very complex. Tarkovsky's way was to cut through it by making pictures, not words. The ambiguity is still there, but it's easier for Tarkovsky to deal with. 'Build your film on white, on silence and on stillness' wrote Robert Bresson (126).

In *The Sacrifice* language is in the foreground. 'Words, words, words' moans Alexander (quoting Shakespeare and speaking in English in the film). The lines are from *Hamlet*: Polonius asks '[w]hat do you read my lord?' and Hamlet answers '[w]ords, words, words' (II. ii. 195). Alexander is surrounded by rustling grass, the sound is like the susurrus of words. His son, temporarily deprived of verbal agency, speaks of the Word at the end of the film. When the boy asks 'why?', Tarkovsky's answer is clear: the camera cranes up the tree, away from the boy, away from the human, chattering realm, into the dazzling whiteness of the sun, sea and tree. If one wants to discover the wonder, Tarkovsky says, simply contemplate this natural glory. (The irony consists in attempting to convey the transcendent or supra-lingual experience via cultural means. Like poets of all ages, Tarkovsky can only use language to point to something beyond language, that mystical realm Wittgenstein evoked. Hélène Cixous remarked that 'everything is language'.[1])

The opening of *Mirror*, with its sequence of the birth (or rebirth) of language (or access to language), can be seen in the terms of Lacanian psychoanalysis. In their study of Lacan, Rob Lapsley and Michael Westlake wrote:

The entry into language and the discovery of lack in the Other therefore precipitates the child into the constitutionally unsatisfiable state of desire. In a further sense, too, the entry into language is the birth of desire. (70)

In a sense, all of *Mirror*, and much of Tarkovsky's cinema and cinema in general, concerns Lacanian *manque à etre*, the lack, the desire. The narrator in *Mirror* goes back to the Lacanian 'mirror phase', in which his mother is the Other, as well as the mirror in which his self-idealization is reflected. So much of cinema replays the œdipal crisis of the entry into the symbolic order of Lacan, with its emotions of lack and desire. As Toril Moi crystallized Lacan's thought so concisely: '[t]o speak as a subject is therefore the same as to represent the existence of repressed desire'.[2]

EIGHT

Sound and Music

When a sound can replace an image, cut the image or neutralize it. The ear goes more towards the within, the eye towards the outer.

Robert Bresson (51)

8 : 1   SOUND AND SPACE

It would be easy to make up an *Andrei Tarkovsky Sound Effects* CD, a compilation of his favourite sounds. It would contain dogs barking, a buzz saw, birdsong, glass tinkling, curtains flapping, wind, thunder, a few rain showers, and twenty different 30 second bursts of water (dripping, running, gurgling, washing).

Generally, Andrei Tarkovsky takes one sound and mixes it high, like Ingmar Bergman, against a background of silence. Tarkovsky praised Bergman's use of sound in *Through a Glass Darkly*, 'a sound on the brink of audibility' in the lighthouse scenes (ST, 159). Tarkovsky admired Bergman's selective sound, singling out a natural sound and enlarging it, making it expressive; Tarkovsky cites the scene in *Winter Light* where the body is found by the stream: '[t]hroughout the entire sequence, all in long and medium shots, nothing can be heard but the uninterrupted sound of the water' (ST, 162). Tarkovsky uses sounds out of context, and lots of off-screen sounds. His sense of the off-screen is highly developed. His films are full of big spaces; they are spacious, for two reasons: 1. his use of off-screen sound, and particularly sounds which enlarge the sense of space, 2. the lack of chatter, of dialogue. Tarkovsky's films have long chunks of silence, or a very few sounds, and these long passages are not kitted out with music, like so many other films. Tarkovsky is quite confident enough to allow many scenes to play in near-silence, whereas more inexperienced directors (or those with producers yelling for more action from the wings) might be inclined to cut to the next action beat or plot point. Tarkovsky uses Robert Bresson's aural ethics: '[w]hat is for the eye must not duplicate what is for the ear' (50).

Tarkovsky's handling of sound is sometimes deliberately ambiguous. 'His sounds destabilize; they make the coherent and comfortable seem suddenly strange and disorienting'.[1] In Tarkovsky's films, sounds sometimes take a long time to become recognizable: the takes are long, and sometimes sounds fade up very gradually, as the camera tracks or zooms slowly. The key to Tarkovsky's ambiguous sound is the way he reveals sound sources, or deliberately obscures a sound's identity, or only selectively reveals a sound's source (ib., 237).

For example, in *Nostalghia* there are off-screen conversations which take some time to be identified. When Andrei and Eugenia visit the St Catherine Baths, the spectator hears a long conversation off-screen. Only after the languorous, slow tracking shot has moved to the far left of the Baths are the sources of the colloquy revealed (the bathers in the pool). In another off-screen conversation, over another tracking shot, as Andrei visits the ruined cathedral, the interlocutors are not revealed at all – perhaps because they are St Catherine and God, or people standing in for them (Tarkovsky has filmed gods before, though: in *Andrei Roublyov* he shot Jesus in the Crucifixion scene).

In *Stalker*, sounds mysteriously appear then vanish: even a small waterfall makes a great din, but when the travellers reach the waterfall and river near the Zone, the sound of it is heard halfway through the tracking shot that reveals it. And when the pilgrims visit the same spot later on, no rushing water is heard at all.[2] Tarkovsky often used parallel sound to interweave reality, dream, memory and fantasy, as when Andrei in *Nostalghia* hears the dripping water or folk singing in the corridors of the hotel in Italy, or when the buzz saw from Domenico's memories invades his own memories. Tarkovsky's use of parallel sound is more subtle than cutting from black-and-white to colour, which indicates a movement from reality to memory, but can be also more insistent. While the eye is dazzled by the memory sepia sequences in slow motion in *Nostalghia* (such as Domenico chasing his son across the steps of the village square), the sound that accompanies the memory makes its presence felt upon the ear just as strongly. Parallel sound occurs in another place in *Nostalgia* when Andrei, thinking of his wife's voice, conjures up her sleeping form and says 'Maria'. She wakes and glances around, as if she had heard his voice in the room. She looks towards the camera, where she thinks the voice has come from.

Dripping water, one of the major Tarkovsky emblems, is a sound not normally audible in everyday life. Certainly during the day in urban or suburban areas, dripping water is not a common sound. The background sounds are too noisy. Only when one is out in the country, or at night, can such quiet sounds usually be heard. The sound of water suggests a 'transcendent, unlocated space', a place that has always been there, like the invisible, sacred, inner world. As such sounds are only heard in moments of quiet and calm, they are linked with states of meditation and repose: in short, religious states of being. A sound such as dripping water is at once relatively ordinary but it's unusual to hear it so often in so many locations, as it occurs in a Tarkovsky film.

Some sounds in Tarkovsky's cinema play once only – such as the sound of the bottle dropping in *Mirror* in the *dacha*, or something (unseen) rolling on the floor in *The Sacrifice*, or the glass falling at the end of *Stalker*, a sound which merges with the rattling approach of the train. There's a kind of poetic genius in the way that Tarkovsky incorporates the sounds of unseen objects, like rolling coins on the floor. Often, these sounds have no onscreen (physical) motivation, but they expand the world of the films immensely. (The sound of coins in Tarkovsky's films hint at bargains, wagers and sacrifices.)

We're always talking about Tarkovsky here, as if the director did everything on a film. But there are plenty of people responsible for the sound in Tarkovsky's cinema. They include: Remo Ugolinelli, Danilo Moroni, Filippo Ottoni, Ivana Fidele, Massimo Anzellotti and Luciano Anzellotti (*Nostalghia*), Owe Svenson, Bosse Persson, Lars Ulander, Christin Lohman and Wikee Peterson-Berger (*The Sacrifice*), E. Zelentsova (*Ivan's Childhood*), V. Krashkovsky (*The Steamroller and the Violin*), E. Zelentsova (*Andrei Roublyov*), Semyon Litvinov (*Mirror* and *Solaris*), and V. Sharun (*Stalker*).

In *Mirror*, in the first of the present-day scenes, at Aleksei's apartment, the camera tracks through empty rooms while Aleksei speaks to his mother on the phone. There is no indication that Aleksei is somewhere in the flat, or where his mother is. The telephone conversation may itself be a memory. There is no insert shot of a phone either, as in the typical Hollywood movie. In *Stalker*, as the characters go into the Zone on the railway car, Tarkovsky, Artemiev and Litvinov use a rhythmic sound of wheels clanking on the tracks; then they add electronic processing of the sounds. This technique – of rhythmic natural sounds or machine-made sounds later processed in a studio – is found in much of 1980s synthesizer pop music – in groups such as Kraftwerk, 'kraut rock', Orchestral Manœuvres in the Dark, Cabaret Voltaire and Depeche Mode. The sound of the railway in *Stalker* is very similar to OMD's *Sealand* (1981) and *The Avenue* (1984).

Tarkovsky's sense of sound is really remarkable, and a major factor in the power of his cinema. In *Stalker*, when the train runs by the Stalker's home, there is: 1. the sound of the train, 2. some metal rattling, 3. a brass band, 4. an aeroplane (this latter is added when the mother weeps on the floor).

8 : 2   SOUND IN *THE SACRIFICE*

In the long and often comical dialogue in *The Sacrifice* between Otto and Alexander, in Alexander's upstairs study, when Otto tells Alexander he must sleep with the witch Maria, the soundscape includes: 1. the creaking of Little Man's bedroom, 2. Swedish folk music, 3. singing from downstairs – a woman, perhaps Alex's wife, and 4. the sea, very quiet. These noises enlarge the screen space immensely, enriching the fictive world Tarkovsky is creating. In the opening two scenes of *The Sacrifice* there are three bangs, like thunder claps or distant explosions, which accompany and underline particular moments: 1. when Otto mentions death, 2. when Alexander speaks of finding the house for the first time, and 3. when little Man jumps on his back. Each of these is a moment of emotional poignancy. The thunder cracks are unexplained – there is no storm, and no rain; they are used to create an atmosphere of unease, of tension before a storm (Alexander, though, does look offscreen as if he's heard one of the explosions. But because they also occur at emotional moments, as when Little Man leaps on Alexander, they also occur in Alexander's mindscreen).[1]

Thunder claps are heard over the image of Christ in *Andrei Roublyov*, where he appears as the Pantokrator. The effect here is of divine power and violence – Christ is portrayed as the stern deity who presides over the Last Judgment, over life and death. In the crowd scene in *The Sacrifice*, only footsteps are heard, not the cries of people nor other noises associated with a crowd (a Hollywood production, for instance, would incorporate all sorts of sound sweeteners for such a big scene). The location and time of the scene is not explained. During it, the sounds of Maria's house and Alexander's house are heard (emphasizing that it is a dream or fantasy).

Ambiguous use of sound occurs in *The Sacrifice*, when the bombers fly overhead. The sounds and images used to suggest the aeroplanes approaching – the maid with the glasses and the sound of vibrating glasses – seem to indicate that the sound comes from above (the maid appears to be glancing up at a chandelier). However, the rattling glasses and low rumble suggests an earth tremor; so when the source of the disturbance is revealed as jets flying overhead, the subversion of a conventional sound/ image association is unsettling (and the aircraft are never shown. A number of jet sounds were mixed together to create the final effect).

Throughout *The Sacrifice* a female folk song is heard, often accompanying Alexander's dreams. By the end of the film, as Maria cycles away from the burning house, the singing becomes a pastoral song, of a woman singing to a herd of cows, or a goosegirl singing to her flock (A. Truppin, 239). The goosegirl's song is linked to the image of the nude Martha chasing some geese in Alexander's house. As in *Nostalghia*, such rural folk songs relate to the memory of the homeland, the realm of the mother.

Occasionally Tarkovsky's cinema features complex mixes and sound-layering: during Alexander's dream, the soundtrack includes the voices of Maria, Alexander and his wife, a crowd's footsteps, the female folk song, Shakuhachi flute music, rattling glass, Alex sobbing (saying 'I can't'), and Maria comforting him like a mother nursing a sick child. The characteristics of these sounds alter as the dream develops. Each sound is mixed high, and the result is frenetic and disorientating. It only takes one or two noises to produce such dissonance, and Tarkovsky usually restricts himself to one or two, instead of five or more.

Among filmmakers Andrei Tarkovsky's deployment of sound recalls that of Ingmar Bergman and Robert Bresson. Near-silence is one of the hallmarks of these filmmakers, and of the art film in general. Jean Cocteau, like Michelangelo Antonioni, will let minutes pass before anyone says anything. This is rare in Hollywood entertainment cinema, where, as in radio, silence is feared. Large parts of Alfred Hitchcock's *Vertigo* (1958, USA) are without dialogue, as Scottie pursues Madeleine obsessively around San Francisco's huge boulevards, but these sequences are overlaid with Bernard Herrmann's ceaseless string music.

Tarkovsky's soundtracks, like Robert Bresson's in *Four Nights of a Dreamer* (1971, France), is a quiet, hypnotic mix of one or two main sounds. Rarely does Tarkovsky go in for a complicated multi-layered mix, such as in the American 'sound designer' films of the Seventies and Eighties (*The Conversation* [Francis Coppola, 1974] or *Nashville* [Robert Altman, 1975]). In the big budget US movies of the late 1970s and 1980s (such as the *Star Wars* trilogy, *Superman* and *Apocalypse Now*), sound designers such as Walter Murch became elevated as mini-*auteurs*. They would spend months preparing the sound mix for a film. They would use four different parts of a helicopter sound to make one sound (as at the beginning of *Apocalypse Now*). Robert Altman's ensemble films were also aurally flamboyant; Altman used deliberately confusing soundtracks consisting a lot of people speaking at once.

Orson Welles also foregrounded the strangeness and sometime incoherence of speech and audibility in films such as *Macbeth* (1948, US) and *Touch of Evil* (1958, US). Some viewers thought Welles' low budgets meant his dubbed sound and overlapping dialogue was crude and cheap. In fact, Welles added the sound in post-production precisely so he could control the sound quality. The large amounts of reverb, for example, are part of Welles' overall cinematic intentions. When critics complained of the 'bad sound quality' in *Macbeth* or *Chimes at Midnight* (1966, Spain/ Switzerland), they seem to have forgotten that Welles was the maker of *Citizen Kane* and *Touch of Evil*, as technically brilliant and virtuosic as any films in cinema's history. Welles was one of the great film directors of sound, with virtually no rivals.

8 : 4   SILENCE

Be sure of having used to the full all that is communicated by immobility and silence... Against the tactics of speed, of noise, set tactics of slowness, of silence.

Robert Bresson (20, 56)

Like Robert Bresson, Michelangelo Antonioni and Ingmar Bergman, Andrei Tark-ovsky uses a lot of silence, or near-silence (sometimes called 'atmosphere' or room tone) in his art (much of the sound in art cinema consists of little more than 'atmospheres'). In this way spiritual resonance can reach a maximum. French philo-sopher Michel Foucault spoke positively of silence:

> I often wondered why people had to speak. Silence may be a much more inter-esting way of having a relationship with people... This is something that I believe is really worthwhile cultivating. I'm in favour of developing silence as a cultural ethos.[1]

Ludwig Wittgenstein, Karl Krauss and John Cage also emphasized silence, while sound designer Walter Murch said he liked to try to get a film to a point of silence, because that was a very interesting place to be in a film. Ursula Le Guin wrote a wonderful short sci-fi story ("The Silence of the Asonu", 1998) about a community which spoke only very reluctantly. The children chatter up until the age of seven or eight, then retreat into continual silence, communicating solely by gesture. Le Guin's story is a poignant, humorous satire on human communication (including how the Asonu people become regarded as religious mystics, their perpetual silence being taken for great knowledge).

> Some visitors to their world are convinced that the lips of these quiet people are locked upon a knowledge which, in proportion as it is hidden, must be valuable — a spiritual treasure, a speech beyond speech, possibly even that ultimate revel-ation promised by so many religions, and indeed frequently delivered, but never in a wholly communicable form. The transcendent knowledge of the mystic cannot be expressed in language. It may be that the Asonu avoid language for this very reason.[2]

There is a further dimension to silence — the mystical aspect. In most historical world mysticisms (Catholicism, Taoism, Buddhism and Sufism, for example) there is a cult of silence. There are three different silences in Christian mysticism — of the

Andrei Tarkovsky   *193*

mouth, the mind and the will. To hear the inner voice of God one must practise all kinds of silence.[3] Religious philosophies of silence included the Christian Quietist movement, which came to prominence in the 17th century, with mystics such as Madame Guyon, Miguel de Molinos and François de Sales. The emphasis was on passivity and reception.

Among modern artists, no one has spoken more passionately about silence than Samuel Beckett. In Beckett's fiction there is a constant tension between the desire to stop talking, for peace and stillness, and the desire to express oneself, to communicate. Beckett's *The Unnameable*, which ends 'I can't go on, I'll go on,' works up to an astonishing plea for silence:

> I can't speak of anything, and yet I speak… if it's possible you can do nothing when you want nothing, who cannot hear, cannot speak, who is I, who cannot be I, of whom I can't speak, of whom I must speak, that's all hypotheses, I said nothing, someone said nothing… The silence, a word on the silence, in the silence, that's the worst, to speak on the silence… the silence, speak of the silence before going into it, was I there already, I don't know… in the end, it's the end, the ending end, it's the silence, a few gurgles on the silence, the real silence…[4]

But perhaps the best precept on silence in mysticism comes from Taoist philosophy, from the *Tao Te Ching*: '[h]e who knows does not speak, he who speaks does not know.' This says it all. In which case, all cinema, art and the media would cease. But in cinema silence is tough – on the viewer as well as the characters – and only rarely implies complete knowledge.

8 : 5   SOUND EFFECTS

Glass tinkling (in many films); a dog barking; the creak of a bucket (in *Mirror*); coins rolling on the floor; wind rustling leaves and bushes; dripping water; running water; the seagulls and skirling birds in *The Sacrifice*; the creaking in Little Man's room; the wind in the grass; behind the cathedral tracking shot in *Nostalghia*, focussed on Gorchakov walking, children and a woman conducting a religious ceremony are heard; the sound of the electrical saw in *Nostalghia* seems to be the perfect sound of a sunny, empty afternoon. Andrea Truppin suggests that the sound of the saw in *Nostalghia* is related to Christianity, to, specifically, Christ the carpenter (this may be stretching filmic analogies a little too far). The sawing sound is introduced when Andrei visits Domenico: Christian motifs abound here (in the Beethoven music, the bread and wine, the discussion of St Catherine, the objects in Domenico's house). Being an *electrical* saw rather than a hand saw (which is associated with Christ as carpenter) may relate to the film's theme of having religious faith in the modern world. The long shot of Rome, for example, one of the great Christian centres of the world, is accompanied by a loud jet passing overhead. Such a shot encapsulates the tension between the old and the modern, the religious and the profane, the (old) world of the spirit and faith, and the (new) world of technology and the machine.

All these sounds add a dimension of mystery, narrative and meaning to the images. They are not narrative sounds in the conventional sense, and often they have nothing to do with extending the physical space. They are not psychological noises either, heard by just one protagonist. They are, rather, the sounds of spiritual states, the noises that accompany religious quests and states of being. Being silent magnifies local sounds so all one can hear is birdsong; or perhaps one hears dripping water. The ear can be as selective as the eye, and Tarkovsky explores the possibilities. Few sounds seem more suited to religious contemplation than running water, or rustling wind. These natural sounds are timeless. Not only have they occurred for millions of years (they must be some of the oldest natural sounds), they also induce a sense of timelessness. Running water or the wind blowing can have a hypnotic quality, suspending experience of time and space, letting the viewer dream while awake. Tarkovsky's cinema often gently nudges the spectator away from the world of words, numbers, rational thought, modern living. Sound is one of Tarkovsky's major tools in accomplishing those psychological and spiritual movements.

When the film comes out of the title credits in *The Sacrifice* and the gorgeous, ancient sound of the sea and the seagulls is heard, a primæval world is evoked, a world that could be from ten million years ago. The soft but relentless beating of the waves induces a sense of tranquillity. Once established, Tarkovsky can go on to gently unveil his images. Tarkovsky also uses many human-made noises, such as the jets in *Nostalghia* and *The Sacrifice*, or the trains that trundle by in *Stalker*. Tarkovsky's ultimate aim, he said, was to use only natural sounds: on the perfectly

realized film (an unrealizable aim as any artist knows) there would be no place for
music at all (ST, 162). He admits that he fails, and uses much music (ib., 159).

8 : 6   SOUNDTRACK MUSIC

*The number of films that are patched up with music! People flood a film with
music. They are preventing us from seeing there is nothing in those images.*

Robert Bresson (126)

Incidental or specially produced soundtrack or theme music in the Hollywood movie
manner is not so common in Andrei Tarkovsky's cinema – no *E.T.* themes or *Star
Wars'* full orchestral extravaganzas for him. Robert Bresson was unequivocal on
this matter: '[n]o music as accompaniment, support or reinforcement. *No music at
all*' (19). In Tarkovsky's cinema, there tends to be classical music and folk music in
the later films, and incidental music in the earlier films: Vyacheslav Ovchinnikov's
conventional screen music for *Ivan's Childhood* and *Andrei Roublyov,* and Eduard
Artemiev's eclectic soundtracks for the subsequent three films (Artemiev suggested
that Tarkovsky employed classical music to make cinema more 'serious' as an art
form; Tarkovsky told Artemiev that cinema was a young artform, so he used
classical music, like the references to the Old Masters in painting, to give his films a
sense of history for the audience). Tarkovsky tries to use music as a poetic refrain, to
parallel the visual image, and maybe open up 'the possibility of a new, transfigured
impression of the same material' (ST, 158). Johann Sebastian Bach in *Solaris* is
deployed in this way: at the beginning, middle and end of the film, it acts as a
refrain of the theme of the film. In *The Sacrifice* Bach is used in the same way.

  Music could be a way of deepening and widening the audience's perception of a
scene, Tarkovsky asserted. It didn't necessarily add anything that wasn't there
already, but it did add a 'new colouring' (ST, 158). But music must always be in
tune with the visual image, Tarkovsky asserted, enhancing it rather than going
against it (ST, 158). And it shouldn't illustrate what was going on, shouldn't prop

up the film.

In his later films, Tarkovsky moved away from employing a conventional score which would underpin the emotion or the action, towards heightened sound effects, and particular pieces of classical music. For Tarkovsky both music and cinema were artforms which dealt with reality, which had an immediate relation to the world, and which didn't require a mediating language (ST, 176). Plenty of cultural critics would violently disagree with that view. For many, both music and cinema are profoundly culture-specific, profoundly mediated, and affected by cultural contexts.

Tarkovsky's main composer, Eduard Artemiev, made some restrained but evocative music for *Solaris*, *Mirror* and *Stalker*. In *Mirror*, as the camera tracks in to the condensation stain on the table there is a tumultuous crescendo in the soundtrack that sounds like Giles Swain's *Cry*, or the György Ligeti music from *2,001: A Space Odyssey*. Similar music, like an orchestra all playing sustained notes at once, occurs in *Solaris*. In *Stalker*, Artemiev's music is really beautiful (his best in a Tarkovsky film): there is a theme tune for the Stalker character (a plangent folk melody played on flute); it begins and ends the film, and comes in at key points, such as the Stalker's dream. The music evokes Russia, combining folk melodies with electronic modernism.

Artemiev said that he composed and recorded a lot of music for *Stalker*, but the maestro concentrated on that one flute piece, using it again and again. There was also supposed to be a music cue for the tunnel (meat grinder) scene, but Tarkovsky didn't use the piece Artemiev had written (Artemiev remarked that every time he saw *Stalker*, there was a hole for him where the music should have been).

In *Sculpting In Time*, Tarkovsky said he was moving towards going without music in *Stalker* and *Nostalgia* (and Eduardo Artemiev would agree with that), but he hadn't yet done without it completely (ST, 162).

During the opening of *Nostalghia* two pieces of music are mixed together – the Russian woman singing and Giuseppe Verdi's *Requiem*. The effect is startling, and states the theme in a grandiose fashion: the folky homeland of peasant Russian is being smothered by the heavier weight of baroque, operatic Italy. A similar juxtaposition of music occurs in *The Sacrifice*, where the Swedish folk song is contrasted with the Japanese flute music.

Eduardo Artemiev remembered that Tarkovsky never went to music recording sessions, which was frustrating for Artemiev, because the film director was for him the only one to have the overview of the film, the only one who could give useful suggestions. So Artemiev tended to compose and record lots of music without knowing how Tarkovsky would use it in the film. Sometimes there were 5 or 6 or even 8 different versions of music that Artemiev wrote and recorded, and most wouldn't find their way into the final film. In *Stalker*, for instance, Artemiev recalled that there was lots more music created, but Tarkovsky only used the flute melody over and over.

8 : 7   FOLK MUSIC

Andrei Tarkovsky generally chooses folk music by solo artists: the haunting flute in *The Sacrifice*, which plays through Alex's nightmare; or the woman singing at the end of *Nostalghia*. This latter film in particular features a selection of women's singing: the praying of the witch-like devotees at the beginning, during the *Madonna del Parto* ritual; the Russian folk music; and, at the end, women talking fades into the single voice singing. The effect of this folk music is really haunting. The music is on its own very beautiful. Coupled with Tarkovsky's sensuous imagery, the effect is sublime.

Pier Paolo Pasolini was particularly brilliant at combining Western classical music with American blues, and folk music from around the world, on films such as *Oedipus Rex*. In his *The Gospel According To Matthew* (1965, Italy), Pasolini used folk and secular music in a similar way to Tarkovsky: the imagery was religious (the Christian miracles), but the music was folky, jazzy, more suited to a film about beatniks hanging out in the Spanish mountains or the Bowery (*The Gospel According To Matthew*'s soundtrack, one of the most remarkable in the history of cinema, included Anton Webern, Mozart, Bach, Sergei Prokofiev, the *Missa Luba*, African spirituals, Leadbelly, Billie Holiday, and Russian revolutionary songs). Yet it worked, adding a dimension of profundity to Pasolini's film. Tarkovsky has this knack too of choosing just the right sound to go with his images.

In some ways Andrei Tarkovsky's use of music is worse than that of Hollywood cinema. Hollywood patches up films with awful sweeping strings and orchestras going at full speed (if everything else in a film has failed to move an audience, music is the last resort: music does so much of the emotional work in a Hollywood film. And Hollywood movies, since the 1970s, have had music cues planted throughout, as if they don't trust the audience to react in its own way to a film, as if the audience has to be told at every stage what to think and how to feel). Tarkovsky goes even further; he selected key classical composers (J.S. Bach, Ludwig van Beethoven, Henry Purcell, Giovanni Battista Pergolesi, Claude Debussy and Richard Wagner), and chose very moving pieces of classical music: J.S. Bach's *St Matthew Passion* (in *The Sacrifice*); the opening of Bach's *St John Passion* (at the end of *Mirror*); Bach's slow, stately *Chorale Prelude in F Minor* (in *Solaris*); Beethoven's *Ode to Joy* (in *Nostalghia*); as well as the opening of Giuseppe Verdi's *Requiem*, with its melancholy double bass sliding ever deeper – a majestic piece of music. Bernardo Bertolucci called Verdi mythic.[1]

So it could be said that Tarkovsky bolsters up his films with such powerful sounds, that he relies on music to do much of the work in his films, as much as Hollywood cinema. The ending of *Mirror*, for example, wouldn't be nearly as moving without those restless violins and clarinets and voices which chase around in the air in Bach's *St John Passion*.

Like film directors such as Ken Russell, Martin Scorsese and Vincente Minnelli, Tarkovsky is a very musical filmmaker. Many sequences are shot with music in mind, and the classical (often choral) pieces fit so well with the visuals. One thinks of the extraordinary endings to Tarkovsky's films.

Among Russian composers, Dimitri Shostakovitch's tragic, bleak music is the aural equivalent of Andrei Tarkovsky's stark imagery. Like the best of cinema, Shostakovitch's music can be piercing in its intensity. In Russian music, the *adagio* from Aram Khachaturian's *Spartacus* (used in *2,001: A Space Odyssey*), like the *adagio* from Gustave Mahler's *Fifth Symphony* (used in *Death in Venice*), is as beautiful a piece of orchestral music as there ever was: the slow, sonorous, deeply emotional phrasing of the strings is of a similar order as Tarkovsky's slow, long, travelling shots. Tarkovsky's images plus such luxurious symphonic music can create cinematic overload. This degree of intensity of beauty is difficult to sustain.

So, thankfully, Tarkovsky is rightly sparing with emotive music (although more austere filmmakers, such as Carl-Theodore Dreyer or Robert Bresson, would no doubt criticize Tarkovsky for indulging himself. Ascetic filmmakers would argue that good films shouldn't need to resort to music in that manner, and so often).

It would be amazing to see and hear Tarkovsky using the religious Minimal composers – the Estonian composer Arvo Pärt, say, or John Tavener. Eastern Orthodox religion and Russian history infuse Arvo Pärt's ascetic, restrained but deeply romantic music, such as his *Cantus* or *St John Passion*. Like Tarkovsky's poetic cinema, Pärt's music contains lengthy sequences where not much seems to happen, where the music hovers on the edge of hearing (what Pärt called 'tintabulation'). When Pärt's music suddenly increases in volume or vigour the effect can be startling (and it can blow up sound systems and hearing with its enormous dynamic range). The ending of the *St John Passion* is a good example of an enormous blossoming into sound, recalling the end of *The Sacrifice* or *Mirror*. John Tavener's music is also deeply entwined with Russian sacred music (such as his *Ikons of Light*), which has affinities with Tarkovsky's cinema.

8 : 9   JOHANN SEBASTIAN BACH

J.S. Bach is the composer for Andrei Tarkovsky's cinema – not Mozart, Beethoven, Brahms nor Ravel. Tarkovsky loves Bach for his highly devout Christian stance, and also because Bach is very emotional (Bach is also a 'musician's composer', like Tarkovsky is a 'filmmaker's filmmaker', a filmmaker beloved of other filmmakers). Bach, though, is Western European and Protestant Christian music, not quite with the same cultural roots as Tarkovsky's Russian Orthodox religion.

What does the use of Bach's music mean in, say, *The Sacrifice*? The music chosen is an *aria* from *St Matthew Passion*. It is musician's music: pure, precise, moving into the abstract. Holy, yes, and a little cold and brittle. The words are in German – not the languages of Swedish or English of the film, nor the sacred language of the Church – Latin. The music is spacious, and very elegant – those emotional strings proceeding so gracefully – so airy and light. This music could be put with many kinds of visuals, it is so universal and abstract. Pier Paolo Pasolini used other parts of Bach's *St Matthew Passion* in his film of Christ's life. Martin Scorsese's employed Bach over the opening credits of *Casino* (1995) and images of a car exploding (the juxtaposition of the sacred and the thoroughly secular (Las Vegas gangsters).)

In *The Sacrifice* the Bach *aria* is played twice – at the beginning and the end of the film, at the times when the Japanese *bo* tree is seen. The connection then is very religious, and very Christian: this pure, abstract classical music and perfect voice, singing of Christ's Passion, set beside the twisted, bare tree, so like Christ's Crown of Thorns, his Cross and the Tree of Paradise, the tree of so many mediæval and Renaissance paintings. The ending becomes a poignant religious statement, backed up by the boy's words: the image deliberately alludes to the *Gospels*, to the Renaissance, to the Old Testament and to Christianity as a whole. But it is also very much an Oriental image – the first words Alexander says are that the tree looks Japanese.

Immediately, then, after the powerful *Western* religious imagery – of J.S. Bach's music and Leonardo da Vinci's paintings, Jesus, the Magi, the Tree of Paradise and the Cross – the film shifts to *Eastern* philosophy, which seems so much better suited to Alexander and Otto and their philosophical debates. They are like a couple of old Zen Buddhist or Confucian monks. Surely there is added symbolism in their names: Alex and Otto, the Alpha and the Omega from the last book of the *Bible*, *Revelations*. Maybe this is going too far with this methodology of symbolism, but Tarkovsky had the *Revelations* in mind when he made this film – that's certain.

NINE

Production

9 : 1   FAST FILMS

Everybody makes films for themselves, really.

Andrei Tarkovsky (1993, 62)

The trouble that Andrei Tarkovsky had to go through to make some of his films *seems* to have been tremendous. The *Diaries* are full of struggles, arguments, set-backs, continual reductions in budget and pay, all kinds of problems. But that's fairly typical of many films, and there are certainly many films which had far, far more troubled routes to and through production (*Cleopatra*, *The Twilight Zone*, *Apocalypse Now*, and so on). Deaths, violence, corruption, endless gestation periods, and schedules that run on for years are not unknown.

In fact, Andrei Tarkovsky enjoyed the protection and support of the Soviet film industry. He was favoured with high quality productions – look at *Andrei Roublyov* or *Solaris*. Those aren't low budget films by any definition of the term. Tarkovsky's epitaph is typical of him: '[t]he only condition of fighting for the right to create is faith in your own vocation, readiness to serve and refusal to compromise'.[1] And

Larissa Tarkovskaya, his (second) wife, said of him in the documentary *Directed By Andre Tarkovsky*: 'he was the only Soviet director to do exactly as he wanted. He was absolutely uncompromising… he did as he wished'. British director Michael Apted (*Coal Miner's Daughter, Gorillas in the Mist, The World Is Not Enough*) said that the hardest part of directing was 'to know when to take advice and when to politely ignore it, what to delegate and what you have to do yourself'.[2] Tarkovsky was clearly one of those filmmakers who preferred to do as much as he could himself, and who only reluctantly delegated tasks. As Larissa Tarkovskaya said of Tarkovsky, 'whatever he could himself, he felt he ought to do'.

In the interview included in the documentary *Directed by Andrei Tarkovsky*, Tarkovsky said that filmmaking was not just a job for him, 'it's my life'; his films and life were a continuum. A film, said Tarkovsky, is 'a fundamental act'. Here's the recurring Tarkovsky mantra of film as art, as a statement, as self-expression, rather than film as mass entertainment, or an industrial artefact, or a team effort. (This is a typical Tarkovsky pronouncement on entertainment: 'I am categorically against entertainment in cinema: it is as degrading for the author as it is for the audience' (D, 367). There must be millions of people who've been entertained by movies who wouldn't know what the hell Tarkovsky is talking about. That was typical of Tarkovsky's austere views of popular entertainment, but millions of punters wouldn't say they felt 'degraded' by watching a film (well, maybe a Guy Ritchie or a James Cameron film, but not every other film).)

For Tarkovsky, commercial cinema and television degraded cinema, turned it into a factory assembly line (ST, 167). Commercial cinema for Tarkovsky debased the artform of cinema, because it cheapened people's tastes and expectations and sensibilities (ST, 179). Entertainment cinema 'extinguishes all traces of thought and feeling irrevocably' Tarkovsky claimed, so that films were consumed like bottles of Coca-Cola. He's completely wrong, of course. Behind his attacks on what he called commercial cinema one can see the complaints of a filmmaker and artist who feels deprived of the big budgets, support systems, publicity, advertizing, and mass distribution networks that the major film production centres enjoy. The 'tragedy' of cinema, for Tarkovsky, was that it was necessary for a filmmaker to have money, resources and a team of people in order to practise their art. 'One has to make money in order to make more films' Tarkovsky complained. 'It's completely different with other arts. One can write a book sitting at home – like Kafka who wrote but published nothing. But the book has been written'.

During Tarkovsky's film career, the Soviet film industry was controlled by a centralized organization, Goskino. It ran the film archives (Gosfilmofond), the storage facility (the Central Film Base), the film school VGIK (All-Union State Institute of Cinematography), film processing laboratories, a script studio, the film actors' studio (Theatre of the Film Actor), a symphony orchestra, and the cinema journals *Iskusstvo kino* and *Sovetsky ekran*. Goskino ran all of the 40 Russian film studios, and all of distribution.

Goskino was led by the chairman (Alexei Romanov and Filip Yermash in Tarkovsky's time), and a governing body which included the heads of department (such as directors, scriptwriters, the board for feature production, the screenwriting board's head, and a KGB official). Mosfilm, the biggest studio in Russia, and the most important, was run by one of the deputy chairs of Goskino; during Tark-ovsky's career, the executive directors of Mosfilm were V. Surin and N. Sizov.

In the Mosfilm hierarchy was a governing body of heads of department (such as scriptwriting, personnel, ideology and production), and an Artistic Council which included party officials, workers and filmmakers.[3] The film production aspect of the Mosfilm studio was broken up into seven production teams, each run by a film director and a production manager. The teams also comprised editors and censors (mostly women), who oversaw the films during production. Each production team had its own script boards, and its own artistic councils (made up of filmmakers), who approved scripts, music, costumes, casts, sets and so on.

In the Russian film system there weren't producers in the Western use of the term; instead, the Goskino and Mosfilm executives acted in a similar manner to film producers in the West. Amongst the crew there were people who functioned something like production managers. On *Andrei Roublyov*, for instance, Tamara Ogorodnikova liaised between the filmmakers and Mosfilm, oversaw health and safety, and allocated the agreed budget (JP, 58). Obtaining additional money from Goskino and Mosfilm could be as difficult as with a Western film studio.

Goskino controlled the release and distribution of films in the USSR. Once a film was completed, it had to be presented to the Goskino authorities. At that stage, Goskino might ask for cuts and alterations. Films would sometimes go back and forth between the filmmakers, the studio and Goskino (similarly, in the Western film system, filmmakers sometimes negotiated cuts or changes with studios, backers and censors that go on for months). Sometimes Tarkovsky would deliberately film scenes knowing they would be cut down (that's a regular practice among filmmakers

– they give the censors something to cut so that other material can slip through).

Only when Goskino was satisfied would the film be approved (and only when a film was accepted by Goskino would the cast and crew receive fees and bonuses). Like many filmmakers, Tarkovsky was very reluctant to agree to the demands for alterations. The bureaucratic film machine (Goskino) had the power to withhold approval to the point where films could be shelved for long periods. This happened with *Andrei Roublyov*. Completed in 1966, it wasn't released in the Soviet Union until 1971.

The art film devotee (Tarkovsky's preferred audience) might rather have one Andrei Tarkovsky film (or one Bergman or Godard or Murnau film) than ten thousand mainstream Hollywood films (which are caricatured by the arthouse crowd as tacky, trashy, shallow and violent films, with enormous budgets, big stars and nothing to 'say' about anything). All films require business as well as art, but from Tarkovsky's point of view (or the art film's point of view), Hollywood entertainment cinema seems to be all business and very little art. To say Hollywood cinema is a money-making industry is merely to state the obvious in a late capitalist, consumerist world.

Violence, sex, beautiful people, guns, cars, exotic locations, visual fx and Arnold Schwarzenegger blowing things up seem to be the order of the day. In fact, Hollywood executives are more likely these days to speak in terms of romance, suspense, jeopardy, conflict, quests, heroes, passion, betrayal, and happy endings, i.e., emphasizing the *emotional* core of the ideal Hollywood movie, not the glitzy trappings that go on top, which critics and detractors tend to latch onto – the women, the cars, the gadgets, the chases, the explosions, the product placement. And studio execs always talk about *story* and *characters*. In short, the Hollywood industry has always known that audiences go to the cinema or rent DVDs and home videos for stories, for the characters and the situations, and to see their favourite stars. And that all-important ingredient: *emotion*. In this respect, Hollywood cinema is supremely successful at delivering what audiences want to see, with a much bigger hit rate than the art film when it comes to providing stories and characters and emotion.

From the art filmmaker's viewpoint, Hollywood films are mediocrity as mass entertainment, loathed for their popularity, yet also curiously fascinating. They trade on speed, the lowest common denominator, the 'lowbrow': quick scenes, quick shots, quick pleasures. Instant gratification. Fantasy and simulcra. For the arthouse acolyte, it's cinema as a McDonald's brunch and popcorn. Jean-Luc Godard dubbed *Schindler's List* (1993), which took on the Holocaust, as a film 'du Max Factor'. Phony history. All glam, no substance. Hollywood colonizing other nation's histories because it didn't have any of its own to exploit. (America as Coca Cola culture, a perpetual Disneyland, with Hollywood as the 'dream factory'). Fast foods, fast lifestyles, fast films.

For the filmmaker working in the European art cinema tradition, the fast films of the Hollywood conglomerates are a kind of death. They have slick plots (films as machines) about shallow people caught in shallow lives. Materialism abounds, consumerism is glossily conspicuous – gadgets, cars, computers, phones, jets, machines, tanned and honed bodies (artificial and part cyborg), great teeth, great hair, instant desire. Money and visible consumerism is the test of the Hollywood movie character – how much money they make and how they display it (if you've got it, flaunt it, as Zero Mostel says in *The Producers*). Or how much sexual desire they can attract. Or how good they are at beating the shit out of other people. Cop thriller, romantic comedy, horror, sci-fi, buddy movie, sword and sorcery, political thriller and costume drama – all made to a formula. Not difficult to see, from a distance (i.e., left-liberal, quasi-Marxist Europe), Hollywood entertainment cinema as a mass of populist, glossy, excessive images, as nothing more than Baudrillardian simulcra. Hollywood as the mirror of late capitalism, reflecting back Western society's excesses.

Many post-New Wave filmmakers in Europe might be inclined to agree with Andrei Tarkovsky's reaction to the film *'Possession'* (Tarkovsky could be referring to *Amityville II: The Possession* [Damiano Damiani, 1982, USA], yet another of the many post-*Exorcist* cash-in horror films, or it could be *Possession* [by Polish exile Andrzej Zulawski, 1981, France/ West Germany]):

> Saw an unspeakably revolting film called *Possession*. An American mixture of horror film, satanism, violence, thriller and anything else you like to name. Monstrous. Money, money, money… Nothing real, nothing true. No beauty, no truth, no sincerity, nothing. All that matters is to make a profit… It's impossible to watch… (D, 323-4)

These commercial movies are Hollywood cinema at its most pure: genre pix in an endless cycle of sequels, cash-ins and franchises: *Nightmare on Elm Street*, *Child's Play*, *Demons*, *Candyman*, *Incubus*, *Scream*, *Basket Case*, *Amityville Horror*,

Friday the 13th, *The Omen* and *Hallowe'en*. Many of these shlock horror films begin with a typical Middle American domestic scene which is then invaded by killers, aliens, mutants, you name it (as in *Gremlins, Shivers, The Exorcist, Scream, Shocker, Hallowe'en*, and so on). The world of the horror film is the psychic, inner realm, in which the fears, horrors, monsters and ghosts and so on are largely psychological. The horror film thus has affinities with the religious film: both look across a troubled interior landscape towards some unknown or other. Ambiguity, alterity, marginality, psychosis and disruption are the marks of both genres, driven along by sometimes intense desire, what Slavoj Zizek called 'the return of the repressed', the undead (sometimes hidden, sometimes gleefully manifest). Both the horror film and the religious film protagonist are sure they've seen or felt something. Their task is to convince others of their interior (supernatural) experience, which is precisely Domenico's goal in Tarkovsky's *Nostalghia* (and, to a lesser extent, the Stalker's task in *Stalker*).

While the Hollywood industry was churning out thoroughly formulaic, mainstream movies (which nevertheless generated tons of money), such as *On Golden Pond, Top Gun, E.T., Kramer vs Kramer, Ordinary People, The Dark Crystal, Footloose, Tootsie, Rambo* and countless sequels, in the mid-1980s, Tarkovsky made his last two films, *Nostalghia* and *The Sacrifice*, which are full of space, silence, restraint and intensity. Tarkovsky's films are 'slow films' – in production and consumption as well as in subject and form.

Andrei Tarkovsky often lamented in the *Diaries* the lengthy gaps between his films (it's a recurring gripe among all filmmakers). There were five years between the releases of *Mirror* and *Stalker*; and four years between *Stalker* and *Nostalghia*. Although this is longer than the usual two or three year turnaround of the Hollywood movie system, it's a better record than, say, fellow art film *auteurs* such as Robert Bresson or Carl-Theodore Dreyer or Sergei Paradjanov. In his diary for April 6, 1972, he wrote: '[h]ere I am forty. And what have I done in all this time? Three pathetic pictures. So little! So ridiculously little and insignificant' (D, 56).

Sometimes Tarkovsky regarded his own films as inadequate, emphasizing their faults above their merits (like many artists do). In his diaries, he wrote that he didn't like his own films – 'there is so much in them that is fussy, ephemeral, false' (D, 174). At the same time, Tarkovsky also felt fairly confident about the value of his own work: 'other people's films are so much worse. Is that pride on my part? Perhaps it is. But it is also the truth' (ibid).

Tarkovsky's output was of a similar rate as Stanley Kubrick's or Lindsay Anderson's. But one of Tarkovsky's heroes, Japanese giant Kenji Mizoguchi, said don't rush: Mizoguchi wrote that '[i]t is essential that one should reflect for 5 or 6 years before beginning to film. Films produced very quickly are never very good'.[4] If Mizoguchi had practiced what he preached, he would have made seven films in his thirty-four year career. In fact he made *ninety* feature films. This astonishing output (more than John Ford but not D.W. Griffith) might suggest that Mizoguchi's films are poor in quality, but Mizoguchi is regarded as one of the greatest of all filmmakers. Other art cinema directors who made a considerable number of films but still maintained high quality over most of them include Ingmar Bergman, Luis Buñuel, Federico Fellini, Claude Chabrol, Yasujiro Ozu, Jean-Luc Godard, Nagisa Oshima, Eric Rohmer, François Truffaut, Andrei Wadja and Rainer Werner Fassbinder. Some of these directors were amazingly prolific: Fassbinder, Ozu, Bergman (as well as directing films, for instance, Bergman found time to direct theatre and opera and TV shows).

By comparison with many of the above filmmakers, Andrei Tarkovsky's output, including his opera, theatre and documentary work, is nowhere near as productive. But while one can lament that filmmakers such as Tarkovsky, Dreyer, Paradjanov and Kubrick didn't make more films, one also wishes that some directors had never started (James Cameron, Guy Ritchie, Paul Anderson [but not Paul Thomas Anderson], Simon West, etc).

It's worth repeating that Tarkovsky fared well in the Soviet film system: he managed to shoot pretty much his scripts as he'd prepared them; he was allowed to film his own scripts (he didn't have to take on 'commercial' properties); he was allowed to take days off or rehearse actors in the middle of shooting; he was able to extensively rewrite his scripts (and even reshoot them from the beginning, as with *Stalker*); he wasn't a 'director for hire'; and his films were released very close to what he wanted (Tarkovsky acknowledged this in an interview published in *Cahiers du Cinéma* in 1987). None of Tarkovsky's films were butchered by Goskino, Mosfilm or censors, for instance.

Compare that with, say, Orson Welles, who had regular run-ins with studios and distributors: *The Magnificent Ambersons* (1942), perhaps the greatest American movie ever made, was re-cut by the studio (RKO) (supervised by Robert Wise and Jack Moss). The ending was re-shot (as well as three other additional scenes), and the film lost some 44 minutes (including the best scenes, Welles maintained).

Accounts of exactly what happened with *The Magnificent Ambersons* while Welles was away shooting in Mexico vary. Welles blamed the preview process (which many filmmakers hate; bad previews help studios justifying reshoots or alterations). Some have suggested that Orson Welles himself participated, perhaps unwittingly, or unconsciously, or deliberately, in the alteration of his films (Universal took *Touch of Evil*, another contender for the greatest American movie ever, away from Welles). Whatever the truth, two of Welles' most important films were drastically altered by the studios (and *The Magnificent Ambersons* was seriously wrecked). That never happened to Andrei Tarkovsky.

9 : 2   SHOOTING

Shooting is really a bore. What is important is the writing of the script and the editing of the footage. It is during the writing stage that I get all my ideas, all my inspiration. Images come to me spontaneously, sometimes completely unrelated to the story line, and I incorporate them into the script. Then I follow my screen-play practically without deviating from it.

Luis Buñuel[1]

Andrei Tarkovsky made two films in foreign languages (foreign to his native Russian, that is): Swedish and Italian (i.e, films shot that were in those languages, rather than dubbed or foreign language versions of films. Pretty much any feature film director has to work these days in foreign languages, when (if) they oversee dubbed or foreign language versions. Some filmmakers, of course, hand over all of that to other companies).

Had he lived to make more films after *The Sacrifice*, it seems inevitable that Tarkovsky would have eventually made a film in English (especially if he had continued with European co-productions, where languages such as French, Italian, Spanish, English and German predominate). Many modern European directors have made English language movies: if they did not move directly into Hollywood, their English language films were acknowledgements of the international power of

English. European art film directors such as Louis Malle, Volker Schlöndorff, Jean-Luc Godard, Wim Wenders, Roman Polanski and Alain Tanner all made films in their native tongue then went on to make English language movies. (And some European film directors made the move to big time Hollywood films: Paul Verhoeven, Roland Emmerich, Wolfgang Petersen and Jan da Bont, just like Fritz Lang, Max Ophüls and Ernst Lubitsch before them).

There are one or two moments in Andrei Tarkovsky's cinema where actors speak in English. Two moments occur in *The Sacrifice*: first where Alexander quotes from the Shakespeare play that Tarkovsky directed, *Hamlet*: 'words, words, words' (this can be in English, because it's by the immortal Bard). The second time is where Susan Fleetwood speaks in English during her panic (Fleetwood's character is not an English speaker, but maybe Tarkovsky liked her delivery of the lines. It's not explained in the film why she speaks in English at that point).

Tarkovsky seemed to be moving further West (culturally as well as physically) from his native Russia: first to Italy, then to Sweden. France or Germany would maybe have been next, then perhaps Britain or America. The thought of an *American* Tarkovsky film is intriguing: what would a Tarkovsky film make of America? One thinks of other modern European filmmakers who have made films in or about America, with an outsider's perspective: Wim Wenders with *Paris, Texas* (1984), an arthouse fave, or Werner Herzog with *Stroszek* (1977).

Unlike other European art film directors, such as Wenders, Godard and Truffaut, Tarkovsky did not exalt American culture or American movies. While the *Cahiers du Cinéma* crowd and the French *nouvelle vague* enshrined Howard Hawks, John Ford, Frank Capra and dominant Hollywood cinema, Tarkovsky hardly mentions it in *Sculpting in Time* or his *Diaries*. If Tarkovsky does mention directors, they are usually of the art cinema tradition: Luis Buñuel, Akira Kurosawa, Federico Fellini and Ingmar Bergman. Not for him the affectionate *hommages* to American cinema of the French New Wave (to Humphrey Bogart and American detectives in Godard's *A Bout de Souffle* [1960], or to Orson Welles in Truffaut's *Les Quatre Cents Coups* [1959]). Tarkovsky was at times sceptical of American movies, and sometimes detested them (although people have described Tarkovsky discussing films like *The Terminator* (1984) passionately; Tarkovsky could never have guessed then, however, that *Terminator* director Cameron would one day be producing a remake of his film *Solaris*).

If Andrei Tarkovsky had gone on to make a film in or about America, it might not have been for some time after 1986: his projects in the planning stages included *The Temptation of St Anthony*, Shakespeare, a Dostoievsky film, and even a New Testament film. However, if a big shot producer like Dino de Laurentiis or Scott Rudin had approached Tarkovsky around 1985-86 with a hands-off, final cut, free rein deal on an American picture, Tarkovsky might have been tempted. Say a version of Dostoievsky, but with an American star. That too, is not unknown: many arthouse directors cast American movie stars in their films: Jean-Luc Godard used Jack Palance in *Contempt* (1963), Wim Wenders cast Dennis Hopper in *The American Friend* (1977), Federico Fellini cast Donald Sutherland in his bizarre *Casanova*, and Bernardo Bertolucci and Luchino Visconti put Burt Lancaster in *1900* and *The Leopard* (but then, Wenders, Bertolucci and Godard are – or were – deeply fascinated by Americana). (Tarkovsky didn't use any American actors in his films).

It's unlikely that we would have seen a Tarkovsky film starring Arnold Schwarzenegger, Vin Diesel or The Rock, with a trailer announcing: 'this season, 20th Century Fox presents Arnold Schwarzenegger in *The Brothers Karamazov*... from the director of *The Sacrifice* and *Nostalghia*'. But a picture with, say, Jack Nicholson or Johnny Depp, would have been a possibility.

Hollywood cinema is continually forging strange new alliances. Nobody could have guessed, for example, that Mel Gibson would make a film about Christ (*The Passion of the Christ*, 2004), that it would be shot (not dubbed) in Aramaic, and that it would be such a success with audiences (despite having no stars). (No doubt Tarkovsky would have had a few things to say about *The Passion of the Christ*, and he might not have completely hated it).

It's common practice to spice up casts of European co-productions with American stars but some European art filmmakers have consciously avoided casting them: Ingmar Bergman, for instance. However, some of Bergman's ensemble went the other way – to Hollywood: Max von Sydow is a classic example. He started at the top, playing Christ in a mega epic, *The Greatest Story Ever Told* (1965), was a brilliantly camp villain in *Flash Gordon* (1980), was Barbara Hershey's artist-lover in Woody Allen's *Hannah and Her Sisters* (1986), and was Tom Cruise's nemesis in the sci-fi flick *Minority Report* (2002).

Among Tarkovsky's regular collaborators were fellow director and scriptwriter Andrei Mikhailkov-Konchalovsky, actors Anatoly Solonitsyn, Nikolai Grinko,

Nikolai Burlyaev, Erland Josephson (a Bergman regular) and Oleg Yankovsky, composers Eduard Artemiev (*Solaris, Mirror, Stalker*) and Vyacheslav Ovchinniko (*Ivan's Childhood* and *Andrei Roublyov*), set designer A. Merkulov (*Mirror, Stalker*), cameraman Vadim Yusov (*The Steamroller and the Violin, Ivan's Childhood, Andrei Roublyov, Solaris, Mirror*), costume designer Nelly Fomina, and editor Lyudmilla Feiginova (*Andrei Roublyov, Solaris, Mirror, Stalker*).

It seems Andrei Tarkovsky often had disputes with his camera people. He disagreed with the cinematographers on *Mirror* (ST, 136) and *Solaris* (D, 62). Most of *Stalker* was re-shot. Tarkovsky controls his camera meticulously, and although his films are full of really stunning imagery, the camera person on a Tarkovsky film needed to be slow, thoughtful and precise. No running around with a Steadicam for Tarkovsky, as seen in the films of Paul Verhoeven, Paul Thomas Anderson and John Carpenter and every Hollywood film of recent times. Not as many big, sweeping, operatic camera movements, as with Bernardo Bertolucci and his director of photography Vittorio Storaro (though Tarkovsky employed some big crane shots: in the apples on the beach shot in *Ivan's Childhood*, for example, or the climb up the tree shot in *The Sacrifice*). No shaky hand-held camerawork, either, as in early French New Wave cinema.

The most beautiful camerawork in Tarkovsky's cinema occurs in *Nostalghia* (shot by Guiseppe Lanci) and *The Sacrifice* (shot by Sven Nykvist), both made with Eastman Colour film. Nykvist is the celebrated cameraman of Ingmar Bergman's films, but Lanci's work on *Nostalghia* was equally gorgeously done. When he viewed the material for *Nostalghia*, Tarkovsky was amazed because it was 'completely homogeneous, both in its mood and the state of mind imprinted on it… the camera was obeying first and foremost my inner state during filming… I was at once astounded and delighted' (ST, 203).

Tarkovsky isn't known for fruitful and long-running collaborations with his director/s of photography like, say, Bernardo Bertolucci and Vittorio Storaro, Martin Scorsese and Michael Ballhaus, Ingmar Bergman and Sven Nykvist, or Oliver Stone and Robert Richardson. And the fact that Tarkovsky's last five films (from *Solaris* onwards) all had different cinematographers says a lot. However, Tarkovsky's first three features were all shot by Vadim Yusov, so there is a continuity of style and a working relationship there.

Sven Nykvist had won Oscars for his photography on Bergman's *Cries and Whispers* (1973) and *Fanny and Alexander* (1982). Nykvist had worked with

Bergman since 1960 (*The Virgin Spring, Winter Light, The Silence, Persona, The Touch, Hour of the Wolf, The Shame, Cries and Whispers, Scenes From a Marriage* and *Fanny and Alexander*. His work with Bergman alone would put him in the front rank of DPs around the world). Nykvist was also DP for other directors: Louise Malle (*Pretty Baby*, 1978), Roman Polanski (*The Tenant*, 1976), Volker Schlöndorff (*Swann in Love*, 1984), Philip Kaufman (*The Unbearable Lightness of Being*, 1988), Richard Fleischer (*The Last Run*, 1971), Jan Troell (*Hurricane*, 1979), Alan Pakula (*Starting Over*, 1979, *Dream Lover*, 1986), Bob Fosse (*Star 80*, 1983), Norman Jewison (*Agnes of God*, 1985 and *Only You*, 1994), Bob Rafelson (*The Postman Always Rings Twice*, 1981), Nora Ephron (*Sleepless in Seattle*, 1993), Richard Attenborough (*Chaplin*, 1992), Paul Mazursky (*Willie and Phil*), 1980), and Woody Allen (*Another Woman*, 1988, *Crimes and Misdemeanours*, 1989 and *Celebrity*, 1998).

By the time Nykvist came to work with Tarkovsky, then, he had already worked with some of Europe's finest filmmakers (Bergman, Malle, Polanski, Schlöndorff), and some of the US's best (Pakula, Kaufmann, Rafelson, Jewison, Fosse). Paul Mazursky said that Nykvist operated the camera himself for about half of *Willie and Phil*, and he employed what he called the 'creeping zoom': '[h]e would do the slightest pan and the slightest move at the same time, so that in a barely perceptible way, you'd get a tiny little bit closer. It was poetic – quite miraculous'.[2]

According to contemporary accounts, Sven Nykvist found it tricky working with Tarkovsky on set of *The Sacrifice* at first, because of Tarkovsky's habit of sitting beside the camera, and directing actors through the camera. As Nykvist liked to operate the camera himself, that could cause tensions. Some film directors never look through the camera, or steer clear of the camera crew. Some sit hunched behind the video monitors, but Tarkovsky was a supremely hands-on director. It was impossible for Tarkovsky to direct from a distance.

In Michal Leszcylowski's documentary on the making of *The Sacrifice* (*Directed By Andrei Tarkovsky*, 1989) a very intense filmmaker is depicted, often lost in thought, or wandering away by himself, or squinting through upraised hands, or discussing set designs, or raking water around on the grass, or moving stones around the model of the house, or carefully directing the actors, or clutching his head in exasperation. During the shoot in the city courtyard (for Alexander's nightmare), Tarkovsky was seen personally directing the dressing of the set, rather than leaving it up to the art director's team (and communicating through the interpreter, as ever on *The Sacrifice*), making sure there was plenty of newspapers and trash strewn about, plus black plastic, all sprayed down with hoses, and getting the car heaved into the correct position, on its side. Tarkovsky acknowledged the contribution of the team members in making a film, but he always insisted that the final word and conception comes from the director (ST, 33).

Tarkovsky is shown in *Directed By Andrei Tarkovsky* looking through the camera a good deal; sometimes he's on the camera dolly during shooting. He is depicted as a director who gets involved in every aspect of shooting. Indeed, Larissa Tarkovskaya quotes a line from his diary: '[d]on't bother other people with things you can do yourself.' Tarkovsky likes to do everything, to make sure everything is done properly. Collaborators said that Tarkovsky was involved with every aspect of filmmaking, down to the tiniest detail (the more the director reproduces the minutiæ of life in 'their concrete sensuous form', Tarkovsky said, 'the closer he will be to his aim' [ST, 154]). For Tarkovsky, the film director was the final force or vision in a film. After all of the pages of script written, the locations chosen, the art director's sketches, and the actors cast, there was, finally, the director: 'only one person' stands alone, the director, 'the last filter in the creative process of filmmaking' (ST, 18).

In Leszcylowski's documentary he is portrayed as an obsessive *auteur*, a genius energized by a religious vision – the artist as shaman and religious hero (like Vincent van Gogh, Arthur Rimbaud and Mark Rothko). Jeanne Moreau tells an interesting story of pre-shooting nerves: François Truffaut used to pace up and down all night; Joseph Losey had an allergy attack; while Luis Buñuel, just before shooting, 'would touch everything, each object to reassure himself'.[3]

Art must take over the artist's life, Tarkovsky asserted, even to the point where it could endanger her/ his existence (ST, 188-9). American artist David Smith is one of many artists who have said the same thing (artists invited to teach in the academy often lecture their students like that, emphasizing the life-or-death necessity of making art). And many of the artists Tarkovsky admired – Vincent van Gogh, Fyodor Dostoievsky – do have that life-on-the-edge live-or-die extremism about them.

Tarkovsky made *The Sacrifice* with many Swedish actors and crew members. He had to speak through an interpreter. This perhaps helped his concentration – he wouldn't be distracted by what people were saying around him (in the same way, different groups of filmmakers communicating via internet, ISDN, broadband or other electronic links, such as a film director in Hollywood and a visual fx team in London or Sydney, have said it was actually a better, more efficient way of working.) Yet despite problems in translating Russian ideas and commands into Swedish or English on the set, *The Sacrifice* is remarkably unified. The shooting seems have been a relaxed and coherent affair, with the crew working well together. It was not one of those sets where some obnoxious assistant director strides around in a padded anorak shouting 'we're going for a take now, loves' in an edgy, weary, seen-it-all-done-it-all voice.

One can fully understand the utter relief the crew felt when the re-take of the very long and complex last shot of *The Sacrifice* was completed, because these things take so long to prepare for, to rehearse, and to shoot. After it, Tarkovsky says 'we all let go: we were nearly all weeping like children' (ST, 226). Tarkovsky's technique was to rehearse difficult shots again and again, so that he often only needed one or two takes. (That's another difference with the Hollywood practice of shooting thousands of feet of film and printing every take. It might be expected, for instance, for Tarkovsky to demand take after take, like Stanley Kubrick, famous for 50 or 60 takes just for simple shots, but that doesn't seem to have been the case.)

During shooting Tarkovsky's aim was to stick as closely as possible to the basic idea of the film, which has been decided by the filmmaker (that means Tarkovsky himself, not a collective of writers, script doctors, co-producers, assistant producers and executive producers. Tarkovsky was co-writer and director on most of his films). He demanded total concentration from the other team members: they are there to make sure the vision is realized (ST, 125f). He was probably hell to work with at times (really, *really* hell).

For Andrei Arsenievich Tarkovsky, the screenplay was not literature (ST, 126) and he moved towards spontaneity, towards allowing things to happen during shooting (127, 131). The script and the shooting script were guides only. For Tarkovsky, the script wasn't a finished work of art, but was only successful in terms of how it could be transformed into a film (ST, 74). For Tarkovsky, 'a screen adaptation, always arises on the work's ruins so to speak. As a completely new phenomenon'.

Yasujiro Ozu was rigorous in his use of actors and direction. He had the film composed in his head before he went on set; the actors were required to follow his precise instructions. He even counted the number of steps an actor would take in going from one room to another, even if the action occurred off-screen.[4] Tarkovsky was as fussy and perfectionist (though in different ways). It's common, too, for filmmakers (not just the perfectionist ones) to have the film already directed in their head before they walk on set. They've already imagined it all when they were writing the script (or when they were reading the original book or play or comic strip or short story if it's an adaption). They re-live it many times again making deals, setting up finance, and again during preproduction (casting, design, tests, scouting locations, storyboarding, etc). So those filmmakers, like Yasujiro Ozu and Alfred Hitchcock, who were famous for knowing every aspect of a film before the cameras rolled, were by no means the only ones.

Tarkovsky said that in the early days, he would plan shots and scenes exactly, but later tried to encourage an element of spontaneity about shooting. So that actors, locations, sets and the like could 'prompt one to new, startling and unexpected strategies' (ST, 127). Tarkovsky said he often thought of the psychology of the characters before shooting a scene, or the inner state of the scene, rather than specifics (ST, 132). Although he said he didn't alter the original conception of a film too much during shooting and post-production (ST, 93), it wasn't until the last stages of post-production that a film's final form became crystallized (this was certainly true on *Mirror*). Sticking too closely to the script could be a grave or even fatal mistake (ibid.).

On *Mirror*, Tarkovsky said the crew used to visit the country house set at dawn just to experience the atmosphere of the place (ST, 106). Tarkovsky often impro-vized and changed his ideas for scenes as he went along (even a film director known for rigorously sticking to the script and the storyboards, Alfred Hitchcock, in fact didn't, but incorporated new ideas and improvizations as he shot his pictures). New ideas were written for Margarita Terekhova in *Mirror*, for instance, 'to make use of her tremendous potential' (ST, 131). She became the present-day wife of the narrator, as well as his mother from the past (the character of Natalia wasn't in the original script). Via Margarita Terekhova came the idea for integrating the past and present scenes.

Andrei Tarkovsky always wrote his own film scripts (Tarkovsky preferred to make films from scripts he'd been involved in writing), but most of his scripts were collaborations; he did not write them alone (unlike, say, Ingmar Bergman or Woody Allen, who tended to write on their own. A writer-director who works with other writers is much more common than a sole writer-director). Tarkovsky co-wrote *Andrei Roublyov* and *The Steamroller and the Violin* with Andrei Konchalovsky; *Mirror* was co-authored with Alexander Misharin; the Strugatsky brothers co-wrote *Stalker*; and Tonino Guerra co-wrote *Nostalghia*. *Ivan's Childhood*, meanwhile, was written by Mikhail Papava and Vladimir Bogomolov (who wrote the original book – the novella *Ivan*).

In the Soviet film system, a proposal was written first, then a longer 'literary script' (written as a story, rather like a treatment in Hollywood). The authorities would comment on each proposal and script draft. The 'director's script' was next (basically this was a shooting script, with notes on camera angles, locations, music, etc).

Tarkovsky was suspicious of talky scripts and films: the dialogue, for Tarkovsky, only accounted for a small part of the overall impact of a scene or a film (ST, 75). The 'meaning' of a scene wasn't to be found solely in the words spoken by the actors; the characters' psychological state, the physical action, the setting, the images and so on were just as important for Tarkovsky (and usually given more significance than the dialogue). The best dialogue for Tarkovsky was that which fused with the *mise-en-scène*, the sounds, the textures, the psychology and the images of a film.

Film critics continue to reduce films to dialogue and stories, as if the impact and experience of a film can rest solely in the dialogue. But dialogue, as Tarkovsky rightly maintained, was only one component of many in a film. Dialogue was literary, and cinema transformed the literary into something else (ST, 134). And cinema wasn't literature: 'it bears no essential relation to literature whatsoever'. Tarkovsky made a distinction between a script written for the cinema, and a script which turned out to be literature. A film script was written specifically so it could be turned into a film, Tarkovsky asserted. That was its only function. Too many screenplays were really literature for Tarkovsky.

'I don't believe in the literary theatrical dramatical construction,' Tarkovsky maintained, because it 'has nothing in common with the dramaturgy that is particular to cinema as art form'. Instead of describing and explaining actions, 'in film one does not need to explain, but rather to directly affect emotions'. His films were about inciting an emotional response, he asserted: 'the only thing I am after is for them to give birth to certain emotions'.

Ivan's Childhood, Solaris and *Stalker* are literary adaptions, but they are very much 'films by Andrei Tarkovsky', with the Tarkovsky stamp all over them (i.e., Tarkovsky's films can boast a far greater degree of authorship than many Holly-wood films possessing the personal credit for the director, which's more about economic status, clout in the industry and agents' percentages than artistry). *Andrei Roublyov* was based on a real, historical figure (though it certainly wasn't the usual 'artist's biopic'). Early on in his career, Tarkovsky had been opposed to film adaptions of classic literature or plays. They existed so perfectly within their own medium, they couldn't be adapted. Later, Tarkovsky altered his views, and con-templated adaptions of Shakespeare, Dostoievsky, Thomas Mann, Tolstoy, and Ven-yamin Bulgakov.

Many of Tarkovsky's unmade films had literary sources. But whether the source book was by Thomas Mann, Hermann Hesse or Fyodor Dostoievsky, one knows the film would have had Tarkovsky's signature everywhere. Tarkovsky was one of those filmmakers with an idiosyncratic style (one thinks of Orson Welles, Robert Bresson, Walerian Borowczyk or Jan Svankmajer) that turned whatever he made into a recognizable 'un film de Tarkovsky'. A Tarkovsky film, like a Borowcyzk or Svankmajer film, could not be mistaken for anything else (which is an *extremely* rare phenomenon). *Auteur* or not, Tarkovsky was a filmmaker who was involved in every aspect of making cinema — from script to post-production and the press con-ference.

Tarkovsky was doubtful whether cinema had thus far had any filmmakers who could be counted alongside the great authors of world literature (ST, 173). It was perhaps because cinema was still developing its language and form. I'd say that any of the great *auteurs* Tarkovsky admired — Bresson, Bergman, Kurosawa, Buñuel — could stand beside the great authors (Dante and Pushkin, say, or Rabelais and Meville).

In *Sculpting in Time* Tarkovsky describes how *Mirror* was transformed from being a series of somewhat unconnected memories and feelings of childhood to complexly interwoven webs of scenes, shots, episodes, gestures, newsreels, past and present experiences (*Mirror* was co-written with Alexander Misharin). He wrote:

> This account of the making of *Mirror* illustrates that for me scenario is a fragile, living, ever-changing structure, and that a film is only made at the moment when work on it is finally completed. (ST, 131)

Mirror only started to become a good film during the editing (according to Tarkovsky), which Tarkovsky spent a lot of time on (however, one imagines that the beauty of the rushes must have been obvious to anyone who saw them). For Tarkovsky, cinema is not literature, as poetry is not prose. Cinema transforms literature into another medium. A film such as *Mirror* is intensely poetic, and lives in a different world from literature, from the printed word. There are incidents in it that are found in literature – the return of the father, for example, to his homeland and family. But this is filmed as one shot (the father in uniform holding his estranged children) in a complex montage which cuts between past and present and two images by Leonardo da Vinci accompanied by the strains of an opera singing of the veil of the temple being rent. Time and space are squashed through the eye of the needle of Tarkovsky's cinematic virtuosity, and changed utterly. The script might be born in prose and literature, but after cinematic transformation it ends up as something else entirely – a series of images and sounds. The poetry of cinema takes over.

Similarly, with *Nostalghia*, Tarkovsky spent ages working on the screenplay with Tonino Guerra, who co-wrote many of Michelangelo Antonioni's films (including *Red Desert*, *L'Avventura* and the excellent *Identification of a Woman*, 1982, Italy). Scenes were shortened, re-written or dropped to make the script attractive to the financers. Every so often, because of the delays and set-backs, Tarkovsky tried to remind himself of the film he was trying to make:

1. *Madonna del Parto*
2. Foyer of the Hotel du Palma. Reminiscences and 'translation'.
3. The windowless room. Eugenia. The well. Conversations. The dream. (D, 289-290)

But the script bears little resemblance to the finished film. As in many novels, all the work of research is buried under the surface. It's there, but one has to dig. In the later films, the written screenplay, outline, treatment or shooting script is completely transcended by the cinematic image. Take Gorchakov's death scene, for example: a man carries a candle across some drained Baths. A simple enough operation. Could be done in a couple of shots, lasting three seconds each. Or even ten or twenty seconds each.

Shot 1: L.S. Man walking across Baths. 15s.
Shot 2: M.C.U. Man placing candle on ledge. 9s.

Instead, there is a nine-minute continuous take, without dialogue, with few sounds, without music, without big acting, without voiceover. The image becomes primary. This is not prose, dance, painting, music or sculpture. The only concrete relation is to a person walking in a drained Italian pool, the actor on the screen. It is the spiritual relation that counts here — the relation to mythic, tragic ritual, to fire symbolism, to the Christianity of the *Gospels*, to mediæval mysticism, to religious faith and self-transcendence.

9 : 4   BUDGET

Andrei Tarkovsky's films seem to have been made under quite different conditions to the Hollywood system. There was a political, ideological and social pressure upon Soviet filmmakers unmatched in Western Europe or America. Tarkovsky felt he was victimized. He hated the Mosfilm system, calling the people who ran the Soviet film industry 'idiots' (D, 14). Yet the repressive institution enabled him to make as his second feature a large-scale historical drama, with many locations, a large cast and hundreds of extras. Produced by Hollywood at the time, such a film might have cost ten or more million dollars (the average Hollywood feature budget for 1965 was $1.5 million), or $80-140 million today (consider comparable epics of the early Sixties such as Nicholas Ray's *King of Kings* [1961, USA] or Anthony Mann's *El Cid* [1961, USA]). William Wyler's *Ben Hur* (1959, USA) cost 15 million dollars, and *Spartacus* (1960, USA) cost $12 million. (In talking about budgets and money, one must always keep in mind inflation, comparisons with the average budget of the time, and not least the socio-economic system of a film's production. United Artists'

The Greatest Story Ever Told, Fox's *The Sound of Music* and MGM's *Dr Zhivago*, for instance, made at the same time as *Andrei Roublyov* in the mid-1960s, were produced in a very different political environment as well as a different film production system.)

Like *Andrei Roublyov, Solaris* has high production values; it is certainly no low budget sci-fi flick like *Dark Star* (1974) or *Plan 9 From Outer Space* (1958), with wobbly sets, scrounged costumes and low power performances. For *Mirror*, which was shot under schedule, the production team went to considerable lengths in the design of the film (you had to on a Tarkovsky film): they rebuilt Tarkovsky's childhood home, as well as re-planting the nearby field with buckwheat so that it would accord with Tarkovsky's memory of the place (ST, 132). 'The average Soviet feature costs about 600,000 dollars to produce, with budgets scarcely ever rising above 1 million dollars' wrote David Cook in 1990, adding '[a]s in other Eastern European countries, both filmmakers and performers are modestly paid by Western standards' (775). The low pay of cast and crew enabled a Russian film like *Andrei Roublyov* to be produced for far less than it would have done if it had been made in the West. In the Russian system, the crew was paid a standard wage during production, having to wait (sometimes for a long time) for the bonuses.

Pretty much most high budget movies in the Hollywood system nowadays have a negative cost of $80-100 million or more, and 'low budget' means $20-30 million. (Tarkovsky didn't get all the money he liked – Goskino wouldn't allow the budget needed to stage the Kulikovo Field battle which would have opened *Andrei Roublyov*).

Tarkovsky estimated that *Nostalghia* would cost about £500,000.[1] Tarkovsky was paid around $100,000; he also tried to dispense with an assistant director and claim the salary for himself, according to Toscan du Plantier (JP, 306). By 1982 prices, this is cheap (the average Hollywood feature budget in 1982 was $10,000,000).

Information on the exact amounts spent on Tarkovsky's films is difficult to find, partly because it's always tricky find out out *exactly* how much a film costs to make, in any system. The Hollywood and Italian film industries are famously impenetrable when it comes to costs, salaries, fees, percentages and accounts. Money is simply never discussed. Sometimes Hollywood films use the enormous production costs as part of the marketing (*Dinosaur* – $175m, *Pearl Harbor* – $145m, *Titanic* –$200m, *Waterworld* – $175m) in that boastful manner of movie producers as cigar-chomping industrial capitalists (which is what they are, of course), but it's rare.

Soviet films of the 1960s and 1970s which used folk material and a poetic approach to movie-making in a way comparable with Andrei Tarkovsky included Sergei Paradjanov's *Shadows of Forgotten Ancestors* (1965), Otar Isoliani's *Pastorale* (1977), Yuri Ilenko's *White Bird with a Black Mark* (1972) and Georgy Shengelaya's *Pirosmani* (1969). The stand-out film of the time was undoubtedly Sergei Paradjanov's *The Colour of Pomegranates* (1969), which Kristin Thompson and David Bordwell describe as 'probably the most shockingly experimental film made in the USSR since the late 1920s' (1994, 638). Paradjanov's treatment by the Soviet authorities was much more savage than their treatment of Tarkovsky: Tarkovsky could complain, but he wasn't treated like Paradjanov, who was forbidden to make films, and was sentenced to years of hard labour and prison.

Filmed in dilapidated warehouses and industrial zones, *Stalker* looks at times like some student post-Holocaust thriller (like Luc Besson's *The Last Battle* [1983, France] or *Mad Max* [George Miller, 1979, Australia] to pick two low budget examples of the same era). Except that *Stalker* wasn't low budget (by Soviet standards). Tarkovsky was able to re-shoot much of the film, which is a luxury granted to few filmmakers (usually only the prestigious ones, like Woody Allen or Stanley Kubrick, can secure extensive re-shoots. Film studios only very reluctantly allow filmmakers to substantially re-shoot films. Often, if the executives think a film can't be salvaged, they prefer to scrap it and write off the loss).

Tarkovsky complained in his diary that it wasn't possible to make films without the permission of the State (D, 10). Tarkovsky felt that the Soviet film system had held him back from making more films. He complained to Filip Yermash, Goskino's chairman, that up until 1983 he had directed only five films in 22 years in the USSR. That's true, but it's not the whole picture, because when Tarkovsky wasn't directing, he was writing scripts (including for other directors), developing films, and directing theatre. He wasn't sitting about waiting for the Soviet authorities to give him the green light.

If Tarkovsky had been working in the Western movie industry (in Western Europe, say), he might have directed even fewer films, as Vida Johnson and Graham Petrie rightly point out (1994, 6), because his films were not commercial, box office-friendly products. They tended to be complex art films, the kind of films which have often found it difficult to find an audience, or even a theatrical release at all (the number of films *not* released outside their country of origin in Europe is depressingly *huge*).

Tarkovsky's films were not historical epics favoured by French-Italian-German co-productions, for example, or cool, hip thrillers with sexy stars aimed at the youth markets in, say, Spain or the Netherlands. Maya Turovskaya reckoned that Tarkovsky might not have made many more films, had he lived longer, because he tended to work very slowly anyway.

Tarkovsky had to fight for much of the budget of *Nostalghia*, because he was outside the Russian film industry (for the first time on a feature, though he had made the documentary *A Time To Travel* in 1981). Tarkovsky realized how difficult other Western filmmakers found film finance. But it could be simply that he moans about the budget of *Nostalghia* so much in his *Diaries*. The film is indeed his most sparse — a few actors, and a few choice locations — Rome, Monterchi, the Milan hotel courtyard, the St Catherine Baths. But Tarkovsky makes the £500,000 he received from Italian television (RAI TV) go a very long way, because *Nostalghia* looks like it cost twenty or even a hundred times its budget. One of the reasons is the use of existing locations: filming in the centre of Rome, for instance, gives a film an instant enormous setting too expensive to build. Another reason is Tarkovsky's luxurious feeling for textures and layers (smoke, rain, snow, backlight), which give the impression of a slick, costly, perfectionist sheen to his films. A shot may only consist of one actor and smoke drifting over a field, but Tarkovsky can make it look like a *lot* more.

The money and resources for *The Sacrifice* came from Argos Film, Paris, Swedish Film Institute, Film Four International, London, Josephson and Nykvist, Sverige Television/ SVT 2, Sandrew Film & Teater — a European co-production, with finance mainly from television companies (the French Ministry of Culture was also involved). This was a typical financing pattern for 1980s art films (and continues to be today). With a complex financial package like that, the producer of a film needs to be a canny negotiator, in order to liaise between so many backers, which will all have their own priorities and stipulations. (In the case of *The Sacrifice*, the producers were Anna-Lena Wibom of the Swedish Film Institute, and Katinka Farago of Farago Film).

One of the producers of *The Sacrifice* was Anatole Dauman, one of the key figures in European art cinema scene of the 1960s and 1970s. Dauman's *resumé* on the art cinema circuit (via his company Argos Films) was impeccable: Alain Resnais (*Hiroshima Mon Amour, Last Year At Marienbad, Muriel*), Jean-Luc Godard

(*Masculin-Féminin, Two or Three Things I Know About Her*), Robert Bresson (*Au Hasard Balthazar, Mouchette*), Nagisa Oshima (*In the Realm of the Senses, Empire of Passion*), Volker Schlöndorff (*Circle of Deceit, The Tin Drum*), Walerian Boro-wczyk (*Immoral Tales* and *The Beast*), Wim Wenders (*Paris, Texas, Wings of Desire*) and Chris Marker (*Sunless*).

All of Tarkovsky's films look as if the director achieved everything he had planned in pre-production. He gets the sets and locations he wants; the right actors and crew members; and final cut (though not always). And he also got to make films which he had originated or scripted himself – a *very* important point. That is, Tarkovsky wasn't a film director for hire, he wasn't assigned to projects he hadn't initated (except for *Ivan's Childhood*, which Tarkovsky was invited to direct, taking over from the director Eduard Abalov). Rather, Tarkovsky originated and developed his projects and scripts himself, and presented them to the studio. That's the paradigm of the classic *auteur*, the film director as artist, rather than the other view, of the film director as hired hand, a jobbing worker. It's important because Tarkovsky could have a sense of ownership of a project, of being the prime mover. He could get excited about making the project, feel motivated to do it, because he initiated it.

A film director like Stanley Kubrick is an interesting comparison on this point: Kubrick spent years searching for film projects he *wanted* to make, and he found that very difficult. There was no point just making *anything*. It had to be something worth doing. And what's also interesting about Kubrick in comparison with Tarkovsky, is that Kubrick wasn't a writer, and did not write his own scripts, and only produced films based on existing material (generally books). Tarkovsky, by contrast, was that very rare thing in the movie world, a director who was also a writer and who co-wrote film scripts from original ideas. Almost everyone else works from some existing material, whether it's a comic book, a computer game, a play, a novel, a newspaper article, a TV sitcom, a cartoon, an opera, a fairy tale, a musical, or whatever. (Actually, Tarkovsky did three films from books, and four movies were from original scripts, about half-and-half).

By the time of *Nostalghia* and *The Sacrifice*, Tarkovsky had refined his filmic technique to the point of maximum clarity and beauty. These two films in particular look really stunning, especially considering their modest budgets. But there are many cases of films looking striking on a tiny budget: *Breathless* (Jean-Luc Godard, 1959, France), *Eraserhead* (David Lynch, 1976, US), *Chimes At Midnight* (Orson Welles,

1965, Spain/ Switzerland), *Effi Briest* (Rainer Werner Fassbinder, 1974, West Germany), *The Blood of a Poet* (Jean Cocteau, 1930, France) and *Un Chien Andalou* (Luis Buñuel, 1928, France).

Peter Greenaway's *Prospero's Books* (1991, GB), a dazzling (if cold-blooded) piece of cinema, cost just £1.3 million, which is peanuts beside the average Hollywood feature budget of $25 million of the time. (*Prospero's Books* did benefit from £2 million worth of video editing time, which was given by Japan's NHK to show off their high-definition television system).

François Truffaut's *The Four Hundred Blows* (1959, France) cost $65,000; Ingmar Bergman's *Prison* (*The Devil's Wanton* [*Føangelse*], 1949, Sweden) cost $40,000, as did Akira Kurosawa's *Rashomon* (1950, Japan). *Mad Max* (George Miller, 1979, Australia) cost $350,000 (and looked it, with its post-punk post-apocalyptic chic), but it made 10 million dollars worldwide.

It's amazing that the *sensei* could produce *Rashomon* – a film regularly in top 10 or top 100 all-time film lists – for $40,000! That amount might cover half a day's shooting on a typical Hollywood movie (not counting above-the line costs or talent). Of all those wonderful filmmakers cited above, I'd chose three – Welles, Bergman and Kurosawa – as object lessons in how to make great films for very low budgets.[2]

How they did it was the same way Tarkovsky did it: by producing great stories, great characters, great situations. In short, great cinema. One can dissect the cinematic techniques (carefully controlling what the camera frames, selective lighting, imaginative staging, powerful performances, sound fx to enlarge the space, music, editing, writing, and so on), but what really counts is an uncanny ability to grab the viewer with a completely compelling cinematic experience. There's no better way of putting it, really. So when you're watching one of their movies you're not glancing at your watch, you're not thinking about doing something else, you're not anywhere else.

Every movie goer has a bunch of film moments which have them transfixed, so they forget to breathe. It'd be easy to cite literally hundreds of examples of cinematic transcendence from the history of cinema. But it's easy just using Welles, Bergman and Kurosawa: the first scenes of *The Magnificent Ambersons* (closest to perfection in American cinema), the whole of *Citizen Kane*, the last reel of *The Seven Samurai*, the river sequence in *Dersu Uzala*, the finale of *Through a Glass Darkly*, the radiant close-ups of Rita Hayworth in *The Lady From Shanghai*, Harriet Andersson and the island idyll in *Summer With Monika*, the statues and puppets that come alive in *Fanny and Alexander*, the battle in *Chimes At Midnight*, the long take (ten minutes) in the murder scene in *Macbeth*, Mike Vargas tracking Quinlan in *Touch of Evil*, Toshiro Mifune's wandering samurai in *Yojimbo* and *Sanjuro*, and the battles at the end of *Ran* and *Kagemusha*.

9 : 5   ANDREI TARKOVSKY'S UNMADE FILMS

One can never make the film of one's dreams, Jean-Luc Godard remarked; it always eludes the filmmaker. 'The film of your dreams never happens. Not for Fellini, not for anyone'.[1] The film that Andrei Tarkovsky most wanted to make but never did was probably the one by or about Fyodor Mikhaylovich Dostoievsky. For a long time he nurtured the idea of filming Dostoievsky. Most of the lists of projects in the *Diaries* feature Dostoievsky. Tarkovsky produced a detailed treatment of *The Idiot*, in which he discussed the problems of adapting Dostoievsky (his 'realism' and 'anti-naturalism', and 'his own affinity to cinema' [D, 375]). Akira Kurosawa said that making his vision of *The Idiot* (*Hakuchi*, 1951, Japan) 'was very hard work. It was extraordinarily difficult to make... Dostoievsky is very heavy'.[2]

A list of possible films for Tarkovsky of 1970 (D, 14) included *Joan of Arc*, *The Plague* (Albert Camus), *Kagol* (about Borman's trial), *A Raw Youth* (Dostoievsky), *Joseph and His Brothers* (Thomas Mann), *Matryona's House* (Anatoly Solhenitsyn), and intriguing titles such as *Two Saw the Fox*, *The House With a Tower*, *Echo Calls* and *Deserters*. Tarkovsky loved Thomas Mann, and likely would have based a film on something by Mann had he lived longer (he calls Mann a genius in his diary [D, 7]). He loved Mann's *Tonio Kruger* and *Doctor Faustus*. He had discussions, in 1970, of shooting *Joseph and His Brothers* in Italy.

Many of Andrei Tarkovsky's ideas for films are literary adaptions: Albert Camus' *The Plague*, Thomas Mann's *Joseph and His Brothers* and *Doctor Faustus*, Anatoly Solhenitsyn's *Martyrona's House* (D, 143), *Hamlet*, Dostoievsky's *Crime and Punishment*, *Hoffmaniana* (D, 153), *A Light Wind* (adapted by Tarkovsky and Friedrich Gorenstein from Alexander Belyaev's *Ariel*), *The Double*, Venyamin Bulgakov's *The Master and Marganita*, L.N. Tolstoy's *The Death of Ivan Ilyich*, and so on (D, 211).

If Tarkovsky had filmed them, some of these films would have been remakes (*Crime and Punishment* and *Hamlet*, for instance). But they wouldn't have been 'faithful' adaptions of the books (if that's possible at all). Tarkovsky's idea for *Hamlet*, for instance, was to do it with almost no dialogue (pretty radical for one of the wordiest plays in history. Shakespeare's characters, if nothing else, talk incessantly, using ten lines where one would do. Taking away their dialogue is already a major departure from the plays). Tarkovsky was still contemplating making *Hamlet* in 1984 (he had also been offered to direct it by the Royal Shakespeare Company in Britain). Tarkovsky's adaption of Dostoievsky's *The Idiot* would run through the narrative twice over, from the point-of-view of two characters (Mishkin and Rogozhin), splitting the narrative into two movies.

Another idea for a film was *Life of Archpriest Avvakum*, which Tarkovsky was considering after making *Andrei Roublyov* (Archpriest Avvakum Petrovich, 1620-1682, was a prominent churchman and leader of the Old Ritualists or Old Believers). In 1959, Tarkovsky co-wrote a script with Andrei Konchalovsky: *Antartica, Distant Land* concerned a Russian expedition of scientists in Antartica, but although it was submitted to two Soviet directors (Grigory Kozintsev and Edmond Keosayan), it was mever made.

E.T.A. Hoffman was a favourite author with other filmmakers – Michael Powell had directed his own version of the *Tales of Hoffman* (1951), a bold, operatic endeavour, which was (like many of Powell's best films) also about the magic of cinema. In amongst Hoffman's fantasia, Powell had been fascinated by the concept of automata – puppets and dolls that come to life. That would doubtless have featured in Tarkovsky's take on Hoffman. According to Michal Leszcylowski, *Hoffmann-iana* was going to be Tarkovsky's next film after *The Sacrifice*, to be started in Autumn, 1986. Tarkovsky had scouted locations (in Berlin, at Charlottenburg Palace), and would have been helped by the Bavarian film programme. (It was going to be a German co-production when it was developed in the 1970s).

Hoffmanniana would have been loosely based on Hoffmann's life, and would have included real-life figures such as Heinrich von Kleist, Novalis, Julia Mark, Theodore Gottlieb von Hippel and Johanna Eunike. It would have blurred bio-graphy, fantasy, dream and fiction, and would have celebrated artistic subjectivity (perhaps even more strongly than *Mirror*), with gaps in memory, fantasies, visions, thoughts and subjective consciousness mixed with reality, as Tarkovsky explained in his 1984 notes on *Hoffmanniana* (CS, 370).

Much of Tarkovsky's cinema has literary origins. Conversely, if writers such as André Gide, Novalis or Dostoievsky had made films, they could have been like those of Bresson or Tarkovsky – austere productions with everything stripped away leaving spiritual faith and the search for truth. In the realm of literary adaption, Tarkovsky's interests chime with those of Luchino Visconti, who made films of Dostoievsky's *White Nights* (*La notti bianche*, 1957, Italy), Albert Camus' *The Outsider* (*Lo straniero*, 1967, Italy) and Thomas Mann's *Death in Venice* (*Morte a Venezia*, 1971, Italy). These three writers (Camus, Mann and Dostoievsky) recur in Tarkovsky's list of potential films.

Versions of books by Tarkovsky's beloved Dostoievsky include MGM's *The Brothers Karamazov* (Richard Brooks, 1958) and a Russian *Brothers Karamazov* (Ivan Pyriev, 1968); versions of *Crime and Punishment* by Josef von Sternberg (1935, USA), Georges Lampin (1958, France) and Denis Sanders (1959, USA); *White Nights* (filmed by Visconti in 1957, and as *Four Nights of a Dreamer* [Robert Bresson, 1971, France]); *The Gambler* (Károly Makk, Hungary-France); *Notes From the Underground* (Gary Walkow, 1995, USA); a Russian interpretation of *The Idiot* (Ivan Pyrliev, 1960), and Akira Kurosawa's *The Idiot* (1951). Thus, there had already been many cinematic adaptions of Fyodor Dostoievsky's books: big Hollywood productions, Russian interpretations, and versions by three of Tarkovsky's heroes: Kurosawa, Visconti and Bresson.

Tarkovsky changed *Stalker* considerably (from the book by the Strugatskys) and one is sure that his adaptions of Dostoievsky, Mann, Shakespeare and others would have been similarly pared down and idiosyncratic. Among the more intriguing but never-to-be Tarkovsky films is *Joan of Arc* – 'a latterday *Joan of Arc*' he called it (D, 153). One wonders how it would compare to the powerful *Joan of Arcs* of Carl Dreyer (1928, France) and Robert Bresson (1961, France). (It probably wouldn't have been like the Hollywood *Joan of Arc* (1948) with Ingrid Bergman, or the ridiculously over-the-top French-US *Messenger: The Life of Joan of Arc* (Luc Besson, 1999)). Perhaps Tarkovsky's interpretation of Dostoievsky would have recalled Bresson's beautiful adaption of *White Nights*, shot so hypnotically in Paris, under the title *Four Nights of a Dreamer* (1971, France).

Other intriguing plans of Andrei Tarkovsky's included a 'film based principally on [Carlos] Casteneda' (D, 166). This could have been something wonderful, a journey into shamanic, magical territory. At one point Tarkovsky toyed with the idea of doing a sequel to *Stalker* (D, 169), with the same actors, in which the Stalker turns into a 'votary', a 'fascist', '[b]ullying them into happiness'. The mind boggles.

A film of Hermann Hesse's fiction – *The Glass Bead Game* or *Steppenwolf* – could also have been tremendous (D, 79). One would imagine Tarkovsky's version of Hesse's Existential, mythic fiction (or Albert Camus, Franz Kafka, Jean-Paul Sartre or Knut Hamsun) to be something like *Stalker*, the most Hesse-like of his films. Tarkovsky raved about *The Glass Bead Game* in his journals: 'brilliant', 'a spiritual symbol of life. A novel of genius' (D, 23). Tarkovsky quoted Hesse in *The Glass Bead Game*: 'truth has to be lived, not taught. Prepare for battle!' (ST, 89)

In 1970 Tarkovsky was toying with the idea of shooting Thomas Mann's *Joseph and His Brothers* (a favourite book) in Italy; Tarkovsky had met Dino De Laurentiis's Italian production manager (Robert Coma) on the Russian-Itallian co-production of *Waterloo* (D, 21). Tarkovsky, though, reckoned the powers that be wouldn't greenlight it (D, 25).

Sardor was written for Uzbek filmmaker Ali Khamraev by Tarkovsky and Alexander Misharin in the early 1970s; the proposal didn't go anywhere, and the full script was written later, at the end of 1978, for another Uzbek director, Shukhrat Abbasov, then head of Uzbekfilm (CS, 420).

Flying was at heart of *Light Wind* (a.k.a. *Ariel*), co-written with Fridrikh Gorenshtein. The people who can fly are used to spread religous beliefs. Although there are sequences where characters fly, Tarkovsky rewrote the script to turn it into an exploration of philosophical and spiritual issues. There are references to Jacob Boehme.

Towards the end of the decade (in 1978), Tarkovsky listed potential film projects as *The Country* (a 16mm documentary of reflections); *Italian Journey*; *The Master and Margarita* (from Venyamin Bulgakov's novel); *The Horde*; and a film based on Carlos Casteneda (D, 160). *The Country* was a low budget 'amateur' film that Tarkovsky contemplated making while waiting for other film projects to bear fruit. It would have been shot in Spring, in April and May, and would have featured actor Alexander Kaidanovsky as Tarkovsky himself (D, 168). A year or so later, another list of movie projects included *The Idiot* (Dostoievsky), split into 2 two hour films; another Dostoievsky project, *The Double* (but this time a biopic); a film about the last years of Lev Tolstoy's life called *The Escape*; *The Death of Ivan Ilych* (from L.N. Tolstoy); *The Master and Margarita* again; and *Nostalghia* (D, 211).

At one time (1980), Ingmar Bergman expressed interest in collaborating with Tarkovsky on a film, according to Tarkovsky in his *Diaries* (248). What they might have done together, however, is mouth-watering but indistinct. For instance, both were perfectionist directors who also originated and wrote their own material. Would one have written and the other directed, or would it have been an anthology piece? Although Tarkovsky did write scripts or ideas for other directors (such as *Sardor*, for Ali Khamraev), he didn't do that much, preferring to spend his energy on his own projects.

But perhaps the most fascinating of Tarkovsky's many unmade films is of Samuel Beckett's novel *Molloy*, the first of *The Unnameable* trilogy. What a meeting of talent that could have been: Beckett and Tarkovsky. In the *Diaries* Tarkovsky jots down a few ideas on *Molloy*:

> A diagram of the life of someone who is seeking (actively) to understand the meaning of life... I. Two actors. 2. Unity of place. 3. Unity of action. 4. It would be possible to be aware of nature in the background now and again (as it grows dark or light. (D, IOI)

Imagine Tarkovsky (or Federico Fellini, Ingmar Bergman or Werner Herzog) trying to get to grips with Beckett's *Molloy*. This is a typical extract from the book:

> But already the day is over, the shadows lengthen, the walls multiply, you hug the walls, bowed down like a good boy, oozing with obsequiousness, having nothing to hide, hiding from mere terror, looking neither right nor left, to crawl, nauseating but not pestilent, less rat than toad. Then the true night, perilous too, but sweet to him who knows it, who can open to it like the flower to the sun, who himself is night, day and night.[3]

However, although Samuel Beckett's art is regularly produced in the theatre around the world, and has been adapted for TV and radio, there are hardly any feature film versions. Camus and Kafka have been filmed a few times – equally 'dark', 'difficult' Existential fictions – but not Beckett. You'd think there'd be a well-known film of *Waiting For Godot* made by now, and used by literature students who are advised to watch the versions of *Romeo and Juliet* (1968 and 1996) or *Henry V* (1945 and 1989).

Although Tarkovsky didn't film Samuel Beckett's fiction, there are elements of Beckett's disaffected, shambling derelicts in Gorchakov (he always appears in a grey overcoat, a very Beckettian costume) and the characters in *Stalker*. The Stalker's home is out of Beckett's fictional world – the run-down building, the family squashed together in the old iron bed, the trains clanging by outside. This could be out of Samuel Beckett's *The Expelled,* or *Molloy.* What Tarkovsky's characters lack is the vehemence and utter despair of Beckett's down-and-outs. Tarkovsky has a spiritual hope which Beckett does not (could not, would not) entertain. The pragmatic negativity in Beckett's art would have to be tempered by Tarkovsky, who would not have been able to embrace the darker, miserable aspects of Beckett's *œuvre.* Even during the most downbeat moments of crisis in Tarkovsky's cinema, there is faith and belief.

9 : 6   CINEMA OF EXILE

Life as an exile from Bulgaria and a 'foreigner' in France may have influenced Julia Kristeva's notion of the 'outsider'. For her, the two things, exile and the feminine, became intertwined. Kristeva has stated that her interest in psychoanalysis arose partly from being exiled from Bulgaria.[1] Being an exile helped Kristeva see both her own country and her adopted country more clearly.[2] Her experience of displacement was an ingredient in the formation of her idea of the 'cosmopolitan' individual, the 'intellectual dissident'. As Kristeva knew, strangeness or otherness (being a foreigner) is fundamental to being human: as Kristeva put it, *étrangers à nous-mêmes* (we are strangers to ourselves). In her book *Strangers to Ourselves* Kristeva describes the foreigner as the 'cold orphan', motherless, a 'devotee of solitude', a 'fanatic of absence', alone even in a crowd, arrogant, rejected, yet oddly happy (1991, 4-5). The stranger is always in motion, doesn't belong anywhere, to 'any time, any love' (1991, 7).

Julia Kristeva's description of the 'writer' is quite different from that imagined by middlebrow newspaper columnists or amateur writers writing for a hobby. Writer can here refer to an artist or filmmaker:

> I shall term "writer" that ability to rebound whereby the violence of rejection, in extravagant rhythm, finds its way into a multiplied signifier. It is not the reconstruction of an unwary subject, reminiscing, in hysterical fashion, about his

lacks in meaning, his plunges into an underwater body. It is rather the return of
the limit-as-break, castration, and the bar separating signifier from signified,
which found naming, codification, and language; they do this not in order to
vanish at that point (as communal meaning would have it), but in order, lucidly
and consciously, to reject and multiply them, to dissolve even their boundaries,
and to use them again. (1986, 187)

Tarkovsky took on the persona of the exile from the early 1980s to his death in
1986: he encouraged the portrait of himself as the Russian genius filmmaker in exile
in Italy and Paris, misunderstood in his homeland, and only appreciated when he
travelled to the West. That's a caricature of Tarkovsky The Martyr Of The Soviet
Political System, but it was a media profile which he often allowed to be per-
petuated. In his diary, Tarkovsky remarked that it wasn't possible for a Russian to
live in Italy, 'not with our Russian nostalgia' (D, 259). Layla Garrett, interpreter on
The Sacrifice, said that Tarkovsky deeply missed his son Andriusha, whom he had
left behind in Moscow in the late 1970s. Garrett recalled Tarkovsky complaining
bitterly after another telephone call to Moscow (where he would even talk to his
dog as well as his son), 'why can't I live together with my own son? I haven't seen
Andriusha for more than three years and I love him more than anything in the
world' (23).

TEN

Andrei Tarkovsky and Painting

Take the mirror as your master — I mean smooth-surfaced mirrors — for when reflected on their surface objects resemble paintings in many ways. Thus, painting shows the object on a level surface, yet they look as if they were in relief, and the mirror does the same. Painting is based on the surface only and so is the mirror.

Leonardo da Vinci.[1]

10 : 1   PAINTING AND FILM

One essential difference is time: the painting can be contemplated for hours at a stretch, while film always takes up the same time each viewing. The painting is physically still, while the film image flickers. Painting and cinema offer different (but related) depictions of death, time, change, being and otherness. Tarkovsky's poetic cinema moves towards the condition of painting, in his nine minute takes, lighting out of Jan Vermeer or Georges de la Tour, vistas out of Pieter Brueghel, and his (often) static presentation (scenes staged as enigmatic, mnemonic *tableaux* served up in Renaissance space for the viewer). Further, painting has a physical presence that can be seen as far more complex than that of film: in painting the spectator considers: the size and the scale of the painting, the nature and colour of the frame, the canvas, the various media, the texture, the relation to other paintings, the relation to the viewing space, the lighting and viewing height, and so on. Cinemas differ as spaces, but once the lights go down, the film is pretty much the same. Theatrical release prints can be tatty or new, sound can be clear, Dolby, surround sound 7.1, loud or muffled, and the screen can be large or small, but the film is essentially the same.

There is something dead about film: it is up there, on the screen, but it was filmed elsewhere; the events flickering up there are over, often long gone. Jean-Luc Godard saw it the other way around: painting is dead, but film is alive, because it shows mortality in motion, death on the screen:

> The cinema is the only art which, as Cocteau says (in *Orphée*, I believe) 'films death at work'. Whoever one films is growing older and will die. So one is filming a moment of death. Painting is static: the cinema is interesting because it seizes life and the mortal side of life. (18)

People move and talk but they are coloured shadows (literally like the shadows in Plato's Cave). A painting, meanwhile, is there in front of the viewer, and *the object is it*. There may be references to things dead and gone in the picture – a landscape, say, or a dead person. But the object itself is still there and, despite some ageing, is essentially the same as it was ten, twenty or four hundred years ago. Further, film is a mass medium. It is not special, not a one-off, like painting. One knows there are seventy (or three thousand or so) other prints, circulating the globe at one time, showing the same film four times daily. Even a special collector's edition' DVD or video of a movie is printed in thousands or millions. But when one stands in front of a painting, one possesses the *only one*. It's as if, if one reaches out and touches a Rembrandt or Duccio painting, there is a direct connection to the artist, but cinema offers a different kind of ghost. But maybe, in the end, both museums and cinemas are full of ghosts and death.

These are material, formal considerations: semantically, painting and film share many things in common. Both are illusions of other realities. Both refer, suggest, allude, compare, indicate, poeticize, evoke and portray things outside of themselves. Both can be seen as Baudrillardian 'simulcra', merely different kinds of writing (*pace* Jacques Derrida). Just more texts cluttering up the cultural imaginary. Both are fictions, stories, allusive even when totally abstract (and they're automatically already wholly 'abstract'). Both painting and cinema operate in social systems of élitism, patronage, and advanced technology. One difference, however, may be fundamental: painting is one of the oldest arts, with a history going back at least forty thousand years. And painting, like all art, has its origin in religion.

Historically, cinema has lagged behind painting, in terms of technique and formalism. Jean-Luc Godard's polemical, cut-up, formally innovative cinema of the early 1960s, for instance, comes thirty years and more after Surrealism, and sixty years after Cubism. Peter Greenaway enshrined painting far above cinema, which he regarded as a 'grossly conservative medium'; painting, on the other hand, Greenaway saw as 'the supreme visual means of communication. Its freedoms, its attitudes, its history, its potential'.[1] One can argue the opposite just as easily.

Many films incorporate images or ideas from painting; from lighting (Cecil B. De Mille's 'Rembrandt lighting' for instance); or how to use *mise-en-scène* to describe character and narrative (Fritz Lang's *Siegfried* [1922-24, Germany] with its Romantic forest out of painting and Grimms' fairy tales); how to visualize epic sets (such as in *Cabiria* [Giovanni Pastrone, 1914, Italy] or D.W. Griffith's *Intolerance* [1916, USA]), which derive from visionary painters such as J.M.W. Turner, Joseph Wright and John Martin. John Martin's gigantic visions of ancient Babylon and Egypt, such as in his *Belshazzar's Feast* (1821, private collection), are clearly the visual ancestors of Hollywood's Biblical epic films.)

Filmmakers often bring in postcards, posters, illustrations from books as research material for the look of films. For instance, 19th century French illustrator Gustave Doré is regularly employed by filmmakers (including many contemporary directors) as an inspiration. The influence of Doré's illustrations for the *Bible*, Dante's *Inferno*, Balzac and Rabelais can be found in the *Lord of the Rings* films (2001-03), Terry Gilliam's films, *What Dreams May Come* (1998) or the *Star Wars* prequels (1999-2005).

Using paintings as a basis for *mise-en-scène* was derided by Andrei Tarkovsky in his writings (ST, 78), although he did just that a number of times in his films. Tarkovsky used painting many times, often incorporating discussions of painters in his dialogues or visuals. There is Leonardo da Vinci in *Mirror* and *The Sacrifice*; Piero della Francesca in *Nostalghia* and *The Sacrifice*; the snowscapes referencing Pieter Brueghel in *Solaris* and *Mirror*; part of Jan van Eyck's *Ghent Altarpiece* in *Stalker*; Albrecht Dürer's *Apocalypse* in *Ivan's Childhood*; Vincent van Gogh is alluded to in the face and hands of Gorchakov; Byzantine icons appear in *Mirror, Andrei Roublyov* and *The Sacrifice*; and *Andrei Roublyov* has the painter's icons crowning it at the end.

Tarkovsky's penchant is for uncluttered artists: he dislikes the Baroque, the mannered, the ornate, the over-rich. Hence his love of Dürer, van Gogh, Leonardo, Piero and Brueghel. One can see in Tarkovsky's cinema affinities with Fra Angelico's simple, lyrical Quattrocento depictions of religious faith – Angelico's art is the culmination of mediæval Christian fervour. One can find the intense mystical feeling of Early Netherlandish painters in Tarkovsky's sacred cinema. Painters such as Jan van Eyck, Rogier van der Weyden, Quentin Massys and Petrus Christus depicted events from the *Bible* in dark but luminous paintings, filled with a miraculous, exquisite, detailed light (the translucence in Early Flemish art is infinitely more enriching than the light in the Impressionists, who're usually celebrated as painters of light but turn out to be opaque and limited).

The famous religious mystics of Northern Europe of this era, Jan van Ruysbroeck and Meister Eckhart, preached the *via negativa*, a devout approach to the Godhead via quiet, interior lucubration. As in Tarkovsky's religious cinema, there are many churches and ecclesiastical buildings in Early Netherlandish paintings. In Jan van Eyck's *Virgin in the Church* (c. 1425, State Museums, Berlin-Dahlem), the Queen of Heaven stands twenty feet tall in an ornate Gothic interior. It is this spiritual grandeur which has gone from modern life, which Andrei Tarkovsky laments. He chose to show a *ruined* cathedral in *Nostalghia* – this in a country (Italy) which abounds in gorgeous, living cathedrals (Orvieto, Siena, Milan, Florence and Arezzo).

But though the Goddess and the Church is broken or decayed, Christ (Christ-like fervour) still burns in Tarkovsky's progatonists: one can see connections between Tarkovsky's Christianity and that portrayed in, for example, Rogier van der

Weyden's stupendous *Descent From the Cross* (1439-43, Prado, Madrid) and the *Crucifixions* by Petrus Christus, Dieric Bouts, Gerard David and Hieronymous Bosch. This Northern European painting tradition is, like Russian mediæval icon painting, Tarkovsky's visual ancestry and inheritance.

Although Tarkovsky does use landmark artists of the Italian Renaissance in his films (principally Piero della Francesca and Leonardo da Vinci) his art is geared to Northern Europe and Russia. The art of the intenser Italian Renaissance artists – Masaccio, Giotto, Andrea Mantegna – chimes with Tarkovsky's visions of the world (but not the blander, airy art of Raphael Sanzio, Francesco Parmigianino, Garfalo (Benvenuto Tisi) or Lorenzo Lotto, nor the later Mannerist, Roccoco and Baroque painters: Annibale Caracci, Guido Reni, Domenichino, Guercino (Francesco Barbieri) and Padre Pozzo).

But no Italian Renaissance painter matches the intensity of the suffering painted by Mathias Grünewald in his *Isenheim Altarpiece* (1515, Musée d'Unterlinden, Colmar). Grünewald's is the Christ to end all Christs as supreme martyr whose agony appears to be trying to suck in all of the world's pain. It's a gruelling, uncompromising depiction of the ultimate sacrifice. This is the kind of angst-ridden torment Tarkovsky would like to portray, and gets close to doing so in *The Sacrifice* (but it was a Hollywood director, Mel Gibson, who achieved it on film in a literal, graphic manner, when he had Jim Caviezel's naked body made up with hundreds of bleeding wounds and lacerations in *The Passion of the Christ*).

In the dark, powerful paintings of Diego Velasquez, Jusepe Ribera and Francisco de Zurbarán, the stars of the Spanish Golden Age, there are also correspondences with Tarkovsky's cinema. The Spanish painters excelled at portraying a fervent kind of Catholicism embodied by monks and saints shrouded in darkness. One can trace a Northern European exaltation of Christian suffering from Mathias Grüne-wald through Albrecht Dürer to Romantic and Symbolist painters such as Caspar David Friedrich, Philipp Otto Rünge, Arnold Böcklin and Edvard Munch, and Expressionists such as Max Beckmann, Georges Rouault, Emil Nolde and Lovis Corinth.

Caspar David Friedrich's images could be ancestors of Tarkovsky's imagery – Friedrich's luminous skies, gnarled trees, ruined abbeys and empty sea shores, not to mention angels (as in Friedrich's *Angels in Adoration, c.* 1834, Kunsthalle, Hamburg). Friedrich painted a house inside a cathedral which is a clear precursor of the closing image in *Nostalghia*.

Tarkovsky is part of this tradition of painting – where spiritual issues are portrayed in an anguished, subjective, expressive fashion. One can see how Tark-ovsky developed the Christian depictions of modern Western art (such as Emil Nolde, Max Beckmann, Egon Schiele and Eric Gill) – each of whom portrayed some event in the Christian story in a modern, Expressionist manner. The tradition of mystical darkness, as found in mystics such as Dionysius the Areopagite (*fl.* 500), St John of the Cross (1542-91), Meister Eckhart (*c.* 1260-1328) and *The Cloud of Unknowing* (14th century), is another ancestor of this approach to spiritual issues.

The typical way in which painting is introduced into Tarkovsky's films is by an actor leafing through a book (in *Ivan's Childhood, Mirror* and *The Sacrifice*). This may have been the way in which Tarkovsky first encountered painting – not at school or in museums, but at home, via a book, in privacy. (In a way, it's a modest, perhaps even too obvious method of weaving in a subplot about painting into the films. But perhaps Tarkovsky's characters are the sort of highly educated people who might look through a book of paintings). Of all the arts, Tarkovsky folds painting and music into his cinema more than any other. He does not, for instance, make references to the history of cinema, or dance, or ballet, or musicals, or sculpture, or opera (Ingmar Bergman's films often reference theatre, for instance, while jazz (and the Marx Brothers) are never far from Woody Allen's films). Both painting and music are significantly non-verbal artforms with a tendency towards lyricism and expressionism (and they're abstract enough to fit into Tarkovsky's cinematic scheme).

10 : 3   JULIA KRISTEVA ON PAINTING

In one of the best readings of the psychology of the Renaissance painter Giovanni Bellini's art, Julia Kristeva's essay "Motherhood According to Bellini", Kristeva makes many points which apply not only to Giovanni Bellini and other Renaissance painters such as Fra Angelico, Sandro Botticelli, Piero della Francesca and Leonardo da Vinci, but also to the artistic project in general, and to Tarkovsky's sacred cinema.

Julia Kristeva discusses the portrayal of the maternal body in Giovanni Bellini's (and Renaissance) art (which is central to films of Tarkovsky's such as *Zerkalo* and *Nostalghia*). In Kristeva's elegant, limpid reading of Renaissance æsthetic philosophy, the woman is simultaneously allowed to be and not to be the mother; she is placed centrally and simultaneously decentred; she is exalted by painters even as she is denigrated (consider the treatment of Eugenia in *Nostalghia*, or Maria the mother in *Mirror*). In Kristeva's theory of semiotics, it is artists, almost more than anyone else, who recognize the importance of the *chora*, of the unrepresentable body (the mother).

> ...craftsmen of Western art reveal better than anyone else the artist's debt to the maternal body and/ or motherhood's entry into symbolic existence – that is, translibidinal *jouissance*, eroticism taken over by the language of art. Not only is a considerable portion of pictorial art devoted to motherhood, but within this representation itself, from Byzantine iconography to Renaissance humanism and the worship of the body that it initiates, two attitudes toward the maternal body emerge, prefiguring two destinies within the very economy of Western representation. Leonardo da Vinci and Giovanni Bellini seem to exemplify in the best fashion the opposition between these two attitudes. On the one hand, there is a tilting toward the body as fetish. On the other, a predominance of luminous, chromatic differences beyond and despite corporeal representation. Florence and Venice. Worship of the figurable, representable man; or integration of the image accomplished in its truthlikeness within the luminous serenity of the unrepresentable. ("Motherhood According to Bellini", 1982, 243)

In her outstanding essay on the Virgin Mary, "Stabat Mater", which refers to the famous painting by Piero della Francesca which Tarkovsky places at the centre of the film), Julia Kristeva wrote:

> Mary's function as guardian of power, later checked when the church became wary of it, nevertheless persisted in popular and pictural representation, witness Piero della Francesca's impressive painting, *Madonna della Misericordia*, which was disavowed by Catholic authorities at the time. And yet, not only did the papacy revere more and more the christly mother as the Vatican's power over cities and municipalities was strengthened, it also openly identified its own institution with the Virgin: Mary was officially proclaimed Queen by Pius XII in 1954 and *Mater Ecclesiae* in 1964. (1986, 170)

Against science, in the Renaissance, there is religion. The Madonna presides over the religious domain, as the maternal presence presides over Tarkovsky's cinema. Kristeva's discussions of the subject are especially pertinent if one remembers

Eugenia's encounter with the sacristan in *Nostalghia*: notice that none of the women involved in the ritual speak to Eugenia: her colloquy is with the sacristan who may be taken to represent the Catholic church and clergy which Kristeva refers to in her discussion).

Kristeva wrote:

There is Christian theology (especially canonical theology); but theology defines maternity only as an impossible elsewhere, a sacred beyond, a vessel of divinity, a spiritual tie with the virginal and committed to assumption.

The Madonna is the primal Mother of all, and her body is the site of so many conflicting feelings. She is both the giver and taker of life, the desired and the loathed object of desire.[1] This is how some of the women are portrayed in Tark-ovsky's cinema (i.e., with barely disguised deep ambivalence: consider, for instance, Gorchakov's dream of his wife with Eugenia, or Andrei Roublyov's attitude of fear and desire toward the pagan woman).

In the Dormition, or the Death of the Virgin, the Madonna becomes a little girl in the arms of her son who is also her father: the roles are reversed, and she becomes a daughter. She is mother *and* daughter, as well as the *wife*: she 'actualizes the threefold metamorphosis of a woman in the tightest parenthood structure' Kristeva remarked in "Stabat Mater" (1986, 169). 'Her replete body, the receptacle and guarantor of demands' commented Kristeva, 'takes the place of all narcissistic, hence imaginary, effects and gratifications; she is, in other words, the phallus' (1984, 101). The Virgin Mary provides a focus for the non-verbal, for those drives and significations which are part of earlier, more archaic processes (what Kristeva termed the 'semiotic *chora*').[2] The Madonna is the Renaissance version of the 'phallic Mother', the site of childhood bliss, site of childhood anxiety. Kristeva explained thus:

The face of his [Giovanni Bellini's] Madonnas are turned away, intent on something else that draws their gaze to the side, up above, or nowhere in particular, but never centres it in the baby. (1982, 247)

What Kristeva's referring to is also a painter's choice common in Renaissance art. Even in paintings when there are many figures (the saints and donors in the *Sacra Conversazione*), very often not one of them will be looking at the baby Jesus, or each other. Instead, they stare off into their own private infinity.

Andrei Tarkovsky   242

Giovanni Bellini's Madonnas present a *jouissance* of maternal space that is, Kristeva suggested, 'beyond discourse, beyond narrative, beyond psychology, beyond
lived experience and biography' (247). But the Kristevan mother also enables
artistic creation.[3] Kristeva interpreted Bellini's art as a secret autobiography in
which the artist tried to displace the father and site himself within the maternal
body, to 'rewrite' the body of the mother in his own fashion.

> Giovanni [Bellini] wanted to surpass his father, within the very space of the lost-
> unrepresentable-forbidden *jouissance* of a hidden mother, seducing the child
> through a lack of being... He aspired to become the very space where father and
> mother meet... Bellini penetrates through the being and language of the father to
> position himself in the place where the mother could have been reached. He thus
> makes evident this always-already past conditional of the maternal function,
> which stands instead of the *jouissance* of both sexes. A kind of incest is then
> committed, a kind of possession of the mother, which provides motherhood, that
> mute border, with a language; although in doing so, he deprives it of any right to
> a real existence (there is nothing "feminist" in Bellini's action), he does accord it a
> symbolic status. (1982, 248-9)

Not every ounce of Kristeva's brilliant reading of Giovanni Bellini and Renaissance art can be applied directly to Tarkovsky's cinema, but many of the points she
makes help to throw light on the relation between creation, the artist, women and
the feminine in Tarkovsky's films: how Kristeva evokes a lost, unrepresentable
mother, for instance, or so intelligently re-imagines the œdipal negotiations every
artist is embarked upon (and in the process, she goes beyond Freud or Lacan,
producing a psychology of artistic creativity far more satisfying than either Freud or
Lacan).

The skillful painter must paint two main things, man and what is going on in his mind.

Leonardo da Vinci[1]

Leonardo da Vinci is the unsurpassed master of darkness, ambivalence and strange beauty. He is the highpoint of figurative art in the West. There are many aspects of Leonardo that single him out as Andrei Tarkovsky's favourite artist: his vast curiosity, his restlessness, his perfectionism, his ambiguity, his solitary outsider lifestyle, his *sfumato* painterly style and the timelessness of his art. (Tarkovsky spoke of Leonardo's ability to observe the world from outside, detached, but accurate.) Leonardo is also one of the supreme examples of the artist-as-hero, something that Tarkovsky identifies with. Tarkovsky portrays Andrei Roublyov as a quiet wanderer possessed by genius. There is a lot of Leonardo's personality in the character of Roublyov (Roublyov as misunderstood genius, as a perpetual exile, as in advance of his era, and so on). (Leonardo's art enjoyed a new surge of interest in the 2000s, following author Dan Brown, *The Da Vinci Code* book and film, and count-less cash-ins).

Like Andrei Tarkovsky, Leonardo da Vinci produced only a few 'finished' works (and every artist can identify with that, the eternal dissatisfaction with one's work, the mind flitting to other projects, the ease of being distracted). But the ones Leonardo did make are the apotheosis of the Renaissance, and the whole Western art tradition, unparalleled in their sense of depth, darkness and mystery. Leonardo is an occult exponent of the invisible — he makes the invisible visible, in the German painter Max Beckmann's sense. Beckmann's aim, like Tarkovsky's, was 'always to get hold of the magic of reality' as he put it.[2] In Leonardo's art one finds a sense of the invisible and the beyond more compellingly rendered than in just about any other painter. Leonardo's occultism is his ability to make manifest the inner spiritual dimensions of things. He investigates his subjects on so many levels — the social, spiritual, physiological, personal, hermetic and scientific.

Leonardo's people — the women, angels, saints, outcasts, children and madmen — inhabit a twilit world of shadows. Leonardo's subjects are half-angels, half-devils, supremely ambiguous, tantalizing, mocking and mysterious. None of Tarkovsky's people are as fully imagined as Leonardo's softly smiling angels and goddesses (as great as Tarkovsky is, I don't think he would put himself on the same level as Leonardo). It's practically impossible to portray a Leonardo face in cinema. The famous Leonardo Gioconda Smile, as enigmatic as Buddha's grin, is also unfilmable. At one point in *Mirror*, Tarkovsky tries to do it: he cuts from the *Portrait of a Woman* (Ginerva Benci?, *c.* 1474-76, National Gallery of Art, Washington) to Natalia, the wife of the narrator. The mythicization stems from the montage, which is bold (ST, 108).

The sitter in *The Young Woman With the Juniper* (used in *Mirror*), Tarkovsky called at once 'attractive and repellent. There is something inexpressibly beautiful about her and at the same time repulsive, fiendish' (ST, 108). Leonardo's portrait was effective, Tarkovsky reckoned, because the viewer couldn't single out any particular aspect of the painting from the whole, it couldn't be grounded in one particular interpretation. Instead, the artwork offered up the 'interaction with infinity', an opening out into infinity (ST, 109). Easy to see how Tarkovsky might like a similar response to his own art: that the viewer wouldn't be persuaded to dissect his films, to take them apart detail by detail, but to apprehend them as a whole. It was the *whole film*, Tarkovsky asserted, that was the work of art, not any particular element. Dividing up a film into components was to miss the point (114, 177). Only a film as a whole can carry the meanings and values that audiences ascribe to them, Tarkovsky said, not the dissection of individual shots or scenes.

An autoeroticism is found throughout Leonardo da Vinci's work. His eroticism is focused on himself. One doesn't need Freud to show that Leonardo's eroticism pivots around repression, masturbation and autoeroticism. Not only did he create many images of that obscure object of desire, the mother figure, who in the Lacanian psychological system is a displaced phallus (the so-called 'phallic mother'), Leonardo also constructed many images around the mirror. There is the *doppelgänger* or 'Other', for instance, in his paintings – the second or double mother, the second or twin Jesus. And of course there is also the famous 'mirror writing' which he used.

Themes common to both Andrei Tarkovsky and Leonardo da Vinci include: the twins, seen in Leonardo's two mysterious *Virgins of the Rocks* (*c.* 1483-86, Louvre, Paris, and *c.* 1503, National Gallery, London and other works). The twins appear in *Mirror*, and the double in *Nostalghia*. The myth of the Two Mothers – in Leonardo's beautiful *The Virgin and Child with St Anne* (*c.* 1510, Louvre) and the London *Cartoon* (*c.* 1498, National Gallery) – are found in *Nostalghia* (the Russian women in Gorchakov's dream); and in *Mirror* (the aunt and the mother). At the end of *Mirror* the matriarchal trinity is seen: the grandmother, mother and (in this case two) children, a familial configuration like that of Leonardo's *St Anne* images, where the grandmother is depicted as a Dark Mother, a Black Goddess figure.

The double or *doppelgänger* is one of the long-standing motifs of cinema, found in Doctor Jekyll, *Kagemusha, The Prisoner of Zenda, Persona, Vertigo* and many other films). One of Tarkovsky's favourite devices, employed on all of his films from *Solaris* onwards, was to put several versions of the same character on screen at the same time, without resorting to cutting or visual effects. This was achieved simply and in-camera by using stand-ins of the lead actors, with the same costumes, hair and make-up, positioned carefully on set. Examples include the multiple versions of Hari in *Solaris*, or Gorchakov's dreams of Russia and his home in *Nostalghia*. Sometimes Tarkovsky cuts back and forth between the same space in different states: the *dacha* in *Mirror*, for instance, is depicted empty and desolate one moment, then as it was in the past in another. Sound effects or music smooth over these transitions.

In Andrei Tarkovsky's and Leonardo da Vinci's art women are exalted — as well as feared and stereotyped. Like Leonardo, Tarkovsky's cinema enshrines the strange power of women (the familiar depiction in masculinist art of women as unknowable, unreachable Other). The scene where the mother Maria flails her arms in the raining room in *Mirror* is like the modern filmic equivalent of a scene from a long lost Leonardo painting (one can imagine Leonardo — or post-Leonardoan artists like Gustav Klimt or Gustave Moreau, artists with similarly ambiguous views of women — applauding Tarkovsky for that scene. To an artist like Michelangelo or Gianlorenzo Bernini it would appear bemusing).

Women in Tarkovsky's cinema recall those in Leonardo's art — there is the same emphasis on ambiguous sexuality, fetishes (long hair), arcane gestures, prominent eyes, swan-like features, serenity, restlessness and strangeness. (Leonardo's women are the precursors of the *femme fatales* in Symbolist and *fin-de-siècle* painting or 1940s *film noir*). It was the memory of his mother, Sigmund Freud wrote of Leonardo, 'that drove him at once to create a glorification of motherhood'.[3] The same could be said of Tarkovsky, in *Mirror*. Both artists glorify the mother: she is a gigantic figure, never fully understood by the child. She is at once dangerous and deeply desired.

An oft-quoted anecdote about Leonardo da Vinci has him painting the head of the

Medusa, the phallic castrating mother, which frightened his father when he glimpsed it in a darkened room. There's something very cinematic about that image of Leonardo's father seeing the head of the Gorgon in a shadowy room. It's a scene with the ambiguity, the visual component, and the œdipal anxiety of the Freudian primal scene. It's all there: the artist son, the father, the darkness, the terrifying image of woman. One can imagine Pier Paolo Pasolini shooting a vivid interpretation of that scene in Leonardo's home (like the modern-day scenes Pasolini created for the prologue of his *Oedipus Rex* [1968], the supreme rendering of the Oedipus myth in cinema).

And the story about Leonardo crafting the Medusa is also wonderfully quaint: the idea that an adult could be frightened by a painting (or by a film). But isn't that also the power of art? And Tarkovsky's films too? There must be viewers who have wept while watching a Tarkovsky film, or laughed, or felt something. Or, to put it another way, is there a filmmaker who's regarded as one of the greats whose films have *not* contained a significant *emotional* component, whose films have *not* deeply affected spectators *emotionally*?

10 : 5   LEONARDO DA VINCI'S *ADORATION OF THE MAGI*

There is something terrifying about Leonardo da Vinci's *The Adoration of the Magi* when one sees it in the flesh, as well as something beautiful and mysterious. The square painting (1481-82, Uffizi, Florence) depicts a moment of maximum religious revelation. Fervent spirituality spirals out from the calm centre of the Madonna and Child. Leonardo pushes back the frontiers of pictorialism. Oswald Spengler called it 'the most daring painting of the Renaissance'.[1] The half-angelic/ half-dæmonic beings slipping through the painting have surely the most beautiful faces in Western art. The event they celebrate is an epiphany, when the Godly nature of Jesus is publicly revealed. Leonardo depicts the manifestation of the divine, the experience of the numinous, the *mysterium tremendum*. Here the deification is enacted, with a host of witnesses, the witnesses being a cross-section of humanity, from the lowly sub-proletariat in the background, around the horses, to the royal figures in the foreground. It is a portrayal of mana:

> Mana [wrote Weston La Barre] is a projection of our awe at the spectacle of the "holy", the uncannily known... Subjectively experienced, the numinous is taken for an external epiphany of mana. (1972, 368)

Tarkovsky aims for such an epiphany in his films, where God-in-nature is mysteriously revealed. This is (partly) what Tarkovsky seems to be going for when he films the rain at the end of *Stalker*, for instance.

Leonardo da Vinci's *The Adoration of the Magi* is revolutionary, artistically, and revelatory, spiritually. Energy resounds off the surface of *The Adoration of the Magi*. It is an amazingly energetic, even chaotic, picture. As Venturi said, 'modelling is swept away on a tide of emotion'. Only the lost *Battle of Anghiari* would have had a similar frenetic energy as the *Adoration*. *The Adoration of the Magi* is one of those rich artworks that can withstand many visits (there aren't as many of those sorts of works as one might think). Leonardo's *Adoration*, like all of his paintings, gives the viewer a plenitude of richness to work on. There are many layers to it, yet each layer can also be seen beside the top layer, so to speak. Leonardo makes the deepest levels visible, as well as the upper levels. If the artwork is a lake, with the deep meanings at the bottom, in the dark, unconscious zones, Leonardo makes these visible. He makes mystery visible, as Paul Valéry said.

The *Adoration of the Magi* genre traditionally depicts the three kings Caspar (or Jasper, the oldest), Balthazar (often depicted as black) and Melchior (the youngest) travelling to Bethlehem (as related in the *Gospel of St Matthew*). In the later mediæval period, the three kings represented parts of the known world: Europe, Africa and Asia, as well as the temporal powers submitting to the Church.[2] January 6, the feast of Epiphany (and the Twelfth Night of Christmas) is traditionally the date of the Magis' visit, as well as Jesus's appearance to the shepherds (also, Epiphany is a bigger deal in the Eastern Orthodox calendar. And Epiphany was the old Christmas Day, and is older than Christmas itself as a festival. Epiphany, originating in the Eastern Church of the 3rd century, coincided with pagan New Year festivities, before the calendars were changed).

No matter how deeply one trawls Leonardo's *Adoration of the Magi*, one never quite explains away its sense of mystery. The mystery remains present to the end. The drawing *suggests* so much, without, finally, being specific about its content. The meanings it suggests change, softly and subtly, exactly like the play of light over its sublime surface. There is the mystery of the tree, rising from roots directly above the head of Christ. The tree is clearly the Tree of Life of ancient mythology, and Christ is the shaman who will later, as a grown man, become the shaman of his tribe, climbing the Cosmic or World Tree, and bringing back news of the other world. Leonardo's picture depicts also, of course, the World Tree on which Christ is crucified. Significantly, there are angels on either side of the tree trunk; the angels are guardians of the tree, and they also remind the viewer of its miraculous nature. There is the mystery of the crowds of figures, interweaving, limbs merging into limbs in the shadows. There is the mystery of the background architecture, with its grand steps and arches, worked out so carefully in the sketch for this work. (New analysis of Leonardo's *Adoration*, has revealed fascinating elments in the under-drawing).

Tarkovsky chose to focus on the Magi, in the first shot of *The Sacrifice* (over the opening credits). The abasement of Balthazar, Caspar (or Jasper) and Melchior is total: one of the kings kneels down so low his head nearly touches the ground. The Child soaks up this adoration, while the Virgin deflects it with her expression of humility. She is absolutely the heart of the painting, visually, although the Child is the centre, spiritually, in the orthodox view. Early Leonardo sketches for an *Adoration* show the Virgin doing all the adoring; she kneels with her arms outspread before the Child, as in the *Adorations* of Early Netherlandish art (it's a moment of adoration before the magi appear, and is known as *The Adoration of the Virgin*, based on an account by St Bridget of Sweden following a visit to Bethlehem in 1370). In the *Adorations* or *Nativities* of Fra Filippo Lippi, Piero della Francesca, and the Early Netherlandish painters, the Madonna holds her hands together in humble prayer before the majesty of the Child. In Leonardo's drawings, her arms are outspread: her awe at the Child below her is also a self-glorification.

The 'spectacle of the holy' is a useful term (from Rudolf Otto); Leonardo makes a spectacle of the revelation of holiness: there is no other picture like *The Adoration of the Magi* in Leonardo's art, and indeed, in all Renaissance art. It is one of the few images that is 'unique'. Yet, this is the point: that Leonardo makes 'special' or 'miraculous' events or emotions that by his day had become tired and well-used clichés. Before his time, there had already been hundreds, if not thousands, of *Adorations of the Magi* painted. There had already been hundreds and thousands of religious images made. Leonardo's task, as a religious painter, was to imbue the religious subject matter with the sense of mystery and transcendence that it first had (making the revelation go back to the First Revelation). He has to re-invent the presence of the eternal and the divine. It's not easy. This is every religious artist's task.

Tarkovsky acknowledged that he was one of those artists who created their own inner world, rather than recreating reality (ST, 118). The innerness or interiority that Leonardo depicts has been the province of poets for centuries. It is the unknown, dark, nighttime, inner space of poetry, symbolized by the night, by stars, blackness (death), and infinite spaces. Novalis, the German Romantic poet, wrote:

> Toward the Interior goes the arcane way. In us, or nowhere, is the Eternal with its worlds, the past and future... The seat of the world is there, where the inner world and the outer world touch... The inner world is almost more mine than the outer. It is so heartfelt, so private – man is given fullness in that life – it is so native.[3]

The figure of the angel is a key element in Leonardo's depiction of the 'invisible'. The angel, as Rainer Maria Rilke noted in his *Duino Elegies*, is that presence that can move between this and the other world, between light and dark, between the living and the dead, between heaven and earth. Leonardo's angels are the most terrifying figures in Renaissance art. They are human and more-than-human (post-human, beyond-human), they are softly smiling, they are sunken in shadow, they are extravagantly androgynous, both male and female, and more than either (trisexual), like the divine being (the hermaphrodite) of alchemy. (Dæmons might be a better term: not 'demons' but 'dæmons' out of Gnostic and hermetic philosophy).

Leonardo's angels are at the height of their mystery in *The Adoration of the Magi*, a truly magnificent drawing, and unsettling in its inexplicableness, its miraculous ability to hypnotize the viewer, its astonishing power and frenetic energy. Leonardo's angels move amongst humans in a shadowy zone below the tree. It is a vision of humanity in a whirlpool of religious energy, the focus of which is the epiphany of the Virgin and Child, who sit so calmly still in the centre.[4]

In the two *Virgin of the Rocks* paintings by Leonardo, the Leonardoan angel-dæmon appears at its most voluptuous. The sketch of Leonardo's angel in pencil for the painting is extraordinary in itself, but when Leonardo's unsurpassed graphic abilities are combined with his deep *sfumato* lighting and oil technique, the result is dazzling. Leonardo's painted angel is, to use Oswald Spengler's term, 'indescribable'. So the art critic moves into superlative overload, as Walter Pater or John Ruskin often did, and comes out with a load of over-lyrical hyperbole. (The gushing style of some art historians helps to emphasize the erotic nature of art and art criticism. Even the most ironic, cool and super-cynical of postmodernist philosophers are always talking about 'desire'. What does the sculptor Carl Andre say about desire?: 'I have very few ideas, but I have strong desires... You can't cut off desires except painfully.[5])

Leonardo's angels certainly have a 'terrifying ethereality', to use a term typical of the more Romantic branches of art criticism. Leonardo's 'genius' is more than a thaumaturgic ability to manipulate paint and line and tone and colour, but that does help. The American painter Adolph Gottlieb wrote: '[p]aint quality is meaningless if it does not express quality of feeling.' Gottlieb pointed out again the connection between the materiality of painting and the emotionalism of it. Certainly Leonardo knows how to modulate expressiveness and feeling through paint and line.[6] Leonardo's unmatched talent for expressivity is one of the aspects of his art that attracted Tarkovsky (Tarkovsky, ever the modernist, never gives up on the belief that art can 'express' something, that it can be emotional).

Tarkovsky used *The Adoration of the Magi* to frame the narration in *The Sacrifice*. He holds his camera on the central portion of the painting for many minutes at the opening of the film. Sometimes in the rest of the film the painting is shot so that the glass over it acts as a mirror. Sometimes it shifts within a shot from being a painting to a mirror. There is a flicker of humour when Alex tells Otto that the painting is a print, not an original. Alex's joke is another reference to the authenticity of religion, religious images and religious faith in a modern, Godless world. The painting presides over Alex's dream. The central gift in the painting, from a King to Christ, echoes the gift of life Alex gives to his mute son at the end of the film – the gift of life as the ultimate sacrifice. Tarkovsky's upward tilt shot, at the opening credits, visually connects the gift of the sacrifice with the tree above. The tree lies vertically above the gift of the King in the painting, connecting father and son together spiritually. (In the secular world of contemporary movies, with Christian values long abandoned, the sacrifice of giving up life remains heroic, one of the hallmarks of a hero. It climaxes films such as *Saving Private Ryan, Gladiator, Armageddon, Braveheart* and *The Poseidon Adventure.* Contemporary Hollywood cinema may be using the heroic sacrifice not so much for its moral or spiritual content, but because it gives a film an emotional or thematic climax at the same time as the action climax). In Kristevan semiotics, sacrifice takes its place as the thetic moment which separates the semiotic from the symbolic. Sacrifice does not, though, let violence loose; rather, it helps to regulate it. When sacrifice is incorporated into religion, violence may be dissipated completely.

Andrei Tarkovsky saw Leonardo's *Adoration of the Magi* in Florence in August, 1979 (D, 200). Two days later he saw Leonardo's *St Jerome* (c. 1480, Vatican, Rome) and noted: '[a]bove all – the Leonardos' (ib.). The tortured image of St Jerome is fixed to the wall in Alex's upstairs study in *The Sacrifice*, like the *Adoration of the Magi*. Alex is clearly identified with St Jerome in the saint's guise as dishevelled penitent – the Jerome who had a vision in the desert of angels announcing the Last Judgement (which is the plot of *The Sacrifice*, except the angelic messenger service is television, and the Last Judgement comes in the form of nuclear war, a common motif in films of the Cold War period). St Jerome is sometimes shown in Renaissance paintings listening to the angels' trumpets blowing over his head. In *The Sacrifice*, the Apocalypse is announced by the missiles or jets screaming overhead – latterday technological angels.

The severe *Self-Portrait* by Leonardo da Vinci (c. 1512, Royal Library, Turin) appears in *Mirror* as the father returns to the homeland. Tarkovsky's father was a poet, an artist, and the appearance of the Leonardo sketch at this point underlines the significance of the father as a creative person, and that the film is an æsthetic construction and inquisition – in part the Story of the Birth of an Artist. The self-reflexivity of Leonardo's art is part of his mystery, and probably one of the reasons that Tarkovsky was attracted to him.

10 : 6   ANDREI TARKOVSKY AND PIERO DELLA FRANCESCA

Piero della Francesca's art makes geometry mystical. It is bright and timeless, like Classic Greek fresco and relief. Piero's paintings fetishize architectonic precision. Piero extends space beyond Euclid and Newton towards an Einsteinian four dimensional worldview. His spatial mysticism looks towards Cubism and modern abstraction, to quantum mechanics and the New Physics. Piero della Francesca is regarded as the first Cubist,[1] a realist,[2] and the 'greatest geometrician of his age'.[3] Piero's large blocks of colour and light are musical, like choral sounds. His art is unified, supremely, by his vision. As in Ludwig Wittgenstein's philosophy, Piero makes mathematics transcendent. Like Leonardo he is a scientific artist, but this is not the reason Tarkovsky puts his work into his films.

Piero della Francesca created two monumental *Madonna* paintings – the *Madonna della Misericordia* (*c.* 1460, Town Hall, Sansepulcro, Italy) and the *Madonna del Parto* (*c.* 1450-55, Cemetery Chapel, Monterchi, Arezzo). It is the latter painting that presides over the opening of Tarkovsky's Italian film, *Nostalghia*. Piero's parthenogenic Goddess exudes a noble magnificence, with her belly pushed forward, her cool, sky-blue dress, her quickened womb and attendant angels. But it is the face, the extraordinary Pieroan face, that turns this *Birthing Madonna* into a Black Goddess, a deity who 'presides especially over marriage and sex, pregnancy and childbirth' (as Marina Warner wrote [1985, 274]). In 1979 Tarkovsky noted in his *Diary*:

> *9 August, Bagno-Vignoni*
> Early this morning there was a thunderstorm, very beautiful. Rain. This morning we looked at the hot water baths – St Katherine. It's a fantastic place for a film.
> Tivoli showed me the stream, and the room with no windows for the 'Companion' and for the film. *Madonna del Parto.*
> We filmed Piero della Francesca's *Madonna of Childbirth* in Monterchi. No reproduction can give any idea of how beautiful it is.
> A cemetery on the borders of Tuscany and Umbria.
> When they wanted to transfer the *Madonna* to a museum, the local women protested and insisted on her staying. (D, 196-7)

Piero's *Pregnant Madonna* is a thaumaturgic image, thought by locals to have magical properties (Piero, 98). The Madonna is a powerful matriarch, an archaic image of Mediterranean motherhood. In *Nostalghia* she is part of a women's ritual, as the local women gather and kneel and pray before the image of the pregnant Goddess: birds are symbolically released from the statue's womb. Eugenia is identified with the Goddess as Tarkovsky cuts from one to the other in a piquant piece of montage (why bother with subtlety, or complex staging, when the point can be made with simple cross-cutting?). The scene plays out with a slow tracking shot moving into the face of Piero della Francesca's austere Earth Mother painting. On May 3, 1980 Tarkovsky explained the scene:

The first episode, in the mist. Madonna del Parto. The pregnant women come crowding here like witches, to ask the madonna to ensure them a safe delivery, and so on. The mist lies in layers around the church. (D, 245)

(That aspect of the women's ritual – that they were pregnant – wasn't quite made clear in the film.)

Austere and unreachable, yet Piero della Francesca's art is more approachable in some ways than Leonardo da Vinci's, and in *The Sacrifice* Otto says, to counter Alex's morbid obsessions with Leonardo, that he prefers Piero to Leonardo.

10 : 7   TARKOVSKY AS RENAISSANCE MAN

To discuss the function of painting at every level in Andrei Tarkovsky's films would require a complete volume in itself. Or maybe two or three essays in *Screen*, *Positif* or *Cahiers du Cinéma*. It is significant that his film of an artist (*Andrei Roublyov*) is about a painter (not a musician, dancer or writer), and not just any painter, but a religious painter, a Renaissance figure. The late Middle Ages and Early Renaissance seems to be Tarkovsky's preferred era – the epoch of Dante Alighieri, Francesco Petrarch, Fra Angelico and Giotto. In *Andrei Roublyov* Tarkovsky charts the change from the fervent God-fearing religiosity of mediæval times to the more world-weary humanism of the Renaissance.

The age of Andrei Roublyov the icon painter was a time when magic and God were still believed in, and when mapmakers still scrawled on the edge of maps *'Here Be Dragons'*. In the Renaissance era and its painters, such as Albrecht Dürer, Leonardo da Vinci and Jan van Eyck, one finds the mixture of magic and realism which fascinates Tarkovsky (art of the time when the Middle Ages were becoming the Early Renaissance, the early modern era). Like Dante and his pilgrim, Tarkovsky (and many a filmmaker) travels in the shadowy world of Purgatory and the Inferno. This combination of Renaissance magic and 20th century cynicism culminates in *The Sacrifice*: the magic occurs when Alex flies above the bed with the witch, or when he peers into the depths of *The Adoration of the Magi*. The science and ratiocination is represented in the fly-passes of the jets and the sombre TV announcement (and the weary submissive passivity of the people in the house, who seem to have already given in to the inevitable holocaust). Alex is a Prosperoan figure, a latterday magus with his *yin-yang* cloak and career in the theatre. He is a Paracelsian wizard inhabiting the dream world of his own creations (Little Man as Ariel, Martha as Miranda, the doctor as Prospero's rival the duke, and so on). *The Tempest* is part of *The Sacrifice*'s deep structure.

Pieter Brueghel (*c.* 1525/30-69) was long one of Tarkovsky's favourite painters, in particular his famous series of landscape paintings, the *Months* series (five paintings all dated 1565, except for one). Clearly influenced by Leonardo da Vinci and Italian Renaissance art (after his journey over the Alps to Italy), Brueghel produced an art that combined the epic and the intimate, the legendary and the anecdotal. His depictions of Winter and Autumn, of people at work and play, of the cycle of the seasons, are instantly memorable, both as landscapes, and classic versions of figures in the landscape. Such was the affection Tarkovsky had for Brueghel, he mounted *hommages* to the painter in his films, staging scenes based on particular paintings. (There's a Brueghel-like scene of figures in a snowy Albanian landscape in *Ulysses' Gaze* [1995], Theo Angelopoulos's exploration of the war-torn Balkans).

10 : 8   ANDREI TARKOVSKY AND MODERN ART

Among modern painters, Andrei Tarkovsky's magic realism is similar to that of Paul Klee, Marc Chagall and Levitan, creators of a private mythology which combined European folklore, the intense interiority of dream images with art's semi-abstraction. Among abstract artists there are similarities between Tarkovsky's cinema and the abstract painting of Piet Mondrian and fellow Russians Wassily Kandinsky and Kasimir Malevich, artists for whom art was spiritual. Tarkovsky is not an abstract filmmaker like say, Malcolm le Grice or Stan Brakhage (and was never as abstract as Malevich or Kandinsky), but there are moments of abstraction in his works (for example, the lengthy journey on the trolley in *Stalker*). For artists such as Wassily Kandinsky and Constantin Brancusi, abstraction was realism; it wasn't 'abstract' in the sense of being separated from reality.[1] (Like Kandinsky and

others, Tarkovsky was interested in Rudolf Steiner and anthroposophy. Tarkovsky
had prepared a film about Rudolf Steiner, to be made with Alexander Kluge.)

The cinematic images of religious filmmakers, such as Ozu, Bergman, Bresson,
Buñuel, Dreyer, Pasolini and Herzog, have equivalents with modern painting. The
self-torture and angsting of Expressionist painters such as Egon Schiele, Edvard
Munch, Max Beckmann, Georges Rouault, Emil Nolde and James Ensor have equivalents in cinema: in Carl Dreyer's *The Passion of Joan of Arc* (1928), for instance,
or the macabre, occult, Mittel European aspect of the Expressionists in *The Cabinet
of Dr Caligari* (1919). The grand, Romantic paintings of the American postwar
Abstract Expressionist painters externalize in oil paint the spiritual yearnings found
in Tarkovsky's films, or those of Bergman and Bresson. The formal breakthroughs
in the art of US painters such as Barnett Newman, Mark Rothko, Frank Stella and
Jasper Johns echoes the rise of the European New Wave cinema, whether in France
or Czechoslovakia. Abstract Expressionism was at its highpoint when Tarkovsky
was a film student, a period when he was formulating his own æsthetic principles.
For painters of the 'Abstract Sublime' (Newman, Rothko, Still, Kline), art was seen
as tragic, religious, passionate. Rothko and Newman spoke in terms of tragedy,
infinity, emotion, religion, the divine. Subjectivity was combined with formal
abstraction and monochromy on a grandiose scale. Colour carried spirit, and
religious anxiety could be portrayed with clouds of paint.

'Abstract art is a mysticism' wrote Robert Motherwell in 1958.[2] Richard
Pousette-Dart wrote in 1952: '[m]y definition of religion amounts to art and my
definition of art amounts to religion'.[3] Painters such as Mark Rothko and Ad
Reinhardt had intensely religious aims. They spoke of painting as a mystical
exercise; they referred to Buddhism, Taoism, Zen, negation (the *via negativa*) and
emptiness. At one point in *Andrei Roublyov* the icon painter flings some mud onto a
white wall — an image straight out of Jackson Pollock and Franz Kline (an image
which could not have occurred without Pollock's example of dripped paint).

In the 1960s the art object itself became as important as what it represented or
alluded to: Morris Louis's colourfield canvases, Richard Serra's metal props, Carl
Andre's bricks and tiles and Donald Judd's wall stacks and hollow metal and
Plexiglas boxes were simply things-in-themselves. As the sculptor Tony Smith said:
'I'm interested in the thing, not in the effects'.[4] Tarkovsky said the same thing in
Sculpting in Time (212). The art critic Clement Greenberg put it like this:
'[p]ictorial space has lost its "inside" and become all "outside".'[5] This is how

Tarkovsky defends his use of rain or fire: the thing is just there, in itself. Frank Stella, the American abstract artist, wrote: '[m]y painting is based on the fact that only what can be seen is there. It really is an object… What you see is what you see'.[6] In a similar way, Tarkovsky aims for simple denotations. But the connotations in his films are endless, and complex. In Tarkovsky's cinema, whatever is there connotes all sorts of things; there is a galaxy of signifieds. The effect Tarkovsky desires is similar to that of the artist William Baziotes, who wrote in 1959:

> It is the mysteriousness that I love in painting… It is the stillness and the silence. I want my pictures to take effect very slowly, to obsess and to haunt. (M. Tuchman, 45)

There are many moments in Tarkovsky's cinema when the viewer is expected to simply contemplate things, as things-in-themselves, as objects of presence and being, in the thereness or *dasein* of Existentialism, or in the Existential phenomenology of Maurice Merleau-Ponty, the world which was 'always "already there" before reflection begins'.[7] But that raises all sorts of intriguing philosophical problems when applied to cinema, because the world is never 'already there' in films, it is always a manufactured, codified, cultured world (and Tarkovsky spends a good deal of time and rehearsal to make sure that the world that reaches the screen is exactly how he wants it to appear). But that's the beauty of Tarkovsky's cinema: it is always completely cultural, never natural; it looks simple but is very complex; it has a mesmerizing surface but also many layers underneath; it appears to derive from a single *auteur* but is always a team effort.

The 1960s saw the rise of Minimal art, a cultural move in the West in painting, sculpture and installation art (as well as music and cinema) towards the 'minimal', the Oriental precept of 'less is more'. Tarkovsky's films are not 'Minimal' in the sense of resembling the cubes and boxes in aluminium, Cor-Ten steel, Plexiglas and mirrors of Minimal artists like Donald Judd, Robert Morris, or Larry Bell. The smooth, unadorned and rectilinear forms of Minimal art are not plastic equivalents with Tarkovsky's *mise-en-scène*. But Tarkovsky does use some of the tenets of Minimalism: the clarification of forms, the reductionism, and the repetition and seriality. Like Minimal artists, Tarkovsky often compels the viewer to contemplate one thing for much longer than they would usually (a wall, a snowfield, weeds in a stream). In both Tarkovsky's films and Minimal art, nothing much seems to be happening (Minimal art was often derided for being 'boring', a blank, anonymous

art). The ascetic and austere elements in Minimal art can also be found in Tarkovsky's cinema, in which going to extremes, being uncompromising, and being true
to oneself and one's ideas are fundamental. Simplicity was one of the goals,
æsthetically, for Tarkovsky, but one of the hardest to achieve. It was very difficult
trying to find a means of simple expression. The 'struggle for simplicity', Tarkovsky
said, 'is the painful search for a form adequate to the truth you have grasped' (ST,
113).

Minimal art, in the works of Robert Smithson, Donald Judd, Robert Morris, Brice
Marden and Frank Stella, also utilized the Oriental move towards emptiness (the
void of Zen Buddhism and *The Tibetan Book of the Dead*), an evocation of
nothingness found in the 'skyspaces' and treated rooms of James Turrell and Robert
Irwin (rooms with special walls, windows and ceilings, with the ceilings opened to
the sky), the apparently 'empty' art gallery spaces of Dan Flavin and Bruce Nauman
(rooms lit by neon or fluorescents lamps with nothing else in them), or the
apparently empty canvases of Brice Marden, Ad Reinhardt, Frank Stella, Jo Baer or
Robert Ryman (all-white, all-gray or all-black paintings).

Another affinity is with the later fiction of Samuel Beckett, his 'fizzles' (short
texts) and novels which evoked emptiness, barren spaces, and derelicts moving
slowly through wastelands (Tarkovsky's films, though, are far more life-affirming
than Beckett's fiction: Tarkovsky's emphasis, for instance, on religious faith, love
and hope, would make Beckett vomit).

The flipside of the Minimal art experience was Process art (and assemblage and
Postminimal art), art that was deliberately messy, unformed, unpolished (what
Robert Morris called 'anti-form'). It found its expression in artists like Robert
Smithson and Morris, Dennis Oppenheim and Hans Haacke. An art of processes, or
experiences, or concepts, or just 'stuff' (like the piles of felt, wood, steel, wire, and
general stuff in Morris's Postminimal sculptures). It led to Robert Smithson's
evocations of quarries, industrial plants, pipes, slag heaps, zones which have a
definite correlation in some of Tarkovsky's cinematic spaces. Basically, these
particular Tarkovsky places are run-down, post-industrial (and sometimes post-
apocalyptic) realms, which civilization has abandoned. Over them one or two
shabby-looking figures move slowly. The prime example is the Zone in *Stalker*, but
this type of space also crops up in *The Sacrifice*, *Nostalghia*, *Ivan's Childhood* and
Mirror. Robert Smithson and his art cronies like Donald Judd and Dennis
Oppenheim would make trips to industrial zones or quarries; those were the places

that interested Smithson (deserts and salt flats were another favourite destination).
The affinity is not only with Tarkovsky's post-industrial, post-everything spaces,
but also the bleak wastelands of science fiction of the 1960s and after, of J.G.
Ballard, William Burroughs and Philip K. Dick.

ELEVEN

Philosophy and Religion in Andrei Tarkovsky's Cinema

11 : 1   PHILOSOPHY AND RELIGION

Few film artists have been so obsessed by religious matters as Andrei Tarkovsky. One thinks of Ingmar Bergman, Yasukiro Ozu, Luis Buñuel, Carl Dreyer and Pier Paolo Pasolini, among others. Tarkovsky is regarded as a religious filmmaker (and Tarkovsky was a believer, unlike Bergman, Buñuel and Pasolini. Indeed, among European and Russian filmmakers of the 1960s to 1980s, Tarkovsky is unusual in believing in God and the redeeming power of spiritual faith. Jean-Luc Godard, Bernardo Bertolucci, Donald Cammell, Paul Verhoeven, Peter Greenaway, Krzysztof Kieslowski, Andrei Konchalovsky – the last thing those cosmopolitan, sophisticated film directors would do is admit to religious beliefs, in their public personas at least. The odd thing, of course, is that filmmakers like Ingmar Bergman, Werner Herzog or Woody Allen spent a lot of time in their films exploring religious and spiritual issues).

But Andrei Tarkovsky made no secret of his religious beliefs, and religious issues lie at the heart of his work. Tarkovsky was fascinated by questions of faith, purity,

Andrei Tarkovsky   2 6 1

integrity, good and evil, doubt, suffering and sacrifice. In part Tarkovsky's notions of faith and hope derive directly from Christianity. *Stalker* was about a man having crises of faith, only to find himself renewed by each bout of despair, Tarkovsky said (ST, 193). For Tarkovsky, the Stalker was 'an extremely honest man, clean, and, so to speak, intellectually innocent. His wife characterizes him as 'blessed'… the last idealist'. The three travellers at the end of *Stalker* become aware for Tarkovsky of the most important thing in life: faith (ST, 199).

At the end of *Stalker*, Tarkovsky aimed to make a genuine affirmation of love (for some, his way of going about it might have seemed eccentric). He has something of the determination and obstinacy of the early Christian fathers in this continual affirmation of notions such as love and faith. Tarkovsky is no fire and thunder Old Testament prophet – or he doesn't seem to be, because of his quiet, serious, scholarly surface (i.e., in his media profile as intense Russian poet-filmmaker). But it's no surprise that some critics have likened Tarkovsky to a saint or martyr, or employed the language of religion to describe his cinema. 'The one thing capable of resisting the universal destruction is love… and beauty. I believe that only love can save the world' Tarkovsky confessed (D, 26).

Remembering the significance of religion in Tarkovsky's cinema (people pray, characters debate theological issues like Buddhist monks, God is overheard talking to a saint, Crucifixions are staged, and so on), it's worth recalling some of the tenets of Christianity, and in particular the fervent sort of belief that Tarkovsky's cinema indulges in (as well as questions). The intensity of Christian religion can be illustrated with a quote from (who else?) the over-zealous and near-psychotic St Paul, who wrote:

> For I am persuaded, that neither death, nor life, nor angels, nor principalities, nor things present, nor things to come, nor powers, nor height, nor depth, nor any other creation, shall be able to separate us from the love of God, which is in Christ Jesus our Lord. (*Romans*, 8: 38-39)

Taking a brief glance at St Paul is as good as looking at anyone to bring out some of the fundamental aspects in Christian religion. St Paul was the most widely influential Christian thinker, the ancestor of most Christian philosophers, saints and prophets (including the prophets and madmen in Tarkovsky's cinema). As such St Paul can be said to have influenced Western art, including Western cinema, as much as any individual (certainly far more than the heroes of contemporary cultural theory – Freud, Marx, Nietzsche, Lacan, Wittgenstein, Benjamin, etc). Or to put it another way: when Western filmmakers, from Griffith and Murnau to Bergman and Tarkovsky, are grappling with religious issues, much of the time they're taking on the influence of St Paul.

A post-Freudian anthropologist, Weston La Barre, described St Paul thus:

> ...the apostle Paul... was a pathetically unprepossessing man, small, bow legged, blind in one eye, and he apparently also suffered from a slight deformity of the trunk. He had a speech defect, was epileptic, and had violently murdered his brother while in an evidently epileptic-equivalent state, and on his own testimony had severe sexual problems (*Romans*, 7: 14). He was unmarried and had nothing sexually to do with women, whom he hated and feared, although he accepted money, food and shelter from them. In personality, Paul was doctrinaire and bigoted... [Paul] achieved only a paranoid identification of the divine Hebraic Father with the divinized Hellenistic Son; it is his own pathology projected... Paul was quite familiar with the platonic Noble Lie (*Romans*, 3: 7) and boldly proclaimed his own: that the Messiah had succeeded by failing, that he had died and not died, that he was actually God sacrificed to God, and that through faith in this new Mystery all mortals would share his immortal godhead. All these fantasies were thoroughly un-Jewish, indeed preposterous and blasphemous in Judaic terms. They were also preposterous and blasphemous in classic Greek terms. (1972, 603, 607-8)

This devastating meeting of psychoanalysis with religion is quoted at length because it offers a picture of the person who has probably had more influence on the theological aspects of Western religion than any other. More than Jesus, even – because Jesus didn't write. It was St Paul who appropriated the figure of Jesus, and filled the world with his version of the messiah.

If Jesus was the novelist who wrote a genius book, St Paul was the producer who decided he would adapt the book (without paying the two thousand year option to the rights), and do it *his* way. He would become producer, director *and* writer, and secretly regard himself as the star. Hell, the messiah had done a good job, but St Paul's movie version would be much bigger, better, louder, sexier, and cooler (well, not sexier). It's a familiar story of appropriation and taking credit in film and entertainment industries the world over, as well as religions of all kinds.

Only one journey is possible: the journey within. We don't learn a whole lot from dashing about on the surface of the Earth... And of course we cannot escape from ourselves; what we are we carry with us. We carry with us the dwelling place of our soul, like the turtle carries its shell. A journey through all the countries of the world would be a mere symbolic journey. Whatever place one arrives at, it is still one's own soul that one is searching for.

Andrei Tarkovsky (1982)

The Tarkovsky character is on a 'vision quest', and each Tarkovsky film is structured on the vision quest of the archaic shaman.[1] The quest is to find the sacred amongst the secular, the timeless amongst the temporal or transitory, the valuable amongst the banal. Sometimes the quest is for being, truth, wholeness, meaning, childhood – the terms change, but the quest remains essentially the same. Pier Paolo Pasolini, in rejecting the conventional fiction film, went instead for the truth. 'My ambition in making films' he wrote, 'is to make them political in the sense of being profoundly "real" in intent'.[2]

Raúl Ruiz's notion of a 'shamanic cinema' offers another approach to poetic cinema:

All these films are sleeping within us. An ordinary narrative movie provides a vast environment in which these potential film sequences disperse and vanish. A shamanic film, on the other hand, would be more like a land mine: it explodes among these potential films and sometimes provokes chain reactions, allowing other events to come into being. In the same way, the shamanic sequence makes us believe we remember events which we have not experienced; and it puts these fabricated memories in touch with genuine memories which we never thought to see again, and which now rise up and march towards us like the living dead in a horror movie. This mechanism is the first step in a process which could permit us to pass from our own world into the animal, vegetable, and mineral kingdoms, even to the stars, before returning to humanity again. (79-80)

In some Tarkovsky films, the quest has an external dimension – *Andrei Roublyov, Solaris, Nostalghia* and *Stalker* contain outward journeys in the world which mirror the protagonist's inner quest (the outer dimension is essential for a dramatic medium). *The Sacrifice* is a seemingly static film; but it is modelled on the Dark Night of the Soul of mysticism (made famous in the writings of Spanish mystic St John of the Cross), on the Night Journey of Muhammad and the ancient shaman's travelling to other worlds (which is the model for all religious journeys or quests or pilgrimages). And within the film there are journeys which reflect Alex's state of mind: to the Japanese tree; to the city in the dream; to the witch's house; to the trees outside the house where he talks with Maria.

The journey in *Mirror* is the complex flight between past and present, between memory, dream and fantasy, between wife and mother, between youth and age, between the family then and the family now. In *Solaris* the journey is ambiguously away from and towards the secular world of the Earth, with its technological cities, cars and televisions, to the sacred, inner world of dreams and the past (embodied by Hari, Kelvin's dead wife). *Solaris* is all about atoning with the past, about guilt, redemption and forgiveness. *Solaris* may represent Tarkovsky's most radical inward turn, an interiorization continued in *Mirror*.

Nostalghia's outer journey is from Russia to the Italian countryside then to Rome. Gorchakov wanders about not so much like a mediæval pilgrim on a quest, as the modern, dispossessed exile. Gorchakov has to be given his quest by Domenico (to carry the candle over the water). In a way, Gorchakov is adrift because he has no quest, no goals, no *desire* left. In a typical narrative film, the aims are often shifting over the course of the story. But in *Nostalghia*, Gorchakov is searching for something, but he doesn't know what it is, or even if he would want it if he found it. (It's not erotic desire or women – Gorchakov spurns Eugenia when she offers herself to him; she mocks him when he declines to take her). When he wanders into the ruined cathedral, God is heard talking about Gorchakov and his uncertain spiritual state, but the man cannot hear him. One imagines that even if God sent an unmistakable sign (a burning bush, say), Gorchakov would still ignore it.

Stalker is modelled on the pilgrimage of the faithful to some shrine, temple or Cathedral, a Rome or Mecca or Lourdes. The film consciously evokes religious pilgrimages, and suggests many other films as well as real pilgrimages undertaken throughout history. Each of the three pilgrims takes a problem or question to the shrine, as in mediæval romances and fairy tales. This recalls the questions in mediæval Arthurian romance, such as 'whom does the Grail serve?' The answer offered in the film is that the Zone or the Room serves life, or the sacred manifested in life. The narrative line of *Stalker* for critic Peter Green plots 'a path that skirts hazardously close to hocus pocus or schoolboy adventure' but manages to rise above them, and the sci-fi component, to attain a metaphysical plane.[3]

Each Tarkovsky film has a mythic structure. *The Sacrifice* has something of *King*

Lear and *The Tempest* about it, consciously elegiac, a film about consciously revaluating one's life and maybe turning one's back on everything that one once was and accomplished (Prospero's breaking of his staff and drowning his books). *Mirror* relates to *Hamlet* and *Oedipus Rex*, with œdipal material particularly prominent. Like *Solaris*, *Mirror*'s about being haunted by the past, about being unable escape the past, or transcend one's origins. *Stalker* has elements of the *Odyssey* and Greek myths in it, as well as many Biblical overtones (for instance, ancient Greek mythological quests such as Jason and the Golden Fleece, or Orpheus in the Underworld, or Odysseus travelling back to Ithaca).

11 : 3   FAITH

Faith, once lost, can never be regained, for it is the nature of authentic belief never to have been questioned; all that is possible now is ever more frantic asservations in the face of doubt, protestations of cultural loyalty, and an attempted nativistic journey back into the sacred past. Each religion is the Ghost Dance of a traumatized society.

Weston La Barre (1972, 44)

Each Tarkovsky protagonist is driven by faith. The faith of the Tarkovsky protagonist is called into question in each film: what does s/he *really* believe in? How important is faith for the individual? Can s/he live without it? By the end of each film personal faith has been challenged. Sometimes the quest is to find it again (while acknowledging the impossibility of such a task). Sometimes it is to encourage its significance for others as well as oneself.

The Stalker frantically re-asserts his faith at the end of the film. In *Nostalghia* the protagonist sinks back into a glamourized past, into a dream-vision of a yearned-for Russia – comprising the *dacha*, the snow, the pool, the dog, the ululating women on the track. In *The Sacrifice*, Alex's faith is tested to the limit, and the resultant shift in his mental state (from neurosis to psychosis) encourages him to burn down his world in a ritual conflagration accompanied by the Japanese flute music, which represents the otherness and religious unity of Eastern mysticism he has always yearned for and now can no longer achieve. The deep breathing in Zen meditation and breathing of the flute was linked; the breath, wind, sound, and spirit were connected. The Japanese flute music is a spiritual music, which emphasized emptiness, the gaps between the sounds and breaths. The mantle of shamanic power is passed on to his son as Alex drives right past him in the ambulance. The first act of the narrator in *Mirror* is to interrogate the past on the telephone to his mother. His last act, while (apparently) on his death bed, is to release the bird, a symbol since time immemorial of freedom and the soul (hinting at metempsychosis, as well as the soul flying to heaven. Whether Tarkovsky gets away with someone releasing a bird on their deathbed is another question. In an MTV pop promo it would be cheesy and silly enough to be accepted in an ironic, playful fashion, and kids in Seattle or Seoul might find it cool when their pop idol goes all arty on them, pretending to die and release a bird. But in a serious art film it's something else: it's meant very seriously).

Faith is blown apart or re-affirmed, or replaced by something else in Tarkovsky's sacred cinema. Few modern artists, and even fewer filmmakers, talk about religious faith. Yet it is a central concept in Tarkovsky's philosophy. There is the æsthetic dimension: one needs faith to make art; and the ontological aspect: without faith life is severely impoverished; 'only faith interlocks the system of images' he wrote (ST, 43). The Tarkovskyan protagonist is marked by her/ his faith – 'people whose strength lies in their spiritual conviction' (ib., 207). In this sense, in his devotion to faith, Tarkovsky is like some mediæval mystic, nurturing his religiosity.

II : 4   TRUTH

Andrei Tarkovsky's philosophic thinking pivots around big metaphysical terms such as Faith, Truth, Time and Experience. The search for 'truth' is, like spiritual conviction or faith, central to his philosophy. For him, art is a noble undertaking, a search 'for the spiritual, for the ideal' (ST, 38). Art is a revelation of the world, an awareness of the infinite, 'the eternal within the finite, the spiritual within matter, the limitless given form' (ST, 37). (It could be Goethe or Thoreau or Pushkin talking). The aim of cinema, said Tarkovsky, must be for truth. This 'truth' is concrete, achieved by getting as close as possible to 'the images of life itself' (D, 355). The artist can only approach the absolute through faith and creativity (ST, 39). Art was not simply self-expression for Tarkovsky; there was always a higher calling – to do with spiritual communication, forging a spiritual bond, and sacrifice (ST, 40). Tarkovsky wrote and directed like someone with complete conviction, someone believing utterly in what he does. In the *Diaries* he noted on March 24, 1982:

> The most important thing and the hardest thing to have is faith. Because if you have faith, then everything comes true. Only it's impossibly hard to believe sincerely. There is nothing more difficult to achieve than a passionate, sincere, quiet faith. (D, 308)

This reaching out for absolute faith and belief in truth is the basis for the narratives of *Nostalghia* and *The Sacrifice* in particular, but it is a theme in all Tarkovsky's films. The films and the protagonists become increasingly desperate and tragic, because it is increasingly difficult to maintain or even search for religious faith in a very secular world, a world in which God has been dead, officially, for a hundred or so years, since Marx, Freud, Darwin and Nietzsche helped to kill him. Films of what Will Rockett called 'upward transcendence' are rare (23). There are many films of sideways (social) transcendence, and of downwards transcendence (the descent into horror and the supernatural).

As with the Christian father and theologian, Quintus Septimus Florens Tertullian of Carthage (*c.* 160-220 AD), the Tarkovsky character believes because it is absurd ('I believe because it is absurd [*credo quia impossible*]' said Tertullian of Christ's life). There is no total nihilism, and even the character who burns himself to death (Domenico), in what seems to be a very desperate gesture, is a passionate believer. 'True poetry goes with a sense of religion. An unbeliever cannot be a poet' says Tarkovsky (D, 321). This might be true for Tarkovsky, but plainly it is not true for many unbelievers who were also brilliant poets: William Shakespeare, Arthur Rimbaud, and Thomas Hardy (or perhaps their belief was in different things – but certainly not God in the traditional sense of the term). Thomas Hardy, for example, said he had been looking for God for fifty years and hadn't found him. On the other hand, poets such as Francesco Petrarch, Dante Alighieri, Emily Brontë and John Donne might agree with Tarkovsky.

We should long ago have become angels had we been capable of paying attention to the experience of art, and allowing ourselves to be changed in accordance with the ideals it expresses.

Andrei Tarkovsky (*Sculpting In Time*, 50)

As with Ingmar Bergman, Robert Bresson and Michelangelo Antonioni, many viewers might say Andrei Tarkovsky's cinema is bleak and pessimistic. In fact, Tarkovsky is very optimistic. 'Artistic creation is by definition a denial of death. Therefore it is optimistic, even if in an ultimate sense the artist is tragic' commented the director (D, 91). Tarkovsky takes his cue from Christianity and Buddhism, which are religions of negation (known as the *via negativa* in mysticism). The greater the denial, the greater the reward. Hence there is in Tarkovsky's sacred cinema an emphasis on the denial of self, ego, personal desire. William James wrote of this self-sacrifice in *The Varieties of Religious Experience*:

They [Buddhism and Christianity] are essentially religions of deliverance: the man must die to an unreal life before he can be born into the real life. (131)

This is the way of the teachings of Jesus: the 'dying-to-self' before the rebirth. As Jesus said in the *Gospel of St John*: '[v]erily, verily, I say unto you, Except that a grain of wheat fall into the earth and die, it abideth by itself alone; but if it die, it beareth much fruit' (*John*, 12: 24). What Tarkovsky's religious cinema tries to do is to film the agony of this dying-to-self, this making oneself into a seed, ready to be reborn ('[a]n image is a grain, a self-evolving retroactive organism' Tarkovsky wrote in 1974 [D, 91]). On a Marxist/ materialist level, it means identifying with the very basic forces of life – killing and eating. As Joseph Campbell put it: '[l]ife lives by killing and eating itself, casting off death and being reborn, like the moon' (1988, 45). At a deeper level, it means cultivating the sense of self – nurturing it in order to lose it. D.H. Lawrence wrote: '[h]ow one must cherish the frail, precious buds of the unknown life in one's soul' (1934, 375). The whole process is difficult, painful and time-consuming. Tarkovsky's films are long and slow partly because of (depicting) this ontological and spiritual difficulty.

(A few critics have interpreted Tarkovsky's films in terms of the 'hero's journey', as Joseph Campbell called it, a myth criticism approach which's very popular in Hollywood screenwriting, and American film criticism. The heroic or single myth has very familiar elements: the call to adventure, the quest or goal, the journey, the obstacles, the acts of sacrifice and catharsis. Each stage in the hero's journey is easy to apply to Tarkovsky's films – and vague enough to be applied to any part of any of the films. Tarkovsky's films, however, differ greatly from contemporary Hollywood cinema's because the journeys are so intensely interiorized. His films don't have Luke Skywalker battling the Dark Father, or Mad Max or Tom Cruise saving a community from villains).

II : 6 RELIGIOUS EXPERIENCE

Part of the problem of the religious film, or the film that uses religious subject matter, is that religion deals with the unseen, the unknown, with absolutes that don't lend themselves readily to being filmed. The problem in cinema is always how to visualize things, no matter how 'real' or abstract. And it's especially tricky when trying to dramatize an inner life. The traditional feature film demands drama and conflict. The Hollywood formula treatment means, in short, extreme dramatiz-ation.[1] Tarkovsky shies away from excessive, expressive treatments, over-deter-mined dramatization and exposition. He relies heavily on the abilities of his actors to communicate his sense of the religious. He also uses many cinematic techniques, ranging from slow motion to special print processing in order to change the texture and colour of the image.

Tarkovsky's poetic cinema *suggests* the religious – in its performances by actors, its narrative structures, in the juxtaposing of images and sounds. Where Hollywood cinema might resort to dialogue, exposition or voiceover to explain a state of mind, Tarkovsky uses very long takes, or one of his motifs (rain, water), or sound. Tarkovsky's sense of the noetic, the divine, is not that of Hollywood cinema, yet he is a psychological director, trading in states of mind (just like any Hollywood film in fact). 'The Truth is not to be spoken but lived' said Hui-Neng, the 8th century Zen Buddhist master (J. Ferguson, 200). As far as cinema is concerned, Truth, Essence, Spirit (or whatever one calls it), must be lived, portrayed, filmed. It must pass through the many gates and filters of the cinematic process. (If it's amazing that any film gets made at all, with so many obstacles to overcome, it's even more extraordinary that a *religious* film can survive the process).

Each of Andrei Tarkovsky's protagonists experiences fully their moments of doubt and pain when their faith is called into question. The agony is wholly internal – the diametric opposite of the conventional narrative film, which always seeks to dramatize experience with external action. Tarkovsky is something of an Existentialist – his religious self-questioning philosophy (some would say self-torture) has similarities with the thought of 20th century theologians such as Nikolai Berdyaev, Paul Tillich, Bernard Lonergan, William Johnston, Karl Barth and others – and also modern philosophers such as William James, Martin Heidegger, Jean-Paul Sartre, Maurice Merleau-Ponty, Edmund Husserl, Claude Lévi-Strauss, Gaston Bachelard and Søren Kierkegaard, not forgetting Friedrich Nietzsche. (Tarkovsky might not personally feel so many affinities with the postmodern cultural theory philosophers and gurus, such as Jacques Derrida, Fredric Jameson, Teresa de Lauretis, Homi Bhabha, Jacques Lacan, Michel Foucault, Jean Baudrillard, Hélène Cixous, Paul de Mann and Umberto Eco. Although some of them – Luce Irigaray and Julia Kristeva, for example – have written lucidly of spiritual issues. In fact, although contemporary cultural philosophers appear at first to be ultra cynical, seen-it-all-before, world-weary thinkers, they write a lot about spiritual and religious matters, and regularly employ the language of religion in their gnomic tomes).

For Andrei Tarkovsky, religion begins with the individual, and is founded upon the individual. His films are (partly) about religious upheavals in individuals. Tarkovsky does discuss wider, societal issues (the world going down the drain in *The Sacrifice*, or the alienation of cities in *Solaris*, or the historical battles and events that formed Russia in *Andrei Roublyov*). But he concentrates on the individual, isolating him/ her from other people and from society. In the late films this is all the spectator sees: the individual alone, stripped of the societies that enculturated them, going through painful existential transformations. The emphasis in Tarkovsky's philosophy is on personal experience, and the importance of the personal response. The personal is not so much political in Tarkovsky's cinema, but tragic, mystical, desperate. 'In cinema, works of art seek to form a kind of concentration of experience, materialised by the artist in his film' Tarkovsky wrote in *Sculpting In Time* (85).

One can't film the divine, so one has to film people who stand at the interface of God and his creation, the natural world. This is where psychoanalysis and anthropology sites its studies – in the human animal. One of the supreme embodiments of the meeting-point of the human and the divine in the West is Christ. Although he filmed Jesus in close-up only once (there was a Calvary scene in *Andrei Roublyov*), Tarkovsky makes many references to him (Hari 'resurrects'; Andrei Roublyov is nearly crucified; and the Writer in *Stalker* dons some twisted twigs as a Crown of Thorns, echoing the *Ecce Homo* image of Christian iconography). Certainly, Tarkovsky was a believer – he invokes God in the *Diaries*, in times of stress. But clearly his faith had been shaken many times – particularly in the early 1980s, when the Americans were talking about a 'limited nuclear war' and global catastrophe seemed very close. In *The Sacrifice* Tarkovsky explored the links between God and nuclear war, embodied in that sinister phrase 'nuclear theology'.

11 : 8   GOD AND THE BOMB, OR RELIGION AND NUCLEAR WAR

Where was God when the bomb fell on Hiroshima? Outrageous blasphemy! It was the holy duty of patriotism!

Weston La Barre (1972, 46)

The moral and religious dimension of the nuclear weaponry debate is problematic. What is the relation of God to nuclear nations? Did God sanction the use of atomic bombs on Nagasaki and Hiroshima? President Truman blasphemously claimed that God was behind America in its use and possession of atomic arms. Christian thinkers have been unable to reconcile the two things: religion and nuclear weapons. Both deal with ultimates: the creation of a world and the obliteration of all human life. A human-made Apocalypse or Last Judgement. For some commentators, the possession of nuclear arms turns people into gods. They now have the power that divinities such as Krishna or Jehovah have: to destroy whole worlds. Robert Oppenheimer looked to the Orient to provide the tropes for the atomic bomb – the 'light of a thousand suns': 'I remembered the line from the Hindu scripture, the *Bhagavad Gita*... 'Now I am become death, destroyer of worlds''.[1] This was a general trend in mid-20th century theology and philosophy – to look to Eastern mysticism. The tendency went hand-in-hand with the Existentialism of Jean-Paul Sartre, Albert Camus, Martin Heidegger and Samuel Beckett.

God has retreated from the worlds of Tarkovsky's films, or at least it looks that way: so many barren or wintry landscapes, full of broken machines, smashed-up buildings, broken hearts, broken egos, shattered psyches and battered souls. Fellow Russian artist Marc Chagall wrote of the death of God:

> God, perspective, color, the *Bible*, form, lines, tradition, the so-called humanisms, love, caring, the family, the school, education, the prophets and Christ Himself have fallen to pieces.[2]

Mircea Eliade wrote of the death of religion and how it relates to contemporary society:

> it is true that the theology of "the death of God" is extremely important, because it is the sole religious creation of the modern Western world. What it presents us with is the final step in the process of desacralization. (1984, 151)

It is this global desacralization that Tarkovsky's sacred cinema explores, coming down on the side of mystery and interiorization. And in *The Sacrifice* Tarkovsky used the reality of nuclear war as an equivalent or embodiment of desacralization on a global scale.

Stalker takes place in a post-holocaust (post-nuclear) landscape; *The Sacrifice* occurs just before an airstrike; the Tokyo freeway sequence in *Solaris* is a hell of noise and light. In Tarkovsky's cinema, God is elsewhere, but yearned for (*how could he abandon us?* is the cry of the religionist facing the horrors of the 20th century). In vain Alex kneels and clutches his hands together and recites the Lord's Prayer as the camera bears down upon him (in *The Sacrifice*). (Orson Welles remarked somewhere that there are two things impossible to film: one was prayer, someone praying. The other was sex.) But after the dream has revealed the pain to be internalized, a figment of Alex's tortured psyche, there is no cut to a balming, life-affirming shot of the clouds. (This occurs at the end, with the final shot, of the tree and ocean). God lies under the surface (a ghost, a memory, a trace): in the icons in the book Alex leafs through, or in Leonardo da Vinci's *Adoration of the Magi*, or in the arms of the 'witch' Maria. God doesn't appear in *The Sacrifice*, and the final, longed-for revelation of God doesn't occur. Instead, Tarkovsky's protagonists learn about their frailties, and capabilities. They learn about altruism and responsibilities; and they learn that nothing is certain; that everything is fragile and in flux; and that religious absolutes do not come from God but are elements of human adaption.

11 : 9   THE SUPERNATURAL IN ANDREI TARKOVSKY'S CINEMA

Two fundamental literary qualities, supernaturalism and irony... The super-natural comprises the general colour and accent — that is to say, the intensity, sonority, limpidity, vibrancy, depth and reverberation in Space and Time. There are moments of existence at which Time and Duration are more profound, and the Sense of Being is enormously quickened.

Charles Baudelaire (12)

What does appear many times in Andrei Tarkovsky's *œuvre* (instead of – or despite – God) is the supernatural. 'Supernatural' is probably the wrong kind of word, being associated now with the kind of films Tarkovsky despised. But the præter-natural, the miraculous or mysterious is central to Tarkovsky's sacred cinema. Doors creak open by themselves (*The Sacrifice*); objects roll around and fall to the floor (*Mirror*); or they rattle (*Stalker*); birds flap in alcoves, or burst from statues (*Nostalghia*); a bird lands on a boy's head like a blessing (*Mirror*); a bird breaks a pane of glass (*Mirror*); a lamp keeps going out and relighting itself (*Mirror*); a candle stays miraculously alight (*Nostalghia*).

Tarkovsky's films are full of objects behaving in strange ways (as if a poltergeist were at work on the sets, but a poltergeist with a star-fixation, who only moves objects when the camera's rolling). The known, empirical world is not everything: behind it lies a vast unknown: the invisible is everywhere; the known world, it turns out, is not known at all, but is full of mystery. Tarkovsky imbues objects taken for granted with mystery. The world of the inanimate has a life of its own, is as dynamic as the human world. Long after the people are dead in those Russian houses, doors will still be creaking open, and glass bottles will still be mysteriously falling to the floor, though with no one, and no camera, to see them, to give their actions value, to mythicize them.

Tarkovsky has an elemental view of the world – like John Cowper Powys or Walt Whitman. Fire, rain, wind, rivers – these are the cosmic, powerful elements in Tarkovsky's filmic world. In this sense, Tarkovsky is something of a magician, and his præternatural sympathies recall the mages and alchemists of old, such as John Dee, Elizabeth I's court wizard who communicated with angels, or Paracelsus, or Cornelius Agrippa, or visionaries such as William Blake or Emmanuel Swedenborg. Like John Dee and Blake, Gorchakov is associated with angels and angelism; and, like Joan of Arc, Gorchakov hears voices, hears God talking to St Catherine.

Tarkovsky's religious cinema doesn't depict Christ or God, but does reveal a world in which the unknown is not in the next country or the next town but right here, in this building, in this room. The filmic world of Tarkovsky is not so much Christian as pagan, not full of God and holiness but the paranormal, the unusual, the unexplained and the strange. Tarkovsky loves, like the writer Bruce Chatwin, the miraculous (Chatwin said his life had been one long search for the miraculous). Tarkovsky's unmade film of St Anthony would have been full of bizarre occurrences. In Tarkovsky's poetic films, a glass of water becomes a strange object, with a magic of its own. Like the motifs of fire and rain, these magical objects are the hallmarks of Tarkovsky's cinematic style. They are devices which enable him to separate his filmic worlds from those of any other filmmaker. The Tarkovskyan magic world exists in its own time and space, far away from Hollywood, but also far away from Beijing, Rome, London, Berlin, Bombay, or any other film capital or industry.

Intense Christian spirituality haunts Andrei Tarkovsky's films – in particular *Andrei Roublyov, Nostalghia, Stalker* and *The Sacrifice*. The imagery of the Russian Orthodox Church recurs in Tarkovsky's films – the candles, icons, fire, crosses, angels and rituals. Elements of the Orthodox Church religion appear in Tarkovsky's sacred cinema: the veneration of icons (with images having divine auras); the lived spiritual life; the Seven Sacraments (Baptism, Conformation, Mass, Confession, Holy Orders, Matrimony and Extreme Unction); celibacy and the monastic way of life; and the belief in the Virgin Mary. There are examples of the Catholic rites of penance, Eucharist, baptism, pilgrimage, sacrifice, resurrection, Crucifixion, purification and apotheosis in Tarkovsky's religious films. These rituals are not always performed in a manner that's obvious or immediately recognizable (such as the snowbound Crucifixion in *Andrei Roublyov*). Domenico hands Gorchakov some bread and wine in *Nostalghia*, a clear reference to the Last Supper and Eucharist. This very obvious piece of symbolism is integrated quite naturally into the film – the actors carry on discussing things as if no gigantic symbol has just been flashed at the audience (and no doubt it went unremarked by many viewers). Domenico's crucifixion is a much more strident ritual, more essential to the plot of *Nostalghia* than the bread and wine which Gorchakov receives, yet it is also self-conscious and contrived (an audience may be more inclined to interpret Domenico's self-immolation in religious terms because just prior to doing it he has been haranguing onlookers about moral, religious matters).

In *Andrei Roublyov* Tarkovsky clearly enjoyed recreating those moments in history when important Christian images (Roublyov's icons) were being made. Here the Christian imagery, of churches, holy men, icons – is required by the subject and the era. In the later films, the Christian images had to be suggested rather than shown directly, in order for Tarkovsky to maintain his realism, his sense of the concrete. *Nostalghia* is full of religious references, yet it remains 'realistic' (although it is a very stylized of realism). The film begins with a religious ritual: there is a Last Supper, a Crucifixion, a ruined Cathedral, a sermon and a baptism. Yet, as in *The Sacrifice*, the religious allusions are integrated with the realistic aspects of the narrative.

Yet Tarkovsky also used fantasy and the fantastical throughout his films – as when Alex and Maria levitate while they make love (On depicting love as flying,

Tarkovsky told Layla Garrett, that 'love is a miracle – it transcends the gravity of the material world. People in love must levitate' (1997, 23).) But Tarkovsky's fantastical reinterpretations of Christian ritual didn't go as far as Luis Buñuel – in *Viridiana* (1961, Spain), for instance, Buñuel savagely parodied the Last Supper.

11 : 11   THE LEFT-HAND PATH

Other religious influences in Andrei Tarkovsky's cinema include: Georg Gurdjieff (D, 277), Rudolf Steiner and anthroposophy (D, 344), Zen Buddhism and Taoism (he mentions Lao Tzu and the *Tao Te Ching*, for instance, and *haiku* poets like Matsuo Basho), the humanism of William Shakespeare, Lev Tolstoy, Arthur Schop-enhauer and Fyodor Dostoievsky, as well as the idealism of Johann Wolfgang von Goethe and Hermann Hesse. Despite his belief in suffering, Tarkovsky is not a Buddhist: he is an idealist and Romantic, and Taoism connects with this Western stance.

Tarkovsky was interested in Rudolf Steiner, telekinesis, ESP, astrology, and Oriental philosophy (Taoism and Buddhism). Tarkovsky also tried meditation (including Transcendental Meditation). Tarkovsky would refer to numerology – the magic of numbers (his birth date, he said – April 4, 1932 – added up to the number five in numerology). 'That is the key to my soul, the key to my character. It stands for temptation, contradictions and extremes. I'm like Leonardo's Man – crucified in a circle of life' Tarkovsky said.[1]

The magical side of Tarkovsky, the side that believes in the miraculous, has much in common with Neoplatonic thought (Philo, Prophyhry, Plotinus), with hermet-icism and the occult 'theory of correspondences' (the 'theory of correspondences' was taken up by poets such as Charles Baudelaire and Arthur Rimbaud, and European Symbolist artists like Gustave Moreau. It's related to the notion of synæsthesia, where colours have equivalents with sounds, or touches with smells, and so on).

Tarkovsky thinks in poetic, intuitive ways, and he continually makes poetic connections. His visual motifs – milk, rain, fire, water – work in this way. The connections are of what hermeticism calls the lunar, left-hand, feminine, unconscious kind (the stuff of nighttime, of dreaming, of the unconscious). In no sense could Tarkovsky be termed a mathematical, scientific and mechanical film-maker. Films are not for him machines (as they are sometimes described by Steven Spielberg, James Cameron or Brian de Palma. However, Tarkovsky had to be very technically proficient in order to control every aspect of production, cinema being an intensely technological medium).

Films for Tarkovsky are anguished, personal spiritual statements that are torn from the depths of one's being. Art itself can create a spiritual experience in the viewer, equivalent to a religious experience, Tarkovsky maintained; 'Art acts above all on the soul, shaping its spiritual structure' (ST, 41). Tarkovsky's films are conceived first on the experiential level – as moments and images and feelings. Werner Herzog said: 'I believe the real power of films lies in the fact that they operate with the reality of dreams' (J. Franklin, 113). Like Herzog's, Tarkovsky's cinema is deliberately anti-intellectual and anti-rational. Their logic is of poetry not science ('art does not think logically', like science, Tarkovsky said [ST, 41]). Tarkovsky mistrusts science: for him, the transcendent lies in the mystical sphere of life. Tarkovsky could not see that science can be mystical, but in the New Physics, cosmology or quantum mechanics, with its talk of black holes, event horizons, superstrings, quarks and babyverses, it can be. (Many writers and scientists have discussed the links between religion and science, God and cosmology, among them: Stephen Hawking, Fritjof Capra, Russell Stannard, Carl Sagan and Arthur C. Clarke).

11 : 12   SAINT TARKOVSKY

In the Tarkovskyan film persona there are elements of a range of religious types: the alchemist, the magician, the shaman, the philosopher, the mystic, the martyr and the pilgrim. The Writer in *Stalker*, for instance, laments the passing of magic from the world: the world is all triangles and numbers now, he claims (his speech is an instance of Tarkovsky being rather clumsy and too-obvious in his denigration of science and logic). Yet the Writer too is a pilgrim, filled despite his world-weariness with yearning (he's searching as much as any Tarkovsky protagonist, perhaps for a miracle which will restore his faith – because only a miracle could do that). In the Tarkovskyan character, in the persona of the *auteur* who made the films, there is something of an alchemist, an arcane searcher for the Philosopher's Stone. In Tarkovsky's magic cinema, the Grail, the goal, the transmutation of base matter into gold or the 'Great Work' of alchemy, is spiritual fulfilment, embodied in a single, beautiful shot. Each film ends in an ecstatic vision or moment which has been striven for throughout the film (and is sometimes achieved despite the death of the character). Here the Tarkovskyan character is like a mediæval saint or martyr at the end of some pilgrimage across wastelands or through a Dark Night of the Soul. The Stalker is something of a chivalrous knight, a guardian of the holy of holies, which's the wish-fulfilling Room (a Grail image, a cauldron of plenty).

11 : 13   THE GOSPEL ACCORDING TO SAINT TARKOVSKY: TARKOVSKY AS PROPHET

What some observers are unsure about is Tarkovsky the Prophet. His films seem to be teaching something. They interrogate spiritual issues. But what, precisely, is he saying? What is *The Gospel According to Tarkovsky*? He is saying that spiritual feelings should be nurtured; that faith is essential; that the modern secular world destroys spirituality; that humility is important; that the individual must test these things for her/ himself; that there are no leaders to tell people what to do; that spiritual feelings can be experienced anywhere, by anybody; that getting in touch with one's spirituality is the most serious business there is; that the process is long and painful, with no promise of completion.

Tarkovsky's films take spiritual doubt and turn it into torment (that's what art does, what drama is). Sometimes the religious journey ends in death (*Nostalghia*, *Mirror*) or in near death (*Stalker*, *The Sacrifice*, *Solaris*, *Andrei Roublyov*). But Tarkovsky, as a prophet, retains a sense of mystery and ambiguity. He is a poet who wishes to remain a little abstract and ambivalent, rather than a prose-writer who has to be much more literal. What Tarkovsky likes about film is its ability to remain ambiguous and mysterious, while also being immensely didactic, concrete and authoritative. Film communicates powerfully, but in Tarkovsky's sacred cinema it communicates mystery. No explanations, no answers, and often only half-formed questions. (However, Tarkovsky did contribute a book of his thoughts, views, ideas and discoveries: the 'gospel' of Tarkovsky was published as *Sculpting In Time: Reflections On the Cinema* in 1986. The book is Tarkovsky's principle æsthetic statement, outside of his films (the collected screenplays and the diaries count as secondary sources).)

TWELVE

Structure and Narration

12 : 1   DIRECTIONS

Andrei Tarkovsky uses many devices of the art cinema tradition, as noted in the introduction: open forms, abstract and formalist approaches to narration and ambiguity. Structurally, Tarkovsky's films are in some ways classic narratives; they begin, they develop, they end (with more closure of narrative strands than one might expect, though usually with ambiguity intact). His films work within the realm of conventional dramaturgical techniques: from exposition through rising action to climax and closure. There are conflicts, questions, journeys, decisions and problems in Tarkovsky's cinema, as well as simile, metonymy, metaphor, synedoche and much figurative discourse.

At the same time, Tarkovsky's films exhibit many elements of Peter Wollen's definition of 'counter-cinema':

Classical cinema	*Counter-cinema*
Narrative transivity	Narrative intransitivity
Identification	Estrangement
Transparency	Foregrounding

Single diegesis	Multiple diegesis
Closure	Aperture
Pleasure	Un-pleasure
Fiction	Reality (P. Wollen, 78)

Taking *Mirror* and *Nostalghia*, for instance, one can see that these films fall into the counter-cinema mould; Tarkovsky's films veer between identification and estrangement, single and multiple diegesis, fiction and reality. Peter Wollen applied his counter-cinema approach to Jean-Luc Godard's cinema and Tarkovsky was not as radical nor as political as Godard. But there are elements in Tarkovsky's lyrical films of demystification, a rejection of spatial, temporal verisimilitude and detachment.

12 : 2   BEYOND TRAGEDY

The typical structure of an Andrei Tarkovsky film is to start with dissatisfaction and end with a partial resolution of tension. There is no classic closure in Tarkovsky's films, because the questions are unanswerable, the problems unsolvable, the attitudes indissoluble. In Tarkovsky's cinema there is no easy way out, and the hard way is nearly impossible to achieve. The gateway is very narrow, and it's closing in. The intensity increases over the course of a film, but it often loses its sense of direction. There are no happy endings to Tarkovsky's fairy tales, because the problems raised in his films are gigantic. There is no hero, no Grail, no Grail knight, no cowboy, no private detective or police chief great enough to rejuvenate the wasteland, to solve the mystery, to reunite estranged people, or find lost souls. There is no woman to be saved and wed. There is no reward. There is no climatic chase or violence or confrontation. There is no villain. There are few (if any) comic moments. No smiles. No laughter. No consolations.

(The lack of a villain or an antagonist, for instance, would be a big problem for a Hollywood studio executive perusing a Tarkovsky film script. There has to be an antagonist driving the plot, causing the initial lack or loss, and creating the obstacles and problems. Hollywood cinema thrives on its Darth Vaders, its Nazis, its terrorists, its *James Bond* megalomaniacs, its serial killers. It reminds me of a conversation Steven Spielberg had with Christopher Hampton when Spielberg agreed to produce David Lean's adaption of Joseph Conrad's *Nostromo* for Warners in the late 1980s. Spielberg liked Hampton's script, but had a question: who was the villain of the piece? Hampton replied: money. Spielberg said: yes, I understand that, but who is the villain? Hampton repeated: there wasn't one.

Tarkovsky's cinema tends to lack the driving force of nearly all fiction films. The 'villain' is internalized, or abstract (an abstract concept like 'loss of faith'), which makes them problematic.

12 : 3   ENDING IN ECSTASY

And yet the endings of Andrei Tarkovsky's films are moments of ecstasy – some of the most rapturous finales in all cinema. It's not just the music that makes these endings so powerful, nor the fact that the bored viewer is joyful because the film is nearly over. No, these are genuine ecstasies, that grow out of the material. They are false in some ways: the music helps to boost the rapture. Yet there is something life-affirming about Tarkovsky's film endings. Tragedies his films are not. The situations of the protagonists are tragic – in their bleak worlds of restlessness and spiritual bankruptcy. Yet the view of the films is life-affirming. The catharsis comes from seeing someone being so close to the edge. The endings are thus transcendent. Not utterly transcendent – there are always ambiguities to grapple with, elements in life that cannot be overcome. Gorchakov's ecstatic placement of Russia in the midst of Italy, for instance, is achieved at a massive cost to his soul (indeed, the ambiguity of the ending of *Nostalghia* has Gorchakov die in the Baths, after carrying the candle, so that his vision of the Russian *dacha* in the Italian cathedral is achieved only in death, in spirit. Perhaps it's the embodiment of his dying moments?).

With his penchant for desperate figures out of Fyodor Dostoievsky's fiction, and his love of Shakespearean tragedy (he directed *Hamlet* for the theatre), Andrei Tarkovsky might be expected to make pessimistic films, like those of Joseph Losey, Erich von Stroheim, Luchino Visconti or Sam Peckinpah. Stanley Kubrick's cinema could be seen as either nihilistic or realistic (but seldom idealistic). At the end of Kubrick's assault on the Vietnam experience, *Full Metal Jacket* (1987, USA), Private Joker says 'I'm in a world of shit, but I'm alive and I'm not afraid'.[1] This is the bottom line in Kubrick's cinema: to be alive not dead. Just survival. Similarly, Rainer Werner Fassbinder's bleaker films (such as *Fox and His Friends* [1974]) or Werner Herzog's dark comedy *Stroszek* (1977), could be seen not as pessimistic but realistic. Tarkovsky is infinitely more positive than modern cinema's pessimists and realists (Fassbinder, Scorsese or Kubrick). Some filmmakers appear to enjoy rubbing the viewers' faces in the dirt.

Words such as 'hope', 'faith' and 'truth' are used without irony by Tarkovsky. In an Alain Resnais or Fassbinder film, these words are used with lashings of irony. Tarkovsky seems to lack the same sense of irony. Tarkovsky, after all, is the artist who wrote in *Sculpting in Time* (his prose testament which enlarges the last will and testament of the films): '[i]n *Stalker* I make some sort of complete statement: namely that human love alone is – miraculously – proof against the assertion that there is no hope for the world' (ST, 199). One could not imagine a similar statement coming from Fassbinder, Roman Polanski, Jean-Luc Godard, Luchino Visconti, Terence Malick or Luis Buñuel. Tarkovsky is rare among filmmakers in his adherence to such notions as 'love', 'faith', 'truth' and 'hope' (for pessimists and realists, these are at best self-delusions).

12 : 4   CULTURAL STRATEGIES:
POLITICS, IDEOLOGY AND CULTURE

Andrei Tarkovsky's films work in a cultural space veering between abstraction and naturalism, between subjective psychology and objective realism, between spiritual asceticism and utterly indulgent Romanticism, between religion and demystification, between formal simplicity and cinematic complexity, between Communist Russia and the capitalist West, between the cinema of the (Soviet) State and the art cinema of Europe. In Tarkovsky's major cinematic device (the long take) there is a tension between stasis and movement, between dramaturgy and duration, between realism and artificiality. Tarkovsky's sequence shots, like those of any filmmaker, draw attention to themselves as pieces of virtuoso cinema, even as they strive for naturalism and verisimilitude. One kind of cinematic sequence shot is a good example of artifice, technofetishism and acute self-consciousness: the long Steadicam shot. There are some famous Steadicam opening shots to films (from the early 1980s onwards), shots that weave in and out of people, furniture, props and doorways, in a way that is meant to wrench a gasp from any audience. Wow! Look at that camera move in *One From the Heart* (Francis Coppola, 1982, USA), *Absolute Beginners* (Julian Temple, 1986, GB), *Hallowe-en* (John Carpenter, 1978, USA), or *The Bonfire of Vanities* (Brian de Palma, 1991, USA). Some filmmakers, such as Martin Scorsese, had sets built specifically for a continuous Steadicam shot (such as the restaurant scene in *GoodFellas* [1990, USA]). Robert Altman sent up the over-dynamic, pompous Steadicam shot in the opening of *The Player* (1992, USA). The *Ur-*Steadicam film is undoubtedly *The Shining* (Stanley Kubrick, 1980, USA), in which camera operator (and inventor of the Steadicam) Garreth Brown showed just what the system of counter-weights could do on a giant hotel set built at Elstree studios. Although Tarkovsky didn't use the Steadicam, it was inevitable that he would have done had he made more films, camera movement being absolutely vital to his cinema (and from his first film, *Ivan's Childhood*, Tarkovsky had showed that he loved to use all of the technical tools of cinema available, such as extreme wide angle lenses, or big cranes, or very lengthy tracks).

Andrei Tarkovsky's sequences are so long they move beyond the self-conscious stage in which the mechanics of cinema are all too obvious, and shift into another realm, where the point of the shot is made clear. Tarkovsky transforms the temporal element alchemically into something spiritual. All the best religious cinema must use a *gestalt* method, a theory of dialectical montage, in which the religious aspect, x, is more than the sum of its parts. In relativity physics, mass is a form of energy; similarly, in the religious film, transformations from secular film material to sacred thought are possible. A film may *be* a religious experience in itself, as well as *depicting* a religious experience (it's not just sci-fi geeks who consider watching *Star Wars* or *Star Trek* a spiritual experience: many filmmakers speak reverently of the first time they saw *Citizen Kane*, or *Fantasia*, or *Persona*, or *The Seven Samurai*, or a Ray Harryhausen film).

Tarkovsky regards his films in this way: he is an alchemist, changing the nature of his subject, just as Hari, who is made up of neutrinos, slips in and out of the quantum realm, and changes herself in *Solaris*. Hari is formed of ripples on the quantum sea; but for Tarkovsky the quantum realm is full of spirituality, not atomic and sub-atomic particles.

Culturally, Andrei Tarkovsky is a Romantic, an inheritor of the Romanticism of Aleksandr Pushkin, Friedrich Hölderlin and Johann Wolfgang von Goethe (and, later, the poetic, dream-haunted *avant garde* Surrealism of André Breton, Jean Cocteau, Joseph Cornell and Luis Buñuel rather than the de Sadean, Freudian aggression of Antonin Artaud, Hans Bellmer and Georges Bataille). De Chirico rather than Picasso; Dostoievsky rather than Tolstoy; Hoffmann and Grimm rather than Charles Perrault and Hans Christian Andersen. And Russian poets such as Blok, Mayakovsky, Mandelstam and Akhmatova. (Tarkovsky was dubious about the idea of the *avant garde*, about progress, and about experimentation. There couldn't be any real experimentation in art, Tarkovsky maintained; and the idea that art was 'progressing', getting better all the time, was false (ST, 97). As Tarkovsky put it, 'how can Thomas Mann be said to be better than Shakespeare?' (ibid.).)

Tarkovsky is a conservative stylist who sometimes resorted to radical formal innovations. He is as anti-rational as an anti-scientific artist can get. He is an artist of the right hemisphere of the brain in the terms of split-brain psychology. Intuition, not rationality; imagination, not reality; sacred, not secular. In Lacanian terms, Tarkovsky goes for the Imaginary realm, not the Symbolic realm, with its psychic unity found in the mirror phase. A cinema of the Kristevan semiotic *chora* by way of the dream realm of the Freudian unconscious. Cinema as dreamwork (post-Freudian psychotherapy). A cinema that eschews the œdipal authority of the Symbolic realm (the Law of the Father), but can never outface it, of course. The suture in Tarkovsky's religious cinema is to reconcile the private, inner dream world and the outer, social world. The films operate at this interface. Tarkovsky holds a mirror up to himself, but the mirror reflects back a personality not pure but severely modified by the demands of enculturation, identity, ambition and œdipal tensions.

Politically, Tarkovsky's cinema is as bourgeois as they come, as seen from a Marxist, materialist ideological perspective. Tarkovsky's films are full of religion (opium), moneyed aristocratic down-and-outs who live in dilapidated splendour (a house next to the sea or a romanticized *dacha* in the woods), stylized poverty and sumptuously filmed settings (it looks like poverty, but it isn't, really. A socialist realist documentary on poor folk living in slums a Tarkovsky film ain't).

The rationale of Tarkovsky's cinema is 'fiction = mystification = bourgeois ideology' (P. Wollen, 89). On one level, Tarkovsky's cinema is all mystification and mythicization. Through Tarkovsky's powerful poetic abilities, everything in his films is romanticized and spiritualized. Nothing is radical; Tarkovsky's politics are conservative and reactionary. Societal change will only occur in Tarkovsky's cinematic world if there is a *spiritual* transformation in the individual. This is a stance Marxists and Maoists find laughable. Tarkovsky's films were criticized by Goskino and Soviet film establishment as being too personal, too religious, and not nationalistic, communist or Russian enough. There was no looking East for Tarkovsky, no looking towards China, Maoism and Communism, as there was with many of Western Europe's intellectual filmmakers in the late 1960s and early 1970s (for example, Jean-Luc Godard, Michelangelo Antonioni and Bernardo Bertolucci). This move to China and the Red East also occurred with the Parisian intellectuals, such as those in the *Tel Quel* group (Julia Kristeva, Roland Barthes, Philippe Sollers, François Wahl, Marcelin Pleynet and others). Meanwhile, at the same time, the West (America) went to war with the Orient.

12 : 5   NARRATIVE DEVICES IN ANDREI TARKOVSKY'S CINEMA

Tarkovsky employed different kinds of narrative forms within in his films. The dream sequences are the most obvious instances, but there are also home movies (in *Mirror*, for example), flashbacks, memories *and* imagined memories (in *Nostalghia*), TV reports (*Solaris*), TV broadcasts (*The Sacrifice*), newsreels, pseudo-documentaries (the hypnotism scene in *Mirror*) and documentary footage.

Consider some of the formal elements in Tarkovsky's cinema: of the many *looks* found in cinema there are few looks of relationship in Tarkovsky's art, of characters looking at each other. Instead, they look down, wearily, or look away from each other (look at the way Tarkovsky blocks a typical two-hander dialogue scene: the actors are standing at right angles, or with their backs to each other. The central dialogue scene between Domenico and Gorchakov in *Nostalghia*, for instance, has the religious proselytizer wandering around the room discoursing while Gorchakov listens). Further, the *network of looks* in conventional editing (shot/ reverse shot) is negated by the sequence shot technique (for instance, Tarkovsky seldom chooses to cut reaction shots into his sequence shots). *Cause-and-effect linearity* is also negated, or used infrequently. The trajectory of the Tarkovsky film is one long digression bound only loosely by œdipal, æsthetic, spiritual, emotional, nostalgic and artistic constraints. *Spatial and temporal verisimilitude* is generally affirmed, but there are times when Tarkovsky deliberately subverts this. For instance, he uses Brechtian *distancing devices* occasionally – a character will look into the camera (like Maria when she kills the cockerel in *Mirror*). In cinema this is regarded as a modernist technique, breaking the fourth wall, though it is ancient in the theatre. Many times in a Tarkovsky film *dramaturgy* is subverted in favour of poetic realism: *continuity* and *sequentiality* are often discarded in favour of a dramaturgy of dream that moves into spontaneity and intuition.

Tarkovsky does employ *foreshadowing* (for example, in *Nostalghia*, Domenico gives a candle to Gorchakov and he uses it at the end of the film). *Visual rhymes* and *puns* are another favourite device.

Classical or *continuity editing* is generally deployed, but again Tarkovsky often subverts it in favour of poetic logic. As noted above, *poetic* or *symbolic montage* is Tarkovsky's main method of cutting. He rarely uses *rapid cutting* (only at moments of crisis, and then rarely). *Cross-cutting* is rare too, as is *parallel action*. A Hollywood editor would have definitely cut the two fire rituals climaxing *Nostalghia* together, in an attempt at maximum drama. Tarkovsky merely places one scene after the other (notice how he delays the reaction shots of Gorchakov's candle-carrying right to the end of the shot: nothing must disturb the intensity and suspense of that nine-minute take. During Domenico's fire sermon, however, Tarkovsky makes good use of the many extras hired for the day, with elaborate tracking/ reaction shots).

Tarkovsky's *découpage* pivots around poetry. Yet Tarkovsky is conservative with his editing techniques, compared to some *avant garde* filmmakers: he does not use *Hollywood montage*, which is ideal, really, for his kind of poetic cinema (he might have been tempted to if he had lived into the age of digital editing on computers, where optical effects and speed ramping are easy to achieve, and don't require optical printers or expensive laboratory processing). Tarkovsky rarely employs *fades* (to white or black). *Jump cuts* are used, but not nearly as much as one might expect from a dream-bound *ciné*-poet (and not as much as in Tarkovsky's New Wave contemporaries, such as Godard, Truffaut and Wenders). Tarkovsky does employ extensive *montage sequences*, though, most obviously in his dreams,

memories and flashbacks. Here his editing style is distinctly modernist and New
Wave.

But Tarkovsky does use many *dream devices: flashbacks, connecting motifs,
refrains, memories, flashforwards* (the end of *Nostalghia* is a kind of flashforward,
of an imagined future), and hundreds of *hypersituated objects* (highly foregrounded
objects, such as the bottles of milk, books, candles and the fires). *Visual rhymes* are
a form of *refrain*. Tarkovsky happily quotes from his own films, just like Godard or
Spielberg. He uses *intermediate spaces*, actionless spaces between scenes. He loves
elaborate *tracking shots* (some are *extremely* complex). He always prefers to have
the camera on a track or dolly and seldom employs *handheld camera*. He's very fond
of extravagant crane and boom shots, like Sergei Paradjanov or Vincente Minnelli
(it's very fitting that the final shot of his final film should be an elegant crane
upwards, echoing the opening shots of his first film, *Ivan's Childhood*). Sometimes
Tarkovsky uses radical camera movements, such as $360°$ *pans* (early on in *Andrei
Roublyov*, for example, there are two very slow three-sixty pans around the interior
of the hut where the monks listen to the jester).

Tarkovsky never wastes an opportunity to move the camera: if there's time (and
money) to rehearse and shoot a complex camera move, he'll do it. One of the great
pleasures of Tarkovsky's cinema is the way he moves the camera (it's the same with
Welles, Angelopoulos or Bertolucci). But while even great film directors sometimes
seem to be moving the camera for the sake of it (Martin Scorsese, Peter Greenaway,
Terry Gilliam), there's never that sense in Tarkovsky's films. Favourite Tarkovsky
camera moves include: craning down with an actor as they bend down to the
ground; craning up trees; and very long tracking shots – the longer the better
(through woods, over fields, over water). Sven Nykvist remarked that Tarkovsky
seemed to be one of those film directors who had been trained at film school to move
the camera where possible (Nykvist had also worked with Roman Polanski and
Stanislav Barabas, who also liked to move the camera good deal).

Tarkovsky's *camera angles* can be as clever, self-conscious and showy as a film
student going out with a camera for the first time (or a bored, jaded pop promo
director trying to spice up another dreary pop act). Tarkovsky never lost his liking
for unusual camera angles: they're everywhere in his films as well as his early films.
Tarkovsky often favours a camera angle slightly above an actor's head, and very
often his camera is tilted down at an actor lying on the ground (in *Stalker*, for
instance).

Dreams are sometimes indicated by treated *colouration*, or black-and-white or sepia-and-white, but just as often by no obvious signs. Tarkovsky enjoys manipulating a variety of filmic codes in order to achieve his results. *Exposition* is dropped in Tarkovsky's cinema in favour of long and slow visual effects which sometimes relate only tenuously to a character's situation or psychology. The horse at the beginning of *Solaris*, for example, does not fit in with the exposition. Unless perhaps it shows that otherworldliness and beauty can be found right here on Earth as well as in space. One doesn't have to travel thousands of miles to distant planets to find authentic strangeness and beauty (beauty and the beautiful was very important for Tarkovsky). The horse perhaps embodies Earth's natural wonder (and it's also, of course, Tarkovsky quoting himself: the slo-mo horse at the end of *Andrei Roublyov*).

Sometimes, Tarkovsky's exposition is clumsy: Alex in the first scene of *The Sacrifice* rattles off pages and pages of exposition during that lengthy tracking shot over the grass, and quite a bit of it is unnecessary, and could've been woven into the film in a more imaginative manner. Many film producers might've been tempted to advise her/ his director to consider cutting it, but perhaps one doesn't do that with Tarkovsky. (Tarkovsky's clearly not that interested in it anyway, and seems to be trying to get it out of the way).

Point-of-view in a Tarkovsky flick is generally very *subjective*, bound up with notions of individual psychology, with a religious search, with spiritual matters. Total *objectivity* (social or ideological) is not found in Tarkovsky's cinema. Nor does he use, like, say, Michelangelo Antonioni, a cool, dispassionate point-of-view. No; like Federico Fellini and Werner Herzog, Tarkovsky is bound up completely in his creation, and the point-of-view in his movies reflects that degree of involvement (Freudians would call it 'emotional investment').

Tarkovsky's *narrative style* owes something to the stream-of-consciousness method (of the literature of James Joyce, Virginia Woolf, D.H. Lawrence and John Cowper Powys, among British novelists). *Mirror*, especially, is a sequence of thoughts, dreams, memories, newsreel and symbols. The film was so open in form Tarkovsky admitted it was edited in twenty different ways (and no doubt, if Tarkovsky had lived on into the age of DVDs and director's cuts, he might have returned to editing the film: *Mirror* isn't 'finished', as no work of art is really 'finished'. Films, especially, can be reworked on so many levels in so many ways – months and months can go by. Some filmmakers, like Stanley Kubrick or Francis

Coppola, were famous for editing their films up to – and beyond – the release date).
What, ultimately, fused these disparate forms of *Mirror* together was probably
Tarkovsky's personal vision, his emotional commitment. The deeply psychological
and poetic nature of Tarkovsky's films nevertheless means that they are very anti-
psychoanalytical, non-deterministic, anti-reductionist and anti-secular in their
world-view. Instead, a post-Orthodox Christian pantheism is advocated, an
affirmation of the God Within, and an inkling of the emergence of a Goddess
Within.

THIRTEEN

Childhood, Family and Character

13 : 1   AFFIRMATION OF THE FAMILY

Each of Andrei Tarkovsky's last five films ends on a note of affirmation of the family, of child-parent relations, of childhood, of the maternal realm, and of familial, emotional bonds. The past in Tarkovsky's cinema is feminized, presided over by powerful matriarchal figures: the mother, grandmother, wife and Spanish lady in *Mirror*; the spouse and changeling daughter in *Stalker*; the wife and mother in *Solaris*; the wife, daughter, maid and witch in *The Sacrifice*; and the powerful Madonnas and matriarchs who surround Gorchakov and his dreams of the Russian motherland in *Nostalghia.* In *Mirror* the familial affirmation is of the classic (archaic) matriarchal trinity: daughter, mother and grandmother (made even more personal by the director's mother, Larissa Tarkovskaya, playing the grandmother, and the same actress, Margarita Terekhova, playing the wife and mother in the different time periods); the endings of *Solaris* and *The Sacrifice* offer an image of patriarchy spanning the generations, as father and son embrace. At the end of *Stalker*, as in *Offret*, the child turns magical and performs a psychic/ spiritual act or ritual. At the end of *Nostalghia* the protagonist is all alone with the family dog, but the homeland is miraculously re-affirmed, with Russia in Italy, the snow and, above all, the female ululations on the soundtracks. (Significantly, none of the Russian women are standing in this 'Russian' landscape, as they have every time this dream, memory or fantasy has been shown throughout the film).

13 : 2   THE MYSTERY OF CHILDHOOD

In films such as *Ivan's Childhood, Solaris* and *Mirror*, Andrei Tarkovsky explored the world of childhood and remembered childhood, always filtered through memory, desire and regret, and never presented without mnemonic filmic devices. Tarkovsky used his films, like many artists, to investigate his own childhood and emergent psychology, to exorcize ghosts and re-experience pains: '[i]f you are serious about your work, then a film is not merely the next item in your career, it is an action which will affect your whole life' (ST, 133). Art was a serious business for Tarkovsky. Like the painters Mark Rothko or Max Beckmann, Tarkovsky took his work very seriously.

Childhood itself is a serious matter, as the illustrator of children's books, Maurice Sendak, noted: '[William] Blake is unquestionably important, my cornerstone in many ways. Nobody before him ever told me that childhood was such a damned serious business'.[1] The sculptor Constantin Brancusi said that the artist must retain child-like qualities to work creatively. Plenty of artists and actors have remarked on the child-like nature of art and performance – of dressing up, of play. One of these child-like qualities is *wonder*.

Maurice Sendak's books (*Where the Wild Things Are, In the Night Kitchen, The Juniper Tree* and *Outside Over There*) generate a sense of mystery of childhood in a similar way to Tarkovsky's films. In many of Sendak's books (and many fantasy and fairy tale books), as in Tarkovsky's films (and many other films), there are fantasy flying sequences. Sendak wrote: '[a]rtists are going to put elements into their work that come from their deepest selves. They draw on a peculiar vein from their own childhoods that is always open and alive' (ib., 125).

Tarkovsky measured his experience of childhood against that of other artists, and against commonly-held beliefs. In *Mirror* he goes back to feel again the ambiguity and pain the absent father caused (Ingmar Bergman and Steven Spielberg revisited their troubled childhoods in films like *E.T.* and *Fanny and Alexander*). Tarkovsky's films act like fairy tales – mechanisms in which the unconscious is uncensored, and anguish can be powerfully expressed (a 'what if?' scenario which's allowed to run unfettered). *Mirror* works as exorcism; but it is also about the birth of the artist, and the experiences that shape the artist's life. The psychoanalyst Alice Miller wrote:

> Children learn about evil in its undisguised form in their early childhood and store this knowledge in their unconscious. These experiences of early childhood form the source of the adult's productive imagination... (A. Miller, 232)

Tarkovsky shows childhood to be something essentially mysterious. The kids in *Mirror* are simply there, out in the garden, or pouring salt onto the cat's head, or running, or watching a fire. There is doing, but being takes precedence. In the Tarkovskyan childhood, everything is strange, but not necessarily threatening. There is none of that occasionally sinister and unsettling treatment of children found in American films, where children are often either sentimentalized in a cloying, gooey manner, or they are soon to be witnesses of meaningless violence.

In Andrei Tarkovsky's cinema, children are closer to the magical, præternatural world than adults: the boy Aleksei in *Mirror* has premonitions; the bell-caster Boriska in *Andrei Roublyov* has magic gifts; in *Nostalghia* the boy asks terrifying questions in all seriousness ('is it the end of the world, papa?'); in *The Sacrifice* the boy Little Man sleeps in a mysterious twilit bedroom, builds houses with witches, lies like Buddha under a bo tree, and utters the divine words of Creation ('in the beginning was the Word'). Significantly, all the important children, from Ivan to Little Man, are boys (except for the daughter in *Stalker*.)

Andrei Tarkovsky's cinematic depiction of childhood has affinities with that of Federico Fellini: the bed, the furniture, the house and its environs are seen as magical spaces, where the individual was first formed, where her/ his first encounters with a larger world took place. In films by both Federico Fellini and Tarkovsky sheets and curtains billow mysteriously in the wind; the house is presided over by a Madonna; words are not spoken, nor remembered – childhood is experienced primarily, sensually, physically, viscerally, and before language.

In Volker Schlöndoroff's wonderful film *The Tin Drum* (1978, West Germany), the boy Oskar is deliberately inarticulate. He lives in an exaggerated, mythical world of erotic, political, domestic and family strife. The ideological and sexual discourses in this great film are portrayed forcefully and graphically, in a way Tarkovsky would have loathed. There is such an intense sense of life, of life being lived, on a multiplicity of levels, in a subtle, crazy, ironic and multi-layered way, rare in cinema. There is the same insistence on magic, again often expressed through the environment, or encounters between the child protagonist and the environment.[2]

Bill Douglas's trilogy (*My Childhood*, 1972, *My Ain Folk*, 1974, *My Way Home*, 1978, GB) presents childhood as a bleak, comfortless ordeal, but one not without moments of startling beauty. Douglas's trilogy is, like *Mirror*, very lyrical, and, like Tarkovsky's film, there is no laughter in childhood at all. Children go about seriously, with no smiles. Children in Tarkovsky's *œuvre* are solemn beings, lonely creatures, often estranged from their parents (think of Little Man, or Ivan, for instance). Like many people, Tarkovsky said he had problematic relations with his parents (he described his relations as 'tortured, complicated, unspoken'). 'It's patently clear that I have a complex about my parents' (D, 19).

13 : 3   RELATIONSHIPS

[Solaris] ends with what is most precious for a person, and at the same time the simplest thing of all, and the most available to everybody: ordinary human relationships, which are the starting-point of man's endless journey.

Andrei Tarkovsky (*Diaries*, 364)

The relationships valorized in Andrei Tarkovsky's poetic cinema include those of children and parents, initiate and guru, follower and leader, husband and wife. The endings of many of the films shows the strength of the child-parent relation: fathers and children (*Stalker*, *The Sacrifice*, *Solaris*) or mothers and children (*Mirror*, *Nostalghia*). The children themselves are strange: they are not regular kids: the fiercely independent orphan in *Ivan's Childhood*, a wartime spy in his tweens, mature beyond his years; the blonde boy in *Nostalghia*, unsettlingly angelic; the mute, injured Little Man in *Offret*; the silent changeling girl in *Stalker*.

The husband-wife or lover relation is rarely seen in the same depth as the child-parent relation (and there are no significant homosexual or gay relationship in Tark-ovsky's cinema). The couples in *Mirror* and *Stalker* argue bitterly. In *Andrei Roublyov* there is the unconscious sexuality in the relation between the chaste monk-like painter and the mute woman. Between Alex and his wife Adelaide in *The Sacrifice* there is hardly any loving contact. In *Solaris*, a man succumbs to loving an artificial woman composed of neutrinos millions of miles from Earth.

Sexual relations between men and women are fraught with difficulties, as in the fiction of Thomas Hardy or Lev Tolstoy. Ambiguity, paranoia, self-doubt and fear reign; ambivalence is the hallmark of the Tarkovskyan human sexual relationship. There is no explicit sexuality, nothing more liberal than a kiss; Tarkovsky's films have the restraint (some call it prudishness) of Japanese cinema (Kenji Mizoguchi, Hiyao Miyazaki and Yasujiro Ozu, but not *animé* like *The Legend of the Overfiend*).

So, no nudity (except in the pagan festival in *Andrei Roublyov*, and one or two other moments).[1] Unwilling or unable to depict explicit sexual encounters, for critics like G. Petrie and V. Johnson, Tarkovsky transferred sexuality to the sensual depictions of the natural world (the swaying weeds in the streams in *Nostalghia* and *Solaris*, for instance, or the Stalker lying back in the grass in the Zone [JP, 249]).

The kiss in *Andrei Roublyov* is a unique instance of a profound erotic gesture: after it the painter and the woman are bound up together. Tarkovsky employs the kiss in the manner of Production Code era Hollywood cinema, as a synecdoche to stand in for sex. He doesn't need to show Roublyov and the woman having sex, because it's clearly signposted in a number of other places too (such as the shot of Roublyov running away to join the revellers, or Roublyov appearing shamefaced to his assistants the following morning, or the way he pointedly averts his eyes as the naked woman swims past his boat).

The central Tarkovskyan character is the white middle-aged Western male: cynical but also innocent; world-weary but also hopelessly idealistic; highly educated but not very wise; sceptical but also religious; an exile from his culture who nevertheless cannot escape his culture (and an exile who can never go 'home'); a drifter; painfully sensitive; a man at a crisis point (not always a mid-life crisis, but with many of the same symptoms); a fallen angel, someone who was once successful but is now in decline.

He is, of course, the classic outsider, the stranger, the loner: solitary, melancholy, a wanderer and nomad. It's a figure found in much of modern literature. In, for example, J.-K. Huymans' Des Esseintes, D.H. Lawrence's Paul Morel, Albert Camus, Jean-Paul Sartre, Franz Kafka, Knut Hamsun, André Gide's Edouard and Lawrence Durrell's Darley. A masculinist, modernist creation fashioned to express the Existential alienation and emasculation experienced by modern men. Often frail, with tragic personalities, Tarkovsky's men have drifted out of Dostoievsky's underground novels. Tarkovsky's men would be at home in the fictional worlds of Kafka's Prague, Gide's Paris or Dostoievsky's Moscow.

Tarkovsky's main characters (apart from all being male, except for Maria/Natalia in *Mirror*), are not action men or heroes in the conventional sense. They are artists (Roublyov), scientists (Kelvin, the Scientist, Domenico), actors and critics (Alexander), and writers (Gorchakov, the Writer). They're usually highly intellectual, and cite Shakespeare, Pushkin or Dostoievsky at the drop of a hat. Tarkovsky said his characters were weak, not tough heroes, but out of their weakness came strength; it was the conflict that was strong, not the characters: 'the central characters are almost always weak persons whose strength is born out of their weakness, out of the fact that they just do not fit in, and are at odds with their surroundings'.

The women in Tarkovsky's cinema, meanwhile, take on stereotypical dimensions. There are virgins (Martha in *The Sacrifice*, the red-haired girlfriend in *Mirror*), whores (the witch in *The Sacrifice*, the pagan woman in *Andrei Roublyov*), crones (the grandmother in *Mirror*), maids and helpers (the aunt in *Mirror*, the maid in *The Sacrifice*), and 'modern', liberal women (Eugenia, Hari, Natalia and others).

Generally, women in the cinema of Andrei Tarkovsky are assigned patriarchically-defined roles – mothers, wives, lovers and grandmothers. They are often seen in a bad light: as seducers, who can easily tease men into submission. The pagan woman, Eugenia, Hari, Natalia, Maria and Martha each play this role. They are often hysterical, or insane, or difficult: there are a high number of hysterical scenes in Tarkovsky's cinema.[1] There are women as mothers, reassuring and bathing their fretful, fearful male charges. And, with their long, Pre-Raphaelite hair, veils, shawls and long dresses, there are the archetypal 'evil woman', the *femme fatale*, the Medusa or Black Venus type,[2] as found in much of Western culture, from Petronius through Dante Alighieri and William Shakespeare to Charles Baudelaire and Gabriel d'Annunzio, to Raymond Chandler, *film noir* and neo-noir films.

(An actress having her hair up or down is a simple but recurring indicator of her personality or intent in Tarkovsky's cinema. In *Mirror*, for instance, Maria as the mother has her hair up; but when her husband visits her, in the raining room scene, her hair is down. And her modern-day counterpart, Natalia, plays with her hair a lot, as does Eugenia in *Nostalghia*. The Italian translator has the most obviously eroticized hairstyle in Tarkovsky's films, in contrast to Gorchakov's Russian wife, whose hair is tied in a demure bun. But Eugenia lets her long, curly hair down at every opportunity. Tarkovsky's fetishism for long hair – preferably wet as well – is immediately apparent).[3]

Often, Tarkovsky's women have magical powers – the mute woman in *Roublyov*, Maria the witch, *Solaris*'s Hari, the grandmother in *Mirror* and the Stalker's daughter all have special abilities. The mythology, politics and ontology of women dominates European art cinema (certainly Godard, Truffaut, Dreyer, Bergman and Kurosawa all evoked women reverently, as well as negatively). Michelangelo Antonioni said:

> I especially love women... Through the psychology of women everything becomes more poignant... They express themselves better and more precisely... They are more instinctive, more sincere.[4]

In Tarkovsky's cinema, women are exalted, exaggerated, denigrated and pigeon-holed. He limits their personalities, their potential, their sphere of action. The men always have a larger world of agency and thought, as in most other arts. The mother in *Mirror* is magnified as an Earth Goddess, a Mother-of-All. She is a working, single parent. Beyond this, her sphere of influence is limited. Although she works, and is seen at work, her chief characteristic is to 'be'. *Mirror*'s modern day wife Natalia is a powerful and independent woman, who keeps the child, despite the narrator's complaints (the narrator in *Mirror*, Aleksei, may be Tarkovsky's most self-critical and honest portrait of a modern, 'feminized' man; but he may also be Tarkovsky's unapologetic criticism of men who were brought up – like himself – mainly by women). Like Eugenia, Natalia can move beyond the man. The narrator, meanwhile, is never seen (except part of his body), but he controls the narration, the action, the whole plot of the film. The film pivots around the mother/ wife's personality, but it is the narrator's drive that sets the film in motion, and shapes its course (the film is his dream, his memory, his life).

13 : 5   ACTORS

Like many theatre directors and some film directors, Andrei Tarkovsky had a group of performers that he used again and again. Anatoly Solonitsyn was his favourite: Solonitsyn's function is similar to Jean-Pierre Leaud's in François Truffaut's films (why are Truffaut and Léaud always trotted out as a classic example of a director and star collaboration? For my money, Jean-Luc Godard and Léaud were far more interesting – consider the marvellous *Masculin-Féminin* for instance).

Tarkovsky liked actors who looked tortured and haunted. His favourite face seems to be something that looks like Vincent van Gogh – thin, pinched, bony, haggard, but also noble, aristocratic, cultured. (He calls attention to Oleg Yankovsky's resemblance to van Gogh in *Nostalghia*). Aleksandr Kaidanovsky (the lead in *Stalker*) has a bony face made even more distinctive because of the shaven head. Erland Josephson brings a maturity to the tragic, tortured Tarkovskyan face – and adds the Ingmar Bergman dimension.

Tarkovsky has a knack of choosing intriguing faces: Nikolai Burlyaev (Ivan), Gudrun Gísladóttir (the witch), and Yuri Nikulin (the Cathedral Treasurer in *Andrei Roublyov*). *Andrei Roublyov* is a panoply of interesting faces (faces out of Hieronymous Bosch or Hans Memling) and different acting styles. (But the undoubted champion of art film *auteurs* who had an uncanny eye for extras and actors is Pier Paolo Pasolini. His films probably have the most extraordinary faces in world cinema of the 1960s and 1970s or any era of cinema).

Andrei Tarkovsky hated vulgar gestures, actors who pander to audiences, and cerebral, analytical actors who have to dissect their roles (ST, 145). He had problems with Donatas Banionis who played Kelvin, because Banionis kept trying to analyze his character (ib., 145). And it shows: *Solaris* is a weaker film because of Banionis's mannered performance (or because of the disagreements between the director and the actor). Tarkovsky prefers psychological truth (ib., 155). Authenticity is essential – an intuitive, emotional realism: '[i]n front of the camera the actor has to exist authentically and immediately, in the state defined by the dramatic circumstances' (ib., 139).

Tarkovsky is not as good with actors as, say, Orson Welles or Jean Renoir (i.e., he hasn't got the reputation of being an 'actor's director'), but he does get some good performances from his cast. Best of all is Margarita Terekhova, who is exceptional in *Mirror* (though Erland Josephson in *The Sacrifice*, Aleksandr Kaidanovsky in *Stalker*, and Nikolai Burlyaev in *Ivan's Childhood* and *Andrei Roublyov* are also marvellous). Tarkovsky wasn't known for holding extensive rehearsal periods prior to shooting like, say, Francis Coppola (Coppola's technique of read-throughs with the whole cast, then video taping rehearsals and editing them as an animatic or 'electronic storyboard' was not Tarkovsky's method. A lot more of the rehearsal time on a Tarkovsky picture was for technical stuff). Tarkovsky tended to give actors only a little direction, like Woody Allen or George Lucas, preferring to cast the right people and hope that they would deliver the goods (although, if an actor was having difficulties, Tarkovsky would patiently advise them).

Tarkovsky's directorial process recalls that of Carl-Theodor Dreyer directing Maria Falconetti in *The Passion of Joan of Arc* (1928). Dreyer had various techniques to enhance the performances in the film: absolute silence on set; erecting screens around the performers, and so on. However, Dreyer wasn't always able to explain exactly what he was after to Falconetti, but she had an intuitive grasp of what he wanted, and was able to express it through performance. The collaboration of Dreyer and Falconetti was one of the most fruitful in the history of cinema, with Dreyer's direction and Falconetti's performing combining to produce one of the great films. (Some of Dreyer's perfectionist methods were more draconian: making Falconetti kneel on stone floors for long periods, shaving her head, playing rushes over and over, giving her a real bloodletting, and even putting her under hypnosis.[1] Tarkovsky never went quite that far with actors in the pursuit of realism. He didn't put his actors under hypnosis, as Werner Herzog did in his amazing, soporific one-of-a-kind film *Heart of Glass* (1976, Germany). Besides, Tarkovsky wasn't after 'realistic' acting).

The directorial approach Tarkovsky took with actors wasn't the theatrical tradition of discussing every fine point of a character's personality, motivation or actions (which some actors found frustrating). Actors found that Tarkovsky was reluctant to explain in detail about their character. He tended to think in images, Donatas Banionis remarked (Banionis complained that at times Tarkovsky was only interested in how an actor looked physically). Tarkovsky told actor Alexander Kaidanovsky on the set of *Stalker* that he didn't need 'your psychology, your expressiveness... The actor is part of the composition, like the tree, like water' (JP, 45). Tarkovsky didn't like his actors to act knowing everything about their characters, or about the whole narrative. Sometimes he would deliberately withhold information about the plot (ST, 140). In a 1966 interview, Tarkovsky said he preferred not to tell actors about motivations or functions within a scene, but what s/he has to respond to, what her psychological or emotional state should be (D, 358).

Instead of giving actors specific and helpful suggestions on how to play a scene, Tarkovsky often preferred to muse on the philosophical aspects of the film. Actors have recalled that Tarkovsky was difficult on set, and something of a tyrant. Working for him could be physically and mentally exhausting. Tarkovsky didn't employ stand-ins for actors, so each actor had to perform the actions for real each time. Tarkovsky would horse around sometimes, but generally the atmosphere on set was fairly serious, about getting the work done.

Actors often do well in a Tarkovsky film for the simple reason that the films are so good (a good film makes everyone look good). Although he may not be one of the celebrated directors of actors like Elia Kazan or Robert Altman, Tarkovsky does have the knack of creating a space where great acting can occur, if the performer is up to the challenge. For instance, Tarkovsky employs plenty of long takes, which (most) actors love: it gives them room to explore a character. Also, Tarkovsky's lead roles are truly leading roles: the characters are in most every scene, and have ample opportunities for serious acting.

Tarkovsky's acting style is most like Robert Bresson's — outwardly impassive, inwardly tormented. His aim is for inner intensity, as exemplified by his favourite artists: Fyodor Dostoievsky, Ingmar Bergman, Vincent van Gogh and Leonardo da Vinci. Robert Bresson called actors 'models', and wrote:

YOUR MODELS MUST NOT FEEL THEY ARE DRAMATIC… It is not a matter of acting 'simple' or of acting 'inward' but of not acting at all. (81, 90)

Tarkovsky asked his actors to suggest inner turmoil but without resorting to over-the-top performances. The most difficult task for a Tarkovsky actor was to portray spiritual crises with minimal means. Tarkovsky asked his actors to carry much of the weight of the spiritual exploration in his films. The camera, the music, the sound fx, the lighting, the costumes, the dialogue and all the rest of it were doing their bit, but the actor was the focus of the viewer's attention.

FOURTEEN

Love, Gender and Sexuality

In the end everything can be reduced to the one simple element which is all a person can count upon in his existence: the capacity to love. That element can grow within the soul to become the supreme factor which determines the meaning of a person's life. My function is to make whoever sees my films aware of his need to love and to give his love, and aware that beauty is summoning him.

Andrei Tarkovsky (ST, 200)

Judging by what Andrei Tarkovsky says, love seems to be at the heart of his philosophy. He wrote that 'human love alone is – miraculously – proof against the blunt assertion that there is no hope for the world' (ST, 199). Here Tarkovsky echoes the mythos of the Western world from early Christianity to 1960s counter-culture: the belief that love is a transformative power in society, political as well as sexual or familial, that 'all you need is love'. Tarkovsky is a romantic idealist, and his sentiments chime with those of artists such as Novalis, Johann Wolfgang von Goethe and Emily Brontë. Yet there are few images of romantic love or expressions of grown-up sexuality in his films. (And Tarkovsky doesn't go anywhere near the wilder sides of sexuality, such as the pornography, S/M, transsexuality and eroticism in the fiction of Georges Bataille, William Burroughs, Marquis de Sade,

Jean de Berg or Pauline Réage, or their equivalents in modern cinema: Walerian Borowczyk, Ken Russell and Pier Paolo Pasolini). No lesbian, gay or homosexual relationships, either, in Tarkovsky's films.

The most erotic moment in Tarkovsky's work is probably when the naked pagan woman kisses Andrei Roublyov on the mouth (there's a biographical aspect to this scene: the nude woman is Tarkovsky's wife, and she's embracing his lead actor, and an actor who was an alter ego on screen for Tarkovsky). Roublyov is tied to a post — his situation deliberately echoes Christ on the Cross (and just so's the viewer doesn't forget, it's mentioned in the dialogue by his captors — narrative signposting as obvious as a Hollywood popcorn movie). The scene has many religious precedents. In the *Song of Songs* in the *Bible* (one of the most erotic religious texts in the Western tradition), there is the line 'let him kiss me with the kisses of his mouth'. Another precedent is Mary Magdalene tending the wounded Christ after he's been taken down from the cross. Tarkovsky echoes this in *The Sacrifice*, when Maria washes Alex's hands; and that scene is itself a re-run of the one in *Solaris*, when Kelvin's mother bathes him. In Renaissance painting, Sandro Botticelli produced two tender *Pietà* paintings, with the Magdalene clasping the dead Christ's feet. And in 20th century art, Eric Gill produced a woodcut, *Nuptials of God* (1922, University of Texas), which exactly prefigures Tarkovsky's image: a naked, long-haired Mary Magdalene kissing the crucified Christ. The set-up — men teased and tempted by naked women — also recalls many Christian saints and martyrs, in particular St Anthony (about whom Tarkovsky planned a film, with assistance from the Pope, no less [D, 345]). The long-haired, sexually predatory woman — this is one of the archetypal Tarkovskyan women — whether it's Maria in *Offret*, Natalia in *Zerkalo*, Hari in *Solaris* or Eugenia in *Nostalghia*.

The sexual act in Tarkovsky's cinema is portrayed by flying or floating. When Alex sleeps with the witch Maria, she strips her clothes off and caresses him like a mother tending a child. They rise off the bed, spinning slowly. The lights dim gradually and the room becomes a womb. It's more like a regression to early childhood than sex between adults, more like a mother comforting a son (look at — or listen to — the way Alex behaves in this scene). The sex act is elevated from the realm of realism to the mythic, transcendent realm. (The links between flying and erection, intercourse and orgasm were pointed out by Sigmund Freud, among others. What's great about Tarkovsky's cinema is that he can take something as obvious as flying = sex and make it work. It could so easily backfire, and come across as a crude joke).

The floating scene in *Mirror* is more explicit. The father turns to the woman floating above the bed and strokes her hand. It is one of the few obvious gestures of affection in Tarkovsky's *œuvre*. The woman says 'it's as though I'm floating in the air.' She looks dreamy, or post-orgasmic, lying on her side, her body twisted, her hair floating behind her.

The scene is made clearly erotic by the moment that precedes it: Maria has just killed a cockerel. She stares into the camera and smiles wickedly, evilly, triumph-antly. Her face is lit starkly from below, accentuating the sockets of her eyes, recalling the manic stares of Stanley Kubrick's alter-egos: Jack Torrance, Dave Bowman and Alex the droog. On a number of occasions, in *2001: A Space Odyssey* (1968, USA), *A Clockwork Orange* (1972, USA) and *The Shining* (1980, USA), Kubrick has his anti-heroes stare at the viewer in close-up, their heads lowered and lit from below, their eyes wide-open and staring intently. This is how Maria looks at the viewer in *Mirror* after her act of violence. The wall behind her drips with water, recalling the hair-washing scene earlier, depicting the child's confused view of the sexual relations between his mother and father. Maria is transfigured – into a wraith. If ever the look of a castrating phallic mother or Medusa was portrayed in cinema, this is it. The sense of this complex montage is ambiguous. Certainly it's about violence, sex, blood, illness and heightened states of perception. The taunting look of Maria just after she's killed the cockerel suggests she's just killed her husband, or his sexuality, or his potency, or his identity, or her memory of it all. She kills the cockerel and it is an act of supremacy. The symbolism of the cockerel is, traditionally, solar, fertile, masculine and phallic. A Freudian analyst might treat the scene as a violent castration, recalling the Indian Goddesses who beheaded their consorts as they copulated with them.[1] Wendy O'Flaherty wrote:

> The Goddess not only dominates her consort but kills him, cutting off his head. In this she resembles the female praying mantis, who bites off her consort's head... By eating his head, the mantis removes her consort's inhibitions and frees him to copulate more vigorously. (81)

Decapitation and castration are symbolically and mythopœically equivalent. The poetic implications of this scene are thus clear. Here the woman is mythicized as a monstrous other, the castrating Goddess, the *vagina denta* or 'phallic mother' of psychoanalysis.

Andrei Tarkovsky was unhappy with the scene: he wanted to cut it because it was too obvious what was going on (ST, 109-110). But it's been known all through the film that the woman Maria (like Natalia, her modern-day counterpart) has been much more powerful, more independent, more dignified, and more valuable than her husband. When the father returns from the war he stands meekly with his children (he's given nothing to 'do' by the director); Maria, meanwhile is a restless, dynamic character. The first time Maria's seen in *Mirror* she is sitting on the fence; then she walks to the house; then she stands in the corner of the room; she walks about; sits and stares out of the window; goes out to the fire. She is not 'motherly' in the usual, stereotypical, traditional sense of the term. She is not shown doing domestic chores, or talking to or cuddling her children (or even being much aware of them). It is the aunt, not the mother, who picks up and looks after the children. The mother is restless, dissatisfied, sometimes portrayed as beautiful, other times as unkempt and ugly. Part of her remains other, a mystery to her children.

In *Solaris*, Hari and Kelvin float languidly together to the strains of Bach's music. But this is a rather chaste scene, and Kelvin and Hari aren't entangled in an erotic embrace. Earlier, Hari had appeared as a dream-made sprite, a succubus out of fairy tale and mythology. Kelvin sleeps and Hari arises out of his unconscious. Outside the ship is the giant unconscious, the Ocean. Hari appears framed against the dazzling white circular window of the space ship. The film is a network of circles. The circle represents the Ocean — on ancient maps, seas were circular, enfolding the known land masses. The circular window also stands in neatly for the planet the space ship orbits above, and for all things to do with space travel. Hari encircles Kelvin — and soon he's orbiting around her, psychologically. In traditional symbolism, the circle is time, eternity, change, cyclical processes (Kelvin repeats his response to his wife to the new Hari, as if he's caught in a circle of repetition, a time loop, a karmic wheel, and the film thus has a tragic, fatalistic aspect to it. Kelvin seems doomed to commit the same mistakes *ad infinitum*).

The second time Hari appears in *Solaris* is also erotic: she cuts off her dress with scissors and embraces Kelvin in bed. Later, Hari writhes on the floor, nipples visible under her wet shirt as she resurrects in an erotic epilepsy. Hari's fit is later replayed by the Stalker's wife, and by Adelaide, the mother in *The Sacrifice*. Instability in women and female identity in Tarkovsky's cinema is equated with sexual arousal. When Eugenia berates Gorchakov in *Nostalghia* she bares her breast. (Tarkovsky is no different from so many filmmakers, who sexualize women through their breasts.) Slavoj Zizek, writing about *Nostalghia*, said that

> for Tarkovsky, the moment a woman accepts the role of being sexually desirable,
> she sacrifices what is most precious in her, the spiritual essence of her being, and
> thus devalues herself, turning into a sterile mode of existence: Tarkovsky's uni-
> verse is permeated by a barely concealed disgust for a provocative woman; to this
> figure, prone to hysterical incertitudes, he prefers the mother's assuring and stable
> presence.

Tarkovsky's female characters are seldom seen as independent, completely free of men (unlike art film contemporaries like Ingmar Bergman, Jean-Luc Godard, Margarethe von Trotta, or Pedro Almodóvar, Tarkovsky never made a film with a woman in the lead role). Rather, Tarkovsky's women are always shown in relationship to men, as mothers, wives, daughters, lovers (and occasionally sisters: Tarkovsky's sister figures, in *Ivan's Childhood* and *Mirror*, for instance, barely make an impression they're so under-written).[2] But Tarkovsky's male characters need their women – whether it's poor Ivan dreaming about his mother, or the Stalker coming back to his wife. In *Solaris*, Kelvin will give up his life back on Earth to be with his wife Hari, knowing full well she is a replica created from neutrinos by an alien intelligence.

Mothers and sons is the more common relationship in Tarkovsky's cinema than fathers and son (fathers tend to be alienated from their sons, or absent, or dead). The mother can be an idealized figure (as in *Ivan's Childhood*), but also somewhat distant and unaffectionate (as in *Mirror*), and occasionally given to hysterical outbursts (in *Stalker* and *The Sacrifice*). There is also a hint that Tarkovsky would prefer women to stay in their roles as nurturing mothers, and not to have a life outside of that.[3] If they do, it is threatening and disruptive (Eugenia in *Nostalghia*, for instance, is not a nurturing mother or passive wife figure, and Gorchakov doesn't know how to treat her).

Tarkovskyan women are sometimes wild, strange, other, with magical powers, only half-understood. Yet Tarkovsky also shows that men living without women are only half-alive (in *Nostalghia*, for instance). Tarkovsky goes along with the Renaissance alchemist of Prague, Paracelsus, who said that the second, spiritual birth had to occur in the Mother; one has to die to/ in the Mother first. The same idea occurs in Goethe's *Faust*, which is a key reference point, philosophically, for Tarkovsky's cinema. All of Tarkovsky's films can be analyzed as investigations into the anxieties of accomplishing the spiritual rebirth, because each of Tarkovsky's characters is struggling to rebirth themselves, to achieve a second growth after the journey into adulthood, a poetry of sacrifice and transformation, in an alchemical, spiritual and magical fashion. The films are full of the neuroses, anxieties, doubts, confusions and pains of rebirth, of loss and renewal, of lack and desire.

The anxiety of being the voyeur in cinema is the pain of separation, exclusion and loss. As Pier Paolo Pasolini said in a 1973 essay "Locations, or the Search for Lost Places", 'the look of someone regarding two nude bodies making love is not self-sufficient, does not resolve itself in oneself'. Instead, it involves, Pasolini said, an identification with one or other of the participants.

> The pleasure in looking at a sexual act reproduced – a sexual act which one has experienced – involves also the pain of realising that one is inevitably excluded from it. Thus, to watch an act of love reproduced is like watching something lost which returns, something dead which comes alive'.[4]

Watching people have sex emphasizes the viewer's isolation, the gulf between desire and the act (between watching something and doing it), and being excluded, outside of life. But it includes watching any act.

The sex scenes in Tarkovsky's films are not like those of mainstream entertainment cinema. In a typical (Hollywood) film, the woman is yielding, inviting, passive; she pulls her top off, without kissing the man. She stares at him; he stares at her body and breasts (typically only breasts are shown in an 'R' rated movie). The audience's look is aligned with the masculine gaze of sexual conquest; the man is the lead character, the hero, the star. Cut to the couple making love under a sheet in pretty backlighting (Hollywood actors' contracts stipulate precisely which body parts can be exposed, or if body doubles'll be used, etc). Always in the missionary position, always the man on top, always the woman gasping, glorifying the man's sexual prowess, always the camera bearing down upon the woman from above, like the man. This is nearly every sex scene in every mainstream film.

For feminists (such as Andrea Dworkin, Catherine Mackinnon and Susan Griffin), here's the whole mechanism of pornography: women as invaded, colonized territory, the eternal victim. (That's a deliberately over-simplified description of a sex scene in Hollywood cinema: there are all sorts of other factors, to do with economics, censorship, politics, ethnicity and gender. Script, story and narrative are often way down the list of priorities).

In the cinema of Andrei Tarkovsky, the women are often on top or above the men, like Tantric Goddesses, like Isis hovering over the dead god Osiris (and being impregnated beyond the grave), like the Madonna in Piero della Francesca's two paintings, the *Madonna della Misericordia* and the *Madonna del Parto*, where the Mother of God shelters, nurtures and mothers humanity below. To simplify things, Tarkovsky shows that if the feminine is not integrated, people are not 'whole', in the Jungian sense, or the integration of *yin* and *yang* in Taoist philosophy. The feminine is essential, and this is embodied in the heterosexist relations in Tark-ovsky's visions (and most cinema and art). Men must live with women, as D.H. Lawrence put it, and this is the only erotic relationship fully sanctioned and sanctified by social institutions such as the church, government, law, marriage, and the family (what feminists such as Adrienne Rich termed 'compulsory hetero-sexuality').

Tarkovsky's cinema does not challenge any of these received notions (or even subtly modify them). His depictions of women simply exaggerate neuroses in differ-ent ways, a little differently from mainstream international cinema, but not much. (But it's the same with art cinema generally: although it appears to be 'cool', 'progressive', more 'liberal' or more culturally 'advanced', it usually promulgates precisely the same gender and sexual relations as mainstream cinema. Or, to put it another way, Jean-Luc Godard, Michelangelo Antonioni and Wim Wenders aren't that much different from George Cukor, Richard Attenborough or Anthony Mann).

In Tarkovsky's cinema, sexuality is restrained, like all emotions. As Tarkovsky remarked in *Sculpting in Time*: '[f]or me the most interesting characters are out-wardly static, but inwardly charged with energy by an overriding passion' (ST, 17). Tarkovsky's cinema is firmly sited within patriarchal, masculinist discourse. The gaze, narrativity, image and subject-object relation in his cinema uphold the patriarchal status quo. Tarkovsky may not be a macho 'men's men' director, like Howard Hawks, Sam Peckinpah or John Ford, but his gender politics aren't a lot more developed (indeed, one could say that the films of a director like Hawks or Ford have a more sophisticated view of women than Tarkovsky's view).

Tarkovsky includes beds in his pictures, which might suggest eroticism (the big iron-framed beds of *Stalker, Mirror* and *Nostalghia*) but the sheets are crumpled as after sleep not sex. The married couple at the beginning of *Stalker* sleep in the same bed, but they have their child between them, and judging by the way they lie awake, and later on argue, they don't seem particularly affectionate, and are not a loving couple.

Only once or twice is Tarkovsky's cinema explicitly erotic. In Gorchakov's dream, Eugenia sits above him, and his hand clutches the mattress. But this is more maternal than erotic, for Eugenia is whispering to him, comforting him in his nightmares, rather like the way the witch in *The Sacrifice* comforts Alex (however, Eugenia's hair is down – a sign of sexuality in Tarkovsky's cinema – and she doesn't look particularly 'motherly'). Just before this shot there's the ambiguous embracing of Eugenia and Gorchakov's wife. It is a fantasy of Gorchakov's of Russia embracing Italy, a reconciliation of nations and homelands. It is more a gesture of feminine and national solidarity than lesbian eroticism, as when Adelaide embraces the maid in *The Sacrifice* (the two women hugging next to the bed in *Nostalghia* recalls a scene in Ingmar Bergman's *The Silence*, where the two sisters, Anna and Ester, embrace beside a window and sitting on a bed).

Tarkovsky is not one of those filmmakers who's that interested in investigating sexuality. He is not like, say, Bernardo Bertolucci or Pedro Almodóvar, who construct whole films around sexual relationships. In Rainer Werner Fassbinder's cinema, love is inextricably bound up with politics, with materialism and exploitation (in the powerful film *Fox and His Friends*, for instance [1974, West Germany]). Fassbinder rigorously explored the blurred boundaries of gender, desire, materialism, homosexuality, class, labour and power structures. Fassbinder said 'love is the best, most insidious, most effective instrument of social repression' (J. Franklin, 142). This is clear from *Fox and His Friends, Lola* (1981, West Germany) or *The Marriage of Maria Braun* (1978, West Germany). Filmmakers such as Fassbinder, Godard, Bertolucci, Almodóvar and Antonioni make incisive explorations of sexuality and its relation to identity, society, politics and destiny. (Godard, in the 1960s, seemed to contrive to have a nude woman in just about every film – somehow there are always naked women drifting about in his films – even in those about Christian saints, such as *Hail, Mary* [1984, France]). But for the Hollywood film machine, sexuality is usually merely another incident in the construction of a formulaic narrative film, dealt with at a superficial, saccharine level... a marketing tool, a tease, something to put in the trailers.

PART TWO

THE FILMS

FIFTEEN

Ivan's Childhood

What's striking about *Ivan's Childhood* (*Ivanovo detstvo*; *My Name Is Ivan* in the US, 1962) is that it is such an accomplished debut feature film. Like many other first features, it has elements of a young graduate filmmaker trying to prove himself, a certain flamboyance and self-consciousness (the complex deep focus compositions, for example, or the 'poetic' slow motion in the dream sequences). However, there is far less of this than in many debuts which are intended by the production team to act as a 'calling card' for Hollywood (on the other hand, Tarkovsky wasn't that young – he was thirty when the film was released, married with a child, and had studied at the national film school for six years). Tarkovsky was aware wanting to test himself, though, of using the making of *Ivan's Childhood* to find out if he could be a film director: it was 'specially important. It was my qualifying examination' he commented later (ST, 27). Tarkovsky said he deliberately 'left the reins slack', and 'tried not to hold myself back' (ST, 27).

Ivan's Childhood is a superb depiction of the loss of innocence in childhood, how youth is robbed of childhood, how the sins of the fathers utterly wreck a young soul. It's also a war movie, and offers a poignant evocation of how war ruins lives. The film lyrically individualizes war, depicts how wars happen to individuals, not just nations or cultures.

Ivan's Childhood is an absolute gem of a movie, with a very strong central performance from Kolya Burlyaev. In many respects it's the easiest of Tarkovsky's films to watch: it's not too long for a start (95 minutes); it has a linear, easy-to-follow narrative; the predicament of the main character is easy to identify with (not so easy for audiences to hook into Andrei Gorchakov's life in *Nostalghia*, for instance); it has an impressive look (with not too many distracting quirks); and it's very moving (it's unusual for a film with a child in the lead role for the character to die. *Home Alone, E.T.* or *Harry Potter* this isn't).

Ivan's Childhood is a modest film, but no less impressive for all that. Steven Spielberg in *Empire of the Sun* (1987) and Volker Schlöndorff in *The Tin Drum* (1979) delivered war films seen through the eyes of children as big budget epics with spectacular set-pieces. But *Ivan's Childhood* holds its own against them (and others).

Ivan's Childhood is a film of the Soviet 'thaw'; films featuring young children were popular at the time, particularly for diploma or first films. The Soviet New Wave arose partly from the 'thaw', the 'opening' and liberalization of the late 1950s and early 1960s, after which Soviet cinema was changed, and could not go back wholly to its old socialist realist ways.

Directors of this Khrushchev era included Grigori Chukrai, Sergei Bondarchuk and Mikhail Kalatozov. Val Golovskoy aligned Tarkovsky with directors such as Tengiz Abuladze, Marlen Kutsiev and Otar Ioseliana, and Lenfilm directors such as Gleb Panfilov, Illia Averbach, Vitali Melnikov, Aronovitch, Dinara Asanova and Alexei German. (It helped Tarkovsky to begin his movie-making career at the time of the thaw; ten years earlier, and his sort of poetic films might not have been so well received.)

After the 'thaw', Western critics had a habit of judging Soviet films in terms of how much they rebelled against the Soviet system; the good/ worthy films were seen as those which transgressed official ideological doctrine; the more non-conformist they were, the better, the more they reacted against Soviet bureaucracy, the better. Tarkovsky's films were judged in this way, and Tarkovsky The Soviet Rebel, the cinema outsider, the ideological non-conformist, was a standard view up until his death.

Ivan's Childhood launched Tarkovsky's career with a bold start when it won the Golden Lion award at the Venice film festival in 1962. Also showing in Venice were films directed by Bernardo Bertolucci (*The Grim Reaper* – his first feature), Frank Perry (*David and Lisa*), and Roman Polanski (his debut, *Knife In the Water*). *The Sacrifice* won awards at Cannes, Guldbagge and BAFTA. *Solaris* and *Nostalghia* also won awards at Cannes.

Ivan's Childhood was based on Vladimir Bogomolov's novella *Ivan* (1957). Originally, the Mosfilm production was going to be directed by Eduard Abalov, who had already shot some scenes, but Mosfilm halted the project in October, 1960 (footage apparently no longer exists of the first version of *Ivan's Childhood*). Part of the budget had thus already been spent, and Mosfilm were going to write off the production. The film eventually came in 24,000 roubles under budget. It was shot in late 1961, on the River Dnieper, at Kanev, with shooting finishing by January 18, 1962 (most of the film was shot on location, but the chief set – the church crypt – was built in the studio). By March 1, 1962, *Ivan's Childhood* had been examined thirteen times by various artistic councils at Mosfilm.

One of the original writers had given *Ivan* a happy ending, with the young military scout surviving the war and having a family; Bogomolov and Tarkovsky kept the tragic ending, with Ivan becoming another of the thousands of casualties of war. Vladimir Bogomolov, who had been a military scout himself in the war, disagreed with Tarkovsky about the director's treatment of his novella, particularly the love story, and how Tarkovsky had downplayed the military aspects.[1]

Tarkovsky and his screenwriting collaborator, Andrei Konchalovsky (who appears in a cameo as a bespectacled soldier who meets up with the doctor Masha in the film), altered writers Bogolomov and Papava's treatment, adding four dream sequences (AT, 67-68), which focussed the film on Ivan's psychological state. (Bogolomov agreed to Tarkovsky's addition of the dreams, even though they significantly transformed his novella. But he did argue with Tarkovsky and co-writer Konchalovsky about the way Tarkovsky wanted to depict wartime. Bogolomov was anxious to have the military aspects accurate to his own memories of the war. But Tarkovsky wasn't interested in delivering a documentary-style depiction of child spies in the war. Some of the arguments between Bogolomov and the co-writers were 'extremely heated').[2]

Mosfilm's executives and advisors requested minor and major changes in *Ivan's Childhood*; one of the objections (inevitably) was the sight of the remains of Goebbels and his family at the end (from a newsreel). In *Sculpting in Time*, Tarkovsky discussed the problems of literary adaptions (he made three: *Ivan's*

Childhood, Stalker and *Solaris*): some works were fully formed, he said, and thus are difficult to film. Other prose works (usually minor ones, not literary 'classics') can contain ideas which are not so æsthetically developed, and have space allowing for cinematic adaption (ST, 15-16). One can see how novels such as *Wuthering Heights, Tess of the d'Urbervilles* or *War and Peace* are so complete in themselves, they seem to resist film adaption. One can see how a director like Tarkovsky would prefer a more open approach to literary adaption, allowing him to explore his own preoccupations (this is what he did on *Ivan's Childhood, Solaris* and *Stalker*, altering the plot and treat-ment to suit his own ends, sometimes to the authors' annoyance). (That Tarkovsky made three literary adaptions out of his seven feature films is a reminder that Tarkovsky wasn't wholly a writer-director hyphenate who directed films only from his own original scripts).

Andrei Tarkovsky was drawn to Vladimir Bogomolov's *Ivan*, he said, by the story of the young scout; and by the character of the boy, tragically denied a proper childhood. The lack of military action and exploits also intrigued him: instead, *Ivan* was about an interval in between forays that had a 'disturbing, pent-up intensity' (ST, 17). *Ivan's Childhood* takes place in the interlude between Ivan's scouting missions behind German lines: at the start of the film he crosses the barbed wire and the flooded forest, moving from enemy territory to the Russian field station after swimming across the river; at the end of the film, he is escorted back through the swamp.

Ivan's Childhood portrays, confidently and poetically, a bleak, war-torn world, of swamps and rivers, muddy tracks, barbed wire, deserted forests, dishevelled people and tired soldiers, ruined buildings, destroyed remains of military hardware (a crashed German plane looming over a riverbank, canons), rain, drifting mist and smoke, fizzling flares descending out of leaden skies. Solitary figures in sodden, broken landscapes strewn with wreckage, the machines of warfare. Roads churned up into mud.

The world of *Ivan's Childhood* is not the brightly-lit, heroic battlefields of Hollywood's World War Two films of the same era, but a dark, sombre, stark and brutal world, recalling films such as Andrzej Wajda's 'Polish School' trilogy, *A Generation, Canal* and *Ashes and Diamonds* (1954-58), made a few years before Tarkovsky's *Ivan's Childhood* (which Tarkovsky had seen at VGIK; Wadja's trilogy is a film school favourite). The tracking shots in the trenches in *Ivan's Childhood* recall the lengthy, *virtuoso* shots in Stanley Kubrick's anti-war film

Paths of Glory (1957). One sequence, where Galtsev and Kholin talk, seems particularly inspired by *Paths of Glory*: they walk along a trench, with the camera first
in front of them, then, as they pass it, dollying behind them, all done in a continuous
take. (*All Quiet On the Western Front*, may have been another influence – that
famous war film has bravura shots where the camera cranes along the top of
trenches).

There are three great eras in Russian historical films: the Napoleonic wars; the
Russian Revolution; and the Second World War. As Sylvie Dallet noted, Tarkovsky's *Mirror* and *Andrei Roublyov* were part of these eras.[3] However, Tarkovsky
has usually rejected history; after evoking the World War II world of *Ivan's
Childhood*, Tarkovsky took

> refuge in the mythical description of suspended time… enabling him to reflect
> upon the individual in all his fragility, crushed beneath the weight of a troubled
> universe. Events are perceived as unacceptable heresies. (ib., 306)

After the opening dream sequence, Tarkovsky establishes the war-time setting of
Ivan's Childhood with some very stylized, Expressionist shots: Ivan waking up in a
windmill, a building out of Gothic horror films and Northern European painting,
portrayed with wide angle, tilted shots. As Ivan walks away from the windmill,
Tarkovsky uses another bravura image: Ivan walking into the sun on a barren
hillside (Maya Turovskaya related the apocalyptic imagery of the sun and sunsets in
Ivan's Childhood to examples in the poetry of Alexander Blok, Sergei Urusevsky
and Mikhail Sholokhov). The images of the bleak, smoky landscape are accompanied by edgy, foreboding music of drums and brass. (Many another debuting film
director might have loaded the opening section with some big scenes, putting the
budget and production values up on screen. Tarkovsky has the confidence to leave
that out, putting it into a much later scene, when Lt-Col Gryaznov talks on the
telephone at the HQ and trucks and extras are glimpsed in the window behind him.)

The German enemy is rarely seen in *Ivan's Childhood*; instead, gunshots and
explosions are heard, plus the signal flares which fall throughout the film against
leaden grey skies. In fact, German soldiers are only shown once or twice – in the
night crossing of the swamp, for example, and in the newsreel footage of Berlin.
However, the Germans are unambiguously loathed, especially by Ivan. For the boy,
the Germans are the enemies of art and culture. As he looks at some Albrecht Dürer
woodcuts in a large art book (having already read all of the magazines and articles

that Galtsev has saved), he remarks that it reminds him of the barbaric Germans, who burn books (Ivan sees a figure riding a horse in Dürer's prints and it reminds him of a German on a motorcycle. Ivan seems to ignore the intense stylization of Dürer's prints, and accepts them as documentary evidence).

Instead of the action-adventure predominating in Hollywood depictions of the Second World War, Tarkovsky's film is full of scenes of near-silence and people waiting. As one of the characters says, the sound of silence is the sound of war. An eerie, unnerving silence, punctuated by sudden bursts of gunfire and explosions (of course, that makes the film a lot cheaper to produce, because the war can be suggested through a library of sound effects. Many filmmakers have resorted to the same devices. There are, though, some combat scenes in *Ivan's Childhood*: a series of explosions, for instance, when the Germans start to bomb the Russians. There's a beautiful moment when the bombardment ceases, and birds start singing again over a memorable shot of dust swirling around a cross stuck in the ground, the light behind it creating a halo effect).

Many of Andrei Tarkovsky's familiar motifs appear in *Ivan's Childhood*: rain, fires, trees, tracking shots over water, sounds of dripping water, birds (the sound of birdsong in the dreams; the cockerel who belongs to the old man), dream sequences, long takes, dream images of mothers, doors opening and closing on their own, references to fine art (the icon of the Madonna and Child; Ivan looking at woodcuts by Albrecht Dürer).

Visually, *Ivan's Childhood* is a stunning achievement, with Tarkovsky conjuring memorable images: Ivan in the flooded forest lit by flares; the handheld shots of the birch wood; the ruined buildings and the mud; the apples spilling over the beach (in one Tarkovsky's very best shots, the swooping crane shot down to the sand); the snow on the river; the cross in the sun in the dust; Ivan 'flying' in the opening dream sequence. Religious imagery is present in *Ivan's Childhood* in the Virgin and Child icon, the Albrecht Dürer wood prints, and the windmill silhouetted against the smoky sky like a cross. Note that Tarkovsky chose Dürer's *Four Men of the Apocalypse* as the main visual art reference, with its suitable Biblical resonances of devastation (and aligning the Germans with the horsemen who bring ruin to the world: they destroy everything, Ivan complains, including burning books in a town square. Throughout the film, Ivan has to remind the young lieutenant Galtsev that he has already seen terrible things in the war, even at his young age, including one of the Germans' death camps).

The use of newsreel footage of the Soviet soldiers in Berlin grounds *Ivan's Childhood*, as with *Mirror*, in a particular historical framework (some of the footage may be shot for the film, but made to look like newsreels). After the newsreel, the Soviet soldiers are seen exploring a half-destroyed German building. Even in this apparently straightforward, though melancholy scene, the Tarkovsky touch is at work: through the gaps in the roof small pieces of burnt paper, like leaves, float down, like the dandelion seeds in *Andrei Roublyov* and the snow in *Nostalghia*.

Although rated 'PG' by the British Board of Film Classification, *Ivan's Childhood* contains some disturbing imagery: the charred remains of Goebbels, for example, and a row of his poisoned children. There is another family shown dead in documentary footage. And in the execution room, in the basement of the bombed German building, is a row of ropes, for hanging prisoners, plus a guillotine. The sight of the guillotine motivates a short montage or vision, for Galtsev, of Ivan's demise, with shots of Ivan rolling over and over, as if he's just been guillotined. (Ivan is definitely dead: a Russian soldier sifts through documents about prisoners, merely grimly noting if they were hanged or guillotined. Galtsev (now scarred and looking much older, and the only survivor among the characters) recognizes Ivan in a photograph, which's shown to the viewer in C.U.). Black ash drifts down from burning papers.

Much of the visual style of *Ivan's Childhood* uses deep focus, wide angle photography, recalling German Expressionist cinema, and films such as *Citizen Kane* (which had impressed Tarkovsky, as it has affected so many filmmakers). Like Orson Welles and Gregg Toland, Tarkovsky and cameraman Vadim Yusov created complex compositions in deep focus, with action in the foreground and middle distance (sometimes racking focus between actors, and often having an actor in a big C.U. in the foreground, listening to an out-of-focus actor in the background). For his single take scenes, Tarkovsky orchestrated his actors meticulously, so they sometimes move into close-up, or into the distance. The scenes in the military post are perhaps the most obviously Expressionist, with Tarkovsky exploring the ways in which the most mundane and common of dramatic scenes – people talking in a room – can be livened up.

As well as deep focus photography, Tarkovsky and Yusov also used tilted camera, and dramatic, *film noir* lighting. In the episode with the old man in the countryside, low angles were employed, with shots of entrapment – Ivan surrounded by charred, broken timbers, for example. In the scene where Ivan enthusiastically embraces Kholin, the bunker is entirely lit with a shadowy light which flickers on the ceiling.

Aurally, *Ivan's Childhood* bears Tarkovsky's idiosyncratic stamp, in its use of selective off-screen sound, such as birdsong, gunfire, and strange noises, such as the creaking wood and door throughout the scenes with the old man in the wrecked village. There is also the deeply emotive Chaliapin singing, which resonates in the scene towards the end of the film, where Kholin and Galtsev sit in the bunker, and are visited by Masha, who has been posted elsewhere (Chaliapin sings 'Masha must not cross the river').

Although the takes are not as lengthy as in Tarkovsky's later work, many scenes are covered in a single master shot: for instance, in the scene where Kholin and Katasonych walk to the boats by the riverbank, examine them, decide which one to take, talk to Galtsev, and carry the boat into the water, Tarkovsky covers the action in a single master shot.

A very long take comes late in the film, when Galtsev and Kholin sit in the bunker, after returning from taking Ivan across the river: it's a wide shot, from above, showing the men sitting at the table; Kholin puts on the gramophone; they listen, then switch off the music; Masha arrives, and stands in close-up, in the foreground; she talks with the soldiers; Kholin approaches her; when Kholin goes to fetch something to show her, she leaves. Instead of breaking up the beats into separate shots, Tarkovsky covers it all in a single lengthy take.

The first shot of Tarkovsky's first feature film was echoed in the last shot of his last feature film: a young boy at the base of a tree, with the camera slowly craning upwards into the branches. This shot in *Ivan's Childhood* is an unusual opener: the crane shot is typically an establishing shot at the beginning of a scene, and usually starts high, with a view of the landscape of the film, craning down to show the protagonist. Here, it cranes up and away from the lead character (the shot also has one of Tarkovsky's favourite devices – the double or stand-in to place a character simultaneously in the foreground and the background). The camera movement upwards relates to the joyous atmosphere of the first scene of *Ivan's Childhood*, where the motion upwards culminates in Ivan seeming to fly. In *The Sacrifice*, too, the crane up shot indicates bliss and transcendence.

Ivan's Childhood is also unusual in opening with a dream sequence; the audience at this point can't know if the images are a dream or 'reality' (though the heightened quality of the images, and the mysterious, shimmering music are clues). Another link with *The Sacrifice* is that both films begin and end with images of a single tree. In *The Sacrifice*, the tree, with its Oriental and Christian associations, may survive and grow; but the tree at the end of *Ivan's Childhood* is a dead, charred, branchless trunk, like the dead tree in *Waiting For Godot*, a symbol of the natural world ruined by humanmade war. The tree is also placed, mysteriously (and impossibly), in the middle of a sandy beach: it's a dark, foreboding image in the midst of the happy, sunlit dream sequence. *Ivan's Childhood* ends with a tracking shot towards the tree, before fading to black. By this time, the audience knows that Ivan is already dead.

The tree symbolism in *Ivan's Childhood* doesn't require much analysis to grasp it: at the beginning of the film (although it's in a dream), Ivan is alive in a world of living trees. At the end of the film, both the tree and the boy are dead. The environment around the Russian's base in the church is a wasteland of mud, holes and dead trees (note how Tarkovsky put the Russians in the crypt of a church, a *mise-en-scène* that doesn't require any complex decoding. No surprise, either, that hints of religious imagery can be glimpsed in the crypt: a bell, an icon). The command base was originally supposed to have been a ceramics factory, Tarkovsky said in 1962, which would have had factory carts shuddering in the shock waves of the artillery attack in narrow tracks. The spies are tied to a dead tree; the river floods a forest of what appear to be dead trees (one falls down). The birch wood, for the ambiguous romantic interlude, is a favourite Tarkovsky space (a wood near Moscow was used, and was reprised in *Andrei Roublyov*, for the scene where the stone masons are blinded. The birch wood took along time to find; the filmmakers had looked at many other groves).

Like his second film, Tarkovsky's first film opens with a flying sequence; in both scenes the flight ends abruptly, with a sudden return to earth: in the case of *Andrei Roublyov*, the flier expires; in *Ivan's Childhood*, the flight is seen to be a dream, with Ivan's actual existence – the rundown windmill, the war-torn landscape, the swamp, his enveloping solitude – becoming all too real. While *Ivan's Childhood* begins and ends with a happy dream, there is no ambiguity about what happens to Ivan, and the difficult, lonely, harsh life he has.

Perhaps the oddest scene in *Ivan's Childhood* is where Kholin meets Masha, the female doctor, in the birch forest (the romance was originally going to be between Galtsev and Masha [CS, 58]). Tarkovsky's films do not contain many scenes of seduction between a man and a woman. There is the mild flirting between the doctor and mother at the beginning of *Mirror*, but more common are images of consummation (Alexander and the witch in *The Sacrifice*, the floating woman in *Mirror*, Eugenia on the bed with Andrei in *Nostalghia*). And there are the images of post-coital reverie ('I feel like I'm floating' says the woman in *Mirror*).

In *Ivan's Childhood*, though, Tarkovsky depicts, in some detail, a man talking and flirting with a woman, offering an interlude from the war drama. The summery birch forest contrasts with the bleak, wintry, flooded forest. There is one kiss in this scene, but not in the rest of *Ivan's Childhood* (compared to Hollywood or European movies, Tarkovsky's films include far fewer erotic kisses, and even less sexual contact). However, the tropes of intercourse are present: Kholin invites Masha to climb a fallen tree. Elaborate, wordless tracking shots follow Masha walking up the tree trunk with Kholin watching her above. When the kiss does come, it is a sudden embrace, as Kholin lifts Masha over a trench, clutching her and holding her in space and kissing her. As in much of the rest of this scene, the mystery derives from the peculiar perspective and visual devices Tarkovsky chooses to employ: as they kiss, the camera cranes down into the trench, looking up at them from a very low angle; when the embrace ends, the camera cranes up, out of the trench, finally resting on Masha in close-up. It is an odd camera movement, with a hallucinatory quality like much of the camerawork in *Ivan's Childhood*. Freudians might see the fallen tree as a phallic object, which Masha climbs; while the trench, especially from the low angle, has a vaginal quality. Another reading of the crane shot into the trench might see it as another image of entrapment, of which there are many in *Ivan's Childhood* (the sides of the trench form diagonals right across each side of the frame). Another view might be of transitions between borders, with the sides of the trench recalling two separate countries, or two separate people. The kiss between Masha and Kholin above the trench was a tragic image for Tarkovsky; he likened it to a 'graveside kiss' (the association of the trench with a grave heightens the Freudian theme of the interchangeability of love and death).

Later, the camera, presumably now embodying Masha's point-of-view, suddenly veers off into the wood. In the birch wood scene, Tarkovsky employs handheld camera, cranes, and tracking shots, with characters moving in and out of the white trees, and the trees sliding in and out of the frame. The motif of the highly mobile camera is reprised later, when Masha enters the wood alone; this time, the handheld camera (her p.o.v., or perhaps an equivalent for her emotional state) swoops around the trees, diving close to a tree trunk, and finally tilting up vertiginously to the tree tops. Emotive string music accompanies this scene.

Kholin acts as the predatory male in the birch wood scene; he knows that Galtsev likes Masha; Masha, meanwhile, is unsure about Kholin (Tarkovsky cast a handsome actor, Valentin Zubkov, for the part, which makes his seduction less threatening), and tries to slip away from him. She seems to succumb at one point (there's a hint, suggested by off-screen movement, that Kholin persuades Masha to touch his genitals); but she breaks free (he also seems to think better of it, and pushes her away). At the end of the scene, Galtsev walks into the woods, trying to find Masha, and eyes Kholin suspiciously.

The two sections of *Ivan's Childhood* that are not as successful as some of the others are the love scene in the birch wood and the old man in the burnt-out house. In *Sculpting in Time* Tarkovsky said this latter scene was shot in two different ways, the one that Tarkovsky preferred afterwards wasn't used. Instead, the scene used was the one that stuck to the script ('a result of meekly following the script' as Tarkovsky put it [ST, 31]). In Tarkovsky's own conception, the scene was to have featured a lonely, desolate, waterlogged field, with 'stumpy, autumnal white willows' along the road, and a scraggy cow pulling Ivan on a cart. When the Colonel's car drove up, Ivan was to have run far away, to the horizon, with Kholin following through the mud (ST, 31-32). Tarkovsky had seriously considered deleting the sequence with the old man in the ruined village. (On further viewings, though, the scene isn't as bad as Tarkovsky makes out).

In the middle of *Ivan's Childhood* is a scene that isn't a dream sequence, but expresses Ivan's feelings and fears, as he plays a game on his own in the military post, while the soldiers go and look for a boat, and cross the river. In Ivan's war game, the realities of military conflict intrude in an exaggerated, psychological manner: in near-darkness, Ivan's flashlight picks out graffiti on the walls – messages from Russian prisoners: 'avenge us!'; German voices are heard, some of them perhaps Adolf Hitler; the sound of people (particularly women) weeping is heard; Ivan rigs up a large bell with a rope; he crawls around with the knife he's borrowed from Galtsev, hunting German soldiers. The lighting is shadowy and Expressionist; whip pans and rapid cutting adds to the unreality; Ivan's mother (played by Tarkovsky's first wife, Irma Tarkovskaya) is briefly glimpsed in the torchlight, as well as a body on the floor, and one or two other characters.

Tarkovsky's cinema has often featured such scenes – not dream sequences, but images expressionistically dramatizing an individual's state of mind. Often the key people in the protagonist's life appear (as when Andrei sees Domenico staring at him in the wardrobe mirror in *Nostalghia*). Ivan crawls on his belly in the shadows, talking to himself as he plays his game of war; he interrogates a coat on a hook on the wall, as if it's a captured German soldier, addressing the camera directly: 'you will pay for everything'.

At the end of Ivan's tortured game of war, he breaks down, weeps, falls to the ground. An icon of the Virgin Mary and Child is uncovered at this point, when an explosion rocks the bunker (as the Germans start to shell the Russians' positions). When Ivan rings the bell, it continues to ring after he's stopped ringing it, and the chimes are joined by the sound of cheering. (Ivan's game was foreshadowed earlier, when he uses seeds, barley ears, wheat grains, pine cones and berries on a piece of paper to remind himself of the Germans' positions; as the camera tracked in close-up over the objects on the paper, German voices, marching soldiers and sounds of war were heard on the soundtrack).

The climax of *Ivan's Childhood*, in terms of action, is the night crossing of the river. In a Hollywood war movie, this scene would be played for maximum suspense. In Tarkovsky's film, the suspense is still there, but much more muted; and the sequence veers off into poetic cinema (with lengthy shots looking down at the water sliding past the boat). (Note how the narrative of *Ivan's Childhood* occurs between Ivan's two expeditions into enemy territory: a Hollywood movie would probably want to show at least one of these adventures).

Tarkovsky confidently enhances the unreality of the nighttime river crossing – firstly by shooting it all at the tail end of the magic hour, which gives the sequence a haunting, melancholy photographic atmosphere. Smoke drifts; flares fall (seen first in reflection in the water). There's hardly any dialogue, as Galtsev, Kholin and Ivan stay as quiet as possible. Suspense is intensified with the quiet but insistent music (which's interrupted by sudden stabs of strings to accompany shots of the two dead spies tied to the tree, and the sound of bullets). The boat sliding past a crashed German fighter plane is another memorable moment. For no particular reason, a tree falls into the water as the Russians pass by. Machine gunfire splashes in the water near the boat. Tarkovsky adds a typical Tarkovskyan moment when it starts to snow on the river (turning the reverse angle of the crashed plane at the close of the sequence into a classically composed image of the aircraft against white sky, grey river and black smoke).

(One of the original ideas was to have the river crossing occurring in thick fog, with black figures glimpsed amidst smoke 'sculptures', shapes which would have

been created with smoke and fog. But the wind on the Kanev flood plain was too
strong for conjuring shapes in the air. There was also going to be a montage of
images lit by the flares (such as figures in the fog, or C.U.s of eyes and branches).)

When Galtsev and Kholin say goodbye to Ivan, Ivan's theme is played softly on
the track. It's a touching moment, because it's the last time that Ivan is seen alive by
his friends (and by the viewer, except in his last dream). There's a hint, created
wholly in the editing, that Ivan doesn't survive the river crossing: a flash cut from a
shot of the river to another close-up shot of the river, with bright light reflected in
the water, accompanied by the sound of gunfire. The meaning of this shot is
ambiguous, but one reading of the film language at this narrative point is that Ivan
has been hit, but the filmmakers have declined to show it (a common device in
cinema). Later, three German soldiers pass very close to Kholin and Galtsev, who
just manage to hide behind some trees (if Ivan's dead, these are probably his killers.
Galtsev wants to shoot them, but Kholin prevents him).

From the river crossing to the end of the film, the tone is unrelievedly grim:
Kholin and Galtsev sit in their base, hardly communicating; the long Berlin sequence
has unsettling newsreel footage, images of execution rooms, Russian sombrely sifting
through the wreckage, and the revelation of Ivan's death. The war may be over, but
there's no sense of victory or joy (Kholin has been killed on the journey to Berlin).
Only Ivan's final dream brings a little lightness into the proceedings, but that dream
has a tragic irony, because Ivan's short, painful life is already over. Tarkovsky
spoke of the characters in *Ivan's Childhood* being doomed and tragic, as if 'the
breeze of the plague' was blowing over them.

Ivan is portrayed throughout the film as a combination of the innocent and cynic,
the vulnerable and the tough. There are touching moments, such as when Ivan uses
seeds, nuts and leaves he's collected to explain the German positions on a piece of
paper. The apparently childish use of leaves and seeds is mitigated by the fact that
in this scene Ivan is wrapped in a blanket, with a blackened face, in a field station,
just arrived from a military mission. There is nothing childlike about Ivan's occupation.

Like the children in fairy tales, Ivan is an orphan, and the soldiers act as
surrogate fathers. Note, though, that Ivan's father does not appear in any of the
memory/ dream sequences, only his mother and sister. The mother embodies Ivan's
œdipal quest, his yearning for familial, domestic sanctuary – associated with images
of nature, she is literally 'mother earth'.

Tarkovsky didn't want to romanticize or sentimentalize Ivan or his predicament. Ivan mustn't be the 'pride and joy of the regiment,' Tarkovsky explained, 'he must be its grief'.[4] For Tarkovsky, Ivan's tragic situation was a child who was living as an adult, a child who was caught up in adult life (the war). But he was still a child, and the film had a scene where Ivan was shown to be a child (the scene where he plays at war, on his own in the base).

Unlike Jean-Luc Godard in his feature debut a couple of years earlier (*Breathless*), Tarkovsky was restrained in his use of music, which generally accompanies the dream sequences (as well as the birch wood scene, Ivan's war game, and other scenes). Here, the orchestral cue (by Vyacheslav Ovchinnikov) is sweet and lyrical, bolstering the sunny, summery images of Ivan's childhood with his mother in the countryside. One or two sudden stabs of music accompany the dramatic revelations in the film: when the two dead scouts are seen tied to a tree with ropes around their necks at the end of a panning shot of the river, for example, or when Ivan's photograph is seen in the ruined building at the end of the film, indicating that he's been killed by the Germans. In the night river sequence, dramatic tension is heightened by jarring strings and low drum beats. In other scenes, slow, sombre and mysterious cues enhance the atmosphere of unreality and threat. The main use of diegetic music occurs in the military post, where Katasonich plays the other soldiers a Chaliapin folk song, which stops them in their tracks.

Nikolai Burlyaev, who plays Ivan, is immensely impressive; convincing at all times, unlike many child actors (a world away from the usual Hollywood child actors). Burlyaev conveys a mixture of innocence and cynicism, enthusiasm and weariness, belief and pessimism. In the dream sequences Burlyaev's Ivan is full of light – clean, mobile and joyful; in the war zone scenes, he is tough, vulnerable, sullen, aggressive, sporting old clothes (speckled grey sweater, black hat, old black pants), dishevelled hair, and a muddy face. (*Ivan* wasn't Kolya Burlyaev's first film – he had already appeared in four films by then).

Ivan's Childhood garnered many favourable reviews, including five front page reviews during 1962. Jean-Paul Sartre came to *Ivan's Childhood*'s defence when it was criticized by the Italian Communist Party newspaper *Unita* for being 'petit bourgeois'. *Ivan's Childhood*, Sartre wrote, used 'socialist surrealism' to portray a 'Soviet tragedy'; Ivan was a combination of 'monster' and innocent, driven by vengeance for his mother's death (J. Sartre, 1965). Antoine de Baecque saw Ivan as a victim, saint and martyr (1989, 53-54). Like other children in Tarkovsky's cinema, Ivan is linked with the infant Christ. Revisiting *Ivan's Childhood*, Maya Turovskaya remarked that it was 'balanced and complete, with each strand of the plot, every visual and other motif carried through to its logical conclusion in total clarity' (95).

One of the elements of *Ivan's Childhood* that should be noted is the casting. From his first film onwards, Tarkovsky got the casting of the lead roles spot-on. The importance of casting is too often overlooked in film criticism, but it's absolutely vital. While the roles of the soldiers, including Galtsev, Kholin, Katasonych, and Gryaznov, would have been relatively easy to cast, the central role offered a huge challenge, because Ivan was in most of the scenes, and would carry the film. Finding a really good child actor is always difficult, but Kolya Burlyaev was stunning.

One of the remarkable elements of *Ivan's Childhood* are the four dream sequences. The dreams are quite separate from Ivan's real life; there is no bridge or interface between the two worlds; instead, there's a gulf which Ivan cannot fuse.[5] And each dream starts out positively, but ends badly. Tarkovsky told Mikhail Romm that Ivan dreams of the life, the normal childhood, he's 'been robbed of' (CS, 57). The first dream sequence begins with a medium close-up of Ivan (wearing only shorts), the sound of a cuckoo, and the slow crane shot up the tree. Images of a sunlit natural world follow: a goat, a butterfly, trees. As he starts to 'fly' (apparently standing on a camera crane), he laughs happily; the music emphasizes that this is meant to be an ecstatic, transcendent sequence. After showing Ivan rising up into the leaves, there is a helicopter long shot, followed by a long panning medium shot along a wall of cracked earth and roots, ending on a pensive Ivan.

Towards the end of the dream sequence, Ivan's mother appears, standing in a track in the wood. As in later dreams, Ivan drinks water from a pail. Kneeling on the ground, he looks up at his mother and says 'mother, there's a cuckoo' (Tarkovsky said these were some of his first words, aged four [ST, 29]). The relaxed intimacy ends abruptly with the sound of gunshots, the mother falling to the ground, the camera tilting, and Ivan calling 'Mama!' As he wakes up, Glatsev is there, and Ivan wonders if he talks in his sleep.

In Ivan's second dream, the motifs of light, water and a peaceful mother-child bond again appear, this time refracted through images of reflections and mirrors. As in *Mirror* and *Nostalghia*, Tarkovsky plays with the viewer's expectations of naturalism: the viewpoint of a low angle shot, looking up at the mother and Ivan leaning over the side of a well, is revealed to be underwater (the camera is situated under glass, with water on it). The second dream begins with the sleeping Ivan being put to bed by Galtsev; there is a characteristic Tarkovsky travelling shot (a big close-up on the stove and flames then moving slowly across the floor, past wood) which ends on Ivan's hand, water dripping on it from somewhere above. The next shots show the chimney of the bunker now as a wooden well: Ivan is shown looking over the well with his mother. As in the first dream sequence, when Ivan said he could hear a cuckoo, they talk about something lyrical and natural: that one can see a star by daylight in a well. The mother's comment – that it is day for us but night for the star – is another view of Ivan's predicament, his life caught between day and night, the ideal, dream world and the actual, war world. Tarkovsky plays with the audience's expectation of naturalism when he has the camera looking up through water at Ivan and his mother, then cuts to images of Ivan at the bottom of the well, his arms in the water, reaching down to a bright light under the water, as if it's a fallen star. The second dream ends, like the first one, in the death of the mother by gunfire; she is shown lying face down, with water flying through the air in slow motion over her body, with the bucket on the left.

The third dream sequence in *Ivan's Childhood* is also hallucinatory, heightened, intentionally unreal, with its back projection of trees and landscape in negative. Such an obviously artificial scene, using back projection, is rare in Tarkovsky's cinema. In this dream, the perennial Tarkovsky favourite motif, rain, is dominant: it makes the apples, the faces, the horses and the beach gleam. Tarkovsky explained in *Sculpting in Time* how it came about: '[q]uite unexpectedly it occurred to us to have negative images in the third dream. In our mind's eye we glimpsed black sunlight sparkling through snowy trees and a downpour of gleaming rain' (ST, 30). Tarkovsky said the content of the dream – the apples, horses and rain – came from his own memories, 'straight from life', not via the distillation of art. Some of the landscapes in *Ivan's Childhood* came from his own memories, Tarkovsky said: the beach, the birch wood, the flooded forest (ST, 28-29).

There are two parts to the third dream: in the first, Ivan is on the back of a truck loaded with masses of apples; his sister (or perhaps childhood friend or sweetheart) sits by him; he offers her an apple; she is shown in a close-up pan, the camera moving past her face three times in succession, in an apparently continuous take. Each time the girl appears, her expression darkens. 'We wanted to capture in that scene a foreboding of imminent tragedy' remarked Tarkovsky (ST, 30-31). (The apple truck is introduced with a L.S. on normal film stock, driving along a country road).

The second section of this dream takes place on a beach; the intention was to link the dream to Ivan's last dream, which occurs on the beach. Tarkovsky introduces the beach scene with one of his extraordinary shots: a descending wide angle crane shot, looking down on hundreds of apples strewn over the sand next to the sea, fallen off the truck, now in the middle distance, and three or four horses visible ('an obvious homage to Dovzhenko's *Earth*' [JP, 75]). In the next shot, a horse is seen in M.C.U. nuzzling the apples on the sand.

In the fourth dream, the dreamer is dead. The viewer has seen the Berlin sequence, the Russians uncovering the grim execution rooms, and Galtsev finding Ivan's document. In the dream (perhaps one of Ivan's last dreams, when he was awaiting execution), Ivan is shown on a huge sunlit beach (actually a riverbank), wearing only shorts, again drinking water from a bucket. He looks up at his mother; she walks away from him and waves to him.

Ivan is then portrayed, in a high angle shot, playing hide-and-seek with some young children on the beach, near a large dead tree. In another shot, Ivan is shown chasing his sister along the sand and into the shallows. As in the first dream, Ivan is laughing joyously. Tarkovsky cuts between the rapid tracking shots of the two running children. Ivan runs on and on, past the girl, into the sparkling shallows. It's as if he can't stop running; his spirit seems to be unstoppable, indomitable. Indeed, it is Burlyaev's Ivan's inner strength that dominates the film.

The dream, and the film, ends with shots of Ivan by the dead tree, raising his arm; then the final shot, a track into the tree trunk, so that it obscures the lens. (Tarkovsky had contemplated having Ivan shot by a stray bullet and dying in the snow, seeing his mother from the first dream before he died. Another idea was to have Ivan discover his double, dressed in his wartime clothes, and chase after him [CS, 60]).

The fourth dream appears at first to be the happiest in the film; it doesn't end with gunshots and the death of his mother, but with ominous drumbeats and shots of the dead tree. However, the viewer knows that Ivan is already dead. As Graham Petrie and Vida Johnson point out, the naturalism and everydayness of this last dream contrasts bitterly and ironically with the viewer knowing that Ivan has in fact been executed by the Nazis 'after a brief life soured by hate and deprivation' (JP, 75). As with the endings of *Mirror* and *Nostalghia*, the protagonist is already dead when the dream occurs (ibid.). In 1962, Tarkovsky stated that the final (fourth) dream was critical, because the viewer knows now that Ivan is dead, and so it takes on a tragic mood. Although the imagery appeared at first to be upbeat (Ivan running along a riverbank in sunlight), that wasn't the intention at all, Tarkovsky said. Instead, it was meant to be poignant: 'this is a cinematic-poetic tragedy'.

SIXTEEN

The Passion According to Andrei Roublyov

Andrei Roublyov was the subject of much discussion in the Soviet Union and was withheld by the authorities for years. It was Tarkovsky's most controversial film, and retains its power to startle viewers. It's easily Tarkovsky's most visceral and violent film, by far the most action-packed (and there's plenty of nudity, too). Nowadays, with the many changes in the political and ideological climate (such as *glasnost*, the end of the Cold War, the dissolution of the Soviet Union), some of the political controversies have faded over time. These days, contemporary audiences might find other aspects of *Andrei Roublyov* more unsettling: the treatment of animals, for instance (a cow set on fire, a horse killed on camera), or the images of torture and barbarity. You can slaughter hundreds of actors and extras on screen, but harming animals disturbs many viewers. Feminists might find the treatment of women in *Andrei Roublyov* equally problematic. There are two significant female characters in *Andrei Roublyov*: the pagan woman Marfa that Roublyov possibly sleeps with, and the fool that he adopts. Simplistic second wave feminist film criticism could argue that Roublyov is a 'feminized' character himself (passive, not particularly pro-active).

There were prints of *Andrei Roublyov* of varying lengths, from a US 146 minute version, to an 'original cut' of 180 minutes, which was shown in the Soviet Union in 1989. The three hour and twenty minute version was the first cut, entitled *The Passion According to Andrei* (the original title of *Andrei Roublyov* was *The Beginning and the Ways*). Tarkovsky said he preferred the 185 minute version which was released in 1971.[1] (Maria Turovskaya said that Tarkovsky cut the film down from 5642 to 5250 metres, and later pruned another 174 metres off it; the Russian release print was 5076 metres [48]). (The original title of *Andrei Roublyov* — *The Passion According To St Andrei* — was rejected by the authorities). Tarkovsky claimed that nobody else had cut *Andrei Roublyov* except him. And his trims were mainly for reasons of length, not meaning or censorship (i.e., he had shortened lengthy scenes, in order to bring down the running time). Tarkovsky also said that the cuts made to the violent scenes actually rendered them more powerful.

The film was defined by a series of negatives by critics and supporters — it was not a historical film, it was not this, not that (L. Anninsky, 191). It was partly the film's avoidance of the usual biographical or historical genre features that made it disappoint audiences, who expected something different. Official Soviet critics debated at length whether *Andrei Roublyov* departed significantly from historical genre and Russian folklore and myth. Tarkovsky was taken to task by Soviet critics for what he had left out, for what he had *not* done. For Lev Anninsky, *Andrei Roublyov* was a typical film of the 1960s in Russia (perhaps *the* film of the Sixties): it looked forward to the films of the Russian soil and village life of the 1970s; it explored the individual's relation to society; it rejected stereotypes; it aimed to mix naturalism with poetry; and it was a 'national film'.[2] The actor who played the Duke twins and the military instructor in *Mirror*, Yuri Nazarov, remarked (on the British DVD of the film) that *Andrei Roublyov* was to Russian cinema what *War and Peace* was to Russian literature.

Marc Ferro compared one of Russia's great historical epics, Sergei Eisenstein's *Alexander Nevsky*, with *Andrei Roublyov*: both are scholarly recreations of the past, but with opposing meanings: in '*Nevsky*, the mortal enemy is the Germans, or Teutons, while in *Roublyov* it's the Chinese, the Tartars. In *Roublyov*, Russia is saved by her sanctity, her Christianity; in *Nevsky*, the hero is deliberately secular-ized'.[3] Ferro compared Tarkovsky's subjective treatment of history with directors such as Luchino Visconti and Hans-Jürgen Syberberg.

For Western film critics, *Andrei Roublyov* was seen (inevitably) as an allegory of

Soviet political repression and how it affects the modern artist (see, for example, Jacques Demeure and Barthélemy Amengual in *Dossier Positif*).[4] For Tarkovsky, *Andrei Roublyov* was about 'the spiritual and moral force of the Russian people', with Roublyov's art being a 'protest against the ruling order of the times, against blood, treachery, oppression'.[5] Western critics, such as Michel Ciment, saw *Andrei Roublyov* as an allegory of Tarkovsky's circumstances as an artist in the Soviet Union (1988, 79). Other Western critics, such as Vincent Canby, found *Andrei Roublyov* ponderous and clichéd (1973); William Paul decried Tarkovsky's 'clumsy 'Scope camera style' (1973). Balint András Kovács and Akos Szilágyi related *Andrei Roublyov* to the Russian icon tradition, Russian history, and to Alexsandr Pushkin and Piotr Yakovlevich Chadayev (1987). For Lev Anninsky, *Andrei Roublyov* was concerned with three major topics: power and history; the human condition; and the divine (1991, 196).

The historical conflicts in *Andrei Roublyov* could be compared to modern political events, such as, most obviously, Russia's involvement in the Second World War (with the invading Tartars as Germans), or the Russian Revolution, or the oppression of Stalinism (which Tarkovsky had alluded to in *Ivan's Childhood*). *Andrei Roublyov* could also be seen as a parable about the birth of a nation, modern Russia.

Very few facts are known about Andrei Roublyov's life. He was born around 1360, and died between 1427 and 1430. His name appeared in historical records beside Feofan the Greek (Theophanes the Greek) and Prokhor of Gorodets, when the Cathedral of the Annunciation was painted in Moscow. Roublyov and Danilo worked on the Cathedral of the Assumption in Vladimir in 1408, which Tarkovsky used as an episode in *Andrei Roublyov*. Roublyov and Danilo also worked on the Church of the Trinity, in 1422, at the Monastery of Troitse Sergiev. Roublyov's painterly style is marked by a tender, 'all-pervading mood of gentleness' (H. Gerhard, 171). Roublyov's *Holy Trinity* icon is one of the few works definitely attributed to the painter (even though it has been painted over three times).

Tarkovsky worked for over two years on the script for *Andrei Roublyov*, with his friend and fellow VGIK student Andrei Konchalovsky (Konchalovsky was a fairly young writer for such a big film – he was 26 in 1963). Tarkovsky acknowledged that it was the actor Vasil Livanov who had proposed making a film based on Andrei Roublyov's life, when he, Tarkovsky and Konchalovsky had been working on *Ivan's Childhood*.

The film treatment of *Roublyov* was passed in December, 1963. Critics dubbed the panoramic script 'The Three Andreis', referring to Tarkovsky, Konchalovsky and Roublyov. The script was published (in the journal *Iskusstvo kino*) before the film came out, when Tarkovsky began work on it (April, 1964): it contained 12 episodes and two prologues, for two parts. The published script contained a prologue to Part One, which contained 9 episodes: *The Buffoon, Theophanes the Greek, The Hunt, Invitation To the Kremlin, The Passion According To Andrei, The Blinding, The Celebration, The Last Judgement* and *The Attack*. There was another prologue, for Part Two: a peasant trying to fly using wings, followed by three episodes: *Indian Summer, Melancholy* and *The Bell*. The finished film had one prologue and 8 parts, with an epilogue in colour.

One of the major scenes to be cut from *Andrei Roublyov* was the Kulikovo Field battle scene, which depicted the Russians victorious over the Tartars. This was an expensive scene, costed at over 200,000 roubles (the Kulikovo battle sequence had to be cut (because of cost) before the Mosfilm authorities would green-light *Andrei Roublyov*). 'The Hunt' was also dropped – the hunting of swans by the Duke's brother. 'Indian Summer' was dropped, in which the fool gives birth to a half-Tartar, half-Russian child. 'The Field of Virgins', the story of Russian women selling their long hair to save Moscow from the Tartars, which interests Roublyov, was left out. Roublyov's memories of his childhood was cut; another vision of a Crucifixion, which Theophanes sees, was dropped (it took place in a desert-like setting, to contrast with Roublyov's vision of a snowy, Russian Cavalry).

However, although various (mainly budgetary) restrictions forced the cuts, Tarkovsky managed to combine elements and scenes. Despite the inevitable compromises on any large-scale undertaking of this kind, Tarkovsky was able to stage some spectacular stuff, including the Tartar raid and battle on Vladimir (which is just jaw-droppingly good), and the eye-opening bell-casting scene, both with thousands of extras, costumes, props, horses, stunts, practical effects, and complex staging. There was also a Crucifixion in the snow and a pagan Midsummer Night festival (St John's Eve) involving many nude extras.

It wasn't as if the restrictions, then, forced Tarkovsky to completely cut out the epic aspects of his project (the budget for *Andrei Roublyov* only ran to 26 horses; the rest (about 90) were borrowed from a hippodrome). Indeed, *Andrei Roublyov* stands as one of the great epic films, alongside *El Cid, Ben-Hur, Kagemusha, Lawrence of Arabia, Spartacus, Quo Vadis,* and *Intolerance*. It has everything one could wish for in a grand epic: spectacle in abundance, extravagant visual style, exotic settings, and serious themes. As a combination of the interiorized (small-scale) art film and the blockbuster historical epic movie, *Andrei Roublyov* is remarkable.

Amazing to think that at the centre of this mediæval epic is no King Arthur, or Alexander the Great, or macho, sword-wielding warrior, but a quiet, introspective painter and monk who's wracked by spiritual and artistic doubt! Almost every historical epic of this type, with a large cast, thousands of extras, multiple locations, expensive location shooting, battle scenes, and so on, has some clearly defined hero, easy to identify with, with easy-to-understand flaws, appetites and goals. Amazing that Tarkovsky was able to produce an epic historical film with such complex psychology and philosophical themes. There are far fewer of the conventional narrative elements of the historical epic in the Hollywood vein in *Andrei Roublyov*: no 'romantic interest', no traditional goals, no family, no villains (the Duke and his henchmen are not conventional villains). (But there is enormous spectacle, costly set-pieces, detailed reconstructions of mediæval times, and so on – the same elements are found in *El Cid, Ivanhoe, The War Lord,* etc).

Tarkovsky said he didn't want the details of a historical film – the costumes, decor, sets, etc, to detract from the drama or the characters or the themes. He didn't want it to be exotic, or decorative or theatrical, like too many historical films, in his opinion (Tarkovsky's models for avoiding exoticism and presenting mediæval life as 'ordinary' were the historical films of Akira Kurosawa). *Andrei Roublyov* wasn't going to be a chronological or logical account of an artist's life, either. It was going to jump about in terms of time and place. It would have the logic of poetry rather than the theatre. Cinema shouldn't simply ape theatre or drama, Tarkovsky maintained: true cinema was a work that could only be made in cinema (D, 67). Tarkovsky consciously avoided showing Roublyov painting icons: he didn't want to make the usual kind of artistic biopic.

It's incredible that this was only Andrei Tarkovsky's second film. It's quite common to put a young director, with a lot to prove, and bundles of energy, someone eager to please, whom the studio can control, at the helm of a big budget film. There are many striking aspects about *Andrei Roublyov*, including: (I) that Tarkovsky created a total masterpiece after only one feature film; (2) that Tarkovsky's powers of filmmaking seem totally accomplished and confident – the image-making, the direction of actors, the staging and blocking of the scenes, the complex camera moves; (3) that a historical epic film of this era could have such a quiet, introspective hero – and an artist, not a war hero!; (4) that the themes of the film could be so unusual, even antithetical to the conventional historical epic (spiritual doubt, artistic integrity, morality and conscience).

While praising Tarkovsky's achievement in *Andrei Roublyov*, one should not forget key collaborators such as DP Vadim Yusov, whose contribution was immense, co-writer Andrei Konchalovsky, art director Yevgeny Chernyaev, editor Lyudmila Feiginova, Vyacheslav Ovchinnikov's music, sound designer E. Zelentsova, wardrobe by L. Novy and M. Abar-Baranovska, and the key players: Anatoly Solonitsyn, Ivan Lapikov, Nikolai Grinko, Nikolai Sergeyev, Irina Tarkovskaya and Kolya Burlyaev.

Andrei Roublyov must count as one of the great horse films, as well as one of the great epics, great historical films, and great mediæval films. Traditionally the preserve of Hollywood, with its countless Westerns and men on horseback, *Andrei Roublyov* is filled with horses, from the opening scenes to the final shot (horses have of course been one of the favourite subjects of painting, from Uccello and Leonardo to Stubbs and Boccioni).[6] Horses were a common sight in the historical films of the 1950s and 60s, in the Roman and Biblical epics, the Italian sword-and-sandal films, historical epics like *Lawrence of Arabia* and *El Cid*, and of course Hollywood cowboy films (since the early days of cinema).

Commenting in 1969 on the horses in the rain image at the close of *Andrei Roublyov* (and on horses in the rest of the film), Tarkovsky said that it was

is a symbolic image as the horse for me is a synonym of life. When I'm looking at a horse I have a feeling I'm in direct contact with the essence of life itself. Perhaps it's because horse is a very beautiful animal, friendly to man, and is moreover so characteristic of the Russian landscape. The presence of horses in the last, final scene means that life itself was the source of all of Rublov's art.

Horses feature throughout *Andrei Roublyov*: the horse rolling onto its back at the beginning; the horses in the rain at the end; the Duke's retainers who arrive on horses to drag off the jester; the riderless horse that trots into the cathedral and startles the fool; the Tartar raid on horseback; the messenger galloping past Roublyov and Daniil on the country road; the Duke's henchmen blinding the stone masons on horseback; the Tartar carrying off the fool on his horse; the Tartars entering the cathedral on horseback; the Duke coming out to inspect the bell on horseback; and the poor horse that falls down the stairs and is killed on screen. As well as horses, there are cats, dogs, birds, snakes, ants, birds and cows in *Andrei*

Roublyov.

Andrei Roublyov can be seen as a late arrival to the period of blockbuster epics of the 1950s and early 1960s (films such as *The Ten Commandments, Ben-Hur, The Fall of the Roman Empire, King of Kings,* and the movie that effectively ended the cycle, *Cleopatra*). One can see from even a few shots of *Andrei Roublyov* that it was produced, conceived, written, staged, shot and edited very much in the manner of the Western historical epics of the 1950s and 1960s.

As well as being a historical epic, *Andrei Roublyov* is one of the great mediæval films, a film with a convincing portrayal of life in the Middle Ages, along with *The Seventh Seal* (1956) and *The Virgin Spring* (1959), the early films of Walerian Borowczyk, Akira Kurosawa's historical epics, and Pier Paolo Pasolini's 'trilogy of life' (*The Decameron* [1970], *Arabian Nights* [1974] and *The Canterbury Tales* [1971]). *Lancelot du Lac* (Robert Bresson, 1974), *The Navigator* (Vincent Ward, 1988) and *Jabberwocky* (Terry Gilliam, 1977) might be added to that list. *Andrei Roublyov* depicts a tough world of famine and plague as well as icons and monks: it is a world away from Hollywood's Robin Hoods, chivalrous knights, sunlit forests, enormous castles, jolly feasts and beautiful princesses.

Filming on *Andrei Roublyov* began in April, 1965, according to Tamara Ogorodnikova, the producer, and Tatyana Vinokurova, head of archives at Mosfilm (though Maya Turovskaya reckoned production started in September, 1964). Shooting ended in November, 1965, due to snow, and continued on location during April-May, 1966. The budget was originally 1.6 million roubles, but was cut down to one million roubles (JP, 80). The return to the location in 1966 raised the budget by 300,000 roubles. *Andrei Roublyov* is one of those films about which legends have grown, as with *Apocalypse Now, Heaven's Gate* or *Cleopatra*, so facts and figures merge into myth-making and hyperbole.

Andrei Roublyov was subject to much scrutiny by the Soviet film authorities, who demanded many cuts, because it was too violent and too long (at 5,642 metres). Tarkovsky said in December, 1966 (in a letter to Goskino's chairman, Alexei Romanov), that he had cut out 390 metres (15 mins) in 37 changes, and that he didn't want to make any more, because they would alter the film profoundly (T. Vinokuroya, 65). The film was seen as too 'naturalistic', especially in its depiction of violence. The authorities also wanted the peasants' appearance to be spruced-up.[7] On December 27, 1966, Tarkovsky agreed to cut out the horse-killing, and make other minor cuts.

Andrei Tarkovsky   *341*

When further cuts were requested after the premiere at Dom Kino in late 1966/ early 1967, Tarkovsky refused to make any more changes. Consequently, the film was shelved for nearly five years, with Mosfilm, Goskino, the critics and Tarkovsky not agreeing on the film. *Andrei Roublyov*'s release was delayed again and again. The Cannes film festival requested the film, but the Soviet authorities refused. An unofficial screening was arranged and *Andrei Roublyov* was given the International Critics' Prize. More cuts in the film were requested (in 1970 and 1971). The film eventually opened on general release in Russia in December, 1971.

Andrei Roublyov looks stupendous, at times extraordinary. Many of the shots are beautiful to look at. *Andrei Roublyov* is shot in widescreen and black-and-white. Widescreen is common, black-and-white is less frequent; the two together are rare, and here they're ravishing. Black-and-white was chosen to create the mediæval world of *Andrei Roublyov*, because colour would have been too pretty. The colour used at the end of *Andrei Roublyov*, when *The Holy Trinity* is seen, was to suggest the way art can transform life, Tarkovsky said. For Anne Lawton, the colour icon ending is a 'true epiphany of mystical splendour' (1992, 129). Of the final section in colour, Tarkovsky said that he 'wanted to bring the viewer to this work through a kind of dramaturgy of colour, asking him to move from certain fragments towards the whole, creating an impressionistic flow'. It was also meant to be a buffer or interlude, between the film and the outside world, so that the viewer could make up their mind about the film. 'I think if *Roublyov* had ended immediately following the 'Bell' episode it would have been an unsuccessful film,' Tarkovsky explained. 'We needed to keep the viewer in the cinema at all cost. It was necessary to add some type of continuation of the artist's life to show how great he was'.

There are many memorable images and sequences in *Andrei Roublyov*: the opening flight sequence, the bell-casting, the fires in the snow, the river sequence, the Crucifixion in the snow, the pagan festival, and the birch wood. The battle, where the Tartars invade Vladimir, is tremendously exciting, violent and visceral, with Tarkovsky moving into spectacle cinema territory more usually associated with David Lean, William Wyler, Sergei Bondarchuk, D.W. Griffith or Cecil B. DeMille (Tarkovsky said he referred to Leonardo da Vinci's *Treatise On Painting* for inspiration on how to stage the battle. That's typical of Tarkovsky: while other filmmakers might refer to earlier films – a John Ford movie, say – Tarkovsky goes to Leonardo da Vinci!).

Tarkovsky demonstrated that he can handle a large-scale film, complex set-ups, practical fx, stunts, and sequences that involve hundreds of extras – like *Ben-Hur* (William Wyler, 1959) or *El Cid* (Anthony Mann, 1961). (Big scenes like this aren't directors' scenes so much as reliant on efficient first, second and third assistant directors, production managers, location managers and great second unit teams). The battle scene involves masses of people, and when the bell is raised up and blessed and finally rings, there are what seems like thousands of people in the vicinity. Tarkovsky creates epic cinema here. Tarkovsky has the confidence to cover many of the big scenes with complex master shots and long takes, very demanding for the crew and the actors, who have to hit marks and rehearse moves, time after time.

The pagan festival, for instance, must have been difficult to shoot: it was shot mainly in the magic hour for a start, which would mean coming back day after day for the light (as well as being a difficult scene to light), there were boats, and water, and people swimming, and stunts, and stacks of practical effects (fires, smoke, torches), and many extras were half or fully naked (and they had to run over rough ground).

Much of *Andrei Roublyov* is shot with long lenses, often with a person's head in M.C.U. against activity behind, as in the bell-casting sequence, with the bell-caster Boriska against the smoke, or often shot through the legs of people and horses (as in the Crucifixion in the snow). Many of the shots in *Andrei Roublyov* last more than two minutes, giving the film an elegant, slow, processional pace, even in the scenes of violence. Some scenes are staged as *tableaux*, with the figures arranged within the frame like paintings (and the long lenses squash the planes of focus together, bringing the background and middle ground to the front). But these are not static *tableaux*, because Tarkovsky's camera is always moving.

As Sven Nykvist pointed out, although the compositions in *Andrei Roublyov* often place a figure in the centre of the frame, they are not mundane. In a number of two-shots, such as when Roublyov and Theophanes or Roublyov and Daniil are talking, Tarkovsky frames one closer to the camera than the other, sometimes they're facing away from each other; the blocking of actors within the widescreen frame is dynamic, always interesting. In the log hut in Part One, Tarkovsky uses a favourite New Wave device: the 360° pan, to show the other people sheltering from the storm, and to show time passing.

The influence of Akira Kurosawa, in films such as *Throne of Blood*, *The Seven Samurai* and *The Hidden Fortress*, and the film many directors have cited as an influence, *Rashomon*, can be seen on *Andrei Roublyov*: in the high contrast widescreen cinematography; the warriors on horseback; the mud and water; the rain; the graphic violence; the drifting clouds of mist and fog; and the minimal interiors. The general harsh muddy, rainy, snowy, misty mediæval look of *Andrei Roublyov* is familiar from the films of Kurosawa and Bergman (*The Virgin Spring, Throne of Blood, Rashomon* and *The Seventh Seal*, for example). Sven Nykvist said that *Andrei Roublyov* 'was a true revelation to me when I saw it for the first time. Pure image magic!' Tarkovsky said they were aiming not for ethnographic, archæological or historical accuracy so much as a 'physiological truth', a poetic truth which would hopefully ring true for a modern cinema audience (ST, 78).

Tarkovsky said he loved *The Seven Samurai* and *Sanjuro*, and reckoned that Kurosawa had achieved more in the historical film genre than anyone else. But Tarkovsky found the concept of *Throne of Blood* lacking, because it took the story of *Macbeth* and applied it to Japanese history, and missed the profound nature of the tragedy.

Of Kurosawa's historical films, Tarkovsky said:

one perceives his Middle Ages without any exoticism. He is such a profound artist, he shows such psychological connections, such a development of characters and plot-lines, such a vision of the world, that his narrative about the Middle Ages constantly makes you think about today's world.

There are eight parts to *Andrei Roublyov*, with a prologue and an epilogue (in colour). The main locations are the Andronik Spasa Nerukotvornogo monastery, Vladimir, founded in around 1360., and the environs of Moscow (the film was shot at the real Andronnikov monastery in Moscow, by the Yaouza River, which now houses the Andrei Roublyov Museum, as well as the Monastery of the Trinity St Sergius in Zagorsk, among other locations).

The film opens with a balloonist rushing up to a church which is surrounded by lakes and a river. A group of peasants are chasing the balloonist; his accomplices are hurriedly preparing the animal skin balloon, filling it with hot air from a bonfire; a fight ensues in which the balloonist's helpers are set upon (one of the peasants yells 'burn them alive!'). A complex tracking shot follows the balloonist around the walls of the church, and through it to the other side.

The approaching crowd is always shot from near the church, not the reverse angle: the viewpoint in this scene is thus always with the balloonist and his helpers (i.e., with the individual dreamer against the mass, the one who imagines flight and the mob who want to destroy his dreams. It's a mini parable about the fate of the artist, if you like, doomed to be misunderstood, to go against the grain, to be an outsider and dissident. Or it's a wonderful sequence which introduces the world of the film in a highly unusual fashion).

The balloonist dashes up to the church towers, and launches himself out into space. Tarkovsky used a big crane to shoot a vertiginous bird's-eye-view, of what the balloonist sees as he looks down, the camera moving away from the church, then swinging back, closer to a row of stone carved heads. There are rapid zooms towards the balloonist too (not from ground level, but from beside the man suspended underneath the inflatible). After a series of helicopter shots (deliberately cantered off the horizontal) of the landscape from the air (people in boats, lakes, trees, animals), the balloonist crashes beside a lake or river. The film freeze-frames at this point, then cuts to a shot of a horse rolling over onto its back in slow motion (the balloonist is seen in M.S. lying next to his contraption, apparently dead; the camera trucks closer to the balloon, the air seeping out into the water).

The horse shot is a Tarkovsky speciality: it does not follow on from the previous action, nor connect with the next episode; there is no one in the frame; it is not any character's point-of-view; its function is a bridge or link between two sections of the film, the prologue and the first episode, but it is a deliberately ambiguous image. It can be interpreted every which way.

The slo-mo horse image also announces to the audience early on that this isn't going to be your usual historical epic film. It tells the audience that *Andrei Roublyov* is going to have poetic moments which aren't necessarily part of the narrative, which may act as interludes or linking images. Filmmakers often put some of the stylistic devices they'll be employing later on in the film early on in the narrative, to allow viewers to get used to them. The horse itself is thus not going to 'pay off' later on, like a shot of the villain hiding a gun under the money in a briefcase in a con-temporary thriller. It's not a plant or piece of foreshadowing, but it does announce early on the direction that the film will take from time to time.

The prologue vividly describes the characteristics of the world of Andrei Roublyov: the mediæval *mise-en-scène*, the earthy, water-logged landscape, the large scope of the film, the elements of magic combining with religion (the magical flight departing from the church), the dreamer and the mob (and how his helpers can be targets for violence too), and the limits of ecstasy and fear (emotions displayed by the balloonist; he cries 'I'm flying!'). (Originally, Roublyov was going to be included in the prologue, helping and burying the peasant flyer).

Tarkovsky, in *Andrei Roublyov*, revels in the creation of a rainy, dirty, muddy, snowy, violent, cruel and sometimes bizarre post-mediæval world. *Andrei Roublyov*, wrote Amos Vogel:

> reeks with the evil odour of the Middle Ages, an era of brutality, human degradation, abject poverty, rape, senseless mass slaughter, mud and pagan orgies, when people were at the mercy of both temporal and 'spiritual' powers. (1974, 150)

The first part of *Andrei Roublyov* ("The Buffoon" or "The Jester") is set in Summer, 1400, and concerns the 'clown' or 'holy fool'. The 'holy fool' figure, which appears in many of Tarkovsky's films, is a familiar aspect of Russian religious culture, going back centuries. The *yurodivy* or 'holy fool' was a gifted individual, tolerated by the authorities to be eccentric and critical about injustice and evil. Like shamans or magicians, the *yurodivye* possessed insights and prophecies about things ordinary people could not apprehend. The *yurodivy* was a loner, an anarchist who broke rules (D. Shostakovitch, xxi). In Tarkovsky's cinema, the *yurodivy* personality is easily discernible in figures such as Domenico in *Nostalghia*, Otto in *The Sacrifice*, and of course the Stalker. Historical recreations of the holy fool are key elements of *Andrei Roublyov*.

Roublyov and his two companion painter-monks are shown arriving at a village. They walk through a rainstorm, and shelter in a log cabin, where the jester is performing a bawdy song about adultery. As the monks (Kirill, Daniil and Roublyov) walk through the landscape, one of them mentions that he has never noticed a particular tree before. The walking monks are covered with lengthy tracking shots through the landscape. Thunder is heard towards the end of the walking sequence, with rain blurring the screen. At this point, very little is offered about these three characters: a messenger approaches them from a distance and asks them to return: all the viewer gleans is that these people are leaving somewhere to go somewhere else, that they have been working together for years, but there are no close-ups of the characters, and not much attempt at differentiating them. Although Roublyov is one of the three characters, he is not really introduced as the main character of the film until the second episode. Throughout the first episode, in the hut with the holy fool, he's just one of the three monk-painters.

In the wooden hut, the holy fool cavorts madly, dancing, doing handstands and tumbles, while the audience laughs (covered in a lengthy take, the camera follows the actor's movements around the hut, with the audience ranged around the walls in various states of enjoyment or passivity). The jester's song is a bawdy tale with beards, shaving, cheeks and buttocks: when the clown walks on his hands, his clothes fall, revealing a face painted on his rear. The monks sit along one wall, staring impassively and hardly reacting to the energetic song and dance of the holy fool. There is a pan around the room, from the centre, showing the jester, children, other onlookers, and the monks, Daniil now asleep. There is a squabble between two peasants outside the hut; they slip in mud; one of them is fairly drunk, and staggers about with a log, as if to strike his opponent. Their brawl is curtailed by the arrival of four horsemen, the Duke's men. After a struggle, the jester is taken away the Duke's retainers. He is thrown against a tree by two of the horsemen and knocked unconscious. He is lugged on a horse, and his lute is smashed. (The last part of the scene is covered in a single long take by Tarkovsky from inside the hut, the view-point again with the audience inside, and the monks; the doorway, the horse, the tree and the lute are all lined up for the single shot).

The end of part one of *Andrei Roublyov* is a soft, painterly shot, filmed with a long lens: Roublyov and his retinue walk from left to right beside the water and some trees. Out of focus, on the other side of the lake, the Duke's horsemen are seen. It is one of those near-silent, beautifully composed shots that makes Tarkovsky such a celebrated director. It is not a shot that furthers the plot or action particularly; in its static beauty it is more like a painting, in which narrative detail occurs in the background as well as the foreground (it brings to mind Renaissance painters such as Paolo Uccello); but it is the epitome of Tarkovsky's cinema.

Part one, "The Jester", serves to show the earthy environment Roublyov and the monks inhabit – lust (in the fool's song), the poverty, performance (an artist, his art and his audience), the cross-section of society (children, the middle-aged and the old in the same space), the oppression and violence of the regime (of the Duke's men), and the harsh surroundings (the hut and the rain).

Part two (set in 1405) is entitled "Theophanes the Greek": Kirill is shown visiting Theophanes in a violent city – people are being tortured on wooden wheels. The scene is a long (6 or 7 minute) two-hander dialogue scene between Theophanes and Kirill. Theophanes the painter is first seen lying on his back on a bench, as if a corpse (he encourages Kirill to come and gape). Kirill, who works with Roublyov, praises Theophanes' paintings above Roublyov's work. Theophanes complains about his working conditions, his assistants going AWOL (to watch the executions).

Theophanes (after hearing Kirill praise his paintings) invites Kirill to paint the Annunciation Church in Moscow. At first Kirill refuses; he agrees on the condition that Theophanes comes to the Andronnikov monastery to ask him in front of Roublyov and the monks. When shouts are heard from outside, Theophanes rushes to the door: a man covered in blood is seen being put on the torturer's wheel. Theophanes wonders if the violence will ever end. Inside, Kirill contemplates Theophanes' icon of Christ (only at the end of the scene does Tarkovsky include a C.U. of the painting that Kirill has been discussing in the scene).

Throughout the scene Tarkovsky employs lengthy takes with the actors moving slowly in a variety of two shots, Kirill now on one side of the frame, the camera slowly panning to Theophanes. It's a technique that Tarkovsky will employ throughout the rest of the film. These early scenes serve to introduce some of the main characters, such as Theophanes, Kirill, Daniil, and Roublyov (and their relation to each other – how the other painters look up to Theophanes, for example). However, Roublyov is still known mainly as one of the group of painter-monks, not as a lead character.

The action moves to the Andronnikov monastery. Kirill is shown in his room with icons stacked against the wall; passages of *Ecclesiastes* (XII) are read out in voiceover ('vanity of vanities, all is vanity'), perhaps an interior monologue. When an assistant enters the dark room, Kirill berates him (a shorthand method of portraying Kirill's dissatisfaction with life in general, but with the life of a painter in particular and the commissions from the Duke). The action moves outside, into the snowbound courtyard of the monastery, where a few scenes will be set (an enormous pile of wooden logs fills one side of the yard). The Duke's messenger arrives on horseback to invite Roublyov and the monks gathered there to Moscow (the level of detail in *Andrei Roublyov* is always impressive. In this short scene, for instance, even the messenger is given a characterization and bits of actorly business to perform. He's not just a stock character, but hints at a life of his own).

But the scene with the Duke's messenger is of course a classic narrative device to set the main dramatic thread in motion (which's the life of Andrei Roublyov). It is *here* that Roublyov makes his first big impression: the first elements of his characterization are introduced (not least the rivalry between the painter-monks: note how the messenger addresses Roublyov not, as Kirill hoped, himself).

There is an emotional, tearful scene between Daniil and Roublyov, in Daniil's rooms. Roublyov visits Daniil and confesses his reliance on him; the painters are reconciled. It's a small, intimate scene, culminating with Roublyov kissing Daniil's hand. Outdoors, in the snow in the courtyard, probably the next day, Kirill leaves the monastery. He complains loudly to the assembled monks about money corrupting their lives. He quotes from the *Bible* (including Jesus and the moneychangers). As Kirill leaves the monastery, alone, trudging off into the deep snow, he shouts at the monks and, exasperated, violently beats a dog with a stick (possibly killing it; this is the first of a few scenes of excessive cruelty to animals in *Andrei Roublyov*. Dramatically, it functions to express Kirill's frustration). The end of the episode, like some of the others, fades to black.

By now, the film has established a vivid, confident *mise-en-scène* of deep snow, flat plains, lakes, rivers, slender trees, dogs, and wooden buildings. Although many scenes are set in Summer, or Spring, I always think of *Andrei Roublyov* as a very Wintry, snowy film (in its way, it's a more suitable movie for Mid-Winter viewing than *It's a Wonderful Life*, *The Wizard of Ox* or *White Christmas*). And in *Andrei Roublyov* the settings and *mise-en-scène* are vital; the film draws so much of its impact from its skilful evocation of place and period.[8]

Part three is titled "The Passion According to Andrei": it's 1406; Roublyov and his assistant Foma are seen walking through a forest by day; Roublyov complains about Foma's lies and dishevelled life. There are shots of nature: a stream, a water-snake, mud, trees, and roots. This introduces the theme of Roublyov's (and Tarkovsky's) deep identification with the natural world, a *participation mystique* as significant as the relation with God. (But the viewer has already seen many beautiful images of the natural world in the film. The extraordinary thing is that although *Andrei Roublyov* is usually considered a film about religion, art, politics and history, and the individual's (the artist's) role in relation to those issues, it is also a film about nature.)

The scene closes with a still-life: a dead swan which Foma prods with a stick. (This is a relic perhaps of the cut scene of the Duke's brother hunting swans). The dead swan may also relate to Dutch still-life paintings, which were also called *Vanitas* or *Memento Mori* paintings, *vanitas* being a reference to *Ecclesiastes* (I: 2), a favourite passage from the *Bible* of Tarkovsky's.

As with most of *Andrei Roublyov*, slow tracking shots run throughout the Roublyov and Foma scene. On *Andrei Roublyov*, the camera team must have laid thousands of feet of tracks and wooden boards (over snow, mud, grass, stones). Ingmar Bergman talks about Tarkovsky's camera flying all over the place, and in

Andrei Roublyov it certainly does. But there's no sense that the camera is being moved just for the sake of it, partly because Tarkovsky blocks his actors in interesting patterns and movements. In many contemporary Hollywood movies, for instance, the camera flies all over the place because a looma or remote crane has been hired for the day (and filmmakers love their toys, and can't resist using them), but the action itself might be fairly static. In *Andrei Roublyov* and other Tarkovsky films, Tarkovsky moves the camera and the actors, so that the staging is dynamic. In the dialogue scene between Roublyov and Theophanes, for instance (the next scene), the camera is drifting or panning, continually reframing the actors. Sometimes they stand facing each other, or at right angles, or facing away from each other, while the camera keeps them in two shots.

Later, Roublyov discusses theology with Theophanes in a sunlight landscape beside a river (accompanied by Foma, who washes Roublyov's brushes in the water). Roublyov talks about human failings, while Theophanes concentrates on the Christian cycle. If Jesus returned to earth, Theophanes says, people would crucify Him again (a point that's been made many times over the centuries).

Tarkovsky intercuts this scene with the superb Crucifixion in the snow. As Roublyov and Theophanes speak, their voices are heard over the Crucifixion sequence. The film cuts to a medium close-up of Jesus drinking water from a river; it's as if he's next to the same river as the painter-monks (but in the snow. Later, he eats some snow — I think that's the first time I've seen Jesus eat snow in a film).

There is no local sound from the Cavalry, no sound of the people weeping, the nails being driven into the Cross, the horses, and so on. The music comprises solemn drum beats and a choir. Christ is shown dragging his Cross up a slope with his followers in attendance. There is a Virgin Mary, a Joseph of Arithemea supporting her, a Mary Magdalene figure and other followers in this scene. Tarkovsky concentrates on these very famous figures, cutting back to them from Christ. Mary Magdalene clasps Christ's legs, weeping, in M.C.U.; the camera follows her as she slumps to the snow, kissing Christ's feet. The camera stays low for the next beat, following Christ's feet in medium close-up as he walks through the snow towards the wooden Cross. He lies back upon it and is bound to it (the Magdalene embracing his feet again). Christ is pulled upright on the Cross with ropes in a very long shot.

During the 'Russian Calvary', Roublyov ponders in voiceover on the suffering of the Russian people under Tartar rule; he wonders if Christ's life was to make a peace between God and humanity. The 'Russian Passion' (it's also 'The Passion

According To Andrei Roublyov') illustrates many moments from the *Gospels* and their depiction in Renaissance painting which Tarkovsky was very familiar with: the Magdalene embracing Christ's feet (Sandro Botticelli), Christ carrying the Cross (Early Netherlandish painters such as Hieronymous Bosch), Christ being nailed to the cross on the ground, the cross being pulled upright, and so on.

The wide shots of Christ and the retinue walking through the snow were composed exactly like a Pieter Brueghel landscape, with figures dotted around the landscape (Tarkovsky would return to this seminal image a no. of times). The cuts from Christ on the Cross to the Virgin Mary recalled Pasolini's *The Gospel According to Matthew*.

One can see the Crucifixion scene as an integral part of the religious themes of *Andrei Roublyov;* but it is also Tarkovsky's chance to mount his own, Russian, snowbound version of the Passion. it's his opportunity to mount a scene which had been portrayed many times in films of the 1950s and 1960s. So the Crucifixion in *Andrei Roublyov* can be regarded as part of the ancient world movie genre. And notice how Tarkovsky employs some of the same techniques as historical epics like *The Robe* or *Ben-Hur* which include Christ, but shoot him from behind or from a distance, or just his hands. Tarkovsky also hides Jesus, concentrating on his legs, for instance (but he does allow two or three medium close-ups).

It is a distinctly *Russian* Crucifixion, with Jesus clad in a Russian peasant's clothes. The setting and the costumes make the Crucifixion a scene seen from Andrei Roublyov's point-of-view: it's not, for instance, dressed and set in the ancient Middle East: it's the same environment that Roublyov and Theophanes inhabit.

At the end of the Crucifixion in the snow, the film cuts back to Roublyov and Theophanes on the riverbank. Part two ends with a shot of Foma cleaning Roublyov's paintbrushes in the river: the shot pans left, away from Foma, over the water. This is a familiar Tarkovskyan motif: shots of water ends parts one, two and three (the "Passion According to Andrei" begins and ends with a shot of a stream).

The pagan festival occurs in part four, "The Celebration" (set in 1408). Roublyov is going to the cathedral in Vladimir by boat, with Foma and his accomplices. Grad-ually the presence of revellers at a Midsummer Night's festival becomes apparent — there are flickering lights, torches being carried about, many bonfires, birds singing, birds fluttering about, distant voices, and figures in the distance flitting around. The naked pagans are filmed as mysterious, ambiguous figures, with long lens shots through the trees. A milky, smoky darkness pervades the scenes, with reality becoming indistinct. The pagan festival is a series of ghostly, luminous shots, brilliantly staged, with full use of the widescreen ratio; the dreaminess is enhanced by Viacheslav Ovchinnikov's rhythmic music and the choir singing, which runs throughout the scene (Julian Graffy (1997) reckoned that Ovchinnikov's music was 'crassly illustrative', and 'seriously damaged' *Ivan*, *Roublyov* and *Steamroller*).

Roublyov leaves his companions, to run after the pagans. In the trees, Roublyov meets a nude woman (Marfa); he stares at her; she is pulled down by a man (off-screen), into the bushes. Tarkovsky makes Roublyov's sexual desire obvious by having his robe catching fire by his feet as he looks at the pagan couple, who're heard, not seen, making love. Roublyov puts out the flames. He moves to a wooden hut and spies on a woman, nude under a sheepskin coat, who is climbing up a ladder and jumping over a bonfire repeatedly (a pagan ritual for purification). For Fran-çoise Navailh, the naked women in films like *Andrei Roublyov* and *The Kinder-garten* (Eugeni Yvetushenko, 1983) – rare in Soviet cinema but not so rare in Tark-ovsky's films – 'express the de-eroticization of woman, rather than sensuality, assim-ilating woman to the Earth/ nature rather to pleasure'.[9]

Roublyov's scopophilia is interrupted when he is captured by some men; they drag him into the hut and tie him to a post, mocking him with references to the Crucifixion – Roublyov is bound with arms raised, like Christ. Roublyov tells them that, for his sins of being with the pagans, he should be crucified upside-down. After the men leave, the semi-nude woman approaches him. Roublyov tells her that the pagans' form of love is sinful and praises brotherly love. The woman replies that all love is one.

The themes of ascetic Christianity fighting sin and sexuality reach their height when the woman takes off the coat and, now nude, kisses the bound monk on the mouth. Then she unties Roublyov and he leaves. A series of atmospheric, misty shots follows, of the pagans waist-deep and naked in the river, holding torches (they were seen earlier, running into the water, in a high angle wide shot). A little boat, with an effigy in it, floats between the rows of worshippers in the river.

Roublyov is next shown running in the forest, scratched and unkempt. There is a cut to a medium close-up of the pagan woman, smiling to herself. The implication is that they have had sex (although it's not made clear what happens to Roublyov on this night).

The next scene is the riverbank, in the morning, with Roublyov sheepishly rejoining his companions, who watch him as he walks to them. Roublyov avoids

Foma's questions about what he has been doing. The group leaves the riverbank in two boats. A scuffle and shouts on the bank draw their attention; two people are shown trying to escape from the Duke's retainers. Tarkovsky cuts between the riverbank fight and Roublyov and his followers as they mutely watch. The man escapes into the river but doesn't get very far, being accosted by the Duke's men. The pagan woman manages to escape, and runs, nude, into the river. Roublyov tells Seryozha, his youngest apprentice, not to watch; one of his group covers the apprentice's eyes. Roublyov and the woman are placed close together visually as she swims past the back of his boat; the episode ends with the camera tilting up to show her swimming far across the river in wide shot.

Part five, "The Last Judgement", which takes place in 1408, concerns the painting of the cathedral in Vladimir for the Grand Duke. Roublyov is shown struggling with his work in the cathedral. In the first scenes, Roublyov is absent from the cathedral: his assistants wait for him to begin his work on the bright, white interior walls. In a flat landscape, on a track, Roublyov tells Daniil why he can't take up the Vladimir commission. A horseman, the bishop's messenger, is shown galloping past the two monks (the horseman, seen in the far distance and approaching along the road, recalls the famous entrance of Omar Sharif in *Lawrence of Arabia*).

The cathedral walls are impossibly white inside, as if taunting Roublyov to make a single mark on them, to convert their virginal whiteness into religious painting. It's the writer and the blank piece of paper, the painter and the blank canvas primed and ready. The whiteness links to the state of the town of Vladimir prior to the Tartar invasion – it will never look this white again after the Tartars have defiled it. (Tarkovsky emphasizes the links too with childhood as a pure state by having milk splashing and feathers or seeds floating, as if the white interior is an equivalence of childhood purity and innocence. (I always thought the images of seeds drifting slowly on the breeze was something that Tarkovsky knew looked good but which never really happened in real life, until I saw floating dandelion seeds back-lit against the sun in a train station in Kent). The white walls also link to the fool's virginal or pure spiritual state (note how Roublyov throwing paint and spoiling the white walls disturbs her).)

The narrative moves to the cathedral, where Foma declares he is leaving Roublyov's group. He packs his bag and departs. There is a short scene of the Duke in his white palace. Roublyov is shown with the Duke's daughter, who has thrown milk at him. The stonemasons travel to another job, for the Duke's brother, who is the Duke's rival. During the scenes with the Duke, Roublyov is seen painting on an icon in the background.

The stonemasons become the victim of the Duke's hate, as they are blinded by the Duke's men, led by his steward Stepan, in a forest. As with other violent episodes in *Andrei Roublyov* (which is Tarkovsky's most violent film by a long way), it takes place in a bright, sunlit space, the pastoral lyricism of the forest setting contrasting harshly with the brutality of the action. A crane shot establishes the stonemasons walking through a birch forest, with Stepan on his horse waiting for them. The Duke's men ride into shot. As in *King Lear*, the blinding occurs right in front of the audience, as the Duke's steward grabs one of the masons with his legs and arms, leaning down to blind him with a knife. Pandemonium follows, as the horsemen hunt down and wound the other stonemasons. Tarkovsky shoots the violence in a series of long lens images, contrasting foreground and middle ground planes of action. The scene ends with a tracking shot which concentrates on a survivor, Seryozha, as the horsemen ride away. There is a brief cutaway to one of the masons with bloody eye sockets.

The final shot is a typical Tarkovskyan motif: a close-up of what seems to be milk leaking out of a flask into a stream. The image of the white liquid spreading into the water is a tranquil coda to the visions of needless brutality. (It's a refrain motif that occurs later on, right after the death of Foma; and Foma was seen earlier washing paintbrushes in water).

The narrative alters abruptly with a shock cut to paint being thrown at a wall, a gesture embodying Roublyov's creative and spiritual frustration with his painting (it's a rare kind of smash cut in Tarkovsky's cinema). Roublyov smears the pigment and sobs; Seryozha is told to recite from the *Bible* by Daniil. The quotation (from St Paul) deals with male-female relations. St Paul says that women going into churches should cover their heads. Roublyov's artistic dissatisfaction is linked directly to the holy fool, when she enters the cathedral (with her head uncovered) and inquisitively touches the paint thrown at the white wall. When the fool smells her fingers, she too sobs (the reason for the fool's distressed reaction to the paint on the wall is not explained). But for Roublyov, the sight and behaviour of the fool throws his own desperation into perspective. Now buoyant, he goes out into the rain (a white sheet of over-exposed light beyond the door). The fool, after a pause, follows him (with the sound of the rain mixed high, the camera tracks gently away from the painter's assistants arranged in a *tableau* in the cathedral).

An idea that didn't make it into the final film was that the pagan woman would have had a child in the course of the story (though not by Roublyov). After it, she would have recovered herself, regaining her normality. (The pagan woman does disappear, inexplicably, before rejoining the narrative. It is not uncommon for characters to do that in a Tarkovsky film; and he wouldn't bother to explain why). (In the script of *Andrei Roublyov*, the pagan woman is called the *durochka* ('little fool'), and sometimes *blazhennaya* ('blessed'). Some critics have linked her to the Russian concept of the 'holy fool'.)

This is the end of Roublyov's lengthy creative lassitude, and the scenes in which Roublyov and his followers sit about listlessly. But, crucially, Tarkovsky elides the act of Roublyov and his followers painting the cathedral: instead, the camera reveals the new paintings as it pans and tracks while following the Tartars entering the church. The paintings are pushed into the background of the action, then, as if they just happen to be there when the enemy rides into the building on horseback. But the paintings, too, are what this film are all about: and the Tartar leader Khan and the Duke's brother discuss them (Khan wonders who the woman is – it's the Virgin Mary the Duke's brother replies. – Who's the boy in the box? – Jesus. When the Duke's brother tells Khan she was a virgin, Khan laughs and retorts that she couldn't have been a virgin if she had a child). The paintings are discussed again in the scene between Roublyov and Theophanes (again, it is not Roublyov who draws attention to the paintings, but Theophanes. Very often, in this film about the life of a painter, it's not the painter himself who discusses his paintings or other paintings).

The Tartar attack on Vladimir occurs in part six, "The Raid" (1408). It is the most violent and action-packed sequence in Tarkovsky's work. The cinematic presence who most influences this part of the film is the *sensei*, Akira Kurosawa (more than Sergei Eisenstein, for instance). It's also a huge challenge for Tarkovsky as a relatively youngish director: he's got the budget, he's got the extras, he's got horses and horse riders, he's got the locations and sets, he's got stunt people, he's got all of the machinery and tools of filmmaking at his disposal: can he come up with some thrilling cinema? Yes, he can.

The opening shot of "The Raid" is a long shot of the Russian camp from the other side of a river. It is held a long time (one minute forty seconds), the camera tracking and craning slowly as the Tartars approach in the foreground. This serves to introduce the Tartars and their leader, Khan (Bolot Ishalenev). Tarkovsky has Khan grin for much of the Vladimir raid sequence, as if all of the carnage is just a game for him. Indeed, like the Duke's brother, Khan seems nonplused and unaffected by the chaos and death occurring all around him. When it's all over, for instance, Khan calmly discusses the paintings in the cathedral — while Roublyov is shell-shocked, trembling in fear, hardly able to believe what's just happened.

The build-up to the raid has many shots of the Tartars on horseback riding through the countryside (pure Kurosawa); the wide shots emphasize the thundering hooves, the dust kicked up by the horses, the speed of the galloping horsemen and their enjoyment of the chase. These images are partly in there for production value (lots of horses, and extras in costume), and to intensify the visceral action of the sequence (the horses' hooves are mixed high on the track). They also serve to evoke the impressive war machine of the invading force, and build them up as powerful foes (the music cue for this scene is a low drone, with drums).

Before the entry into the undefended city occurs, though, Tarkovsky inserts a character-building flashback, concerning the rivalry of the Duke and his brother: they are seen in a candlelit church, making peace with each other. The flashback scene is revisited twice more during the Vladimir raid sequence (with a choral cue on the soundtrack).

Tarkovsky used a series of lengthy and complex sequence shots to portray the attack, some of them very elaborate, the camera constantly on the move, framing and reframing, tilting, panning, tracking and craning. The lengthy takes cover many rehearsed fights, beats, gestures and stunts. Some of the shots follow Tartars on horseback hunting down and killing the townspeople, including Foma. Another of Roublyov's apprentices is cut down by a horseman as he escapes on foot and he dies next to a woodsaw (which wobbles up and down, making a warbling sound, ridiculous amongst the carnage). An old woman pursues a cow which's on fire and trapped, running around with its back on fire, until she's killed with a spear hurled by a Tartar soldier. (The cow was protected by asbestos, Tarkovsky said. Maybe, but you wouldn't want to be that cow in that shot). (Cattle on fire occurred in 1996's *Mars Attacks!*, though they were computer generated; actually the cow on fire image preceded *Andrei Roublyov*: it appeared in the *Mars Attacks* cards of the early 1960s that the Tim Burton film was based on).

On the battlements (or a wooden walkway on a wall), in a lengthy, complex tracking shot, a woman struggles to escape from Tartar soldiers. She's dragged along the ground by her hair, until the camera pans to the right, past her, and her screams are heard off-screen. The camera continues to pan right to the cathedral front and the Duke's brother and the Tartars on horseback. The repetitive thud of a battering ram hitting the doors of the cathedral runs through the following shots, of the horsemen gathering around the cathedral.

Here Tarkovsky utilizes a brutal (even crude) symbolic equivalence between the body of the woman being raped (off-screen) and the cathedral building being attacked by the battering ram (the equivalences are between the woman's body and the body of the cathedral, of the Church itself, the Church and Christianity as Mother, as protector of its flock of children or worshippers). In this instance, the Church (religion) cannot protect its flock from the enemy, and the Tartar soldiers enter the church (on horseback – an added defilement) as they rape and enter the body of the woman (another cruel equivalence is made between the battering ram and the phallic invasion of the woman – the Tartar soldiers are invasive on many levels, not just the social or political but also physical, sexual and spiritual. Not only are the people of Vladimir killed or maimed, the cathedral is wrecked, the women are raped, and Roublyov's art is damaged).

The scenes of violence culminate when a riderless horse falls quite far down some steps, onto its back. The animal was killed with a spear in the first version of the film, which Tarkovsky cut (in some versions it's retained, occurring at the end of the sequence with the horse. Tarkovsky said that the horse had been taken from the slaughter-house, so it would have died soon anyway).

There is some deeply traumatic imagery in this section of *Andrei Roublyov*: a cow on fire, a horse speared to death, torture, and much slaughter, by sword, spear, axe and arrow. It's striking just how visceral and violent this part of *Andrei Roublyov* actually is, how many murders Tarkovsky portrays, and how graphic the violence is. It's far from the received view of Tarkovsky as a maker of slow, spiritual, introspective films. Here, he's as aggressive and muscular as other action and epic directors of the time, such as Sam Peckinpah, Anthony Mann, David Lean or Richard Fleischer.

The violence in *Andrei Roublyov* can be justified on a number of narrative levels, to do with the tough world of the mediæval era, the oppression of the political system (represented by the Duke and his men), and so on. But it's also in *Andrei Roublyov* because it's a spectacular movie, and Tarkovsky is no different from countless other filmmakers who relish portraying violent acts on screen (filmmakers have always denounced violence even as they throw themselves into depicting it).

Some of the stunts and action sequences in *Andrei Roublyov* might appear a little mild compared to the more outrageous stuntwork of a contemporary Hollywood or Hong Kong action movie, but they also have a pathos rare in such big, noisy expensive scenes. That's real fire the actors and stunt people are narrowly avoiding; that's really a cow on fire, not CGI; that's a horse really being speared to death right in front of the camera.

Tarkovsky shows the townspeople cowering on the floor of the cathedral, and the Tartars outside assaulting the doors with a battering ram. Roublyov is seen with the fool, pulling her down beside him – only now, quite late in the Tartar invasion sequence, is Roublyov introduced (a more typical editorial approach would involve cross-cutting between the people inside the church, and to Roublyov in particular, and the carnage outside).

The Tartar soldiers ride their horses into the cathedral and loot it. As they enter the church, Tarkovsky shoots the Tartars from a low angle, so that Roublyov's completed paintings can be seen above and behind the horsemen, their quiet serenity contrasting vividly with the invading soldiers – the sacred penetrated by the secular, politics overcoming religion.

During the chaos in the cathedral, a Tartar soldier hauls the fool from Roublyov, presumably to rape her. Roublyov pursues them up some wooden stairs at the side of the cathedral. He kills the soldier (off-screen) with an axe (the soldier tumbles down the steps). Instead of Roublyov or the fool or the monks, it is the sacristan who is tortured by the Tartars. It is a lengthy and gruesome and very ugly sequence: he is bound to a stake, is manhandled around, has fire pushed at his face, is bandaged up, then has a hot liquid poured into his mouth (this horrific moment is shielded from the viewer by one of the soldiers). Finally, the sacristan is dragged by a horseman by his feet along the ground, out of the cathedral, presumably to his death.

Dramatically, the long torture scene functions to evoke the cruelty of the world that Roublyov and his followers inhabit (it's a common dramatic device in films and plays to use a secondary character to portray an aspect of the narrative. The sacristan is not particularly important as a character in the rest of the film; he's introduced partly so that he can be the subject of the torture, as with the jester in the opening scene.)

Wide and high angle shots follow of the battle, with the townspeople fleeing in slow motion, and birds flying across the frame (these very high crane shots echo the ones in the prologue, of the balloonist). Tarkovsky cuts back to the Duke's brother's face repeatedly (so that the aftermath of the raid is seen from his point-of-view), sometimes implying that the brother reacts impassively to the devastation, at other times the brother appears to be in two minds about the raid, and would prefer to be elsewhere. Roublyov is shown inside the cathedral, trembling in a shell-shocked state. Tarkovsky includes some vivid details: a burnt book; corpses everywhere; and the fool plaiting a dead woman's hair (a brilliant touch).

Foma is shown fleeing from the city; he makes it to the woods nearby, but he is shot by an arrow in the back. He collapses in a slow motion death that recalls Sam Peckinpah (although the model is clearly Akira Kurosawa and *The Seven Samurai*). Foma falls into a stream; the camera films in white liquid in the water (presumably milk), a refrain used earlier.

In the aftermath of the Tartar raid, Roublyov talks in the ruined church with Theophanes, who is dead, but appears not as a ghost or vision; Roublyov vows he will never paint again. At this point, for his sins (he killed a Russian soldier), Roublyov takes a vow of silence. Inside the cathedral, it snows (as at the end of *Nostalghia*). 'Nothing is more terrible than snow in a church' (the snow, though, looks more like feathers or the dandelion seeds seen earlier). A horse trots into the ruined church. Bells toll mournfully throughout the scene. The dialogue is covered entirely with close-ups and medium close-up two shots, the actors moving slowly to and fro, in front of the wall (a favourite way for Tarkovsky to shoot a dialogue scene). Shot with a long lens, against the wall, the images have the flatness and frontality that Sergei Paradjanov and Walerian Borowczyk are so fond of. Nigel D'Sa (1999) suggested that the compositions in *Andrei Roublyov* reflect icon painting: the way characters are positioned centrally, frontally, and lost in thought.

Part seven, "The Silence", depicts the suffering of the people in 1412 at the Andronnikov monastery at the hands of the Tartars. In the snow, Roublyov walks about in silence, coming upon the fool, who is hunting for food on her own and picks something growing on the pile of logs (a mushroom or a plant) in the centre of the courtyard. (Like many film directors, Tarkovsky could be extremely picky about details at times. For instance, shooting on *Andrei Roublyov* was halted when Tarkovsky insisted that the log pile was built from birch not aspen). When Roublyov sees this, he forces her to let go of the plant, and spit it out. The fool, disturbed, moves away from Roublyov and the camera lingers on her. But fairly soon she's stamping in the snow with Roublyov, happy again. The whole scene has been played out without dialogue (like so much of the film). The *mise-en-scène* of this part of the film is of poverty and hardship – the cold, the snow, a bonfire, people dressed in rags.

The narrative moves indoors, to a group of people sitting at a table and eating scraps of food and mouldy apples (barrels of apples are placed on either side of a whitewashed corridor). This's another dialogue scene, and is shot largely from a low angle beside the table in a long take. Time has taken its toll on the monks in the monastery – apart from the famine, which's one of the chief topics of conversation, everyone is older. Roublyov now looks middle-aged, with grey in his beard, and Kirill turns up, maimed and dishevelled (Kirill begs the abbot to be able to stay in the monastery, and is given a cell). The dialogue between the group of survivors also serves the narrative function of describing Roublyov's new state of penitential silence, and how he has taken up the fool, to remind him of his sin. Towards the end of the scene, Roublyov enters and takes some apples from the barrels.

Roublyov's silence had a 'very broad, abstract, and even symbolic meaning' for the filmmakers, but they didn't necessarily agree with it, and tried to show that it was also a rather pointless response. Indeed, Roublyov's non-reaction and vow of silence makes him appear as uncaring, rather stupid and even inhuman. When the fool is carried off by the Tartars, it was to show the 'absurdity of the situation', because 'no sane person would have done this', Tarkovsky explained. 'But Andrei should have reacted and not allowed this offence to his charge's honour'. Roublyov doesn't react in the way a normal person would do, Tarkovsky said, and it was Boriska's example which eventually snaps him out of it, who shows him the value of perseverance, and creativity, and faith.

Roublyov dips out of the film for half-an-hour or so when Boriska takes centre stage. Roublyov becomes merely an observer (a role he has already undertaken at length anyway). It gives *Andrei Roublyov* an unusual structure, which isn't wholly successful. It might make more narrative sense to put the Boriska episode in earlier, but it is used to throw a different light on the creative process, and on the role of the artist. The Boriska and bell sequence offers a different view of the artist and how s/he operates within society (what her/ his art is *for*, how it works, who gets to see it, and so on).

In the second half of part seven, a band of Tartars on horseback arrive at the monastery, loud, laughing and jeering. They taunt the dogs, throwing them scraps of meat. The camera lingers on the dogs fighting for the food in a series of shots; dramatically, the starving dogs are an equivalence with the hungry population, how food is now scarce and people are fighting for it (it also shows the Tartars' scorn).

The performance of the actors, and the staging and blocking of the scene, serve to illustrate the uneasy relationship between the Tartars and the Russians: the Tartars are bellicose, confident, laughing, vain. In some ways they are caricatures of invaders and colonizers. They could be a Roman legion in an ancient world epic, or American grunts in a Vietnam movie.

The holy fool is fascinated by a piece of meat left on the large pile of logs in the centre of the courtyard (it's apt, in a time of famine, that food should be the lure that puts the fool in amongst the Tartars, and gets her noticed by the chief solder. The dialogue in the previous scene had established that the fool is good at hunting out food). The Tartar chief stops her from eating it, saying it's dirty meat. She is adopted by the chief of the Tartars (as a joke, it appears, at first). In front of the cathedral, she's interested in his armour, and polishes his breast plate, looking at herself reflected in it. He jokes about making her his eighth wife. He takes off his helmet and the fool tries it on; he puts a cloak around her. She cavorts in the middle of the snowy courtyard, while the Tartar soldiers laugh. Roublyov attempts to pull her away a number of times but the fool keeps resisting. Roublyov tries to drag her away, but she breaks free again. Finally, she climbs up beside the Tartar and gallops off with them. Roublyov is distraught; Kirill assures him the fool will be well-treated by the Tartars, and might be returned.

It's ironic in this scene, where Roublyov loses his closest companion, that he has taken a vow of silence and cannot reason with the soldiers; it's ironic too that the fool is unable to communicate with either Roublyov or the Tartars, that she seems to abandon him because the Tartars have shiny, pretty objects, and she's beguiled like a child by them. So it's not an abduction scene, with a cowboy's woman being taken off by American Indians in a Western movie. It's not *The Searchers*. The fool goes willingly, and fights with Roublyov to be able to go.

The bell-casting is the centrepiece of part eight, "The Bell", set in 1423-24. It introduces a major character, Boriska, late in the film: another creative person to mirror Roublyov. What's striking is just how much Boriska dominates the last part of *Andrei Roublyov;* he's in virtually every scene, and he is driving the narrative. Roublyov, meanwhile, is reduced to the role of a bystander: he watches Boriska from afar, often looking down at the youth from the edge of the bell pit. But Roublyov doesn't do anything to shape the plot in this section, and Boriska displaces him completely as the central character. Only at the end of the sequence does Roublyov act – he comforts Boriska and tells him that he will paint and Boriska will cast bells.

So *Andrei Roublyov* is not only about one creative personality, but at least two (there are others, such as the other painters). 'I wanted to use the example of Rublyov to explore the question of the psychology of artistic creativity' Tarkovsky commented in *Sculpting In Time* (34). In the figure of Roublyov the artistic journey is from activity to doubt and anxiety, a creative block or impasse, and a self-imposed abstinence. His observation of Boriska's intense struggle with the bell, the workers and the whole project, the film suggests, is instrumental in inspiring him to start painting again. For Boriska, the creative arc moves from having nothing to gaining everything, doing it all by sheer determination, which seems to come from nowhere. Boriska doesn't know the secret of bell-making (he says his father wouldn't tell him), so he's an example of an artist making it up on the fly: total improvization or spontaneity.

One can see how Boriska's mode of spontaneously reacting to the moment is in tune with Tarkovsky's theory of cinema. What's striking about *Andrei Roublyov* is how Tarkovsky was, by a relatively early age, already dealing with creative inertia and self-doubt. Tarkovsky has made a film about middle-age crisis (and it's the first of a few; indeed, each of Tarkovsky's subsequent films can be regarded as playing out middle age crises — and films like *Nostalghia* and *The Sacrifice* are primarily middle years crisis narratives).

No one could miss the link between the role of the bell-maker and that of the film director: the ordering and the bullying, the praying and the pleading. The team work, the common goal, the combination of technicalities and æsthetics, are further comparisons (with the Duke and his cohorts as the studio executives and financiers). And, not least, the necessity of creative (perhaps divine) inspiration.

'The Bell' opens with a medium close-up of Boriska leaning against a wall. He looks glum, and about eighteen. Only the youth seems to be up and about; the landscape (of snow and hills) reveals no other soul. The Duke's retainers visit Boriska's house, to find the bell-maker for a commission. Boriska tells the men on horseback that his father and family have died of the plague. Boriska says he can make the bell — his father gave him the secret. Shouting and pleading with the men in desperation (they have left off-screen), Boriska manages to convince them to take him along.

Boriska is next shown leading the bell-making party to some ground outside the city (which can be seen beyond). Boriska continually overrides the doubts of his workers, dictatorially. When one of his men refuses to continue working, Boriska orders him to be beaten. Boriska weaves webs of lies about bell-making, in order to convince himself as much as his workers about his ability to cast bells. Images of Boriska in a circular pit in the ground come next, and handheld shots of Boriska following a root to a tree. He discusses the clay they've found: they have to keep looking. Boriska argues with Stepan about the clay.

In the rain, alone, Boriska is shown searching for the right kind of clay needed in making the bell. At this precise moment Roublyov is re-introduced: passing nearby on a track with a cart and horse, he observes Boriska's joy at finding the correct material by accident (after slipping down a slope). Boriska calls out to the others. Until this point, Roublyov has been absent from the film for a while.

Boriska is shown in various stages of artistic creation: from nervous exhaustion, through absent-minded musing, to excitement. Boriska's unquestioned faith in his abilities inspires Roublyov to start painting again. The next scene, which begins the bell-casting sequence, opens with a huge shot: workers are in the deep pit on the hill; Boriska is in the centre; the camera cranes up to reveal hundreds of extras — digging soil, chopping wood, and hundreds more in the valley beyond. There's another argument among the bell-founders, in the pit beside the bell. Boriska orders a worker to be flogged; his cries of pain are heard off-screen. Roublyov is above, on the edge of the pit, watching Boriska. Boriska rests on some fur.

A close-up of Roublyov segues into a flashback of the beginning of the film, an image of the three monks sheltering under an oak tree from the rain. The music is soft. Boriska is woken up to find the bell is on fire; the baking's begun. Boriska discusses silver and the secret of making bronze. At this point, the jester (or buffoon) returns from the past, and in a big group scene accuses Roublyov of betrayal many years ago. Most of this ghost-from-the-past scene is covered with a single long lens shot, without cutaways or reaction shots — the *tableau* style of staging in the film (with Akira Kurosawa's shooting style as an obvious influence).

One of the most impressive sequences in Tarkovsky's cinema follows, a brilliant handling of cinematic spectacle: the bell-casting scene. Boriska presides over the furnaces; rows of workers operate the giant bellows; buckets, enormous machinery, wooden beams, rope, planks, water, smoke, molten metal and sparks. It's nighttime (it doesn't have to be, but the fire and sparks look much better in the dark). A large crowd is gathered up on the hill around the pit. There's a stunning backlit shot of Boriska against smoke and flame as the metal runs down channels towards the bell.

There isn't any music at all in these spectacular scenes, just local sound effects (many another director would have been tempted to intensify the drama of these scenes with music. But they are so breathtaking, they don't need it).

Next morning. The bell is now cooling; the foreman checks the bell. The bell-founders start to chip away at the casing, with Boriska chopping at it in the foreground. As before, Roublyov is watching from above. The next scene switches back to Roublyov again, a flashback to the monastery, with a fellow monk (Kirill) berating Roublyov for wasting his talent, for keeping silent, for refusing invitations to paint.

The bell-raising sequence is the last big scene in *Andrei Roublyov*, and it does not disappoint. Every extra for many miles around has been commissioned to add to the spectacle. The sequence opens with an incredible *wow* shot of hundreds and hundreds of extras, long lines of ropes which lead up to the bell, the crowds gathering to watch, the scaffolding holding up the bell; the shot winds up with an overhead image of the giant bell below and the ropes crisscrossing it. It's the kind of shot that takes months to prepare, and days to rehearse. Workers are busying about, and Boriska stands near the bell. (he's still as nervous as ever — this's close to his moment of truth). (It's an odd coincidence that Columbia's cartoony 1964 Viking romp, *The Long Ships*, also contained an enormous bell, though this time as the standard Hollywood McGuffin, as treasure).

The bell-raising scenes comprise big, long takes — a crane up move to show the workers readying to haul the bell into the air; Boriska giving the signal; and a track past the workers holding the ropes to Boriska, with the bell behind him. Loud creaking sounds accompany a long lens shot of the arrival of the Duke and his retinue. People bow on either side of the road as he passes. Priests bless the bell in the next scene. The camera again lingers on Boriska, who's pacing about, mute, pensive, withdrawn, nervous — he barely says a single word during the whole bell-raising sequence.

Ambassadors in rich robes chat in Italian. The crowds are silent, expectant. With the bell in place, a worker pulls an enormous hammer to and fro. When it finally sounds (after quite a long build-up), there is a cut to a C.U. of Roublyov, and to a woman in white leading a horse (this appears to be another of Tarkovsky's mysterious images, an angelic presence, although Graham Johnson and Vida Petrie reckon it's the holy fool, now in ordinary clothes). The bell continues ringing over the next shots. The climax comes with a boom up and out from Boriska sitting in the mud beside the bell, showing the crowds cheering and waving. Bells in the town ring in answer.

The following scene shows Boriska weeping beside a wooden post in a landscape of mud and pools (Tarkovsky said he didn't see mud in his films, he saw earth mixed with water, 'the source from which things grow'.)[10] Roublyov appears, and comforts him, taking the youth in his arms (reminiscent of Christian *Pietà* imagery). Roublyov speaks for the first time in what seems ages (in the film's terms, it is literally years or decades). Boriska admits that he never knew the secret of bell-making, that his father hadn't told him. The woman in white is shown again, in the distance.

After the conversation on the muddy riverbank between Boriska and Roublyov, the camera pans left to a small log fire and cuts to colour. Then follow the series of pans in close-up over Roublyov's paintings (dissolving from the fire to a portion of painting which is red). The paintings in the colour epilogue by Roublyov (or attributed to him) include the *Trinity, The Nativity, The Entry Into Jerusalem, The Apostle, The Death of the Virgin, The Redeemer Lives* and *Raising of Lazarus.*

Choral music accompanies the close-ups of the real Roublyov's paintings. At first, abstract shapes predominate, before the camera goes wider to include figurative forms, which include Christ, his halo, angels, Mary Magdalene, the Holy Spirit (as a dove), churches, the Virgin Mary, the Nativity, and three angels (the Trinity). Instead of showing all of Roublyov's *Holy Trinity* at the end of the film, Tarkovsky used details of the icon, because, he said, the way a painting is apprehended is different from cinema. The audience was meant to construct the picture from a series of segments.[11] (Some of these rostrum camera shots, it has to be said, are a little messy, and the editing too isn't completely polished).

The sequence closes with the sound of thunder and rain. After the shots of Roublyov's icons, there are shots (in colour) of Christ's face; rain appears to be running down the paint (it's meant to be on one of Roublyov's icons, but it's a surface standing in for the real thing). Then a dissolve to rain falling beside a river and four horses (the rain's in focus, the horses are out of focus). The end. (Tarkovsky acknowledged (in an interview with Michel Ciment in *Positif*) that the horses at the end of *Andrei Roublyov* were symbolic of life.)

Andrei Roublyov is a passive and often mute personality: a watcher, the observer through whom the events of the film are seen. The meditations in *Andrei Roublyov* are on the role of the artist in society, the artist in relation to the state, to politics, to religion, to God, to sexuality, to purity, to vision, to suffering, to life. Each sequence, each part (from one to eight) illustrates an ideological, moral, artistic, and biographical point. Roublyov frames the film, provides the axis around which the film revolves. In many ways, *Andrei Roublyov* is the clearest filmed statement of Tarkovsky's position on art and spirituality, and the relation between the two.

His films were about people who possessed an 'inner freedom', as Tarkovsky described it, while around them are people 'who are inwardly dependent and unfree' (ST, 181). The apparent weakness of his protagonists was in fact an inner strength, he said. Amos Vogel, in his book *Film As a Subversive Art*, wrote of *Andrei Roublyov* as a significant plea for personal freedom:

> More important than its massive beauty, the sensuous plasticity of its images, and extraordinary fusion of ideological, narrative and æsthetic structure, is its message of human freedom: the pre-eminence of the suffering, questioning individual, as against the mass, of the indomitable spirit of self-realization and the delineation of relations between individual and temporal power. (150)

Art is seen as holy, as holy as religion in *Andrei Roublyov*. Art has a sense of the numinous as powerful as religion. Art is seen as a cult, with fetish objects, monastic precepts, followers like pilgrims and mystics, and images of divinity. Constant connections are made in *Andrei Roublyov* between holiness, madness and creativity, embodied in different ways by the figures of Roublyov, the holy fool and the bell-caster Boriska. These three figures are linked in one scene, as if they are three sides of the same person, the same phenomenon: belief and faith in life, with artistic creativity as the ultimate affirmation of life. The theme of three-in-one or the trinity is taken up by Roublyov and his two companions, Daniil and Kirill; and by the subject of Roublyov's most famous painting, *The Holy Trinity* (later, in *Solaris*, there are three men on the space station, and in *Stalker* three men enter the Zone).

The artists in *Andrei Roublyov* offer different views on one of Tarkovsky's recurring themes: the problem of the artist and her/ his relation to society. Daniil is the conformist, the follower of social trends; Kirill is the untalented artist, too proud and jealous; Theophanes is a real artist, an older generation. Boriska is the untutored youth, working from an intuition that seems divine. Like Roublyov, Boriska veers from self-confidence to self-doubt, from faith to frustration, from ecstasy to despair (JP, 91). Roublyov is a version of the Tarkovskyan artist: humane, humble, sometimes confused, sometimes difficult, sometimes too passive, but with a fundamental faith.

One of the most troubled depictions of the artist struggling with society and political authority was the blinding of the stonemasons: their 'crime' is to assert their independence from their masters. Such a scene might have had personal reson-ance in a society (the Soviet Union of the mid-20th century) which had imprisoned, silenced and exiled artists and writers.

The bell-casting sequence in *Andrei Roublyov* provides another look at creativity, this time through a young boy's experience. He is an initiate, a neophyte, a young shaman-in-the-making. Here creativity is seen in religious and shamanic terms, because the boy doesn't really know the alchemical secret of making bells – he uses his intuition, his blind faith as the Stalker would put it. He feels his way into his creative role and his public post. Boriska is a believer, believing from his deeper self, working from his unconscious. One sees this happening very clearly – in every facial expression of the boy as he storms about the bell-casting site, in an obsessive state of nervous energy. The workers get caught up by the boy's excited vision, just like the followers of shamans and preachers – and religious fanatics. When the molten liquid pours into the bell, it is filmed as a religious transformation – the channels of hot metal are blinding; smoke billows up; the boy stands in the foreground, transformed. It's like a religious vision, all that smoke and light – there is something Baroque about it, a vision of angels, clouds and cascades of light, like the ceiling of a Baroque church. It is kinetic and ancient. The boy is like the young Merlin the magician of Arthurian legend creating Stonehenge, or a young Paracelsus or Cornelius Agrippa, alchemists trying out their magic.

When Andrei Roublyov throws some mud at a white wall, in his frustration, the image recalls modern art, the paintings of Jackson Pollock or Franz Kline – an image out of Abstract Expressionism. The moment when the holy fool comes into the Cathedral and starts to touch the mud, as if it is something special, is moving. *Andrei Roublyov* is full of white spaces, of white-on-white imagery: white walls, white landscapes, white milk, white rivers, white skies, white snow, a white Crucifixion, white seeds and white feathers drifting over people's faces. Andrei Roublyov and Boriska are spiritually linked when Roublyov witnesses the bell-maker making his important discovery of the right kind of clay. From that moment, the two are bound up together, and Roublyov is often shown watching Boriska, as if observing the birth of an artist. At the end of the film, before the zoom into the fire and the change into colour, Roublyov clutches the exhausted Boriska and says 'you'll cast bells, I'll paint icons'. Art and spirituality are welded together. Life suddenly comes alive: the film itself catches fire. The fire here is clearly symbolizing purification and rebirth.

After the montage of paintings, in colour, the climax to the film, there is a zoom into the face of Christ as the Pantokrator, and a sound of thunder cracking. This is a violent image: Christ plus thunder. It speaks of the Last Judgement, of the Apocalypse, of global transformations. But after this there is a shot of wood with paint faded on it, and rain runs down it – a typical Tarkovskyan image. Then the last shot: four horses stand beside a river. They are shot slightly out of focus: the rain, a sheet of water in the foreground, is in focus (it's a self-consciously painterly shot). It's an image of refreshment, rebirth, the world made clean as after a Spring shower, as after the Flood, after Noah's Ark has landed on Mount Ararat. The sound of the choir has faded now: there is just the sound of rain. Then a fade to black.

SEVENTEEN

Solaris

17 : 1   *SOLARIS*: BACKGROUND

Andrei Tarkovsky had developed *Solaris* from early 1968 onwards (Andrei Konch-alovsky was going to collaborate on the script, but the two filmmakers disagreed about the adaption). It wasn't his first choice to follow up *Andrei Roublyov* (he wanted to make *Bright, Bright Day*, the script which became *Mirror*) and a film about his mother (parts of this also went into *Mirror*). Tarkovsky said, before he made *Solaris*, that what attracted him to Stanislaw Lem's 1961 book was the story of a man who can't escape his past, who regrets what he's done, and wants to relive his life in order to make amends for it. It was the morality, psychology and philosophy of the book that appealed to Tarkovsky, not the hard science, the technology, or the conventional sci-fi elements. When he applied for money from Mosfilm, though, Tarkovsky emphasized different aspects of the project: '[t]he plot of *Solaris* is taut and sharp, full of unexpected twists and turns and exciting confrontations…We can be sure from the start that the film will be a financial success' (M. Turovskaya, 52). Despite the success in the West of films such as *2001: A Space Odyssey* and *The Planet of the Apes*, sci-fi was still a genre at this time (the early 1970s) that was not a guaranteed box office winner. *Star Wars* and *Close*

Encounters of the Third Kind were still some years away.

Tarkovsky complained in his diaries about the shoot, which was, as usual on a Tarkovsky movie, fraught with problems (many, as usual, stemming from conflict between the filmmaker and his backers – but it's the same story with thousands of filmmakers, who routinely complain they don't have enough money, enough time, enough support, enough film stock, enough technicians, etc). The budget was red-uced by Goskino, from the approved 1,850,000 roubles to 900,000. Tarkovsky dis-agreed with Vadim Yusov, his DP; 'Yusov and I are constantly arguing. It's very hard to work with him now' he wrote in his diary for August 10, 1971 (D, 39). Falling out with the director of photography on any film can be problematic for the director (the cameraman and director often being the two people usually having most influence on a film set), but for an *auteur* like Tarkovsky, who liked to control every aspect of filmmaking, and especially the visuals, it would have been frustrat-ing (in his diaries, at least twice, he mentions that he wants to shoot with a 50.75mm lens, but Yusov insisted on a 35mm lens). Tarkovsky must have been happy working with Yusov going into *Solaris*, though, as he'd used Yusov on both previous features, and Yusov had been his main DP thus far in his career.

Tarkovsky wrote an early draft of the *Solaris* script in 1968 (with Friedrich Gorenstein); he cast the film in May, 1970. The scenes of the *dacha* and environs were shot at Zvenigorod, about 40 miles from Moscow, from March to Summer, 1971. The River Ruza was another location. Tarkovsky chose to shoot some of the scenes in black-and-white (such as Kris burning his papers on a bonfire; though, as these take place, like the others, in the present day, there seems to be no really good reason for using black-and-white). The Japan shoot (consisting of cityscapes and car shots in Tokyo) took place in late September/ early October, 1971. Getting towards the end of cutting the film, in December, 1971, Tarkovsky said in his diaries he was pleased with some scenes (the suicide, Tokyo, the mother, the lake, the night conversation, Kris's dreams), but wasn't sure if the film would work as a whole (D, 45).

The film was shown to Mosfilm at the end of December, 1971. Unfortunately, Mosfilm requested many changes (35 in all), and then further changes. The comments from Mosfilm and Goskino, detailed in Tarkovsky's diary for January 12, 1972, included: produce a clearer image of Earth in the future, including some landscapes; clarify the society of the future, whether it's socialist, communist, capitalist; drop the concept of God and Christianity; cut out the foreign executives at the conference; delete the mother scene; shorten the Earth scenes; shorten the bed scene; cut out the shots of Kris without his trousers; clarify the time for Kris's journey out and back, and his work; show the space journey; make it clear that Kris completed his mission; the encephalogram should be shown at the end; Gibarin should have committed suicide for the benefit of his friends and colleagues; make the necessity for contact more explicit; Hari 'ought not to become a person', and why does she vanish?; Sartorius lacks humanity as a scientist; put the scene back in of Berton and Kris's father talking about their youth; and clarify Solaris and the visitors (D, 49-50).

As Tarkovsky bemoaned in his diary, these changes could not be completed without ruining the film (D, 51). Tarkovsky agreed to make small changes, which he thought wouldn't damage the picture, but resolved to fight further demands. On February 25, 1972, Tarkovsky related the requests for further alterations: shorten the film by 300 metres; cut out Hari's suicide (which isn't shown); cut out Tokyo; cut out the mother scenes; delete the scene with Hari's dress; and the end scene with the flowing water (D, 55). Tarkovsky, his sister and Vadim Yusov have all commented that they deliberately shot some scenes too long, knowing they would be asked to be cut.

The film was released on March 20, 1972, and was chosen to go to Cannes in May, 1972. After the debacle of *Andrei Roublyov*, *Solaris* received a proper release, which must've gratified Tarkovsky. Natalia Bondarchuk remarked that she visited many places to promote the film. (Akira Kurosawa, in Russia at this time, recalled how he and Tarkovsky had gone to a restaurant after a late night screening of *Solaris* in Moscow, drunk lot of vodka, and sang the theme from *The Seven Samurai* together).

The various versions of *Solaris* range from the 2 hours 45 minutes Cannes film version; a 2h 30m French release version (Tarkovsky said he cut 12 minutes from *Solaris* in Paris for the French version [D, 61]); a 1h 50m Italian version; a UK release version, at 2h 45m; and a US (dubbed) version of 2h 12m. There was apparently a longer version, at over three hours, which Tarkovsky cut down before he took the film to Cannes.

The scenes which were probably dropped were the 'mirror room' scene (photos show the director posing in the Minimal art room, with Kris Kelvin and Hari (Rheya in Lem's book) in a bed beside him), and a scene between Kris and his father. (The mirrored room was made in 1966 by Conceptual artist Lucas Samaras, and installed in the Albright-Knox Art Gallery in Buffalo. *Mirrored Room* was also used by Robert Fripp and Brian Eno for the album cover of *No Pussyfooting* (1972). It's unlikely that Tarkovsky and his crew would travel to New York state to shoot that scene, so it's probably a version of the *Mirrored Room* built for the film.)[1]

Tarkovsky praised Natalia Bondarchuk in his diaries (D, 46); he had considered using Ingmar Bergman regular Bibi Andersson for the part of Hari (as well as his first wife, Irma Rausch, which would've added another layer of autobiography to the project). But Tarkovsky was unhappy with Donatas Banionis, something of a Method actor, who had to know the motivation for his scenes. This wasn't what Tarkovsky wanted from an actor at all. For him, the actor had to be the servant of the film, to fit in with the grand scheme of the film. Tarkovsky didn't want to spend too much time going through explanations or motivations. The idea of working with actors like Robert De Niro or Dustin Hoffman, performers who spend weeks preparing and researching and practising for a role, would be anathema to Tarkovsky.

Solaris was Andrei Tarkovsky's first feature film in colour (*The Steamroller and the Violin* had been shot in Sovcolor). Tarkovsky said he wasn't entirely happy with his use of colour in *Solaris*, and one can see that in some scenes, where the colour is not as controlled as in the later films (the use of the widescreen format, though, is excellent). After *Solaris*, however, Tarkovsky's films were mainly in colour, though with many black-and-white sequences, and many in the twilit borderland between full colour and black-and-white. (The use of colour is not tied in to the psychological narrative in the film, as it would be in *Mirror* and later films, and the switches to black-and-white seem somewhat arbitrary).

The dichotomies in *Solaris* are between the present and the past, the past as it really was and the past as one'd like it to be, the human and non-human, age and youth, reality and wishes and dreams, inside the station and outside, the individual's unconscious and the Ocean, Earth and Solaris.

By 1990, Stanislaw Lem's books had been translated into 30 languages, with over 6 million of his books in circulation (2.5 million of these were in Russia). Around 30 new translations of Lem's books were made per year. Lem's works often concern failures of communication, and how social and political changes affect the individual.[2]

Solaris was published in 1961. The major motif is the implacable but conscious and intelligent planet, with its vast sea which produces 'mimoids', solid phantasms. Like the Zone in the Strugatsky brothers' *Roadside Picnic* or the monolith in *2001: A Space Odyssey*, Solaris remains a mystery throughout the book. The Ocean responds to the humans' bombardment by X-rays by invading their unconsciousness and recreating their secrets and shames (the sea being *the* classic symbol of the unconscious, the id; Solaris is the Thing, the blind libido embodied, remarked Slavoj Zizek, while the Zone is the void which sustains desire). As long as the space station stays over Solaris the humans on board will be haunted by their human frailties and failures. Tarkovsky announces his divergence from traditional sci-fi fare early on after Kelvin's arrival on the station, when Gibarin introduces the idea of conscience.

Kris is the centre of the novel: the planet Solaris finds out that Kris once had a wife (Hari) who committed suicide when he spurned or neglected her (Kris blames himself for this; in both film and novel, Hari is not specifically defined as Kelvin's wife, though in dubbed versions she is; it's easier, here, to refer to her as such). After Hari mysteriously appears in his room when he is asleep on the bed, Kris leads her into the rocket launching room, tricking her like a child and locking her in a missile. This scene is not wholly convincing; Kris survives the launch and being on fire, for example, by simply rolling himself in a blanket (he's unable to open the doors; Snaut wryly suggests he tries launching the rocket from the corridor next time). (The fires lit on the very costly rocket set in *Solaris* apparently started a fire that nearly wrecked the studio.)

A new Hari, made by the Ocean, returns to haunt Kris (again appearing when he's lying on his bed), after he has launched her into space. The planet exposes human weaknesses, the moral and emotional confusion underneath the scientific methodology and the crusading exploration of space. While the Ocean is at peace with its inner life, the humans are not. Towards the end of *Solaris*, Hari realizes she isn't human, and that her life is a deception. She commits suicide in Sartorius's Matter Disintegrator (this's not shown, but is related to Kris by Snaut — a curious elision), after trying to kill herself earlier by drinking liquid oxygen.

In "The Thing from Inner Space", Slavoj Zizek wrote that 'this fragile specter, pure semblance, cannot ever be erased — [Hari] is "undead", eternally recurring in the space between the two deaths'. For Zizek, Hari is doomed because is a phantasm created by the man, doomed to embody *his* psychology:

the tragic position of Harey is that she becomes aware that she is deprived of all substantial identity, that she is Nothing in herself, since she only exists as the Other's dream, insofar as the Other's fantasies turn around her...

'Is there anything more tragic than such a scene of failed self-erasure' remarked Zizek. For Kris, Hari's appearance offers the 'cruel miracle' of a second chance (even at the end of the novel, Kris is still hoping against hope that 'the time of cruel miracles was not past' [195]).

Again, the differences between Hollywood's sci-fi films and Tarkovsky's is immense. In the scene where Hari first appears, for example, Kris reacts warily but in a very restrained manner; a Hollywood film, starring Bruce Willis, Brad Pitt or Mel Gibson, say, would emphasize the drama, with the suspense and strangeness greatly exaggerated; the ensuing erotic contact between Kris and Hari – just a kiss in the first scene – would likely be more passionate in a Hollywood version. For Tarkovsky, *Solaris* was about the 'new morality arising as a result of those painful experiences we call 'the price of progress''. Kelvin's 'tragic dilemma' is that he doesn't change when given the chance.

It was the 'moral problems' in Stanislaw Lem's novel that attracted Tarkovsky, not the technology, the science or speculative questions (D, 362). For Tarkovsky, Khari (Hari) represented Kelvin's conscience. As Tarkovsky put it: 'in simple terms, the story of Khari's relationship with Kelvin is the story of the relationship between man and his own conscience. It's about man's concern with his own spirit, when he has no possibility of doing anything about it' (D, 363). The whole point was that Kelvin wasn't able to do the right thing even when he had a second chance, Tarkovsky explained. Because if he had been able to live the second time around differently, he wouldn't have been guilty the first time (D, 363).

Kris begins *Solaris* detached from people, his face blank, unresponsive, apparently uncaring; his emotional trajectory in the film is towards love, sympathy, conscience. He comes back to life. The tragedy of *Solaris* is that, by the time Kris has learnt to become more fully human, or human once again, it is too late. He repeats the same mistakes in his relation to the Ocean-made Hari that he made with the real person.

Tarkovsky fused mother and wife, as he will do to even greater lengths in *Mirror*. Both Kris's mother and wife are depicted in similar ways, as distant, beautiful, blank (with the Leonardo smile). They share the same patchwork dresses and shawls.

The credits for *Solaris* are simple, white on black, accompanied by Johann Sebastian Bach's *Choral Prelude in F-minor* (which's one of the major music sounds in *Solaris*, the other being the low drones and rumbles that go with shots of the Ocean).

Scene 1 can be broken down thus:

Shot 1. Water, green weeds in the shallows, an autumn leaf floats by, the camera pans left. Very clear water: images of translucency and tranquillity.

Shot 2. The river again, tilt down, pan right, past reeds, onto the land, then up to Kris. The camera moves leisurely but deliberately from nature to humanity. It is typical of Tarkovsky's cinema to evoke the natural world first, then humanity in the midst of it. Kris seems to be immersing himself in the natural world, to soak it up before he travels into space. He stands quietly and still.

Shot 3. The reeds in M.C.U. again, zooming in.

Shot 4. Leaves, crane up to show Kris in the landscape. Birdsong. Kris walks off to the right.

Shot 5. L.S., treescape, Kris walks left to right.

Shot 6. Kris walking to a lake; the camera tilts up to show his father's *dacha*.

Shot 7. Lakeside, Kris walking along the bank.

Shot 8. A horse canters by.

Shot 9. As shot 7, pan right, Kris washes his hands in the lake; sound of a car; he looks up, cut to:

Shot 10. Cars and people in L.S. on a bridge (his p.o.v.). They call to him.

Scene 1 in *Solaris* evokes a tranquil, pastoral world: all greens, browns, blues, images of soil, water, mist, plants and sunlight. It's an unusual, but not unique beginning to a science fiction film. In Kris's father's home is a bird cage, a Greek bust, and pictures of early ballooning on the wall: images of flight (which relate to his journey into space; these sorts of objects will appear later, in the library on the space station). A reproduction of Andrei Roublyov's *The Trinity* is on the mantel-piece (the painting also appears in Tarkovsky's next film, *Mirror*, and it's in Kris's room at the space station). Like many filmmakers, Tarkovsky quotes from his earlier films. The poster for *Andrei Roublyov* appears in the Moscow apartment of the narrator in *Mirror*, for instance. Music from *Ivan's Childhood* crops up in

Andrei Roublyov (and sounds from *Andrei Roublyov* are heard in *Solaris*).

When Berton, a fellow scientist and astronaut, arrives with his son (or grandson), this initiates the exposition, where the quest or goal of the film is set out, via the lengthy video playback (a typical messenger figure in sci-fi movies): to investigate the strange goings-on at Solaris, an ocean-planet (Berton's maybe twenty years older than he appears in the televised investigation into Solaris and 'solaristics'). In the black-and-white video programme, the nature of the planet Solaris is discussed at a conference or investigation with various officials, with Berton being cross-examined (the setting — a long white interior stretching away behind the actors — recalls the space station in *2001: A Space Odyssey*).

In the report, the younger Berton (in pilot's uniform) recounts how he flew over the Ocean on Solaris and filmed it. Clips from his film are shown, but they reveal little except a very bright sky, and vague shots of clouds taken from high altitude. The scientists and delegates at the inquest exclaim that the pilot has filmed nothing but clouds. Berton, meanwhile, claimed he saw a 'garden' below the Ocean, as if made from plaster, as well as a naked child four metres tall.

Next, Kris's familial relationships are evoked; in a scene between Kris and his father, after the video playback, Tarkovsky cuts to a photograph of Kris's mother. Kris burns his papers, in a symbolic renunciation of home, the family and childhood. But these things haunt him later on, in the spaceship. He takes a film of himself as a boy with him into space, shot (mainly) by his father. This is the equivalent of Tarkovsky's own father's poems, which represent homeland in Tarkovsky's cinema. As well as Berton's child, there is a young girl, anonymous and unexplained (perhaps a neighbour), near the *dacha*, recalling the girl in the dreams in *Ivan's Childhood*.

Before the Solaris video is played in the house, there is a sudden rainfall, a typical Tarkovskyan motif; Kris stays outside, letting himself get wet. In one shot he stares at a Tarkovskyan still life consisting of tea cups, saucers, and fruit on a table on the balcony outside the house. The camera closes in on the rain dropping into a cup (it's a circular image of water: the Ocean in microcosm. This scene of Kelvin staring at the cup in the rain was inspired by the Italian Renaissance painter Vittore Carpaccio, in particular a picture of boats departing in Venice, in which each figure seemed absorbed in themselves, not looking at anyone else.)

Solaris's a slow film. At the beginning, there's no dialogue until nearly three minutes from the end of the credits. There's no exposition or real conversation for 6 minutes. The exposition of the video tape playback lasts up until 20 minutes (it's far longer and talkier than a contemporary Hollywood movie, which would want to move the story along much swifter; a Hollywood screenwriter might also be encouraged to find a more compelling method of delivering the scientific exposition. It's as if Tarkovsky is simply getting the sci-fi bit out of the way, and being deliberately dull in doing so). *Solaris* doesn't reach the space station until some 36 minutes.

For Tarkovsky, too much of science fiction cinema concentrated on the physical details of the future. For Tarkovsky, speaking in 1971, *2001: A Space Odyssey* fetishized technology into something exotic, which missed the point. *2001* was like a science museum for Tarkovsky, a place where technological developments are displayed. Tarkovsky wondered if it would have been better to dispense with the science fiction *mise-en-scène* of *Solaris* – the rockets and space stations – completely (ST, 199).

Tarkovsky said if he wasn't interested in sci-fi or fantasy, he was in the moral or spiritual problems the genre sometimes tackled. And real life didn't need the spectacular glow of fantasy to make it extraordinary: 'ordinary life is also full of the fantastic. Life itself is a fantastic phenomenon,' Tarkovsky said in 1972. 'Fyodor Dostoievsky knew it well. That's why I want to focus on life itself everyday, ordinary. Because within it anything can happen'.

The Earth scenes were meant to be beautiful and mysterious, to represent what Kelvin is leaving behind (and revealing his homesickness). For Akira Kurosawa, the early scenes on Earth haunted the rest of the film with their beauty: 'they almost torture the soul of the viewer like a kind of irresistible nostalgia toward mother earth nature, which resembles homesickness'.

In the Earth scenes, the main (emotional) relationship is between Kris and his father, and the visiting astronaut Berton, who brings the videotape of the investigation into the Solaris problem with him for Kris, who's leaving for the planet the following day, to look at. A middle-aged woman, aunt Anna, is also present at the *dacha* but she has little to say, and acts primarily as an observer. Berton has brought a boy with him.

Before the Tokyo sequence, Anna (the aunt), and Kris's father watch a TV programme (a different one) about Solaris, in which more (rather mundane) exposition occurs (about the survivors on the space station, Snaut, Sartorius and Gibarian). Before the journey to the ocean planet, there is an extraordinary sequence of driving around modern-day Tokyo, shot from a car, through many freeways, bridges, tunnels and under-passes. Tarkovsky had already established that this was Berton's view from the car, as he drove away from the country back to the city: his video phone message had interrupted the TV programme that Kris's father and his aunt Anna were watching. Tarkovsky cuts a few times from the views out of the car windscreen to Berton's thoughtful face; his child is seen moving around in the background.

There is a mass of electronic whirrs and hums on the soundtrack: industrial noises, many not synthesized. Tarkovsky makes a city look other-worldly, and driving a car becomes a strange journey in an unreal, human-made, technological landscape. Black-and-white and colour is used here, with colour coming towards the end of the sequence (the variations between colour and black-and-white seem mainly for visual beauty, rather than any logical pattern). The final shot is of a Tokyo cityscape, a high angle wide shot showing intersecting freeways at twilight, crammed with traffic. Akira Kurosawa praised the Tokyo scenes for their horror:

> what makes us shudder is the shot of the location of Akasakamitsuke, Tokyo, Japan. By a skillful use of mirrors, he turned flows of head lights and tail lamps of cars, multiplied and amplified, into a vintage image of the future city.

The Tokyo sequence ends abruptly with a cut to a beautiful black-and-white shot of the lake, mist and trees near the *dacha*; sound and movement suddenly ends (one of the most delicious shots in Tarkovsky *œuvre*). A slow pan right, showing Kris in L.S. beside a bonfire, in front of the *dacha*, burning old papers. In this scene, Anna and his father are shown pensive and saddened about Kris's impending departure (Anna walks off on her own). Sounds of dogs in the background; a dog was shown beside his aunt; when Kris was in the house, the horse from *Andrei Roublyov* trots by. In one of the close-ups of Tarkovsky's beloved motif, fire, a photograph is seen, of the woman who materializes on the space station, Hari.

Kris wanders around his family home, before the journey into outer space. In another slow pan across a still life – which includes, as in most Tarkovsky still lifes, books – Kris's metal box is seen, with the plant in it, that he takes on his journey, a link with Earth. Snaut suggests another link in Kris's room – he puts pieces of torn paper on the air conditioning ventilator, which sounds, he claims, like leaves. There is also an illustrated copy of *Don Quixote*.

The planetary voyage is announced with a cut to a (static) starscape, contrasting the ambiguous warmth of home with the infinity and inhumanity of space. A similar cut occurs in the sequel to *2001: A Space Odyssey*, *2010* (Peter Hyams, 1984, USA). The journey sequence inevitably has Stanley Kubrickian connotations: Kris is framed head-on: a C.U. of his eyes, echoing the shots of Bowman at the end of *2001: A Space Odyssey*. This is a standard Kubrick motif (critics call it the 'Kubrick stare'). There are exotic, ominous sounds, throbs and hums in this sequence. It is typical sci-fi, really. Apart from the simple starfield, Tarkovsky concentrated on Kris's experience of space travel: a close-up on his eyes, pulling back slightly, and rotating the camera, suggesting the strangeness of the journey. Superimposed on this shot, as Kris spoke to the Solaris station and said the signal was breaking up, were shimmering shapes. Then a shot of Kris's view out of the window of the spaceship, descending towards the station, which's seen as a circular island in the middle of the Ocean (one of the few special effects shots in *Solaris*).

A contemporary Hollywood film would make much more of this journey to Solaris; there isn't even an exterior shot of the spaceship; it doesn't interest Tarkovsky much at all, and he doesn't waste much time on it. Stella Bruzzi (1995), commenting on the costumes and look of science fiction films, noted how in *Solaris* Tarkovsky stressed the ordinary, everydayness of life in space, his 'downbeat, depressive approach to the myth of space travel', his 'stark and deflating vision'. The costume designer on *Solaris*, Nelly Fomina, recalled that Tarkovsky didn't want the usual futuristic and exotic clothing of sci-fi films, but something more timeless, and connected to Earth (Hari's beige and cream costume and white and brown crocheted shawl certainly do that).

After his odd, perfunctory arrival at the Solaris station – no welcoming party, no message, no voice on an intercom – Kris meets the main characters and their neutrino 'mimoids'. The scientist Sartorius (Tarkovsky regular Anatoly Solonitsyn) is shifty, cynical, a latter-day Dr Faust with a rational explanation for everything (Snaut calls Sartorius Faust in his laboratory). Sartorius spends most of his time in his lab (which's only shown from the outside). Sartorius's 'visitor' is a dwarf who bursts out of his room (while he's talking to Kris in the corridor) whom he forces back inside (in the book it's a child; there are photographs of children on the wall outside the laboratory, which Sartorius shiftily covers up).

Sartorius, as a scientist, doesn't believe in the mimoids, yet he too is haunted by them. Another scientist, Snaut (Yuri Yarvet), has a much bigger role than Solon-itsyn's Sartorius; Snaut acts as something of an intermediary between the extreme views of humanism and science represented by Kris and Sartorius. Snaut seems to have tired of the whole problem of the Ocean and 'mimoids' a long time ago, and would prefer to simply retire to his room. And, via a video playback, there's the dead Gibarin (Sos Sarkissian), Kris's one-time mentor, whose 'visitor', a teenager in a blue nightdress, is still haunting the corridors to the sound of jingling bells.

The film, when it reaches the space station, is harsh and empty, full of white spaces, hard edges, metal, and synthetic materials (plastics, PVC). (The design is still late 1960s – the high-key lighting, the Minimal decor; as in films like *The Knack*, *THX-1138* or *2001: A Space Odyssey*, or John Lennon's *Imagine* music video, rooms are painted all in white). The long curving corridor, the silvery metal doors, the rows of round windows (one large, with smaller ones on each side), the small shiny mirrors, with the Ocean beyond.

There are two main corridor sets in *Solaris*: the red one, lined with doors to the living quarters, and plastic buttons and boxes, and the white one, with the large circular windows, upright metal cabinets leaning over, and doors leading to the laboratories. Kris's room has white, padded plastic on the walls. Black, blue, grey and white are the predominant colours on the station (apart from the library, which stands out with its green carpet, wooden panels and earth colours). Slow zooms or tracking shots in the silent, empty rooms; the spartan room Kris chooses, with its bed covered with a plastic sheet, chairs, a desk (contrasting vividly with the untidiness of Gibarian's room). Kris places objects he's brought from home in it: the metal box of soil on the window sill; his reproduction of Andrei Roublyov's *Trinity* on a shelf.

Tarkovsky covers the action with lengthy takes, the camera zooming in and out or tracking slowly crabwise. As in *Andrei Roublyov*, in dialogue scenes, actors drift slowly to and fro behind other actors. When Kris lies on the bed, Tarkovsky and Yusov employ very low angle shots, looking along Kris body from his feet (and recalling the Renaissance paintings of Christ in the tomb – Andreas Mantegna's being one of the most famous. A Hollywood movie would probably opt for high angle, overhead shots here).

Early on in Kris's visit to the station, Tarkovsky introduces the strangeness of the Ocean: the large round windows are at first black; Tarkovsky tracks past Kris's shoulder, into the darkness, then back out again (he repeats this later). In a subsequent scene, as Kris explores the spaceship, the windows change quickly from dark to light over a cut. In the following shots through the windows, the swirling mass of the Ocean is seen. The Ocean's depicted as a vortex of liquid slowly spiralling, directly recalling Douglas Trumbull's Stargate effects in *2001: A Space Odyssey*; some shots evoke the 'slitscan' process Trumbull developed for the 1968 film, with spiralling movements in the upper and lower half of the frame; in some shots, there's a sky and sun above the Ocean; the Ocean images are accompanied by Eduard Artemiev's synthesizer and strange sci-fi noises and drones (which's again another link with *2001: A Space Odyssey*, in particular the Stargate sequence, which was accompanied by low rumbles and electronically treated sounds).[1]

Tarkovsky's favourite motifs are here aplenty: fire (bonfires, candles, rockets, and so on); childhood; floating; horses; dogs; water. Kris takes a bit of Earth with him on his journey: a plant in soil in a metal tin (first seen in a still-life just before Kris leaves Earth); the other scientists have mechanisms for reminding them of Earth (Snaut has a butterfly collection in his room, and, early on, he shows Kris how to put strips of paper over the heating duct, so it sounds like leaves).

The spirits on the spaceship recall the sprites in Shakespeare's *The Tempest*: Gibarian's spirit (a giant topless black woman in the book) is a white teenage girl in a blue nightdress accompanied by tinkling bells (recalling Caliban who hears sweet music; many filmmakers tackling *Solaris* would also alter the black topless giantess to something more politically correct; needless to say, a tall black woman didn't appear in the 2002 remake of *Solaris*); there is also Sartorius' dwarf (recalling Ariel), kept in the laboratory.

Kris's wife is the most fully realized spirit in *Solaris*, a long-dead Miranda to Kris's perplexed Prospero. These beings are only partially glimpsed by Kris – he sees the girl in a blue dress walking in front of him in the corridor (the camera catches her at the edges of the frame, or glimpses her behind frosty glass); Sartorius's dwarf runs out of the door of his laboratory, only to be pushed back inside by the scientist. There is also something in Snaut's room: as Kris talks to Snaut, just after he's arrived on the station, a hammock and sheet behind him shakes. As Kris leaves the room, he looks back, there is a cut to an extreme close-up of an ear and part of someone's head (ears feature prominently in the library scene).

Further backstory and exposition occurs in *Solaris* when Kris explores Gibarin's room, and plays the video Gibarin made just before he committed suicide (the eerie Ocean music comes in for the first time here, when Kris stops the tape and there's a zoom into the black round window). The chimes which accompany Gibarin's girl visitor are heard on the soundtrack of the tape and outside the door of Gibarin's room as Kris plays the tape (Tarkovsky would revive the tinkling chimes for the angelic effects in *Nostalghia*). Kris glimpses the girl in a blue nightgown a few times (she's also in Gibarin's video), in the distance (curiously the 'visitor' persists on the space station after Gibarin's death). In one short scene, he follows the visitor into a refridgeration compartment where Gibarin's corpse is kept (the low angle shot of Gibarin looks forward to the way Kris's filmed in bed later, making the age-old connections between sleep and death, which're cited in the quote from Miguel Cervantes).

When Kris resumes playing Gibarin's final message, the film goes to black-and-white. It's here that Gibarin tells Kris that the situation on Solaris 'is all about conscience'. (Towards the end of the video tape, voices are heard off-screen, and knocks on the door; in a nice touch, Kris, standing in Gibarin's room, glances towards the door, as if convinced for a moment that someone's there. Tarkovsky often plays with the audience's perception during the video playbacks by maintaining the sounds from the tapes off-screen while filming the actors watching them).

Suicide features prominently in *Solaris*: Hari repeats the suicide of her real-life counterpart, while Gibarin's suicide, which looms over Kris's arrival at the space station, is never properly explained (the motives offered include shame, hopelessness and cowardice). Gibarin insists that he's not mad, and that Kris will eventually understand him, and why he killed himself. And Kris does realize fairly rapidly that all is not well with the inhabitants of the space station.

One of the key motifs in *Solaris* is the circle or globe, which appears many times: the circular space station and corridors, the spiral swirls of the Ocean, the planet Solaris, the circular windows of the station (with circular pools of white light on the floor), the circular rocket launch room, the apples, balls, chandeliers, balloons, clocks, Earth globes, cups, bowls of water, the spherical lamps and vases, the concave mirrors, the circular table in the library and *dacha*. The globes, circles and circuits act as mirrors, lenses and viewing devices (it seems as if it's the Ocean that studying the humans, rather than the other way around – as if they're in a giant laboratory).

The set-up of *Solaris* is that of a spaceship orbiting above an enormous planet-sized mirror, the Ocean itself. In a film so chock full of mirrors, it's no surprise that Tarkovsky's next film would be entitled *Mirror*. (Tarkovsky is not particularly interested in the Ocean itself, but only in the way it acts as a giant mirror for the humans, reflecting and exaggerating and subverting their desires and demons).

The circle motifs are another link to *2001: A Space Odyssey*, which concentrated at length on giant circular images of planets, orbiting spacecraft, the globe of the *Discovery* ship, extreme close-ups of eyes (Bowman and the Star Child), and spinning space stations like vast wheels. One of the selling points used in the marketing of *2001* was the enormous centrifuge constructed in a London studio to emulate artificial gravity in deep space (famously used with the camera dollying beside Frank Poole jogging).[2]

Another recurring motif has Kris leaving Hari on her own, and Hari being unable to bear it. In one scene Hari smashes through a metal door while Kris's on the other side, unable to open it (she breaks through it in slow motion, and collapses, her limbs blooded); in another, Kris rushes back to her in the bedroom, but she's asleep (the bed covers are awry); he embraces her, all contrite; finally, when Kris has left Hari alone again, she commits suicide by drinking liquid oxygen. (Actress Natalia Bondarchuk recalled that the first time she tried to get through the specially constructed door, she couldn't do it; part of that was kept in the scene).

The scenes replay Kris's past, when he left his real wife alone, felt guilty about her, and returned to find she'd poisoned herself. In this film of conscience, shame and guilt, Kris seems unwilling or unable to learn from his past mistakes, and persists in (or is doomed to keep) repeating the same actions, which led to his wife's suicide in the past, and leads to Hari's suicide in the present.

Ivor Montagu likened Hari's appearance in *Solaris* to the folk tales of seal-wives appearing to Orkney fishermen, or djinn princess brides in Arabic tales (1973, 94). Certainly Hari's mysterious, erotic presence recalls all of those characters from fairy tales (the mermaids, nymphs, dyads, mænads, elves and sprites who entice and seduce mortal men).

During the scenes leading up to Hari's suicide and its aftermath, the film seems more interested in Hari and her predicament than Kris (she, rather than he, is leading the narrative, and he is reacting to her behaviour). This may reflect Tarkovsky's own dislike of Donatas Banionis and admiration of Natalia Bondarchuk, and subsequent emphasis on Hari's character.

Memory and the past is a recurring theme in *Solaris*, mediated through the modern technology of sci-fi, the video tape (in the book, the video tapes are written reports). There are three video tapes: the account of Berton's visit to Solaris; Gibarin's suicide note to Kris; and Kris's father's home videos. (The home videos are pretty accomplished, with slick camerawork – these are not amateur films). The home videos include images of Kris's mother in a fur coat, in the snow, and later beside the lake; Hari at the *dacha*, waving to the camera (and dressed in her familiar shawl and beige and brown dress); Kris as a five year-old boy, and very briefly as a teenager.

Kris shows Hari a film his father made when he was younger (shot in Zvenigorod) as a test, to gauge her reactions to seeing herself. Tarkovsky said that Kris's father's films should be poetic (perhaps using Tarkovsky's father's poems as a starting-point [D, 37]). They were shot in a style that Tarkovsky had developed from *Ivan's Childhood* onwards: wordless, silent imagery of family members in rural settings: Ivan in the forest setting in *Ivan's Childhood*, for instance, or the images of the red-haired girl with the chapped lip in *Mirror* (*Mirror* consciously expanded upon the home movies in *Solaris* – in particular the Brueghelian snowscapes).

Kris sinks deeper into himself, into the isolation (approaching autism) brought on by the solitude and melancholy of space travel, the empty spaceship, and the ghosts of his past. When Hari appears to Kris he is, significantly, asleep. At first Hari is like a succubus, a dream-made spirit. A few times she is framed against the dazzling white circular window, like a halo, or body aura; when she is first seen she is shot near the round window, on a chair (her pose and demeanour, as well as the cut from a C.U. of Kris, asleep, to Hari's mouth, recall Leonardo da Vinci's paintings, in particular the *Portrait of a Woman (Ginerva Benci?)*, referenced in *Mirror*). There's a wonderful gold lighting scheme in the room. She approaches Kris slowly, lies beside him and kisses him. (As well as an extreme C.U. of Hari's mouth, there's a dolly shot into Kris's ear, which's followed by a cut to an aerial image, flying over the Ocean; Kris talks in voiceover.)

In many shots Hari is framed next to or looking into mirrors, especially in scenes where she is wondering about herself (Tarkovsky uses the classic staging of two actors looking at each other in a mirror, a double two-shot). In one wonderful moment, Hari picks a photograph of Kris's wife, but doesn't know who it is; when she looks at herself in the full-length mirror, holding the photo, she recognizes herself.

The second time Hari appears to Kris is also charged with eroticism: she cuts off her dress with scissors and embraces him in bed. She is ten years dead. This is what fascinates Tarkovsky – these beings created by the unconscious – not the daylight conscious mind, which he dislikes, but the unconscious desires. So the film could take place anywhere: in one view, the sci-fi element is practically superfluous (it is often deliberately negated).

The library in *Solaris* is a capsule of Earth history and culture: it is painted in earth colours (green walls, green carpet, lots of wood); there are books, pictures (such as the series of Pieter Brueghels, including Brueghel's famous *Months* series and *The Tower of Babel* [1563]), photographs, busts, china, a death mask, 'ethnic' masks, telescopes, stained glass windows, candles, brass scientific instruments, musical instruments, globes, mirrors, guns and a Venus de Milo statue. Brueghel's *Hunters in the Snow* (1565, Vienna, a.k.a. *February*), pervades the library scene. Tarkovsky cuts back to it a number of times. There are lengthy exploration of the painting – the iced-over pools, the skaters, the hunters and their dogs, the stark, leafless trees, the birds, the towns and churches, the distant snow-covered hills – as the camera pans over it (recalling the end of *Andrei Roublyov*, like a mini art history lesson).

The library scene is central to *Solaris*; it crystallizes many of the themes of the film, and includes the characters discussing Hari's 'humanity', Snaut offering Tarkovskyan philosophy (on issues such as love and morality), a speech from Snaut (taken from Stanislaw Lem's book) about humanity's need to see everything in human terms, a discussion of science and rationalism vs. morality and art, the thirty seconds of weightlessness, and the lengthy contemplation of Brueghel's paintings.

Both Snaut and Sartorius offer sceptical, detached views of Kris's involvement with Hari; when Hari speaks up, she says Kris is being the most 'human' of the lot. Hari also introduces a concept alien to the scientists – love. Sartorius's response is to remind her that she is not real, that she's a copy, a reproduction of the real Hari, who's dead (Sartorius challenges Kris to give her a blood test). Sartorius berates Kris for not being interested in anything but lolling around in bed with Hari (a surprising number of the scenes in *Solaris* are set in and on the bed in Kris's room). For Stanislaw Lem, the emphasis on human love and morality is made redundant by the total indifference of the universe. In the book, Kris comes to the conclusion that 'the age-old faith of lovers and poets in the power of love, stronger than death... is a lie, useless and not even funny' (194).

The weightlessness of Kris and Hari is stunning, but not overdone. Tarkovsky begins the short sequence with some movie magic *à la* Jean Cocteau: a candelabra floating in space, past a chandelier, which trembles and tinkles. As Hari and Kris start floating (on chairs), a book (*Don Quixote*) flies past in the foreground. In an extraordinary shot, Kris and Hari clasp each other as they float in front of the display of Brueghel paintings on the curved bay.

After Hari has been staring at the Brueghel painting of *Hunters in the Snow*, the camera follows her gaze and meditates on the painting for some three minutes in a series of C.U. pans over the painting joined by lap dissolves, to the sound of J.S. Bach's *Choral Prelude* (this's one of the few instances of Hollywood montage in Andrei Tarkovsky's cinema). There are also sound effects that match the images in Brueghel's painting (such as the sound of birds, bells chiming, dogs barking and voices, all favourite Tarkovsky off-screen sounds). At the end of this montage there is an image from Kris's father's amateur film of Kris as a boy beside a swing and fire in the snow in a Brueghelian setting (this image/ memory was fleshed out and used again in *Mirror*). The montage ends with a lengthy shot of the Ocean, and moves directly into Hari's suicide (with a cut on sound, of the shattering metal oxygen flask).

Kris has a white streak in his hair, like the Stalker, and Gorchakov in *Nostalghia*. Hari, meanwhile, has an ethereal beauty, like a Leonardo da Vinci model. Kris's wife took poison when he left her – and the replica wife drinks liquid oxygen. Naturally, in this re-run of his life, Kris doesn't want to abandon her this time. There are all sorts of intriguing questions posed here – about real and imaginary/ dreamed life, about morality and the past, about guilt and self-deception, about ambition and regret. Given this second chance, Kris wants to do the right thing (but seems doomed to repeat his mistakes). The way out for the characters in *Solaris*, Tarkovsky said, was in dreams, in illusions (ST, 199).

It is significant that most of the replicas (or 'mimoids', as the script has it) are women – and that the main replica made by the Ocean is a woman. There is an allegorical, metaphorical agenda here: some post-colonial or feminist critics might wish to see the replica or spirit as a slave, or an ethnic minority, or women in general, or any decentred, disenfranchised class of people. 'My feelings are not inferior to yours', Hari tells the three men in the library (she speaks up after listening to their cynical, materialistic accounts of what is going on in the space station. This is not only the cry of a replica woman, but of a real woman. The irony – the tragedy – of *Solaris* is that Hari becomes more fully 'human' than the real humans. Critics such as Jean Baudrillard, Jacques Derrida and Fredric Jameson have pointed out the ambiguous relation between what is 'real' and the 'imagined'. Kris and Hari (and the film itself) can be seen as existing partially in a Jamesonian or

Baudrillardian 'hyperspace'.

The sense of time passing is ambiguous in *Solaris*. The interval between scenes could be a few hours or days or weeks. In the Earth scenes, a day and a night seems to pass; the lengthy journey to the planet Solaris is compressed into a few shots; when Kelvin reaches the station, his stay appears to last a few days, but it could be much longer (presumably, the Ocean affected the scientists already there over weeks and months). But time passing has usually been vague in Tarkovsky's films, as it is in so many fiction films.

Oddly, key narrative developments in *Solaris* are not shown: Hari's conversation with Sartorius, the bombardment of the Ocean, Kris's encephalogram being beamed at the Ocean and, crucially, Hari's death in the Matter Disintegrator while Kris's asleep. The viewer sees Hari appear for the first time, and is intimately involved with her for much of the film, yet, when the time arrives for her to die, it's not shown. It's another of Tarkovsky's subversions of dramatic conventions (the Soviet film authorities wanted Hari's death to be off-screen).

Later in *Solaris*, Hari commits suicide by drinking liquid oxygen in the corridor, right after the library scene. Kris (clad in underwear and a cream pyjama shirt, suggesting they've made love) kneels over her frozen form. Snaut, hearing the commotion, comes out into the corridor and remarks: 'don't turn a scientific problem into a bedroom story.' A good line, a scriptwriter's line, which accurately sums up Kris's propensity for melodrama, for reducing what is really an extraordinary encounter (between humanity and the sentient alien Ocean) to a domestic drama. (Snaut also mutters that he can't get used to the mimoids' resurrections.) During her 'resurrection', Hari writhes on the floor, nipples visible under the wet shirt, in an erotic epilepsy, a machine-made convulsion in which orgasm, madness and death are all visible.

In an earlier scene, terrified of being left alone, like a child, Hari bursts through a metal door, after beating on it. When Kris tends her wounds, they are already healing (the transformation's accomplished in a long take, as are many of the unreal events in *Solaris*; Tarkovsky likes to use cinema's tricks of the trade to show something magical. So he had Kelvin tending Hari's arm, going to a closet for medication, and returning to find the wounds nearly gone, all done in one shot.)[3] In a later scene, Kris feels guilty about leaving Hari on her own, and rushes back to her from the laboratory, but finds her asleep in bed.

Hari's cardigan or shawl appears in many scenes; it's her signature, part of her personality; when she isn't there, Tarkovsky cuts to a shot of the shawl; after she's been annihilated it appears on a chair in the library, as Kris talks to Snaut. When Hari materializes again, she puts her shawl on the back of a chair, where there is already another one. (It's a neat piece of visual shorthand, to suggest that this could go on and on. As Snaut reminds Kris, Hari could come back hundreds of times).

A dream/ memory sequence occurs when Kris is in a delirious state; he's filmed in bed, then staggers out into the corridor; by the round window in the white corridor, the main place for viewing the Ocean outside, he meets Snaut and talks about love and mankind; cut to a shot of the Ocean, swirling, in white and green; then a tracking shot of Hari and Snaut seen from behind on either side of Kris, supporting him, walking along the corridor. A bright light, behind their heads, sometimes flares into the lens, turning the screen white. This same action, of the three people walking, is repeated in similar shots, with match cuts on the light flaring the lens. Loud music comes in; then the scene moves to Kris's house on Earth, in deep sepia. There is a shot from an unusual angle, accompanied by a loud organ sound, of Kris on his bed in the station; it tilts and pans down to a vase of flowers and a mirrored floor – a reflection of Kris is seen on the floor (plastic sheets are hung up – echoing the sheeting in the *dacha*). This is the remnant from the mirror room scene which was cut from *Solaris* (Kris takes his bed with him on his dream journey, which's seen in the mirror room, and in the *dacha*). Then a shot of Hari, crouching beside Kris's head, comforting him; she looks up, into the camera; another light flares the lens. Then one of Tarkovsky's continuous dream shots in which multiple versions of Hari are seen, plus flowers, fruit, Kris's mother and the dog from the *dacha*, all in the same shot (achieved with stand-ins all dressed and made-up the same as Hari). The Haris are shown walking around Kris's room, or standing by the window (the music is mixed very loud). The shot ends on Hari sitting in a chair, staring at the camera. Cut to: a black-and-white shot of Kris rising from the bed; he stands up and embraces Hari. The ominous music fades, the camera tilts down to a chair, upon which a glass vase is rattling then becomes still. Kris seems to be back on Earth, in his *dacha*, but it's not Earth. Cut to: a black-and-white image of Kris back on Earth (dressed in the pyjamas he wears in bed in the station), in his father's house, but the furniture, walls and windows are covered in plastic. It is an image of familiar yet altered surroundings, the distant future, or perhaps the past, after his wife's (or mother's) death, or where he really wants to be, in his anxious delirium. The scene's full of circular imagery and Tarkovskyan still lifes (the table, the glass vase, the apple, the bowl, the cup). A reproduction of the Brueghel painting which Hari and Kris gazed at in the station's library is taped to the video screen. Kris's mother is the age she would be when he was a boy. His mother reads a book; eats an apple; then, like the witch in *The Sacrifice*, she bathes a wound on his arm, with a white jug of water and a bowl (the jug appears in Kris's bedroom later); she kisses him, and moves out of shot; he weeps, murmurs 'Mama'; the sound of dripping water continues past the local sound of the water pouring into the bowl. Kris's delirium ends with a zoom into black, past his mother, a cut back to a shot of Kris in bed, in colour (there's a curious wipe effect between the two shots, with a black shade wiping across the frame).

After the long dream or memory sequence, involving Kris and his mother, Hari dies, offscreen. Kris wakes up to find Snaut in his room, but no Hari. Hari leaves a suicide note, like the one Kris's real wife left. The Ocean is changed: Snaut tells Kris that it is starting to form islands – islands of memory. Snaut says maybe it's time for Kris to return to Earth. In the subsequent scenes, all the filmic signals are that Kris is returning to Earth, but then the ominous music comes in – a little like Ligeti's music in *2001: A Space Odyssey*. The music is the main clue that all is not as it was before – this is the music that has been used with the visual effects shots of the Ocean. It is finally seen that Kris has created himself an island out of the dreamstuff of the Ocean on Solaris, and out of the ocean of the unconscious inside him.

The ending of *Solaris* looks like this: on the spaceship J.S. Bach's organ music starts up. Zoom in to Kris's little plant, set against the white circle of the window. This is a poetic link to the opening shots of the film, of the reeds in the river. Then Kris is seen beside the lake, as at the beginning of the film. It is now wintry, though (the lake is frozen – a wonderful touch, but apparently not intentional). Dead, bare trees. Mist. The *dacha*; the dog; the fire (which's still burning, as if Kris hasn't been away for long). The music ends. Kris approaches the house and looks inside. His father is there, lost in himself, sorting through books and papers. It is raining on him (but he doesn't notice), steam rising from his shoulders. Kris's father sees Kris staring in at the window, and goes to the front door: Kris kneels before him and embraces him, just as he did with his imagined wife. The scene conflates issues such as love, family, œdipal relationships, dreams, memories, wish-fulfilment, patriarchy and death. The scene recalls the Biblical Prodigal's Return (as in Rembrandt's famous painting). The ending was partly about, Tarkovsky explained, returning to the source, to the cradle, to home, to the place that can never be forgotten (D, 364).

And it has even more significance for Kelvin, because he has travelled so far on the road of technological progress to reach that realization.

The final shot of *Solaris* (actually three shots blended together): in extreme wide angle, a crane up away from and above the house and the embracing father and son. Two dissolves: to a helicopter shot of the house, rising away from it; then to a very distant visual fx view of the house, the lake and the island amid the green Ocean. The electronic music reaches a crescendo, the frame goes white, then fades to black — credit: 'the end'. It is a stunning ending, bigger indeed than *2001: A Space Odyssey*. At the end of *2001: A Space Odyssey*, humankind is reborn as a superbeing, but for what purpose? The ending of *Solaris* is deeper: humanity is shown as being on the point of learning that its purpose is really love, to love and be loved. This is what Kris concludes, or that the film concludes for him. It is one of Tarkovsky's central messages.

The Christian overtones in *Solaris* are many — the name Kris, the bathing of hands, the mother, the themes of patriarchal lineage and the father, the quest, the moral questions, the mimoid Hari as a Mary Magdalene (the virgin/ whore duality), the real wife as a martyr, a Virgin Mary, Hari's materialization as an incarnation, her 'resurrections' back to life, Kelvin redeeming himself, and so on. *Solaris* has a standard science fiction theme, though, which has been seen in space soaps, such as *Star Trek*, *Space 1999*, *Lost in Space*, *Stargate*, *Farscape* and *Dr Who*, and in cult sci-fi films such as *The Forbidden Planet* (Fred Wilcox, 1956, USA), *Mission To Mars* (2000), and *Alien* (Ridley Scott, 1979, GB). The scenario is: people visit a seemingly ordinary planet or meet some alien presence which slowly effects them. It is *Robinson Crusoe*, the islomania theme. Each person is an island. One is alone inside oneself. One makes one's own world. One creates things, one's own meanings, which are constantly changing. But relationship, with someone, is the best way out: back to love again, as at the end of *Stalker* and *The Sacrifice*. One can't deny society, enculturation and relationship, and Kris reconnects.

Kris imagines and 'makes' Hari, the 'wife' made of neutrinos. She becomes more human, more like his vision, his version of reality — or, rather, of what he would like reality to be. His wish kills him; desire is a killer. *Solaris* is based on a classic idea in science fiction, but also a classic idea in Western literature. The film works with mythic, archetypal elements. This man has been encountered a billion times before. He is single, heterosexual, white, bourgeois, highly educated, disenchanted, an outsider. He voyages into the unknown, in true heroic fashion, to solve a mystery. Kris is a protagonist that embodies significant aspects of the modern world: he's, appropriately, a psychologist (the postmodern shaman, the psychologist as a technological witch doctor). (One could see *Solaris*, as Maya Turovskaya does [123], as the only occasion in which Tarkovsky explored a love story. But it's more like going over the remains of a ten-year-dead love relationship, and when Kris revives the emotional bond with Hari, it is deeply ambiguous. Not least because the rational part of Kris realizes that his beloved is created from neutrinos by an alien presence).

For some critics, *Solaris* is a disappointing film – as a Tarkovsky film, or as a sci-fi film. Perhaps if *Solaris* had been conceived and lit and set in a *Stalker*-sort of future world – in a run-down, shabby space station, it might have been better for those critics and viewers expecting that. The actor who plays Kris, Donatas Banionis, is the weakest central performance in Tarkovsky's cinema; unfortunately, so much depends upon his performance – to carry the philosophical and spiritual weight of the film.

Tarkovsky added a new character, Maria, Kris's wife, in scenes set on Earth. Stanislaw Lem's novel took place entirely on the space station. Lem rejected Tarkovsky's first script, in which some two-thirds of the film would be set on Earth. While Lem's book emphasized that human values and emotions are dwarfed by the immensity, indifference and hostility of the cosmos, Tarkovsky's film enshrined those human qualities to the maximum, clinging onto them up until the last shot. Tarkovsky added many of his own references to Lem's novel, too: to *Faust* (the scientist Satorius); Fyodor Dostoievsky; Lev Tolstoy; Miguel de Cervantes (*Don Quixote*); Greek mythology (the myth of Sisyphus); and Pieter Brueghel. *Solaris* is in part a compendium of Tarkovsky favourites from high Western culture.

After he'd completed it, Andrei Tarkovsky said he was pleased with *Solaris*, preferring it to *Andrei Roublyov*: '[i]t's more harmonious than *Rublyov*, more purposeful, less cryptic. More graceful, more harmonious than *Rublyov*' (D, 53). His adaption of Lem's novel couldn't be faithful, Tarkovsky asserted: 'I attempted to put on screen my own reader's version of *Solaris*. In order to remain faithful to the author I had to deviate from the novel now and then in search of visual equivalents for certain themes'.

But Stanislaw Lem was not happy with Tarkovsky's interpretation of his book. Lem disagreed with the lengthy prologue on Earth and the emphasis on Kris's mother. These were more Tarkovsky's concerns rather than those in the novel.

Among Tarkovsky's additions were lines such as Snaut's to Kris: 'all these heart-rending emotions are pure Dostoievsky, nothing more'. Lem tried to persuade Tarkovsky to change the shooting script, but later withdrew from the project.

In 1979 Lem said he had only seen parts of *Solaris* on Polish television. Lem remarked that he had expected to see contrasts between 'home, sweet Earth' and the 'cold cosmos', between the gigantic Ocean outside and the enclosed space station inside. 'Unfortunately Tarkovsky took sides and favoured 'home sweet Earth' against the 'Cold Cosmos'', Lem said in an interview. Instead of the 'drama of cognizance', Lem said, Tarkovsky made *Solaris* a 'moral drama *par excellence*, which in no way relates to the problem of cognizance and its extremes. For Tark-ovsky the most important facet was Kris's problem of 'guilt and punishment', just as in a Dostoievsky book'. Tarkovsky said that one of the drafts of *Solaris* had half the script taking place on Earth, which was reminiscent of *Crime and Punishment*. Stanislaw Lem complained to Tarkovsky that he hadn't made Solaris at all, he made *Crime and Punishment*. 'What we get in the film is only how this abominable Kelvin has driven poor Harey to suicide and then he has pangs of conscience which are amplified by her appearance; a strange and incomprehensible appearance'.

Tarkovsky said he was intrigued by the idea that Kelvin was an average guy, so ordinary he was also a bore, but something happened to him on Solaris, when he encountered Hari. Unfortunately, Stanislaw Lem didn't share Tarkovsky's take on the story: 'as soon as he [Kelvin] begins to feel something or suffer – he becomes a human being. And this was leaving Lem completely unmoved. Totally unmoved. And I was deeply moved by this'.

Even so, Tarkovsky did not present his emotional, moral, natural and religious preoccupations in a one-sided manner: the sceptical, rational side of science was also represented, in the figures of both Snaut and Sartorius (though it's clear where Tarkovsky's sympathies lie). Later, in films such as *Stalker* and *The Sacrifice*, Tarkovsky further explored the oppositions of science and religion, rationality and creativity. In the laboratory in *Solaris*, for example, Sartorius suggests that Hari should be used for a scientific experiment, an idea which Kris strongly objects to. Sartorius scornfully says that Kris has got involved on a shallow, emotional level.

And Lem would have liked to have seen the planet Solaris itself. Lem complained that Tarkovsky had radically altered many elements in his novel, which Lem wanted to see on screen. Lem also said that he realized that Tarkovsky was ungovernable, that he was going to make his own version of *Solaris* anyway, so he gave up trying to alter the adaption.

Despite Stanislaw Lem's misgivings about the changes Tarkovsky made to his book, he must have realized that *Solaris* was a superlative piece of filmmaking, and also that, up until 1972, apart from *2001: A Space Odyssey* it was one of the very few really good sci-fi films. Tarkovsky had seen *2001* before he directed *Solaris*, but he didn't like it. Tarkovsky thought Kubrick's film to be too cold and sterile, and vowed to make his film the opposite, with its lived-in, messy space station, and richly furnished library. Tarkovsky said he was trying to make the future world of *Solaris* realistic; he was 'striving to make this imagined world as concrete as possible, especially in its purely external manifestations. Reality shown in *Solaris* must be materially tangible, almost graspable'. The lengthy spaceship sequences, which formed large chunks of *2001: A Space Odyssey* were reduced to a brief space travel scene which was mainly a C.U. of Kris, and a visual effects L.S. out of the spacecraft's window as it approached the circular station floating above the Ocean. In *Solaris*, Tarkovsky wanted to make the technology ordinary and everyday. 'I would like to film *Solaris* in such a way that the audiences are not faced with something technologically outlandish' (M. Turoskaya, 59).

Solaris is sometimes mentioned in books on science fiction and fantasy films, and aligned with sci-fi films of the same era – *2001: A Space Odyssey*, obviously, but also John Carpenter's quirky *Dark Star* (1974), George Lucas's bleak, brilliant *THX 1138* (1970), Douglas Trumbull's environmental odyssey *Silent Running* (1973), Peter Weir's consumer fantasy *The Cars That Ate Paris* (1974), and Michael Crichton's dystopian *Westworld* (1973).

Solaris is nearly always compared unfavourably with *2001: A Space Odyssey*, although Tarkovsky was keen to distance himself from Kubrick's film, and *Solaris* clearly had very different aims and themes. *The History of the Movies* guidebook offered a typical view: that it 'was an error for Tarkovsky to have attempted to follow *2001: A Space Odyssey*, a cinematic cul-de-sac, especially with a less dramatic use of decor and technology' (1988, 419). David Thomson was scathing of *Solaris*: '[a]n episode of *Star Trek* explored this theme with more wit and ingenuity, less sentimentality, and a third of the length' (in ib., 419). For Thomson, the 'visualisation of *Solaris* is as senselessly elaborate as in *2001: A Space Odyssey*, and the philosophy as mediocre' (1978, 597).

Solaris achieved a kind of cult status, being regarded as one of the more serious and important (but not necessarily enjoyable) sci-fi films. It was featured in a few critics' top ten lists, and was top of British sci-fi writer Brian Aldiss's top ten (above *Things to Come, A Clockwork Orange, Alien, Metropolis, Capricorn One* and *West-world*). Some film critics saw *Solaris* as an allegory (or reflection) of contemporary Soviet society, a critique of scientific Marxism, and a way of addressing the crimes of the Stalinist era.[4]

17 : 3   *SOLARIS* AND *BLADE RUNNER*

There are affinities between the replicas in *Solaris* and the replicants in *Blade Runner*, the hugely influential sci-fi film of 1982.[1] *Blade Runner*'s replicants have been likened by film critics to various ethnic minorities; marginalized, they have to live off the planet; the police boss Bryant refers to them as 'skin jobs', evoking the racist policemen in other films referring to 'niggers'. The replicants are slaves, and work in the 'Off-World colonies', recalling the slave trade of the West.

For some critics, the replicants are at the centre of *Blade Runner*'s exploration of reality and dream, the imagined and the real past, real and implanted memories, themes which are reflected in the tensions between the modernist and postmodern look of the film, its 'retrofitting', the evocation of the future using elements of the past.[2] The themes of time, mortality, memory and reality/ artifice are taken up in the photographs the replicants collect (in *Solaris*, as in most of Tarkovsky's films, paintings, rather than photographs, are the psychic touchstone, indicating Tark-ovsky's more traditional modernism, preferring painting over photography. But Tarkovsky does use photographs of Kris's mother, and of Hari, at key moments). For Deckard in *Blade Runner*, the photos are fakes provided by genetic engineering boss Tyrell to aid the implanted memories of the replicants, and thus control them (in a way, Kris uses the home videos he shows Hari as a way of humanizing her, of helping her to become more 'human'. It's as if he's educating her, rebuilding her). Deckard also collects photographs, which are 19th and 20th century images, of people he could not have known personally, suggesting that these too are fakes. The photos are little pieces of history and the world, whether faked or not, and they are needed by humans or cyborgs to fill in missing gaps in their lives (one of the first things the mimoid Hari does is to study closely a photograph of the real Hari that Kris has brought with him). In a totally postmodern world, where surface is everything, photographs (or home movies) may stand in for memories, may have as much weight and resonance as real memories. Much of *Blade Runner* concerns a nostalgia for 'real life', for something beyond mere image and surface, for something beyond the flashing, swivelling lights, the layers of rain and smoke, the huge wedding cake of artifice, an escape into reality; and always with the sense that time is running out — for Rachel as well as for the murderous replicants. 'Too bad she won't live', says Gaff at the end of the film, 'but then again, who does?'

Like Deckard in *Blade Runner*, Kris in *Solaris* finds himself falling in love with a replica of a woman, something synthetic (half-human, half-cyborg in *Blade Runner*, and a woman made of neutrinos in *Solaris*), manufactured by a higher intelligence (the Tyrell Corporation and the Ocean). And, importantly, both Deckard and Kris begin not to care if the women they love are not 'real'; the *feelings* they have for them, the bonds between them, have more significance than their flesh-and-blood materiality. Also, both Rachel and Hari begin to ask questions about their origins and real selves, and Deckard and Kris muse on what is real and what isn't. The journey of both Deckard and Kris is to learn to become more human, more humane and compassionate.

Thus, although *Blade Runner* is a piece of mainstream Hollywood entertainment, it is also in the category of the metaphysical sci-fi film (of which *2001: A Space Odyssey* is the obvious example), though it is nowhere near as meditative and introspective as Tarkovsky's Soviet classic. (For Gothic strangeness and the authentic tingle down the back with regard to replicas and automata, *Blade Runner* was outdone by another film made at the same time: Ingmar Bergman's *Fanny and Alexander* (1982), which contained an unforgettable sequence set in the back of an antique shop, where the young boy, Alexander, wanders into a world of puppets and dolls that come alive.)

Cyborgs, robots and human 'hybrids' have been a standard component of science fiction since the first great classic book of sci-fi and horror, Mary Shelley's *Frankenstein*.[1] Since then, popular culture has been awash with cyborgs, androids and robots: the robot Maria in *Metropolis*, Gort in *The Day the Earth Stood Still*, *Forbidden Planet*'s Robbie, *2001*'s HAL, R2D2 and C3PO, the 'droids in *Star Wars* (partly based on the peasants in Akira Kurosawa's *The Hidden Fortress* [1958]), Lee Majors in *The Six Million Dollar Man*, Yul Brynner in *Westworld*, the replicants in *Blade Runner*, Arnold Schwarzenegger in the *Terminator* series, Judge Dredd, RoboCop, Tetsuo, Ash in *Alien*, Number Five in *Short Circuit*, the Mark 13 cyborg in *Hardware*, *Max Headroom*, Data and the Borg in *Star Trek*, the military cyborgs in *Universal Soldier*, Arny's Quaid in *Total Recall*, Max in *Dark Angel*, Haley Joel Osment's David in *A.I.*, television sci-fi (*Dr Who, Stargate SG-1, Farscape, Babylon 5, Blake's 7, Futurama, Total Recall 2070, The Bionic Woman, Quantum Leap*), and so on, not to mention children's toys (such as War Planet, Transformers, Digimon, Beast Wars, Warhammer, and the thousands of characters in comic books, cartoons, TV series, films and computer games which are turned into merchandising: *Teenage Mutant Ninja Turtles, The Mighty Morphin Power Rangers, Pokémon, The Mask, Tank Girl, X-Men, Men in Black* and *Judge Dredd*).

For some commentators (D. Bell, 2000), the cyborg is not limited to the characters in *The Terminator* or *Star Trek*, but texts can be cyborgian, or founded on a cyborgian consciousness (transgressing Cartesian epistemologies and Western philosophy's dualisms). For critics such as Hal Foster, Mark Dery, Claudia Springer, Anne Balsamo and Scott Bukatman, cyborgs in contemporary cinema are 'a last bastion of overdetermined human, masculinist definition, bodies armoured against the malleability and invisibility of the present'.[2] They reaffirm bourgeois, dominant ideology, conventional notions of good/ evil, male/ female, human/ machine, self/ other (A. Balsamo, 1999).

Of course, contemporary Hollywood cinema doesn't get much further than the sensational image of humans inter-acting with cyborgs at the most extreme levels: sex, violence and death. Even movies enshrined by the critical academy, such as *Blade Runner*, don't go much beyond the titillating question: 'what's it like to fuck an android?'

Associated with the cyborg or robot are the many monsters in the horror genre, Slavoj Zizek's 'return of the living dead': Leatherface in *The Texas Chainsaw Massacre* (with his trademark mask and chainsaw extension). Anti-heroes with knives for fingers (Freddy Krueger in *A Nightmare On Elm Street* and the eponymous youth in *Edward Scissorhands*). 'Jaws' in the James Bond films of the 1970s, with rows of metal teeth. *Hellraiser's* Pinhead. Ghosts (*The Sixth Sense, What Lies Beneath, The Others*). Demons and the Devil (*The Exorcist, The Devil's Advocate, Spawn, Angel Heart*). Vampires (*Dracula, Buffy, Van Helsing, The Lost Boys, Interview With the Vampire*). Sub-humans or mutants (*The Fly, Basket Case*). Zombies (George Romero's films). Werewolves (*An American Werewolf in London, Wolf, The Howling*). Devilish aliens (*Gremlins, Critters, Independence Day*, the *Alien* series). Poltergeists (*Poltergeist*). Killer dolls (*Magic, Child's Play*). Witches (*Salem's Lot, The Craft, The Blair Witch* films). And psychopaths and serial killers (the *Friday the 13th, Candyman, Scream* and *Hallowe'en* films). While *Solaris* seems to be a long way from those Hollywood films, there are many affinities between Hari and the other neutrino-based replicas in *Solaris* and Hollywood's cyborgs and robots.

For critic Donna Haraway, the cyborg represents the possibility of new identities, moving beyond binaries, boundaries, universalisations. Transgression is a key theme in Haraway's thinking. New sutures, new borders. For Haraway, the technological revolution is as significant as industrial capitalism (1985). In "A Manifesto For Cyborgs", Haraway offered a chart of transitions 'from the comfortable old hier-archical dominations to the scary new networks I have called the informatics of domination'.

Here, simulation replaces representation, biotics replaces organisms, surface replaces depth, obsolescence replaces decadence, replication replaces reproduction, genetic engineering replaces sex, robotics replaces work, 'fields of difference' replaces the nature / culture binary, and 'cyborg citizenship' replaces the public and private (we are all cyborgs claimed Haraway; Haraway has famously proclaimed herself a cyborg, a quintessential technological body) (1985).

In Harawayan cyborg culture, the boundaries of the 'self' are increasingly becoming blurred (many cultural theorists have concerned themselves with borders and marginality: Homi Bhabha, Paul Gilroy, Julia Kristeva). New terms are required: the 'trans-human' is halfway between the human and the 'post-human', a site of suture, and marginality; the 'post-human' is an enhanced human (who may be 'post-biological'), with neurological, biological, psychological and technological enrichments.

The moment of the construction of the cyborg is a vital scene in the horror genre, whether it's in *Metropolis, Frankenstein* (Victor Frankenstein cries 'it's alive!'), *The Fifth Element* or implied in the title sequence of *The Six Million Dollar Man* ('we can rebuild him' – no one asks 'why bother?'). For Raymond Bellour, movies concentrate on this primal birth scene because this is what the cinematic apparatus is always doing, substituting a simulcra for reality.[3] The reanimation of the monster, the cyborg or the human is one of cinema's specialities. It's one of cinema's (and sci-fi's) primal scenes. Cinema is, physically, a continuous resurrection: people photographed eighty years ago at 16, 18 or 24 frames per second seem to come back to life. It's the flipside of Jean-Luc Godard's remark that cinema literally films death, that the people one films will die. Also, actors speak of enjoying playing death scenes, pantomiming the mysterious, perennially fascinating moment of ultimate transition.

There are many fascinating areas of discourse born from exploring cyberculture which there isn't space here to discuss: film animation, puppetry, dolls, toys, automata, fairy tales and fantasy. (With regard to cinematic animation, for instance, the possibilities for critical analysis are vast, covering early pioneers such as Georges Méliès, Emile Reynaud, Winsor McCay, Ladislaw Starewich and Willis O'Brien, through *avant garde auteurs* such as Jan Svankmajer, Alexander Ptushko, Jiri Trnka and the brothers Quay, to the puppeteers and stopmotion geniuses who went to Hollywood: George Pal, Ray Harryhausen and Henry Selick.) And a topic like puppetry goes back a long way, and takes in Punch and Judy by way of the *Howdy Doody Show* and *Thunderbirds* to *Spitting Image* (and any contemporary kid's TV show). Related to puppets are automata (which have enjoyed a resurgence in 'high art' circles with practices such as 'kinetic art' and the contemporary art installation), and dolls and toys, with or without batteries.

There were rumours in 2000 of James Cameron (*Titanic, Terminator, Aliens*) being involved in a remake of *Solaris*. The idea of Cameron, of all people in Hollywood, directing a remake of an Andrei Tarkovsky film was depressing for Tarkovsky fans (and not just remaking a Tarkovsky film, but a very good film, and a classic science fiction film). Somehow, the fusion of the brash, Republican showman of Hollywood blockbusters and a holy icon of art cinema seemed unlikely and unwelcome (my first reaction was: get your filthy hands off Tarkovsky!). Subsequent reports (in early 2001) had Steven Soderbergh (*Sex, Lies and Videotape, Erin Brockovich, Ocean's Eleven*) attached to the project. The film emerged from 20th Century Fox in late 2002, with Soderbergh directing and writing, and Cameron, Rae Sanchini and Jon Landau producing. George Clooney and Natascha McElhone starred, with Jeremy Davies, Viola Davis and Ulrich Tukur supporting. James Cameron remained an important presence – not just as producer, he also appeared in the marketing, the HBO Special, and featured in the commentary on the DVD release. Cameron also contributed to the production, including the editing.

20th Century Fox's *Solaris* was the first Tarkovsky film to be remade (although the producers insisted their film was a new and different approach to Stanislaw Lem's novel from Tarkovsky's film). Indeed, the 2002 *Solaris* was a very different animal: it was a dissection of a love affair between Chris Kelvin and his wife Rheya, containing numerous flashbacks which depicted the various stages of the romance, up to Rheya telling Chris she had been pregnant and had aborted the child, unsure how he would react. The 2002 *Solaris* kept the film at the level of a psychodrama between two people, while Tarkovsky had moved towards moral, ethical and philo-sophical explorations.

The Fox 2002 *Solaris* made other alterations to the novel, such as cutting out a lot of the scientific discussions (and the metaphysical speculation) of Lem's book, changing the sex of another character (turned into a black woman, played by Viola Davis), and had the space station orbiting above the planet Solaris, rather than on it.

The 2002 *Solaris* had a similar ending to Tarkovsky's film, in the sense that Kelvin remains on Solaris, but it unfolded in a very different way from Tarkovsky's ending. In the 2002 *Solaris*, Kelvin appears to have returned to Earth, going about his daily routine (riding on trains, walking rainy streets, etc), but, in the final scene,

Rheya appears in his kitchen. Thus, Kelvin never left Solaris at all (a fact emphasized by three images of the planet as the final shots of the film). At the end, then, Kelvin decides to stay on Solaris because it means he can spend more time with Rheya, even if she is an alien, constructed from anti-matter out of his memory. As the 2002 *Solaris* is primarily a love story, the film closes with Kelvin and Rheya being reunited in a tear-filled, emotional scene (i.e., Hollywood melodrama – muted and minimal, admittedly, but very much about heterosexual, bourgeois love). Tark-ovsky's ending, meanwhile, emphasized homecoming, Earth, Russia, the *dacha*, the father, the family, and the return of the prodigal son to the childhood home.

All fears of Hollywood tarnishing the legacy of Tarkovsky with a tacky remake were allayed: the 2002 *Solaris* was a smart, minimal take on the novel, but wasn't a patch on Tarkovsky's film (like Steven Soderbergh's other films, the *Solaris* remake came across as a filmed treatment of what the final film would look like, a script in progress, rather than a rounded, accomplished film on its own). And it didn't dent Tarkovsky's reputation one bit.

EIGHTEEN

Beyond the Mirror

Mirror

We celebrated every moment
Of our meetings as epiphanies,
Just we two in all the world.
Bolder, lighter than a bird's wing,
You hurtled like vertigo
Down the stairs, leading
Through moist lilac to your realm
Beyond the mirror.

Arseny Tarkovsky, 'First Meetings'[1]

18 : 1   MIRROR AND POETRY

Mirror (*Zerkalo* o r *The Bright, Bright Day*) is a poem. This is the key to understanding the film. It is a *ciné*-poem, complete with metaphors, allusions, references, historicity, lyricism, concrete and abstract images, a number of voices, motifs and symbols, autobiography, stanzas and refrains. Some images correspond to a line in a poem, while the refrains and links are the shots of fire which fade to black. If one thinks of *Mirror* poetically, then the form — the overlapping, the montages, the merging of imagery and events from the past and present – becomes clear. The spectator has to make an effort to unravel the components of the film, has to fill in gaps and re-order the events, but it makes sense in the end.

Mirror begins with one of the most poetic ten or fifteen minutes in cinema: from the moment where Maria is sitting on the fence, to the house on fire, then after that to the hair-washing and rain-filled room sequence. There is so much going on, so much that is startling. Only a film like *The Magnificent Ambersons* has a similarly miraculous first reel. Oliver Assays reckoned that the post-credits sequence is 'one of the most beautiful things I had ever seen in the movies' (1997, 24).

Mirror is Tarkovsky's beloved project, one he (seems to have) wanted to make for a long time (it remained his favourite film, and closest to his concept of cinema [CS, 255]). It is loosely autobiographical, and combines many elements, from poetry read in voiceover by the director's father, to dream sequences, flashbacks, newsreel and mnemonics (memory devices). The film is a poetic exploration of childhood: the long dolly shots around the old house in the country and the Moscow apartment explore the spaces of childhood, the geography of memory: the table was there, the chair was here, the window was there, and so on. A film of acutely remembered places. Film as personal psychogeography, self-reflexive, even indulgent, recalling Federico Fellini's *Otto e Mezzo* (1963) and *Amacord* (1973), classics of the autobiographical or personal film genre (Theo Angelopoulos's *Ulysses' Gaze* (1995) is another). For Oliver Assayas, *Mirror* was about film perception, a film which went *beyond* cinema, into 'issues of memory and remembrance, and the relationship between memory and perception' (1997, 24).

One of the fan letters (which Tarkovsky quoted in his diary) enthused about *Mirror*:

> it is your best film, it is a film about life, the most truthful and realistic film at life that we have ever seen. How is it that you have such amazingly subtle under-standing of all the confusion, complexity and splendour of life? (D, 213)

'I believe if one tells the truth, some kind of inner truth, one will always be understood' Tarkovsky commented, *pace Mirror*. In cinema, Tarkovsky said he wanted both the documentary, factual approach, in which every detail must be accurate, and the emotional, subjective, inner truth.

(But although *Mirror* would be 'a film built in its entirety on personal experience [D, 13], it wouldn't, as Tarkovsky maintained in *Sculpting In Time*, be Tarkovsky talking about himself. It was, rather, ultimately a film about feelings: about his feelings towards his loved ones and relatives, and about his own inadequacy – 'my feeling of duty left unfulfilled' [ST, 134]).

In a 1975 interview, Tarkovsky said that, *pace Mirror* that 'there are no entertaining moments in the film. In fact I am categorically against entertainment in cinema: it is as degrading for the author as it is for the audience.' That's a typical Tarkovskyan comment (but he's wrong about entertainment, I think). Tarkovsky also took a dim view of art's ability to educate, too: 'art cannot teach anyone anything, since in four thousand years humanity has learnt nothing at all' (ST, 50). Art shouldn't explain, or prove, or answer questions, Tarkovsky said (ST, 54).

The film had a number of titles. It was *The Bright, Bright Day* (or *The White, White Day*) for a long time (this title comes from one of Arseny Tarkovsky's poems). In February, 1973 Tarkovsky wrote: 'I don't like *The Bright Day* as a title. It's limp. *Martyrology* is better, only nobody knows what it means; and when they find out they won't allow it. *Redemption* is a bit flat, it smacks of Vera Panova. *Confession* is pretentious. *Why Are You Standing So Far Away?* is better, but obscure' (D, 69). It's not just in pre-1989 Soviet Russia where filmmakers were forbidden to use a title by state institutions. In the West, titles are not copyrighted (at least in the UK), but it would be a foolish company, however, that tried using names such as 'Disney', 'McDonald's' or 'Coca Cola' on a product or service, those corporations being notorious for the number of litigations they pursue). But Tarkovsky is not to referring to another studio, company or artist who might prevent him from using a title, but to the Soviet authorities.

Mirror started to take shape around 1968, when Tarkovsky worked with his co-writer, Alexander Misharin (Tarkovsky had asked Misharin to help him edit the script of *Andrei Roublyov*, which Misharin had been reluctant to do, because Andrei Konchalovsky was the writer, but wasn't around at the time. Misharin helped Tarkovsky to cut out a whole section of *Andrei Roublyov*).

Tarkovsky had originally planned filming interviews with his mother with a concealed camera, using questions such as 'when did you begin smoking?', 'do you like animals?', 'are you superstitious?', 'are men or women stronger, do you think?', 'do you ever have friends outside your circle?', 'do you always speak the truth?', 'what would make you especially happy now?', 'have you ever envied youth?', 'which are your favourite poems?', 'are you capable of hatred?', 'which part of your life would you say was happy?', 'what do you think about space travel?', 'do you like Bach?', 'what do you remember about the war with Spain?', 'what was the funniest thing that ever happened to you?', 'are you a good swimmer?', 'do you remember the day when you sensed you would become a mother for the first time?', 'which is your favourite season?', 'have you ever starved?', 'what do you think about war?', 'what is freedom?', 'how many years did you work at the printers?', and 'are you scared of the dark?'

Mirror, according to the script *A Bright, Bright Day* (Mosfilm, 1973), was going to have less documentary footage and more memories of Tarkovsky's childhood. The narrator was going to quote from Aleksandr Pushkin's 'The Prophet' (a favourite Tarkovsky text) and walk past a funeral at a cemetery, encouraging the narrator to muse on life and death.

The Bright, Bright Day screenplay had opened with a scene in a cemetery, and a funeral. Scenes included the demolition of a church in 1939; the mother selling flowers in a market; a horse riding lesson; a scene at a ractrack; and a forest scene at night (M. Turovskaya, 63).

I wanted to tell the story of the pain suffered by one man because he feels he cannot repay his family for all they have given him [Tarkovsky wrote in *Sculpting In Time*]. He feels he hasn't loved them enough, and this idea torments him and will not let him be. (133-4)

The film would be about a mother, Tarkovsky said: 'any mother capable of arousing an interest in the authors,' Tarkovsky and Alexander Misharin wrote in their proposal for *Mirror* (when the film was called *Confession*): 'as all mothers, she must have had a full and fascinating life. This must be the ordinary story of a life, with its hopes, its faith, its grief and its joys' (CS, 257). The concept, according to Misharin and Tarkovsky, was to trace the 'spiritual organization of our society' through 'the rightful fate of one person; a person whom we know and love, who is called Mother' (CS, 258).

The narrator in *Mirror* is strictly a *narrator*, in the technical, literary sense of the term. Rather than being the narrator of a novel, however, *Mirror*'s narrator is the narrator of poetry, because *Mirror* is a *ciné*-poem, rather than the cinematic adaption of a novel. (And, to reinforce that, *Mirror* quotes from poetry far more than novels). So, although he is heard off-screen, interacts with characters (chiefly with Natalia), and is glimpsed briefly on his death bed, he is still not really meant to be a flesh-and-blood character like Maria, Ignat or Natalia. He is the narrator of the poem that is the film.

The script continually evolved, with daily rewrites (that's normal on many films, but *Mirror* had a loose structure, which could accommodate all sorts of additions or alterations.[1] As Tarkovsky wrote in *Sculpting In Time*, 'a great deal was finally thought out, formulated, built up, only in the course of shooting' [131]). Tarkovsky acknowledged that *Mirror* was the most complex of his films structurally and dramatically. The stuttering and hypnotism scene (which opens the film) was probably going to be put somewhere in the middle of the film, because the twelve year-old Ignat is seen turning on the television in the present-day Moscow apartment. Ignat would thus have been introduced differently. A likely opening of *Mirror* would have been: (1) the titles followed by (2) the long tracking shot around the narrator's apartment, establishing the present-day location, and the narrator, then (3) the printing works scene, then (4) the mother and doctor scene in the field.

The post-production of *Mirror* was troublesome because the first rough cuts of the film didn't work (and it wasn't simply a case of the filmmakers hating the first rough cut, as they so often do). *Mirror* was '*extremely difficult* to edit' Tarkovsky confessed (my emphasis). The film, as Alexander Misharin noted, had too many scenes and too many themes, and they couldn't be arranged into a form that satisfied everyone. If the scenes were arranged in a particular pattern, Misharin said, some other scenes would be left out. There was a moment of revelation when the 34 or so scenes fell into the final form. As Misharin told it, Tarkovsky's wife Larissa had sewn a kind of sack with pockets in it, which they hung on the wall and placed the scenes in each pocket. As if by a miracle, Misharin remembered, both he and Tarkovsky had seized the scenes at the same time and shuffled them into the same order. After that, the post-production of *Mirror* continued without problems.

Alexander Misharin recalled that the writing process on *Mirror* had been intense for a time: he and Tarkovsky had shut themselves away for three or so weeks and wrote every day. They employed a common practice among co-writers: they wrote scenes on their own, then swapped them and edited the other's scenes. Misharin said people reckoned they knew which were the scenes Tarkovsky had written and which were his, but often the opposite was the case. *Mirror* was not only about Tarkovsky's past and family; there was plenty of Misharin's background in there, too. Misharin recalled that he and Tarkovsky only fell out seriously once or twice.

According to Tarkovsky's diary, *Mirror* was allocated 622,000 roubles (a small budget; about \$2.5 million) and 7,500 metres of Kodak film. Filming began in

September, 1973 and finished in March, 1974. *Mirror* was not sent to Cannes (Tarkovsky and co-writer Alexander Misharin blamed Filip Yermash, Goskino's chairman, for this). It was released in the Soviet Union in early 1975 at a third (then second) distribution category.

The newsreel footage in *Mirror* is a substantial element in the film. It is gathered from all sorts of sources, the result of anonymous camera teams, and from so many places – throughout Russia, but also in China, in Berlin, in Spain, in Prague, and in Hiroshima. A lot of the footage is familiar from the countless documentaries on World War Two, on Russian history, on Nazi Germany, and on 20th century history (there are whole cable and satellite channels now dedicated to airing this kind of material).

But Tarkovsky deploys it in quite different manner from the typical TV documentary. There are no captions and no voiceovers identifying the many images and historical events. And none of the characters in *Mirror* refer to the footage, or even to the events depicted in the newsreels. Instead, Tarkovsky relies on the viewer's knowledge of history to fill in the gaps. Some of the newsreel will be familiar (the nuclear bomb explosions require no gloss). But much of it will be unknown to many in the audience. At the same time, viewers will not need to know where and when some of the newsreels were shot. The remarkable footage of the Soviet balloonists, for example, or the moving images of soldiers trudging doggedly through mud and water do not require the viewer to know all the details. (Tarkovsky does employ one of the standard devices of TV news and documentaries: he adds studio sound effects to footage that was shot silent (as a lot of it was).)

Some viewers and critics were confused by the use of the same actors for different roles in *Mirror* (even though this is is a not uncommon strategy: it's used in the *Back To the Future* series [1985-90], for instance, and other time travel movies. A famous instance occurs in *The Wizard of Oz* [1939], although that's not time travel).

Part of the point of using the same actors and actresses for the mother/ wife and narrator/ son is to show that the past and present are connected and interfuse. The present exists beside the past, not only in dreams and memories, but also in people, in their faces, personalities and actions. There is a historical, social and personal continuity. One cannot escape the influence of the past, and the same situations are re-enacted (for example, the 1930s family is broken, and the present-day husband and wife have parted). Cinema works at the point of viewing in a continuous present, yet it is always, as Jean Cocteau said, 'filmed death'. The past and present are bound up tightly together in the last shot of the film: Maria is there, and Maria as an old woman with Maria's two children (the old woman doubles as a grand-mother). Matriarchy and female solidarity is affirmed, as is generation-to-generation contin-uity, ambiguity and sadness.

'I should like to ask you all not to be so demanding, and not to think of *Mirror* as a difficult film' Tarkovsky asserted in 1975. It is no more than a straightforward, simple story. It doesn't have to be made any more understandable.

Structurally, there are two moments in the past that are explored in *Mirror*: 1935-36, 1942-43, and the present (*c.* 1974). The film principally takes place in these *three* time zones (discounting the newsreels), and in, primarily, *two* locations: a modern day apartment in Moscow, where the narrator lives (but is not seen); and the *dacha* (house) in the country, where the narrator lived as a boy with his mother, while his father was away at war or in the services. Characters are compared to each other, while others are irreconcilably opposed. (The newsreels, though, are roughly chronological).

Past (1935 and 1942)		*Present (about 1974)*
Maria, the mother	›	Natalia, the modern wife/ mother
Children's grandmother	›	Maria as an old woman (*and* the narrator's mother)
Aleksei, aged 5		
Aleksei, aged 12	›	Ignat, aged 12
Father (soldier)	›	Aleksei, the narrator

The mother and the boy of the past also dwell in the present. There are further complexities: Tarkovsky's real father reads his own poems (but the poetry in the film is not identified as by Arseny Tarkovsky), while Tarkovsky's own mother appears as the grandmother (Maria as an old woman), *and* the grandmother in the 1935-36 scenes (or she is Maria as an old woman transposed to the past).

Pier Paolo Pasolini had cast his mother to play the aged Virgin Mary in *The*

Gospel According To Matthew (and Martin Scorsese liked to use his mother in minor roles). Tarkovsky's own step-daughter was the red-haired beloved of the teenage Aleksei, and Tarkovsky's second wife, Larissa Tarkovskaya, played the doctor's wife. The *dacha* of the past is built on (the foundations of) Tarkovsky's real childhood home (it was important for Tarkovsky to build his childhood home in the *exact* spot it had once stood). The film is one long evocation of one person's childhood. It might have turned out self-indulgent and pretentious. Instead it is magnificent and profound.

18 : 2   *MIRROR*, SCENE BY SCENE

In the following notes on *Mirror* the film has been broken down into scenes, but individual shots (there are some two hundred) would be a better (but much lengthier) method. Some scenes, as often in Tarkovsky's cinema, consist of only one shot. (200 shots is a very small amount for an average-length feature film; Tarkovsky reckoned 500-1,000 would be average [ST, 117]; *Nostalghia* and *The Sacrifice* are much longer, and contain even fewer shots: between 115 and 120).

Mirror scene-by-scene:

Scene I. Prologue. Documentary. (1974).

In colour, Ignat (Ignat Daniltsev) switches on the TV in his father's Moscow (modern day) apartment. The TV doesn't tune in straight away. The programme shows a hypnotist/ therapist curing a shy boy's stutter, in *cinéma verité* style (the youth is a lanky teenager). There is no indication of what TV show this is, if it's a documentary, or part of some other programme. It's as if Ignat has just switched on in the middle of a TV show.

Vida Johnson and Graham Petrie relate the stutterer's desire to speak to the repression of the artist in the Soviet Union (JP, 116). The woman commands the teenager: 'you will speak loudly and clearly, freely and easily, unafraid of your voice and your speech'. The whole scene is covered in a single lengthy take, zooming out from the faces to show the two people in medium shot, then zooming back in; the shadow of the mic boom is visible. The style of the TV clip, though, has affinities with the rest of *Mirror*; there are no devices of TV (captions, voiceover, introductions) to indicate that this is a TV documentary.

The hypnotist tries a number of devices to put the youth into the correct mental state (including having him lean back on her hand, which she takes away). It's familiar hypnotism stuff. Finally, she concentrates on the boy's hands, creating tension through verbal suggestion then releasing the tension in his hands and in his voice at her command. As soon as he speaks clearly, cut to:

Main titles, with organ music (Bach), sombre white out of black.

Scene 2. The past (1935). The *dacha*.

In colour, Maria (Margarita Terekhova) sits smoking on a wooden fence between the field and the *dacha* behind her in the trees (we are presumably in the Russian countryside around the middle of the 20th century). She wears a white embroidered dress and a black cardigan, her hair in a bun (Tarkovsky used pictures of his mother' clothes as references for Terekhova's costumes). She's in her thirties. The camera tracks from a wide shot up to and past Maria, from behind her; the doctor (Anatoly Solonitsyn) is visible in the distance. The prologue is shot at the magic hour (of course). Off-screen sounds enlarge the space (a train; birds; dogs barking).

The doctor approaches. The narrator (Innokenty Smoktunovsky), in voice-over, talks about the *dacha*, the surrounding area and his father appearing: instead the doctor appears (which sets up further œdipal tensions). He is a surrogate father, and wistfully flirts with Maria, knowing she lives alone. They share a cigarette. The boy (who is the narrator, aged five) watches from a hammock tied between two trees, where he dozes next to his sister. (If he was asleep before, he isn't now; to emphasize that the young Aleksei is watching them, Tarkovsky includes a reverse angle of Maria and the doctor, taken from Aleksei's point-of-view). (No need to note the echoes of the voyeur of the Freudian primal scene).

When the doctor sits beside Maria on the fence, it breaks, and they both fall backwards. Maria rises quickly and dusts herself off, stepping away from the man, but the doctor remains on his back, the camera pushing in on him slowly. The doctor says that some living things fell with them. The doctor, philosophical now, talks about nature, trees, bushes, plants; 'trees don't rush about, fussing... We don't trust nature anymore.' He says 'visit us' and Maria does, later, at the end (in scene 30). (The doctor's not a nature freak, however: he mentions a nut tree nearby, but Maria tells him it's an alder).

The doctor walks away across the field, turns, and the bushes and field of buckwheat blow in the wind (Tarkovsky didn't want the actor Anatoly Solonitsyn to simply look back here, he wanted a reason for him to do so. If he had simply turned and looked back at her, it would have been false [ST, 111]). He waits a moment, as if pondering returning to Maria (the wind blows a second time, but less strongly), but he turns and leaves.

Maria turns away and goes inside the house, the camera tracking behind her, framing her against the house (the first reveal of this important setting – not only significant in the narrative, but one of the big expenses in the production). The poetry, read by Arseny Tarkovsky, begins here for the first time (the poem is 'First Meetings' [ST, 101], which begins '[e]very moment that we were together | Was a celebration, like Epiphany'). The poem celebrates love, where the woman leads her suitor into her world 'beyond the mirror'.

In this scene, Tarkovsky has introduced a number of elements, including a scene set in the past, voiceover narrating that scene, some of the key characters, and another slab of voiceover, but a different voice, this time reciting poetry (with yet another layer of meaning added, because it is the director's father reading one of his own poems). So already *Mirror* is fairly complex, narratively. And the viewer doesn't know yet who the narrator is. Add to that the two spaces of the opening scene, both set in modern-day Russia.

Scene 3. Inside the *dacha* (1935).

In colour, the mother, Maria, is shot in glowing sunlight. She looks transfigured. The actress looks like a Madonna out of Piero della Francecsa – the eyelids are rounded, heavy, clearly defined; the round face has slightly protuberant eyes (later the actress is deliberately compared with a Leonardo da Vinci portrait).

Outside, the aunt picks up Marina, who's half-asleep. There's a fire in the garden. A marvellous C.U. of the children sitting at the table in the room with Maria combines a Tarkovskyan still-life with actors: one of the children pours salt onto a cat's head, and there's spilt milk on the table. The children seem to be whispering about some secret or game.

Maria wanders around the room, with the poetry still being read in voiceover (the poem speaks of the transfigurations of love). The camera follows her (standing in the corner, then sitting down); in another shot, the camera dollies to the open window, with Maria sitting beside it, revealing the trees and ground around the house. It's raining; there's a table below with a Tarkovskyan still-life arrangement on it; the camera tilts up to show the field beyond the trees. Dogs bark loudly, and off-screen a man's voice calls out 'Dunya!', and a woman's voice answers him ('Pasha!').

Maria goes out to see the fire, and returns to tell the children. As they run out, a complex shot follows (one of the most complex in Tarkovsky's cinema): it begins with a track and pan away from a bottle mysteriously falling off the table, to a mirror on the wall (the first of many mirrors in the film); pull focus to the boys looking at the fire; a track with another boy (identified as Klanka) who appears next to the mirror, out of the door to show the barn on fire, seen beyond a wall of rain water dripping off a gutter. The final framing is a composition in deep focus, from the rain dripping in the foreground, through the middle ground of the garden and figures, to the burning barn beyond. A continuous shot of pure mystery: the first of many startling images in *Mirror*. It's a shot that would likely have taken an afternoon or perhaps all day to rehearse, to light and to shoot. The camera is hitting many marks, and props, actors and practical effects have to be co-ordinated with split second timing (and young child actors add further complications).

Cut to a shot of Maria against the trees; she walks to a well and drinks some water from a bucket. The camera tilts up to show the burning building. The creaking sound of the bucket at the well is as loud as the burning barn (an example of heightened sound fx).

Scene 4. Aleksei in bed at night (1935).

Shot 1. In black-and-white, the 5 year-old boy Aleksei (i.e., the narrator as a child) is in a large brass bed with an ornate headboard (no sign of Marina). Near-silence, a distant bird or owl. Faint (choir?) music. Another subtle sound effect here is the clink of metal, perhaps to indicate his father's uniform.

Shot 2. Trees and bushes rustle in L.S. The owl hooting, the trees blowing, a dark forest — these are the primæval and timeless expressions of otherness and strangeness. Lines from Dante Alighieri are quoted in *Mirror*, where the poet spoke of being halfway through life and entering a dark forest. The dark forest or *selva oscura* comes out of the *Divine Comedy*, at the start of Canto I of *The Inferno*. Apart from Dante, *Mirror* also alludes to Aleksandr Pushkin, the *Bible*, and Dostoievsky's *The Devils*. At the end of *Mirror*, the camera retreats into the darkened wood.

Shot 3 (as shot I). The boy says 'Papa'. The boy gets out of bed (he's dressed in a white nightshirt), moves a chair, and walks towards his mother's room. A piece of white clothing (a shirt?) is thrown across the doorway.

Scene 5. Maria's bedroom (1935).

The dream or memory sequence, also in black-and-white, is continuous temporally with the previous scene. The mother (Maria) and the returned father (Oleg Yankosvky) wash her hair, in a large bowl, in slow motion (the father is shown first, pouring some water). Maria is sexualized through her hair: it is often wild, in strands before her face, or wet with rain, or tied up; she often touches it and fiddles with it.

In this scene, she looks odd, her head bent down, face obscured. She stands, moves back slowly and flails her arms mysteriously. The camera pulls back too. A near-match cut shows the same room from a slightly different angle, but now empty. The walls and ceiling are dripping with water. Flames from a gas stove flicker. Lumps of wet plaster and water fall from the ceiling in slow motion, with the sound of it hitting the floor (which's wet). Eduardo Artemiev's electronic music wells up. There is no local sound (and no dialogue) in this scene, but the heightened sound of water dripping, and the sound of the bits of plaster and ceiling hitting the floor.

This could relate to the Freudian primal scene — the boy's remembered glimpses of the sexual relations between his mother and father. A child's fantasy of adult sexuality, perhaps, a memory of something he never saw, but thought about (or it's the narrator recreating it through a boy's eyes). But the room switches from the room in 1935 to a room transfigured by memory: now it's deteriorating, raining, falling apart (perhaps it's some decades later). Or perhaps the father's return disrupts the boy's psychological equilibrium, which's dramatized in this vivid fashion. Certainly the scene is abstract and ambiguous.

Maria walks to a mirror (back to the room in 1935, but now it's still raining

inside it). A lengthy C.U. of Maria follows her as she walks dreamily beside dripping walls. In a later shot, she's wrapped in a white shift and towel. Post-coital atmospheres are evoked here, as after the later cockerel-killing scene. Maria looks in the
mirror, sees herself as an old woman (played by Tarkovsky's own mother, Maria
Tarkovskaya, dressed similarly to the young Maria). A landscape is seen reflected in
the mirror (the shot has the obscure power of a Leonardo da Vinci painting – the
landscape in *The Virgin of the Rocks*, for example). The old woman wipes the
mirror, as if exploring the glassy interface between illusion and reality. The lighting
changes in the middle of shots here too, to bring out the reflections in the glass and
the mirrors (and adding to the theatricality). This scene ends with a colour bridging
shot, a poetic refrain, of a hand warming itself on a gas flame.

In the scene, the narrator imagines himself back in 1935, aged five, waking up to
find his father returned and with his mother. The film then leaps into the future, in
a fairy tale manner, as Maria looks in the mirror and sees herself forty years later
(this's the narrator mother Maria as she is now – in the next scene, the narrator is
talking with her on the phone). So if *Mirror* was fairly complex in terms of
narration by the end of the *dacha* scenes (scenes 3 and 4), it's more complicated now,
with these leaps between the past and the present, and the introduction of dream or
memory sequences.

Scene 6. The present (1974), in the narrator's Moscow apartment.

In colour, the camera pans right from some lace curtains, which link up with the
curtains in the *dacha* of the past. One very lengthy shot, tracking around the
apartment, which contains: a French film poster for Andrei Tarkovsky's *Andrei
Roublyov* on the wall; many mirrors; curtains half closed; plants; a sparse
environment, with little furniture and few comforts (and it has the flaky, scumbled,
textured walls that Tarkovsky loves, as if he's painting with walls). (According to
Tarkovsky, people used to visit the apartment set, designed by Nikolai Dvigubsky,
because it eerily recreated a sense of decay and damp).

The Moscow town apartment is a maze of mirrors, a labyrinth. Especially in the
later shots of Natalia, where she is framed against a wall, there are many mirrors
behind her; sometimes she stares into a mirror, playing with her hair, while
conversing with the narrator.

A telephone is heard ringing. In voice-over (presumably the man is somewhere off-camera, in the apartment), the narrator talks with his mother about the past, about 1935, and a woman (Lisa) at the printing works who died that morning (that's why his mother is calling him). The narrator says that he has been ill, hasn't spoken to anyone for three days, and has been dreaming about his mother as if he were a child. That line of dialogue clarifies the previous scenes for the viewer).

The dialogue about Lisa and the printing works leads the spectator into the next scene. The camera continues to track towards the long dark curtains at the end of the apartment. The telephone dial tone is heard, and this sound is blended the tram conductor in the next scene.

Scene 7. The past. The print works, Moscow (1935).

In black-and-white, Maria is rushing to the printing works, in heavy rain, in daytime. A tram and a conductor announcing stops is heard passing by, overlapping the previous scene. The camera, mounted high on a truck, seems to be pursuing her, as if running her down (or as if at tram height; neatly, the tram is heard but not shown, a cheap but effective way of introducing the idea of a city with trams without having to show it). The camera follows Maria in a tight long lens shot behind a fence, still tracking (these close mobile shots recur throughout the printing works scenes). Bleak, grey streets, rain, shabby corridors, a sparsely furnished office, bare lightbulbs. It's Stalinist Russia.

Maria thinks she's made a mistake in a State (Stalinist) publication. Evocations of work in Stalin's regime in the Thirties (which relates to the opening hypnotism scene, where the youth is encouraged to speak in his own true voice, evoking freedom of speech and the freedom of the artist and the creative voice). A young secretary (who's only been there a week) whimpers nervously about having a mistake in a State document. She goes out of the office to find Lisa; Maria is searching through the papers on her desk; Lisa (Alla Demidova) enters (taller, a little older and more efficient than Maria).

The three women leave the office and head for the printing presses. Lengthy, intricate tracking shots follow Maria as she walks past the noisy printing machines to find the proofs in a cupboard (photographs of Stalin and other politicos are on the walls). Her boss (played by Tarkovsky regular Nikolai Grinko) looks on wearily, and makes somewhat sarcastic moments (such as 'let some work and let others be afraid'). (The threat and repression of the Stalin era is deftly evoked at the level of the regular worker. This is a long way from the State-endorsed cinema of Sergei Eisenstein – *Alexander Nevsky*, for instance, made in 1937).

Maria moves to a spot on her own, by the window, to examine the proofs at length. Co-workers gather around. One of them says they've been printing throughout the night. Eventually, Maria finishes up checking the proofs.

Scene 8. Printing works.

Arseny Tarkovsky's poem "From morning on I waited yesterday" (ST, 123) is read by the poet over black-and-white tracking shots of the mother Maria as she walks along a corridor, followed by Lisa in the distance. Some of the corridor shots in the printing works are in slight slow motion (though for no obvious reason, except perhaps to enhance the unreality of this particular memory of the narrator's mother's. Tarkovsky said in *Sculpting In Time* that the slight slo-mo was employed to suggest 'a vague feeling of something strange' in the audience [ST, 110]).

The black-and-white photography changes colour with each shot in the print works scenes – it is tinted pink, sepia, blue – created by different film stocks and processing times, perhaps. Or from printing from colour film stock. Or perhaps it's intentional. (In *Stalker*, Tarkovsky said the alterations in the hue of the black-and-white shots were intentional. Georgy Reberg, *Mirror*'s cameraman recalled that black-and-white film stock was used to make up for the lack of colour stock; and the DP on *Solaris*, Vadim Yusov, said the same thing; which makes the use of black-and-white in Tarkovsky's movies partly the outcome of economics, not only the poetry of cinema).

Scene 9. Printing works.

Maria discusses the mistake with a colleague, Lisa, back in their office. She whispers the mistake in Lisa's ear; they laugh about it (Mark Le Fanu reckoned the misprint is 'sralin', related to the verb 'to shit', a misprint of Stalin; according to Neil Sinyard, the 'man of shit' episode caused everyone involved with the mistake to be arrested [1992, 157]). Unless the audience has foreknowledge of Soviet history, they won't have any idea what all the fuss is about. So Tarkovsky withholds the reason why Maria is so upset, but when it comes to revealing it, it's whispered to Lisa. (Also, Tarkovsky doesn't even make it clear that the printing house scene occurs in the repressive Stalinist era).

Maria's colleague (Nikolai Grinko) appears, bringing some alcohol (but he has little to do in this scene except to be a bystander). Maria is then severely dressed down by her fellow worker Lisa, as an over-dependent wife, with damaging emancipated ways, and is compared to Captain Lebyadkin's sister, Maria Lebiadkina, in Fyodor Dostoievsky's *The Devils*, the mysterious woman who has a small mirror, and who unmasks Nikolai Stavrogin as an usurper and pretender (the Dostoievsky reference is pure Tarkovsky).

Maria doesn't really understand the reference to Dostoievsky, but she finds Lisa's attack disturbing, and weeps. Tarkovsky concentrates the viewer on Maria, and the effect of Lisa's attack on her, not on Lisa, or the colleague, or the secretary. Big close-ups of Maria show her at her worst and most vulnerable (few Hollywood stars would like to be photographed like that).

Lisa's diatribe is overwritten, too literal — and goes on for too long. The emotion isn't out of place in *Mirror*, but the length and content of the speech is. At the end of the scene, Maria rallies, tells Lisa to grow up, and leaves the room. Lisa follows her.

Scene 10. Maria in the shower at the print works.

Maria runs ahead of Lisa, locking herself in the shower; the camera dollies along behind them (as it does a few times already in these scenes), then turns about to follow Lisa as she walks off, and sings, and jumps in the air.

In the shower, the water won't run. The shower running out emphasizes not only the harshness of the Stalinist environment, but also the lack of affection and love (or understanding, or companionship) in Maria's life. The abundant water of the earlier hair-washing scene, which was aligned with Maria's sexual relations, has now run dry. Maria laughs at first, but then is downcast.

Scene 11. A connecting image.

A large fire in a field in L.S., perhaps a different, distant view of the neighbour's burning building, or perhaps another fire. A short colour shot which fades to black — signifying the end of a memory sequence.

Scene 12. The narrator's Moscow apartment (1974).

Natalia, the narrator's estranged wife (who's also played, like Maria/ Masha, by
the excellent Margarita Terekhova), talks of her son Ignat, families and parents. She
is filmed in front of a mirror (of course). The narrator Aleksei, the boy's father and
her ex-husband (off-screen, as he is throughout the film) says she reminds him of his
mother. Then a flashback, as an insert: Maria in the past walks away from the
camera; the aunt carries the boy.

Cut back to Natalia and the narrator (who's also the now grown-up son) talking
about repeating the same mistakes of their forebears. (Cinema can simply cut from
the past to the present, and this scene is a visualization, via editing, of the concept of
the 'sins of the fathers' influencing the subsequent generation. It is constructed, in
other words, in the editing room, and the lines of dialogue about repeating mistakes
help to underline the issues being explored. Off-camera dialogue can be added during
editing, as new ways of cutting the film emerge).

Scene 13. The narrator's apartment in Moscow (1974).

Some Spanish exiles visit the apartment and talk of Spain in the old days —
bullfighting and flamenco dancing (in colour). One of the Spanish men describes a
bullfight and the action of a matador. A young woman starts a flamenco dance, but is
stopped abruptly by being slapped by one of the older men. They are guests of the
narrator (he refers to them in his conversations with Natalia). The scene acts as a
meditation on being exiled in space (Spaniards in Russia) which reflects on the
narrator's exile across time, from his own memories. Note also how the Spaniards
evoke the past nostalgically. And the film's emotional thread takes up the journey
into the Spanish past with the next scene.

Scene 14. First newsreel. Spain.

A montage of black-and-white newsreel, of a Spanish bullfight (with the sound of
the bullring), followed by a Spanish Civil War newsreel. The footage of the civil
war is from *Native Land* (1942), a film made by Leo Hurwitz and Paul Strand, the
American photographer. The images are of human suffering (bombs, crowds,
parents being separated from children, children looking lost and forlorn). The

subtext is spiritual longing and the nostalgia of the exile, later explored in *Nostalghia*. Like the Spanish refugees, the Russians are also exiles (exiles in their own country – a modern, Existential version of an ancient condition). Tatiana Panshina noted that *Mirror*'s heroine 'recalls that Moses led his people out of captivity. But who will lead us, Russians, out?' (1978, 11). *Mirror* doesn't offer explanations for some of the suffering the narrator and his family undergo. There are no reasons given for the breakdown of the narrator's marriage, nor for the failure of his parents' marriage.

More newsreel follows: Soviet balloonists ascending into the stratosphere – graceful images of flight, with men suspended from small balloons, and larger balloons (silence on the soundtrack at first; then choral music – Pergolesi's *Stabat Mater*?). Then the tickertape May Day parade of 1939. Tarkovsky said he wanted to include the footage of the balloonists simply because it was extraordinary material.

Scene 15. The Moscow apartment (1974).

C.U. of Ignat leafing through a large picture book of Renaissance paintings (a favourite Tarkovsky device, which introduces a different world into the film, as well referencing some of his beloved painters): beginning with Leonardo da Vinci's *Self-Portrait* as an old man with a beard (which turns up later in the film), and also showing some of Leonardo's masterpieces: *The Virgin and Child With St Anne* (c. 1510), *Portrait of a Young Women (Ginerva Benci?)* (c. 1474-76) and the *Mona Lisa* (1503-05), accompanied by choral music. The book is an old-fashioned art book, with tissue paper covering each illustration (only costly art books are printed like that these days. The book was a Broghaus edition which Tarkovsky knew from his childhood).

Scene 16. The Moscow apartment (1974).

Some time later. Natalia and Ignat sit on the floor and pick up some money when the mother drops her handbag on the floor as she prepares to go out. The boy gets a shock from one of the coins... of *deja-vu*, he says, as if he's done this before. Intimations of reincarnation here, and cyclical mythologies (as well as the physical world not being the limits of the world, a recurring theme in Tarkovsky's *œuvre*). It's also a rather clumsy piece of dramaturgy in sustaining the nostalgia and memory theme.

Natalia, before she leaves, says his grandmother, Maria Nikolayevna, might call at the apartment. Tarkovsky said (in 1985) that even he wasn't sure why the mother at the door thinks she's got the wrong place (it wasn't explained in the script, either, and it was too late for Tarkovsky to invent a subplot explaining it).

Scene 17. The Moscow apartment (1974).

Some time later the same day, in colour. Ignat is left alone by Maria. The boy has a visitor in a semi-dream or memory sequence (or he is transported back in time), after moving from the front door: a severe-looking Spanish woman (Tamara Ogorodnikova), sitting in an adjacent room in the apartment, is being served tea by a maid; she commands Ignat to find a particular notebook. Ignat obliges by finding the book on the nearby shelves. Ignat starts reading aloud from Jean-Jacques Rousseau, but the woman asks him to find another passage. Ignat reads aloud from Alexander Pushkin's 1836 letter to Piotr Yakovlevich Chadayev about the Christian schism that helped form Russia. Russia here is described as a buffer between the Christian West and the Mongol East.

The Spanish woman doesn't introduce herself, and isn't named; and she wasn't one of the group of Spaniards who were in the apartment earlier. (The Spanish lady was interpreted as the poet Anna Akhmatova by some viewers. Tarkovsky said it wasn't, but she was played by Tarkovsky's production manager, Tamara Ogorodnikova). She commands the boy to go to the front door. Ignat's grandmother (played by Tarkovsky's real mother, Maria Tarkovskaya) is there, but thinks she's got the wrong apartment and moves away. A bizarre occurrence, because she must have been to the apartment many times (the scene also fuses the time travel aspects of this part of the film, the Spanish woman from the past connecting with what's happening outside the apartment in the present). Tarkovsky acknowledged that this scene was not successful, but was created to convey the confusion and shyness of the old woman.

Ignat turns back, and finds that the Spanish woman and her maid have disappeared, along with the tea cup. Slowly the camera pushes in to the table: the music, the original score (by Eduardo Artemiev), wells up to a crescendo of impossibility: the boy has had a phantom visitor, yet her cup has left a condensation mark on the table, which gradually disappears.

At the end of the scene, Ignat's father (the narrator) calls him on the telephone, asks if his mother called, and mentions a red-haired girl from the past he once desired, which leads neatly into the following scene.

Throughout the phantom visit from the Spanish woman and her maid, Ignat acts at first surprised to see them, though not particularly afraid. This's no Hollywood horror flick, no Stephen King or Clive Barker outing, where many another twelve year-old kid would be freaked out if these two figures suddenly materialized out of nowhere in the otherwise empty apartment. Ignat doesn't spend any time trying to work out how they got there, either; he is no ghosthunter or supernatural detective. This isn't *Ghostbusters* (1984), *The Goonies* (1985), *The Ninth Gate* (1999) or *Van Helsing* (2004). Finally, the *impetus* for the visit doesn't seem to come from Ignat, but from his father, the narrator. The film is really about the narrator and his memories and dreams, not about Ignat. But Ignat is, if not the catalyst, sometimes the vehicle or carrier or observer of the narrator's life and memories. He experiences parts of his father's memories (again, without explanation in the film).

Some of the dreams in *Mirror* are anxious: the boy wandering alone in the *dacha* in the later memories or dreams, for instance, with his mother distant or behind a locked door, are not comforting evocations of the maternal realm of the past. The memory of the return of the father from the war is not particularly warm, either, and neither is the flashback to Maria at the printing works.

It isn't explained exactly who the Spanish woman is, nor why she is there, nor her relation to Ignat or the narrator. The group of Spanish exiles, too, might be guests of the narrator, but might not be (Natalia, his estranged wife, interacts with them, but the narrator does not; like Gatsby, he is always elsewhere, and especially at his own gatherings). But if the viewer recognizes that the film is really interweaving big historical events with the personal lives of the characters, from the past (1930s and 40s) and the present (1970s), it makes sense. But Tarkovsky introduces such elements at first without signalling their precise function within the whole film; Tarkovsky steers the film back and forth through time, and between the local and personal and the historical and political, without always clearly marking each transition (further layers are heaped up with dream and memory sequences). It is simply assumed that the viewer will be able to keep up.

Scene 18. Practice gun range. The past (1942-43).

In the Russian countryside in the snow, in colour. This is a memory sequence of the father's childhood (but the narrator is not at the centre of this particular section), which follows on from his telephone call in the previous scene (although the narrator is now some seven years older). The redhead girl with the chapped lip (Olga Kizilova) that the narrator/ father desired, is seen (she remains a mysterious, elusive object of adoration, smiling shyly like the Mona Lisa, and she doesn't have a line of dialogue).

A Leningrad orphan, Asafyev, is the focus of this sequence: he weeps when commanded to about turn by a wounded veteran officer; Asafyev takes him literally and turns through 360°, facing the other way from his cohorts. The officer berates him. The youths stand around in the snow at the end of the shooting range in the daytime.

Another boy terrifies the group of would-be soldiers when a practice grenade is picked up and then thrown (probably by Asafyev). The officer hurls himself on top of the grenade which rolls down the shooting range, to protect the boys. The camera tracks in to the man and a heartbeat is heard on the soundtrack. Time is stretched out – the explosion of the grenade is expected, but doesn't happen. In a slow tilt-up shot from the prone officer to the youths in the distance, one of them says it was only a practice grenade. The veteran soldier wearily gets up and sits on a stool, in a C.U. follow shot. The red-haired girl is seen again, touching a cold sore on her mouth (chapped or sore lips are a recurring motif in Tarkovsky's child characters, and nose bleeds are frequent, too).

This scene is not straightforward, either. For a start, Aleksei (the narrator) at age twelve is played by the same actor (Ignat Daniltsev) who also plays the narrator's son Ignat. So the same actor plays both the narrator at age 12 and the narrator's son (who also happens to be 12). But that's not the only complicated thing about this scene: although the scene is the *narrator's* memory, it actually features the boy Asafyev more than the narrator (which's also true of the following few scenes). In which case, these memories are not so much personal ones of the narrator, but more generic ones, of kids growing up at this particular time and in this particular place. But the film moves into a big historical framework when it intercuts these scenes in the snow at the practice range and near the shooting range with more newsreel footage.

Scene 19. Newsreel. Crimea, 1943.

Then follows a complex montage of cross-cutting: between the memory sequence
in the snow of 1942-43 (the personal) and newsreel images (the political and social):
Soviet troops crossing Lake Sivash in the Crimea, 1943, with overdubbed local
sound, in black-and-white – first water noises, drumbeats, then troops wading
through water, with Tarkovsky's father's poetry read over the images towards the
end of the sequence (the poem is 'Life, Life' [ST, 143]). The shallow, muddy lake
recalls the flooded forest of Tarkovsky's other World War Two film, *Ivan's
Childhood*.

Tarkovsky recalled that the footage of the people dragging themselves through
the mud had a 'piercing, aching poignancy' (ST, 131). Apparently, only a few
survived the ordeal, and the cameraman was killed the same day (ibid.)[1]

Scene 20. A hillside in the snow (1942-43).

Same space and time as Scene 18. A Pieter Brueghel *mise-en-scène* in colour (his
painting of *Winter*): people sledging, other figures dotted about the snowscape. A
lakeside. The boy, Asafyev, walks up the hill towards the camera, into medium
close-up. He is weeping, but also whistling.[2]

It was limiting, Tarkovsky reckoned, to employ the techniques and devices of
older artforms in cinema, such as painting or theatre. For a filmmaker who so often
referred to paintings, and created images from paintings, Tarkovsky was also suspicious of using too much from the history and theory of painting, which could make
cinema too derivative (ST, 22).

Scene 21. Newsreel. World War Two, 1945.

Black-and-white newsreel, consisting of: (1) Soviet troops in Prague in 1945; (2) a
Moscow victory parade, with fireworks; (3) people on crutches; (4) bombs and air
raids, accompanied by loud explosions; (5) the Hiroshima bomb, with a loud electronic cue; (6) another atomic bomb (which looks like a nuclear test on an ocean
atoll). All these images from the Second World War (mainly 1945) are accompanied
by timpani and symphonic music.

Scene 22. Hillside (1942-43).

As Scene 18. Asafyev on top of the snowbound hill in M.C.U.: he looks into the camera, as if contemplating the scenes that the viewer has just witnessed, then walks away a little; a bird lands on his head. There are three tiny ellipses in this shot, to shorten it in the editing (Asafyev's briefcase moves slightly, as do the figures in the background). He reaches up and holds the bird. It's one of those sequences in a Tarkovsky film which sound dumb on paper, but make sense when you see them. It's magical, but not cute or sentimental (Asafyev's solemn expression steers it away from something Disneyesque).

Scene 23. Newsreel. China, 1959.

Black-and-white footage of China, 1959. Maoism. Crowds with the *Red Book*, pictures of Mao, a vast Chinese demonstration (Damansk Island in 1959). One can see how big *Mirror* is as a narrative, how it can leap from quiet, intimate moments, like Asafyev with the bird in the snow, to China and Maoism in the late 1950s. Tarkovsky and his team developed a structure and cutting pattern that could accommodate such immense leaps across space and time.

Scene 24. The past and present mixed together (1942-43 and 1974).

Shot 1. In the modern-day, Moscow apartment, Natalia is cutting wood on the floor. She looks up. The narrator, off-camera but within her eye-line, addresses her, and says 'what about the children?'

Shot 2. Aleksei's father, looking down, dressed in a soldier's uniform, in the past (1943), returned from the war. He's standing near the house in daytime, and looking down, as if at Natalia in the present. (An eyeline match, in other words, that arches across thirty years).

Shot 3. The two children, brother and sister (Ignat and Marina), now aged 12 and about 10 (i.e., in 1942-43), talking in the wood, near the *dacha*. Their father calls them from a distance (off-screen). (It's another return of the father sequence, echoing the one earlier). The book. The camera tracks into the girl, who's crying.

Shot 4. L.S. of the two kids. Their father calls them again. They run. The camera tilts down to Leonardo da Vinci's *Self-Portrait* (*c.* 1512) in the large picture book on a table.

Shot 5. L.S. of children running towards the camera (Ignat trips over, which appears to be a mistake that was left in).

Shot 6. Natalia, in the present day Moscow apartment, thinking, as if looking at the scene in the past.

Shot 7. The 1942-43 past again: C.U. of father holding the children. Operatic music (J.S. Bach) comes in loudly, singing of the Resurrection and the veil of the temple being rent from top to bottom. Ignat hides his face in his father's chest, as if cowering from the loud music.

Shot 8. Leonardo's *Portrait of a Woman (Ginerva Benci?) (c. 1474-76), with a bright light reflected on it. Tarkovsky says the painting was used as a 'timeless element' cut into the flow of moments in *Mirror* (ST, 108).

Shot 9. In black-and-white, Natalia, deliberately juxtaposed with the Leonardo image, talks to the narrator (who remains off-screen). Natalia is lit harshly from the side. There are two tall mirrors against the wall. This is a present-time echo of the scene from the past – the father returning to see the children. They discuss parental rights, who should have the child, and marital relations. The families of then and now are compared. The father/ narrator is repeating the mistakes his own father, the soldier, made.

Ignat walks into frame, and the camera pans left to follow him. The narrator/ father asks Ignat if he'd like to come live with him and Ignat looks very surprised, and says, no, there's no need. Natalia also showed surprise a moment earlier that her ex-husband would suggest that. At the end of the shot, the camera zooms into a mirror.

Cut to Ignat wandering in the apartment, on his own (and still in black-and-white). The narrator/ father and Natalia are heard in voiceover.

During this scene, Natalia is looking at some large black-and-white photographs, which include Aleksei's mother. Natalia comments that she does look like Aleksei's mother (not surprising, since the same actress also played Maria). In the photo, the actress Terekhova is wearing the mother's dress of forty years ago.

Scene 25. The Moscow apartment (1974).

Natalia is framed in C.U. against a mass of books as she is interrogated by the narrator (and listens while the narrator talks about himself). She is lit from below (the kind of harsh lighting a Hollywood star would hate). In the same lengthy shot, she walks slowly next to two mirrors, and leans against one; she moves into a brightly lit spot, then into shadow; then she's framed against a window, playing with her hair; it's raining outside; the camera tracks to Ignat outside, who's burning a bush in the courtyard. This is a very lengthy take (the longest shot in the film, at 3 minutes 55 seconds). The movement of Natalia, leaning on the wall or moving slowly along it, from right to left, recalls the shot and motion of Maria in the raining room, in the earlier memory scenes. Natalia leans down and her hair is seen, as before, like Maria's. An abrupt cut to:

Scene 26. The past. Around the *dacha* (1935-36).

A linking shot of the trees in the past at night, darker than before, in black-and-white (the imagery of the scene (scene 5) where the five year-old Aleksei climbs out of bed).

Scene 27. The past (1935-36). The *dacha*.

Interior of the old house (now in colour), with the narrator's voiceover but no local sound (the narrator speaks about the cherished spaces of his grandfather's house). The narrator's memories are shown here: the boy (the narrator a child) sits on a bed on the floor; Marina plays with water by the door, beside a large glass vessel, another with fire (he lights a match in darkness). Maria moves through the *dacha* in a white summer dress. A big vase of flowers on the table.

The action is covered in a complex sequence shot which has many moves and beats.

Scene 28. The past (1935-36). Around the *dacha*.

The five year-old Aleksei is outside the house in the trees, in black-and-white. A zoom into the house. The boy is at the door. Slow, eerie music.

V. Johnson and G. Petrie suggest that this black-and-white sequence is the narrator's dream of not being able to re-enter the house (JP, 127).

Scene 29. The past (1935-36).

Shot 1. The boy says 'Mama!'. In black-and-white, the boy is seen at the door, outside the house. The door opens by itself, mysteriously.

Shot 2. A pane of glass falls out of a window in slow motion: a bird (a cockerel?) breaks it.

Shot 3. The trees again, but by daylight. A fierce wind blows them: track left to a low table, with objects such as apples, bread, a spoon and a glass vessel on it. Some of these items fall off the table in slow motion (another take of this shot occurs later on).

Shot 4. House and trees, in slow motion: the boy runs into the house. It snows.

Shot 5. Aleksei moves past some washing, blowing in the breeze and goes to the door. He tries it; it's locked. He comes back, out of frame. The door opens. The mother is crouched behind the door, staring off camera, as if at the boy, picking up some potatoes, in slight slow motion; behind her is rain seen through a window (but it's not raining in her doorway). A dog pads out of the house.

This scene collages images of Aleksei age five and the *dacha*, the shots made mysterious and ambiguous by the slight slow motion. The sequence has the unreality of a dream, as if the narrator of 1974 (aged 44) is trying unsuccessfully to rebuild a fragmented memory of 1935 (when he was five). It's as if he can remember the spaces of the house clearly, and that his mother was there, but not the exact emotion of the moment.

Scene 30. The past (1942-43). The doctor's house.

In colour now, Aleksei (aged 12) and his mother Maria visit the doctor's house (the doctor, significantly, is absent – as is Aleksei's sister Marina, from this and the following scenes, though no explanation is given).

It is dusk, near a river. The boy walks in bare, muddy feet. After some hesitation, and awkward talk with the doctor's wife (played by Andrei Tarkovsky's second wife, Larissa Tarkovskaya, who was also assistant director on *Mirror*), the two are eventually invited in to the house. (A predominantly wooden structure, lit by yellowy light; lamps; old wooden furniture; rain drips over the front door. The doctor's wife wears a silky, elegant, damson dress which's meant to look out of place). No music in this part of the film, but the sounds of water dripping.

While the two women talk in an adjoining room about the earrings Maria's brought to sell for food, Aleksei starts to dream. The light changes. String music comes in (Henry Purcell, from the opera *The Indian Queen*?). A slow zoom in to a C.U. of Aleksei's face looking at himself, reflected in an elliptical mirror; another angle follows.

A succession of odd images: a C.U. of milk dripping onto the floor; an oil lamp that keeps going out and re-lighting itself;

Three different fires are seen, in succession: a woman, not Maria but the boy's father's one-time girlfriend, the red-haired girl with the chapped lip, is sitting next to and warming herself beside one fire. The man in the scene is not Aleksei's father, but the military officer, who also loved the girl. Aleksei seems to be having visions of the instructor's sexual relations (and perhaps his father's). There are echoes also of his father's relation with his mother, because the hand seen warming itself on the flame is in, apparently, the parents' bedroom or a similar room (an image from the erotic raining room sequence in scene 5). A mirror in a wardrobe.

The hand in front of the fire in *Mirror* as a motif connecting the past, memories and the present recalls a similar motif in Alain Resnais' *Hiroshima Mon Amour* (1959): there is a shot in Resnais' film of the Japanese lover's hand followed by a shot of the hand of her previous (German) lover.

Aleksei stares at himself in the oval mirror, in a slow zoom. This could be a dream within a dream (i.e., the narrator in the present is remembering himself in the past having a dream, and perhaps a dream within *that* dream). Cut to: the two women next door, in C.U., talking, with the sound of water dripping. The doctor's wife is trying on the earrings. She comes in to find Ignat sitting in the dark; she relights the lamp. (Maria looking into the mirror at the earrings Tarkovsky thought was the kind of shot Ingmar Bergman might have done.)

Scene 31. The neighbour's house again, in the past (1942-43).

A continuation of the previous scene. Colour. The mother and son are shown the woman's child in another room; a slow zoom into the sleeping child. The doctor's wife talks over reaction shots of Maria and C.U.s of the baby. A low, mysterious music cue.

The child is clad all in white, in a luxurious cot with a white canopy and white sheets, like a vision of Christ in the manger. Perhaps this is an alternative life or the future as it could have been, for Aleksei, to have a wildly affectionate mother. His own mother, Maria, is not affectionate – or at least not physically. Mother, son and daughter very seldom (if ever) touch. Throughout the scene Maria's poverty and emotional aloofness is contrasted with the doctor's wife's comparable luxury and demonstrative affection (for such a revered figure, *Mirror*'s mother figure is surprisingly unmotherly).

The scene connotes ovulation, wombs, pregnancy, nurturing (the doctor's wife says she is in her fourth month, and wants a daughter this time), and intense, over-whelming motherly love. Smug, indulgent, proto-bourgeois domesticity and matern-ity. Maria reacts by wanting to leave quickly, and says she feels sick.

Scene 32. The doctor's house (1942-43).

Cockerel killing sequence (in colour). The doctor's wife persuades Maria to do it, as she feels nauseous, being pregnant. Maria sits against a wooden wall, lit from below.

The bird is killed off-screen, but some feathers flutter around the doctor's wife in C.U. After Maria's killed the bird, water runs down the walls; she lifts her head, stares into the camera and smiles, her face lit luridly (and unflatteringly), from below. It looks like the most fun Maria's had for some time.

Cut to the father, shot in black-and-white and slow motion, staring straight at the camera, and, by implication, at Maria. He turns, and strokes a woman's hand as the camera zooms out (accompanied by J.S. Bach on the track). Maria is apparently ill and floating above a bed; she wear a white cotton dress (many other European film directors of the early Seventies would've had Maria naked) She says 'it's as though I'm floating in the air.' This could be Maria's dream of her former sexual life with her husband, as well as the narrator's memories or imagined evocations of his mother's and father's sexual relations. (The link with Maria's sexual life with her husband is reinforced by the rain running down the wall behind her, a refrain of the 'raining room' scene earlier in the film).[3] The scene certainly illustrates the height of the love between Ignat's parents, so it may be a vision of an erotic union which produced a child – the narrator.

The erotic components of the scene are unusually explicit in Tarkovsky's cinema (sex and death are bluntly brought together, with the cut from the cockerel killing to the orgasmic floating above the bed. The additional symbolism of blood, sacrifice, ritual, cockerels, beheading and all the rest don't need any glossing).

Cut back to the doctor's house: Maria and Aleksei swiftly take their leave of the neighbour, without waiting to be paid for the earrings.

Scene 33. A riverbank in the past (1942-43).

Maria and her son walk beside a river, coming back from the earring and cockerel scene, in a dollying two shot. Maria, smoking and thinking, moves into M.C.U. Poetry is read over this scene (there's no local sound); the poem is 'Eurydice' (by daddy Tarkovsky), which contains images of birds, fire, souls, skies and freedom:

> And I dreamt of a different soul
> Dressed in other clothes:
> Burning as it runs
> From timidity to hope.
> Spiritous and shadowless
> Like fire it travels the earth,
> Leaves lilac behind on the table
> To be remembered by. (ST, 157)

Scene 34. The trees around the *dacha*.

The trees and bushes again, in black-and-white and slow motion (similar to shot 3 in scene 29). The camera tracks left to a table with bread and a lamp on it. No sound of the wind, just the poetry in voice-over.

Scene 35. The house in the past (1935-36).

In slow motion and black-and-white Aleksei enters the now deserted house (it's a continuation of scene 29). Giant spherical bottles of water are on the table. The camera pans left. The poetry voiceover stops, and there is a strange sound of wind. The room is filled with hangings and clothes on lines, veils and lace curtains, blowing in the breeze. The windows are open. This image is spectral, very lyrical (and Felliniesque). The camera becomes the wandering spirit of the narrator evoking his past, exploring and tracking around the dim room: the camera dollies into a mirror: the reflection shows the 5 year-old Aleksei holding a large glass bottle filled with milk (all covered in what appears to be a single sequence shot; there may be an invisible cut when the camera moves into the mirror). There is the distant sound of a dog barking, and a train whistle (a great touch); echoes of childhood.

'Films should be experienced, not explained, thought Tarkovsky, and no film-maker surpassed him in being able, as it were, to film the human spirit' wrote Neil Sinyard (1992, 158).

There's a nice quote by Federico Fellini in a documentary talking about how impressed the Italian was by Akira Kurosawa's *Rashomon* (1951). Somehow, Fellini said, Kurosawa was able to photograph air itself. Fellini was referring to the unsurpassed technique Kurosawa developed of portraying the elements, such as rain and mist. It's the same with Tarkovsky (who was deeply influenced by Kurosawa's elemental techniques).

Scene 36. The past (1935-36).

The five year-old boy swimming in a river, in colour, shot from behind, with the camera following him in a boat.

Scene 37. The past (1935-36).

Inside the *dacha* (in colour), the camera tracks through the living room (which's empty) towards the window. The room looks art directed by Tarkovsky to look like a still-life painting: a vase of flowers; a cat; some eggs and a book on the window sill.

Outside the *dacha*, in bright sunshine. Birds sing. It is Summer. Seen through the window, the five year-old Aleksei walks out to his sister and grandmother, but the latter is played by the same actress (Maria Tarkovskaya) who plays the aged Maria in the modern-day scenes. She sits in the same pose as Maria did in the opening scenes: looking out at the field and forest, and smoking. Aleksei says the lamp is smoking. The past and present are mixed together here.

Scene 38. The present (1974). A Moscow apartment.

In colour, a doctor (in a white coat) comments upon his patient: the patient is the narrator, seen in the shadows of the next room (Tarkovsky himself played this part, though not his voice, which was by the usual narrator, Innokenti Smoktunovsky). He is ill in bed. A variety of mirrors line the walls. The doctor tells the people in the room (oddly, and impossibly, the Spanish women of the earlier Pushkin reading scene, and an old woman) that people can die of yearning, when their life falls apart. The narrator's illness in *Mirror*, Tarkovsky said in 1985, 'was necessary in order to convey the author's spiritual crisis, the state of his soul'. And it was a narrative device, so that the narrator could be recollecting his life.

Ultra-symbolically, the narrator picks up a tiny bird beside him on the bed. In voiceover, he tells the people in the next room that 'everything will be all right'. He releases the bird into the air in slow motion (the camera moves ahead of him, anticipating his gesture, and the shot moves into slow motion). (Tarkovsky played the dying narrator himself, and, according to the DP, Georgy Reberg, had wanted to have his face on screen as well as his body. Reberg had persuaded him not to, arguing that it would have made *Mirror* 'uncomfortably, and unacceptably, personal' [JP, 304]). The hero of *Mirror*, Tarkovsky explained, was fatally selfish and self-absorbed: he was unable to appreciate those around him, incapable of loving them without wanting something in return (ST, 208).

Scene 39. The past and present.

The final sequence in the film, in colour, which cuts between three time zones. Maria is lying down with the soldier father: this is the oldest image in the film, because Maria is pregnant with her first child, the narrator (thus the film moves at this point from the narrator at the end of his life to before the narrator was born). So it must be about 1930.

The man and woman lie in the grass at the edge of the forest, as young lovers, before the house has been built. The second time zone is the present day, when the grandmother (or Maria as an old woman, some 44 years later) visit the childhood home, which is now a ruin. The third time zone is suggested by Maria standing alone in the field, which could indicate the 1942-43 time zone (or it could be 1935-36).

The final scene of *Mirror* is lit by a beautiful, warm magic hour light, and the action is covered with complex tracking and panning shots.

Shot I. A slow pan around the landscape surrounding the old house, the Ignatievo Forest. The music is at a low volume: Johann Sebastian Bach's *St John Passion*, the opening passages of strings and clarinets. Tilt and crane down to the couple lying down in the grass.

Andrei Tarkovsky *431*

Shot 2. Aleksei/ Ignat (aged 5) and the old woman are walking in the wood – this is in the present (Maria as an old woman revisiting her old house).

Shot 3. C.U. of the ruins of the house, bits of wet wood, a hole full of crockery, in a tracking shot and zoom.

Shot 4. The trees around the *dacha* of the whole film, but seen now in L.S. from a new perspective: the grandmother walks out of them. This is the only time a human being has been seen in this sacred space, in amongst the trees. It has to be the grandmother who is associated with such a place, the dark forest, because she is (the aged) Maria, the centre of the film and of the narrator's life, the heart of all the mythopœia. She takes hold of the boy's hand; they survey the smashed house.

Shot 5. As shot 2: Maria deep in thought, perhaps watching the people of the future, perhaps imagining the future, and how she will be in the future – as an old woman and grandmother. The father asks her whether she wants a girl or a boy. This sets her thoughts racing: the actress shows her inner turmoil brilliantly: she cries, bites her lip, sighs, smiles, looks heavenward, then turns, as if to look at:

Shot 6. The grandmother with the boy and girl, walking through the field, away from the ruined house. They walk in the direction of the place where the doctor was first seen emerging at the beginning of the film. The music suddenly surges up to full volume. Significantly, Maria is standing in the distance in the field, watching the grandmother and children walking. Maria has seen into the future, and seen herself returning as an old woman to the smashed house which hasn't yet been built behind her. This is one interpretation. Or it's a curtain call, a final appearance.

Shot 7. A lengthy L.S.: the grandmother and children walk through the fields while the Bach choral music carries on playing loudly. The opening movement of Bach comes to its abrupt ending; the boy hollers; then he runs and catches up his grandmother; they walk away from the camera, which tracks steadily into the wood, receding further and further; it is sunset; the sky is orangey purple; the forest gets darker; the birds at twilight are heard (the camera zooms in towards the end of the shot – almost certainly a mistake, but it doesn't detract from the beauty of the scene). A stunning, lyrical ending.

The function of the image, as Gogol said, is to express life itself, not ideas or arguments about life. It does not signify life or symbolise it, but embodies it, expressing its uniqueness.

Andrei Tarkovsky, *Sculpting In Time* (111)

As an evocation of childhood, the yearning, mystery and pain of it, *Mirror* is unsurpassed in cinema. True, Tarkovsky does simplify things by missing out the agony of adolescence. Instead he chooses two ages, five and twelve, in which children are still children, and not restless, disaffected, disappointed teenagers. The film could be extended indefinitely through a variety of age ranges: 2, 8, 15, 19, 26, and so on. Tarkovsky also excludes a crucial part of childhood – education and school; also, the child's relations with other children. By leaving out school and friends, Tarkovsky presents a highly selective view of childhood. For Tarkovsky, childhood is largely a lonely experience, with parental affection a rarity.

Mirror also acts as the spiritual biography of an age: the eras of 1935-36 and 1942-43 are so poignantly evoked by the newsreels. These images, seemingly a world away from an intimate portrait of childhood, fuse beautifully with the rest of the film. There are moments of forced symbolism – the narrator releasing the bird, for instance, which is intended to relate to his death. It is a motif out of the tackiest pop promo (don't Queen have a video where Freddie releases a white dove?). The film, though, soars above pretension and artifice by the magnitude of its passion. There is no denying the lucidity and poetic authenticity of these mnemonic images. *Mirror* is the closest thing in cinema to a poem by Rainer Maria Rilke, Arthur Rimbaud or C.P. Cavafy, those masters of the poetry of nostalgia. Like the poems of Rilke, Cavafy and Rimbaud, *Mirror* is a dense mesh of constellations of images and memories, a veritable mnemonic banquet. It is a film of fierce self-reflexive intensity – something like Rimbaud in his poem of childhood 'Le Poëtes de sept ans'. Among the thousands of mainstream (Hollywood) films that try to depict children and childhood, very few come close to the luminous authenticity of *Mirror*. Yet *Mirror* never slips into easy sentimentality (although it does come close once or twice). It never becomes complacent or banal. It is marvellously self-reflexive, yet avoids all the traps of inwardly-looking art. Though unashamedly introspective, *Mirror* virtually achieves a universal transcendence.

Michael Dempsey called *Zerkalo* 'intractable', 'ineffable' and 'enigmatic' (1981). 'Enigmatic' *Mirror* certainly is. Some critics said it was 'a crossword puzzle'. Herbert Marshall reckoned that *Mirror* was very unusual in terms of mid-Seventies Soviet cinema, and was difficult for Soviet critics to understand (1976, 95). Nothing like it had been seen in Soviet cinema before, Marshall asserted. *Mirror* is

> not only told entirely subjectively, but from a subjective point of view at different periods of life both in reality and in memories and dreams, from a boy, a teenager, to a man, the director himself, and his father and mother. Such a film has hitherto never been seen on the Soviet screen. (ib., 95).

According to John Dunlop, *Mirror* 'encountered a wall of opposition on the part of the Soviet film industry'.[1] Some critics (Turoskaya, Elmanovits, Bakhtin, Solovyov) saw *Mirror* as the record not of one's person's life, but of a generation. V.I. Solovyov caught the spirit of the film right when he said that *Mirror* seemed to be portraying 'not film images but *my* thoughts, *my* memories' (1989, 11). Maurice Clavel wrote of *Mirror* that there is 'no other film like it. One can see how little subjectivist this film is. Perhaps it itself is sacrificial, like Russia according to Pushkin'.[2]

Viewers wrote to Tarkovsky about how much *Mirror* had affected them. Tarkovsky subsequently quoted some of these letters in *Sculpting in Time*. For Leonid Bakhtin, part of *Mirror*'s power is precisely its puzzling, mysterious elements. Bahktin wrote:

> As we reach to grab phrases and shots which seem to openly give us the key to the whole, we come to understand that one cannot exhaust the whole, that we must, like the hero, who exists behind the mirror, go over memories, strain our conscience and impressionability over Aleksei's life and our own. (1988, 79)

Jacques Grant noted that *Mirror* is not so much an anti-Marxist as an 'a-Marxist' film; Tarkovsky avoids confronting politics; Grant saw the motif of the mirror as a barrier, 'placed by the filmmaker between himself and a world which he refuses to see and to discuss' (1978, 68). That's a common criticism among film reviewers, castigating the director for *not* making the film they thought he should have made. Why *should* a personal film be about memories of childhood deal politics or the so-called 'real' world? But of course, Tarkovsky *does* address social, historical and political issues throughout *Mirror*, not only by including the many newsreel images, but also evoking a moving scene of Stalinist repression. There are many other films of childhood which completely avoid references to historical events. In fact, *Mirror* is *very* unusual in being both a film of personal memories *and* wider historical and social issues.

Gilles Deleuze wrote of *Mirror* in terms of the metaphors of crystals, seeds and mirrors: '*Mirror* is a turning crystal', offered Deleuze, which

> turns on itself, like a homing device that searches an opaque environment: what is Russia, what is Russia? The seed seems to be frozen in these sodden, washed and heavily translucent images, with their sometimes bluish, sometimes brown sur-faces, while the green environment seems, in the rain, to be unable to go beyond the condition of a liquid crystal which keeps its secret. (1989, 75)

NINETEEN

Into the Wasteland:

Faith and the Quest in Stalker

19 : 1   *STALKER*

Stalker' s *mise-en-scène* is roughly-hewn, broken-down, burnt-out and long-forgotten: buildings and machines lie derelict, areas are grassed-over, distinctly post-apocalyptic (or at least – at best – post-industrial). The Stalker's home is a derelict place, with bare floorboards, sparsely furnished, the daughter's crutches lean against a wall, pills and a glass of water on a round bedside table, and lightbulbs that burn out. In the last shots, hundreds of books on shelves are shown in the Stalker's bedroom. The preamble text, after the opening credits, tells how the Zone was caused by an alien presence. The film may be taking place in some present or near-future, but Tarkovsky's post-industrial desuetude could be 1879 or 1939 or 2079, as well as 1979, when the film was released (and it could be set, like *The Sacrifice*, with not that many changes, in A.D. 85, as well as 1979 or 1985). The landscape of *Stalker* is, as usual in Tarkovsky's cinema, not confined to any

Andrei Tarkovsky   437

particular time frame.

Critics have aligned the world of *Stalker* with Stalinist Russia. For Balint Anrdás Kovács and Akos Szilágyi, the Zone represents the secrets a society withholds to maintain itself. It's an area of the past (and collective memory) which's officially closed off (except to the outsiders who have to explore it continually). Reviews in the US (such as by Janet Maslin and Vincent Canby) were much less excited than European critics (by the time of *Stalker*, the Tarkovsky cult was growing in Europe). Maya Turoskaya spoke of *Stalker*'s 'minimal' look (1989, 109); for John Orr, because *Stalker* is

> sparse and minimal – it *is* largely about three men and a dog – it evokes a world in macrocosm, as if the boundaries of the Zone are the physical boundaries of the Soviet Union itself. Moreover it matches its political concerns to a delirium of form. (1998, 47).

For David Wingrove, in *Science Fiction Film Source Book*, the Zone is 'the spiritual heartland, the imagination, life itself in the midst of non-life', whose sinister, alien nature is suggested with no special effects at all, making *Stalker* true science-fiction, as well as

> pure cinema – a wonderful succession of multiple expressive images which accumulate in the viewer's mind and attain deep significance… not merely an exceptional science fiction film, a great work of art, and perhaps the most memorable experience in sf [sci-fi] cinema. (1985)

Scott Bukatman linked the Zone with other sci-fi zones, such as the 'Interzone' of William Burroughs, the zonal geography in Jean-Luc Godard's film *Alphaville*, and the segmented Germany in Thomas Pynchon's *Gravity Rainbow* (1993, 163). John Moore asserted that *Stalker* is 'arguably the most sophisticated science fiction film to be made to date' (1999, 121).

Stalker could have been shot in any of a hundred different countries: the grassy meadows, the bushes and trees, the derelict apparently industrial buildings, and the empty warehouses, could be found in Germany, France, Scandinavia, Canada, Argentina, New Zealand, India, Japan, etc.

As a title *Stalker* now has even more negative connotations, with stalkers making the news. But *Roadside Picnic*, the English title of the Strugatskys' book, isn't satisfactory, either. (And in 1979, the title '*Stalker*' sounded like a cheap 'n' nasty horror flick, of which there were plenty in the wake of 1978's *Hallowe'en*. They were also dubbed 'stalk 'n' slash' movies).

When Tarkovsky got his hands on the *Stalker* project, Maya Turovskaya remarked, the sci-fi element was pruned back to just a few elements (the Zone, the daughter, the journey, the wishes). 'Nobody now died, nobody reached their goal, nobody even crossed the threshold' (107). In the original proposal, there were two stalkers – 'Carrion Crow' and 'Red' (the latter was basis for the Stalker in the film). Inside the Zone there were visions of people who were caught in time-warps, mirages, dangerous marshes. and the Writer wanders into a house and decides to stay there (CS, 378).

The dangerous aspects of the Zone exist primarily in the Stalker's dialogue: the Writer and the Professor and the viewer do not get to *see* what the Zone can do. The threats, the traps, the hardships seem to exist only in the Stalker's mind. The Writer and the Professor only have his word to go by. Only rarely does the Zone actually offer something dangerous, and even then it is ambiguous: when the Writer approaches the Room via a direct route, a voice calls out to him, telling him to stop and go back. But even this may just be a Wizard of Oz moment, because it's only a voice, and nothing more, which threatens the Writer. There's nothing tangible (no sci-fi monsters here, no arrows, no gunshots). And even this voice, it is suggested, could have been produced by the Writer himself.

But the Stalker walks about as if he's being watched all the time, as if he's in someone's gun sight, as if the Zone will sprang a new trap at any moment. The Stalker's behaviour is paranoia encapsulated: he's always telling the other two not to touch things, or to stay away from certain areas.

Stalker was intended to have a unity of time and space and action, Tarkovsky said, to take place within a space-time close to real time (ST, 193). 'I wanted it to be as if the whole film had been made in a single shot' Tarkovsky wrote in *Sculpting In Time* (193). David Russell remarked that Tarkovsky's films together make 'one great film', which motifs, images, events, characters and themes echoing each other.[1]

According to Anne Lawton (1992), *Stalker* was seen by three million people in a year, while *Moscow Distrusts Tears* (Vladimir Menshov, 1980), which won Best Foreign Film Oscar, was seen by 75 million (three million may be a small audience for a Russian film in its homeland, but that's not a complete flop – especially since *Stalker* was really an art film. A typical Hollywood film might be seen by 30 million viewers after it's finished its cycle through theatrical, satellite, airlines, pay-TV, cable, DVD and video, network and syndicated television markets). Tarkovsky said *Stalker* wasn't his favourite film: 'it was very difficult to make it, almost impossible to edit it'.[2] At other times, the maestro said he was very pleased with it.

The locations for *Stalker* included: Dolgopa in Russia; Tallinn in Estonia; Isfara in Tajikistan; and Chernobyl / Pripyat in Ukraine (the whole film was going to be shot in Tajikistan at one time — but an earthquake scuppered that idea). *Stalker* was shot twice. The problems with the imported Kodak film stock were sensed from day one of the shoot (the editor, Lyudmila Feiginova, explained that Russian labs were not so good at processing Kodak stock. Three other films had problems with the faulty film stock). *Stalker* was shot in I.37:I aspect ratio. Tarkovsky had to wait some time before he saw the rushes, and shooting continued until the fault was made official. By that time, about half of the film had been made, and two thirds of the budget had been spent. Tarkovsky said in his journal that the footage shot at Tallinn had to be scrapped twice — because of faulty equipment as well as Mosfilm's laboratory processing (D, I46). A later diary entry had the film being defective three times (D, I54).

Accounts differ on exactly how the film was closed down and re-started a month later. Tarkovsky apparently used the technical fault to stop the shoot and rethink the film — it wasn't the total disaster it might have been to other filmmakers. If Tarkovsky had been *really* happy with the film as it was being shot, he would have kicked up a big fuss if the stock was faulty. Goskino was considering writing off the film as a 'creative accident'; Tarkovsky was happy to write off the film already shot, but wanted to begin again from scratch. He got his way.

Goskino and chairman Filip Yermash gave the green light for the maestro to start over — if he agreed to make *Stalker* as a two-part project (which he did); it was a way of exploiting the technicalities. And it meant that Tarkovsky could rewrite the film (which he did), hire a new cinematographer (Georgy Reberg was out, Leonid Kalashnikov was in) and a new set designer (Boym was out, and Shavkat Abdusal-amov was in). (Tarkovsky had had problems with both his DP and set designer, both crucial roles on a Tarkovsky production. Odd, because Tarkovsky had got on with Reberg during *Mirror*, which had been one of the happier shoots for Tarkovsky; and Reberg's contribution to *Mirror* is immense. But Tarkovsky had also replaced his regular cinematographer for *Mirror*, Vadim Yusov. Even so, some of the scenes that Reberg shot — such as the waterfall scene — made it into the final cut, according to editor Feiginova, DPs Reberg and Knyazhinsky and actor Kaidan-ovsky).

So shutting down *Stalker* was also a way of hiring new crew members, as well as rewriting the script. There were eventually some ten versions of the script, according to actors Alexander Kaidanovsky and Nikolai Grinko. It also meant new money, and more film stock.

The crew had been shooting in Estonia for some three and a half months (from May to August, 1977) before the production was halted. The budget for *Stalker* was originally (in 1977) planned to be 650,000 roubles according to some estimates (about $2.6 million). It went up to a million roubles.

Shooting continued in late August, 1977. When the film was planned again, this time as a two-part project, it was put into the 1978 slate of productions, and shooting resumed in June, 1978, in Tallinn. A third DP was hired (Alexander Knyazhinsky), with Tarkovsky now taking over as production designer. Post-production continued through December, 1978 into early 1979, with Goskino accepting the film in May, 1979 (and — a first for Tarkovsky — no major cuts or alterations were requested). (Tarkovsky fired some of the *Stalker* crew, such as Boym and Shavkat Abdusalimov, but some — like Kalashnikov — had walked out.) The Soviet authorities (including military officials) didn't like the film, and it had a limited release (only 196 prints were struck, for instance). Within Russia, *Stalker* was negatively reviewed in general — or simply ignored. Its positive reputation in the West — to the point of now being a cult movie — really began with a showing at Cannes in 1980.

In the first version of *Stalker*, the Stalker had been 'some kind of drug dealer or poacher' Tarkovsky said (D, 147). Tarkovsky had toyed with the idea of having a woman in a leading role in *Stalker* (D, 105). The production designer on *Stalker*, A. Merkulov, said that the second version of *Stalker* was quite different from the one made and abandoned a year earlier. Merkulov said the two films differed in many respects. Kaidanovsky's performance, for example, altered. According to Merkulov, none of the shots were repeated in the second version: Tarkovsky shot the second film as if it were a new film.

A. Merkulov also remarked that the budget of the second film (300,000 roubles) only covered the first part, so that Tarkovsky had to stretch the budget for half of the film over the whole film. Merkulov noted how, a year earlier, they had had many tanks and vehicles for the scene in the Zone, but had to make do with three tanks second time around. Merkulov spoke movingly of how devastating it must have been for Tarkovsky when the film shot was ruined. But set-backs, projects begun and uncompleted, projects that never get past the script stage, are common occurrences for the professional filmmaker. It wasn't the first time that a film was shot then abandoned, but the fact that it was a technical fault with experimental film stock must have seemed frustratingly stupid (and avoidable) to Tarkovsky and the production team. Merkulov even suggested that the film stock may have been deliberately wrecked.

Despite the financial and logistical difficulties, the personality clashes, the hirings and firings, the stops and starts, and the lengthy production cycle, *Stalker* wound up as one of Tarkovsky's most accomplished and hypnotic films.

Stalker was based on the Strugatsky brothers' novel. (Tarkovsky said that Georgy Kalatozisvili had considered making *Roadside Picnic* into a film, but hadn't been able to come to an agreement with the Strugatsky brothers.) The Strugatskys' books (Boris, b. 1931, and Arkady, 1925-1991) were concerned with issues such as technology, social change, nuclear power, relativity, and how science affected the individual. Their work included *Destination: Amaltheia*, *Far Rainbow*, *Second Invasion*, *Monday Begins On Saturday*, *Tale of the Troika*, *Snail On the Slope*, the *Maxim Trilogy*, *Definitely Maybe* and *The Ugly Swans*. The Strugatskys' novels, including *Roadside Picnic*, explored social and individual morality.[3]

The Strugatsky brothers had another film made in the Soviet Union, *The Dead Mountaineer Hotel* (Grigori Kromarov, 1979), set in the snowy Kazakhstan hills, about a detective investigating a hotel of guests who are aliens. Alexander Sokurov's *Days of the Eclipse* was based on the Strugatskys' *A Billion Years Before the End of the World*. *Letters From a Dead Man* (Konstantin Lopushansky, 1986), also had a post-nuclear theme; Lopushansky co-wrote the film with Boris Strugatsky and Vyacheslav Rybakov. There is a reference to *Stalker*'s Zone in Chris Marker's 1982 film *Sunless*.

Most of the script collaboration on *Stalker* was between Arkady Strugatsky, Boris having withdrawn from the project (not everyone could work with Tarkovsky; Arkady Strugatsky said that Tarkovsky would work on the script late into the night, then shoot the next day. The break on *Stalker* after the film stock was ruined gave Tarkovsky an opportunity to rewrite the film yet again. Tarkovsky took out the references to multiple zones in the book, the detailed descriptions of the zones, and the precise explanations of them; he altered the character of the stalker (called Red in the book; Tarkovsky toned down his more ruthless personality); Tarkovsky also lost the Golden Ball, the object of the quest in the Zone (which grants wishes); Monkey is more mutated in the book (her mutations are caused by Red's journeys in the Zone, and Red's wish is for his daughter to be cured).

But Tarkovsky did keep plenty of elements from the book (such as the 'Plague Quarter' borders around the Zone, the gun, the nuts thrown to test the terrain, the trains and flatcars, and the fundamental narrative of the quest to the heart of the Zone). An early draft of (entitled *The Wish Machine*) had the Stalker going into the Zone to ask for a cure for Monkey.

The Stalker, the spiritual as well as physical guide to the Zone, explains the Zone: how it's difficult to traverse it; how direct routes are not always the best or quickest; how new traps are created and old ones abandoned; how one can't go back the same way; how one mustn't go into the Zone with the wrong intentions (such as bringing a weapon); how the wretched, those who have lost all hope, are let through. The Stalker explains the Zone all the way through the film, not just in a preliminary piece of exposition. It's his favourite subject of conversation, he reveres it as well as being terrified of it.

Tarkovsky stressed the physical, non-allegorical nature of the Zone, saying it didn't stand it for anything else; it was not a metaphor. The Zone is clearly a 'mindscreen', to use Bruce Kawin's term (1978), but it is also the 'mindscreen' of the Writer and Scientist as well as the Stalker, and also a collective mindscreen. It is a mysterious, dystopian, forbidden and forbidding place. Critics have linked *Stalker*'s Zone to Chernobyl, the site of the 1980s nuclear accident; to Mayak, the guarded radioactive city; and to the Gulags (the Stalker looks like a Gulag or concentration camp inmate). The Stalker was related by critics to an inmate (a 'zek') of the labour camps, and the Zone to the camps, the Gulag, to Russia, and to the Eastern Bloc nations.

Slavoj Zizek said the Zone in *Stalker* might have five possible meanings for a Russian audience: a prohibited area; a Gulag or prison; land poisoned by technology (such as nuclear or biological warfare, Chernobyl); forbidden foreign territory (like Berlin within the GDR); or a meteorite impact zone (like Tunguska in Siberia).

Certainly the Zone evokes nuclear disaster areas (the Stalker throws metal nuts to uncover radioactive waste), but it is not any specific site. It could be the site of any disaster (such as a virus or plague, or a former war zone). The tiled floor and hypodermic needles evoke 'an abandoned laboratory of deadly experiments'.[4] It seems to post-industrial, a one-time factory or power plant; but it might also be a scientific research centre. There are few dramatic spaces in *Stalker*: the Zone, the Stalker's home, the bar, the factories where they climb aboard the railway truck.

Cleverly, Tarkovsky makes the Zone appear a more complicated place than it at first looks. There is a gulf between the Zone as it appears to the viewer and as the characters (particularly the Stalker) react to it. The camera pans to a waterfall and a great surge of white water – one imagines it to be deep and dangerous. But then the actors step through it: it's only ankle-deep. The pipe (called the 'meat-grinder' by the Stalker) seems innocuous enough, but the Stalker is terrified of it (and his fear infects the others). In the script, the pipe scene is only 3/8ths of a page (CS, 405); in the film, it's a major sequence. In *Stalker*, it becomes wearying just to walk a few yards. This is a wasteland in miniature.

One might see the *Stalker* landscape as Freudian and over-eroticized: the long tunnel, for instance, which can be seen as a vaginal image, followed by the flooded room at the end of it, which is suitably uterine. The Room itself, the goal or Grail of the whole film, can also be seen as a womb motif, recalling mythological motifs of plenitude, such as Eden or Paradise, or the Holy Grail and the Celtic cauldron over-flowing with life.[5] (Tarkovsky's films contain many elements of mythology and Classic Greek tragedy, which enable them to transcend their eras.) The climax of the film has the protagonists sitting down on the floor of the Room. There is a pool in front of them, and the major element in the climactic shot is rain falling. The imagery of the rain, the pool and the Room can be seen as relating to rebirth, women's mysteries, a 'return to the Mother', and natal themes (rain as life-giving, orgasmic *jouissance*, the re-affirmation of primal, natural reality). The rain shatters the mirror of the pool, which has reflected back the protagonist's male narcissism and fantasies for much of the film. The shattering of the mirror destroys the men's slide into narcissistic fantasy, abstraction and idealism, and restores the real, mobile, changeable, transient natural world. But it could have any other interpretation: the never-ending nature of a quest, say, or that the travellers can't avoid bringing their own neuroses and worldviews with them which are reflected back at them. (In the script of *Stalker*, the climax is only a quarter of a page of stage directions [CS, 414]).

Stalker is the first film of Tarkovsky's late, mature style, which's marked by the long, slow sequence shot, the long and slow zoom in or tracking shot. Time expands softly, slowly. The film itself is long (some 160 minutes), but contains only about 142 shots, an extraordinarily low number for a film of the late 1970s (and this is even more amazing, because it's 142 shots in a film of two hours and forty minutes, not a conventional one hour and thirty or forty minute feature film). This makes an average shot length of over a minute (the equivalent in a Hollywood film from the 1970s onwards would be less than four or five seconds). A typical Hollywood feature of the time might have 800-1,000 shots (or more, in a film of 2 1/2 hours-plus). By the 1990s and 2000s, 1,500 was not uncommon.

So *Stalker* is a film constructed from lengthy sequence shots, many lasting several minutes. The camera tracks just above surfaces: a sewer pipe strewn with refuse, a water-logged interior, the human body as a landscape. The shots dazzle with their dynamic cinematography, and they fit together seamlessly. The tension in each shot seems to hang precariously on the edge of something – as if something extraordinary or puzzling is going to happen, or as if the film itself is going to burn in the projector, as in a candle or a fire. Or perhaps it might be swept away or dissolved by the dripping water. Tarkovsky's later films have this quality of being on the edge of destruction – or transfiguration. A film in the process of melting away into itself. A film burning to ashes like the book of poems in *Nostalghia* or the house in *The Sacrifice*, or melting into a clear mountain stream. Nothing left in the darkness but the sound of running water. The film ends, you shut your eyes in the dark – but still hear running water.

Most of the sets in *Stalker* appear to be adaptions of existing locations (Tarkovsky is credited as art director – after two previous designers had been fired. In the Hollywood system, the production designer and the art director are not the same people as the ones who actually dress the sets). High on the art department's list of props and equipment on *Stalker* must have been hoses, rigs and trucks for rain and creating puddles, smoke and fog machines, greens (plants), scrapped military vehicles, and the entire contents of junkyards and cast-offs from factories and hospitals, for the machinery and detritus strewn over the Zone (the newspapers, the cables, the bits of metal, the trash of whole towns). At times, the dressing of the sets in a Tarkovsky film looks as if a flood or tidal wave has receded, leaving pools of brackish water, grass permanently damp or dewy, and trash strewn everywhere.

When the travellers halt in the middle of the film, they lie or sit beside a shallow pool; the Stalker is isolated on a little island, his hand lying in the water. (Sometimes the water in *Stalker* looks stagnant and lifeless, appropriate for the post-apocalyptic environment of the story). As well as pools in *Stalker*, there are rivers, lakes, flooded warehouses, dripping tunnels, rooms of water, and waterfalls. The only obviously artificial set, and the least successful example of production design, because it looks so self-consciously 'futuristic' or weird, is the room of mounds of sand (Tarkovsky designed this set).

Musically, *Stalker* focusses on one of Eduardo Artemiev's compositions: the lyrical, haunting flute theme (also known as the Stalker's theme). There was plenty more music written by Artemiev for *Stalker*, but Tarkovsky opted not to use it. The idea of using classical music behind the sound of the train, in the Stalker's house scenes that open and close the film, derived from Tarkovsky telling Artemiev that he heard music behind the rhythmic sounds of trains. Thus, Beethoven and Ravel can be discerned underneath the rattle and rumble of the train. (Using classical music was also part of Tarkovsky's project of grounding cinema in something historically recognizable to the audience. The same approach was used in *Star Wars*).

Stalker is a film, like *Nostalghia*, in which hardly anything happens. There is no 'action' in the traditional, Hollywood sense of the term. *Stalker*'s 'action' is deeply interiorized and contemplative, bordering on the mystical. No car chases, multiple explosions, drugs, gadgets, spaceships, special effects, techno-fetishism, fist fights, sex scenes, or 500 uses of the word 'fuck'.

The film is itself (and for its maker) a religious quest. Making the film becomes a prayer and re-making the film (on viewing it) becomes a pilgrimage. The quest of the three main protagonists is also religious (or at least philosophical). As in fairy tales and mediæval pilgrimages, characters set out to find what they've always desired (or feared). As the Stalker puts it, what you've desired brings you most pain in life. Your desire defines your life. As Tarkovsky rightly realizes, it is not the goal, not this or that particular sacred site or Holy Land that matters to the pilgrims, but the journey itself. Each traveller has different motives and goals, and each re-evaluates their lives by the end of their journey near the end of the film (the Writer seems to be re-evaluating his goals throughout the film. Unlike the others, the Writer is continuously psychoanalyzing himself – and everything else around him). *Stalker*, Tarkovsky said in *Sculpting In Time*, was about 'human dignity, and how a man suffers if he has no self-respect' (ST, 194).

The three men can be seen as:

Art	Science	Religion
Writer	*Scientist*	*Stalker*
Poetry/ anti-rationalism/ cynicism	rationalism/ unbelief/ industry/ war	magic/ intuition/ pure faith

Only the Stalker can see (or feel) the danger in the Zone (but when the others disobey his orders, they don't seem to suffer any significant consequences). He has faith/ belief/ God. He believes, wholeheartedly. He does not question his belief, nor the Zone and its properties. The other two veer from naïve, ever-hopeful primitive belief, to world-weary cynicism: at times they despise the Zone and their reasons for being there. Sometimes both the Writer and the Professor offer bored cynicism in response to the Zone, but they also fear it, and respond swiftly to the Stalker's awed reaction to the Zone.

As in *Nostalghia*, there are the familiar Tarkovskyan motifs in *Stalker* of a dog, fire, water, birds, milk, and so on. There are many passages of near-silence. There is less and less dialogue as the film progresses. (The family members may also represent principles: Monkey is the mystical, the Stalker is the religious or spiritual, and the Stalker's wife is the social or ethical principle). In the script, the Professor tells the Writer that the Stalker was crippled in the Zone by a bad accident, and has been in prison twice (CS, 397). He also used to work for the Professor as a lab technician.

There are Christian themes in *Stalker*: aside from the religious nature of the quest and the 'miraculousness' of the Zone, the Stalker himself is linked with Christ. He looks like a suffering saint and martyr; he is called 'one of God's fools'; he quotes, in voiceover, from the *New Testament*, and is associated with Christ at Emmaus. In one shot, the Stalker's voice is heard over a shot of the prone Stalker by the waterfall; a cut shows the other two listening with eyes closed; the camera pans from the Scientist to the Writer, who rests leaning on him; the Writer opens his eyes, looking at the Stalker; the camera pans back to the Scientist, who is also now looking at the Stalker, whose further Christian affinities have been revealed. At the end of the 'telephone room' scene, the Writer mocks the Stalker's religiosity by putting on a crown of thorns (and the Stalker asks him to desist).

Desire is a recurrent theme in *Stalker* – note that one of its titles was *The Wish Machine*. The Stalker tells the other two that their dreams and their desires will come true when they reach the Room. *Stalker* is all about desire, and the desire to desire, the daring to desire. Gradually the motivations for each character are developed, from the superficial to the more profound. When they reach the room next to the Room, the Stalker says that it is the greatest moment in their lives, when their deepest wish will come true. *Stalker* has affinities with many quest narratives, including the important notion that when the endpoint is attained, each individual's desires have been changed by the journey, and the goal of the quest is not what they expected at all.

19 : 2 *STALKER*, SCENE BY SCENE

A scene-by-scene breakdown of *Stalker*:

Scene I. The Stalker's home

Shot I: after the opening credits over a M.S. shot of the bar (in black-and-white), with its flickering fluorescent lamp and bartender, the film begins in the Stalker's home (Eduard Artemiev's music plays over the credits). A short piece of exposition, in white titles on black, scrolling up the screen, explains the Zone after the opening credits.

Shot 2: in black-and-white the camera tracks forward slowly, up to some partially-open doors to reveal the large brass family bed in a large, dirty, damp, bare room. It has the pockmarked and uneven walls that Tarkovsky liked (recalling the textured walls of the raining room in *Mirror*).

Shot 3: a noisy train passes by, causing the objects on a round table, which include pills and a glass, to tremble; the glass of water moves (looking to the final scene with Monkey). Then a slow lateral tracking movement, looking vertically down on the three people in the bed, with Monkey (Natasha Abramova) in between her parents. Both the Stalker (Alexander Kaidanovsky) and his wife (Alyssa Freindlikh) are awake, staring into space silently.

In the next shot (a continuation of shot 2), the Stalker gets up to leave for the Zone, careful not to disturb his sleeping family; he dresses (in very worn, dirty clothes); in the same shot he walks towards the camera, into C.U., a technique used throughout the film, partially closing the doors behind him; his wife is seen rising up in the bed between the doors. These two shots establish the slow pace of *Stalker*: we are many minutes into the film, but there have only been two shots (disregarding the shot of the bar over the credits).

The Stalker prepares himself to leave for the Zone – lighting a fire, brushing his teeth, eating some food. The Stalker's wife comes in, switches on a lamp that burns too bright then breaks, and harangues him for leaving. Like the men of so much of Western literature, the man tries to escape domesticity and the matriarchal rule of the homestead.

The wife collapses on a chair then falls to the floor, sobbing loudly and writhing, arching her back. It is the most hysterical outburst in Tarkovsky's cinema, aside from Adelaide in *The Sacrifice*. It seems out of proportion with the scene (and film) thus far, but establishes the depth of the wife's feeling for the Stalker (Adelaide's hysteria is understandable in the run-up to a nuclear attack). It is also a brief scene, and the narrative leaves the woman on the floor to follow the Stalker. The sound of a train passing occurs again, this time mixed with Richard Wagner's *Meistersinger*. (Nothing is said in *Stalker* until eight some minutes into the film.)

Scene 2. The bar

Outside the bar, the Writer (Anatoly Solonitsyn) talks with a young woman beside a newish white sports car at a dockyard about belief, God, and the Middle Ages. The Writer speaks about how boring the real world is, a world where triangle ABC equals triangle ABC.

There is no mystery, the Writer says (he's dressed in a long black coat, and has a plastic carrier bag). The Stalker, approaching over railroad lines, listens from a distance. The Stalker and the Writer enter the bar, after the woman drives off when the Stalker says something harsh to her (which the viewer doesn't hear). (The Writer has a number of props in his armament which he has to discard through the film: cigarettes, a woman (in the sports car), and so on.)

Andrei Tarkovsky   *449*

Inside, they meet the Scientist (Nikolai Grinko). Preliminary character exposition: the Stalker is looking for life, for positive goals; the Writer is cynical at this point: he hates the lack of mystery in the world. He is bitter. The Scientist is pragmatic.

After introducing the Scientist, that's all of the major characters in *Stalker* accounted for: five people: the Stalker, the wife, Monkey, the Writer and the Scientist. After the bar scene, the film stays with just three characters for two hours, until the end. It's not the only movie to do so: *Hell In the Pacific* and *Cast Away*, for example. But you have to have a great script, and great performers.

The suspicion of science and technology that's found in the Writer's view of the Scientist comes out in Tarkovsky's writings. In his diary, for instance, he remarks that the formula $E = MC^2$ cannot be true, 'because there can be no such thing as positive knowledge'. True knowledge was intuitive, non-rational, *felt*, Tarkovsky asserted. 'True knowledge is achieved in the heart and in the soul' (D, 284). Or again: 'I can accept faith, but not knowledge' (D, 289).

The Stalker is silent for most of the scene, as the camera tracks in slowly to the three men sitting on stools at a high table (in a 4 1/2 minute take), listening to the Writer and Scientist talk – of art and science (this establishes a debate between art and science, creativity and rationality, which will run throughout the film).

The Stalker is framed between the Writer and Scientist. The Scientist says he is curious about the Zone; the Writer says he is going for inspiration (a view he later changes). There are off-screen sounds of foghorns and train whistles, suggesting that there is still some industrial activity in this dilapidated harbour area.

Scene 3. Factories

Driving around in the Landrover. The sound of the vehicle (the engine, the tyres in the mud) and the trains is mixed very high, emphasizing the unreality of this post-mechanical wasteland, a no-go zone, a border checkpoint between ordinary/ safe/ domestic life and the unreality/ spirituality/ danger of the Zone. *Mise-en-scène* of overgrown railway tracks, flooded factories and warehouses, wise mesh fences, spotlights, emptiness: Franz Kafka's Prague after a holocaust, or Stalin's Moscow after a hundred years of military curfews.

The Stalker drives the Landrover around muddy tracks, through alleys in between disused factories, and over rubble, avoiding a policeman on a motorbike.

There are complex tracking shots and single takes, following the three men in the Landrover. In some shots, the vehicle disappears from view, then reappears when the cop has gone; sometimes the camera tracks rapidly with the vehicle; sometimes the Landrover is driven by the Stalker along narrow alleys, reappearing in a different place. Continuity is disrupted in some of these shots.

A worker opens some metal gates above a railroad to let a train towing a couple of trucks pass. A shot of the border control point reveals a mass of lamps, posts and fences, with white-helmeted and uniformed guards on each side of the railway track as the train approaches and is let through. Swiftly, the Landrover drives onto the tracks from off-camera and skids, following the train; the camera shoots the action tracking behind the car. Lights are switched on and the guards open fire with machine guns on the Landrover, smashing part of the railroad trucks' load, breaking glass in windows, but the men in the vehicle cross the border unscathed.

The Scientist is instructed by the Stalker to find the nearby rail car; he walks carefully through a desolate engine shed; gunshots disrupt the pool behind the Scientist, as the camera zooms in at the end of the shot. Echoey sound of water dripping.

In a slow lateral tracking shot the Scientist approaches the rail car, pushes it to the right, and the Landrover enters the scene in the distance, behind him. The Stalker and Writer climb onto the rail car.

Scene 4. The rail car

On the railway tracks they ride into the Zone. Lengthy C.U.s of each protagonist, to the sound of electronically-treated railway noises. This sequence goes on much longer (3 1/2 mins) than might be expected from the narrative up to this point. All other sounds die away quickly, with just the rhythmic sound of the rail car on the tracks dominating. Sometimes the camera pans from one person to another; often the C.U. shots linger on the back of the protagonists' heads. (This is one of the most famous sequences in Tarkovsky's cinema, which viewers often thought of as a single shot, but it is five).

Scene 5. Arriving in the Zone

Sudden cut to full colour, no gradual change (the Zone is all in colour). L.S., panning slowly to the right, of trees, bushes and odd abandoned items (trash, but also industrial machinery). Then a very lengthy tracking shot moving slowly to the left, of the men climbing off the rail flatcar and looking around the Zone. It seems to be mid-Summer, June or July, with the green leaves and birdsong making a dramatic contrast to the desolate greys and blacks of the warehouses and dockyard (plants and grass were sprayed to enhance their colour – a not uncommon practice in cinema, and quite common in Tarkovsky's films). There are no trees, for instance, in the world outside the Zone (which automatically renders it negative in Tarkovsky's eyes).

The Stalker says of the Zone: it's as if 'we've made it by our state of mind'. He says the Zone is so still, and that there's no one there. Decivilization. Solitude. He says the flowers don't smell. He is happier. The Stalker talks about his teacher, Porcupine, who committed suicide.

A river gradually becomes visible, behind the men, in a valley, with a hill beyond. They are startled by the sound of dogs howling. The Scientist ties some cloths around metal nuts at the Stalker's request.

The Stalker goes off on his own to lie face-down in the bushes, to commune with the nature spirits of the Zone; Eduardo Artemiev's Stalker flute theme music is heard, the first music for some time. Slavoj Zizek remarked:

> in Tarkovsky's universe, we enter the spiritual dimension only via intense direct physical contact with the humid heaviness of earth (or stale water) – the ultimate Tarkovskyan spiritual experience takes place when a subject is lying stretched out on the earth's surface, half submerged in stale water.

The Scientist tells the Writer about the Zone and the Stalker's mutant daughter (who is rumoured to be legless): this comes across as rather humdrum exposition. Tarkovsky's sense of cinematic style seems low-power here, in this monotonous dialogue. It's a talky scene that might have benefitted from some pruning. The Scientist explains about the meteorite, the 'Room' in the Zone, and the strange events that have occurred in the Zone.

Scene 6. In the Zone

The three travellers start walking. The Scientist carries a knapsack; the Writer has a plastic bag. The Stalker throws metal nuts wrapped in white cloth ahead of them, into the grass, as if they're gingerly traversing a minefield (he doesn't clearly explain what the dangers are, nor how the metal nuts could uncover them. It's one of the triumphs of *Stalker* that the audience buys into this idea, that three men traverse what appears to be quite unremarkable terrain very slowly and gingerly, a few yards at a time). After throwing the metal nut, the Stalker tells the Scientist to go first, followed by the Writer.

The *mise-en-scène* is of thick, long grass, tall cowslips, gently rolling countryside, trees in the distance, mist drifting over the meadows (as in *Nostalghia*), bits of wreckage dotted about (a group of smashed tanks and military vehicles in one long shot). A distinctly summery atmosphere, despite the dour Dostoievskian tone, the desperation of the Stalker and cynicism of the Writer, and the forbidding post-apocalyptic situation.

There are huge spaces around the characters, empty spaces filled with wood pigeons cooing; wind; few words; sudden outbursts from the Stalker about the dangers of the Zone (the audience needs to be reminded of this constantly, other-wise, it's three guys going for a walk in the country); the protagonists moving in long shot through long grass and cowslips. An atmosphere of intense yet tranquil mystery, full of foreboding yet also quietly hypnotic. There is no other film like this.

The images of figures amongst lush vegetation, captured in gentle tracking, boom or zoom shots, recurs many times in Tarkovsky's cinema – Kris at the beginning of *Solaris*, Roublyov in the forests, the mother in *Mirror*.

Scene 7. In the Zone

The Writer wants to go on ahead, but something holds him back (the Stalker says he has created his own barriers). There is a lengthy track (then zoom) up to and looking through the open doors of a wrecked car; the Stalker ignores the vehicle; the other two look at the car (and towards the camera); sound of the wind at the end of this shot.

The Writer argues with the Stalker about taking a direct route to the Room, which the Stalker says lies ahead. The Stalker tries to persuade him to take a longer, safer route.

The Stalker, who has warned the Writer not to drink, takes the Writer's bottle and pours the liquid away (the Writer has to manage without the props of his trade – alcohol and cigarettes – in the Zone. Earlier, in the bar, the Writer wanted to go back for cigarettes, but the Stalker dissuaded him). The Writer ignores the warning and walks on ahead.

As the Writer approaches an abandoned building the wind rises; the camera zooms out (from the viewpoint of the building) and a harsh voice says 'Stop! Don't move'; at the end of the zoom out, the sides of a doorway are revealed; a cloth or veil falls in front of the lens (like the veils in *Mirror*) before the shot cuts.

Scene 8. The Stalker's exposition

In a lengthy, complex shot, with the camera tracking, panning and craning, the Stalker tells the others about the Zone, its traps and mutability. The shot begins with the Writer returning hurriedly from the ruined building; the Stalker moves away slightly from the others, and explains the dangers of the Zone, in M.C.U., the camera dwelling on the back of his shaven head. Still in the same shot, the Stalker moves back nearer the others; the camera cranes up slightly, back to its original angle; now the building is shrouded in mist.

The Zone was created by people's state of mind, explains the Stalker (compare this with the Ocean in *Solaris*). Thus, during the Stalker's 'dream', dream and reality blur, and the dog from the dream also exists in 'real' life; the dog in *Nostalghia* similarly blurred the boundaries between dream and reality. Normally, the Zone is quiet, but when people arrive, things start to happen (this recalls Heisenberg's Uncertainty Principle, where the observer alters what is observed, and also quantum physics. In psychoanalytic film criticism, the viewer watching the film with their particular characteristics and in their particular circumstances alters the film. *Stalker* plays all the time with subjectivity and objectivity).

Scene 9. The waterfall

Beside a waterfall and a tiled wall. The Stalker and the Writer lose the Scientist, after wading into the water, but find him again, sitting calmly eating and drinking beside a small fire on the ground. He explains that he went back for his rucksack (and had to crawl back); the Stalker is surprised that he is unharmed.

Tarkovsky plays with the viewer's perception of off-screen space and sound in these scenes: the Professor sits beside a wall of water, but it can't be heard; in a later tracking shot in the same location, lamps creak in the breeze, although the water would drown out almost any other sounds.

The Stalker says the Room, the goal of the quest, is only 200 yards away, but they can't get there in a straight line. Obvious metaphors of life itself as the quest. Before this scene, there's a shot looking down on what seems to be a circular well, to a pool of water which's disturbed, perhaps by the object heard falling offscreen (there seems to be a meniscus of oil on the water, which undulates and shines); atmospheric music is played, and poetry spoken in voiceover. The shot recalls the dream sequences in the well in *Ivan's Childhood*.

In another shot, a complex track and zoom, the Stalker is seen edging carefully around something the viewer can't see, just below the bottom of the frame – presumably a well shaft (maybe the one just seen). The Stalker climbs through a circular opening, and converses with the others. Climbing out again, the Stalker tells the Writer to start climbing down a ladder.

Another shot at this point prefigures the Stalker's 'dream': it begins on some embers and tracks laterally over objects such as a hypodermic needle and a book (a still-life motif that will recur in *Nostalghia*).

Scene 10. By the waterfall

The pilgrims rest, and talk. The Stalker is shown in various poses, lying face-down, or face-up, or on his side; some of these discontinuous shots are in full colour, others are sepia/ gold-tinted (in some prints, the sepia shots appear black-and-white). In one shot, the Stalker is lying on a tiny island of soil and grass, surrounded by shallow water, with the dog near him (critics have – inevitably – linked the dog with Cerebrus, guardian of the Underworld in ancient Greek mythology. If one's looking for symbolism attached to the appearance of the dog, I'd suggest it's more like a spirit animal, in the shamanic sense, rather than a guardian).

The space and time of this scene is ambiguous. Multiple interpretations suggest themselves: these could be scenes from the film's present tense, or flashbacks to the Stalker's earlier journeys in the Zone, or the Stalker dreaming of the Zone. Alternatively, the viewpoint could be with the other two travellers (in any combination of the above). The gold-hued (black-and-white) shots are accompanied by the Stalker's theme music.

The shots of the three resting men with their eyes shut are low angle M.C.U.s, slowly zooming in, as they talk. The continuity 'errors' don't appear as 'mistakes' at

all, as they occasionally do in a conventional movie. The Stalker might appear
surrounded by water at one point, or not at all in another; he might be shown lying
on his back, or his side, or face-down, but it doesn't matter one bit. (If the viewer is
still worrying about continuity glitches at this stage in a film like *Stalker*, they've
completely missed the point).

The Writer criticizes the Scientist; they argue – about science and art. The
Writer says (sounding very much like Tarkovsky): 'mankind's sole purpose is to
create works of art.' The Writer digs at the Professor for wanting to be famous and
respected, for wanting to discover the Zone and gain the Nobel Prize. The Scientist
is equally dismissive of the Writer's haughty, idealized conception of art.

In some ways, these scenes, in the middle of the film, contain the essence of
Stalker, and are some of the most compelling in Tarkovsky's cinema. Yet he's
working with seemingly very static elements: three men lying down on the ground,
and a dog. No 'action' in the traditional sense whatsoever. No 'drama', nor even
storytelling. Yet the combination of the visual compositions, the slow zooms, the
tracking shots across the water-logged landscape, the mysterious cuts between colour
and black-and-white, the voiceover by the Stalker's daughter or his wife, and
Eduard Artemiev's plangent music, makes these scenes absolutely hypnotic. (The
voiceover quotes from the *Bible* (*Revelations*, 6: 12-17), talking about the sixth seal.
At the end of the quote, she laughs softly.)

Scene II. The Stalker's 'dream'

One of the most mesmerizing shots in Tarkovsky's cinema: the long tracking shot
in C.U. looking down into shallow water, moving slowly forwards, on a tiled floor,
at a myriad of carefully positioned objects: a machine gun, coins, fish in a glass bowl,
a mirror, paper, a metal spring, a syringe, a calendar, paintings (one looks like a
Claude Lorraine pastoral landscape; the other is from Jan van Eyck's apocalyptic
Ghent Altarpiece).

The 'dream' shot begins on the Stalker's head, near the water, and ends on his
hand in the water. This is an intensely lyrical sequence, with poetry read in voiceover (presumably by the Stalker's daughter or his wife) and Artemiev's haunting
Stalker theme music.

Before this shot, during the waterfall interlude, the Stalker provided some of the
voiceover; some of this comes from the *Bible*, from Christ at Emmaus (*The Gospel of*

Luke, 24: 13-18), the passage where the resurrected Christ is not recognized by two of his disciples. There are also shots of a lake and trees, and a field with wind swirling in it, like a mini-tornado, sending up dust (the ground, dry mud like a ploughed field, moves up and down as if there's water underneath it. It's one of those shots in Tarkovsky's cinema in which something is happening, but it takes the viewer a moment or two to identify the mysterious elements).

Scene 12. Same setting. Some time later

The Stalker talks about music. This is the end of the lengthy middle section in *Stalker*. More than an interlude or digression, these scenes contain (the essence of) the whole film.

Scene 13. In the pipe

The tunnel is full of debris, dripping water, and many roots hanging down from man-holes (which offer the principal light source). It looks like a sewer (a favourite setting for chases and monsters in movies). The pipe, which the Stalker calls the 'meat-grinder', presents another kind of test (this scene appears particularly like a mediæval adventure, a test in a Grail quest). Distance is mysteriously expanded.

The Stalker takes some matches and they choose them to see who must go first, in a lengthy discussion scene (all captured in a single take). The Writer loses and walks gingerly into the pipe. Meanwhile, the Stalker and Scientist stand back from the entrance to the pipe, as if they fear something terrible is going to happen to the Writer. The scene is covered by dazzingly good, slow, eye-level tracking shots, looking forwards and backwards along the pipe, often from right behind the Writer. The sound is of echoey water dripping and footsteps. When he thinks it's safe, the Writer calls to the others to follow. They do so, but slowly, carefully, and always hanging back from the Writer, and hugging the walls.

It's impossible to gauge accurately how long this section of concrete sewer is (50, a 100 metres?), but it's another testament to Tarkovsky's genius that this short, gently curving tunnel could be the setting for such a suspenseful scene (and the suspense is created with none of the Hollywood back-up of enhancements, such as music, or visual effects, or rapid cutting, or dialogue).

The Writer stops at the other end of the pipe and takes out a gun before entering the next space, a small room with chest-deep water. The Stalker yells at him to leave the gun — 'who are you going to shoot at?' The Writer drops the gun, climbs through the doorway, down some steps, and wades into the water, up to his shoulders (it looks freezing), and climbs the steps on the other side; the other two follow him (it's all done in a single, difficult-to-repeat shot).

Scene 14. The room of mounds of sand

The large room of small sand dunes looks artificial, too obviously like a film set. A short jump-cut sequence shows a bird flying into the room and disappearing, followed by another bird which flies in and lands on the mounds (kicking up dust). This is one of the few 'sci-fi' or 'surreal' sequences in *Stalker*. There is also a slow motion shot of the metal nut and white cloth landing and bouncing on the sand.

The Writer delivers a long speech about how people don't take notice of the artist, and how they rape him/ her for everything they can get. This speech is performed into the camera, though he appears to be addressing the others (who are some way off, however). The Writer sits next to a deep well (perhaps related to the earlier shot of a well). The Writer drops a rock into the shaft, which, after a long pause, creates reverberating noises.

The direct address of the camera is unusual in Tarkovsky's cinema (though not in New Wave cinema — Jean-Luc Godard, for example, employed it often — probably more than of his contemporaries. In this case, Tarkovsky may have used a shot from a different place in the script, as he did with the shot of the Stalker's wife at the end of the film talking about living with the Stalker). The Writer's views can again be seen as echoing those of Tarkovsky (one of Tarkovsky's perennial themes was the artist's relationship with society, which the Writer discusses here).

Scene 15. The telephone room

The interior of the building changes, from the underground pipe to a series of large dilapidated rooms, dominated by pools of water and piles of refuse. The mysterious dog reappears, trotting into the interior. The Stalker, leaning against a window in profile, recites a poem, supposedly by Porcupine's sensitive brother (it's actually "Now the summer is gone" by Arseny Tarkovsky [ST, 191]).

The three men are then seen talking in a smaller room off one of the larger rooms.

Behind them is a window. Water is glimpsed moving under the floorboards. The Writer finds some sleeping pills on the window sill (a link with the Stalker's home, as is the lamp that suddenly flares up then goes out, a typical Tarkovskyan moment). A telephone on the floor rings, unexpectedly. The Writer answers it and says no, this isn't the clinic.

The Scientist then takes up the phone and dials a number. He talks to someone at the laboratory; the other voice is heard also. The Scientist tells the man, who's a work colleague from the laboratory, that he's stolen the device from Bunker Four and is going to use it. The man in the laboratory offers another motivation for the Scientist wanting to destroy the Room: it's not for fame and glory, but because he slept with his wife twenty years ago. This barb seems to be really hurt the Scientist, who crumples.

All this is covered in a lengthy take (6 mins 50 secs): it begins in M.S., with the men framed in the doorway; it zooms in to the Scientist when he walks forwards and crouches down with the telephone; zooms out after the phone conversation's over; then the men come out of the room; the Writer puts on the crown of thorns and walks into M.C.U. The Stalker is taunted by this image of the Writer as Christ.

Scene 16. On the threshold of the Room

Before entering the room next to the Room, there are some curious shots: one is of a corridor with a door (off-screen) to the left which opens and shuts on its own, letting in light. On the floor are two skeletons which seem to be embracing, and a plant (which may be growing out of their remains).

Now the travellers're next to the Room, the Stalker, deeply moved, tells the other two that their greatest desire will come true. When it comes to the crunch, the Writer backs out of entering the Room, saying he doesn't want to debase himself by praying (the Writer is perennially sceptical, but always defers to the Stalker at the last moment, or when he has a difficult choice to make). The Writer denounces the Zone, as if he's been cheated. The Stalker then asks the Scientist if he wishes to go first into the Room.

The Scientist pulls out a 20-kiloton atomic bomb, a small metal cylinder. He calls it a soul-meter, for measuring the human soul. The Scientist says he wants to blow up the room, to stop it getting into the wrongs hands — of megalomaniacs and politicians. The Stalker grapples with the Scientist, trying to grab the nuclear device. The Writer pulls him off repeatedly, throwing him violently to the floor.

The Stalker then confesses (in a high angle C.U. as he kneels on the floor) what the Zone is and what his mission means to him. He is utterly dejected – the Zone is for people who have lost all hope. The Room represents hope for those who have lost all hope, the Stalker says; he can't bear the Scientist wanting to destroy the last possibility of hope (*Stalker*, Tarkovsky maintained, was an optimistic film: art, for Tarkovsky, should foster a sense of faith and hope). The Writer still sees the Stalker cynically, denouncing him as hungry for power and money, saying he can be tsar and God in the Zone. Moving into close-up, still in the same shot, the Stalker denies the Writer's accusations.

After refusing to enter the Room, standing on the edge of it, the Writer nearly topples into it; the Stalker grabs his coat and pulls him back (it's a nice touch of comedy, like something out of a *Bugs Bunny* cartoon or Buster Keaton).

Then, in a lengthy long shot, the climax of the journey, the Scientist dismantles his bomb and throws parts of it into the pool nearby. He sits beside the others, and it rains. The *mise-en-scène* recalls Domenico's derelict dwelling in *Nostalghia*. The view is from inside the Room, a different angle from the previous shots, looking out to the three men sitting together on the floor, who look into the Room. They are framed in a large opening, recalling a proscenium arch. The Room itself is flooded, like the tiled area of the middle section scenes.

It rains, then stops; the water from the roof drips. The sound is of dripping water (no music). The Scientist throws other bits of the bomb towards the camera, into the pool. The lighting changes: as the camera zooms out, the room becomes gold-tinted; white lights are faded up above the group of men; the orangey light inside the Room is faded down.

The Stalker says maybe he could give up and come to live in the Zone. The rain decreases to drips. This climax is the opposite of Hollywood entertainment cinema. The characters sit still, hardly moving or speaking; the camera is static; it is a single shot, lasting minutes; there is no music, no voiceover, little dialogue, just the sound of dripping water and birdsong. The re-affirmation of nature and elemental life is powerful.

After this lengthy shot, there is an overhead (linking) shot of a fish (a carp?) next to the bomb in the tiled pool; black oil or ink is seen spreading over the water (recalling one of the earlier shots of the flooded tiled floor). Nature and science are shown together here, with the natural world winning out ultimately. The fish has

Christian connotations (Christ as the Ichthus, the Fish-God), and also relates to the astrological water sign Pisces: the two thousand year period from Christ's birth to the year 2000 is called the Age of Pisces. The fish symbolism can thus relate to the themes of apocalypse and the end of the millennium. The world of *Stalker* shows a post-industrial, post-atomic wasteland that needs refreshing: the fish could relate to this sense of millennial, cosmic rebirth (and maybe the fisher king in Grail mythology). It is odd, in discussing the symbolism of the fish in *Stalker*, that Tarkovsky should maintain he is not courting symbolism. Yet he places a fish right next to the atomic bomb in a shot. Maybe Tarkovsky is only stressing materiality and the concrete, but in the context of this particular film, with its myriad religious imagery and themes, its metaphysical discussions, the reverse is more likely. Andrzej Wajda remarked that in *Stalker* was Tarkovsky 'throwing down the gauntlet' to those filmmakers who lived in the materialistic world.

The sound of a train is heard over this shot: it is a bridging shot, which takes the film back to the bar, outside the Zone. But the music behind this particular shot, behind the train noise, is Maurice Ravel's *Bolero*, of all things, not, as one might expect from Tarkovsky at this point, a Bach *aria* or choral music (there were going to be more classical pieces at this point underneath the train noise).

Scene 17. Back in the bar

The Stalker's wife and daughter Monkey are seen in black-and-white near the dockyard, with a power station behind them on the other side of the water. The wife comes in to the bar to claim the Stalker. The Writer marvels at her.

After such a long and arduous journey the three men have returned from the Zone with a simple cut, from the fish and the bomb and Ravel's *Bolero*, to a shot of the wife and daughter near the dockyard, and then the men in the bar, in almost the same position, sitting around the tall circular table (suggesting that they haven't been changed much by their experiences, or maybe haven't even travelled anywhere at all; the journey has been more internal than external and physical, though the film, and the journey, definitely hasn't been 'just a dream'). The Stalker tells his wife about the dog (which trots into the scene). The family leave the bar and the Writer and Scientist, who are not seen again in the film.

Scene 18. A river bank

The Stalker carries his daughter home on his shoulders by a wide river with a power station in the background, in colour. Monkey is first seen in C.U., moving against the water; the camera then zooms out and tracks the other way when the family move down the riverbank and walk nearer the water's edge, a reveal that shows Monkey being carried on the Stalker's shoulders in a wide shot.

Scene 19. Stalker's house

The Stalker's wife tends the Stalker on the bed (recalling similar scenes in Tarkovsky's *œuvre*), in black-and-white. A few dandelion seeds float down in this scene, as in *Andrei Roublyov*, but even more float over the final shot of the film, of the Stalker's daughter.

Before the bed scene, there is a C.U. shot of the dog lapping (loudly) at a bowl of milk with the Stalker lying on the floor next to it (the Stalker on the floor in his home is a visual rhyme with the earlier scene of the wife lying down, but now the woman is the strong one).

The Stalker moans vehemently that the intelligentsia (the writers and the scientists) do not believe in anything. They have no faith; but *he* has faith (Tarkovsky called the Stalker 'one of the last idealists'). In the Zone, in scene 16, just outside the Room, the Stalker said that the most important thing was 'you must believe…' For him, this is the crucial thing: pure belief. The Stalker's actions here — arriving at his house and undressing and lying in bed — mirror his first ones in the film (in reverse order).

The wife delivers a speech in M.S. direct to camera (this shot was apparently going to be put in the previous scene in the bar) — saying she prefers a life with sorrows because a life without sorrow would also be a life without happiness or hope. The nobility of Christian, Nietzschean suffering. Suffering as the burning-point of Existential consciousness. Pain = life. In this Schopenhauerian, Dostoievskian and somewhat Buddhist view, suffering is essential because it means life has hope. In *Sculpting In Time*, Tarkovsky preferred to talk about spiritual potential or achieving freedom than happiness or satisfaction (239). In his 1984 lectures in London, Tarkovsky stated that artistic activity wasn't about happiness:

I have never been able to understand how an artist can be in a state of happiness during the creation process. Man does not exist for the purpose of being happy. There is a much, much higher purpose to life than merely being in a state of happiness.

In *Sculpting In Time*, Tarkovsky remarked that the scene where the Stalker's wife has her speech in the bar was partly meant to show to the Scientist and the Writer how loyal and compassionate and devoted she was, how she could still love her husband after all she has gone through, and despite also having a sick child (ST, 198). The Stalker's wife explains that she sticks by her husband, despite his being a Stalker and potential prisoner, and despite the 'mutant' offspring of stalkers.

But the significance of the Stalker's wife's impact on the two men isn't at all clear in the film. Tarkovsky claimed that the Writer is 'startled' by the Stalker's wife's 'faithfulness' and 'the strength of her human dignity', but that's not really the unambiguous interpretation of the bar scene.

The Nietzschean, Exisential view of life as eternal struggle was often propounded by Andrei Tarkovsky: the idea that there was always a striving after complete happiness, but never an achievement of it. It's the concept that aspiration, and becoming, and struggle, was the journey. As the Buddhists said, suffering was the norm: 'there has to be suffering, because it's through suffering, in the struggle between good and evil, that the spirit is forged' (D, 297). In Buddhism, according to Gautama Buddha, suffering is one of the Four Noble Truths: suffering is everywhere in life (the first truth); it is caused by desire; and suffering ceases when desire ceases; and the fourth truth says that the path to salvation and the ceasation of pain is the eightfold path. In the Western world, though, and in Tarkovsky's life-philosophy, desire is very difficult to eradicate.

Scene 20. The Stalker's daughter

A single shot, in colour, zooming and dollying out from C.U. to M.S., viewed from the end of a table. Monkey is reading a book, expressionless, in profile, wearing a golden headscarf. She looks out of the window, then back. In voiceover (in what is assumed to be Monkey's voice), a poem about eyes is heard (Fyodor Tyutchev's "How I love your eyes, my friend" [ST, 197]). The camera tracks slowly back. Dandelion seeds drift. Then three glasses on the table start to slide down the surface, as Monkey stares at them, her head on the table (which shakes). The tall glass falls off but doesn't smash. (This scene wasn't in the original treatment, which had closed with the Stalker, his wife and Monkey walking from the bar through factories and puddles).

The three glasses could refer to the three protagonists who went into the Zone, the tall one being the Stalker (with milk), who has fallen over the edge of faith, into unbelief, or perhaps into life, or it's an apotheosis of his life, or he has reached tranquillity. The three glasses are aspects or themes which could refer to the holy trinity of the family; and also to the Holy Trinity (as some critics have maintained), or they could just demonstrate the daughter's magical facility (or that there are still things occurring outside of normal life, even after the Stalker seems disillusioned and hope seems lost).

In the opening shots, when the train goes by, its movement rocks the bedside table and a glass moves. This would be a commonsensical reason for the moving glasses (but Monkey moves the glasses *before* the train is heard. Technically, although the train might have been able to shake the table before it was heard, that isn't how movies work). The symbolism is unclear: the scene could mean whatever one likes, really; but there is no doubt that the child's magical abilities are powerful.

The sound of the train (from the opening shots) is heard (and a fog horn), and behind the noise choir music, the *Ode to Joy* from Ludwig van Beethoven's *Ninth Symphony*.

End of the film, with a fade to black (but the sound of rattling continues for a few seconds).

19 : 3   CONCLUSION

At the end of the film the Stalker is changed most. He frets and groans about the intelligentsia, the faithless. His own faith has been shattered. He goes through an Existential crisis. His wife nurses him like a Madonna in *Pietà* paintings, with the dead Christ at the foot of the Cross. She says she'd like to go into the Zone, but this doesn't pacify the Stalker.

The Writer remains as cynical as ever. He says soul-searching is an invention of the mind. He puts a Crown of Thorns on in the Zone and mocks the Stalker and his faith. He says the Stalker is like a shaman, enjoying the sense of power, of being able to order people about, to say who lives and who dies in the Room or the Zone (the power of a deity). The Writer is halfway between the Stalker's position (maximum faith) and the Scientist's (total disbelief). The Writer wants to believe, but is severely disappointed when the pilgrimage fails to deliver. The Scientist says he doesn't understand anything anymore. Tarkovsky explained that his interpretation of Fyodor Dostoievsky's *The Idiot* would be about someone who wanted to believe, but could not. For Tarkovsky, Dostoievsky 'dealt with the tragedy of the loss of spirituality. All his heroes are people who would *like* to believe, but cannot'.[1]

The film ends with a transference of power, like *The Sacrifice*: from the Stalker to his daughter. It is a religious ending, the hopeful image of the child, the future, of the cyclical nature of life. Note that the two main scenes with Monkey – Monkey on the Stalker's shoulders, which begins with a close-up of Monkey in her golden headscarf, and the last table scene – are both in full colour, suggesting hope, a way out and transformation from the squalor of the black-and-white scenes. Only the two scenes with the Stalker's daughter are in colour, outside of the central scenes set in the Zone, suggesting that Monkey has a magical connection with (the powers of) the Zone. (Three endings to *Stalker* were shot, and each was included in the film, though not in the way originally scripted. The Stalker's wife's monologue, for instance, was going to occur in the bar, to the three men. Tarkovsky and editor Feiginova shifted it to the Stalker's house, which alters its resonance. The magical act of Monkey's and the lament of the Stalker were added to the script later).

The film is perfectly circular: at the beginning the Stalker gets out of bed, pulls on his trousers, talks to his wife, then leaves. At the end these actions are precisely reversed. In *Stalker* Tarkovsky makes an unambivalent statement about faith and belief over cynicism and unbelief, of love and relationships over hatred and chaos, of hope and the future over despair and death. (But it is also ambiguous: the three men appear in the bar in the same positions, as if they haven't been anywhere; their journey has been psychological and spiritual. Similarly, the events in *The Sacrifice* might all have been a dream of Alex's, a product of the insanity which overwhelms him at the end. And Kelvin, at the end of *Solaris*, seems to have travelled back to Earth and been reunited with his father. But, as the camera flies higher and higher, it's revealed that, no, he is still on the planet Solaris after all, and his journey has been into the interior).

TWENTY

The Angel Under the Water

Nostalghia

20 : 1   TARKOVSKY IN ITALY

Andrei Tarkovsky might have gone the whole way in his new (Italian) spelling of
the word *nostalgia*: he included the 'h'. Including the 'g' turns the word into its
Greek original: *gnostalghia*, which means 'homing-pain': *gnostos* = home, and
alghia = pain. The film is full of gnostalghia; mainly for Russia, Russia in Italy.[1]
The story concerns a man in exile, adrift from his homeland and family life. The
situation echoes Tarkovsky's exile at this time (late 1970s to early 1980s). 'I wanted
to make a film about Russian nostalgia,' Tarkovsky explained, 'about the particular
state of mind which assails Russians who are far from their native land' (ST, 202).
And at times that nostalgia, that inability to escape from the past, can seem like a
sickness (ST, 206).

Nostalghia came about partly because Tarkovsky wanted make a film in Italy
(which he had visited a few times), and because of his friendship with Tonino
Guerra, Michelangelo's Antonioni's regular screenwriter (Antonioni himself had
visited the Moscow film festival in 1975). Guerra had met Tarkovsky in 1962 (at

the time, he was married to a Russian).

Tarkovsky had previously made a documentary on Italy, *Tempo di Viaggio* (*A Time To Travel*), which he created with Tonio Guerra, who scripted *Nostalghia*. Many of the places Tarkovsky filmed in the 63-minute Italian television documentary were used in *Nostalghia* (including the St Catherine Pool, the region around Piero della Francesca's *Madonna del Parto* at Monterchi near Arezzo, and the hotel room). In writing his Italian travel film, Tarkovsky said he wrote the script in Russian, then had Lora Yablochkina (Guerra's Russian wife) translate them into Italian for Guerra; he would rewrite them, then Yablochkina would translate them back into Russian for Tarkovsky (D, 194). This would be one of the sources (like other elements in *Time To Travel*) of the translation theme in *Nostalghia*.

In the documentary by Donatella Baglivo about the making of *Nostalghia* (*Andrei Tarkovsky Directs Nostalghia*, a.k.a. *Un Poeta nel Cinema*, 1983, CIAK; which's essential viewing for Tarkovsky), the maestro is shown at the height of his powers, but on foreign soil, surrounded by an Italian crew and shooting in the heart of Italy. Interpreters were required on set at all times – not just to translate from Russian to Italian, but also from Russian and Italian to English. The three lead actors of *Nostalghia* were different nationalities: Oleg Yanovsky was Russian, Erland Josephson was Swedish, and Domiziana Giordano was Italian. A script reading, for example, between Tarkovsky and his three leads, required a translator to go from Russian into Italian, and another interpreter to translate that into English (for Josephson's benefit). Yankovsky seems to have been one of Tarkovsky's few Russian speakers on set. Sometimes, although there were many reasons for Tarkovsky's exile from Russia, it appeared as if Tarkovsky was deliberately creating challenges for himself. From the documentary one can see that some of the Italian crew had difficulty adapting to the working methods of the Russian genius, just as he had trouble working in the Western, European film industry.

In *Andrei Tarkovsky Directs Nostalghia*, one sees Tarkovsky taking great care with every detail of the shoot: he's often at work around the set, adjusting a curtain, arranging candles, re-adjusting the lighting, and so on. He's seldom seen losing his temper or acting the prima donna, and appears to have infinite patience with the technical process of filmmaking. He will wait and wait until he gets exactly what he wants. Tarkovsky appeared to be actually a relatively quiet presence on set, not loud or joking or acting the clown or the dictator. However, it is always clear who is boss, who is requesting this or that from the crew or the actors, and who is driving the show.

The painter in Tarkovsky comes to the fore in the *Nostalghia* documentary – so many of Tarkovsky's shots are constructed like paintings (still life paintings, or portraits, or landscapes). Tarkovsky is shown adjusting props and sets as if he's art directing the location or set to look like some vision in his head. Tarkovsky told his co-writer Tonino Guerra that

> starting with *Solaris*, and then in *Mirror*, and in *Stalker* there are the same objects, always the same. Certain bottles, certain old books, mirrors, various little objects on shelves or on windowsills. Only that which I would like to have in my home has the right to find itself in a shot of one of my films.

Although *Nostalghia* focusses on three main characters, and appears to be a 'small-scale' film, there are quite a few big scenes: the speech in the square in Rome, and the procession of religious devotees in the church, for instance. These scenes demanded a good deal of organization, animals and extras to look after, and plenty for the first and second assistant directors to do. The evocations of Russia were also elaborate scenes, requiring smoke, rain, wind and complex lighting, as well as extras and animals.

The *Nostalghia* 'making of' documentary also reminds the viewer how much Tarkovsky relied on the practical (physical) effects team, who provided smoke, rain, mud, fire, wind and other effects on set. Thus, even apparently 'simple' Tark-ovsky shots often needed all sorts of practical effects as well all the other filmmaking apparatus. A Tarkovsky shoot would demand hoses, rain nozzles, water trucks, buckets, brooms, plastic sheeting, tarpaulin, wind machines, smoke machines, ladd-ers, etc, as well as the usual gear.

In Donatella Baglivo's documentary, Tarkovsky is seen patiently working with his actors, going over lines and actions, rehearsing action, or showing his actors what he wanted by stepping in and performing the blocking himself. In the scene where Eugenia has a long speech in the hotel bedroom, actress Domiziana Giordano took a while before she understood what Tarkovsky wanted and was able to deliver it. Tarkovsky took lots of time to go over the kind of thing he was after and shot take after take until Giordano's performance came close to his vision. Giordano later said that she was nervous about working with Tarkovsky, but that he was actually pretty easy to act for. She remarked that he had tons of ideas about how to shoot a

scene, but would often compress those ideas, cutting out variations, when it came to
shoot. Tarkovsky was absolutely meticulous in terms of paying attention to every
aspect of filmmaking, Giordano said. (Tarkovsky considered casting Jill Clayburgh
in the lead role in *Nostalghia* (she had starred in Bernardo Bertolucci's *La Luna* the
previous year, which Tarkovsky had hated).)

In the TV documentary *Tempo di Viaggio*, Tonino Guerra asks Tarkovsky about
his key influences among film directors. Tarkovsky cites Alexander Dovzhenko (in
particular, *Earth*, for its poetry of cinema), Robert Bresson (for his radical
simplicity), Federico Fellini (for his humanity and generosity), Michelangelo
Antonioni, Jean Vigo (Tarkovsky calls him the father of modern French cinema,
including the New Wave), and Ingmar Bergman (Tarkovsky says he watched
Bergman's films before beginning his own films).

Tarkovsky's *Tempo di Viaggio* consists largely of Tarkovsky and Tonino Guerra
travelling around Italy visiting sites that Guerra introduces to Tarkovsky with a
view to including them in the film *Nostalghia*. Tarkovsky and Guerra visit
Ravello, Lecce, San Sepulchro, St Catherine Baths and the Amalfi coast, among
other Italian spots. These location scouting trips are intercut with conversations
between Tarkovsky and Guerra in what is presumably Guerra's home in Rome.
Tarkovsky and Guerra discuss their film project, Tarkovsky's favourite filmmakers,
fiction films, and Tarkovsky offers advice to young filmmakers. Although there's
plenty in *Tempo di Viaggio* to interest a Tarkovsky fan, it isn't a particularly
distinguished work. It doesn't really get to grips with his subjects – Italian art and
culture, the differences between Italian and Russian culture, being an exile or visitor
from Russia in Italy, and so on. *Tempo di Viaggio* seems rushed, unfinished, messy,
and confused.

In *Nostalghia*, the central character, Gorchakov, a Russian, goes to Italy to
research an 18th century musician called Pavel Sosnovsky (that's just the pretext for
the visit, and it's not particularly important). He meets an Italian interpreter,
Eugenia, and the religious fanatic, Domenico (Domenico in the film was meant to be
a teacher of mathematics from a village in Tuscany. Domenico's character was
developed and strengthened during shooting, Tarkovsky said at Cannes). All the
time he yearns for Russia. Gorchakov cannot relate to the people around him in
Italy, nor can he share his impressions of the new country with them (ST, 202). And
he cannot escape his own past. *Nostalghia* is unequivocally a film about alienation:
it is about 'someone in a state of profound alienation from the world and himself'

(ST, 204).

There are two places and two main time zones in the film: past and present, Russia and Italy; that is, sepia-and-white dream/ memory sequences of rural Russia of the past (and also Domenico's past); and the colour present day Italian sequences. To confuse things, Italy is also shown in sepia-and-white, as if in the past, but actually these are dream, fantasy or memory sequences. Tarkovsky said in an interview in *American Film* that he was searching for a kind of montage which had the subjective logic of dreams or memories or thoughts. Hardly anything is said: the film is even more spacious than *Stalker* or *The Sacrifice*. The film is full of a soft light and mist.

Most of the shots in *Nostalghia* are slow tracking shots, either forwards or backwards, or sideways. The Baths are filmed with crabwise dolly shots, low down, with the wall that surrounds the pool moving across the bottom of the frame. There are many interiors, too, of corridors: hotel corridors, the arcades of the churches; and the Milan hotel courtyard. At times the sepia-and-white and colour shots merge: it's difficult to tell which is which. The mist smooths over the jumps between the two (Tarkovsky fills his visions of both Russia and Italy with mist).

While he was thinking about the film (during 1978-79), Tarkovsky toyed with other ideas which didn't make it into the film: having the lead character marry an Italian woman; the hero telling the story of the film to a blind man; close-ups of hands; the hero dies from a stray terrorist's bullet; a Dostoievsky scene; and a psychiatrist (D, 188f). With Guerra, Tarkovsky mused what occupation to give his hero, settling on a writer (who's interested in architecture). Interpreters were included to cut down on the amount of Russian in the film (the interpreter and the Italian woman were combined in the character of Eugenia).

Other scenes that didn't make it into *Nostalghia* included a lunch with Gorchakov, Eugenia and one of her friends; Gorchakov wandering around Rome in the early morning; a lecture and Q & A session at the Russian-Italian Society; a scene taken from *The Devils*, a conversation between Stavrogin and Kirilov about God; the mirror episode from *A White, White Day* (where a man looks into a mirror and sees someone else; it was there, but altered); and a scene from *The Idiot*, between Myshkin and Rogozhin (CS, 466-7).

In the first draft of the script for *Nostalghia*, Eugenia and Gorchakov were in Venice, in a boat; there were Russian scenes, in snowy St Petersburg and Moscow; Gorchakov speaks to his wife by phone and argues with her; and there's a scene from *Crime and Punishment* (between Svidrigailov and Raskolnikov). *Nostalghia* would thus contained many scenes straight out of Fyodor Dostoievsky's *œuvre*, and in some ways it's Tarkovsky's most Dostoievskian film (Tarkovsky was still very keen on making *The Idiot* at this time).

In the script, Gorchakov is still alive after the candle-carrying scene – he's checking out of his hotel, and talking with Eugenia, who's in Rome, on the phone; she tells him about Domenico's demonstration (CS, 498f). The film alters the sequence of events: Gorchakov dies in the screenplay from a heart attack in the hotel. After his death, he dreams of being with his family in Russia, and waking them up to see the moon rise. After that came the final scene, of the Russian *dacha* in the Italian cathedral. The moonrise sequence was put earlier in the film (with Gorchakov dreaming of it, but not appearing in his dream), and only the cathedral scene followed Gorchakov's death. It makes more dramatic sense to cut straight from Gorchakov dying at the end of the candle and baths scene to the final dream.

When the film was being set up with RAI TV in Italy, three months of preproduction, two months of shooting and three months of postproduction were being talked about. Part of the film was going to be shot in Russia (the Russian flashbacks/ dream sequences), but that was logistically too difficult. The Soviet authorities dragged their feet, and were reluctant to co-operate with RAI TV. The deal was eventually set-up between RAI, Gaumont/ Italy and Sovinfilm.

In his *Dairies*, Tarkovsky wryly noted that 'the impossibility of being alone in beautiful Italy does not amount to an idea' (D, 193), and the film needed a much stronger narrative to sustain it. In *Sculpting In Time*, Tarkovsky stated: 'I was not interested in the development of the plot' (204). So that's that.

Scene I. Credit sequence. The past. Russia.

L.S. of a hillside next to a river in muted colour. Early morning. Mist drifts slowly over the field. A white horse is down below. A young boy (Alyosha) and three women in white dresses and black shawls walk down the slope. There is an old woman (the grandmother), a youngish woman with dark hair (Gorchakov's wife, played by Patrizia Torreno), and a younger woman (16 year-old Anna). The three women relate to the trinity of women in earlier Tarkovsky films, and also to the three Jungian archetypes of the feminine principle (virgin, bride/ mother and crone, the Triple Goddess of ancient times, and so on).

The camera tracks slowly towards the edge of the hill. Later this gently sloping vale in Russia is identified as Gorchakov's home, or his memory of (an idealized) homeland. Music: Russian folksong: women singing. The sombre opening bars of Giuseppe Verdi's *Requiem* fade in over the folk music. Titles roll up the screen: white, superimposed over the image.

Scene 2. Italy. Present day.

Verdi's *Requiem* fades as the picture fades to black.

Shot 2 of the film: L.S. Early morning; misty again; the Italian countryside: Tuscany, in the Arezzo region. A Volkswagen Beetle drives into frame. Camera pans. Car stops. Two people get out: Eugenia (Domiziana Giordano) and Andrei Gorchakov (Oleg Yankovsky), a glamorous, long-haired Italian interpreter in her thirties and a glum middle-aged Russian writer in an overcoat. She says the light reminds her of 'certain Autumn afternoons in Moscow'. The remark seems calculated to make Gorchakov squirm with nostalgic yearning. Gorchakov says he is sick of seeing beautiful sights, even though he instigated this trip to the Arezzo area.

Eugenia walks away from the camera, up the hill. The camera tilts slowly to reveal behind the mist a church. Here is the primary nostalgia of the film: the yearning in Italy for Russia. Later on, in the hotel foyer, they discuss the artistic icons of the two countries (Tolstoy and Pushkin, Dante, Petrarch and Machiavelli).

Scene 3. In the chapel.

Eugenia in the chapel – a vaulted undercroft or crypt, presided over by Piero della Francesca's magnificent *Madonna del Parto*. Rows of columns. Masses of candles glow in front of the painting. The slow, crabwise tracking shots throughout the scene emphasize a sense of awe and worship. The *Madonna del Parto* in the film is not the original painting in Monterchi, needles to say, but a reproduction shot in the crypt of San Pietro (a Romanesque church about 120 kilometers from Monterchi).

Eugenia meets a sacristan who looks like the men out of *Stalker*: very short cropped hair and a haunted expression. Eugenia asks the sacristan why more women than men pray. This seems to be true: go to any Italian church or cathedral, and one sees many more women than men. The man replies in a patriarchal fashion (it is the woman's role to sacrifice herself). The sacristan suggests that Eugenia try to pray: she cannot and will not kneel (she is wearing high-heeled shoes and says it's difficult to kneel).

Then a ritual procession comes in. Tarkovsky says they are meant to be like witches. They carry candles and a large statue of the Virgin Mary. It is set down in front of the painting.

The master shot of this part of the scene is a slow zoom in from M.L.S. to M.S. Then a kneeling, praying woman, muttering to the Mother of God, opens the clothes over the belly of the statue and many birds fly out, chirping madly. They flutter around the church. The sounds of the birds become echoey, enlarging the sense of space in the undercroft. Shots of feathers landing on the candles. A shot of Eugenia, in C.U. is followed by a slow push-in to the face of Piero's *Madonna of Childbirth*.

Scene 4. Russia.

Shot 1. A Russian country setting in sepia-and-white: a gently sloping vale, with a path, telegraph poles, a small pool, a *dacha* and trees, behind the house. Gorchakov stands near the *dacha*, dressed the same as in scene 2.

Shot 2. A white feather flutters down out of the sky and lands in some water, in C.U.: the camera tilts and cranes slowly up Gorchakov's body as he bends down and picks up the feather. Gorchakov has a white dash in his dark hair. He is a 'marked man', something of an angel, like the Stalker.

Sound of running water. Chimes are heard softly jangling and Gorchakov looks up: the implication is that an angel is passing by, letting loose a feather. (Later an angel is seen under water.) The camera pans to the right and the *dacha* is seen, presumably his home in Russia. An angel walks in front of the house. This is a dream/ memory sequence. (Angels here, angels there — well, this is Italy, after all, the birthplace of the Renaissance).

Scene 5. A hotel foyer in Italy.

Gorchakov and Eugenia talk at night about exile, frontiers, translation and art. A long scene (in colour) of dialogue and exposition. Eugenia is reading the poems of Arseny Tarkovsky (what a coincidence!). Gorchakov says that poetry cannot cross borders, is untranslatable (this opinion casts an ironic light on Tarkovsky's own situation: a Russian making a film in Italy).

During this scene there is an insert of Gorchakov's wife, Maria, in sepia-and-white, as Gorchakov turns to look at Eugenia. Eugenia is often the link for Gorchakov back to Russia: through Eugenia, Gorchakov looks to his wife, Maria.

Gorchakov then explains about Pavel Sosnovsky, a music composer who lived in Italy: Gorchakov is supposedly researching Sosnovsky's life (Sosnovsky was also known as Maximilian Sasontovich Beryozovsky, 1745-77).

When the concierge arrives to show them their rooms, Gorchakov walks towards the camera, which tracks backwards. Dripping water and a dog barking is heard: Russia is impinging again. Cut to:

Scene 6. Russia. The *dacha*.

In the Russian landscape of Gorchakov's memories — a child (presumably his daughter, Anna) — runs in slow motion down to a pool accompanied by a dog (the dog's called Dak in the script). Over this memory sequence the sound of the concierge is heard showing the guests to their rooms.

The pattern of the rest of the film is set in motion now: cuts between Russian sepia-and-white or muted colour dream/ memory/ fantasy sequences, and present day Italy. Often it's difficult to tell the two landscapes apart. Dripping water is often heard throughout the film.

Scene 7. The hotel bedroom in Italy.

Gorchakov explores his room, switching on lights (a lengthy shot, 2 minutes 45 seconds). Eugenia arrives and asks Gorchakov if he wishes to telephone Maria in Moscow. In the corridor, Eugenia now kneels, playing at running a race. She falls, laughs, and goes upstairs. (Characters who stumble or fall over are so common in Tarkovsky's films as to go beyond just giving an actor something to do in a scene. Sometimes it appears to have no extra meaning; at other times − as when Otto collapses in *The Sacrifice*, or Boriska falling down the muddy bank in *Andrei Roublyov* − it has a dramatic point).

Scene 8. The hotel bedroom in Italy.

In a very lengthy shot, one of the central scenes of *Nostalghia*, a track and zoom in the hotel bedroom, Gorchakov watches the rain then lies on the bed. The room gets steadily darker. It is still raining. A dog appears (in both the Russian and Italian scenes: it is, like the fire in *Mirror*, a connecting poetic motif). On the soundtrack a glass rolls about, as do coins. The lighting changes again: Gorchakov's face is illuminated.

There are many light sources in this scene (it's a lighting cameraman's dream scene): 1. outside the window, 2. in the bathroom, 3. in the room − from the side windows, 4. the shadow of rain through a window on the wall behind the bed, 5. strong side lighting, on Gorchakov's face. These light sources fade up and down during the shot, a self-consciously theatrical effect, quite rare in cinema (there is no 'realistic' reason for the alterations in light).

The movement of the shot is towards dreams, memories, the past, and Russia. It's a shot in which the motion from 'objective', third person reality to first person subjectivity and interiority is achieved without cuts, rippling dissolves, music, visual effects, sound effects, voiceover or other cinematic devices which conventionally cue changes of states like this.

Time passes. The sound of water and the barking dog remind him of Russia: they are dreaming links to his heartland. Gorchakov dreams:

The Russian woman from the earlier scenes, dark-haired, impassive, appears: his wife, Maria, filmed in black-and-white. She walks slowly, shot against what is taken to be the wall of the hotel bedroom (but in brighter lighting). She embraces

Eugenia, who is crying. Both women look similar: both have their hair tied up; both look like Piero della Francesca's *Madonna del Parto* (Gorchakov tells Domenico later that his wife looks like Piero's *Madonna*). (Tarkovsky realized this shot echoed one from Ingmar Bergman's *Persona*, and apologized for it, not liking influences to be too obvious).

The women here are seen as doubles or twins, just as Gorchakov is doubled by Domenico later. In the next shot, Eugenia is lying/ sitting above Gorchakov in a semi-sexual embrace. Cut back to the Russian wife and Eugenia embracing. Dreams here of adultery, marriage, the family, the *doppelgänger* and exile. The two women embracing is also an image of conciliation, in Gorchakov's mind, of Russia and Italy, and the two women in his life who embody those countries. Nations are symbolized by women or Goddesses in art (consider the figure of Liberty or Freedom in French history, and of course the figure of 'Mother' Russia, Russia as the primal 'motherland').

After this, Gorchakov's wife appears in L.S. lying face-up on the bed (which's in a different position) in the hotel room (the only time in *Nostalghia*, with the previous embrace, that Maria appears visually in Italy). She is fully pregnant, echoing very visibly Piero della Francesca's painting of the pregnant Virgin Mary.

Gorchakov is dreaming of the conception, of pregnancy, and his wife and children: the chimes are heard again, which are angelic links. Recall that the Virgin Mary was miraculously impregnated by the Archangel Gabriel.

Cut back to Gorchakov lying on the bed: end of the dream. Eugenia is knocking on the door outside his room, telling him they are due to visit the St Catherine Baths. The scene reverts to colour and daylight.

Scene 9. The St Catherine Baths.

Eugenia and Gorchakov meet Domenico, at the St Catherine Baths. Domenico (Erland Josephson) is a shabby eccentric figure in his fifties; throughout the film he sports a dark woolly hat and dark sweater, and baggy trousers. He has white hair and a grizzled look. He resembles a drifter, a hobo.

Domenico is a latter-day shaman, a politico-religious fanatic who locked his family up in a house for eight years (this was one of the early seeds for *Nostalghia*). Gorchakov and Domenico are doubles, twins, in the tradition of Fyodor Dostoievsky and William Shakespeare.

Some of Tarkovsky's most carefully orchestrated tracking shots and blocking of actors occurs here, during the lengthy lateral tracking shots. It is not clear where the off-screen voices are coming from for some moments. The conversation describes Gorchakov as a Russian poet researching the Russian composer Sosnovsky. The camera, tracking slowly all the time, reveals a group of bathers in the misty pool.

After discussing Gorchakov, the bourgeois people in the pool fill in the background about Domenico: about his 'madness', his religious fanaticism, his desire to carry a candle across the Baths (in other words, this is clunky exposition).

Domenico tells Eugenia about a conversation between St Catherine and God (which pays off later, when God and St Catherine talk about Gorchakov). Domenico talks to his dog about the people who are languishing in the Baths. They are treated as vain, decadent bourgeoisie. 'Listen to them,' Domenico says to his dog; 'we mustn't be like them. We must live differently.'

Scene 10. The hotel foyer.

Gorchakov appears to be considering Eugenia erotically for a moment (which she likes), but he soon starts to ask about Domenico and why he locked up his family (when she realizes that, she turns cold).

Scene 11. At Domenico's house.

Domenico is seen on an exercise bike outside his run-down dwelling (is he riding an exercise cycle because it signifies a character travelling but getting nowhere, or is it just to give an actor something to do?). A scene cut from the film had Eugenia and Gorchakov meeting an old woman, who told them about Domenico (CS, 486).

There is a lengthy (4 minutes 40 seconds) lateral tracking shot which runs back and forth between Domenico and Gorchakov, following Eugenia as she mediates between the two men. This shot directly looks forward to the shot of Gorchakov carrying the candle across the drained pool. The camera tracks back and forth here three times: the third time is the successful one, where Gorchakov makes contact (Gorchakov is successful with the lighted candle on the third attempt).

Scene 12. The model landscape.

There is a model landscape (which presumably Domenico has made), which resembles Russia, in a side room in Domenico's kingdom. In a slow zoom-in, in black-and-white (which relates this landscape to Russia), the camera moves over this model riverscape (recalling the low angle tracking shots over the landscape in *Stalker*) to the Tuscan hills beyond. Birds sing. Gorchakov looks at it as if it is Russia.

Nostalghia is a richly structured film. Much of it works beyond language, beyond verbal expression. For example, Gorchakov silently stares at the model of Russia, framed with the Tuscan hills behind it, but it's impossible to say precisely what this scene means, how Gorchakov feels, beyond saying that it is filled with yearning.

Scene 13. In Domenico's house.

Domenico's house is a strange place of water, rain, shadows and dilapidation (recalling the *mise-en-scène* of *Stalker*). It's a huge empty warehouse, with flagons and spherical bottles set on the floor to catch the rain that pours through the many holes in the roof. The glass bottles evoke those in *Mirror*. The rain through the roof recalls the interior rain of *Stalker*, *Mirror* and *Solaris*. Even though it is sunny outside, the rain comes and goes. It is seen outside a window. As the sun moves into clouds, sometimes the screen darkens. There are many C.U.s of the bottles and water.

Domenico's home is like a water-soaked alchemical laboratory, recalling the cells of St Jerome in Renaissance paintings. Beethoven's *9th Symphony* is heard. There are some odd objects in Domenico's realm: a photo of a broken doll amongst some dead leaves (a little like a Hans Bellmer doll); an iron-framed bed with a big plastic sheet above it to collect the rain water (this odd piece of production design may have been inspired by artist Sadamasa Motonoga's *Water* [1956], where water was collected in plastic sheets suspended from trees); a door frame without walls; graffiti on the wall which reads: 'I + I = I'. This is later taken up in dialogue by Domenico: 'one drop plus another drop makes one big drop,' he says. Does he mean energy, spiritual feeling, faith, madness?

Both Domenico and Gorchakov look into or are filmed against mirrors. While they talk, Domenico hands Gorchakov some bread and wine (a reference to the Catholic Mass and the Last Supper, of course, and also perhaps to the *Memento Mori* o r *Vanitas* images in Dutch still-life paintings, in which bread, wine, and water feature).

Domenico says the world must be saved. The lengthy dialogue scene here sets out the quest of the film: Domenico asks Gorchakov to carry a lighted candle across the St Catherine Baths, because he hasn't been allowed to do so himself. ('You must cross the pool holding a lit candle in your hands' Domenico tells Gorchakov in the script [CS, 490]).

Throughout the long meeting of Domenico and Gorchakov the sound of an electric wood saw is heard. This becomes the emblem of the sunny/ rainy Italian afternoon: all that's heard over Domenico's slow motion dream sequence is the sound of the saw (though where it comes from isn't explained. Is there a woodyard nearby? More likely, it's a sound that Tarkovsky found expressed the dream logic of the sequence. In *Sculpting In Time*, Tarkovsky spoke of 'extraneous sounds that don't exist literally', but are put in the film 'for the sake of the image' [162]).

Scene 14. Domenico's house.

As Gorchakov prepares to leave, there is a lengthy crabwise tracking shot. Domenico's strangeness is underlined when he chooses to step through a free-standing doorframe instead of walking past it. In the partially flooded room Domenico asks Gorchakov about his children. Gorchakov says that his wife is like Piero della Francesca's *Madonna del Parto*, 'but all in black'. Domenico announces that he's planning a political event that's going to take place in Rome.

As the camera continues to track, Gorchakov leaves, to Domenico's bewilderment. The camera begins to dolly the other way and zoom in to Domenico face as he starts to recall the past. (Tarkovsky also employs stand-ins for Oleg Yankovsky, so that he appears be in two places at once, a favourite technique of the maestro's to suggest dreams or hallucinations).

The flooded room of Domenico's in *Nostalghia* has an ancestor in the bridge guard house over the stream in Ingmar Bergman's *The Virgin Spring*. The amount of water symbolism in that film, too, might have inspired Tarkovsky (in *The Virgin Spring* there are many streams, including the miraculous appearance of the spring from under the virgin's corpse; and the sound of water is predominant throughout the film).

Scene 15. Domenico's memory.

A slow motion memory sequence occurs of the family being released. There are shots from the inside the house of the family emerging. Domenico's wife (Delia Boccardo) is seen embracing the feet of a policeman. There is a spilt bottle of milk beside her on the ground. Like Gorchakov's dreams and memories, Domenico's are in sepia-and-white. Domenico is shown chasing his son across the steps of the square in slow motion, watched by a crowd. The boy is also depicted looking up at the camera, as if from Domenico's point of view, and asks 'Papa, is this the end of the world?' (Tarkovsky called this section of the film *The End of the World,* and it wound up in the film pretty close to Tarkovsky's description of the sequence in his diaries in April, 1979 [D, 180]).

The boy who plays the son in Domenico's memory/ dream sequence is also the same actor in Gorchakov's Russian dream sequences: the connections between the two men are very deep. Both men live estranged from their loved ones, their families (they also share the same dog). At this time, in the *Diaries,* Tarkovsky says how much he yearned for his own son while he was in Italy.

Scene 16. The town square.

Gorchakov is shown getting into a taxi in L.S. in colour. The camera pans to the right to follow the car moving off down a narrow street.

Scene 17. Domenico's memory. The town square.

In sepia-and-white, there is a shot of the little town piazza from the same viewpoint as the previous scene, linking past and present.

Scene 18. An Italian town.

A L.S. in colour of a car driving down a steep road from a hilltop town is the coda to the lengthy visit to Domenico's house. This is one of the few concessions in Tarkovsky's film to the beauty of the Italian countryside, this long shot of an Italian hilltop town in the mist.

Scene 19. Gorchakov's bedroom.

Back at the hotel, Eugenia is drying her hair, sitting on Gorchakov's bed. She berates Gorchakov in a lengthy take (4 minutes 5 seconds) for not wanting her sexually, for being different from the rest (of men). This dialogue recalls Mary Magdalene talking to Christ. In anguish she bares her breast and taunts him: isn't this what you (men) all want? she says (meaning sex, women). Then, distraught, she says 'Why can't I meet the right person?'

Each of the three main characters in *Nostalghia* are haunted by their pasts, which are full of anguished sexual relationships. Eugenia then speaks about a nightmare she's had. She weeps. (In the script, Gorchakov strokes Eugenia's hair and kisses her wet eyes [CS, 494]).

Eugenia says she's going to India with Vittorio. She says he's 'interested in spiritual matters'. But Eugenia's telephone conversation with Gorchakov is shown in voiceover — over the tracking-in shot of the businessman Vittorio at his desk in a huge room in Rome. All the signs here are of secularization and materialism: the business suit, the desk, the maid, the lackey, the indifferent way he eats and ignores Eugenia. He is certainly not the man she yearns for: he is the opposite of spiritual. This is an image of Eugenia's future life.

Significantly, she walks away from him, saying she's going to buy some cigarettes: she is walking out of his life (there are already cigarettes on the table). Her deep connection is perhaps with someone like Gorchakov, for all his faults, despite their arguments.

Scene 20. The hotel corridor.

Gorchakov and Eugenia argue in the corridor. She slaps him and makes his nose bleed. Eugenia returns, with a suitcase, as if ready to leave. She starts reading a letter, written by the Russian composer Pavel Sosnovsky. A voiceover in Italian describes Sosnovsky's feelings of nostalgia for Russia. The camera tracks backwards away from Eugenia and follows Gorchakov moving onto a seat in the corridor.

Scene 21. Gorchakov's memories or dreams.

Gorchakov is seen lying on his back, holding his bleeding nose. The light dims, there is the sound of running water and a dog barks: then Maria is shown, his wife, in the familiar Tarkovskyan brass bed. Gorchakov's heard saying 'Maria'. She wakes, as if she's heard him in a dream, as if he's there, in spirit. She looks round, to a point near the camera. But he is far away in a hotel in Italy.

Maria moves around the room, to the window and pulls back a curtain to reveal a bird on the window sill which flaps its wings (linking Maria with the Madonna in the church ritual). She goes out to the space of the first shot of the film, the Russian vale. She is joined by the young woman (Anna) and the older woman (the grand-mother) from the beginning of the film. The dog and the white horse is also there. Doubling occurs here, as in Alex's dream in *The Sacrifice*: the three women, clad in white dresses and black shawls, stand apart from each other during a long, slow crabwise tracking shot: the three woman are seen again, in the same shot, standing a little further away from the camera and nearer the old Russian house. (This scene originally followed Gorchakov's death, and occurred as the penultimate scene in *Nostalghia*).

This is a relatively silent shot; at the end of it, as a foghorn sounds, the women turn around to see the moon rising behind the house. In the script, Guerra and Tarkovsky describe it as:

It is rare that the rising of the moon is such a beautiful sight!
Dumbfounded, they watch its emergence, as though it were a miracle, and their faces reflect the full strength of their expectation of this improbable, over-whelming fortune. (CS, 503)

Then, faintly, what sounds like an Arabic pop song is heard on a tiny, tinny radio in a bathroom. This is only one of many extraordinary sounds in the film.

Scene 22. The flooded church.

The scene of Gorchakov's soliloquy is announced by the incredible imagery of a statue of an angel under water. The shot begins with a slow tilt up to reveal Gorchakov wading through a stream, on his way to the flooded church. The stream, fringed with long grass, recalls the opening shots of *Solaris*. Gorchakov, in voiceover, recites Arseny Tarkovsky's poem "As a child I once fell ill" (ST, 91), a scene originally meant to go in *Mirror*. A young girl, called Angela (another reference to angels), is seen climbing around the walls of the flooded church (in the script, it's a 12 year-old boy, called Marco [CS, 494]). Gorchakov's long sermon, partly in Italian, partly in Russian, is delivered from the centre of the pool in the drowned church. He stands knee-deep in water. The place is full of dripping water. It starts to rain.

Afterwards he lies down. Beside him is a still-life: a bottle of vodka, bread, a fire, the book he has burnt. Significantly, it is a copy of Tarkovsky's father's poems (that's not a very nice thing to do to Dad's poetry; one wonders what Arseny Tarkovsky thought of seeing his book of poems burning on screen in his son's film. Maybe it was included to demonstrate that poetry is spiritual, not reliant on materiality. Gorchakov does say earlier that poetry cannot be translated. Burning a book seems a particularly violent way of expressing that idea: historically, the only people who are well-known for burning books are fascists and tyrants).

There are two books in the film associated with Gorchakov: the *Bible*, which's shown in the prolonged shot as he explores his hotel bedroom (with a comb covered in hair lying on it), and the Tarkovsky poetry book. More Arseny Tarkovsky poetry is heard in voiceover as Gorchakov lies down on his back on the wall of the church.

Scene 23. An Italian street.

In a litter-strewn Italian street, possibly during a dream sequence, in sepia and white, there is a large wardrobe. But when Gorchakov looks in the mirror on the wardrobe, he sees Domenico (who's dressed like Gorchakov). It's a scene intended for *Mirror*. Tarkovsky makes one of his switches here between actors (focussing on a C.U. of a hand on the door handle of the wardrobe). The sound of the buzz saw is heard, associated with Domenico's house. (Gorchakov speaks in voiceover in Russian, but the words concern Domenico).

This short, strange scene reveals the depth of identification between Gorchakov and Domenico, and how they are interchangeable at this point. Gorchakov says: 'why this tragedy? How could I do it to my own flesh and blood?' He seems to be talking more about Domenico's family than his own, or voicing Domenico's thoughts.

Scene 24. A ruined cathedral.

Gorchakov visits a ruined cathedral (which is probably the ruined Cistercian abbey (1224) at S. Galgano, near Siena. The script says it's at Chiustino). This is the site of the final shot. In a black-and-white lateral tracking shot, Gorchakov is seen walking in the cathedral. The sound of kids crying is heard; a woman conducting a religious ceremony; and the voices of God talking to St Catherine, no less. The saint asks God to let his presence be known to the lost individual, Gorchakov. God replies: 'I always do, but he doesn't listen.' (A reference to Gorchakov's self-absorption, which eventually turns fatal).

Scene 25. The flooded church.

As scene 22. Gorchakov looks up; a feather drifts down from above. Gorchakov is shown lying in the flooded church beside the fire and the book, now nearly all burnt. The previous scene in the ruined cathedral, and the one before that in the town street, may both be flashbacks, or memories, or dreams. They don't occur in parallel time with Gorchakov in the flooded church.

Scene 26. Rome.

The film changes in mood as the narrative moves to Rome: there is an establishing L.S. of St Peter's Church accompanied by the sound of a jet.

Scene 27. A hotel courtyard in Rome.

In L.S., Gorchakov is shown waiting for a taxi with his suitcases. Eugenia telephones him and says she is going to India with Vittorio. She says Domenico is speaking in Rome.

Scene 28. Vittorio's place, Rome.

In Rome the decadence of Eugenia's other life is shown – her relation with her lover, Vittorio. Eugenia's telephone call to Gorchakov is heard over this scene. There is little evidence of communication between Eugenia and her lover Vittorio.

Eugenia might be interchangeable with any number of women for Vittorio.

Scene 29. A hotel courtyard.

As scene 27. Gorchakov says he has to delay leaving Italy. A slow backwards tracking shot as Gorchakov walks through the gateway of the hotel. He looks up at the sky. Sounds of the city.

Scene 30. Capitoline Hill, Rome.

Tracking shots show the scene of Domenico's speech on top of Michelangelo's Marcus Aurelius equestrian statue. Domenico is dressed in his black woolly hat and donkey jacket. The act is witnessed by hundreds of motionless people – a cluster of cast-offs from a Federico Fellini movie: old men, a fat circus lady, a madman who jerks his body about, another who mimes Domenico's every movement. Perhaps they were bussed over from nearby Felliniville (the Cinecittà studios where Fellini made many of his films).

There are shots of people dotted around the huge flight of steps at the Capitoline Hill, recalling Alain Resnais' *Last Year in Marienbad* and Giorgio de Chirico's Surrealist paintings of sunlit Italian piazzas.

Scene 31. St Catherine Baths.

Cut to Gorchakov arriving by car at the now drained St Catherine Baths. This scene cuts back to Domenico's speech then back again, to emphasize that both events are taking place at the same time. There are shots of the detritus that is being cleared from the pool by some workers: an oil lamp, bottles, a cycle wheel, a doll. As in the hotel courtyard scene, Gorchakov looks haggard. A dark-haired woman is seen cleaning the Pool; her face recalls Piero della Francesca's *Madonna del Parto* (and Gorchakov's wife Maria).

Scene 32. Capitoline Hill, Rome.

Back with Domenico's speech. Master shots include a slow zoom from a wide shot, and a M.S. craning up Domenico's body. He invokes his mother – 'O madre,

madre'. The word *madre* is the same that is used earlier in the film, when the women address the Virgin Mary during the religious ritual; and also in the final dedication of the film, 'To my mother'. 'O mother, O mother!' cries Domenico; 'the air is that light thing that moves around your head and becomes clearer when you laugh'.

After haranguing the crowd about global catastrophe, Domenico calls for music and douses himself with petrol. He lights his zippo, flames leap up. Tarkovsky cuts to the dog, barking; to Eugenia and the police arriving; to the people watching; to the mimic man below the statue. The music, Beethoven's *Ninth Symphony*, goes awry in the tape machine (in the script, it was the overture to Wagner's *Tannhauser*). Domenico falls from the scaffolding, crawls along the floor in flames and cries out in agony, watched by the mute people. He lies face-down on the ground in a parody of the Crucifixion. The death is pathetic, tragi-comic. In the script, Eugenia comes up close to Domenico, and can hear him still speaking. (The violence – and pathos – of the fire ritual was foreshadowed by the scene where Gorchakov burns the poetry of Arseny Tarkovsky).

Scene 33. St Catherine Baths.

Cut back to Gorchakov and his mission to cross the drained pool with the lighted candle. The climax of the film, and done in one continuous 8 minute and 45 second take. As he carries the lighted candle, Gorchakov is heard sighing and gasping; he sniffs; looks around from to time, as if to check if anyone's watching him; he shields the flame with his hand, then his coat, and later with his body from the wind.

The first time this is seen it is really riveting. He succeeds on the third attempt. As he places the candle on a stone ledge, pouring some wax to stick the candle to the ledge, Verdi's *Requiem* starts up (as at the opening credits). Gorchakov's hands are whipped out of the frame, as if he's collapsed. He's heard gasping. A line of people are seen watching him die, but his body is not shown at all. The dark-haired worker is shown in M.C.U. staring at what is presumably Gorchakov's collapsed form. The death remains ambiguous, though it is assumed he has died of a heart attack (which was presaged in the Rome hotel forecourt scene).

(Note that Gorchakov carries the candle when the pool is drained; but Domenico tried to do it when the pool was full, which would have been much harder. Maybe it was simply a practical decision: Gorchakov wading through shoulder-height water could have looked silly, as well being difficult to achieve. Maybe the pool has lost its regenerative powers, or perhaps it needed to be drained so that it can be replenished with fresh water, fitting in with the rebirth theme. Note that it's not completely dry, but looks like the familiar Tarkovsky muddy and watery landscape).

Scene 34. The Russian vale.

Cut to, in sepia and white, the Russian landscape. The sound of women crying or murmuring is heard, recalling the women in the chapel scene at the beginning of the film, and the sounds heard in the ruined cathedral scene (scene 24). Gorchakov's wife and child are there (though Maria's head is not shown: the focus is on the boy, the child as a continuation of the father, which's also how *The Sacrifice* ends). Russian folksong comes in. Cut to the final shot:

Scene 35. The *dacha* in the ruined cathedral.

A slow zoom out from M.S. to a wide shot of Gorchakov sitting on the grass next to a pool in front of the Russian house, looking into camera. (There was a house brought into Loreto cathedral, supposedly it was from Nazareth – the house where Jesus was born). Trees in the background. The dog sits next to him. At the end of the lengthy zoom snow starts to fall in the Italian cathedral. A dog is heard barking. Tarkovsky lets the camera linger on this scene as the Russian folksong fades. The snow continues to swirl; other filmmakers would probably have cut the shot much earlier. A dedication over the shot reads: 'To my mother'. Fade to black.

The ending seems at once miraculous, astonishing, contrived, false, profound and pretentious – too much, too poetic, too wonderful. Slavoj Zizek remarked that

one is tempted to take the last shot of *Nostalghia* not only as the hero's dream, but as an uncanny scene which, since it follows his decease, stands for his death: the moment of the impossible combination of Italian countryside in which the hero is adrift with the object of his longing is the moment of death.

For critic Anne Lawton, the ending goes on for longer than expected, drawing attention to its duration then, as the snow falls, it suggests 'both divine blessing and a congealed state of harmony. The artist has attained the absolute. He has created eternal life existing simultaneously inside and outside of time' (1992, 130).

Tarkovsky acknowledged that the shot was constructed and too literal. What Tarkovsky was aiming for was something like the scene he greatly admired in *The Virgin Spring*, where snow falls on the dying young woman. A piercing, stunning moment for Tarkovsky in Ingmar Bergman's film, which seemed to go beyond symbolism or meaning (ST, 213).

20 : 3   FURTHER THOUGHTS ON *NOSTALGHIA*

Nostalghia works on many levels, and there are many components in this seemingly sparse film. There is the sexual antagonism between Gorchakov and his wife; between Gorchakov and Eugenia; between Eugenia and her past; there are the symbols of fire and water; the letter of Pavel Sosnovsky; the poetry of Arseny Tarkovsky; the dream sequences; Eugenia's nightmare; the model landscape in Domenico's house; the setting of the Bagno Vignoni, with the objects of civilization being dredged up; the Cathedral; Piero della Francesca; childbirth; poetry and translation; Russia and Italy and exile; and spiritual bankruptcy.

Critic Neya Zorkaya suggested that Gorchakov was not just rejecting Eugenia because of indifference or fear of her sexuality, but because she embodies the past (the glory of the Renaissance in particular, in her affinity with Renaissance madonnas), but without the all-important spirituality.[1] She represents material beauty without the spiritual underpinings. Eugenia thus embodies the spirituality that Gorchakov is searching for (which has also gone from his homeland, Russia).[2]

Tarkovsky recognized just how deeply *Nostalghia* reflected his situation, and felt uneasy about that. For some critics, that was part of its problem: *Nostalghia* was too self-indulgent, too much of Tarkovsky going the Federico Fellini route of mythologizing one's own life. 'I love and admire the filmmaker Tarkovsky, and believe him to be one of the greatest of all time' Bergman confessed. 'My admiration for Fellini is limitless,' Bergman continued, 'But I also feel that Tarkovsky began to make Tarkovsky films and that Fellini began to make Fellini films. Yet Kurosawa has never made a Kurosawa film'.[3] Certainly a few film critics have also viewed

Fellini's later films as self-parodies (Tarkovsky said much the same), as Fellini 'doing Fellini' (and filmmakers such as Steven Spielberg and George Lucas are routinely accused of rearranging collections of their greatest hits). In some respects, Tarkovsky hadn't made enough films to be guilty of that kind of regurgitation, but one or two critics (including Tarkovsky's fellow filmmaker Andrei Konchalovsky), have seen Tarkovsky's later films (they are referring specifically to *Nostalghia* and *The Sacrifice*) as Tarkovsky 'doing Tarkovsky'. (One indication of Tarkovsky's new self-conscious style was Gorchakov's weary treatment of a book of Arseny Tarkovsky's poems, which he takes from Eugenia in the script [CS, 477]. The Tarkovsky of *Mirror* would not have treated his father's poetry like that).

Tarkovsky found it a little difficult to adapt to working conditions in the Western film industry (and the Italian film industry has its own particular modes of operating. Some other visiting filmmakers have found it exasperating and corrupt). *Nostalghia* caused problems also because the Russian genius worked slowly, and didn't like to keep to the agreed schedule.

20 : 4   DEPRESSION, ART, JULIA KRISTEVA AND *NOSTALGHIA*

Andrei Gorchakov is a difficult and somewhat unappealing personality: he is with-drawn, an outsider, a loner and exile. He's not an easy person to be with (as Eugenia finds out). He's way too self-absorbed, and unable (and unwilling) to make connect-ions with other people. (The film confines Gorchakov to interiors, enclosed spaces, and subjects him to repetitive actions; his life doesn't seem to go anywhere; his dreams, like his habits, are circular and repetitive.) He doesn't try to get in touch with his family back in Russia once (unlike Tarkovsky, who rang his family regularly when he was in Italy in the late Seventies). Although Gorchakov suffers terribly from nostalgia (*nostos-alghia* = the 'homing-pain'), he doesn't really do anything about it. He doesn't attempt to contact his family; he doesn't seek help.

And, although he's a writer, he isn't shown writing once. One of the things that writers do is write, and Gorchakov never does. The Greek definition of the word *poet* (*poeitas*) is *maker*; the poet is a maker. But Gorchakov doesn't make anything.

(Gorchakov winds up close to suicide: Gorchakov's one truly significant act in *Nostalghia* – carrying the candle across the Baths – costs him his life. What Gorchakov does could be regarded as a kind of suicide; he really does seem to be someone who's giving up living).

Gorchakov's the classic Existential outsider in every respect (instantly recognizable from the fictions of Knut Hamsun, J.-K. Huysmans, Aldous Huxley, Albert Camus, André Gide, Franz Kafka, Rainer Maria Rilke and Tarkovsky's faves: Fyodor Dostoievsky and Hermann Hesse). As V. Johnson and G. Petrie point out, even Gorchakov's identification with Domenico is dubious, because Domenico is someone who's locked up his family for years and is a religious madman. Domenico is not a regular guy you could go for a beer with.

Gorchakov is the classic depressed creative personality. He cannot escape his depression. If art comes out of the 'crises of subjectivity' as Julia Kristeva suggested – and any number of artists' work could be cited to support her theory – then melancholy and solitude is inevitable. Melancholy is indeed the natural state of many poets and writers (among poets, Hölderlin, Keats, Shakespeare, Petrarch and Sappho, for instance).

Kristeva aligned this depressive poetic melancholy with the metaphoric expression of the repressed maternal element. Kristevan melancholy is aligned with the mother and death: melancholia derives in part from an unsuccessful separation from the mother (mothers, and Tarkovsky's own mother, haunt *Nostaglhia*).[2] The artist writes of love (or life) to bring back love (life). Writing (art) not only enlarges life, it is central to the life of some writers (artists).

> It is, very simply [remarked Julia Kristeva], through the work and the play of signs, a crisis of subjectivity which is the basis for all creation, one which takes as its every precondition the possibility of survival. I would even say that signs are what produce a body, that – and the artist knows it well – if he doesn't work, if he doesn't produce his music or his page or his sculpture, he would be, quite simply, ill or not alive. (1984, 131-2)

For Julia Kristeva, lovers, like artists, create from a sense of lack, loss or pain. The lover, like the artist, is a wounded creature in Kristeva's reading. On one level, artistic creation counters Lacanian lack and Kristevan absence: the act of writing staves off emptiness and loneliness by filling up the psychic space. As Kristeva wrote in "Freud and Love: Treatment and Its Discontents":

> If narcissism is a defence against the emptiness of separation, then the whole contrivance of imagery, representations, identifications and projections that accompany it on the way towards strengthening the Ego and the Subject is a means of exorcising that emptiness. (1987, 42)

In her psychoanalyst mode, Kristeva reckons that art is born out of the pain of loss (Tarkovsky's cinema certainly supports this, as well as the output of the artists he revered: Dostoievsky, Hesse, Pushkin). Kristeva asserted that:

> the creative act is released by an experience of depression without which we could not call into question the stability of meaning or the banality of expression. A writer must at one time or another have been in a situation of loss – of ties, of meaning – in order to write.[3]

In this intriguing reading of the artistic act, Julia Kristeva presents the artist not as a 'technician of ecstasy', as Mircea Eliade called the archaic shaman, but as a technician of melancholia. Tarkovsky's characters tend to be both shamanic and melancholic (*Nostalghia* is full of them). The people on the edge – hysterics, obsessionals, lovers, artists – are often sufferers of depression. Underlying many of the complaints of our time, Kristeva said, is depression (ib., 133). Writing and art may be one way in which the writer writes or paints or dances her/ his way out of depression. Certainly one can look to plenty of artists to see this counter-depression at work (consider Hölderlin, Novalis, Coleridge and Goethe among Romantic poets, for starters). The angst-ridden artist may be a cliché of modern times (Vincent van Gogh, Lautréamont, Mark Rothko, Ludwig van Beethoven, Arthur Rimbaud), but it also fits the facts.

In *Soleil Noir*, her study of melancholy and depression, Kristeva developed her psychoanalysis of melancholy (consider Tarkovsky's protagonists again in the following discussion). For Kristeva, the melancholic is reduced to one basic meaning – despair and pain (*douleur*), rather than a search for meaning. The melancholic fails to develop a sense of the imaginary and symbolic. The inability to mobilize the imaginary and symbolic in the melancholic makes melancholia a kind of living death. Kristevan melancholia is not neurosis, for melancholia does not eroticize the death drive, which results in hatred, and melancholia prevents an eroticization of the separation from the mother. The mother is not the lost object – instead, the subject dies in her place. The artist, though, is able to deal with states such as melancholia because s/he can control signs. The artwork, Kristeva suggests, can be the mark of a 'vanquished depression' (1989, 76). This throws light on the work of so many artists, including Andrei Tarkovsky.

Nostalghia seems to be a work of depression, a work of working out depression. Yet Tarkovsky said, *pace Nostalghia*, that the film was really also supposed to show the hopefulness in contemporary life – that one is never alone, that there are countless threads linking the individual with the past and the future (ST, 205). You're never really alone, Tarkovsky asserted, but part of a web that spreads into the past and the future.

TWENTY-ONE

The Ultimate Act

The Sacrifice

21 : 1   THE WORLD OF *THE SACRIFICE*

The Sacrifice (a.k.a. *Offret* or *Sacrificiatio*) takes place in the present (1985) on the coast in Sweden. It is set before what is taken to be a limited nuclear war (i.e., a conflict that escalates to nuclear attacks, but not a full-scale nuclear exchange). Alex bargains with his life, makes a pact with God to sacrifice himself so as to avoid the catastrophe. But Tarkovsky seems to have forgotten, or not taken into account, that Sweden, like Switzerland, is one of the nations best prepared for a nuclear attack.[1] There are hints in the film, such as references to missile bases, that this isn't Sweden (Sweden doesn't have missile bases, but Russia at the time – as now – has plenty). There are 5.5 million shelter places for the 8 million souls in Sweden. If *The Sacrifice* was really a factual, rather than a spiritual or metaphysical, film, then the people in the country house would almost certainly be sheltered. Victor, being a doctor, would be part of a priority relief system. The TV announcement is inaccur-ate – the Swedish government is much better prepared than that. Further, as the mainstream nuclear films demonstrated,[2] a nuclear attack coming so suddenly and unexpectedly, without a build-up of conflict, is highly unlikely (*The Sacrifice* takes place over a day and a night, with the finale of the burning house occurring the next morning; pretty much most conflicts or wars build up over weeks or months, rather than being suddenly sprung upon the population out of nowhere. Following the terrorist attacks of September 11, 2001, though, the conflict depicted in *The Sacrifice* takes on a new meaning: a large-scale attack without warning could happen).

But it doesn't matter: Tarkovsky's is a spiritual film, and the nuclear catastrophe is a dramatic means of having someone's life thrown upside-down, forcing an onto-logical re-evaluation (and Tarkovsky is not interested in the details of a limited nuclear war). A nuclear war is a very extreme narrative device. In literature it is often an individual's murder (in André Gide, Albert Camus, Shakespeare or Sophocles), or a suicide (in Dostoievsky), or love-making (in Thomas Hardy), or loss of love (in Petrarch).

Tarkovsky is deliberately ambiguous about the oncoming holocaust: it would have made the film silly if it was totally clear that Alexander had saved the world via a prayer and sleeping with the 'witch' Maria. Then it would be relatively easy for anyone to save the world. (Some people would be queuing up to sleep with a witch. But that's a different movie). At the same time, the atomic onslaught cannot entirely be seen as a dream of Alexander's, or a group dream involving the main protagonists at the house, because it makes the actions in the later part of the film motiveless and confused. Alexander's going to extreme (burning down the house) is rendered pointless if his 'dark night of the soul' has all been a dream. Alexander's conscious act of despair in a way proves (or demonstrates) his religious faith (P. Christensen, 1987). *The Sacrifice*'s narrative is metaphorical and metaphysical, because an unethical (and un-Christian) act such as sleeping with Maria cannot save the world in conventional terms. However, if the events seen are 'real', then making love with Maria rescues the planet, and burning the house saves Alexander's soul (ibid.). Producer Anna-Lena Wibom said of *The Sacrifice* that it was 'clear as daylight and quite obvious in its message to contemporary people everywhere'.

Film critics have related *The Sacrifice* to Ingmar Bergman (*Shame* and *Through a Glass Darkly*), Luis Buñuel (*The Exterminating Angel*) and Anton Chekhov (*Uncle Vanya*). *The Sacrifice* had a Bergman location and setting, a Bergmanesque story, was shot in Bergman territory, used some of Bergman's regular (and key)

collaborators (Sven Nykvist, Erland Josephson, Allan Edwall, production designer
Anna Asp), and so on.[2]

The Sacrifice was originally intended for Tarkovsky's regular actor Anatoly
Solonitsyn, but he was too ill (and not much later died), so the role was rewritten
for Erland Josephson (Tarkovsky also rewrote the role of Otto for Allan Edwall).
(Elements of the character Josephson played in *Nostalghia* – the religious fanatic
Domenico – found their way into the new characterization of Alexander).

Sven Nykvist was a major contributor towards *The Sacrifice*. He had also been
offered *Out of Africa*, directed by Sydney Pollack. Nykvist said that Tarkovsky
wasn't much interested in lighting: of primary importance were composition, camera
movements, the literally moving image'. Nykvist said it could take hours for
Tarkovsky to decide how to shoot a scene when he first visited a location. Only
when he had made his decisions could Nykvist come in to light the scene. This could
also take a long time because many of the set-ups were lengthy tracking shots
(which can often be tricky and time-consuming to light).

Anna-Lena Wiborn produced *The Sacrifice* for the Swedish Film Institute.
Tarkovsky complained that the film production process in Sweden treated filmmaking like going to an office, where all that mattered was starting and finishing
shooting at particular times, whereas for Tarkovsky filmmaking was an artistic
undertaking (D, 342). Wiborn found Tarkovsky's working methods difficult to deal
with. He really wasn't used to working with a Western crew, in the Western film
system. For instance, Tarkovsky had a habit of ordering rehearsals or improvizations which weren't agreed beforehand in the budget and schedule. He could be
vague about exactly what he required, and wouldn't stick to agreements already
made. There were clashes, inevitably, but in the West, the film director is usually
king (on the film set, if nowhere else) – and Tarkovsky was also a renowned
director.

'From the Kierkegaardian standpoint, the film may be about a miracle' wrote
Peter Christensen. 'Should Alexander really be the knight of faith, then the laws of
time have been suspended. The film then serves as a parable on the idea that faith
can move mountains' (1987). What is at first confusing, as often in Tarkovsky's
cinema, is that the parable, the miraculous and the metaphysical aspects are shot in
a naturalistic fashion. Tarkovsky wants to have it both ways, both naturalism and
dream-logic, or to have the film interpreted on multiple levels. He doesn't want the
audience to be too literal or dogmatic in its interpretation of what's on screen

(filmmakers like Tarkovsky are constantly battling against viewers decoding images and sounds literally, with everything requiring a motive or explanation). According to some critics, though *The Sacrifice* has less to say about nuclear apocalypse than *The Day the World Ended* (1955), 'several of its stretches are undeniably fascinating and resonant' (P. Hardy, 411). Naturalism and realism wasn't the objective in cinema, for Tarkovsky: rather, the image is 'based on the ability to present as an observation one's own perception of an object' (ST, 107).

There are many Christian images and references in *The Sacrifice*: Alex is a troubled saint or mystic, suffering a Dark Night of the Soul. His journey is like the mythic hero's: from pain to enlightenment. He visits a Goddess – incarnated in the 'good witch', Maria. There is a mythic return – not in the saint/ father/ artist, but the pupil/ neophyte/ initiate, Little Man. Maria is explicitly linked with Mary Magdalene, while other names, such as Martha, speak for themselves.[3] Maria represents dark, nighttime, the feminine, menstrual creativity, witchy powers; while Adelaide is bright, daylight (i.e. known), ovulatory (maternal) domesticity. Maria's quiet sexuality and self-containment is opposed by Adelaide's loud hysteria, the mother as smotherer. Maria is the strongest woman in the film, though she lives alone; Adelaide, surrounded by people, is the weakest. Maria and Alex are linked visually: they both wear black garments with white patterns: Alex has his *yin-yang* sign on a dressing gown; Maria her patterned headscarf (their task is to become whole, to unite the dichotomy of black and white). All the women have noisy shoes, that sound so clear on the polished wooden floor of the house.

(Although Maria is called a 'witch' by Otto, she doesn't do anything 'witchy' in the film, doesn't cast spells or ride around on a broomstick. Indeed, as Vida Johnson and Graham Petrie point out, Maria doesn't even seem to know what Alex is talking about when he says mentions saving the world and the war (JP, 175). Maria seems more pious and moral than a 'witch'. Then there's the problem of squaring sex with a witch with God's mercy. In horror, fantasy and the supernatural film genres, for instance, the last thing sleeping with a witch is going to do is save the world).

In the *New Testament*, Martha and Maria were the two women who followed Christ and were present at the Crucifixion. Other Christian references in *The Sacrifice* include the tree, related to the Legend of the True Cross (so wonderfully painted by Piero della Francesca in Arezzo), in which the Tree of Adam and Eve becomes Christ's Cross. Alex's Cross, his wooden house, burns beautifully. The boy can be seen as a New Adam.

Adelaide is Maria's opposite in the struggle for Alex; but Maria's other opposite is Martha (Adelaide's daughter): it is the virgin/ whore dichotomy. Both women undress, both sleep with their men: Alex on screen with Maria; Martha (perhaps) off-screen with Victor. Victor injects Martha and Adelaide, mother and daughter, with his science, with tranquillizers. The injection is phallic, and also shows how he exacts his patriarchal authority over them. Later, mother and daughter argue over Victor going to Australia. (Adelaide is an unflattering portrait of what Tarkovsky described as a self-assertive, aggressive woman, someone who wants to smother and dominate other people, who won't allow them individuality or independence, and whose lack of spirituality enhances her destructiveness [ST, 223]). Some critics saw Adelaide as an unflattering portrait of Tarkovsky's wife, Larissa.

The characters are aspects of Alex, the actor/ writer. Victor, the doctor, is the rationalist/ scientist, the public voice of reason; he is opposed by Otto, who is something of a jester, a fool, something of a historian and mystic, and something of an occultist – he collects supernatural tales. The opposition of Victor and Otto recalls the Stalker and the Professor in *Stalker*. Adelaide is, like Victor, part of Alex's public persona – and is also linked to his past, his work in the theatre. Adelaide is shown as standing outside the trinity of women figures: Martha, Maria and Julia (the maid).

Inner/ magical/ secret world		*Outer/ scientific/ public world*
Otto		Victor
Maria	Alex	Adelaide
boy		Martha
		Julia

Alex is stuck in the middle of these characters and tensions. Throughout the film he associates himself with the pagan and magical characters, Maria, Otto and the boy (Maria and the boy 'move in a world of the imagination, not that of 'reality'', Tarkovsky asserted; their world is 'filled with unfathomable wonders' [ST, 228]). He moves away from the public/ social/ rational/ reasonable people, Victor and

Adelaide, towards the præternatural, possessed souls. His descent into madness is outwardly destructive, but inwardly regenerative.

Alexander voices laments about contemoprary society which are familiar from Tarkovsky's off-screen pronouncements, as well as characters such as the Stalker and Domenico. He tells his son, 'the Kid':

> We have reached a terrible disharmony, discord, that is, in our material and spiritual development. Our culture – civilization, rather – is wrong, deep down, sonny. You may say that it is possible to examine a problem and, together, come to a conclusion. Perhaps. If it weren't too late. (CS, 523)

Alex is a typical modern bourgeois character, an artist, deeply dissatisfied by an artistic career that has amounted to nothing (he tells Otto this). His literary antecedents are Knut Hamsun's Nagel, Albert Camus' Meursault from *L'Étranger* and Samuel Beckett's Molloy, the Northern European/ alienated/ Existential characters. Alex's personality is also similar to some of André Gide's creations (Gide's protagonists in turn derive in part from Fyodor Dostoievsky, one of Gide's – and Tarkovsky's – favourite writers), in particular Gide's Lafcadio in *The Vatican Cellars*, Marcel in *The Immoralist* and the weary modernist novelist Edouardo in *The Counterfeiters*. Gide's characters' dissatisfaction is intense and involves the 'gratuitous act', which is a way of aiming for freedom, by throwing a spanner into the works of the universe, to stop and jolt life, to aim for something higher and richer. All of Tarkovsky's characters derive from this kind of post-Romantic, post-Dostoievskian culture, the Renaissance/ Romantic concept of the artist, of the primacy of art, as espoused by the characters of William Shakespeare, Johann Wolfgang von Goethe, Thomas Mann and Dostoievsky.

One reading of the form of the film is structured around a classic narrative, with semblances of acts and rising action:

1. Vague but deep-seated dissatisfactions which

2. Crystallize suddenly and violently when the End of the World is announced, forcing

3. The pact with God and the journey towards the total sacrifice after

4. Various thresholds have been crossed, resulting in

5. Death of the self and, finally, after so long

6. Rebirth.

The Sacrifice contains the whole portfolio of Tarkovsky's motifs: fire, milk, candles, icons, water, glass, magical objects, childhood imagery, floating, hysteria and decay. There are the typical Tarkovskyan cultural references – to Bach, Leonardo, Nietzsche, Shakespeare and Dostoievsky. The bicycle is another connecting object: each of the three main people of the central quest (the quest to sleep with a witch and save the world) ride on the bike: Otto at the beginning (the messenger who brings/ sets the quest); Alex in the middle, the (anti)hero riding out on the quest, like a knight of Arthurian romance; and Maria at the end, the object of the quest/ the saviour/ magical agent. In this film horses are absent (except the wild horses of Leonardo's *Adoration of the Magi*).

The autobiographical elements in *The Sacrifice* have been pointed out by critics: the resemblance of Adelaide to Tarkovsky's wife Larissa, for instance (both have a daughter from a previous marriage), or the links between Alex and Tarkovsky, or the similarity of the *dachas* in *Solaris* and *Mirror* and *The Sacrifice*, or Little Man's affinity with Tarkovsky's own child, Andrei, who at the time wasn't allowed to join his family outside Russia.

21 : 2   *THE SACRIFICE,* SCENE BY SCENE

Scene I. Opening titles.

A tight shot of Leonardo da Vinci's *Adoration of the Magi*, framed on the King, Christ and the gift. A long, static shot. Sound of seagulls fades in; then the sea. Bach's aria fades down. The camera tilts upwards, past the people and the angels, to the top of the tree (this shot is echoed in the final shot, when the camera cranes up the 'Japanese' tree).

Scene 2. The Swedish shoreline. Day.

A very lengthy sideways tracking L.S. of Alexander (Erland Josephson), Little Man (Tommy Kjellqvist) and Otto (Allan Edwall). About eight minutes long

(Johnson and Petrie time it as 9m 26s). Bright sunlight. A hut on the left. The shot contains a grassy field, a track, and the sea beyond. It is an empty though not bleak space.

The camera tracks slowly to the left for most of the shot, which begins with Alex and the boy finishing off putting up the 'Japanese' tree. Otto arrives on his bike, along the track, from the distance. The actors are on a converging course with the camera, and gradually move closer to it, from L.S. to M.S. The shot ends with Little Man tying up Otto's bicycle to a bush.

The first words of the film are: 'Come and give me a hand, my boy'. Next sentence: 'Once upon a time…' Then follows Alex's story of the monk and the tree. Sounds of cowbells; a distant explosion.

The lengthy dialogue of Alex and Otto includes the following points:

1. The monk's story of the withered tree (after three years it blossoms).

2. Daily ritual – going to the bathroom at 7 a.m. each morning, and tipping a glass of water down the toilet. A trivial example of how ritual can become holy.

3. Reading of telegrams and birthday greetings.

4. Otto asks: 'what is you relation to God?'

5. Otto sums up Alex's life (the acting, the Shakespearean parts, and so on).

6. Otto says: 'we're all waiting.'

7. Otto talks about his own life – he's always been waiting.

8. Otto mentions Friedrich Nietzsche. Alex talks of Gnosticism and the demiurge.

9. Otto says people live and die and it's the same each time, or perhaps a little different. Reincarnation.

10. Otto says it's late and he must think of a gift, another sacrifice.

11. Alex says: 'in the beginning was the Word, but you are mute as a fish' (this to the boy). The reference to fish recalls Christ as the Fish-God, the Christian age which is the Age of Pisces, and the fact that, 'in the beginning', i.e., millions of years ago, all animals including humans were fish.

(Despite being a master of cinema, one could say that Tarkovsky wasn't being particularly 'cinematic' with this long dialogue scene. Coming from a lesser film director, it would be laughed at as a clonky, simplistic solution to exposition. It's not the easiest introduction to the film, its characters and its themes. Scriptwriting manuals deride too-obvious exposition scenes: A: 'so, you are the doctor?'; B: 'yes, that's right, I am the doctor'; A: 'and you've lived here about ten years, haven't you?'; B: 'that's right, since my wife died'; and so on)

Scene 3. In the trees near the house.

Way over ten minutes into the film, and this is only the *third* shot of the film. Incredibly, there are only about 120 shots in *The Sacrifice*.

Another lengthy sequence. A car pulls up: Alexander's wife (Adelaide – Susan Fleetwood) and the doctor (Victor – Sven Wollter) get out and meet Alex and Little Man in some trees.

It's revealed that the boy is mute after an operation. The doctor compares him to Gandhi. The father talks of the first time they found the house, and of death. The boy crawls away. Shepherd song fades in, very quietly (the distinctive music is associated with strange events in the film, or premonitions; at the end of the film, though, it accompanies the pastoral *dénouement*, with Maria on the bicycle and Little Man beside the tree).

Shot 4. The boy crawling through the trees; Alex's voice is still heard. Pan right to Alex.

Shot 5. Grass and wind and trees, tracking left.

Shot 6. As shot 4, a continuation. 'If only someone could stop talking and do something instead' moans Alex. (That's an ironic comment in the talkiest of Tarkovsky's films. There is a tendency in *The Sacrifice* towards making philosophical pontifications, as if *The Sacrifice* were the film version of Tarkovsky's book *Sculpting In Time*. And some critics find that book a bit pompous and self-indulgent).

Shot 7. Trees. Pan left to C.U. of Alex. Little Man jumps on him playfully. Alex throws him off violently.

Shot 8. M.S. of boy and man, through the trees. A loud crack of thunder on the cut. More premonitions of the oncoming violence.

Shot 9. Little Man, wiping blood from his nose.

Shot 10. Alex in M.S.; he falls to the grass and says 'what's wrong with me?'

Scene 4. A city courtyard. Alex's dreamscape.

A tilt down shot (in black-and-white) of an empty yard, with a car on its side and bits of junk lying about. Shepherd folksong music over this, and the sound of water.

Scene 5. A book of icons.

A C.U. of Alex looking through a book of icons. 'Fantastic' he says. He exalts the pictures, then says: 'we can't even *pray* anymore.'

In L.S. the interior of the house is shown: the large room, the polished floor, the light blue painted walls, the spiral staircase, the large fireplace, the lace table cloth.

The sound of birds flying low over the house: one of the key sounds of the film, very atmospheric. There are extraordinary sounds throughout the film: the creaking in the bedroom, the wind in the grass and the seagulls.

The witch, Maria (Gudrún Gísladóttir), appears at the door, but the housekeeper (Julia – Valérie Mairesse) turns her away. The daughter, Martha (Filippa Franzén), reads the book of icons (she's a child from Adelaide's first marriage). These three women are like the women who followed Christ (Mary, Martha and the other Mary of the *Gospels*). They step about in long, floating dresses and high-heeled shoes. A cupboard door opens, squeaking.

Scene 6. The supernatural story.

Otto brings the framed map (carried on the pedals of his bicycle). The action moves from outside the house to the living room. The people gather around and examine the large map. 'Every gift involves a sacrifice' Otto says, 'if not, what sort of sacrifice would it be?' Tarkovsky considered using Seneca (his *Letters To Lucilius*) as an ingredient in Otto's character in *The Sacrifice* (D, 292).

Maria comes in and is discussed by the women of the house. She looks directly into the camera and says 'The plates, the candles, the wine.' This is a Last Supper film, with Jesus surrounded by his disciples. 'We are blind, we see nothing' says the postman Otto. Then, walking away from the gathering, he suddenly falls over. A C.U. of his face: his pocket watch ticking is heard: intimations of mortality and time passing. Otto tells his story of the supernatural (he collects stories).

Scene 7. Impending war at the house.

Shot 1. Exterior. The witch Maria crosses the landscape near the house at dusk.
Shot 2. Interior: Julia the maid holding up a glass. A tray of glasses vibrates.
Shot 3. The living room. Sounds of jets flying overhead. The women rush to and

fro, looking upwards. The camera tracks towards a cupboard: a large bottle of milk shatters and spills.

Shot 4. Alex, outside the house. Crane down to show the model house by the puddles, built by the boy and the witch (in the script, 'the Kid' has built a castle). Loud, reverberating sound of jet engines.

Shot 5. Alex meets Maria. Sound of distant foghorns as they converse desultorily. Flute music fades in (The Japanese flute music was by Watazumido Shuso.)

(Now, the area around the house has become an unreal, dream-place like the Zone in *Stalker*: pools of water appear, which weren't there before, and the light and the colour hovers between full colour and black-and-white).

Scene 8. Little Man's bedroom.

Shot I. A large, dark bedroom. Creaking is heard (sound of the window?). Flute music. There is a bed, a chair and a chest of drawers set out along one wall, so they can be viewed in one shot, flattened out, a little like Vincent van Gogh's famous bedroom painting. The curtain on one side breathes softly in and out; the light goes up and down.

Shot 2. Leonardo da Vinci's painting of the *Adoration of the Magi*, showing the Virgin and Child, behind glass. Otto and Alex discuss it. Otto leaves by climbing down the external ladder (for no obvious reason).

Scene 9. Living room.

The TV flickers (like a strobe); lamp swings; curtains blow. People are hypnotized. The TV is heard, but not seen. Sound of jets. It's all very vague and confusing. The mother's hysterical reaction is long and drawn-out and traumatic. She clings to the doctor, Victor. Her legs clad in silver stockings, open. She is in a mockery of intercourse and the birthing position, a travesty of the feminine. She is tranquillized, with drugs.

Alex goes out into the twilight; sounds of chandeliers or glasses tinkling; running water; the flute music again.

Scene 10. Living room, some time later.

Still night, but it's light outside. It seems to be eternal dusk, a Northern Summer night. Adelaide confesses to Otto her thoughts on love. She says she's loved the wrong man (Alex) and when Alex comes down the spiral staircase, he's framed between the doctor and the mother. This is a classic composition, the eternal triangle of love and adultery.

The family decide to stay put (the 'stay-put' policy was popular in nuclear civil defence at the time). Julia, the maid, stands up to Adelaide; but Adelaide forgives her and embraces her. Alex looks on. Echoes of *Nostalghia* here, in the women embracing. Alex picks a revolver out of the doctor's bag.

Scene 11. Upstairs in the house.

Leonardo da Vinci's painting presides over the next scene. Alex checks on Little Man in his bedroom. Significant that Leonardo's *Adoration of the Magi* should be in Little Man's room: the father giving the gift of the painting to his son is echoed by the figures of the Magi and Christ in the painting (it's not the usual gift a parent might give to a six year-old child).

Then Alex sits on the floor and there's a long and intense prayer sequence. Alex looks up, perhaps at God, and the camera tracks in and looks down on him. Philosophical pressure in this scene, both cinematic and dramatic. Alex vows to give up everything in a pact (this echoes Goethe's *Faust* – but the pact there was with the Devil). Alexander crawls to the couch and the dream begins. The shepherd folksong starts.

Scene 12. Martha's bedroom.

Martha says, off-screen, 'Victor, help me'. She looks directly into the camera (like Maria), undresses and walks to the bed nude. Cut to:

Scene 13. A town house.

A deserted building. All the doors are open. A vista of receding rooms. A man flees in slow motion over rain-drenched floors. The building recalls Domenico's water-soaked warehouse in *Nostalghia*.

Scene 14. Alexander's dream.

Shot 1. Alex in the run-down house. Water drips. The folk singing on the track continues.

Shot 2. Alex outside, picking cloth out of the mud.

Shot 3. Snowscape and house; slow tracking shot, left to right. Water dripping high on track.

Shot 4. Mud, coins, water, soil and snow in C.U. in a dolly shot angled down at the ground. Tilt up. A boy's naked feet. Alex (offscreen) says: 'my boy.' Wind blows the snow. Alex's breathing loud in voiceover. Sound of bombers; some battered doors blow in the wind.

Shot 5. Alex wakes up on the sofa.

Shot 6. Otto, in silhouette, walks up to the window outside Alex's room, in slow motion.

Shot 7. Alex, reflected in the glass of the Leonardo reproduction, walking to the glass door.

Scene 15. Alexander's room.

Otto offers Alex the quest: to sleep with Maria the witch ('you've got to go to Maria and sleep with her'), who lives behind the church (a typical reference to paganism and religion). Otto's parting shot is that he prefers Piero della Francesca to Leonardo da Vinci. (From Otto's tone of voice, it's as if he's muttering about some dark foe, rather than an artist).

Scene 16. Leonardo's *Adoration of the Magi.*

C.U., with the trees reflected in the glass of the reproduction. Alex moves into the reflection. Sound of the sea, recalling the opening credits.

Scene 17. Balcony of the house.

Alex on the balcony. Sound off-screen of Otto talking about Alex's 'poetic striving'; he also says that an actor is his own work of art. The family are down-stairs eating dinner. Alex creeps around; goes out; gets the gun; looks in at his son (Little Man spends the whole film asleep, like a seed in soil, waiting to grow, to be reborn. He is awake at the beginning and end of the film).

Scene 18. A track in the countryside.

Alex rides from the distance towards the camera in L.S. Dusk, nearly night. He falls off the bike, turns back, then rethinks and carries on. Inexplicably, the camera pans right to a car, its door open, a shawl strewn on the grass. Is this a reference to Adelaide's adultery with Victor the doctor (it looks like Victor's car), as if justifying Alex's act, or Alex's own soon-to-be adultery?

Scene 19. Maria's house.

Inside the witch Maria's house is: an icon; a crucifix; family photos; a dog barking; clocks ticking; a large room; a table; a lamp. The past and religion weigh heavily in Maria's house. The furnishings are largely 'old-fashioned'. For example, rather than a sink, Maria has a bowl and a jug. The organ Alex plays is not electrically powered.

Maria washes Alex's hands. Maria is likened to a mother as well as a lover. Lying with Maria is linked to a return for Alex to the maternal realm. After Alex has played the organ, he talks about his mother's garden. When Alex, as a boy, re-made the garden and tidied it, it looked 'so disgusting'. A tale of œdipal conflicts and regret.

There are cuts between Alex and Maria as he tells his story. Tarkovsky rarely indulges in such obvious reaction shots. Alex then talks of his sister and her hair. A M.C.U. follows of Maria and her long hair. Alex has come here to sleep with Maria, but instead talks of his mother and sister.

Eventually, they sleep together. All the time he is like a child, sobbing, while Maria caresses him and talks soothingly, like a mother. 'Don't be afraid,' she says. They revolve slowly as they float over the bed. Folk singing fades in. Light dims. Cut to:

Scene 20. City courtyard.

People running, with echoey footsteps, folk music, flute music, and Alex sobbing on the soundtrack. The (mainly young) extras run in random directions, bumping into each other. Tarkovsky originally wanted this scene to contain more people, and was disappointed when he couldn't have the amount of extras he wanted (the extras look like students).

The camera tilts down and tracks backwards to a boy lying down asleep on the roof of a building over the courtyard. This is perhaps Alex as a young boy, as well as Little Man. Alex sobs in voiceover: 'I can't, I can't.' (In the script, Alexander is flying over a coastal town, and sees a 'blue-black cloud with a swirling, yellow belly fill the sky', a vision of an atomic apocalypse which engulfs the town [CS, 554]).

Scene 21. The dream continues.

Maria and Alex are in the woods near Alex's house, in daylight. Alex lies down; Maria sits next to him, as if they are lovers. Maria and Adelaide are seen as doubles, like the women in *Nostalghia*. Maria wears Alex's wife's dress, and wears her hair like Adelaide's: a vision of the time when Alex and Adelaide first saw the house, but with Maria instead of Adelaide. A vision, perhaps, of life as it might have been for Alex – a life with Maria.

Scene 22. Leonardo da Vinci's *Adoration of the Magi*.

Scene 23. The landing of the house.

Martha, nude, drives some hens along in slow motion on the landing. An ambiguous sexuality, perhaps referencing her night with Victor. The camera tracks slowly laterally. Adelaide lurks in the shadows. Her voice asks, what has troubled him (Alex). Alex wakes up, and says: 'Mama?' There is another version of this tracking shot in the documentary *Directed by Andrei Tarkovsky*, which's much more elaborate, with many more people and beats (see below). Tarkovsky only used sections of it in the final cut.

Everything seems to be back to normal for Alex in the house: he tries his tape player, it plays; he tries the light, it works; the telephone works; Alex calls his agent or an office in a city, to reassure himself the world still works (the man on the other end of the telephone says it's chaos here); the birds flying overhead are heard again; Little Man's room is as before, with its creaking window; he bangs his knee; a mirrored cupboard creaks open. Everyday reality asserts itself again, with the quick of life and all the difficulties of the human condition.

Scene 24. Outside the house.

Martha and Adelaide talk at a table. Victor says he's going to Australia. Adelaide weeps. They are sitting outside, just as Alex left them, before the dream. They go for a walk. The action is covered partially from Alex's point-of-view as he observes them from a distance.

Scene 25. Interior of the house.

Alex prepares the fire in the conservatory. He stacks up chairs on a table. This recalls the same actor (Erland Josephson), as Domenico, lighting a fire at the end of *Nostalghia* (it is curious that in both films Josephson lights a fire at the climax).

Alex starts the fire, goes upstairs, then switches on the music in his room. He leaves by climbing down the external ladder, after taking a swig of wine from a glass on a table.

Scene 26. Exterior. The burning house.

Throughout this climactic scene the camera tracks back and forth, panning left and right throughout the shot. The action is carefully orchestrated so the camera pans or dollies to follow people. The first take of the burning house was unusable, because the A camera lost speed, and there was a pause before the second camera was set up.

The shot begins with Alex sitting and watching the conflagration; he gets up; the others run towards him, shouting; 'say nothing, ask nothing' says Victor; a telephone rings; noises of the fire and crashes; Alex walks towards the fire; then he runs to Maria; he kneels at her feet, like Kelvin does at the end of *Solaris*; Victor and Adelaide pull him away from Maria; the car near the house explodes; Alex runs back to Maria; Victor and Adelaide pull him away again; Maria runs to him; Adelaide yells 'don't touch him!' to Maria; they take Alex by the arms to the ambulance; Otto appears; Alex runs off; they chase him; he runs to the house; to Adelaide; to the ambulance (Per Källman and Tommy Nordahl play the ambulance men); he's put in the back of it; he gets out, to embrace Otto; he climbs in again; Adelaide opens the doors; he pushes her away and closes them; the ambulance drives off, slowly; Maria runs, picks up the bicycle and rides away; Adelaide walks to the house and sits in the water, exhausted; the house collapses, noisily. Sudden cut to scene 27.

The film magazine had eight minutes and 10 seconds, so the house had to burn down within that time. The scene was shot before sunrise, because it was decided not to shoot in sunlight. When one camera started to lose speed, Nykvist ordered the spare camera to be set up. About 30 seconds were lost.

Two hundred metre wooden rails were set up, for two cameras for the re-take. Just before calling action, the sun came out. Nykvist advised Tarkovsky to start filming anyway: as Nykvist remarked:

'Look, there's nothing you can do...! The sun is coming out, the house is already on fire – and we're on our second house!' But the sunlight worked well with the smoke, and Tarkovsky was exceedingly pleased.

The continuous take of the house burning down and Alex's capture is not meant to be taken literally or naturalistically. The ambulance, for example, comes out of nowhere (no vehicle could reach a remote rural location like that in such a short time), and the other characters, like Maria and Otto, seem to turn up by magic. And Tarkovsky adds sound effects which are beyond realism (like the telephone ringing).[4]

There have been plenty of celebrated fire scenes in cinema: Tarkovsky's in *The Sacrifice*, though impressive, is by no means the most spectacular (David O. Selznick torching Atlanta in *Gone With the Wind* must rank close to the top of a list of Best Movie Burns). A very memorable climactic burning building occurs in Akira Kurosawa's incredible adaption of *King Lear* (*Ran*, 1985).

Scene 27. The tree by the sea.

Shot 1. Little Man walking with the bucket, to water the tree.
Shot 2. Maria on the bike, with cows behind her. The camera tracks right. The ambulance drives by. All three people are linked spatially here: Alex, Little Man and

Maria.

Shot 3. L.S., high viewpoint: Little Man watering the tree; fulfilling his father's prophecy of ritual. J.S. Bach's stately music begins (the *aria* from *St Matthew Passion* that opened the film).

Shot 4. L.S. Maria climbs on the cycle and rides off up the track.

Shot 5. The tree; Little Man sits beneath it, his head against the tree trunk. The last shot of the film. Sound of birds and water; Little Man asks: 'in the beginning was the Word: why is that, Papa?'

Set against the light, the image of the tree is sublime after such profound darkness throughout the film. An image of brilliance and clarity after such agony and uncertainty. Slow crane shot up the tree. Water ripples behind, dazzling in the sunlight. The camera lingers on the top of the tree for some fifty seconds. The image gets brighter; it is like an ascension, or a transfiguration.

The dedication over the shot reads: 'This film is dedicated to my son Andriosha, with hope and confidence, Andrei Tarkovsky.'

21 : 3 THE SACRIFICIAL ACT

The meaning of the sacrifice in the film is clear: the father dies (or gives up his life) to give life to his son and his loved ones. His ego or self is destroyed in the fire. He becomes part of the larger, collective life, of society. The fire ritual unites Alex with all rites of dying/ killing and birthing. Alex says his life changed after the birth of his son. As Joseph Campbell wrote: '[t]he son is primary, and you're there as a fostering presence. You are no longer number one. His birth is death to your primary existence' (1989, 85). Love involved sacrifice for Tarkovsky: they were part of the same thing: 'love is always the gift of oneself to another' (D, 378). A gift, a giving, a sacrifice.

The bigger the thing sacrificed, the bigger the reward. The bread and wine of the Catholic Mass is a symbolic sacrifice: but the sacrifice of living flesh and blood (animals or humans, which the Mass refers to) is infinitely more powerful. Historic-ally, the most significant sacrifices were those of kings. The old king was sacrificed to the deities, to add virility and life to the new king (and to the land). Alex is clearly an old king – he played Shakespeare's King Richard, and the opening shot of *The Sacrifice* is of the Magi offering gifts to Christ, in Leonardo's painting. (There are also allusions to *King Lear*, with the squabbling family members as Gonerils and Regans).

Historically and mythographically, the sacrifical act is to enable something else to live. 'The past must be killed so there can be a future' as Campbell put it (1989, 84). Death creates life: the chain of birth –> life –> death –> rebirth is realized and valorized. The agricultural society's top figure (the king) becomes a god, and the god becomes the food of the people.[1] Alex's culture is a Northern European Protestant/ Christian one, and naturally he is identified with Christ. Christ sacrificed is a version of the older (corn/ oak/ vegetable) gods, such as Osiris, Tammuz, Dionysius, Odin and Cerunnos, who were slaughtered at Midsummer. They were reborn in a blaze of light at the Winter Solstice – born from the Earth Mother (Maria can be seen as a priestess of deities such as Isis, Ishtar and Inanna). (The same myth was used in *Apocalypse Now*, *The Wicker Man* and *Excalibur*).

Tarkovsky's Little Man is reborn – after the bright flames of the conflagration, he is born into the sun's brilliance on the ocean. Tarkovsky is clear about the boy's role as a god, as a god-child born of a magical union between the old god (Alex) and the Goddess (Maria the witch, and the witch as emissary of the Goddess. Tarkovsky called the love of Maria a gift from God [ST, 225]). It is only by giving himself over totally to the Goddess that Alex can be saved. Tarkovsky originally made more of the woman's role in this sacrifice, in the early version, called, significantly, *The Witch* (ST, 219-220).

The sacrifice also, symbolically, involves the whole of Creation. There is a cosmic dimension to Alex's sacrifice, which is pointed out by the rich symbols – of the tree, the Leonardo da Vinci image, the Chinese *yin-yang* motif, and the metaphysical speculations of Otto and Alex. Tarkovsky explores the traditional notions surround-ing the sacrifice – atonement, blood, offering, submission, expiation – but it is the spiritual exchange that he is really interested in: 'I am interested above all in the character who is capable of sacrificing himself and his way of life' Tarkovsky wrote in *Sculpting in Time* (217). Alex says to Otto: '[w]hat if you feel your whole life has been useless?' So Alex renounces everything around him. He is certainly surrounded by many precious things: his wife, son, daughter, friends, Western comforts and a successful career. But it all amounts to nothing in his eyes. Maria the witch standing at the door early on in the film (scene four) represents something beyond: there is Maria and her magic (and the wilderness of the landscape behind her – the darkening plain, the Outside, which becomes the meeting-ground for Alex and Maria). This is the feminine 'wild zone', which encircles the masculine house; it is nature surrounding (patriarchal) culture.

Peter Christensen (1987) suggested that 'possibly the most relevant reference' in *The Sacrifice* is to Søren Kierkegaard's essay "Fear and Trembling", written in 1843. Christensen related *The Sacrifice* to Kierkegaard's exploration of faith, religion, sacrifice and risk, with Alexander acting as a Kierkegaardian 'knight of faith'. For Pascal Bonitzer, *The Sacrifice* is a religious apology, in which the super-natural is 'by necessity secret and uncertain' (1986).

There is a Shakespearean connection too: Alex is like Prospero, with his magical *yin-yang* cloak, in Prospero's cell, the house-island, surrounded by the witch Maria. In *The Tempest* the female power enclosing Prospero on his island is the witch Sycorax. Again, in *Solaris*, wild, feminine nature surrounds a male island, with allusions to *The Tempest*, where the Ocean is aligned with primæval, fecund, feminine nature.

Alex's ontological disaffection is a common occurrence in many modern Existential novels: the hero/ anti-hero/ anti-heroine becomes increasingly dissatisfied with her/ his life (*The Rainbow, Perfume, Mysteries, Steppenwolf, Nausea, The Happy Death, The Black Book* and *Tropic of Cancer*). The threshold is reached and the question is whether or not to cross the threshold, to ride the wave of the crisis, to get to the new world beyond. Has Alex the courage and the strength?

There are Biblical ancestors of Alex's fire ritual (it also recalls the Buddha's 'Fire Sermon'). God burns up the sacrifice as Elijah's altar on Mount Carmel; and there is the Pentecostal fire which descends upon the apostles at Whitsuntide after Christ's death and resurrection. The film takes in the whole of the *Bible*: *The Sacrifice* opens with an image of a God (Alex) planting the Tree of Life, which is an image of God creating the world, a Paradise. In *Sculpting In Time*, Tarkovsky discusses the film as if Alex really has communicated with God, as if God really did answer his prayer, as if God really has chosen Alex (ST, 227).

Alex is something of a Moses, an Abraham, a Hebraic patriarch who is here a modern shaman – an artist. The film contains many machinations which reflect the events of the *Bible*, ending on an Apocalyptic note, as well as a note of Resurrection and Ascension (the crane-shot up the tree, and the rebirth of Alex/ Tarkovsky in his son). The camera flies up into the light. It can be seen as a classic ending of narrative closure and also philosophical openness. Like the ending of *Solaris*, the ending of *The Sacrifice* opens out onto a field of wider meanings. The metaphysical binding-up is of patriarchy, father-to-son hereditary and regeneration, the mythic return, paradise regained, the re-affirmation of the Goddess, the feminine principle. All these things, and more, are indicated in this scene.

21 : 5   STYLE/ SPACE/ SOUND

The external world of history, the personal past and culture come into the house (and Alex's world) from clearly marked outside culture bearers: Victor brings Alex a book of icons; Otto brings the map and telegrams. They are both kings, Magi to Alex's Christ. The Leonardo da Vinci painting is a central emblem in the film. The picture frightens Otto, who prefers Piero della Francesca. The whole film is shot by Sven Nykvist in a Leonardo *sfumato* style, where objects are shrouded in shadows. The Leonardo print is seen in a dim room. When Alex and Otto discuss it they are shot against the light, their faces, like Leonardo's faces, melt into the darkness.

The house is a Leonardo da Vincian world. Objects are seen in a new way: things become sinister — like the cupboard door that creaks, or the glass that rattles. The filmic darkness also recalls the Early Netherlandish painters, particularly the dark but luminous interiors, the detailed and shiny surfaces in the paintings of Rogier van der Weyden, Hans Memling, Jan van Eyck, Petrus Christus and Quentin Massys. Anna Asp said the house in *The Sacrifice* was designed to be timeless, as if the film could have been set in the 19th century or in the future; there was a 'God's face' on one side of the house (comprising windows for eyes and a door for the mouth); the interior was twice the size of the exterior; Asp said that they 'agonized about whether this would be a problem; but ultimately, no one who saw the finished film commented on it' (P. Ettedgui, 115). Tarkovsky was incredibly particular about the design and decoration of the house, Asp explained. 'He wanted to discuss every detail, for example, the distance between the top of a chair to the sill of a window' (ib., 114).

Objects are beautiful in *The Sacrifice*. Tarkovsky's sense of space and surface is sublime here. His grasp of space, light, volume and mass is highly developed. Cinema has never been so beautiful. Tarkovsky controls movements, colour and sound so dynamically. He is a Prospero, charming the viewer with cinematic enchantment, orchestrating his angelic/ dæmonic devices like a Renaissance wizard. The sound of fighters overhead, for instance, is a roar that fills up all the frequencies, from the lowest to the highest (the sound was created from a combination of a number of Swedish military aircraft, plus some low rumbles and other noises). The wind noise in the trees is another mysterious expression, of a Total Other. Alex sits in the Baudelairean 'forest of symbols'. The wind is a mass of voices, stretched out into breaths of sound.

Owe Svensson was part of the sound team on *The Sacrifice* (he had worked with Ingmar Bergman, Bo Widerberg, Liv Ullmann and Jan Troell, among others). The sound in *The Sacrifice*, Svensson pointed out, was more subtle and multi-layered than in Russian films of the time, which tended to be stripped-down and rather heavy-handed. Russian movies (and Italian) tended to add music and only a few heavy sound effects, rather than building up atmospheres with a range of sound fx.

Owe Svensson recalled that Tarkovsky wanted to find some old recordings of cow herding calls (O. Svensson, 2003). He didn't want songs that had been set to music, and eventually Svensson found a shepherd's recording that had been recorded on a wax cylinder, via a telephone link from Rättvik in rural Sweden to Swedish Radio in Stockholm. (As the quality of the recording was poor, reverb was added, and the song was mixed with outdoor sounds.) Tarkovsky asked Svensson to mix the cow songs with the Japanese flutes (taken from a vinyl album). Foghorns (some from ships, some from lighthouses) were also added.

A lot of the sound on location was looped in *The Sacrifice* – partly because the sound of birds was deafening, as the house set had been built in a bird sanctuary, and the production was shooting in May. Some of the actors (such as Erland Josephson and Allan Edwall) loathed dubbing their voices, so Svensson set up a post-syncing studio in a Stockholm soundstage, rather than, as usual in a dubbing theatre, to make the actors feel at home. (He installed a U-matic machine to play back the film, some TV monitors, a lamp, and some microphones). Josephson was persuaded to rehearse his lines prior to recording, and soon delivered performances which improved on the original. (Even so, the ADR in *The Sacrifice* isn't always brilliant, and disturbs credibility a number of times. Some filmmakers loathe looping, while others – Orson Welles most famously – brilliantly exploited adding all of the sound in post-production). Two other (Swedish) actresses helped to voice the part of Adelaide, as well as Susan Fleetwood.

For the sound of the interior of Alexander's house, with its distinctive wooden floorboards, Owe Svensson did all of the foley work himself, in his own country cottage in Sweden (even, he remembered, down to wearing ladies' size 45 shoes). Svensson ensured that the footsteps sounded different in different parts of the rooms.

21 : 6   THE TREE

The tree symbolically is the whole of life – 'the synthesis of heaven, earth and water' (J. Cooper, 176). Tarkovsky shows heaven and earth and water in the final image of *The Sacrifice*. The tree is the Tree of Life, the axis of the world, the tree of growth and regeneration. It is communication between Heaven and Earth. Also, the tree symbolizes the feminine principle, the life-giving Mother Goddess, with her roots in the waters of life. The tree in *The Sacrifice* may have phallic, Christian connotations: but behind the tree is the vastness of the Mother Ocean. Alex says the tree looks Japanese, a peaceful image from some secret Zen Buddhist garden. The Buddhist symbolism of the bo, fig, pipal or bonsai tree is the Great Wisdom Tree under which the Buddha sat. In the film the boy lies under the tree — he's linked to a Buddha-in-the-making. The Buddhist tree is also the Great Awakening at the Sacred Centre. Certainly Tarkovsky films his tree and flatted landscape like a flat Japanese print. The sparseness of the landscape and the limpid light recall Oriental landscape painting (A scene in *Andrei Roublyov* of the prince and a Tartar on horseback, reminded Tarkovsky of director Kenjo Mizoguchi's films, like a Chinese landscape painting).

This image, of the tree, is not an epilogue, as has been suggested, but a cinematic climax, the highpoint of the film. The watering of the tree is a life-affirming ritual, but a more peaceful act than Alex's Promethean/ Romantic rebellion. The way in for Alex is through a woman: 'it is also a spiritual regeneration expressed in the image of a woman' (ST, 220).

If the tree is watered often enough and the ritual performed with complete faith, then the tree will 'burst into life' says Tarkovsky (ST, 229). And so it does: the boy speaks for the first time. This is a moment of profound rebirth. The boy realizes Creation and Paradise in those words. The words begin the *Gospel of St John*. The Word referred to here is the Creative Word of God, the Act of God the Artist, who can remake the world, and make the Word into flesh (*John*, I: 14). The image of the earth, sea and tree occurs in *Revelations* (7:3). The film has many Apocalyptic over/ undertones: the nuclear holocaust is an Apocalypse in modern terms — a thoroughly secular, utterly un-sacred death. The image at the end of *The Sacrifice* also contains the re-assertion of primal elements: earth, tree, sea, sky, soil, stones and water. Disregarding the boy's clothes, the image could be two million years old. It is intentionally timeless.

Alex tries to abolish profane time and re-instate sacred time. He wants a return to the holy, to unify the opposites, the black and white, male/ female, ego/ shadow and self/ world, past/ present, present/ future, and so on. A nuclear war is the most anti-poetic and anti-sacred of all acts. It is an abomination which demands serious retaliation. Alex's gesture of the sacrifice does not work. So he burns his house, his whole world, down. This is an act of Gnostic defiance (Alex mentioned the Gnostic demiurge in the opening scene of the film). The Gnostics believed that this world was a false one, created by a false deity – the Devil or demiurge. The real God is elsewhere, which is what André Breton said about existence ('existence is else-where'). Alex's act is a Promethean act of rebellion, an attempt at a Gnostic/ Cathar rejection of this false, profane world.[1]

Ultimately and ironically, the same society that created the (threat of) nuclear war, the men in suits, in governments and institutions, arrive to cart Alex away. The grey-suited politicians have become white-suited ambulance drivers. Patriarchal institutions swallow up abnormalities, erase them – and Alex gets driven away. His ethic of Gnostic, Romantic rebellion is passed on to his son. His sacrifice is bound up with his yearning for rebirth. Alex dies (spiritually) so the boy can live (physically).

21 : 8   REBIRTH

The motif of rebirth in *The Sacrifice* is pointed up in many motifs: tree, fire, ocean, milk, Leonardo and *yin* and *yang*. The boy is the phoenix who rises from the ashes of his father's funeral pyre. In traditional symbolism, the house is the body: the house-body dies so the boy can be reborn. Like the Magi with Christ, Alex is the guardian of his son. Osiris the father takes second place to Horus his son in ancient Egyptian mythology. But in his symbolic death Alex is also glorified (not least by the dynamics of cinema itself). He reaches an apotheosis, a glorification, at that moment. As Joseph Campbell put it: '[g]oing to your sacrifice as the winning stroke of your life is the essence of the early sacrifice idea' (1988a, 108). This idea is embodied supremely in the West in the figure of Christ (and movies have employed the heroic sacrifical act many times). The sacrifice of love meant total giving, Tarkovsky asserted. Anything less wasn't real love (ST, 217).

This final transformation and rebirth in *The Sacrifice* occurs on the mythic/ spiritual plane – or the poetic, as I've have termed Tarkovsky's kind of approach. But on the psychological level the father-to-son transformation is full of problems and ambiguities. The father-son relation, in Freudian psychoanalysis, is bound up with œdipal conflicts. Little Man clearly suffers from the abstract, often ambiguous and violent love of the father. This is crystallized in the early woodland scene where Alex throws off Little Man and hurts him. The pain and blood (blood is spilt early on in classic mythological stories) foreshadows the later crucifixion by fire of Alex, but also of the film: 'in the beginning was the Word – why is that, father?' The asking of the question (from the *Gospel of St John*) is more important than its answer. Significantly, Little Man doesn't witness the father's fire death, fate has kept him away from that. He is the only major character who is not in the house-burning scene. (Director Alexei German, whom Tarkovsky admired, reckoned the ending of *The Sacrifice* was banal, and wouldn't have got a student into a film school).

The œdipal conflicts, ambiguities and pain suffered by the boy at this endpoint are huge: his father, though he can dance with fire and cavort like the trickster gods of mythology, is only half a shaman. The modern shamans, the representatives of science, the ambulance men, come to claim him (although it takes them a long time to exert their authority over him). The father, too, is no God, no powerful authoritarian figure – not anymore. Once he was, maybe. Tarkovsky sidesteps further (and much deeper) psychic complexities by having the boy a prepubescent eight or nine year old. A fifteen or eighteen year old son would have made that final transformation much less credible.

For the boy *is* the father: 'the father is oneself, complexly and ambivalently, imbricated into one's very character' wrote Weston La Barre in *The Ghost Dance* (1972, 105-6). The father's traumatized death-by-fire and (somewhat ridiculous) capture is also the boy's own experience. There is a huge cost to Alex's sacrifice, for the boy ends up surrounded by the legacy of his father's past and mistakes, as well as his hopes and dreams (embodied in the tree).

For Tarkovsky, the sacrifice involves 'total giving' (ST, 217). It is an act that upsets the rational/ materialist universe, like the 'gratuitous act' of André Gide's anti-heroes. The film is about love, 'love [which] is at once ultimate thrall and ultimate freedom' (ST, 218). People today have a choice, Tarkovsky explained, between blindly following materialism and technology, or choosing to pursue 'spiritual responsibility', and turning to God (ibid.). There needs to be a balance between the material and the spiritual (ST, 233).

The film, and Tarkovsky's own position, is anti-rational, anti-social, anti-authoritarian, anti-establishment. It is a parable, Tarkovsky says, open to interpretations. Tarkovsky's own reading is clear: each of the characters is dramatically changed by the end of the film – Alex most of all. He demonstrates that 'he is able to rise to extraordinary heights' (ST, 223).

21 : 9   ENDINGS

The Sacrifice is a film of its time – the political climate of the mid-1980s, when the fear of a 'limited nuclear war' between the superpowers (probably taking place in Europe) was at its height, and arms escalation at its most terrifying. A nuclear psychosis had set in, with nuclear scares occurring frequently. In Britain there were productions such as *Threads* (Mick Jackson, 1984), *Defence of the Realm* (David Drury, 1985), BBC TV's *Edge of Darkness* (1985), *Pravda* (David Hare/ Howard Brenton, 1985, National Theatre), to name a few of the items with a nuclear politics content.

One scene seems over-the-top in *The Sacrifice*: where Alex goes to Maria's house. He sits down and plays a tune on an old organ. The music is too obviously melancholy and pathetic. But what seems really wrong is Alex's lengthy story of his mother and the ruined garden. This is all so obvious. Tarkovsky has already done it all, visually. He has already shown that going to Maria is like going back to the mother, to the past, to childhood. Her house is full of icons, an old vase, old photos of relatives, a crucifix, and mementos of past lives. Alex's over-long and over-blown soliloquy is unnecessary. The emotional enmeshing of father, mother, son and sister is obvious anyway, in the structure and implications of this scene and its place in the film. In the dream Maria wears Adelaide's clothes: in the next shot, Adelaide is seen wearing the same clothes.

Out-takes: there was another part to the above shot, not used, where Little Man was leading a white horse (here's where a horse might have been woven into the tapestry of *The Sacrifice*). The outtake was shown in Michal Leszcylowski's documentary. There was also a long (six minute) scene of Alex typing a valedictory letter to his family (which Adelaide later reads out); this was the only scene deleted in its entirety, according to Leszcylowski.[1] Leszcylowski also recalled there was 'a scene of the boy practising Japanese gymnastics in very slight slow-motion. It was a long, beautiful tracking shot among the small bushes, but it was too theatrical, too artificial — he [Tarkovsky] was happy to get rid of it'.[2] Another scene dropped was an earlier piece of exposition.

In his contract, Tarkovsky had agreed with the producers to bring *The Sacrifice* in at 2 hours 10 mins, but he wanted it to be 149 minutes (and that's how long the film finally was. The first rough cut was 190 minutes). Editing *The Sacrifice* didn't mean simply joining together all of the long takes (there were only 120 cuts in *The Sacrifice*). It meant six months of very difficult work, according to Michal Leszcylowski. Each cut was 'subject to deep critical scrutiny'.[3]

The most elaborate unused shot in *The Sacrifice* was the end of the dream sequence: C.U. of Alex lying down, with Adelaide beside him (he appears to be waking from a dream): the camera tracked left to show his upstairs room; he is on the sofa, surrounded by fifteen or so people, including the housekeeper and the boy; they all kneel; the tracking shot continues to show various women in long dresses; another woman reflected in a mirror; three men in dark suits; the track left continues to show the upstairs corridor: a man (Otto) rides through it on a bicycle; birds flutter down from above; Martha, nude, runs in slow motion, chasing along the chickens. Thankfully, this shot, perhaps most over-the-top sequence in all of Tarkovsky's cinema, was cut.

The Sacrifice ends on a note of extraordinary beauty, profundity — and optimism. Despite being a difficult film for some to sit through (except for art film addicts) and despite the gloomy plot and the dark *mise-en-scène*, it is a supremely positive, life-affirming film. The last scene is a pastoral one: the herd of cows, the grass, the ululations of what sounds like a shepherdess, the bright sky, images recalling Classical/ Greek pastoralism and Arcadia. (No surprise that the cow is, symbolically, the great Moon Goddess, a symbol of procreation and plenty, the sacred animal of India, a powerful image of the matriarchal and feminine realm.)

With the sublime, abstract music of Johann Sebastian Bach swelling, and the slow crane-shot up the tree, and the imagery – of the tree against the sky, against the sun shining on the glittering sea, the spectator seems to be rising bodily into Heaven. The crane shot points the spectator towards heaven, quite literally and physically, just as at the end of Dante Alighieri's *Divina Commedia*, or Francesco Petrarch's *Canzoniere*. In mediæval times the glorification was of Christ and the Virgin Mary; in Andrei Tarkovsky's cinema, in this last scene of *The Sacrifice*, the apotheosis lies in Maria, in the cows, in the pastoral imagery, in the tree, in the ocean. The achievement is of life itself, life and death, the whole of existence and experience. So it is *life itself* that is being glorified – not the viewers, not the boy, not nature, but life as a whole. This is why *The Sacrifice* is one of the most joyous of films. Few films are as exhilarating as this.

TWENTY-TWO

Critical Responses to Andrei Tarkovsky's Cinema

For me, Tarkovsky is a phenomenon... amazing, unrepeatable, inimitable and beautiful... I consider Tarkovsky the No. 1 film director of the USSR... He is a genius.

Sergei Paradjanov[1]

22 : 1   CRITICAL RESPONSE

The critical response to Andrei Tarkovsky's films has been varied. For some Tarkovsky is a genius, and his films are some of the best in cinema; for others, his films are pretentious, boring, indulgent, irrelevant and obscure. Jay Leyda, in *Kino*, his magisterial history of Soviet cinema, said that Andrei Tarkovsky learned to bypass the mass audience, making beautiful puzzle films from which 'each flattered spectator could take away his interpretation as the only possible one' (403). Certainly, Tarkovsky flatters his audience, as well as exasperating them. I have said throughout this study that one of the most important aspects of Tarkovsky's films is their openness, enabling the viewer to manoeuvre.

Tarkovsky wanted his films to be seen and admired: an audience was essential for the artist 'to fulfil his personal spiritual mission', as he grandly put it (ST, 165). Although he did not deliberately try to please his audience (in the Hollywood manner), and hated the commercial pandering to their tastes (ST, 174-5), he also hoped 'fervently that my picture will be accepted and loved' (ST, 170). Of course, that's what most artists want (and especially with something like a feature film, which can soak up years of a filmmaker's life).

Tarkovsky's view of criticism was that it was too often illustrating an idea, or confirming an opinion or private aspiration or personal position of the critic (ST, 46). To grasp an artwork properly, the viewer should cultivate 'an original, independent, 'innocent' judgement' (ibid.). (Tarkovsky spoke dismissively of the people who study to become film directors and actors – i.e., who become critics – but who are destined to wind up on the edges of the industry, lacking the strength to give up and start another profession [ST, 88]).

Because cinema is an art, Tarkovsky maintained, it's wrong to expect it to be easy to understand. 'Nobody demands that of the other arts' Tarkovsky said.[1] Tarkovsky sometimes appeared wilfully obscure – in not providing clear information on characters or events, or signposting clearly what are dreams, memories, wishes, and other kinds of realities. Sometimes it's not clear *who* is having the dreams or memories (in *Nostalghia*, for instance, Gorchakov seems to dream from Domenico's memories). For Tarkovsky, it doesn't always matter whose mindscreen the sequences represent – it's the images and sounds that count.

For Ivor Montagu, Andrei Tarkovsky is 'one of the best things to happen in world cinema for a long time'.[2] Giovanni Buttafava called Tarkovsky's films 'complex heterodox individual works', 'a series of films that turned the ambiguity of everyday life into the subject of severe subtle investigation'.[3] Of Tarkovsky's *œuvre*, Peter Green wrote: 'this handful of completed works is individually of such weight and vision that each one of them alone might have secured him a place in film history' (1987). Maybe not *Ivan's Childhood*, but any one of Tarkovsky films from *Andrei Roublyov* onwards would guarantee him a place in the cinematic pantheon. This sentiment was typical of the obituaries British critics wrote, such as Ian Christie and David Robinson. They waxed lyrical about Tarkovsky. In "Raising the Shroud", Christie noted, though, that 'there is an urgent need now to resist a premature canonisation' (38). (Obituaries for Tarkovsky appeared in January, 1987 in *Pravda*, *Literary Gazette* and *Soviet Culture* in the USSR, written by Goskino and the Filmmakers' Union).

Arthur Aristakisian, a rising star in Russian cinema (he attended VGIK, and his *The Palms* won a Nika for Best Documentary in 1994), was asked if Tarkovsky had been privileged, in receiving large budgets, and replied '[t]oday it's not a question of money as much as that people have changed. They are corrupt. They find it more and more difficult to think'.[4] Sentiments Tarkovsky would probably agree with.

Andrei Tarkovsky's films were often dismissed as élitist puzzles by the Soviet authorities and critics: his were regarded as films for minorities. Nikolai Sizov, director of the Moscow Film Studios, said *Mirror* was 'too complex'.[5] For the film-maker V.N. Naumov, *Mirror* was 'un-understandable' (ibid.). Sergei Gerasimov, the veteran director who was for years chief of the Joint Acting and Directing Workshops at VGIK, where Tarkovsky studied, said that Tarkovsky was 'a man of very serious talent' (ibid.). Of *Mirror*, Herbert Marshall wrote that it was very sophisticated and new:

> Such a film has hitherto never been seen on the Soviet screen... here for the first time is the 'subjective history' of a Soviet filmmaker in his own film. (ib., 95)

When Soviet films of the time were expected to be 'social realist', it's under-standable why *Mirror* should have seemed so radically different. (Some Russian critics – and filmmakers – couldn't quite accept the idea that Tarkovsky was making a film about his own life, rather than a larger, social subject).

Up until the mid-1990s, Tarkovsky was usually given a few lines in histories and encyclopaedias of cinema, but not much more than that. Tarkovsky was usually placed next to Sergei Paradjanov and his *The Colour of Pomegranates* in film guides (but being put beside Paradjanov means being in very good company indeed). Usually *Andrei Roublyov* was discussed (it was probably the Tarkovsky film that created the most fuss in the Soviet Union). *Mirror* was the next film cited in the film guides and history books, but the rest of Tarkovsky's cinema was rarely analyzed.

In critical books on cinema, Andrei Tarkovsky often emerges as a talented but obscure or minor figure: *The Oxford Companion to Film* said Tarkovsky's films 'are intense, personal works, often disconcerting in the violence they portray' (L. Bawden, 679). In the British Film Institute's *Encyclopaedia of European Cinema*, the entry on Tarkovsky described him as 'a filmmaker's filmmaker'; *Mirror and Stalker* were classed as 'two deeply personal and somewhat obscure films, which

were partly autobiographical'.6 For *The Film Handbook*, *The Sacrifice* suffered
from 'a somewhat contrived religiosity and a morbid disenchantment with human
aspiration and achievement'.7 Tarkovsky has a sizeable entry in the weighty
International Dictionary of Films and Filmmakers, in the *Directors* volume. G.C.
Macnab stated that his work 'can verge on the inscrutable. Too opaque to yield
concrete meaning, it offers itself as sacral art, demanding a rapt, and even religious
response from its audience' (L. Hillstrom, 1997).

In *Halliwell's Film Guide*, one of the popular British cinema guides, *The Sacrifice*
was described as a 'brilliantly filmed but obscure and confusing parable that does not
easily yield its meaning', and *Nostalghia* was an '[i]ndescribably doomladen,
occasionally beautiful, stylistically interesting and for the most part very boring
parable of a kind unique to its director' (L. Halliwell, 1993). *Solaris* for Leslie
Halliwell was 'heavy-going but highly imaginative', technically superb but 'the
whole thing is rather humourless' (L. Halliwell, 2000). Reviewers for the London
listings magazine *Time Out* have generally been big fans. Tarkovsky was given just
a few lines in *The History of the Movies*, mentioning *Nostalghia* and *The Sacrifice*
only (A. Lloyd, 1988).

Vincent Canby, reviewing *Nostalghia* for the *New York Times*, called Tarkovsky a 'film poet with a tiny vocabulary' (quite a few of the US film critics found
Nostalghia disappointing, a repetition of Tarkovsky's established symbols and
themes: 'flawed plot', 'overloaded metaphors', 'banal and lofty generalization', 'a
kind of theatre of gibberish', 'heated melodrama').

In *Elliot's Guide To Films On Video*, *The Sacrifice* was seen as 'mostly an intense
examination of various angst-ridden obsessions, and is sustained by excellent
performances, Sven Nykvist's outstanding camerawork and some truly memorable
sequences', while *Nostalghia* was 'an oppressive and doomladen meditation,
sustained by a few images of great beauty and opaque symbolism, but too stylized
and sluggish to be really effective' (J. Elliot, 1993). Another popular film guidebook,
by Leonard Maltin (one of the better US reviewers), was a fan: *Mirror* was
'superbly directed'; *Nostalghia* was 'a provocative, insightful epic, lovingly
rendered by one of cinema's true poets'; and *Andrei Roublyov* was a 'magnificent
film worthy of comparison with the best of Eisenstein's historical dramas' (L.
Maltin, 2000). While Maltin acknowledged that films like *Solaris* and *The Sacrifice*
were not for all tastes, they were *tour-de-forces* from the director.

Geoff Andrew wrote that Tarkovsky's later films are 'deeply flawed by self-indulgence [and] tend towards obscurantism and a cold, intellectual aloofness' (G. Andrew, 280). There is some truth in this: Tarkovsky's films, despite their intense poetry, can seem cold. But he is not intellectual: he is very anti-intellectual (Tarkovsky wasn't a fan of intellectualized or literary filmmaking, *mise-en-scène* and staging which illustrates an intellectual or literary idea). He makes few concessions to his audience, however. He forces the viewer to work – suffer even, but in most cases his artistic rigour is justified.

The Bloomsbury Foreign Film Guide claimed *Nostalghia* contained 'scenes of an almost perverse obscurity and the final sequence is tedious beyond belief' (R. Bergan, 411). The final sequence, the nine-minute take, is either fabulous or monotonous for the viewer: it either works or it doesn't: if the viewer doesn't identify with Gorchakov's fate, and the big themes of the film, the whole sequence is pointless.

Many critics have disliked the length and slowness of Tarkovsky's films (reviewers hate long movies, for good reasons), the pomposity and self-indulgence of his art. But there have been many self-indulgent filmmakers (such as Charlie Chaplin, Orson Welles, Alfred Hitchcock, Jean-Luc Godard, Maya Deren and Walerian Borowczyk. However, Tarkovsky has usually made much longer films than those directors. On the other hand, he only made seven features, far less than Hitch, Godard or even Welles).

In the 1982 *Sight & Sound* critics' poll, *Andrei Roublyov* was joint tenth (with *2001: A Space Odyssey*); above *Andrei Roublyov* in the poll were the usual 'classic' films: *The General* and *The Searchers* (joint 8th); *Vertigo, The Magnificent Ambersons* and *L'Avventura* (joint 7th); *Battleship Potemkin* (6th), *8 1/2* (5th), *Seven Samurai* and *Singin' in the Rain* (joint 3rd), *The Rules of the Game* (2nd), with *Citizen Kane* at the top. (But that was Tarkovsky's only appearance in the *Sight & Sound* top ten films). Twenty years later, in 2002, Tarkovsky wasn't on the list of films, or of the top ten film directors. The filmmakers topping the list, polled from film directors (not critics) were Welles, Fellini, Kurosawa, Coppola, Hitchcock, Kubrick, Wilder, Bergman, Scorsese, Lean and Renoir). The favourite films of film directors in the same poll were the usual suspects: *Kane, Godfather, 8 1/2, Lawrence, Strangelove, Bicycle Thieves* and so on).

Film critics and filmmakers did cite Tarkovsky's films many times as among their favourite films, but not often enough to put them in the top ten lists, and compete with the *Kanes*, the *Rashomons*, the *Generals* and the *Godfathers*. Other critics and filmmakers who put Tarkovsky in their top ten included in the *Sight & Sound* poll Richard Allen, Russell Campbell, Li Cheuk-To, Malgorzata Dipont, Lalitha Gopalan, Peter Hames, Dina Iordanova, Nick James, Kim Ji-Seok, Andrey Plakhov, M.K. Raghavendra, Donald Richie, Philip Strick, Leonard Tsao, Aruna Vasudev, Alexei Balabanov, Roy Andersson, Gore Verbinski, Ann Hui, Clare Law, Lukas Moodysson, Pawel Pawlikowski, and Sanosh Sivan.

Film directors such as Oliver Assayas, John Boorman, Vincent Ward, Jonathan Glazer, Gilles Mackinnon, Michael Haneke, Scott Hicks, George Sluizer, Jaco van Dormael and Joel Schumacher put a Tarkovsky film in their list of top ten films. And one or two filmmakers put Tarkovsky at the top of their lists: Vincent Ward, George Sluizer, Jaco van Dormael, Clare Law, Gilles Mackinnon and Scott Hicks.

Another British poll, conducted by the *Guardian* newspaper in 1993, was for the top 100 films made between 1980 and 1993. *The Sacrifice* was number 17, and *Nostalghia* was number 49 (not a great poll, really: it also placed dreary flicks like *Truly Madly Deeply* (1990) at no. 63 and *Mona Lisa* (1986) at no. 71).

The Hollywood trade magazine *Variety* raved about *Andrei Roublyov*, calling it 'brilliantly-fashioned' from a director of 'exceptional talent' (D. Elley, 1996). *Ivan's Childhood* was sympathetically reviewed ('lyrical', 'flamboyant', 'rich use of camera'), as was *Solaris* ('Tarkovsky spins a strange, slow but absorbing parable'.) The visual fx may not have been spectacular for *Variety*, but the 'playing is intense and effective'.

Quite often film critics neglect Tarkovsky's films, although they will discuss contemporaries such as Luis Buñuel, Robert Bresson or Ingmar Bergman at length. For instance, in his excellent study of mediæval films, *A Knight At the Movies*, John Aberth explores in detail the usual Hollywood Middle Ages films (*El Cid*, *The Adventures of Robin Hood*, *Joan of Arc*), and some of the European and Russian films (*The Seventh Seal*, *The Passion of Joan of Arc* and *Alexander Nevsky*), but doesn't even mention *Andrei Roublyov* once (although he does look at non-American Middle Ages pictures that are much more obscure than *Andrei Roublyov*).

As he made two films that can broadly be termed 'sci-fi', Tarkovsky is often mentioned in sci-fi guidebooks and sci-fi encyclopaedias. It's much easier for Tarkovsky's films to stand out in a genre like science fiction, where plenty of films are not exactly high quality. Generally, *Solaris* and *Stalker* are regarded as two worthy, significant works of science fiction, as well as being somewhat obscure and too long. The view of *The Aurum Encyclopaedia of Science Fiction* is typical:

If it were not for the intensely cinematic and fascinating *mise en scène* [of *Solaris*], the intellectual content of the film would be seen as a set of very antiquated romantic clichés. However, the cinematic power of the representations is such that the brilliance of the imagery and the skillfully controlled rhythm is all absorbing, making the content merely a minor irritant.[8]

The visualization of *Stalker* is what arrests *The Aurum Encyclopaedia of Science Fiction*, which speaks of the

desolate landscapes causing unspecified anxieties expertly conveyed with eerie lighting and slow, menacing camera movements alternating with uncomfortably long fixed shots, constantly suggesting a sense of an observing presence which may or may not be malignant. (ib., 353)

Bill Warren and sci-fi writer Brian Aldiss put *Solaris* in their list of top ten sci-fi films.[9] Not surprisingly, neither of Tarkovsky's sci-fi films features in *Variety*'s list of the top 130 or so science fiction films in terms of US film rentals (as expected, the top twenty films in the *Variety* sci-fi films list are all Hollywood entertainment features: *E.T., Star Wars, Return of the Jedi, Batman, The Empire Strikes Back, Superman, Close Encounters of the Third Kind, Back to the Future, Star Trek* and *Alien*). Films comparable with *Solaris* and *Stalker*, the more 'thoughtful' or explorative sci-fi movies, such as *2001: A Space Odyssey* and *Westworld*, come much further down the *Variety* list.

Critic John Baxter voices a typical view of sci-fi cinema among critics. Of directors such as Steven Spielberg, George Lucas and Joe Dante, often cited (completely wrongly) as being responsible for the 'juvenalization' of Hollywood since the late 1970s (with films such as the *Star Wars* series, the *Indiana Jones* series, *E.T., Small Soldiers, Gremlins*, the *Jurassic Park* films, and so on), John Baxter said they were like big kids, building their own personal companies which were 'little private worlds', where they 'confect fantasies of childhood. They're basically lonely kids. They're *nerds*. They're nerds who grew up, were given a camera, fifty million dollars and told to make movies', refusing to grow up (*viz.* Spielberg as a 'Peter Pan' figure, holding onto his childhood), acting out fantasies of power and superheroes in films. For John Baxter, there were no real science fiction ideas in these films, they were years behind sci-fi writing, they were infantile. Baxter added that mature science fiction films hadn't been made yet, 'with the exception of someone like Tarkovsky'.[10] (There isn't space here to get into the many reasons for the shift in the content of Hollywood cinema since the mid-1970s, but it's not due to Spielberg, Lucas *et al*). Tarkovsky is thus seen by some critics has having made some of the very few adult sci-fi films to date. (Science fiction cinema has always been decades behind sci-fi writing – contemporary Hollywood sci-fi movies are still hawking the same ancient ideas going back to the comics and pulps of the 1930s, or further back, to Arthur Conan Doyle, Jules Verne and H.G. Welles).

John Brosnan disagreed:

> I am well aware that Tarkovsky's *Stalker* is rated by some as one of the best sf [sci-fi] movies ever made, but not by me. Besides, it would look very out of place in the above line-up. It doesn't even star Arnold Schwarzenegger. (ib., 389)

Brosnan's list of best sci-fi films included *Mad Max 2, Blade Runner, Total Recall, The Thing, Aliens, The Abyss* and *Back to the Future 2*, all mainstream Hollywood sci-fi films, and the sort of films Tarkovsky loathed (and of those films, only the 1951 *Thing*, and maybe *Total Recall* and *Blade Runner*, could compete with *Stalker* or *Solaris* as a great sci-fi movie).

Andrei Tarkovsky was cited in a review of *Liquid Sky* (1982), directed by the Soviet Slava Tsukerman, a supremely dire sci-fi black comedy about sex 'n' drugs 'n' rock 'n' roll: 'the saucer's dinky, the sex is kinky, and you could never imagine Tarkovsky having this much fun in the forbidden zone' (P. Hardy, 376). *Liquid Sky*, though, doesn't deserve a mention in even the most comprehensive books on science fiction cinema, except as a warning to filmmakers (don't do it like this!) or viewers (don't bother!).

Although Tarkovsky said in his writings that he hated much of (particularly American) contemporary culture, of the mass-produced McDonald's, Coca-Cola, Disney kind, he could, according to Layla A. Garrett, 'talk for hours about *The Terminator*' (L. Garrett, 1997). (Tarkovsky's interest in the Arny flick *The Terminator* was partly, according to Garrett, because of his interest in time travel. It's no surprise that Tarkovsky could discourse at length on cyborg fantasy films like *The Terminator* – one reason is that, although he said he wasn't that interested in science fiction, he was a director who made not one but two science fiction film. Two out of his seven feature films were sci-fi. That's a big proportion).

David Cook noted in his excellent *A History of Narrative Film* that *Nostalghia* was 'perhaps Tarkovsky's most mysterious and inaccessible film, but it was a great success at Cannes in 1983' (1990, 769). Cook added that 'to many Western observers even [Tarkovsky's] films made abroad bear the marks of careful, covert Soviet censorship' (770). Many critics have been sympathetic to the humanism underlying Tarkovsky's poetic, determinedly non-social-realist films. David Quinlan said that *Solaris* was 'really a plea for love and peace under its enigmatic surface' (1985), while Jack Ellis said that *Ivan's Childhood* has 'a strong and clear humanist message carrying along its unusual display of technical virtuosity' (344).

In another doorstop guidebook to cinema, *The Story of Cinema*, David Shipman admitted he was sent to sleep by Tarkovsky's films, and left the cinema showing both *Solaris* and *Mirror* before an hour was up. Of *Ivan's Childhood*, Shipman said that its 'exquisite photography… represents nothing but exquisite photography', and the often-used story of a young boy being taught by an older solder 'has never been so unfeelingly projected' (1048). Shipman reacted even more violently to *Mirror*, which he said contained no plot, 'nor the slightest resemblance to human behaviour or connection with imaginative thought' (1049); an extraordinary view. For Shipman, Tarkovsky was cultured but not necessarily intelligent enough to make a successful film.

After his death in 1986, retrospectives of Tarkovsky's films were organized in Moscow in 1987. There have been Tarkovsky film seasons (and Tarkovsky conferences) since then, not only in Moscow and St Petersburg, but in many major cities. Tarkovsky's version of Mussorgsky's opera *Boris Godunov* was staged in London in the mid-1980s and in St Petersburg in 1990.

All of Tarkovsky's films have been available on video and DVD for many years. Tarkovsky is a significant presence on the internet. There's a Tarkovsky Society (founded in 1989, at the time of the first Tarkovsky International Symposium), a Tarkovsky Prize for filmmakers, and a Museum of Andrei Tarkovsky opened in 1996, based in the house where Tarkovsky lived. Andrei Tarkovsky turns up in some unusual places. For instance, in a 1998 book on animation in cinema by Paul Wells, Tarkovsky is quoted at length on poetry.[11]

Few critics have seriously addressed the religious content of Andrei Tarkovsky's
cinema. Yet it is at the religious level that Tarkovsky wished to be understood most
clearly. The religious, ethical and emotional level is Tarkovsky's cinematic province. Critics and filmmakers have all talked about the beauty of Tarkovsky's
images. Critics gushed wildly about Tarkovsky's visuals, using similar terms as art
historians did about the paintings of Caspar David Friedrich, Vincent van Gogh and
Mark Rothko. Words such as 'tragic', 'serene' and 'magical' are frequently employed.

Alan Pavelin discussed five Tarkovsky films in his *Fifty Religious Films*, but he
found little more to say about *Nostalghia* than 'a film of exceptional beauty' (52),
calling *Stalker* 'an intensely beautiful and rewarding experience' (80) and *Andrei
Roublyov* a 'monumental work, a landmark in religious, Soviet, and world cinema'
(9).

Some critics said that Tarkovsky's films lack an awareness of an ideological
structure as do Ingmar Bergman's; Tarkovsky does not seem to consider politics or
ideology as important enough to put into his films. Although historical events such
as the Tartar attack on Vladimir in *Andrei Roublyov* or Domenico's speech in Rome
in *Nostalghia* could easily be given a political or ideological slant (as they might be
if filmed by Sergei Eisenstein), Tarkovsky declines, and, in the case of Domenico's
'demonstration', goes for the Existential and spiritual angle.

Up until Vida T. Johnson & Graham Petrie's 1994 book, there were two book-
length critical studies of Andrei Tarkovsky readily available in English, by Mark Le
Fanu and Maya Turovskaya. Both were disappointing. They do not get to grips
with the passionate artist that Tarkovsky was and is. They were too reverent.
Tarkovsky, though, does seem to inspire hero worship among the critics that admire
his work. One problem with Tarkovsky studies has been the emphasis on the
'tragic', 'suffering' artist and man, at the expense of his cinema. The same prepond-
erance of biographical criticism occurs also in filmmakers such as Pier Paolo Pasolini,
Rainer Werner Fassbinder, Roman Polanski, Orson Welles and Jean Cocteau, where
the filmmakers' life and times threatens to obscure the achievement of the films. As
Pasolini, Polanski, Welles, Fassbinder and Cocteau led such (apparently) colourful
lives, it's easy to see how irresistible biographical criticism is for the film critic.

With Tarkovsky's cinema, the biographical approach becomes hagiography – or, to use Tarkovsky's term, 'martyrology'.

Mark Le Fanu's 1987 book on Tarkovsky was rather mundane, though it did have some unusual insights into some aspects of Tarkovsky's cinema (such as its symbolism). Maya Turovskaya's 1989 book concentrated, like Le Fanu's book, on the seven feature films, but also included chapters on the cinema of poetry, the motifs, and the sense of space and time in Tarkovsky's films. Turovskaya's reading of Tarkovsky's cinema was one of the most sympathetic amongst all critics. Turovskaya had the advantage of being involved with the film scene in Moscow.

Most of the critical articles on Tarkovsky's cinema have been praiseworthy (*reviews* in magazines and newspapers may be negative, but journalists and critics don't usually bother to write an *article* or *essay* which's wholly negative, although sometimes they will to debunk something, or reply to another critic. In other words, if a critic bothers to write about Tarkovsky at all, they're usually fans).

Articles and essays on Tarkovsky's cinema include: Gilbert Adair, 1980; Peter Green, 1984; Timothy Hyman, 1976; A. Heidi Karriker (in G. Petrie, 1990); Herbert Marshall, 1976; Tony Mitchell, 1982, 1984; Ivor Montagu, 1973; Vlada Petric, 1990; Lin Yan Pin, 1991; Maria Ratschewa, 1983; Philip Strick, 1987, 1989; Olga Surkova, 1991; Tatyana Vinokuroya, 1989; and Neya Zorkaya, 1977.

It is also worth noting that many books and special numbers of journals have appeared on Tarkovsky's cinema that haven't yet been translated into English: among them, *Dossier Positif* (ed. Gilles Ciment, 1988); *Etudes cinématographiques* (ed. Michel Estève); *Cahiers du Cinéma*, (ed. Antoine de Baecque, 1989); Guy Gauthier, 1988; Balint Kovács and Akos Szilágyi, 1987; V.I. Mikhalkovitch, 1989; A.M. Sandler, 1991; Marina Tarkovskaya, 1989; Mark Zak, 1988; and *Andrej Tarkovskij*, 1987.

Vida T. Johnson & Graham Petrie's superb *The Films of Andrei Tarkovsky: A Visual Fugue* (1994) takes the now standard seven films as the centrepiece of an approach to Tarkovsky's cinema. There are also sections on Tarkovsky's use of time, space, camera, editing and motifs; on dreams, literature and art in Tarkovsky's cinema; and illuminating chapters on Tarkovsky's life, career and working methods. *The Films of Andrei Tarkovsky* is destined to be one of the key works in Tarkovsky studies for some time. It is the most detailed book yet to appear, and is augmented by the authors' many interviews with people who collaborated with Tarkovsky.

These are some of the common criticisms that are levelled against Andrei Tarkovsky and his films.

(1) *The films are obscure.* True, they can be very obscure, and also *deliberately* obscure and 'difficult'. Tarkovsky doesn't have any problem with making audiences look deep.

(2) *They are vulgar and over-bold.* True, but not vulgar or bold enough to be glaringly obvious to everybody. There are still plenty of viewers who come aware confused – if they manage to reach the end of one of his films at all.

(3) *They are élitist.* Yes, Andrei Tarkovsky's films are undoubtedly designed for minority audiences. This is clear from the stories (no dinosaurs, aliens or space battles for him), the choice of actors (the avoidance of stars), the music (no market-friendly soundtracks), the narrative techniques (lengthy takes), the subjects (a poet adrift in Italy, for instance), the allusions, and the cultural references (to Renaiss-ance painting, say).

The élitism is also reflected in the marketing of the films, and in the way in which they are consumed (consider the video and DVD packaging – by Artificial Eye and Criterion in the UK). The home entertainment audiences for Tarkovsky's films are likely to be highly educated, culturally sophisticated and affluent. They probably consume opera and classical music, visit cinemas and art galleries, read literary and current affairs magazines, and so on. Or consider the way Tarkovsky's films are presented on television (Channel Four's 1989 Tarkovsky film season emulated the auteurist approach taken by the repertory cinemas such as the National Film Theatre in London).

(4) *The films are self-indulgent.* But take many 'great' films – *Intolerance, Citizen Kane, Vertigo, City Lights, Greed* – or most 'great' filmmakers – Welles, Godard, Dreyer, Keaton, Visconti – they are also 'self-indulgent'. The same goes for 'great' artists such as Sappho, Homer, Friedrich Hölderlin, Leonardo da Vinci, William Shakespeare or Emily Dickinson. In fact, it is a way of becoming critically acclaimed: the more self-indulgent the better (think of James Joyce's endless *Ulysses*, Francesco Petrarch's over-the-top romanticism in the *Rime Sparse* or Marcel Proust's epic soap opera *Remembrance of Things Past*, to name a few examples from literature).

(5) *Tarkovsky the man was pompous, arrogant, difficult, blinkered, too*

idealistic, and a control freak. Definitely – all of those. Here was a man with a spiritual mission to fulfil. The slide (ascent?) into pomposity is inevitable (even in the humblest religious teachers, such as Lao-tzu or Buddha), or the humblest of films (such as Robert Bresson's *The Diary of a Country Priest*). Certainly Tarkovsky's views could be too idealistic – and simplistic. He could be difficult. And nobody could doubt that, when it came to making films, Tarkovsky was a classic control freak.

(6) *Tarkovsky's films are too long.* True, he could've pruned his films and still achieved everything he aimed for. *Mirror*, at 106 minutes, is beautifully judged and doesn't feel at all rushed; *Solaris*, meanwhile, at 165 minutes, may be too long for some viewers. But because he only completed seven films, every minute is precious.

Perhaps he should have tried to make a film in one continuous 90-minute shot, to really drive the critics crazy. (Alexander Sokurov, sometimes dubbed Tarkovsky's successor, did just that in *The Russian Ark*, and critics loved it).

(7) *The films are too slow.* Yes, but the slowness was inextricably enmeshed with Tarkovsky's sense of style and the sacred. Speeding up the pace of his films would be impossible without turning them into something very different.

(8) *His films are manipulative.* Yes, but all films (all artworks) are manipulations, from the obvious ones (mainstream international cinema) to the most decentred and deliberately open or vague.

(9) *Tarkovsky's characters are cyphers, one-dimensional, vehicles for his obsessions.* Yes, his characters can appear too flat, too one-sided, too schematic. That's a fault of scriptwriting – and the script is where films fail more than in any other single aspect of filmmaking.

(10) *His films are boring.* Undoubtedly, set next to *The Terminator*, *Jurassic Park 2: The Lost World*, *Star Wars 3 (Return of the Jedi)*, *Jaws IV*, *Rocky V*, *Police Academy 6: City Under Siege*, *Hallowe'en H20* (a.k.a. *Hallowe'en 7*), and *Friday the Thirteenth Part VIII: Jason Takes Manhattan*. Actually, compared to many of those films, Tarkovsky's films are not boring at all.

(11) *Tarkovsky's approaches are limited and repetitive.* True, Tarkovsky did confine himself to a very channelled approach, making the same film (or a very similar one) again and again. But he also showed he could create any cinematic effect there is, if required, from pornography to science fiction visual effects to epic historical spectacle involving a cast of thousands.

(12) *Tarkovsky and his films are humourless.* Yes, and this is a serious failing,

even in films dealing with 'serious' issues such as religious quests and moral crises. There aren't many laughs in Tarkovsky's films, that's true. Yet *Mirror* was emotionally warm and tender. And his films can have profoundly uplifting effects.

(13) *Tarkovsky was pretentious.* Not at all. Tarkovsky didn't 'pretend'. He was *doing it*, for real. He was the real thing, no question. He wasn't pretending to tackle big themes. Perhaps that's what some people dislike about Tarkovsky: such sincerity and artistic committment can be off-putting to non-artists, especially when it is not leavened by postmodern irony and self-deprecation. Filmmakers such as Orson Welles, Federico Fellini and Peter Greenaway still suffer the same attacks of being pretentious. It's one of the film critics' lazy labels.

(14) *Over-ambitious?* Yes, but beautifully so. Maybe Tarkovsky's films might have been improved had he been less ambitious. But it's just not in his artistic make-up to produce modest films.

(15) *Tarkovsky's films display a lack of humanity.* Yes and no. In the later works he wanted to strip everything away, to leave just the individual and the problem with nothing cluttering up the film or things getting in the way: a film of clarity and transparency, luminous as clear water in sunlight. This is a dream of Stendhal, Gustave Flaubert, André Gide and Samuel Beckett among writers (which can lead to an abstraction which some viewers might find obscure).

(16) *Tarkovsky's films are sexist and biased towards masculinism.* True, Tarkovsky didn't explore female characters, the feminine, identity or gender issues deeply enough for some critics. Other filmmakers (such as Pedro Almodóvar, Bette Gordon, Susan Seidelman and Krzysztof Kieslowski) went far beyond Tarkovsky in this respect. Also, as a Christian believer, and a conservative reactionary, politically, Tarkovsky was not so much scared of challenging the patriarchal socio-political establishment, as not interested in such an exploration: he was unpolitical (or apolitical) because it suited his spiritual investigations (although the context in which he produced his films was highly politicized, with politics often thrust into the foreground).

Among American filmmakers of his generation there are few comparisons to make with Andrei Tarkovsky. Consider Brian de Palma, John Carpenter, Robert Zemeckis, George Lucas, John Landis and Alan Pakula: Tarkovsky seems to be a world away from these filmmakers. Even American directors such as Francis Coppola, Philip Kaufman, Terence Malick, Peter Bogdanovitch, Robert Altman and Martin Scorsese, whose films sometimes share some similar qualities with Tarkovsky's, are actually a world away from Tarkovsky's cinema.

One could look at the alienation of modern man in contemporary society in, say, Francis Coppola's *The Conversation* (Gene Hackman wandering about in a raincoat on his own is a bit of a Tarkovskyan figure) or Terence Malick's *Badlands*, but it's not really the same cinematic field. On the other hand, one could see the exploration of the darkness at the heart of Western culture in *The Godfather* as far superior in its way than, say, *Nostalghia*. But what American cinema seldom does is tackle the same issues as Tarkovsky – spiritual quests and Existential alienation – or approach cinema in the same poetic fashion.

Andrei Tarkovsky's fellow Moscow student (and co-writer of *Andrei Roublyov, Ivan's Childhood* and *The Steamroller and the Violin*) – Andrei Konchalovsky – went to the United States to make Hollywood entertainment feature films, such as the odd and superficial *Maria's Lovers* (1983), which had a heavyweight cast (Robert Mitchum, John Savage, Natassja Kinski) but was a puerile, sexist story. 1985's *Runaway Train* was an absolutely stunning thriller, from an idea by Akira Kurosawa. Konchalovsky also made *Tango & Cash* (1989, USA), a violent, formulaic dumb but fun cop buddy movie starring Kurt Russell and Sylvester Stallone. Hard to believe, looking at *Tango & Cash*, that Konchalovsky had worked with Tarkovsky on *Andrei Roublyov* and *Ivan's Childhood*.

In 1997, Konchalovsky directed a wonderful, all-star version of Homer's *Odyssey* for NBC, with Armand Assante as Ulysses, Greta Scacchi as his wife Penelope, and stars such as Eric Roberts and Geraldine Page. Tarkovsky's regular composer, Eduard Artemiev, turned in a powerful score, blending haunting Russian folk melodies and instrumentation with the more conventional Hollywood symphony orchestra. *The Odyssey*, clearly aimed at the international (not necessarily US) market, reworked the subject matter of the Biblical and sword-and-sandal epics of the 1950s and 1960s, with heroes, gods, monsters, adventures, romances and epic voyages.

One wonders what Tarkovsky would have made of his friend's helming of a conventional, starry, big budget movie, which employed many visual effects sequences, such as computer generated imagery, morphing, model shots, mattes, explosions, and the like. Perhaps Tarkovsky would have secretly enjoyed this kind of Hollywood-style, large-scale filmmaking (one recalls how Tarkovsky could talk at length of films like *The Terminator*). One wonders, too, what Tarkovsky might have done with computer generated imagery and digital technology, in which the potential for what can be put on screen is changed, if not actually increased (a film such as Vincent Ward's *What Dream May Come* [1998], a fantasy journey through heaven and hell with many Tarkovskyan moments, was visualized largely through CGI). Tarkovsky may well have employed such visual effects, had he lived longer to be able to use them (he loved to use cinematic tricks and machines), but very likely sparingly. In his writings, Tarkovsky expressed distrust of filmic tricks in portraying dreams, memories and fantasies (ST, 30), even though in his films he used *loads* of trick devices.

Alexander Kaidanovsky, star of *Stalker* (who died in 1995) went on to become a writer and director, producing films such as *Jonah, or the Artist At Work* (1984), *The Visitor* (1988), *Maestro* (1993), *A Simple Death* (1987), starring the actress who played his wife in *Stalker* (Alisa Freindlikh), and *The Kerosene Seller's Wife* (1988). Kaidanovsky acted in *At Home Among Strangers* (1974), *Gold River* (1976), *Povorot* (1978), *El Aliento del Diablo* (1993) and *Magic Hunter* (1994).

Tarkovsky wasn't a fan of the action or adventure type of movie, embodied in American cinema. Rather, Tarkovsky wanted to avoid outward movement, and explore inner worlds (ST, 204). Tarkovsky does seem to be the polar opposite of an action film director, his conception of the European art film being at odds with films like *Titanic*, *Jurassic Park*, *Pirates of the Carribean*, *Spider-man* or *Men In Black*. There were times, though, when Tarkovsky could have benefited from a greatly increased budget: on *The Sacrifice*, for example, for the apocalyptic scene of the crowd milling around in the courtyard, when there weren't enough extras contracted for the scene, and the crowd looks thin on the ground (literally). And multiple cameras would have helped with the climactic single take of the burning house, so that, if one failed, another might have got the shot. (Multiple cameras have been commonplace on Hollywood sets for decades – especially with a once-only take, like the burning of Atlanta in *Gone With the Wind*).

Orson Welles, D.W. Griffith, Sam Peckinpah, Howard Hawks, Nicholas Ray, Elia Kazan – Tarkovsky is like few American filmmakers. Tarkovsky was compared with Steven Spielberg earlier, as an example of apparent opposites. It could be said that Spielberg missed the experience of childhood (deemed his province, in films such as *E.T.* and *Empire of the Sun*), while Tarkovsky got very close – to the mystery, sensuality and violence and inexplicable nature of it (in, for example, *Mirror* a n d *Ivan's Childhood*). Actually, Spielberg is brilliant at depicting childhood and child-like states; he's just very different from Tarkovsky (*Empire of the Sun* and *E.T.*, for instance, are phenomenal films of childhood).

Tarkovsky on Spielberg:

> a director like Spielberg has an enormous audience and earns enormous sums and everybody is happy about that, but he is no artist and his films are not art. If I made films like him – and I don't believe I can – I would die from sheer terror. Art is as a mountain: there is a peak and surrounding it there are foothills. What exists at the summit cannot by definition be understood by everyone.

The links between Tarkovsky and the American *avant garde* too are tenuous (with, for instance, Stan Brakhage, Michael Snow and Maya Deren), though Brakhage's insistence on cinema's poetics and his lyrical films of birth and motherhood chime with the spirit of *Mirror*. In terms of production cycles, Tarkovsky is somewhat like Stanley Kubrick and Robert Bresson – making a meticulously planned film every few years. (Though Kubrick was in a very different economic place from Tarkovsky: Kubrick was generously supported by Warner Bros. from the early 1970s onwards, and had an extraordinary amount of freedom in choosing subjects and making films. Kubrick's problem was in finding material for films that he really wanted to produce and direct. He would search for years trying to find something with all the right elements. Tarkovsky, meanwhile, struggled with each individual project, and wasn't backed by a big corporation like Warners).

Like Erich von Stroheim (on *Greed*), Michael Cimino (on *Heaven's Gate*) and Jacques Tati (on *Playtime*), Tarkovsky was sometimes allowed to go over budget, to film as much as he liked (in general), sheltered by the Soviet film system. On *Nostalghia*, for example, made outside the Soviet industry, Tarkovsky was given 150,000 metres of film stock and $1.5 million (the shooting ratio on an average 35mm feature film might be 6:1. A 90 minute film uses 8,100 feet of film, so, shooting at a ratio of 6:1, 50,000 feet of stock would be required. So the 450,000+

feet Tarkovsky had for *Nostalghia* was a more generous shooting ratio. Some directors, of course, still shoot more than that).

Like certain other *auteurs* (such as Woody Allen, Federico Fellini and Bernardo Bertolucci), Tarkovsky had a knack of getting pretty much what he wanted from his film deals. Or, if not exactly what he desired, then a lot more production help and artistic control than many film directors. The scale of *Andrei Roublyov*, for example, is amazingly large for a second feature (although it's not uncommon for youngish directors to be given the reins of a big project, which is often really controlled by producers and studios). Like Federico Fellini and Ingmar Bergman, Tarkovsky was allowed to pursue his very autobiographical projects with a relatively large amount of investment and resources (Bergman worked with far less money than Fellini, but he was still able to be fairly prolific, at least compared to his contemporaries). The budgets Tarkovsky was given for his films were small by general Hollywood standards: there was no $31 million anti-war extravaganza (*Apocalypse Now*) for him, and no months spent in the Italian countryside making a six-hour Marxist history of Italy (Bernardo Bertolucci's *1900*).

What is certain is that Andrei Tarkovsky joins the ranks of the Soviet and Russian greats: Alexander Dovzhenko, Vsevolod Pudovkin, Dziga Vertov, Sergei Eisenstein and Lev Kuleshov. Tarkovsky is probably now the most celebrated postwar Soviet/ Russian filmmaker (though not the most representative), rising above Grigory Chukrai, Andrei Konchalovsky, Mikhail Kalatozov, Sergei Parad-janov, Grigory Kozintsev, Emil Lotianu, Elem Klimov, Alexander Sokurov and even Sergei Bondarchuk. But only time will tell if Andrei Tarkovsky finally enters the hallowed realm of his passionately admired cinematic heroes and gurus: Bergman, Bresson, Buñuel, Vigo, Mizoguchi, Antonioni and Kurosawa.

No one can follow Andrei Tarkovsky (or has yet). He's a one-off, like Walerian Borowczyk or Jan Svankmajer. You can see where he came from, you can explore his influences, his education, his background, his alliances and collaborations, but he's a unique voice in cinema. Irreplaceable.

But there are some filmmakers who've taken up *some* of his ideas, devices and approaches to cinema (though not so often his themes). Vincent Ward, Alexander Sokurov, Gilles Mackinnon, Krzysztof Kieslowski and the Quay brothers have acknowledged Tarkovsky's influence on their own filmmaking. Influence is one thing (a diffuse, vague term), but only a few filmmakers have deliberately and directly evoked Tarkovsky's style or motifs or ideas in their films.

Tarkovsky's images are intensely memorable – the fires, the dripping water, the streams – all those things that have, from the Eighties onwards, been used in pop videos and self-consciously 'stylish' films such as *Blade Runner* (Ridley Scott, 1982, USA) and *Angel Heart* (Alan Parker, 1987, USA). One can see Andrei Tarkovsky's influence in Derek Jarman's films (he admired *Mirror*). Jarman's *The Tempest* (1980, GB) and *Edward II* (1991, GB) use lengthy takes, and Tarkovskyan fire and water. Neil Jordan acknowledged Tarkovsky's influence.[1]

Tarkovskyan imagery can also be seen in David Lynch's *Blue Velvet* (1986, USA), which is like Tarkovsky on acid; in Luc Besson, in his *Stalker*-like *The Last Battle* (1983, France), with its black-and-white deteriorated interiors and skies raining fish; in Paul Shrader's remake of *Cat People* (1982, USA); and in Peter Greenaway's films – the recurring motifs, the sense of surface, the painterly allusions, the classical music and the esoteric, metaphysical speculations. Greenaway is Tarkovsky made mathematical, like J.S. Bach's music with the passion coldly extracted. The end of Greenaway's *The Belly of an Architect* (1987, GB), where the protagonist throws himself off the 'wedding cake' in Rome (the Vittorio Emanuele II Monument) repeats Domenico's suicide in *Nostalghia* on another landmark of Rome, Michelangelo's Marcus Aurelius statue. (The similarities between *The Belly of an Architect* (1987) and *The Sacrifice* include the concentration on a middle-aged intellectual going through a crisis; the threat of death; the long take; a contemporary European setting; and theatricality.)[2]

The Zagreb video artists Aleksandar Marks and Vladimir Jutrisa cited Tarkovsky as an influence (as well as Bresson, Straub and Dreyer). They referred to the sequence in *Nostalghia* where Andrei carries the candle over the pool in their own *Taking On a Name* (1987), where a woman stands in the sea holding out her arms with flames in her palms, waiting for the sunrise.

Among Russian/ Soviet filmmakers, Tarkovsky's influence was seen in Sergei Paradjanov, Konstantin Lopushanksy's *A Dead Man's Letters* and *A Museum Visitor*, Ivan Dykhovichny's *Black Monk*, and Alexander Kaidanovsky's *The Kerosene Seller's Wife*. After Tarkovsky's death, a number of Russian film directors were hailed as 'the new Tarkovsky'. One of these was Alexander Sokurov, whose films included *Mother and Son* (1997), *Anœsthesia Dolorosa* and *The Russian Ark* (2001). The very Tarkovskyan film *Mother and Son* concerned a man caring for his old mother who's dying; as far as 'action' goes, *Mother and Son* features only the man carrying his mother around country tracks, or sitting on a bench, or tending her in a *dacha*. *Mother and Son*'s really a lyrical evocation of landscape, a pantheistic hymn to nature, a series of mainly static, glowing images of trees, fields, hills, clouds (the shot of a field of grass blowing in the breeze recalls the beginning of *Mirror*), accompanied by the sound of wind, rain, thunder and birds (some of the shots are treated with filters, distorting devices and superimpositions).

Sokurov made a film about Tarkovsky – *Moscow Elegy* (1987; it was blocked by the Moscow House of Cinema), which 'seemed over-awed by its subject'.[3] Paul Shrader much admired Sokurov; Sokurov said that he, Shrader and Tarkovsky were each like 'one step in the staircase' (ibid.). 'Tarkovsky is in the line of Russian artists who see their vocation as like that of the Biblical prophets'.[4]

At the end of Wim Wenders' *Wings of Desire* (1987), a film which arthouse buffs rave about, Tarkovsky receives a dedication, which runs something along the lines of: 'to all the angels, but especially to the departed angels Yasujiro, François and Andrej', which presumably refers to Ozu, Truffaut and Tarkovsky, who had all died in the years before 1987. There is a reference to Tarkovsky's *Stalker*'s Zone in Chris Marker's astonishing poetic travelogue, *Sans Soleil* (1982).

But while Wim Wenders and Chris Marker tipped their hat to Tarkovsky, a filmmaker like Vincent Ward has consciously used Tarkovsky's influence – in films such as *What Dreams May Come* (1998) and *The Navigator* (1988). It was no surprise, as the New Zealand director's favourite film was *Andrei Roublyov*. (Peter Jackson, director of *The Lord of the Rings*, may have eclipsed Ward – and Jane Campion and Lee Tamahori too – as important Kiwi directors, but Ward is infinitely more interesting than Jackson).

In *What Dreams May Come* (1998, US), Robin Williams journeys through the underworld to rescue his lover, aided by Max von Sydow as The Tracker (recalling the Stalker). *What Dreams May Come* was Hollywood fantasy at its grandest, and its visuals were as extraordinary as anything in Tarkovsky's cinema. The story and theme of *What Dreams May Come* – about the redemptive power of love – was also distinctly Tarkovskyan in flavour, but the handling was too sentimental and cloying. That aspect of *What Dreams May Come* turned it into another New Man touchy-feely weepie film (which was Robin Williams' speciality: *Hook* (1991), *Awakenings* (1990), *The Fisher King* (1991) and *Mrs Doubtfire* (1993).)

What Dreams May Come is now regarded as a failure (actually, it grossed $55.4 million theatrically in the States). But because it cost $80 million it's seen as a flop (although it wasn't as a big a turkey as many other movies – *Battlefield Earth*, *Speed 2* and *Lara Croft* spring to mind as frighteningly bad). As a cinematic vision, though, *What Dreams May Come* is staggering (the brilliant Eugenio Zanetti was production designer, Eduard Serra was cinematographer, costumes were by Yvonne Blake, vfx supervisor was Ellen Somers, with art direction by Jim Dultz, Joshua Rosen, Tomas Voth and Christian Wintter).

It's the same with Hollywood films like *Battlefield Earth* (Roger Christian, 2000) and *Batman and Robin* (Joel Schumacher, 1997). No one would pretend that *Battlefield Earth* was a satisfying movie on almost every level, but the visual fx and miniature work (by Louis Craig and Marcel Pierre Dussol) was awesome. And *Batman and Robin* is often cursed for seriously damaging Warners' *Batman* franchise, but I reckon the vision of a Gothic futuristic city in *Batman and Robin* is superior to any of its competitors, including 'classics' like *Blade Runner*, *The Fifth Element*, *Minority Report*, *A.I.* or *Star Wars* (production designer on the third *Bat*-sequel was Barbara Ling, Stephen Goldblatt was DP, wardrobe by Ingrid Ferrin and

Robert Turturice, art director was Geoff Hubbard, and vfx supervisor was John Dykstra, one of the top two or three vfx supervisors in Hollywood).

What Dreams May Come evoked a fairy tale world in brilliant colours, where everything was made of squishy oil paint, an electronic *Wizard of Oz* cinemascape done up in Post-Impressionist washes of oil. Max von Sydow's Tracker recalled the Stalker in Tarkovsky's *Stalker*. The casting of Max von Sydow inevitably suggested Ingmar Bergman (as did the spiritual quest of the film) – Bergman was another of Ward's favourite directors. Andrei Tarkovsky was evoked in another scene, in which the lovers' dream home (now dilapidated) is located in an upside-down cathedral (recalling the image in Tarkovsky's *Nostalghia* of a Russian *dacha* in a ruined Italian cathedral).

What Dreams May Come out-did Tarkovsky when it came to drawing inspiration from the history of painting. No other recent Hollywood film has been so stuffed with references to painters: John Martin's extraordinary Romantic visions of heaven and hell with their epic sense of scale; the Post-Impressionists (such as Claude Monet and Vincent van Gogh – the latter is one of Tarkovsky's favourites); the American Hudson River school of painters (such as Thomas Cole and Albert Bierstadt); Théodore Géricault's *Raft of the Medusa*; Gustave Doré's illustrations to Dante's *Divine Comedy* (rather than Sandro Botticelli's; Doré was an inspiration for many filmmakers); Hieronymous Bosch; Francisco di Goya; and William Blake.

As well as the history of painting, and European architecture, *What Dreams May Come* also drew, like Tarkovsky's films, on Classical mythology, and the history of literature: it contained conscious evocations of Homer (*The Odyssey*), Dante's *Divine Comedy*, John Milton's *Paradise Lost*, and Orpheus's descent into the Underworld to rescue Eurydice.

And Vincent Ward seemed to be as obsessive about his visuals as Tarkovsky: the visual fx team remember Ward coming to them with notebooks full of just skies, and Ward talking about exactly what kind of sky he wanted in the background of a scene.[1]

Ward's *The Navigator, a Mediæval Odyssey* (1988) is an absolute gem of a movie. Shot in New Zealand, set in mediæval Britain (in Cumbria), during the Black Plague of 1348, *The Navigator* concerns a visionary boy in a Northern mining village who has a dream which shows that the village might be saved from the plague by undertaking an odyssey through a chasm in the Earth, to the other side, to a city of light, and planting a new cross on the spire of the cathedral.

But *The Navigator* is also Ward's *hommage* to *Andrei Roublyov*, and contains many affinities with Tarkovsky's epic – the earthy, snowy *mise-en-scène*, the detailed evocation of a rough, peasant Middle Ages (and a similar period of the Middle Ages), the visionary quest, and a shaman at the heart of it (and the brilliant performance by Hamish McFarlane recalls Nikolai Burlyaev in both *Ivan's Childhood* and *Andrei Roublyov*).

As in Vincent Ward's other work, there are plenty of religious elements in *The Navigator*. Ward built on the mediæval worlds of directors such as Ingmar Bergman (*The Seventh Seal* and *The Virgin Spring*) and Tarkovsky: snowy, rainy, muddy, grimy, harsh. Ward also developed the spiritual quests of those *auteurs*, the search for religious meaning in the contemporary, Godless age of the atom bomb. In Tarkovsky's *The Sacrifice*, made two years before *The Navigator*, a man undergoes a kind of spiritual transformation and death as a bargain with God in order to avert nuclear war. In *The Navigator*, a group of men leave on a journey to save their village from the Black Plague (led by a visionary youth, recalling the shamanic Stalker in Tarkovsky's 1979 film, a role later reprised in Ward's *What Dreams May Come*). Like Tarkovsky, Ward makes many references to mediæval religion in his work; like Tarkovsky, Ward also dips in and out of black-and-white in *The Navigator*; and there are further Tarkovskyan moments in *The Navigator*: the prophecies, the crazy quest, the church, the horse, fire, water, etc.

The Navigator is a curious hybrid. Like other English-speaking film cultures (such as the UK and Oz), Hollywood cinema looms large over New Zealand filmmaking. But although it has a Hollywood-style narrative, it is set in England, but made in New Zealand, with a largely Kiwi cast and crew. And it just happens to be a film, if not made along Tarkovskyan lines, which owes a huge debt to Tarkovsky (and Ingmar Bergman).

Another director who has employed some of the methods of Andrei Tarkovsky is Polish director Krzysztof Kieslowski, who died in 1996. Kieslowski was best known for his marvellous *Dekalog* series of TV films (1988), and his *Three Colours* trilogy of 1993-94. Kieslowski greatly admired Tarkovsky, calling him one of the 'greatest directors of recent years', who hadn't lost his ability to create miracles. 'Unfortunately, he died,' Kieslowski added; 'Probably because he couldn't live any more. That's usually why people die. One can say it's cancer or a heart attack or that the person falls under a car, but really people usually die because they can't go living' (1993, 33-34).

Krzysztof Kieslowski took up the way Tarkovsky used hyper-situated objects and motifs, things that went beyond dialogue to express how characters are feeling. Like Tarkovsky, Kieslowski liked to stretch himself, to see how much of a story he could communicate visually or aurally, without resorting to having characters explain or narrate what's going on. Both Kieslowski and Tarkovsky liked to fill their films with long stretches where nothing much happens.

Another link between the two film directors is a penchant for highly selective sound effects, which carry a good deal of the dramatic force of their films. Another link was a self-conscious cultivation of ambiguity, prevalent in much of European art cinema, a deliberate withholding of an over-arching, God-like point-of-view.

The solitary, outsider figures in Kieslowski's films were another link with Tark-ovsky's cinema: both *auteurs* made films about people cast adrift from their culture and society, existing apart from others. The lead characters in *The Double Life of Véronique* (1991), the *Dekalog* series or the *Three Colours* trilogy could wander into a Tarkovsky film and not be too out of place (however, Kieslowski had a penchant for casting very beautiful young European actresses in the lead, such as Juliette Binoche or Irène Jacob, whereas Tarkovsky generally cast middle-aged male actors, and never made a movie with one of those arthouse sirens).

The rather desolate, cold, wintry *mise-en-scène* of Kieslowski's Warsaw in the *Dekalog* films is a similar mind-space to Tarkovsky's Rome in *Nostalghia* or Moscow in *Mirror* (in both filmmakers it always seems to be snowy Winter or rain-swept Autumn, even when it's Summer or Spring). And Binoche in *Three Colours: Blue* or Jacob in *The Double Life of Véronique* may be living in a beautiful city like Paris, but it's a city of disaffected, disconnected people, with the famous vistas consigned to the edges of the frame.

The *spiritual* aspect of Krzysztof Kieslowski's cinema is perhaps the one really important aspect that he developed from Andrei Tarkovsky's art. As well as being loners, Kieslowski's characters are on a spiritual quest; they're all looking for something, and it's not bourgeois romance, or lots of money, or self-esteem, but something they can't define. And they're doomed to fail, like Tarkovsky's protagonists, from the start.

Both Kieslowski and Tarkovsky appeared to make downbeat, slow-moving films, but both were actually optimistic and life-affirming. The *Three Colours* trilogy, for instance, climaxes with an uplifting, life-affirming and miraculous occurrence, when all of the major characters survive a catastrophe at sea. And Tarkovsky would close his films with quiet but deeply-felt spiritual affirmations. The ambiguity was still in place, and the characters probably wouldn't 'live happily ever after', but there was also a positive assertion of spirituality. Tarkovsky was perhaps more inclined than most art film directors to be didactic, and to see himself as a kind of leader or teacher in ethical or religious matters. Kieslowski was highly suspicious, even afraid, of people who claimed to show you the way – teachers, politicians, priests. 'Because really – and I'm deeply convinced of this, I firmly believe it – nobody really knows, with a few exceptions' (1993, 36).

22 : 8   THEO ANGELOPOULOS AND ANDREI TARKOVSKY

The Greek master of European art cinema, Theo Angelopoulos, is another link with Andrei Tarkovsky. Like Tarkovsky, Angelopoulos is a favourite among highly educated cinema audiences, though much less known outside Greece (or Europe) or those intellectual film circles. Again, Angelopoulos explores some of the same psychological, social and spiritual territory as Tarkovsky – a cinema of displacement, migration, exile, history, and spiritual anxiety. (Though Angelopoulos has much more to say than Tarkovsky about the contestation of national and cultural borders, about the agony of exile, about the effects of politics on people's lives).

Angelopoulos's films include *The Travelling Players* (1975), *Alexander the Great*

(1980), *Landscape In the Mist* (1988), and *Ulysses's Gaze* (a.k.a. *The Gaze of Ulysses*, 1995). In some ways, Angelopoulos has taken Tarkovsky's cinema and developed it more than any other director. (Another connection is screenwriter Tonino Guerra, co-writer of *Nostalghia*, who co-wrote *Landscape In the Mist* with Angelopoulos and Thanassis Valtinos, and *Ulysses' Gaze* with Angelopoulos, Giorgio Silvagni and Petros Markaris).

One of the obvious affinities between Theo Angelopoulos and Andrei Tarkovsky is the use of the long take. This is no minor stylistic device: it is the foundation of the whole of Angelopoulos's cinematic style – even more than with Tarkovsky. While Tarkovsky constructed scenes around long takes many times, Angelopoulos employs the device far more than Tarkovsky. And, it has to be said, some of Angelopoulos's sequence shots are even more impressive than Tarkovsky's (and Tarkovsky's are about the best in contemporary cinema).

Angelopoulos builds whole films around long, stately takes that sometimes go beyond even earlier masters, such as Orson Welles or Alfred Hitchcock. One of Angelopoulos's regular techniques is to withhold information, beats, actions or characters until quite a way into a long take. A Tarkovsky long take, meanwhile, usually gives most of the information the audience requires early on, often from the start of the shot. In other words, a long take in a Tarkovsky film is a lengthy depiction of a single action or image within a single space: Gorchakov carrying the candle in *Nostalghia*, for instance, or the Stalker's dream. In Angelopoulos's films, meanwhile, a long take will begin with a single character in a room or on a road, walking, and will move onto an encounter with somebody, which's really a second scene. But that won't be the end of the sequence shot: the camera will still be tracking, zooming, panning, past walls, or windows, say, or following an actor walking, and a street procession will go by, or a crowd of people will emerge from a hotel. Tarkovsky talked about time filling the space of a shot, and Angelopoulos makes that into magnificently realized cinema. It's acutely self-conscious, it unfolds in 'real time', it's slow-moving. And it's showy too (organizing and rehearsing the actors, props, cars, entrances, exits, lighting cues, and extras in an Angelopoulos shot must take hours, days, weeks – there's no quick and easy way of shooting the kind of very long takes Angelopoulos prefers).

And Angelopoulos sometimes outdoes Tarkovsky in evoking a sombre, melancholy mood, where it's always raining, and dusk, where streets are always empty of life, where characters wander about listlessly. In Angelopoulos's vision, the rich history of Greece is hardly ever mentioned; instead, it's a Greece of gas stations and lonely roads, cheap hotels and train stations. Tarkovsky romanticized Italy in *Nostalghia* far more than Angelopoulos romanticizes Greece in *Landscape In the Mist*, for instance. A Hollywood studio financing a film set in Greece and shot by Theodore Angelopoulos would probably want to fire the director when they saw the rushes: no sunshine, no beaches, no islands shimmering in the heat, no blue skies, no rocky countryside, no Greek temples, no whitewashed Greek monasteries, and no locals sitting outside cafés under olive trees. On the other hand, Tarkovsky at least turns in one or two classic images of Italy (hilltop villages, mountains, churches, a long shot of Rome, the Campidoglio square). Tarkovsky's romanticism (and optimism) prevents his films from falling into the downbeat pessimism of some European art cinema.

Notes

INTRODUCTION

0 : 1   LIFE

1. H. Marshall, in A. Lawton, 1982, 179.
2. In A. Lawton, 1992, 338.

0 : 2   THE TARKOVSKY INDUSTRY

1. In V. Johnson, 1994b, 45-46.
2. Julie Delphy said that '[i]t took me years to watch a whole Tarkovsky movie because I found them hard to follow. Then, when I was finally able to watch one, I was blown away, because it's wonderful and deep, it makes you think as much as any book. It transports you somewhere else' (M. Figgis, 278).

0 : 3   THIS BOOK

1. Luis Buñuel, Tarkovsky enthused in *Sculpting In Time*, was a poet of anti-conformism, an uncompromising, furious protest which was expressed in the 'sensuous texture' of his films (ST, 51). Buñuel's approach to cinema wasn't political, or conscious, or cerebral, Tarkovsky maintained, but emotional and poetic. And that, combined with the sensuality of his films, made his works very appealing for Tarkovsky.
2 G. Deleuze, 1989, 68.
3. C. Paglia, "Interview", in K. French, 42.
4. See H. Cixous, *The Newly Born Woman*, Manchester University Press, Manchester, 1986.
5. L. Mulvey, 1989, 25-26.
6. In other words, Tarkovsky is valued precisely because his cinema appears to be the opposite of (or a refreshing alternative to) mainstream filmed entertainment: it employs non-Hollywood actors; it has a lack of banal dialogue and didactic (Hollywood) music; it does not seem to compromise; does not pander to or patronize audiences; it doesn't use gratuitous violence or sensation; it's not formulaic; it's not overblown by massive budgets, and so on.
7. I. Bergman, in J. Graffy, 18.
8. I. Bergman, in D. Robinson.

PART ONE : THE ARTIST

ONE : THE POETRY OF CINEMA

1 : 2   EMOTION AND SPECTACLE: VISCERAL CINEMA

1. In *The New Decade*, Whitney Museum of Art, New York, NY, 1955, 36.

2. C. Hussey, *The Picturesque*, Putnam's, New York, NY, 1927.

3. E. Burke, in *The Philosophy of Edmund Burke*, University of Michigan Press, Ann Arbor, MI, 1967, 256.

I : 3   THE POETICS OF CINEMA

I. R. Durgnat, 238

2. J. Cocteau, in *Mid-Century French Poets*, ed. W. Fowlie, Grove Press, New York, NY, 1955, 121.

3. S. Rohdie, 1995, 52.

4. M. Antonioni, 1986, xiii.

5. J. Godard, 1986, 234.

6. T. Mitchell, 1984, 56.

I : 4   ANDREI TARKOVSKY AS POET

I. In N. Sinyard, 1992, 47.

2. B. Amengual: "Andrei Tarkovski après sept films", in M. Estève, 1983.

3. In 1947, quoted in H. Chipp, 549,

4. G. Bataille, *Literature and Evil*, tr. A. Hamilton, Calder, London, 1973, 65.

5. P.P. Pasolini, in V. Fantuzzi, "La visione religioso", in F. Di Giammatteo, ed. *Lo scandalo Pasolini Bianco e Nero*, 37, I, Jan, 1976.

I : 5   ANDREI TARKOVSKY AND THE HISTORY OF POETRY

I. M. Turovskaya, 15.

2. A. Pushkin, in D. Obolensky, 108.

3. R.M. Rilke, *Duino Elegies*, 151.

4. R.M. Rilke, 1963, 34-35.

I : 6   *HAIKU*

I. M. Buson & M. Basho in L. Stryk, ed., *The Penguin Book of Zen Poetry*, Penguin, London, 1981, 89, 96.

TWO : RELIGION AND CINEMA

I. I. Bergman, 1986, 167.

2 : I   SACRED CINEMA

I. In C. Greenberg, 174.

2. M. Eliade, 1984, 168.

3. J. Godard, 1986, 187.

4. J. Leyda, 347.

2 : 2   LESS IS MORE: THE METAPHYSICS OF EMPTINESS

I. P. Wollen, 91.
2. J. Ferguson, 133.
3. H. Rosenberg, *Barnett Newman*, Abrams, New York, NY, 1978/ 1994, 59.
4. M. Allott, 128, 312.
5. E. Conze, 163.
6. A. Reinhardt, 82
7. *Art International*, magazine, Dec, 1967, 18.
8. E. de Antonio, 163.

2 : 3   THE PHILOSOPHY OF BEING

I. A. Watts, *Tao: The Watercourse Way*, Cape, London, 1976, 96.

2 : 4   TIME AND TIMELESSNESS

I. M. Heidegger, *On Time and Being*, Harper & Row, New York, NY, 1972, 2-5.

2 : 5   INVESTIGATING THE TRANSCENDENT

I. L. Durrell, *Quinx*, Faber, London, 1985, 53.

2 : 6   CINEMA OF LIGHT

I. From the *Pampattic Cittar*, early 15th century, in K. Zvlebil, 117.

2 : 7   EPIPHANY AND TRANSCENDENCE

I. J. Campbell, 1988a, 220
2. J. Campbell, 1988b, 40.
3. R. Barthes, *Image Music Text*, 39.

2 : 8   THE MODERN RELIGIOUS FILM

I. On Pier Paolo Pasolini, see S. Rohdie, 1995; M. Mancini, 1982; R. Rinaldi, 1982; J. Duflot, 1983; A. Panicali & S. Sestini, eds., *Pier Paolo Pasolini*, Nuovo Salani, Florence, 1982; P. Willemen, ed., *Pier Paolo Pasolini*, British Film Institute, London, 1977; B. Schwartz, *Pasolini: Requiem*, Pantheon Books, New York, NY, 1992; S. Snyder, *Pier Paolo Pasolini*, Twayne, Boston, MA, 1980.

By Pasolini: *Entretiens avec Pier Paolo Pasolini*, Belfond, Paris, 1970; *Con Pier Paolo Pasolini*, ed. E Magrelli, Bulzoni, Rome, 1977; *Il dialogo, il potere, la morte: la critica e Pasolini*, ed. L. Martellini, Cappelli, Bologna, 1979; *Empirismo eretico*, Garzanti, Milan, 1972.

2 : 9   HORROR, FANTASY AND SCIENCE FICTION CINEMA

I. A. Billson, in S. Jaworzyn, ed. *Shock: The Essential Guide to Exploitation Cinema*, Titan Books, London, 1996, 45f.

Andrei Tarkovsky   *5 5 7*

2 : 11   HYSTERIA AND MYSTICISM: ANDREI TARKOVSKY AND INGMAR BERGMAN

1. J.-L. Godard, in *Godard On Godard*, 76.
2. I. Bergman, 1994, 249.
3. P. Redgrove & P. Shuttle, *Alchemy For Women*, Rider, London, 1995, 81.
4. Lloyd Rose, in L. Giannetti, 404.
5. I. Bergman, 1994, 249.
6. L. Irigaray, *Speculum*, 20.
7. C. Duchen, ed. *French Connections*, Hutchinson, London, 1987, 85.
8. In E. Marks, 1981, 247.
9. T. Moi, 1985, 136.
10. E. Grosz, "Lesbian fetishism?", *Differences*, 3, 2, 1991.

THREE : ANDREI TARKOVSKY AND THE RELIGIOUS FILM

1. Films which can be seen as allegorical Christian stories include *Cool Hand Luke* (1967), *The Shawshank Redemption* (1995), *Superman* (1978), *One Flew Over the Cuckoo's Nest* (175), *The Good, the Bad and the Ugly* (1966), *Pale Rider* (1985), *Cries and Whispers* (1973), *The Elephant Man* (1980), *The Hunchback of Notre Dame* (1939, 1996), *Spartacus* (1960), *Serpico* (1973), *The Fugitive* (1947), *Strange Cargo* (1940), *The Face* (1958), *The Fisher King* (1991), *The Lion King* (1994), *RoboCop* (1987), *Whistle Down the Wind* (1961) and *E.T.* (1982).
2. G. Forshey, 46. 'When Hollywood does Christ,' wrote film critic David Thomson 'whether it's Jeffrey Hunter or Max von Sydow or Willem Dafoe, the result is not just ridiculous and embarrassing and tedious and about as atmospheric as a paper cup. It is also the complete expurgation, elimination and eradication of any hint of the spirit.' (1998)
3. T. Aitken. "The Greatest Story – Never Told", *The Tablet*, Dec 23, 1995.
4. B. Babington, 104.
5. B. Babington, 5.
6. B. Babington, 16.
7. D. Cook, 1996, 470.
8. M. Wood, *America in the Movies*, Basic Books, New York, NY, 1975.
9. *The Passion of the Christ* did exceptionally at the global box office, considering its subject matter and treatment: it was the fifth top film in 2004, ahead of blockbusters like *Troy, The Day After Tomorrow, I, Robot, Shark Tale* and *Van Helsing*.
10. Sequels swiftly followed: *Hercules Unchained* (1959), *Ulysses vs. the Son of Hercules* (1961), *Hercules, Samson and Ulysess* (1965), *The Challenge of the Giant* (1965), *Hercules in the Haunted World* (1961), *Hercules Against Rome* (1960), *Hercules and the Conquest of Atlantis* (1961), *The Loves of Hercules* (1960), *Hercules of the Desert* (1960), *Hercules Against the Mongols* (1960), *Hercules Against the Barbarians* (1964), *Hercules Against the Sons of the Sun* (1964), *Hercules and the Black Pirate* (1962), *Hercules and the Masked Rider* (1963), *Hercules and the Captive Women* (1963), *Hercules Against the Moon Men* (1964), and *Hercules in New York* (1970), which starred a young Arnold Schwarzenegger.
Most of the *Hercules* muscleman films were made in Italy between 1959 and

1965. Further *Hercules* films were made in the 1980s (*Hercules*, 1983, and *Hercules II*, 1985), starring Lou Ferrigno, and then a group of *Hercules* TV films in 1994 (*Hercules and the Lost Kingdom, Hercules and the Amazon Women, Hercules and the Circle of Fire, Hercules in the Underworld* and *Hercules and the Maze of the Minotaur*), the spin-off TV series *Hercules*, another spin-off, *Xena: Warrior Princess* and another, *Young Hercules*, and a TV series. Then Disney made a big budget animation of *Hercules* in 1997, which led to a spin-off TV cartoon series. Another live action *Hercules* appeared on TV in the early 2000s.

The components of the *Hercules* and muscleman epics included: chases (horse-back, chariot, on foot); a wrestling match; fights with a monster or two (usually in a cave); lengthy treks through deserts or forests; sword fights; training sessions; ransacked and burnt villages; cliffhangers; a brawl in a local inn; seductive sorceresses (including a scene in her bedroom); torchlit tunnels; a variety of technology and weaponry; sexy heroines; corrupt wizards; comic sidekicks; saving the sidekick, father or girlfriend from the tyrant at the end; the hero beating count-less warriors single-handed; and over-the-top costumes (usually courtesy of Casa d'Arte Firenze).

11. Although *Cleopatra* isn't among the most satisfying of ancient blockbusters, and despite the emphasis in the reception of the film on its budget and production problems (the hype preceded the movie by months and years), it's by no means a bad film. Indeed, parts of *Cleopatra* are truly monumental. The viewer marvels at the big scenes, real accomplishments for the assistant directors and second units. The big sets are very, very big, with Cleopatra's palace, where much of the action takes place, as gargantuan as one of the big European palaces, like Versailles or the Schonbrunn. One couldn't call *Cleopatra* a great film, but it is very enjoyable. Some sections are literate (Caesar quotes the erotic Roman poet Catullus, for instance). The acting lets it down, and too many scenes are too talky. Liz Taylor may not be the world's greatest actress, but she does bring enormous star power to the film.

12. B. Babington, 205.

13. *Waterloo* (Sergei Bondarchuk, 1970), *Barry Lyndon* (Stanley Kubrick, 1975), *Napoleon* (Abel Gance, 1927), *War & Peace* (Sergei Bondarchuk, 1967, and King Vidor, 1956), and *The Pride and the Passion* (Stanley Kramer, 1967).

14. *Our Sunday Visitor*, in *The Critic*, 20, Jan, 1961; *Commonweal*, 75, Nov, 1961.

15. *King of Kings* programme, University of Southern California Press, Los Angeles.

16. *Time*, 78, Oct, 1961, 73.

17. W. James: *The Varieties of Religious Experience*, Penguin, 1982, 131.

FOUR : THE FILM IMAGE

4 : 1   CAMERAWORK

1. Quoted in J. Boorman, 1997, 128.

4 : 3   THE TRACKING SHOT

1. 1970, in J. Leyda, 35.

4 : 4   DISTANCE AND VIEWPOINT

I. A. Hitchcock, in *Hitchcock On Hitchcock*, Faber, London, 1997, 125-7.

4 : 7   SURFACES

I. In V. Stoichita, 15.
2. P. & L. Murray, *Art and Artists*, Penguin, London, 1976, 256-7.

4 : 8   DECAY AND TRASH

I. The relation between the excremental and the ecstatic realms has been analyzed by writers such as G. Wilson Knight (see Knight's study of Powys, Lawrence, Joyce and other writers in *Neglected Powers*, Routledge & Kegan Paul, London, 1972).

FIVE   THE MYSTERIES OF SPACE AND TIME

I. In G. Mast, 76.

5 : 2   TIMELESS TIME

I. In E. de Antonio, 73.

5 : 4   TIME IN ANDREI TARKOVSKY'S CINEMA

I. S. Eisenstein, in D. Cook, 190.
2. Quoted in F. Trebbi, *Il testo e sguardo*, Parton Editiore, Bologna, 1976, 51.
3. P.P. Pasolini, in S. Rohdie, 1995, 52.
4. Quoted in P. Kolker, 1985, 83-84.
5. Quoted in P. Strick, 1989.

5 : 5   SCULPTING IN TIME

I. In M. Tarkovskaya, 1983, 233.
2. See V. Nizhny, *Lessons With Eisenstein*, Hill & Wang, New York, NY, 1969, 93f. On the long take in cinema, see V.F. Perkins: *Lessons With Eisenstein*, Hill & Wang, New York, NY, 1969; D. Thomson, *Movie Man*, Stein & Day, New York, NY, 1967; B. Salt, "Statistical Style Analysis of Motion Pictures", *Film Quarterly*, 28, I, Autumn, 1974; B. Henderson, "The Long Take", *Film Comment*, 7, 2, Summer, 1967.
3. B. Bertolucci, in J. Leyda, 35.
4. S. Brakhage, in J. Leyda, 46.
5. D.H. Lawrence, *Reflections on the Death of a Porcupine*, in *A Selection From Phoenix*, 456-7.
6. Peter Redgrove wrote to me:

this 'strangeness' is 'strange' because reality is so fucking extraordinary, and

strange too because most of us try to live without strangeness, and construct
something called the 'ordinary' which never existed. Actually, the strangeness is
so ordinary as to be quite natural. The strangeness is wonder and what is
wondered at is so wonderful that it is strange we do not wonder more.

(P. Redgrove, in J. Robinson, *Here Comes the Flood: The Poetry of Peter
Redgrove*, Crescent Moon, 1994.)

7. Chuang-tzu, *Basic Writings*, tr. B. Watson, Columbia University Press, New
York, NY.

5 : 6 THE SACRALIZATION OF SPACE

1. P. Klee, *The Thinking Eye*, Lund Humphries, London, 1961, 340.

5 : 7 SPACE AND ABSTRACTION

1. W. Kandinsky in *Der Blaue Reiter*, in H. Chipp, 157.
2. W. Kandinsky, *Concerning the Spiritual in Art*, Wittenborn, Schultz, Inc,
New York, NY, 1947, 23.
3. G. Matthieu, *Vers une structuration nouvelle des formes*, Les Études
Carmelitaines, De Silea De Bronwer, Bruges, 1958.
4. E. Husserl, *Cartesian Meditations*, Marintus Nijhoff's, The Hague, 1960, 57.

SIX SYMBOLS AND MOTIFS

6 : 1 ON SYMBOLISM

1. Alain Robbe-Grillet maintained that cinema has its own being, separate from
'reality':

I don't think either the cinema or the novel is for explaining the world... I don't
believe a work of art has reference to anything outside itself. In a film there's no
reality except that of the film, no time except that of the film... The story of
Marienbad [*Last Year at Marienbad*, Alain Resnais, 1961, France] doesn't exist
apart from the way it's told. The only reality is the film's, and as for the criterion
of that reality, for the author it's his vision, what he feels. For the spectator, the
only test is whether he accepts. (1962, in J. Leyda, 396)

6 : 2 RAIN

1. J. Hull, *Touching the Rock*, SPCK, London, 1990, 22f.

6 : 3 WATER

1. In R. Graves, *The White Goddess*, Faber, London, 1961, 218-19.

6 : 4   FIRE

1. W. La Barre, *Muelos*, ib, 107, 130.

SEVEN   THE WORLDS OF ANDREI TARKOVSKY

7 : 1   TARKOVSKY'S WORLDS

1. *Time*, Mch 20, 1978, 20.

7 : 5   FOREST OF TREES, FOREST OF SYMBOLS

1. R. Harrison, *Forests: The Shadow of Civilization*, University Press, 1992, 81.
2. J. & W. Grimm, *The Complete Fairy Tales of the Brothers Grimm*, tr. J. Zipes, Bantam, New York, NY, 1987, 104.
3. D. Obolensky, 397.

7 : 8   LANGUAGE

1. H. Cixous, in V. Conley. *Hélène Cixous*, University of Nebraska Press, Lincoln, 1984, 57.
2. T. Moi, 1988, 99-100.

EIGHT : SOUND AND MUSIC

8 : 1   SOUND AND SPACE

1. A. Truppin, 237.
2. A. Truppin, 241.

8 : 2   SOUND IN *THE SACRIFICE*

1. Similar off-screen explosions are used in *The Bounty* (Roger Donaldson, 1984, GB), here sounding like canon fire and emphasizing Captain Bligh's rage.

8 : 4   SILENCE

1. M. Foucault, *Politics, Philosophy, Culture*, Routledge, London, 1990, 4.
2. Ursula Le Guin, *Changing Planes*, Gollancz, London, 2005, 18.
3. J. Ferguson, 171.
4. Samuel Beckett, *The Beckett Trilogy*, 375-8.

8 : 8   CLASSICAL MUSIC

1. P. Kolker, 1985, 61.

NINE : PRODUCTION

9 : 1   FAST FILMS

1. Quoted in D. Robinson, Jan 3, 1987.
2. In G. Petrie, 1996, 62.
3. V. Johnson, 1994, 8.
4. J. Leyda, 318.

9 : 2   SHOOTING

1. L. Buñuel, *Action*, Nov-Dec, 1974, in J. Leyda, 56.
2. In M. Figgis, 25.
3. J. Moreau, 1976, in J. Leyda.
4. D. Bordwell, 1988, 85.

9 : 4   BUDGET

1. T. Mitchell, 1983, 54.
2. Because of the availability of some of the actors (Jean Moreau, John Gielgud, Margaret Rutherford), some scenes in *Chimes At Midnight* were shot with stand-ins, and, as with *Othello*, sometimes months or miles apart. (Welles said the budget of *Chimes At Midnight* was $1.1 million, but producer Emiliano Piedra said it was more like $800,000.) The battle scenes in *Chimes At Midnight*, regarded by some as the best battle ever put on film, were shot in a park in Madrid. Horses were only available for a few days: much of the battle was shot with a few actors, some weapons, and lots of mud and smoke.

9 : 5   ANDREI TARKOVSKY'S UNMADE FILMS

1. J.-L. Godard, in *Godard On Godard*, 227.
2. In 1969, in J. Leyda, 251.
3. S. Beckett, *Molloy*, 62.

9 : 6   CINEMA OF EXILE

1. J. Kristeva, *Partisan Review*, 1986, 216.
2. Julia Kristeva has written lucidly, for example, of her 'mother tongue'. John Lechte remarked: '[s]he is hypersensitive to the maternal, the familiar, and the same. Such may well be the source of her legendary 'difficulty': what she is talking about is so close to us that it becomes difficult to grasp intellectually' (in J. Fletcher & A. Benjamin, eds. *Abjection, Melancholia and Love: The Work of Julia Kristeva*, Routledge, London, 1990, 81).

TEN : ANDREI TARKOVSKY AND PAINTING

1. In V. Stoichita, 12.

10 : 1   PAINTING AND FILM

1. In S. Rodman. *Conversations With Artists*, Devin-Adair, New York, NY, 1957, 37.

10 : 3   JULIA KRISTEVA ON PAINTING

1. For Julia Kristeva, the Virgin Mary was a compromise solution to the problem of women's paranoia; the Virgin Mary was a sublimation of the woman's murderous desires through the valorization of her breast, and the pain, a fantasy of eternity (in the *Assumption*), a denial of other women, including the Virgin's own mother, a denial of men's part in procreation (the virgin birth). Susan Suleiman wrote:

> the mother, according to Kristeva, the Other is not (only) an arbitrary sign, a necessary absence; it is the child, whose presence and whose bodily link to her are inescapable givens, material facts. If to love (her child) is, for a woman, the same thing as to write, we have in that conjunction a modern secular equivalent of the word made flesh. (*Risking Who One Is*, MIT Press, Cambridge, MA, 1995, 27)

2. M. Jacobus, *Reading Woman: essays in feminist criticism*, Methuen, London, 1986 169).
3. Or as Mary Jacobus put it, '[t]he discourse of maternity gives birth to Kristevan poetics' (1986, 170).

10 : 4   ANDREI TARKOVSKY AND LEONARDO DA VINCI

1. In V. Stoichita, 10.
2. In H. Chipp, 188.
3. S. Freud, 155.

10 : 5   LEONARDO DA VINCI'S *ADORATION OF THE MAGI*

1. O. Spengler, *The Decline of the West*, tr. C.F. Atkinson, ed. H. Werner, A. Helps, Allen & Unwin, London, 1961, 155.
2. J. Hall, 1984, 6.
3. Novalis, *Pollen and Fragments: Selected Poetry and Prose*, tr. A. Versluis, Phanes Press, Grand Rapids, 1989, 26, 121.
4. As Robert Payne wrote:

> A bomb is dropped. Everything is uprooted and hurled into the air... There has been an explosion of spiritual energy, and the people are jolted, alarmed, terrified, happy, wildly joyful, and swept outside of themselves by the appearance of the Virgin and Child... In Leonardo's *Adoration* we are made aware that an event of unprecedented and incalculable importance is taking place and the people are excited beyond measure. (36-37)

5. C. Andre, in L. Lippard, 1973, 157.
6. Nowhere is this more apparent than in the famous Leonardo Smile. Many painters attempted the Leonardo Smile – Correggio, Luini, Sodoma, Boltraffio,

Solario and many anonymous artists – but only Leonardo could make it work successfully.

10 : 6   ANDREI TARKOVSKY AND PIERO DELLA FRANCESCA

1. A. Stokes, *The Stones of Rimini*, in Piero della Francesca: *The Complete Paintings of Piero della Francesca*, intr. P. Murray, notes by P. de Vecchi, Penguin, London, 1985, 11).
  2. R. Vischer, *Luca Signorelli and the Italian Renaissance*, 1879, in ib., 10.
  3. R. Alberti, *Tratto della Nabilta dello Pittura*, 1585, in ib., 10.

10 : 8   ANDREI TARKOVSKY AND MODERN ART

1. H. Chipp, 157.
  2. In H. Chipp, 564.
  3. In M. Tuchman, 1971, 156.
  4. In G. Battock, 1995, 385.
  5. C. Greenberg, *Art and Culture*, Beacon Press, Boston, MA, 1961, 134f.
  6. In G. Battock, 1995, 158.
  7. M. Merleau-Ponty, in *The Phenomenology of Perception*, Routledge, London, 1945, vii.

ELEVEN : RELIGION AND PHILOSOPHY IN ANDREI TARKOVSKY'S CINEMA

11 : 2   VISION QUEST

1. W. La Barre, 1972, 140, 171.
  2. J. Leyda, 1977, 346.
  3. P. Green, 1985, 54.

11 : 6   RELIGIOUS EXPERIENCE

1. B. Kawin, 1987, 63.

11 : 8   GOD AND THE BOMB, OR RELIGION AND NUCLEAR WAR

1. In L. Giovannitti & F. Freed, *The Decision To Drop the Bomb*, 1967, 197.
  2. M. Chagall, *Bridges of Understanding*, University Publishers, New York, NY, 1964, 113.

11 : 11   THE LEFT-HAND PATH

1. A. Tarkovsky, in L. Garrett, 1997, 23.

TWELVE : STRUCTURE AND NARRATION

12 : 3   ENDING IN ECSTASY
1. N. Kagan, 1997, 230.

THIRTEEN : CHILDHOOD, FAMILY AND CHARACTER

13 : 2   THE MYSTERY OF CHILDHOOD

1. S.G. Lanes, *The Art of Maurice Sendak*, Bodley Head, London, 1980, 185.
2. Other films of childhood made since *Mirror* include *Waterland* (Stephen Gyllenhaal, 1992, GB), from Graham Swift's novel, Terence Davies' *The Long Day Closes* (1992, GB), *Hope & Glory* (John Boorman, 1987), *E.T.* (Steven Spielberg, 1982), *Empire of the Sun* (Steven Spielberg, 1987), *Cinema Paradiso* (Giuseppe Tornatre, 1988, Italy), and Bill Douglas' autobiographical trilogy.

13 : 3   RELATIONSHIPS

1. A kiss is regarded by some people as more intimate than intercourse; in pornographic films characters don't always kiss, as with prostitutes, and focus on genital contact, whereas in Tarkovsky's work, on a different level of intimacy, the most people do is kiss.

13 : 4   CHARACTER TYPES, ARCHETYPES, STEREOTYPES

1. Hysteria, or womb-madness, is connected with the powers of women during menstruation, according to Penelope Shuttle and Peter Redgrove, powers which men traditionally do not understand, and try to suppress (*The Wise Wound*, Paladin, London, 1986).
2. M. Praz, *The Romantic Agony*, tr. A. Davidson, Oxford University Press, Oxford, 1933, 50, 320.
3. As G. Petrie and V. Johnson point out, the story Alexander recounts in *The Sacrifice* when his sister cut off her long hair 'makes Tarkovsky's own ideas on this subject almost too transparent' (JP, 221).
4. M. Antonioni, in S. Rohdie, 183.

13 : 6   ACTORS

1. See J. Aberth, 285.

FOURTEEN : LOVE, GENDER AND SEXUALITY

1. W. O'Flaherty, 46-47, 81-87.
2. Tarkovsky had a strained relationship with his own sister, Marina Tarkovskaya.
3. See V. Johnson and G. Petrie, JP, 246.
4. In M. Mancini, 23.

PART TWO : THE FILMS

FIFTEEN : *IVAN'S CHILDHOOD*

1. Mosfilm, 1962, 39f.
2. M. Turovskaya, 32.
3. In A. Lawton, 1992, 304.
4. Tarkovsky, quoted in M. Turovskaya, 35.
5. M. Turovskaya, 7.

SIXTEEN : *ANDREI ROUBLYOV*

1. M. Ciment, 1988, 93.
2. L. Anninsky, *Shestidesyatniki i my*, VTPO 'Kinotsentr, Moscow, 1991.
3. In A. Lawton, 1992, 231.
4. M. Ciment, 1988.
5. 1988 interview, 75f.
6. Mark Le Fanu remarked that the 'wonderful cameos of animals' in *Andrei Roublyov* were 'as noble and mysterious as anything in Rubens or Géricault' (48).
7. V. Johnson & G. Petrie, 1994b, 12.
8. Wood and trees are a prominent motif in *Andrei Roublyov*, from the birch wood where the stone masons are attacked and the trees in the rain storm at the beginning, to the log pile at the monastery, the pagan dancers in the woods, the tree Foma dies beside, and the root Boriska pulls up. Christ pulls the Cross, Roublyov and Boriska sit below a post, and the fool is tortured on a log.
9. In A. Lawton, 224.
10. In M. Ciment, in G. Ciment, 92.
11. M. Ciment, 1988, 90f.

SEVENTEEN : SOLARIS

17 : 1   *SOLARIS*: BACKGROUND

1. Lucas Samaras was best known for deliberately subverting the eroticism of art by furnishing his sculptures and assemblages with pins, nails, razor blades, knives and scissors, as in his vicious *Book 4*, which is stuffed with knives, nails and razor blades. An art of sadomasochism, fetishized pain.
2. On Stanislaw Lem, see Lem's *Microworlds*, Secker & Warburg, London, 1985; J. Jarzebski, "Stanislaw Lem", *Science Fiction Studies*, 4, 2, July, 1977; C. Tighe, "Kozmik kommie konflikts: Stanislaw Lem's *Solaris*", in P. Davies, 1990.

17 : 2   *SOLARIS*: THE STORY

1. Using electronic music fits the sci-fi genre, but it was also employed because Eduard Artemiev composed in that field. It is so different from the trees, grass and woods of *Mirror* or *Nostalghia*, and from the natural world at the beginning of the

film. The music also evokes emptiness and isolation.

2. *2001*'s centrifuge was 10 metres tall and weighed 30 tons. It was built by Vickers Engineering Group, and cost $750,000. The Solaris station is *2001*'s centrifuge laid on it side – a giant horizontal circle. (That spaceship design was reprised in the sci-fi thriller *Sphere* [1998, USA], among others).

3. Natalia Bondarchuk remembered in a DVD interview that she had to hold her breath for about a minute while wearing the special frozen make-up while they shot the scene. She had to communicate with the director using hand signals. Unable to tell the crew she couldn't hold on any longer, she took up a bucket of water and poured it over herself. The stiff, frozen shirt was accomplished with sugar solution.

4. See P. Kenez, *Film Quarterly*, Winter, 1972-73.

17: 3   *SOLARIS* AND *BLADE RUNNER*

1. The amount of academic and cult interest that *Blade Runner* has initiated is substantial. There are collections of essays on *Blade Runner* (*Retrofitting Blade Runner*, edited by Judith Kerman); monographs on *Blade Runner* (such as Scott Bukatman's British Film Institute Modern Classics book); and very detailed explorations of the film, such as Paul M. Sammon's *Future Noir: The Making of Blade Runner*. Some prominent critics have studied *Blade Runner*: Kaja Silverman, Slavoj Zizek, Scott Bukatman, Andrew Ross, Vivian Sobchack and Guiliana Bruno.

There have been many articles and essays on *Blade Runner* and sections in books on *Blade Runner*, such as on postmodernism in *Blade Runner* (for ex, Guiliana Bruno's "Ramble City"), on the androids/ cyborg theme (such as Donna Haraway's *Simians, Cyborgs and Women* and J.P. Telotte's *Replications: A Robotic History of the Science Fiction Film*), or the design of the film (such as D. Neumann's *Film Architecture: From Metropolis to Blade Runner* and Syd Mead in Danny Peary's *Omni's Screen Flights, Screen Fantasies*), or on the director's cut, and so on. Chapters on *Blade Runner* appear in books such as L. Goldberg *et al*'s *Science Fiction Filmmaking in the 1980s*, Jim Collins *et al*'s *Film Theory Goes to the Movies*, V. Sobchack's *Screening Space: The American Science Fiction Film*, L. Cook and Peter Wollen's *Visual Display*, and Annette Kuhn's *Alien Zone: Cultural Theory and Contemporary Science Fiction*.

Then there are pieces and chapters on the special effects in *Blade Runner* (such as Herb Lightman's articles, and in Christopher Finch's *Special Effects*), comic book tie-ins, novel sequels (K.W. Jeter's *Blade Runner 2: The Edge of Human* and *Replicant Night*), a fanzine (*Cityspeak*), a computer game (1997), and souvenir magazines (ed. Ira Friedman). There are, inevitably many internet sites and newsgroups dedicated to *Blade Runner*, including Murray Chapman's *Blade Runner FAQ* page and Jon Van Oast's *2019: Off-World* page, Dan Hentschel's *Blade Runner* Homepage, Paul Brians' "Study Guide for Philip K. Dick: *Blade Runner*", Christian Rohrmeier's "Official *Blade Runner* Online Magazine", and Stephen Bowline and Michael Perkhofer's worldwide web page on Vangelis. The *Alien* series also have their own fan websites (such as *The Unofficial Alien 5 Website* and *The Alien 5 Discussion Forum*).

On *Blade Runner*, see J. Telotte, 1996; S. Bukatman, 1997; A. Kuhn, 1990 and 1999; V. Sobchack, 1987; J. Collins, in J. Collins, 1993; D. Neumann, ed: *Film Architecture: From Metropolis to Blade Runner*, Prestel-Verlag, N.Y., 1996; J. Orr: *Contemporary Cinema*, Edinburgh University Press, 1998; J. Kerman, ed.

Retrofitting Blade Runner, Bowling Green State University Popular Press, 1991; P. Sammon: "Do Androids Dream of Unicorns? The 7 Faces of *Blade Runner*", *Video Watchdog*, 20, Dec, 1993, 1996, and *Ridley Scott*, Orion, 1999; W.M. Kolb: "*Blade Runner*": An Annotated Bibliography", *Literature/ Film Quarterly*, 18, 1, 1990 (*Blade Runner* issue); "*Blade Runner* and Genre", *Literature/ Film Quarterly*, 14, 2, 1986; N. Gader: "The Return of *Blade Runner*", *Perfect Vision*, 3, 12, 1992.; P. Fitting: "Futurecop: The Neutralization of Revolt in *Blade Runner*", *Science Fiction Studies*, 14, 3, 1987; D. Desser: "*Blade Runner*", *Literature/ Film Quarterly*, 13, 3, 1985; M. Dempsey: "*Blade Runner*", *Film Quarterly*, 36, 2, 1982; Y. Chevier: "*Blade Runner*", *Science Fiction Studies*, 11, 1, 1984; R. Lofficier & Jean-Marc, in Goldberg, 1995; H. Lightman: "*Blade Runner*", *American Cinematographer*, 63, 7, July, 1982; M. Webb: ""Like Today, Only More So": The Credible Dystopia of *Blade Runner*", in D. Neumann, 1996; S. Doll & G. Faller: "*Blade Runner* and Genre", *Literature/ Film Quarterly*, 14, 2, 1986; P. Ruppert: "*Blade Runner*", *Cinéaste*, 17, 2, 1989; H. Lightman & R. Patterson: "*Blade Runner*", *American Cinematographer*, 63, 7, 1982; G. Bruno: "Ramble City: Postmodernism and *Blade Runner*", *October*, 41, 1987; S. Mead: "Designing the Future", in D. Peary, 1984; M. Kellner *et al*: "*Blade Runner*", *Jump Cut*, 29, 1984; K. Turan: "*Blade Runner*", *Los Angeles Times*, Sept 13, 1992; P. Strick: "The Age of the Replicant", *Sight & Sound*, 51, 3, 1982; S. Bukatman, in P. Cook, 1995; W. Fisher: "Of Living Machines and Living-Machines: *Blade Runner* and the Terminal Genre", *New Literary History*, 20, 1, 1988; S. Gravett: "The Sacred and the Profane", *Literature/ Film Quarterly*, 26, 1, 1998; R. Instrell: "*Blade Runner*", in J. Orr, 1992; N. Klein: "Building *Blade Runner*", *Social Text*, 28, 1991; P. Lev: "Whose Future? *Star Wars*, *Alien* and *Blade Runner*", *Literature/ Film Quarterly*, 26, 1, 1998; E. Marder: "*Blade Runner*'s Moving Still", *Camera Obscura*, 27, 1991; K. McNamara: "*Blade Runner*'s Post-individual Worldspace", *Contemporary Literature*, 38, 3, 1997; R. Morrison: "*Casablanca* Meets *Star Wars*", *Literature/ Film Quarterly*, 18, 1, 1990; S. Neale: "Issues of Difference", in J. Donald, 1989; and J. Slade: "Romanticizing Cybernetics in Ridley Scott's *Blade Runner*", *Literature/ Film Quarterly*, 18, 1, 1990.

2. Ridley Scott said *Blade Runner* was 'a film set 40 years hence, made in the style of 40 years ago' (Warners press release). *Blade Runner* is thus part of a trend in Hollywood movies to raid the past, and particularly the history of cinema, then mix the elements together. Simultaneously *hommage* and parody, in which old films are used more than real history to recreate the future. In this respect, *Blade Runner* is a nostalgic film, lovingly evoking the history of cinema, exploring the viewer's nostalgia for cinema, the memory of Forties *film noir* (*Blade Runner* was shot on the Warner's lot where *The Maltese Falcon* and *The Big Sleep* had been filmed).

17 : 4   *SOLARIS* AND CYBER-CULTURE

1. On cyborgs, cyberspace and cyberpunk, see: S. Bukatman, 1993; J. Wolmark, 1995, 1999; D. Haraway, 1985, 1989, 1991, 1992; L. McCaffery, 1991; E. Rabkin, 1987; C. Springer, 1991, and "Muscular Circuitry", *Genders*, 18, 1993; T. de Lauretis, 1987; J. Rusher, 1995; B. Rux, 1997; P. Schelde, 1993; F. Botting, 1999; A. Balsamo, 1988; J. Telotte, in N. Ruddick, 1992; J. Bergstrom: "Androids and Androgyny", *Camera Obscura*, 15, 1986; A.R. Stone, "Will the Real Body Please Stand Up? Boundary Stories About Virtual Cultures", in M. Benedikt, ed.

Andrei Tarkovsky   **569**

Cyberspace: First Steps, MIT Press, Cambridge, MA, 1991; V. Hollinger, "Cybernetic Deconstructions", in L. McCaffrey, 1991 and "Cybernetic Deconstructions", *Mosaic*, 1990; R. Barringer: "Skinjobs, Humans and Radical Coding", *Jump Cut*, 41, 1997; D. Larson: "Machine and Messiah", *Genders*, 18, 1993; G. Schwab: "Cyborgs", *Discourse*, 9, 1987; P. Warrick: *The Cybernetic Imagination in Science Fiction*, MIT Press, 1980; N. Friedman: "*The Terminator*", *Journal of Popular Culture*, 28, 1, 1994; C. Fuchs: "Death Is Irrelevant: Cyborgs, Re-production, and the Future of Male Hysteria", *Gender*, 18, 1993; F. Glass: "The 'New Bad Future': *Robocop* and 1980s Sci-Fi Films", *Science as Culture*, 5, 1989; T. Foster. "Meat Puppets or Robopaths?", *Genders*, 18, 1983; N. Nixon: "Cyberpunk: Preparing the Ground For Revolution or Keeping the Boys Satisfied?", *Science Fiction Studies*, 19, 1992; S. Brewster *et al*, eds., *Inhuman Reflections: Thinking the Limits of the Human*, Manchester University Press, Manchester, 2000; J. Prosser, *Second Skins: The Body Narratives of Transsexuality*, Columbia University Press, New York, NY, 1998; N.K. Hayles: "The Life of Cyborgs", in M. Benjamin, ed: *A Question of Identity*, Rutgers University Press, N.J., 1993. Z. Sofia, "Virtual Corporeality", *Australian Feminist Studies*, 15, Adelaide, 1992; C. Sandoval, "New Sciences: Cyborg Feminism and the Methodology of the Oppressed", in C. Gray, 1995; K. Woodward, "From Virtual Cyborgs to Biological Time Bombs", in G. Bender, 1994; L. Levidow & K. Robins, eds., *Cyborg Worlds: The Military Information Society*, Columbia University Press, N.Y., 1989; J. González, "Envisioning Cyborg Bodies", in C. Gray, 1995.

2. S. Bukatman, 1993, 17.

3. R. Bellour: "Ideal Hadaly", in C. Penley, 1991, 127.

EIGHTEEN : BEYOND THE MIRROR: *MIRROR*

1. A. Tarkovsky, *Life, Life*, 42.

18 : 1   *MIRROR* AND POETRY

1. The *Bright, Bright Day* version of the screenplay contained scenes which did not make it into the final film (though the ending was much the same): the cemetery scene; the mother selling flowers in the war; the demolishing of a church cupola; the mother and sister at a hippodrome; and the father's description of battle casualties.

18 : 2   *MIRROR*, SCENE BY SCENE

1. Mark Le Fanu remarked on the beauty and refulgence of the images which Tarkovsky introduced (rightly) without explanation. 'The sequence is as close as possible in Tarkovsky's work to absolute cinema' (77).

2. Olivier Assays said that Pieter Brueghel's *Winter* 'reproduced' in *Mirror* gave him 'a very powerful reaction', which had to with

a certain way of looking at nature, when winter has reduced it to a state of pure transparency, to its essence; in winter there is a sort of simplification, translucency of the world, the light is more transparent, the cold renders our perceptions more acute. (1997, 25)

3. Olivier Assays suggested that this scene depicted the conception of the filmmaker (1997, 24).

18 : 4   CRITICS ON *MIRROR*

1. In A. Lawton, 1992, 241.
2. In J. Passek, 284.

NINETEEN : INTO THE WASTELAND: FAITH AND THE QUEST IN *STALKER*

19 : 1   *STALKER*

1. D. Russell, *Sight & Sound*, 1990.
1. A. Tarkovsky, in "Ispoved", *Kontinent*, 42, 1984.
2. See C. Pike, "Change and the individual in the work of the Strugatskys", in P. Davies, 1990, 90f.
3. J. Orr, 1998, 50.
4. David Wingrove called the approach to the Room

one of the most genuinely tense sequences in cinema, a tension created not through over-the-top Hollywood special effects, but by tapping some level of ourselves which is universal and unchanging. It is a sequence which, in its final stages, is almost unbearable – the journey down the tunnel which leads to the Wishing Room is not matched in cinema, even by Hitchcock, for its creation of an intense, almost nightmarish sense of anticipation. (1985).

19 : 3   CONCLUSION

1. A. Tarkovsky, quoted in M. Turovskaya, xxii.

TWENTY : THE ANGEL UNDER THE WATER: *NOSTALGHIA*

20 : 1   TARKOVSKY IN ITALY

1. Ian Christie noted that in Russian nostalgia means a longing for home, rather than for the past (M. Turovskaya, 159).

20 : 3   FURTHER THOUGHTS ON *NOSTALGHIA*

1. N. Zorkaya, in JP, 162.
2. V. Johnson and G. Petrie suggest that Eugenia doesn't really work as a character because she has to carry too many concepts: threatening sexuality, the wife and family he's escaped from, contemporary materialism, secular society, the death of spirituality of the past, Gorchakov's self-imprisonment, and his inability to connect (JP, 163).
3. I. Bergman, 1994, 334.

20 : 4   DEPRESSION, ART, JULIA KRISTEVA AND *NOSTALGHIA*

1. J. Kristeva: *Revolution in Poetic Language*, 131-2.
2. J. Lechte, *Julia Kristeva*, Routledge, 1990, 34.
3. J. Kristeva: "A Question of Subjectivity: an interview" [with S. Sellers], *Women's Review*, 12, 1986, in P. Rice & P. Waugh, eds. *Modern Literary Theory: A Reader*, Arnold, London, 1992, 133.

TWENTY-ONE : THE ULTIMATE ACT: *THE SACRIFICE*

21 : 1   THE WORLD OF *THE SACRIFICE*

1. See D. Campbell, *War Plan UK*, Burnett, London, 1982, 461.
2. *The War Game*, Peter Watkins, 1965, GB; *Dr Strangelove*, Stanley Kubrick, 1963, USA; *War Games*, John Badham, 1983, USA; *Threads*, Mick Jackson, 1984, GB; *When the Wind Blows*, Jimmy T. Murakami, 1986, GB; *DefCon 4*; *The Day After*, Nicholas Meyer, 1983; *Special Bulletin*, Edward Wyck, 1983; *Countdown to Looking Glass*, Fred Barzyk, 1984; *The Terminator 2*, James Cameron, 1991, USA; *Testament*, Lynn Littman, 1983.
3. Tarkovsky may have chosen the name Alexander in *The Sacrifice* because it begins with an 'a', like the names of many of his other protagonists. Alexander is also the first name of some of Tarkovsky's cultural heroes: Alexander Pushkin, Alexander Dovzhenko, Alexandre Astruc (there is also Alexander Solonitsyn and Alexander Blok).
4. Sound editor Owe Svensson remarked that the telephone is 'an unrealistic sound, but it's extremely effective. It performs the same function as a music cue, but it is, I think, more subtle' (2003, 117).

21 : 3   THE SACRIFICIAL ACT

1. J. Campbell, 1988a, 107.
2. Anna Asp had worked on Bergman's *Autumn Sonata*, *After the Rehearsal* and *Fanny and Alexander*); she also worked on *Pelle the Conqueror*, *Les Misérables* and *The House of the Spirits*.

21 : 7   NEW TIME

1. Sacrifice takes its place in the semiotics of Julia Kristeva as the thetic moment which separates the semiotic from the symbolic. Sacrifice does not, though, let violence loose; rather, it helps to regulate it. When sacrifice is incorporated into religion, violence may be dissipated completely.

21 : 9   ENDINGS

1. M. Leszcylowski, 1987, 284.
2. Quoted in P. Strick, 1989.
3. M. Leszcylowski, 1987, 284.

TWENTY TWO : CRITICAL RESPONSES TO ANDREI TARKOVSKY'S CINEMA

1. Quoted in H. Marshall, 1976.

22 : 1   CRITICAL RESPONSE

1. M. Turovskaya, 69.
1. Ivor Montagu, 1973, 92. According to Philip French, Ivor Montagu was 'the most extraordinary person ever to review movies'; he was a friend of Eisenstein, had edited Hitchcock's *The Lodger*, wrote the rules of table tennis, was a producer at Ealing and Gaumont, a lifelong communist, and son of a peer (J. Boorman, 1998, 6).
2. In A. Lawton, 1992, 276.
3. In J. Boorman, 1998, 347.
4. In H. Marshall, 1976, 94.
5. G. Vincendeau, 1995, 419.
6. G. Andrew, 1989, 282.
7. P. Hardy, 1991, 304.
8. In ib., 461-4.
9. In J. Brosnan, 1991, 387.
10. P. Wells, *Understanding Animation*, Routledge, London, 1998, 94.

22 : 5   CINEMA IN THE WAKE OF ANDREI TARKOVSKY

1. J. Park, 114.
2. Further correspondences have been noted by John Orr (1998, 55-56).
3. I. Christie, 1998.
4. In A. Lawton, 1992, 243.

22 : 6   VINCENT WARD AND ANDREI TARKOVSKY

1. Vincent Ward gathered a huge amount of reference material. As Cheryl Bainum, CG supervisor at POP Film (an fx house) remarked: 'Vincent uses tearsheets like you wouldn't believe. He had a 12-page folder containing nothing but sky images. He wanted one piece of this sky, a cloud from another – then he'd reference a third piece to show how these elements could be blended' (C. Bainum, in K. Martin, "The Sweet Hereafter [*What Dreams May Come*]", *Cinefex*, no. 76, Jan, 1999, 116).

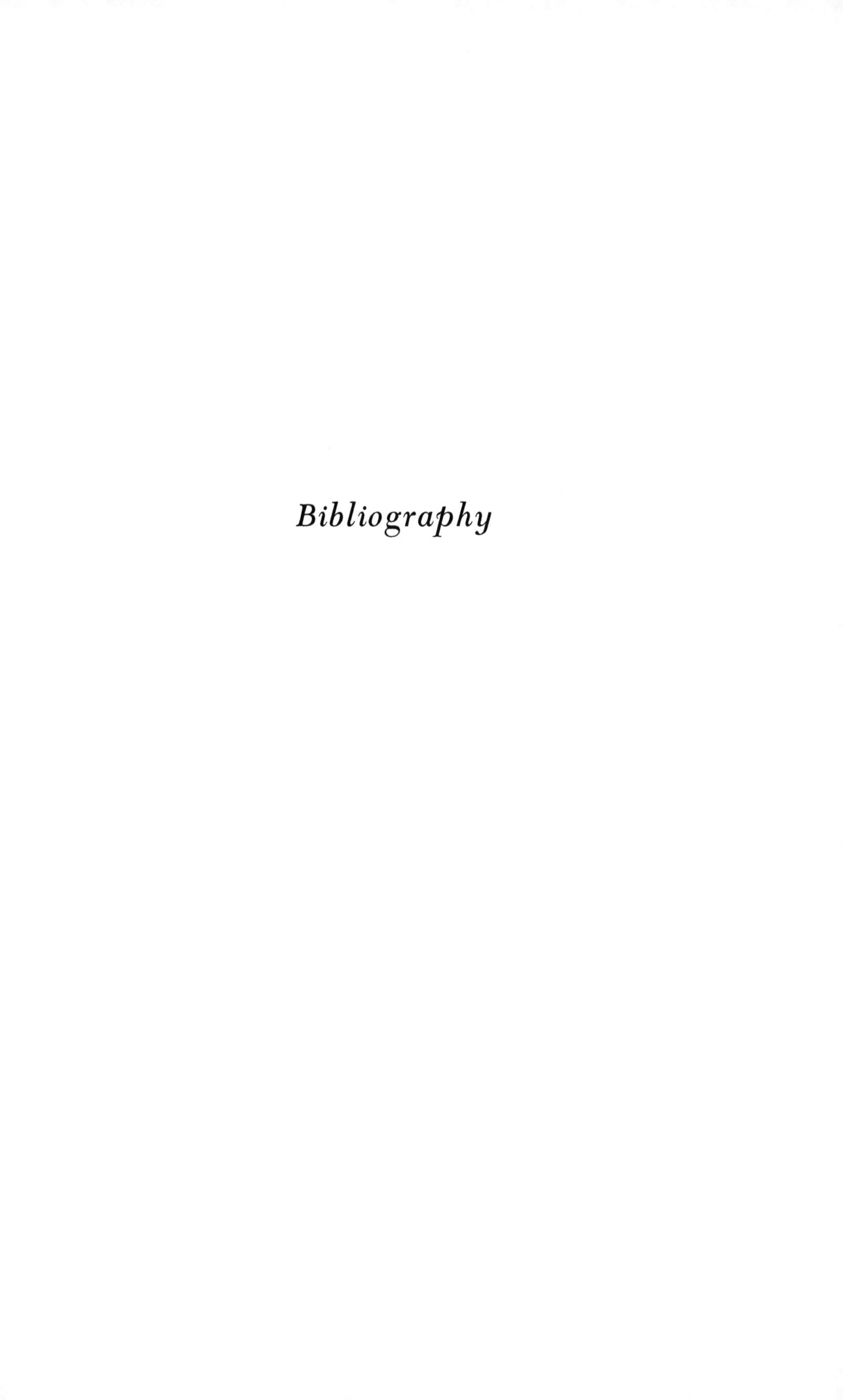

Bibliography

BY ANDREI TARKOVSKY

"Tarkovsky", *Kogda film okonchen* [*When the film is finished*], *Iskusstvo kino*, Moscow, 1964

interview, *Ekran*, 65, Sbornik, Iskusstvo, Moscow, 1966

"Zapechatlennoye vremya [Imprinted time]", *Iskusstvo kino*, 4, 1967

interview, M. Ciment, *Positif*, 109, Oct, 1969

"Vsesoyuznaya pereklichka kinematografistov" [An All-Union Filmmakers' Discussion]", *Iskusstvo kino*, 4, 1971

"Zachem proshloye vstrechayetsya s budushchim? [Why does the past meet the future?]", *Iskusstvo kino*, 11, 1971

Bely, bely den [*Bright, bright day*], Mosfilm, Moscow, 1973

"O Kinobraze [About the film image]", *Iskusstvo kino*, 3, 1979

"My delayem filmy [We make films]", *Kino*, Lithuania, 10, 1981

interview, *Time Out*, 568, Mch, 1981

interview, *Time Out*, 686, Nov, 1981

"Between Two Worlds", interview, *American Film*, Nov, 1983

interview, *Time Out*, 729, Aug, 1984

interview, *The Listener*, Aug, 1984

"A Propos du *Sacrifice*", *Positif*, 303, May, 1986

"Entretien", *Cahiers du Cinéma*, 392, Feb, 1987

"Ya chasto dumayu o vas [I think of you often]", *Iskusstvo kino*, 6, 1987

Le Sacrifice, Schirmer, Munich, 1987

"Strasti po Andreyu [The passion according to Andrei]", interview, *Literaturnoye obozreniye*, 9, 1988

Zerkalo [*Mirror*], Kinostsenarii, 2, Goskino, 1988

"Krasota spasyot mir" ["Beauty will save the world"], *Iskusstvo kino*, 2, 1989

"Vstat na put [Taking the right path]", *Iskusstvo kino*, 2, 1989

Lektsii po kinorezhissure [Lecture on film directing], ed. K. Lopushansky, Lenfilm, Leningrad, 1989

Martyrolog: Tagebücher, 1970-1986, tr. V. Schutz-Bischitzky & M. Milack-Verheyden, Limes, Berlin, 1989

Sculpting in Time: Reflections on the Cinema, tr. K. Hunter-Blair, Faber, London, 1989

Time Within Time: The Diaries, 1970-1986, tr. K. Hunter-Blair, Seagull Books, Calcutta, 1991

Andrei Rublev, tr. K. Hunter-Blair, Faber, London, 1991

Der Spiegel. Filmnovelle, Arbeitstagebücher und Materialien zur Entstehung des Films, Limes Verlag, Berlin, 1993

Collected Screenplays, Faber, London, 1998

Andrei Tarkovski: Récits de jeunesse, Paris, 2004

Diaries, tr. C. Giroldi, ed. P. Rey, Cahiers du cinéma, Paris, 2004

Instant Light: Tarkovsky Polaroids, Thames & Hudson, London, 2004

Interviews (Conversations with Filmmakers), 2006

OTHERS

J. Abert. *A Knight At the Movies: Medieval History On Film*, Routledge, London, 2003

N. Abramov. "Dialog s A. Tarkovskim o nauchnoy fantastike na ekrane [Dialogue with A. Tarkovsky about science fiction on the screen]", *Ekran, 1970-1971*, Moscow, 1971

G. Adair. "Notes From the Underground: *Stalker*", *Sight & Sound*, Winter, 1981

M.J. Affron. "Bresson and Pascal", *Quarterly Review of Film Studies*, 10, 2, Spring, 1985

H. Agel. "Andrej Tarkovski", in *Le visage du Christ à l'écran*, Desclée, Paris, 1985

C. Akesson. *The Sacrifice: The Film Companion*, I.B. Tauris, London, 2000

J. Alexander. "Tarkovsky's Last Vision", *Cinema Papers*, Melbourne, May, 1987

M. Allot, ed. *Novelists on the Novel*, Routledge, London, 1963

R. Altman, ed. *Sound Theory, Sound Practice*, Routledge, London, 1992

C. Anderson. *Science Fiction Films of the Seventies*, McFarland, Jefferson, NC, 1985

Andrej Tarkowskij, Reihe Film, 39, Carl Hanser Verlag, Munich, 1987

D. Andrew. *Concepts in Film Theory*, Oxford University Press, Oxford, 1984

G. Andrew. *The Film Handbook*, Longman, London, 1989

L. Anninsky. *Shestidesyatniki i my [The Sixties Generation and We]*, VTPO Kinotsentr, Moscow, 1991

E. de Antonio & M. Tuchman. *Painters Painting*, Abbeville Press, New York, NY, 1984

M. Antonioni. *The Bowling Alley on the Tiber*, tr. W. Arrowsmith, Oxford University Press, Oxford, 1986

—. *Tales of a Director*, tr. W. Arrowsmith, Oxford University Press, New York, NY, 1987

W. Arrowsmith. *Antonioni: The Poet of Images*, Oxford University Press, New York, NY, 1995

O. Assayas. "Tarkovsky: Seeing is Believing", *Sight & Sound*, Jan, 1997

L. Atwood, ed. *Red Women On the Silver Screen: Soviet Women and Cinema*, Pandora, London, 1993

G. Austin. *Contemporary French Cinema*, Manchester University Press, Manchester, 1996

H. Baba. *The Andrei Tarkovsky Films*, Misuzu Shobou, Tokyo, 2002

B. Babington & P. Evans. *Biblical Epic and Sacred Narrative in the Hollywood*, Manchester University Press, Manchester, 1993

G. Bachmann, interview, 1982

A. Balsamo. "Reading Cyborgs, Writing Feminism", *Communications*, 10, 3, 1988

—. *Technologies of the Gendered Body: Reading Cyborg Women*, Duke University Press, Durham, NC, 1996

M. Barr, ed. *Future Females, the Next Generation: New Voices and Velocities in Feminism Science Fiction Criticism*, Rowman & Littlefield, Lanham, MD, 2000

R. Barthes. *The Pleasure of the Text*, Hill and Wang, New York, NY, 1975

—. *S/Z*, Hill and Wang, New York, NY, 1974

—. *Image, Music, Text*, tr. S. Heath, Fontana, London, 1984

L. Batkin. "Ne boyas svoyego golosa [Unfraid of one's own voice]", *Iskusstvo kino*, 11, 1988

G. Battock, ed. *Minimal Art: A Critical Anthology*, Studio Vista, London, 1969/ 1995

C. Baudelaire. *Intimate Journals*, tr. C. Isherwood, Picador/ Pan, London, 1990

L. Bawden, ed. *The Oxford Companion to Film*, Oxford University Press, Oxford, 1976

A. Bazin. *What is Cinema*, 2 vols, University of California Press, Berkeley, CA, 1960

F. Beaver. *On Film: A History of the Motion Picture*, McGraw-Hill, New York, NY, 1987

S. Beckett. *The Beckett Trilogy: Molloy, Malone Dies, The Unnamable*, Picador/ Pan, London, 1979,

M. Beja. *Film and Literature: An Introduction*, Longman, London, 1979

D. Bell & B. Kennedy, eds. *The Cybercultures Reader*, Routledge, London, 2000

R. Bellour. *Jean-Luc Godard: Son + Image 1974-1991*, MOMA, New York, NY, 1992

G. Bender & T. Druckley, eds. *Culture On the Brink*, Bay Press, Seattle, 1994

N. Berdyaev. *The Beginning and the End*, Harper & Row, New York, NY, 1957

R. Bergan & R. Karney. *Bloomsbury Foreign Film Guide*, Bloomsbury, London, 1988

A. Bergesen & A. Greeley. *God In the Movies*, Transaction, 2000

A. Birkos. *Soviet Cinema*, Archon, Hamden, CT, 1976

I. Bergman. *Bergman on Bergman, Interviews with Ingmar Bergman*, by S. Björkman *et al*, tr. P.B. Austin, Touchstone, New York, NY, 1986

—. *Images: My Life in Film*, Faber, London, 1994

J. Bernardoni. *The New Hollywood*, McFarland Press, Jefferson, NC, 1991

B. Bertolucci & Franco Arcalli. *Last Tango in Paris: The Screenplay*, Plexus, London, 1976a

—. "Bertolucci's "1900": A Preview", *Cineaste*, 7, 4, 1976b

—. *Bertolucci by Bertolucci*, with E. Ungari and D. Ranvard, Plexus, London, 1987

R. Bird. *Andrei Rublev*, BFI, London

E. Blank. "*The Sacrifice*, trapped by its monologues", *Pittsburgh Press*, Jan 2, 1987

M. Bleiman. *On Cinema*, Iskusstvo, Moscow, 1973

J.M. Boggs. *The Art of Watching Films*, Benjamin/ Cummings, Menlo Park, CA, 1978

P. Bondanella. *The Cinema of Federico Fellini*, Princeton University Press, Princeton, NJ, 1992

P. Bonitzer. "L'Idéeprincipale", *Cahiers du Cinéma*, 386, Aug, 1986

J. Boorman & W. Donohue, eds. *Projections 1*, Faber, London, 1992

—. *Projections 2*, Faber, London, 1993

—. *Projections 3*, Faber, London, 1994

—. *Projections 4*, Faber, London, 1995

—. *Projections 4 1/2*, Positif Editions/ Faber, London, 1995

—. *Projections 5*, Faber, London, 1996

—. *Projections 6*, Faber, London, 1996

—. *Projections 7*, Faber, London, 1997

—. *Projections 8*, Faber, London, 1998

D. Bordwell. "Art cinema as a mode of film practice", *Film Criticism*, 4, I, 1979

—. & K. Thompson. "Space and narrative in the films of Ozu", *Screen*, 17, 2, Summer, 1976

—. *The Films of Carl-Theodor Dreyer*, University of California, Berkeley, CA, 1981

—. et al. *The Classical Hollywood Cinema: Film Style and Mode of Production to 1960*, Routledge, London, 1985

—. *Narration in the Fiction Film*, Routledge, London, 1988

—. *Ozu and the Poetics of Cinema*, British Film Institute, London, 1988

—. & K. Thompson. *Film Art: An Introduction*, McGraw-Hill Publishing Company, New York, NY, 1990

—. *The Cinema of Eisenstein*, Harvard University Press, Cambridge, MA, 1993

F. Borin. *Andrej Tarkovsky*, Venice, 1987

F. Botting. *Making Monstrous: Frankenstein, Criticism, Theory*, Manchester University Press, Manchester, 1991

—. *Gothic*, Routledge, London, 1996

—. *Sex, Machines and Navels: Fiction, Fantasy and History in the Future Present*, Manchester University Press, Manchester, 1999

R. Bresson. *Notes on the Cinematographer*, tr. J. Griffin, Quartet, London, 1986

A. Briggs & P. Cobley, eds. *The Media*, Longman, London, 1998

M. Broderick. *Nuclear Movies*, Post-Modern, Northcote, 1988

P. Brophy. *100 Modern Soundtracks*, British Film Institute, London, 2004

J. Brosnan. *Future Tense: The Cinema of Science Fiction*, St Martin's Press, New York, NY, 1978

—. *Primal Screen: A History of Science Fiction Film*, Orbit, London, 1991

D. Brown. *Soviet Russian Literature Since Stalin*, Cambridge University Press, Cambridge, 1978

R. Brown, ed. *Focus on Godard*, Prentice-Hall, NJ, 1972

S. Bruzzi. "Space Looks", *Sight & Sound*, Sept, 1995

S. Bukatman. "Postcards From the Posthuman Solar System", *Science Fiction Studies*, 55, 1991

—. *Terminal Identity: The Virtual Subject in Postmordern Science Fiction*, Duke University Press, Durham, NC, 1993

—. "The Artificial Infinite", in L. Cooke, 1995

—. *Blade Runner*, British Film Institute, London, 1997

—. "The Ultimate Trip: Special Effects and Kaleidoscopic Perception", *Iris*, 25, 1998

N. Burch. *Theory of Film Practice*, Secker & Warburg, London, 1973

T. Burckhardt. *Sacred Art in East and West*, Perennial Books, Middlesex, 1967

I. Butler. *Religion in the Cinema*, A.S. Barnes, New York, NY, 1969

I. Cameron, ed. *The Films of Robert Bresson*, Studio Vista, London, 1969

—. ed. *The Films of Jean-Luc Godard*, Praeger, New York, NY, 1969

J. Campbell. *The Power of Myth*, with B. Moyers, ed. B.S. Flowers, Doubleday, New York, NY, 1988a

—. *The Hero With a Thousand Faces*, Paladin, London, 1988b

—. *This business of the gods...*, Windrose Films, Ontario, 1989

—. *The Hero's Journey: Joseph Campbell On His Life and Work*, Harper & Row, San Francisco, CA, 1990

R. Campbell & M. Pitts. *The Bible On Film*, Scarecrow Press, Metuchen, NJ, 1981

V. Canby. review of *Andrei Roublev*, *New York Times*, Oct 10, 1973

J. Carey. *Spectacular! The Story of Epic Films*, London, 1974

N. Carroll. *Mystifying Movies: Fads and Fallacies of Contemporary Film Theory*, Columbia University Press, New York, NY, 1988

—. *The Philosophy of Horror*, Routledge, New York, NY, 1990

J. Caughie, ed. *Theories of Authorship: A Reader*, Routledge, London, 1988

—. & A. Kuhn, eds. *The Sexual Subject: A Screen Reader in Sexuality*, Routledge, London, 1992

P. Cazals. *Sergei Paradjanov*, Cahiers du Cinéma, Paris, 1993

J. Chambers II & D. Culbert, eds. *World War II, Film, and History*, Oxford University Press, Oxford, 1996

S. Chatham. *Antonioni, or The Surface of the World*, University of California Press, Los Angeles, CA, 1985

H.B. Chipp, ed. *Theories of Modern Art*, University of California Press, Los Angeles, CA, 1968

P. Christensen. "Kierkegaardian Motifs in Tarkovsky's *The Sacrifice*", *Soviet and East-European Drama, Theatre and Film*, 7, 2/3, Dec, 1987

I. Christie. "Raising the Shroud", *Monthly Film Bulletin*, Feb, 1987

—. & J. Grafty, eds. *Yakov Protazanov and the Continuity of Russian Cinema*, British Film Institute, London, 1993

—. & R. Taylor, eds. *Eisenstein Rediscovered*, Routledge, London, 1993

— & P. Dodd. *Spellbound: Art and Film*, British Film Institute, London, 1996

—. "Returning to Zero", *Sight & Sound*, Apl, 1998

M. Ciment, ed. *Dossier Positif*, Editions Rivages, Paris, 1988

E.M. Cioran. *Tears and Saints*, University of Chicago Press, Chicago, IL, 1995

J. Clute & P. Nicholls, eds. *The Encyclopaedia of Science Fiction*, Orbit, London, 1993

—. ed. *The Illustrated Encyclopaedia of Science Fiction*, Dorling Kindersley, London, 1995

P. Coates, ed. *Lucid Dreams: The Films of Krzysztof Kieslowski*, Flicks Books, London

J. Collins *et al*, eds. *Film Theory Goes to the Movies*, Routledge, New York, NY, 1993

E. Conze, ed. *Buddhist Scriptures*, Penguin, London, 1959

L. Cooke & P. Wollen, eds. *Visual Display*, Bay Press, Seattle, 1995

J.C. Cooper. *An Illustrated Dictionary of Symbols*, Thames and Hudson, London, 1978

D.A. Cook. *A History of Narrative Film*, W.W. Norton, New York, NY, 1990

P. Cook, ed. *The Cinema Book*, British Film Institute, London, 1985

R. Corliss: "*The Last Temptation of Christ*", *Film Comment*, 24, Sept-Oct, 1988

B. Creed. "Horror and the Monstrous-Feminine: An Imaginary Abjection", *Screen*, 27, 1, 1986

C.K. Creekmur & A. Doty, eds. *Out in Culture: Gay, Lesbian, and Queer Essays on Popular Culture*, Cassell, London, 1995

A. Crisanti. "Le décor de *Nostalgia*", in G. Ciment, 1988

J. Crowder. "A *Sacrifice* worth making", *Santa Barbara News-Press*, Feb 28, 1987

J. Cuineen. "Film and the Sacred", *Cross Currents*, 43, 1993

A. de Baecque. *Andrei Tarkovski*, Cahiers du Cinéma, Paris, 1989

P.J. Davies, ed. *Science Fiction, Social Conflict and War*, Manchester University Press, Manchester, 1990

A. de Jonge. *Stalin and the Shaping of the Soviet Union*, Morrow, New York, NY, 1986

T. de Lauretis & S. Heath, eds. *The Cinematic Apparatus*, St Martin's Press, New York, NY, 1980

—. *Alice Doesn't: Feminism, Semiotics, Cinema*, Indiana University Press, Bloomington, IN, 1984

—. *Technologies of Gender*, Macmillan, London, 1987

G. Deleuze. *Cinema 1: The Movement Image*, Athlone Press, London, 1989

—. *Cinema 2: The Time Image*, Athlone Press, London, 1989

J. Delmas. "'…comme une fleuve': *Andrei Roublev*", *Jeune Cinéma*, 42, Dec, 1969

M. Dempsey. "Lost Harmony: Tarkovsky's *The Mirror* and *The Stalker*", *Film Quarterly*, Autumn, 1981

L. Denham. *The Films of Peter Greenaway*, Minerva Press, London, 1993

J. Derrida. *Writing and Difference*, University of Chicago Press, Chicago, IL, 1987

—. *Of Grammatology*, Johns Hopkins University Press, Baltimore, MD, 1976

T. Dickinson. *A Discovery of Cinema*, Oxford University Press, Oxford, 1971

M.A. Doane. *The Desire to Desire: The Woman's Film of the, 1940's*, Macmillan, London, 1988

S. Dohan & I.R. Hark, eds. *Screening the Male: Exploring Masculinities in Hollywood Cinema*, Routledge, London, 1993

G. Dolmarovskaya & I. Shilova. *Who's Who in the Soviet Cinema*, Progress, Moscow, 1979

J. Donald, ed. *Fantasy and the Cinema*, British Film Institute, London, 1989

A. Dovzhenko. *Alexander Dovzenko*, MIT Press, Cambridge, MA, 1973

C.T. Dreyer. *Letters About the Jesus Film: 16 Years of Correspondence Between Carl Theodore Dreyer and Blevins Davis*, University of Copenhagen Press, Copenhagen, 1989

N. Savio D'Sa. "Andrei Rublev: Religious Epiphany in Art", *Journal of Religion and Film*, 3, 2, 1999

J. Duflot. *Il sogno del centauro*, Riuniti, Rome, 1983

R. Durgnat. "Epic", *Films and Filming*, 10, Dec, 1963

—. *Films and Feelings*, Faber, London, 1967

A. Dworkin. *Pornography: Men Possessing Women*, Women's Press, London, 1981

A. Dzenis. "The Passion According to Andrei: *Andrei Rublev*", *Metro*, 110, 1997

R. Dyer & G. Vincendeau, eds. *Popular European Cinema*, Routledge, London, 1992

H. Eagle. *Russian Formalist Film Theory*, University of Michigan Press, Ann Arbor, MI, 1981

M. Eagleton, ed. *Feminist Literary Criticism*, Longman, London, 1991

A. Easthope, ed. *Contemporary Film Theory*, Longman, London, 1993

E. Edelson. *Great Movie Spectaculars*, New York, NY, 1976

S. Eisenstein. *Film Form*, tr. J. Leyda, Harcourt, Brace & Co, New York, NY, 1949

—. *The Film Sense*, tr. J. Leyda, Harcourt, Brace Jovanovich, New York, NY, 1974

—. *Notes of a Film Director*, Dover, New York, NY, 1978

—. *Immoral Memories*, tr. H. Marshall, Houon Mifflin, Boston, MA, 1983

M. Eliade. *From Primitives to Zen*, Collins, London, 1977

—. *Shamanism*, Princeton University Press, Princeton, NJ, 1972

—. *Patterns in Comparative Religion*, Sheed & Ward, London, 1958

—. *A History of Religious Ideas*, I, Collins, London, 1979

—. *Ordeal by Labyrinth*, University of Chicago Press, Chicago, IL, 1984

—. *Symbolism, the Sacred and the Arts*, Crossroad, New York, NY, 1985

D. Elley. *The Epic Film*, Routledge & Kegan Paul, London, 1984

—. ed. *Variety Movie Guide*, Hamlyn, London, 1996

J. Elliot. *Eliot's Guide to Films On Video*, Boxtree, London, 1993

T. Elmanovits. *The Mirror of Time: The Films of Andrei Tarkovsky*, Eesti Raamat, Tallinn, 1980

T. Elsaesser. *New German Cinema: A History*, Macmillan, London, 1989

M. Estève, ed. *Etudes Cinématographiques: Andrei Tarkovsky*, 135-138, Lettres Modernes, Paris, 1983

P. Ettedgui. *Production Design & Art Direction*, RotoVision, 1999

L. D. Ettlinger. *Leonardo da Vinci*, Weidenfeld & Nicolson, London, 1969

G. Faraday. *Revolt of the Filmmakers: The Struggle for Artistic Autonomy and the Fall the Russian Film Industry*, Penn State University Press, 2000

F. Fellini. *Fellini on Fellini*, Delacorte, New York, NY, 1976

J. Ferguson. *An Illustrated Encyclopaedia of Mysticism*, Thames & Hudson, London, 1976

E. Ferlita & J. R. May. *Film as a search for meaning*, Veritas, Dublin, 1976

Film Review Annual 1985, Jerome S. Ozer, NJ, 1985

M. Figgis, ed. *Projections 10*, Faber, London, 1999

J. Finler. *The Movie Directors Story*, Octopus Books, London, 1985

—. *The Hollywood Story*, Wallflower Press, London, 2003

L. Fischer. *Shot/ Countershot*, Princeton University Press, Princeton, NJ, 1989

—. *Cinematernity: Film, Motherhood, Genre*, Princeton University Press, Princeton, NJ, 1996

W. Fisher. "Gorbachev's Cinema", *Sight & Sound*, 56, 4, Autumn, 1987

G.E. Forshey. *American Religious and Biblical Spectaculars*, Praeger, Westport, CT, 1992

M. Foucault. *Politics, Philosophy, Culture: Interviews and Other Writings, 1977-1984*, ed. L.D. Kritzmon, Routledge, New York, NY, 1990

J. Franklin. *New German Cinema*, Columbus Books, 1986

G.M. Fraser. *The Hollywood History of the World*, Michael Joseph, London, 1988

J.G. Frazer. *The Golden Bough*, Macmillan, London, 1911-15

C. Freeland & T. Wartenberg, eds. *Philosophy and Film*, Routledge, London, 1995

K. French, ed. *Screen Violence*, Bloomsbury, London, 1996

P. French *et al. The Films of Jean-Luc Godard*, Blue Star House, 1967

S. Freud. *Leonardo da Vinci*, tr. A. Tyson, Penguin, London, 1965

S. Frieden *et al. Gender and the German Cinema: Feminist Interventions*, Berg, Providence, RI, 1993

N. Galichenko. *Glasnost: Soviet Cinema Responds*, University of Texas Press, Austin, TX, 1991

L. Gamman & M. Marshment, eds. *The Female Gaze: Women as Viewers of Popular Culture*, Women's Press, London, 1988

L.A. Garrett. "Der rätselhafte und geheimnisvolle Andrej Tarkovskij", *Soviet Film*, 7, 1989

—. "Never Be Neutral", *Sight & Sound*, Jan, 1997

G. Gauthier. *Andrei Tarkovski, Filmo*, 19, Edilig, Paris, 1988

J. Gelmis. *The Film Director as Superstar*, Penguin, London, 1974

H.G. Gerhard. *World of Icons*, John Murray, London, 1971

J. Gerstenkorn & S. Strudel. "La quête et la foi", *Études cinématographiques*, 135-8, 1983

L. Gianetti. *Understanding Movies*, Prentice-Hall, NJ, 1996

A. Gibson. *The Silence of God: Creative Response to the Films of Ingmar Bergman*, Harper & Row, New York, NY, 1969

P. Gibson & R. Gibson, ed. *Dirty Looks: Women, Pornography, Power*, British Film Institute, London, 1993

J.-L. Godard. *Godard on Godard*, eds. J. Narobi & T. Milne, Da Capo, New York, NY, 1986

L. Goldberg *et al*, eds. *Science Fiction Filmmaking in the 1980s*, McFarland, Jefferson, 1995

R. Goldwater & M. Treves, eds. *Artists on Art*, John Murray, London, 1976

V. Golovskoy & J. Rimberg. *Behind the Soviet Screen*, Ardis, Ann Arbor, MI, 1986

W. Goodman. "Tarkovsky dies at 54", *New York Times*, Dec 30, 1986

J. Goodwin. *Eisenstein, Cinema and History*, University of Illinois Press, Urbana, IL, 1993

—. ed. *Perspectives On Akira Kurosawa*, G.K. Hall, Boston, MA, 1994

D.J. Goulding, ed. *Post New Wave Cinema in the Soviet Union and Eastern Europe*, Indiana University Press, Bloomington, IN, 1989

—. ed. *Five Filmmakers: Tarkovsky, Forman, Polanski, Szabó, Makavejev*, Indiana University Press, Bloomington, IN, 1994

J. Graffy. "Tarkovsky: The Weight of the World", *Sight & Sound*, Jan, 1997

D. Graham, ed. *Film and Religion*, St Mungo Press, 1997

J. Grant. "Andrei Tarkovsky", *Cinéma*, 231, 1978

C. Gray, ed. *The Cyborg Handbook*, Routledge, 1995

P. Green. "The Nostalgia of the Stalker", *Sight and Sound*, Winter, 1984-85

—. "Andrei Tarkovsky", *Sight and Sound*, 56, 2, Spring, 1987

—. *Andrei Tarkovsky: The Winding Quest*, Macmillan, London, 1993

A. Greenberg. *Heart of Glass*, Munich, 1976

N. Greene. *Pier Paolo Pasolini*, Princeton University Press, Princeton, NJ, 1990

R. Grenier. "A Soviet New Wave?", *Commentary*, July, 1981

N. Grinko. "Talisman Andreya Tarkovskogo [The talisman of Andrei Tarkovsky]", interview, *Sovetsky ekran*, 2, 1990

K. von Gunden. *Postmodern Auteurs*, McFarland, Jefferson, NC, 1991

J. Hacker & D. Price, eds. *Take 10: Contemporary British Film Directors*, Oxford University Press, Oxford, 1991

L. Halliwell. *Halliwell's Filmgoer's Companion*, 7th edition, Granada, London, 1980

—. *Halliwell's Film Guide*, ed. J. Walker, HarperCollins, London, 1993

—. *Halliwell's Film Guide 2000*, ed. J. Walker, HarperCollins, London, 1999

S. Hancock. "Andrei Tarkovsky: Master of the Cinematic Image", *Mars Hill Review*, 4, 1996

L. Hanlon. *Fragments: Bresson's Film Style*, Farleigh Dickinson University Press, Rutherford, 1986

F.C. Happold. *Mysticism: A Study and an Anthology*, Penguin, London, 1970

D. Haraway. "A Manifesto For Cyborgs", *Socialist Review*, 15, 2, 1985

—. *Primate Visions: Gender, Race and Nature in the World of Modern Science*,

Routledge, London, 1989

—. *Simians, Cyborgs, and Women*, Routledge, London, 1991a

—. "Cyborgs At Large", *Social Text*, 25, 1991b

—. "The Promises of Monsters", in J. Wolmark, 1999

P. Hardy, ed. *The Aurum Encyclopaedia of Science Fiction*, Aurum, London, 1991

H. Hart. "The Dialogue of Theology With Film", *Encounter*, 51, 1990

R. Hayman. *Fassbinder: Filmmaker*, Simon & Schuster, New York, NY, 1984

M. Hayward. *Twentieth-century Russian Poetry*, London, 1993

M. Healy. "Cinematography is the major attraction of humorless sermon", *Denver Post*, Feb 20, 1987

S. Heath. "Narrative Space", *Screen*, 17, 3, Autumn, 1976

—. *Questions of Cinema*, Macmillan, London, 1981

M. Heaton. "In films, life, Tarkovsky spurned compromise", *San Francisco Examiner*, Jan 30, 1987

S. Hill. "Soviet Cinema Today", *Film Quarterly*, 20, 4, Summer, 1967

J. Hillier, ed. *Cahiers du Cinéma: The 1950s, New-Realism, Hollywood, New Wave*, Harvard University Press, Cambridge, MA, 1985

—. *The New Hollywood*, Studio Vista, London, 1992

L.C. Hillstrom, ed. *International Dictionary of Films and Filmmakers: Directors*, St James Press, London, 1997

F. Hirsch. *The Hollywood Epic*, Barnes, New York, NY, 1978

S.L. Hoagland & J. Penelope, eds. *For Lesbians Only: A separatist anthology*, Onlywomen Press, London, 1988

R. Holloway. *Beyond the Image: Approaches to the Religious Dimension in the Cinema*, World Council of Churches, 1977

D. Holmes & A. Smith, eds. *100 Years of European Cinema*, Manchester University Press, Manchester, 2000

L. Horn. "Tarkovsky's *Sacrifice* charged with images", *Miami Herald*, Nov 21, 1986

A. Horton,& M. Brashinsky. *The Zero Hour: Glasnost and Soviet Cinema in Transition*, Princeton University Press, Princeton, NJ, 1992

—. ed. *Inside Soviet Film Satire*, Cambridge University Press, Cambridge, Cambridge, 1993

—. *Theo Angelopoulos: A Cinema of Contemplation*, Princeton University Press, Princeton, NJ, 1999

A. Huxley. *The Perennial Philosophy*, Chatto & Windus, London, 1969

T. Hyman. "*Solaris*", *Film Quarterly*, Spring, 1976

E. Hynes. "Stalker", *Reverse Shot*, Spring, 2004

J.J. F. Iaccino. *Jungian Reflections Within the Cinema: A Psychological Analysis of Sci-Fi and Fantasy Archetypes*, Praeger, Westport, CT, 1998

P. Iden *et al. Fassbinder*, Tanam, New York, NY, 1981

Iskusstvo kino, 2, 1989

W. Jacobsen *et al. Andrej Tarkovsky*, Munich, 1987

W. James. *The Varieties of Religious Experience*, Penguin, New York, NY, 1982

I. Jarvie. *Philosophy of the Film: Epistemology, Ontology, Aesthetics*, Routledge and Kegan Paul, London, 1987

A. Jefferson & Robey, eds. *Modern Literary Theory*, Batsford, London, 1982

V.T. Johnson & G. Petrie. "Andrei Tarkovskii's Films", *Journal of European Studies*, 20, 3, Sept, 1990

—. *The Films of Andrei Tarkovsky. A Visual Fugue*, Indiana University Press, Bloomington, IN, 1994

—. "Tarkovsky", chapter in D. Goulding, 1994b

—. "Ethical Exploration" [*Solaris*]", *Sight & Sound*, 2002

G.A. Jonsson & T.A. Ottarsson. *Through the Mirror: Reflections on the Films of Andrei Tarkovsky*, 2006

C.G. Jung. *Memories, Dreams, Reflections*, Collins, London, 1967

N. Kagan. *The Cinema of Stanley Kubrick*, Continuum Publishing, New York, NY, 1991

W. Kaoru. *St. Tarkovsky*, Japan, 2003

E. Ann Kaplan. *Women and Film: Both Sides of the Camera*, Methuen, New York, NY, 1983

—. ed. *Psychoanalysis and Cinema*, Routledge, London, 1990

A.H. Karriker. "Patterns of Spirituality in Tarkovsky's Later Films", in D. Petrie, 1990

R. Katz & P. Berling. *Love Is Colder Than Death: Rainer Werner Fassbinder*, Paladin, London, 1989

B. Kawin. *Mindscreen: Bergman, Godard and First-Person Film*, Princeton University Press, Princeton, NJ, 1978

—. *How Movies Work*, Macmillan, New York, NY, 1987

S. Kemal & I. Gaskell, eds. *Landscape, natural beauty and the arts*, Cambridge University Press, Cambridge, 1993

P. Kenez. *Cinema and Soviet Society*, Cambridge University Press, Cambridge, 1992

H. Kennedy. "Tarkovsky: A Thought in Nine Parts", *Film Comment*, 23, 3, 46, 1987

V. Kepley. *In the Service of the State: The Cinema of Alexander Dovzenko*, University of Wisconsin Press, Madison, WI, 1986

—. *Wide Angle*, "Contemporary Soviet Cinema" number, 12, 4, 1990

G. King. "The Scientist as Pioneer Hero: Hollywood's Mythological Reconciliations in *Twister* and *Contact*", *Science as Culture*, 8, 3, 1999

—. *Spectacular Narratives: Hollywood in the Age of the Blockbuster*, I.B. Tauris, London, 2000

—. & T. Krzywinmska. *Science Fiction Cinema* Wallflower, London, 2000

T. Jefferson Kline. *Bertolucci's Dream Loom: A Psychoanalytic Study of Cinema*, University of Massachusetts Press, Amherst, MA, 1987

R. Jewett. *Saint Paul At the Movies*, Westminster/John Knox, 1993

K. Kieslowski. *Kieslowski On Kieslowski*, ed. D. Stok, Faber, London, 1993

R. Kinnard & T. Dasvis. *Divine Images: A History of Jesus On the Screen*, Citadel Press, New York, NY, 1992

Kinovedcheskiye zapiski, 9, 1991; 14, 1992

J. Knight. *Women and the New German Cinema*, Verso, London, 1992

R.P. Kolker. *A Cinema of Loneliness: Penn, Kubrick, Coppola, Scorsese, Altman*, Oxford University Press, New York, NY, 1980

—. *Bernardo Bertolucci*, British Film Institute, London, 1985

—. *The Altering Eye: Contemporary International Cinema*, Oxford University Press, New York, NY, 1983

—. *A Cinema of Loneliness: Penn, Stone, Kubrick, Scorsese, Spielberg, Altman*, Oxford University Press, New York, NY, 2000

R. Koszarsky, ed. *Hollywood Directors, 1941-1976*, Oxford University Press,

New York, NY, 1977

B.A. Kovács & A. Szilágyi. *Les Mondes d'Andrei Tarkovski*, tr. V. Charaire, L'Age d'Homme, Lausanne, 1987

P. Král. "Tarkovsky, or the Burning House", *Screening the Past*, 12, Mch, 2001

L. Kreitzer. *The New Testament in Fiction and Film*, JSOT, 1993

—. *The Old Testament in Fiction and Film*, Sheffield Academic Press, Sheffield, 1994

J. Kristeva. *Desire in Language: A Semiotic Approach to Literature and Art*, ed. L. Roudiez, tr. T. Gora, *et al*, Blackwell, Oxford, 1982

—. *Revolution in Poetic Language*, tr. M. Walker, Columbia University Press, New York, NY, 1984

—. *The Kristeva Reader*, ed. T. Moi, Blackwell, Oxford, 1986

—. "A Question of Subjectivity: an interview", *Women's Review*, 12, 1986

—. *Tales of Love*, tr. L. Roudiez, Columbia University Press, New York, NY, 1987

—. *Strangers to Ourselves*, tr. L. Roudiez, Harvester Wheatsheaf, Hemel Hempstead, 1991

A. Kuhn. *Women's Pictures: Feminism and the Cinema*, Routledge & Kegan Paul, London, 1982

W. La Barre. *The Ghost Dance: The Origins of Religion*, Allen & Unwin, London, 1972

—. *Muelos: A Stone Age Superstition About Sexuality*, Columbia University Press, New York, NY, 1985

J. Lacan. *Ecrits: A Selection*, tr. A. Sheridan, Tavistock Publications, London, 1977

R. Lapsley & M. Westlake, eds. *Film Theory: An Introduction*, Manchester University Press, Manchester, 1988

V. Lasareff. *Russian Icons*, Collins, London, 1962

R. Lauder. *God, Death, Art and Love: The Philosophical Vision of Ingmar Bergman*, Paulist Press, 1989

D.H. Lawrence. *The Lost Girl*, Penguin, London, 1980

—. *The Letters of D.H. Lawrence*, ed. A. Huxley, Heinemann, London, 1934

—. *A Selection from Phoenix*, ed. A.A.H. Inglis, Penguin, London, 1971

A. Lawton. *Kinoglasnost: Soviet Cinema in Our Time*, Cambridge University Press, Cambridge, 1992

—. *The Red Screen: Politics, Society, Art in Soviet Cinema*, Routledge, London, 1992

J. Leach. *A Possible Cinema: The Films of Alain Tanner*, Scarecrow Press, Metuchen, NJ, 1984

M. Le Fanu. *Sight & Sound*, Autumn, 1986

—. *The Cinema of Andrei Tarkovsky*, British Film Institute, London, 1987

P. Lehman, ed. *Close Viewings*, Florida State University Press, Tallahassee, FL, 1990

—. ed. *Defining Cinema*, Athlone Press, London, 1997

S. Lem. *Solaris*, Penguin, London, 1981

L. da Vinci. *Selections from the Notebooks*, Oxford University Press, Oxford, 1952

J. Lewis. *Whom God Wishes to Destroy: Francis Coppola and the New Hollywood*, Duke University Press, Durham, NC, 1995

J. Leyda. ed. *Film Makers Speak: Voices of Film Experience*, Da Capo, New York, NY, 1977

—. *Kino: A History of the Russian and Soviet Cinema*, 3rd ed, Allen & Unwin,

London, 1983

M. & A. Liehm. *The Most Important Art: Eastern European Film After 1945*, University of California Press, Berkeley, CA, 1977

P. Livington. *Ingmar Bergman and the Rituals of Art*, Cornell University Press, Ithaca, NY, 1982

Rafael Llano. *Andrei Tarkovsky*,

A. Lloyd, ed. *The History of the Movies*, Macdonald Orbis, London, 1988

R. Long. *Ingmar Bergman*, Abrams, New York, NY, 1994

Y. Loshitzky. *The Radical Faces of Godard and Bertolucci*, Wayne State University Press, Detroit, MI, 1995

L. Lourdeaux. *Italian and Irish Filmmakers in America: Ford, Capra, Coppola and Scorsese*, Temple University Press, Philadelphia, PA, 1990

J. MacBean. "Godard and the Dziga Vertov Group", *Film Quarterly*, 26, I, Autumn, 1972

C. MacCabe. "Principles of realism and pleasure", *Screen*, 17, 3, Autumn, 1976

—. *Godard, Images, Sound, Politics*, Macmillan/ British Film Institute, London, 1980

R.D. MacCann, ed. *Film: A Montage of Theories*, Dutton, New York, NY, 1966

L. Maltin. ed. *Leonard Maltin's 2001 Movie & Video Guide*, Penguin, London, 2000

M. Mancini & G. Perella. *Pier Paolo Pasolini: corpi e luoghi*, Theorema, Bologna, 1982

E. Marks & I. de Courtivron, eds. *New French feminisms: an anthology*, Harvester Wheatsheaf, Hemel Hempstead, 1981

C. Marsh & G. Ortiz, eds. *Explorations in Theology and Film*, Blackwell, Oxford, 1997

H. Marshall. "Andrei Tarkovsky's *The Mirror*", *Sight and Sound*, Spring, 1976

—. *Masters of the Soviet Cinema*, Routledge, London, 1983

J.W. Martin & Conrad E. Ostwalt, eds. *Screening the Sacred: Religion, Myth, and Ideology in Popular American Film*, Westview Press, Boulder, CO, 1995

S. Martin. *Andrei Tarkovsky*, Essential Books, London, 2005

T. Martin. *Images and the Imageless: a Study in Religious Consciousness and Film*, Bucknell University Press, 1981

G. Mast *et al*, eds. *Film Theory and Criticism: Introductory Readings*, Oxford University Press, New York, NY, 1992

J.R. May & M. Bird, eds. *Religion in Film*, University of Tennessee Press, Knoxville, TN, 1982

—. *Image and Likeness: Religious Vision in American Film Classics*, Paulist Press, 1992

—. *New Image of Religious Film*, Sheed & Ward, London, 1996

J. Mayne. *Kino and the Woman Question: Feminism and Soviet Silent Film*, Ohio State University Press, OH, 1989

L. McCaffery, ed. *Storming the Reality Studio: A Casebook of Cyberpunk and Postmodern Fiction*, Duke University Press, Durham, NC, 1991

M. McCormick. *Model of a House: An Essay on Andrei Tarkovsky's The Sacrifice*, 2006

M. McEver. "The Messianic Figure in Film: Christology Beyond the Biblical Epic", *Journal of Popular Religion and Film*, 2, 2, 1998

L. Menashe. "Glasnost in the Soviet Cinema", *Cineaste*, 16, 1/2, 1988

A. Mengs, *Stalker*, Ediciones Rialp, Spain

J.C.J. Metford. *Dictionary of Christian Lore and Legend*, Thames & Hudson, London, 1983

C. Metz. *Film Language: A Semiotics of the Cinema*, tr. M. Taylor, Oxford University Press, New York, NY, 1974

R. Meyers. *The Great Science Fiction Films*, Carol Publishing, New York, 1999

D. Miall. "The Self in History: Wordsworth, Tarkovsky and Autobiography", *Wordsworth Circle*, 27, 1996

V.I. Mikhalkovich. *Andrei Tarkovsky*, Znaniye, Moscow, 1989

M. Miles. *Seeing and Believing: Religion and Values in the Movies*, Beacon, Boston, MA, 1996

A. Miller. *Thou Shalt Not Be Aware: Society's Betrayal of the Child*, tr. H. & H. Hannum, Farrar, Straus & Giroux, New York, NY, 1986

F. Miller. *Censored Hollywood: Sex, Sin and Violence On Screen*, Turner Publishing, Atlanta, GA, 1994

J.-A. Miller *et al.* "Dossier on suture", *Screen*, 18, 4, Winter, 1977/78

T. Mitchell. "Tarkovsky in Italy", *Sight and Sound*, Winter, 1982-83

—. "Andrei Tarkovsky and *Nostalghia*", *Film Criticism*, 8, 3, 1984

T. Moi. *Sexual/Textual Politics: Feminist Literary Theory*, Methuen, London, 1985

— ed. *French Feminist Thought*, Blackwell, Oxford, 1988

J. Monaco. *The New Wave: Truffaut, Godard, Chabrol, Rohmer, Rivette*, Oxford University Press, New York, NY, 1977

I. Montagu. "Man and Experience: Tarkovsky's World", *Sight and Sound*, Spring, 1973

J. Moore. "Vagabond Desire: Aliens, Alienation and Human Regeneration in Arkday and Boris Strugatsky's *Roadside Picnic* and Andrei Tarkovsky's *Stalker*", in D. Cartmell *et al*, eds., *Alien Identities: Exploring Differences in Film and Fiction*, Pluto Press, London, 1999

M. Morris. "Of God and Man: A Theological and Artistic Scrutiny of Martin Scorsese's *The Last Temptation of Christ*", *American Film*, Oct, 1988

Mosfilm artistic council. *Stenograma zasedaniya khudozhestvennogo soveta* [TS of *Artistic Council Meeting*, Mch I, 1962], First Creative Meeting, Mosfilm, 1962

L. Mulvey. *Visual and Other Pleasures*, Indiana University Press, Bloomington, IN, 1989

M. Mulvey-Roberts, ed. *The Handbook of Gothic Literature*, New York University Press, New York, NY, 1998

S. Munt, ed. *New Lesbian Criticism: Literary and Cultural Readings*, Harvester Wheatsheaf, Hemel Hempstead, 1992

L. Nead. *Female Nude: Art, Obscenity and Sexuality*, Routledge, London, 1992

J. Nelmes, ed. *An Introduction to Film Studies*, Routledge, London, 1996

T.A. Nelson. *Kubrick: Inside a Film Artist's Maze*, Indiana University Press, Bloomington, IN, 1982

G. Nowell-Smith, ed. *The Oxford History of World Cinema*, Oxford University Press, Oxford, 1996

S. Nykvist. "Entretien" (with H. Niogret), *Positif*, 324, Feb, 1988

—. & B. Forslund. *In Reverence of Light*, Albert Bonniers Publishing Company, Sweden, 1997

D. Obolensky, ed. *The Penguin Book of Russian Verse*, Penguin, London, 1965

G. Oritz. "Jesus At the Movies", *The Month*, Dec, 1994

J. Orr & C. Nicholson, eds. *Cinema and Fiction*, Edinburgh University Press, Edinburgh, 1992

—. *Cinema and Modernity*, Polity Press, Cambridge, 1993

—. *Contemporary Cinema*, Edinburgh University Press, Edinburgh, 1998

—. & O. Taxidou, eds. *Postwar Cinema and Modernity: A Film Reader*, Edinburgh University Press, Edinburgh, 2000

C. Ostwalt. "Religion & Popular Movies", *Journal of Religion and Film*, 2, 3, 1998

—. "Armageddon at the Millennial Dawn", *Journal of Religion and Film*, 4, I, 2000

J. Pallasmaa. *The Architecture of Images: Existential Space In Cinema*, Rakennustieto Oy

J. Panshina. "Rossia v ozhidanii chuda", *Russakaia mysl*, Feb 23, 1978

J. Park. *Learning to Dream: The New British Cinema*, Faber, London, 1984

P.P. Pasolini. *Il Vangelo Secondo Matteo*, Garzanti, Milan, 1964

—. *Pasolini on Pasolini*, ed. O. Stack, Thames & Hudson, London, 1969

J.-L. Passek, ed. *Le Cinéma russe*, L'Esquerre, Paris, 1981

A. Pavelin. *Fifty Religious Films*, A.P. Pavelin, Chiselhurst, Kent, 1990

W. Paul. review of *Andrei Roublev*, *Village Voice*, Nov I, 1973

R. Payne. *Leonardo*, Robert Hale, London, 1987

D. Peary, ed. *Omni's Screen Flights, Screen Fantasies*, Doubleday, New York, NY, 1984

C. Peavy. "The Secularized Christ in Contemporary Cinema", *Journal of Popular Film and TV*, 3, 2, 1974

R. Peck, ed. "Myth, Religious Typology and Recent Cinema", *Christianity and Literature*, 42, 1993

C. Penley, ed. *Feminism and Film Theory*, Routledge, New York, NY, 1988

—. *et al*, eds. *Close Encounters: Film, Feminism and Science Fiction*, University of Minnesota Press, Minneapolis, MN, 1991

G. Perry. *Life of Python*, Pavilion, London, 1983

S. Petraglia. *Andrej Tarkovskij*, Edizioni A.I.A.C.E., Turin, 1975

V. Petric, ed. *Film and Dreams: An Approach to Bergman*, Redgrave, South Salem, 1981

—. *Constructivism in Film*, Cambridge University Press, Cambridge, 1987

—. "Tarkovsky's Dream Imagery", *Film Quarterly*, Winter, 1990

G. Petrie & R. Dwyer, eds. *Before the Wall Came Down: Soviet and East European Filmmakers Working in the West*, University Press of America, Lanham, 1990

—. "Andrei Tarkovsky", in G. Nowell-Smith, 1996

K. Phillips. *New German Filmmakers*, Ungar, New York, NY, 1984

P. della Francesca. *The Complete Paintings*, Penguin, London, 1967/85

L. Pietropaolo & A. Testaferri, eds. *Feminisms in the Cinema*, Indiana University Press, Bloomington, IN, 1995

L. Yan Pin. "Simvolika Tarkovskogom i daoizma [The symbolism of Tarkovsky and Taoism]", *Kinovedcheskiye zapiski*, 9, 1991

A. Plakhov. "Soviet Cinema in the Nineties", *Sight & Sound*, 58, Spring, 1990

S. Porter *et al*, eds. *Images of Christ*, Sheffield Academic Press, Sheffield, 1997

C. Potter. *Image, Sound and Story: The Art of Telling in Film*, Secker & Warburg, London, 1990

M. Pye & L. Myles. *The Movie Brats: How the Film Generation Took Over Holly-*

wood, Faber, London, 1971

J. Pym. *Film On Four*, British Film Institute, London, 1992

—. ed. *Time Out Film Guide, 1996*, Penguin, London, 1995

D. Quinlan. *The Illustrated Guide to Film Directors*, B.T. Batsford, London, 1983

E. Rabkin & G. Slusser, eds. *Shadows of the Magic Lamp: Fantasy and Science Fiction in Film*, Southern Illinois University Press, Carbondale, IL, 1985

—. *Aliens: The Anthropology of Science Fiction*, Southern Illinois University Press, Carbondale, IL, 1987

M. Ratschewa. "The Messianic Power of Pictures: The Films of Andrei Tarkovsky", *Cinéaste*, 13, I, 1983

T. Reeves. *The Worldwide Guide To Movie Locations*, Titan Books, London, 2003

K.J. Reiger. *The Spiritual Image in Modern Art*, Theosophical Publishing House, Wheaton, IL, 1987

A. Reinhardt. *Art-as-Art: The Selected Writings*, ed. B. Rose, Viking, New York, NY, 1975

A. Reinhartz. "Jesus in Film: Hollywood Perspectives on the Jewishness of Jesus", *Journal of Religion and Film*, 2, 2, 1998

E. Rentschler. *West German Film*, Redgrave, New York, NY, 1984

—. ed. *West German Filmmakers on Film: Visions and Voices*, Holmes & Meier, New York, NY, 1988

D. Richie. *The Films of Akira Kurosawa*, University of California Press, Berkeley, CA, 1965

C. Rickey. "Starkly, a director explores materialism and spirituality", *Philadelphia Inquirer*, Feb 4, 1987

R.M. Rilke. *Duino Elegies*, tr. J.B. Leishman & S. Spender, Hogarth Press, London, 1957

—. *New Poems*, tr. J.B. Leishman, Hogarth Press, London, 1963

—. *The Selected Poetry*, ed. & tr. S. Mitchell, Picador/ Pan, London, 1987

R. Rinaldi. *Pier Paolo Pasolini*, Mursia, Milan, 1982

P. Robertson. *Guinness Film Facts and Figures*, Guinness Superlatives, 1985

D. Robinson. *World Cinema*, Methuen, London, 1981

—. "Sculptor in Time, Master of Spirit", *The Times*, Jan 3, 1987a

—. "Testament to a Powerful Will", *The Times*, Jan 9, 1987b

W.H. Rockett. *Devouring Whirlwind: Terror and Transcendence in the Cinema of Cruelty*, Greenwood Press, New York, NY, 1988

S. Rohdie. *Antonioni*, British Film Institute, London, 1990

—. *The Passion of Pier Paolo. Pasolini*, British Film Institute, London, 1995

G. Roheim, ed. *Psychoanalysis and the Social Sciences*, III, International University Press, New York, NY, 1951

J. Romney. "Future Soul [*Solaris*]", *Sight & Sound*, 2002

J. Rosenbaum. "Inner Space: Exploring Tarkovsky's *Solaris*", *Film Comment*, 26, 4, Aug, 1990

B.G. Rosenthal, ed. *The Occult in Russian & Soviet Culture*, Cornell University Press, Ithaca, NY, 1997

N. Ruddick, ed. *State of the Fantastic*, Greenwood Press, Westport, CT, 1992

R. Ruiz. *The Poetics of Cinema*, Dis Voir, Paris, 1995

J. Rusher & T. Frentz. *Projecting the Shadow: The Cyborg Hero in American Film*, University of Chicago Press, Chicago, IL, 1995

B. Rux. *Hollywood vs. the Aliens*, Frog, Berkeley, CA, 1997

T. Sabulis. "Director's final *Sacrifice* truly a gift", *Dallas Times Herald*, Jan 16, 1987

D. Salynsky. "Rezhissyor i mif [Director and myth]", *Iskusstvo kino*, 12, 1989

A.M. Sandler, ed. *Mir i filmy Andreya Tarkovskogo* [*The World and Films of Andrei Tarkovsky*], Iskusstvo, Moscow, 1991

J. Sanford. *The New German Cinema*, Da Capo Press, New York, NY, 1982

J.P. Sartre. *Situations VII*, Gallimard, Paris, 1965

P. Schelde. *Androids, Humanoids and Other Science Fiction Monsters*, New York University Press, New York, NY, 1993

G. Scholem. *On the Kabbalah and Its Symbolism*, Routledge, London, 1965

D. Schwartz. *Pasolini Requiem*, Pantheon, New York, NY, 1972

M. Scorsese. *Scorsese on Scorsese*, ed. D. Thompson & I. Christie, Faber, London, 1989

D. Shipman. *The Story of Cinema*, Hodder & Stoughton, London, 1984

D. Shostakovitch. *Testimony: The Memoirs of Dmitri Shostakovitch*, ed. S. Volkov, tr. A.W. Bouts, Hamish Hamilton, London, 1979

P. Shrader. *Transcendental Style in Film: Ozu, Bresson, Dreyer*, Da Capo Press, 1972

—. *Shrader on Shrader*, ed. K. Jackson, Faber, London, 1990

E. Siciliano. *Pasolini*, Random House, New York, NY, 1982

L. Sider *et al*, eds. *Soundscapes: The School of Sound Lectures 1998-2001*, Wallflower Press, London, 2003

K. Silverman. *The Subject of Semiotics*, Oxford University Press, New York, NY, 1983

—. *The Acoustic Mirror: The Female Voice in Psychoanalysis and Cinema*, Indiana University Press, Bloomington, IN, 1988

—. *Male Subjectivity at the Margins*, Routledge, London, 1992

—. & H. Farocki. *Speaking About Godard*, New York University Press, New York, NY, 1998

N. Sinyard. *Children in the Movies*, Batsford, London, 1992

P. Adams Sitney, ed. *The Film Culture Reader*, Praeger, New York, NY, 1970

—. ed. *The Avant-Garde Film: A Reader of Theory and Criticism*, New York University Press, New York, NY, 1978

—. *Visionary Film: The American Avant-Garde, 1943-1978*, 2nd ed., Oxford University Press, New York, NY, 1979

—. "Landscape in the cinema: the rhythms of the world and the camera", in S. Kemal, 1993

—. *Vital Crises in Italian Cinema*, University of Texas Press, Austin, TX, 1995

B. Sklarew *et al*, eds. *Bertolucci's The Last Emperor*, Wayne State University Press, Detroit, MI, 1998

T. Slater. *Handbook of Soviet and East European Films and Filmmakers*, Greenwood, Westport, CT, 1992

G. Smith. *Epic Films*, McFarland, Jefferson, NC, 1991

V. Sobchack. *The Limits of Infinity: The American Science Fiction Film*, A.S. Barnes, New York, NY, 1980

—. *Screening Space: The American Science Fiction Film*, Ungar, New York, NY, 1987/1993

—. "Cities On the Edge of Time: The Urban Science Fiction Film", *East-West Film Journal*, 3, 1, Dec, 1988

—. *The Address of the Eye: A Phenomenology of Film Experience*, Princeton University Press, Princeton, NJ, 1992

—. ed. *The Persistence of History: Cinema, Television, and the Modern Event*, Routledge, London, 1995

J. Solomon. *The Ancient World in the Cinema*, London, 1978

—. *The Ancient World in the Cinema*, Yale University Press, New Haven, CT, 2001

V. Solovyov. "Semeynaya khronika ottsa i syna Tarkovskikh [The family chronicle of Tarkovsky's father and son]", *Novoye russkoye slovo*, 12 May, 1989

C. Springer. "The Pleasure of the Interface", *Screen*, 32, 3, 1991

—. *Electronic Eros*, Athlone Press, London, 1996

B. Steene. *Ingmar Bergman*, Twayne, Boston, MA, 1968

—. ed. *Focus on The Seventh Seal*, Prentice-Hall, NJ, 1972

A. Stanbrook. "The Return of Paradjanov", *Sight & Sound*, 55, 4, Autumn, 1986

N. Steimatsky. "Pasolini on Terra Sancta: Towards a Theology of Film", *Yale Journal of Criticism*, 11, 1, 1998

L. Stern. *The Scorsese Connection*, British Film Institute, London, 1995

V.I. Stoichita. *Leonardo da Vinci*, Abbey Library, London, 1978

P. Strick. "*The Sacrifice*", *Monthly Film Bulletin*, Jan, 1987

—. "Tarkovsky's Lost Minutes", *The Times*, July 12, 1989

—. "Releasing the Balloon, Raising the Bell", *Monthly Film Bulletin*, Feb, 1991

A. & B. Strugatsky. *Roadside Picnic*, Pocket Books, New York, NY, 1978

J. Sudek. *Photothek*, U. Bar Verlag, Zurich, 1985

O. Surkova. "Avtobiograficheskiye motivy v tvorchestve Andreya Tarkovskogo [Autobiographic motifs in the creative work of Andrei Tarkovsky]", *Kino-vedcheskiye zapiski*, Moscow, 9, 1991

—. *Tarkovsky and I*, Zebra E, Dekont, 2002

D. Suvin. "Arkady and Boris Strugatsky", in J. Clute & P. Nicholls, eds. *The Encyclopaedia of Science Fiction*, Orbit, London, 1993

O. Svensson. "On Tarkovsky's *The Sacrifice*", in L. Sider, 2003

N. Synessios. *Mirror*, I.B. Tauris, London, 2001

P. Taggart. "Weighty Film", *Austin American-Statesman*, April 3, 1987

M. Tarkovskaya, ed. *O Tarkovskom [About Tarkovsky]*, Progress Publishers, Moscow, 1989

Arseny Tarkovsky. *Stikhotvoreniya [Poems]*, Khudozhestvennaya literatura, Moscow, 1974

—. *Poems*, Greville Press Poetry, 1992

—. *Blagoslovennyi svet*, St Petersburg, 1993

—. *Sobranie sochinenii [Collected Works]*, 3 vols, Moscow, 1991-93

—. *Life, Life: Selected Poems*, tr. V. Rounding, Crescent Moon, 1999

R. Taylor & I. Christie, eds. *The Film Factory: Russian and Soviet Cinema in Documents*, Routledge, London, 1988

—. *Inside the Film Factory: New Approaches to Russian and Soviet Cinema*, Routledge, London, 1991

—. & D. Spring, eds. *Stalinism and Soviet Cinema*, Routledge, London, 1993

—. et al, eds. *The BFI Companion to Eastern European and Russian Cinema*, British Film Institute, London, 2000

J. Telotte. "The Movies as Monster: Seeing in *King Kong*", *Georgia Review*, 24, 2, Summer, 1988

—. "The Tremulous Public Body", *Journal of Popular Film & Television*, 19, 1,

1991

—. *Replications: A Robotic History of the Science Fiction Film*, University of Illinois Press, Urbana, IL, 1996

—. *A Distant Technology: Science Fiction Film and the Machine Age*, Wesleyan University Press, NH, 1999

—. *Science Fiction Film*, Cambridge University Press, New York, NY, 2001

V. Terras, ed. *Handbook to Russian Literature*, New Haven, CT, 1985

K. Thompson & D. Bordwell. *Film History: An Introduction*, McGraw-Hill, New York, NY, 1994

D. Thomson. *A Biographical Dictionary of the Cinema*, Secker & Warburg, London, 1978

—. *Beneath Mulholland*, Little, Brown, Boston, MA, 1998

C. Tonetti. *Luchino Visconti*, Columbus Books, 1985

—. *Bernardo Bertolucci*, Twayne, Boston, MA, 1994

E. Törnqvist. *Between Stage and Screen: Ingmar Bergman Directs*, Amsterdam University Press, Amsterdam, 1995

F. Truffaut. *The Films in My Life*, tr. L. Mayhew, Penguin, London, 1982

A. Truppin. "And Then There Was Sound: The Films of Andrei Tarkovsky", in R. Altman, 1992

M. Tuchman. *The New York School*, Thames & Hudson, London, 1971

M. Turovskaya. *Tarkovsky: Cinema as Poetry*, tr. N. Ward, ed. I. Christie, Faber, London, 1989

P. Usai *et al*, eds. *Silent Witnesses: Russian Films 1908-1919*, British Film Institute, London, 1989

"*Sacrifice* Rolls in Sweden Next May", *Weekly Variety*, Sept 12, 1984

J. Verniere. "A beautiful *Sacrifice*", *Boston Herald*, Nov 7, 1986

D. Vertov. *Kino Eye*, ed. A. Michelson, University of California Press, Berkeley, CA, 1984

G. Vincendeau, ed. *Encyclopaedia of European Cinema*, British Film Institute, London, 1995

T. Vinokuroya. "Khozhdeniye po mukam *Andreya Rublyova* [The tormented path of *Andrei Rublyov*]", *Iskusstvo kino*, 10, 1989

A. Vogel. *Film as a Subversive Art*, Weidenfeld & Nicolson, London, 1974

Y. Vorontsov & I. Rachuk. *The Phenomenon of Soviet Cinema*, Progress, Moscow, 1980

J. Vronskaya. *Young Soviet Film Makers*, Allen & Unwin, London, 1972

A. Wadja. *Double Vision: My Life in Film*, Faber, London, 1989

B. Walker. *Gnosticism*, Aquarian Press/ Thorsons, Northants, 1983

J. Walker. *Art and Artists on Screen*, Manchester University Press, Manchester, 1993

J. Wall. *Church and Cinema*, Eerdmans, 1971

M. Warner. *Alone of All Her Sex*, Picador/ Pan, London, 1985

G. Watkins. "Seeing and Being Seen: Distinctively Filmic and Religious Elements in Film", *Journal of Religion and Film*, 3, 2, 1999

E. Weiss & J. Belton. *Film Sound: Theory and Practice*, Columbia University Press, New York, NY, 1989

P. Willemen, ed. *Pier Paolo Pasolini*, British Film Institute, London, 1977

L.R. Williams. *Sex in the Head*, Harvester Wheatsheaf, Hemel Hempstead, 1995

D. Wilson, ed. *Sight and Sound: A Fiftieth Anniversary Selection*, Faber, London,

1982

D. Wingrove, ed. *Science Fiction Film Source Book*, Longman, London, 1985

L. Wittgenstein. *Tractatus-Logico Philosophicus*, tr. D.F. Pears & B.F. McGuiness, Routledge & Kegan Paul, London, 1974

P. Wollen. *Signs and Meaning in the Cinema*, Secker & Warburg, London, 1972

J. Wolmark. *Aliens and Others: Science Fiction, Feminism and Postmodernism*, Harvester Wheatsheaf, Hemel Hempstead, 1993

—. "The Postmodern Romances of Feminist Science Fiction", in Pearce, 1995

—. ed. *Cybersexualities: A Reader on Feminist Theory, Cyborgs and Cyberspace*, Edinburgh University Press, Edinburgh, 1999

M. Wood. *America in the Movies*, London, 1974

R. Wood. *Ingmar Bergman*, Praeger, New York, NY, 1969

—. "'80s Hollywood", *CineAction!*, I, Spring, 1985

—. *Hollywood From Vietnam to Reagan*, Columbia University Press, New York, NY, 1986

W. Hastings. "Walt Disney and the roots of children's popular culture", *The Lion and the Unicorn*, 20, 2, Dec, 1996

F. Yermash. "On byl khudozhnik [He was an artist]", *Sovetskaya kultura*, Sept 9, 1989 & Sept 12, 1989

V. Young. *Cinema Borealis: Ingmar Bergman and the Swedish Ethos*, Avon, New York, NY, 1971

D. Youngblood. "Post-Utopian History as Art and Politics: Andrei Tarkovsky's *Andrei Roublev*", in V. Sobchack, 1995

R.C. Zaehner. *Mysticism, Sacred and Profane*, Oxford University Press, Oxford, 1957

M. Zak. *Andrei Tarkovsky: Tvorchesky portret* [*Andrei Tarkovsky: an artistic portrait*], Soyuzinformkino, Moscow, 1988

F. Zeffirelli. *Franco Zeffirelli's Jesus*, Harper & Row, San Francisco, CA, 1984

N. Zorkaya. "Zametki k portretu Andreya Tarkovskogo [Remarks towards a portrait of Andrei Tarkovsky]", *Kino panorama*, 2, 1977

—. *The Illustrated History of the Soviet Cinema*, Hippocrene Books, New York, NY, 1990

S. Zizek. *Looking Awry*, Verso, London, 1991

—. *Enjoy Your Symptom Jacques Lacan in Hollywood and Out*, Routledge, New York, NY, 1992

—. *Tarrying With the Negative: Kant, Hegel, and the Critique of Ideology*, Duke University Press, Durham, NC, 1993

—. *The Metastases of Enjoyment*, Verso, London, 1994

—. *The Indivisible Remainder*, Verso, London, 1996

—. *The Fright of Real Tears: The Uses and Misuses of Lacan in Film Theory*, British Film Institute, London, 1999

—. *The Fright of Real Tears: Krzysztof Kieslowski Between Theory and Post-Theory*, British Film Institute, London, 2001

K.V. Zvlebil. *The Poets of the Powers*, Rider & Co, London, 1973

Filmography

This is a short filmography of films directed by Andrei Tarkovsky: there are other, more detailed filmographies available elsewhere

There Will be No Leave Today
(Segodnya uvolneniya ne budet)

Short made at VGIK in 1959

The Steamroller and the Violin
(Katok i stripka)

Production company – Mosfilm; *script* – Andrei Mikhalkov-Konchalovsky and Andrei Tarkovsky; *photography* – Vadim Yusov in Sovcolour; *editor* – L. Butuzova; art director – S. Agoyan; *music* – Vyacheslav Ovchinnikov; *sound* – V. Krashkovsky

VGIK Diploma project, 1960. Length – 46 minutes

Sasha – Igor Fomshenko; Sergei – V. Samansky; Girl – Nina Arkhanelskaya; Mother – Marina Adzhubey.

Ivan's Childhood (Ivanovo destvo)

Production company – Mosfilm; *script* – Mikhail Papava and Vladimir Bogomolov, based on Bogomolov's book *Ivan*; *photography* – Vadim Yusov in black-and-white; *editor* – G. Natanson; *art director* – Evgeni Cherniaev; *music* – Vyacheslav Ovchinnikov; *sound* – E. Zelentsova.

Released in 1962. Length – 95 minutes.

Ivan – Kolya Burlyaev; Captain Kholin – Valentin Zubkov; Lieutenant Galtsev – E. Zharikov; Corporal Katasonych – S. Krylov; Lieutenant-colonel Gryaznov – Nikolai Grinko; Masha – L.Malyavina; Ivan's mother – Irma Tarkovskaya.

Andrei Roublyov

Production company – Mosfilm; *script* – Andrei Mikhalkov-Konchalovsky and
Andrei Tarkovsky; *photography* – Vadim Yusov in Scope and black-and-white,
part in Sovcolour; *editor* – Ludmila Feganova; *art director* – Evgeni Cherniaev;
music – Vyacheslav Ovchinnikov; *sound* – E. Zelentsova.

Production – 1964-66. Domestic release – 1971. UK release – 1973. Length – 185
minutes. Other versions: 146 minutes, and one 6 minutes longer than the previous
longest known, shown in Moscow, 1989.

Andrei Roublyov – Anatoly Solonitsyn; Krill – Ivan Lapikov; Daniel – Nikolai
Grinko; Theophanes the Greek – Nikolai Sergeyev; mute girl – Irma Raush
Tarkovskaya; Boriska – Nikolai Burlyaev; Buffoon – Rolan Bykov.

Solaris

Production company – Mosfilm; *script* – Andrei Tarkovsky and Friedrich
Gorenstein, based on Stanislaw Lem's book; *photography* – Vadim Yusov in Scope
and Sovcolour; *editor* – Ludmila Feganova; *art director* – Mikhail Romadin; *music* –
Eduard Artemiev, J.S. Bach's *Chorale Prelude in F minor*.

Production – 1969-72. Release – 1972. Length 165 minutes (some versions 144
minutes).

Chris Kelvin – Donatas Banionis; Hari – Natalia Bondarchuk; Snaut – Yuri
Jarvet; Sartorius – Anatoly Solonitsyn; Burton – Vladislav Dvorzhetsky; Kelvin's
father – Nikolai Grinko; Gibaryan – Sos Sarkissyan.

Mirror (Zerkalo)

Production company – Mosfilm; *producer* – E. Vaisberg; *script* – Andrei
Tarkovsky and Aleksandr Misharin; *photography* – Georgy Rerberg in Sovcolour
and black-and-white; *lighting* – V. Gusev; *editor* – Ludmila Feganova; *art director*
– Nikolai Dvigubsky; *music* – Eduard Artemiev.

Domestic release – 1974. UK release – 1980. Length: 106 minutes.

Aleksei's mother/ Natalia – Margarita Terekhova; Ignat. aged 5 – Filipp
Yankovsky; Aleksei/ Ignat, aged 12 – Ignat Daniltsev; father – Oleg Yankovsky;
print worker – Nikolai Grinko; Lisa – Alla Demidova; military instructor – Yuri
Nazarov; passer-by – Analtoly Solonitsyn; voice of Aleksei the narrator – Innokenti
Smoktunovsky; Aleksei's mother as an older woman – Maria Tarkovskaya.

Stalker

Production company – Mosfilm; *script* – Arkady and Boris Strugatsky, based on their story *Roadside Picnic*; *photography* – Aleksandr Knyazhinsky, colour; *lighting supervisor* – L. Kazmin; *editor* – Ludmila Feganova; *production designer* – Andrei Tarkovsky; *music* – Eduard Artemiev; *sound* – V. Sharun.

First screened – 1979. Length – 161 minutes.

The Stalker – Aleksandr Kaidanovsky; the Writer – Anatoly Solonitsyn; the Scientist – Nikolai Grinko; Stalker's wife – Alisa Freindlikh; Stalker's daughter – Natasha Abramova.

Nostalghia

Production company – Opera Film (Rome)/ RAI Television Rete 2 and Sovinfilm; *producer* – Francesco Casati; *script* – Andrei Tarkovsky and Tonino Guerra; *photography* – Guiseppe Lanci, in Eastman Colour; *editor* – Erminia Marani, Amedeo Salfa; *art director* – Andrea Crisanti; *sound effects* – Massimo Anzellotti, Luciano Anzellotti; *sound mixer* – Danilo Moroni.

Production, 1981-83. Release – 1983. Length 126 minutes.

Andrei Gorchakov – Oleg Yankovsky; Domenico – Erland Josephson; Eugenia – Domiziana Giordano; Gorchakov's wife – Patrizia Terreno.

The Sacrifice (Offret)

Production company – Swedish Film Institute (Stockholm)/ Argos Film (Paris), with Film Four International (London), Josephson & Nykvist, Sveriges Television/ SVT 2, Sandrew Film & Teater, with the participation of the French Ministry of Culture; *producer* – Katinka Farago; *script* – Andrei Tarkovsky; *photography* – Sven Nykvist, Eastman Colour and black-and-white; *editor* – Andrei Tarkovsky and Michal Leszcylowski; *art director* – Anna Asp; *music* – J.S. Bach's *St Matthew Passion*, Swedish and Japanese folk music; *sound* – Owe Svensson, Bosse Persson, Lars Ulander, Christin Lohman, Wikee Peterson-Berger.

Release, 1986. Length – 149 minutes.

Alexander – Erland Josephson; Adelaide – Susan Fleetwood; Otto – Allan Edwall; Julia – Valerie Mairesse; Maria – Gudrun Gísladóttir; Victor – Sven Wollter; Martha – Filippa Franzén; Little Man – Tommy Kjellqvist; Julia – Valerie Mairesse.

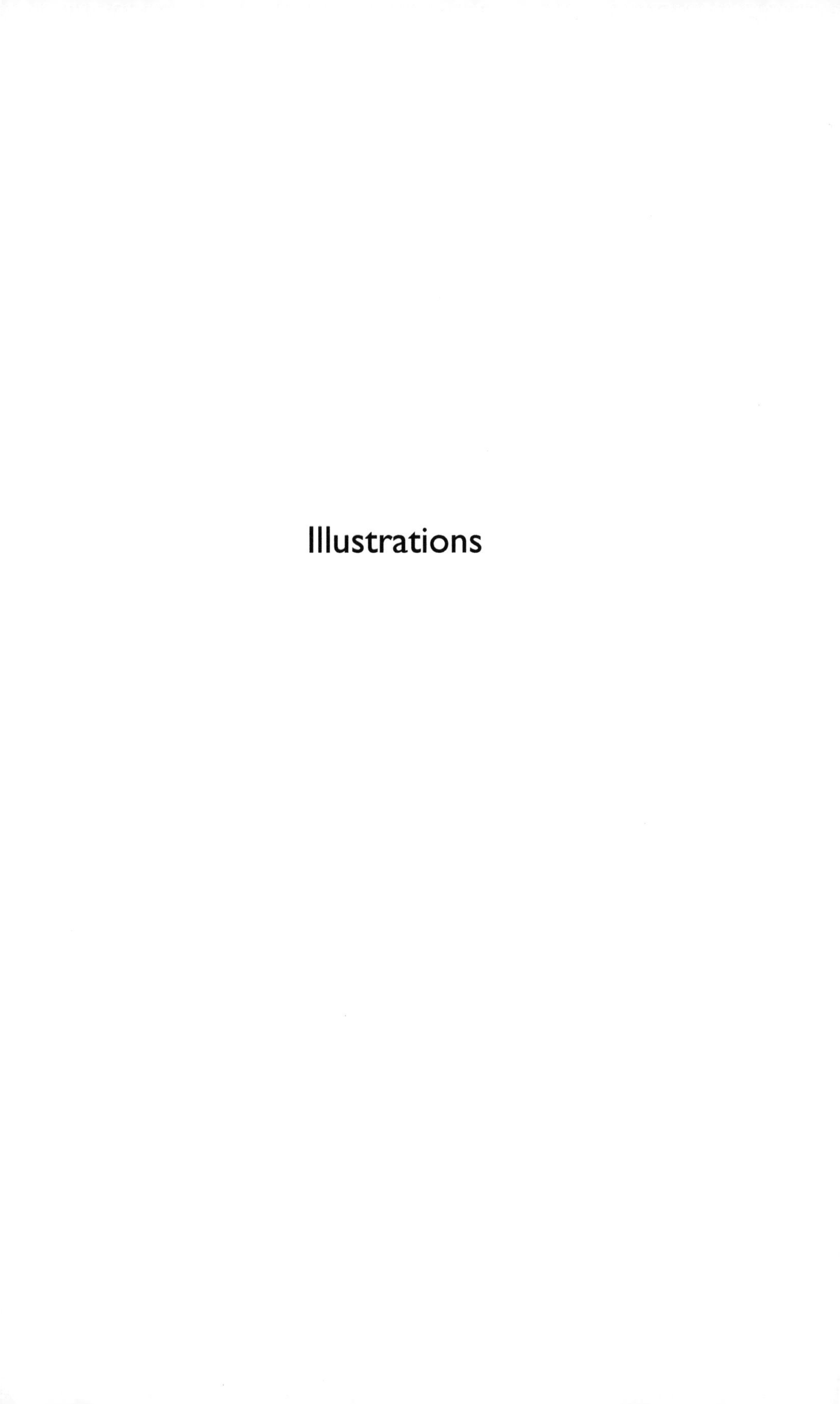

Illustrations

Some of Andrei Tarkovsky's
favourite painters

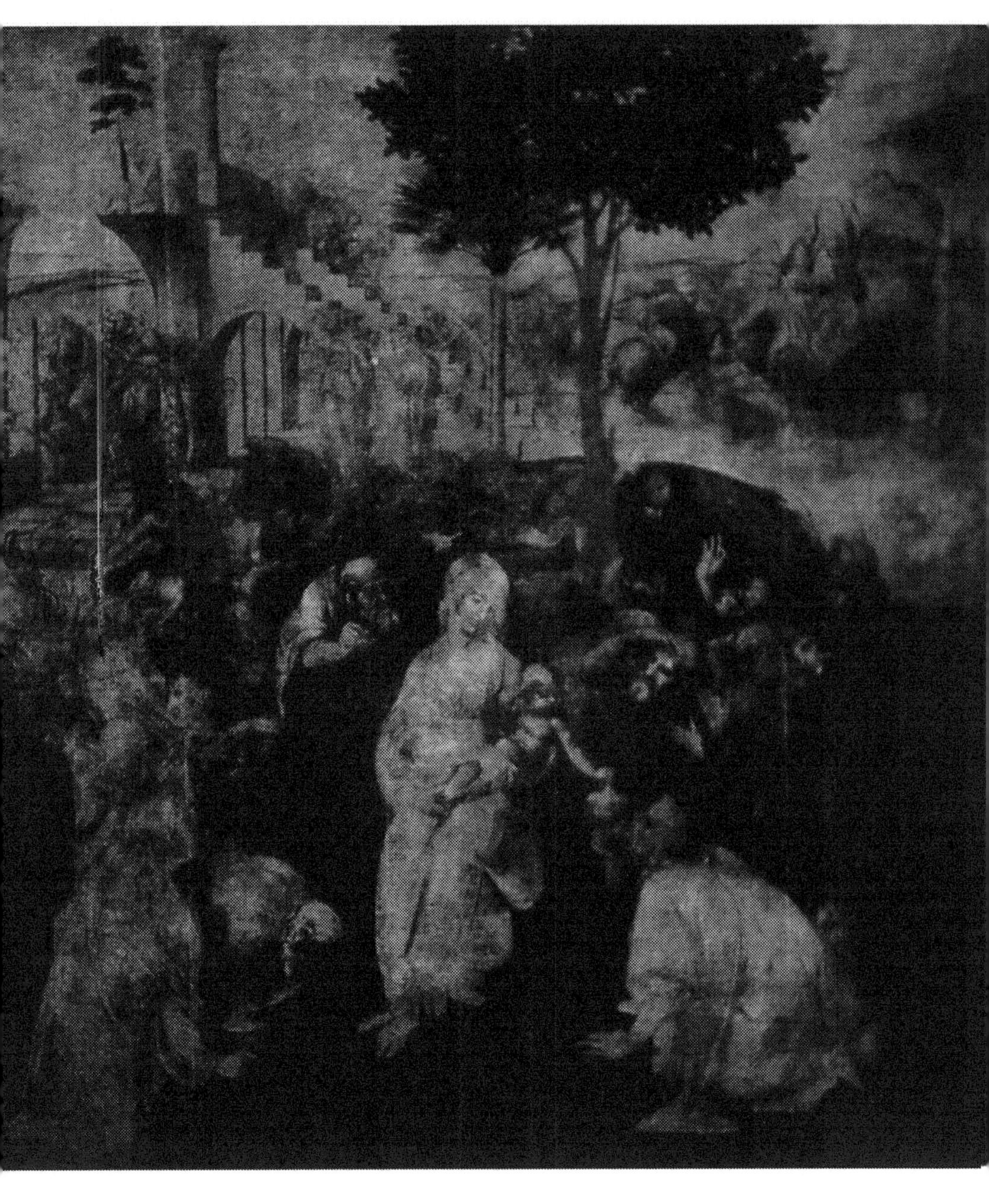

Leonardo da Vinci's beyond beautiful *Adoration of the Magi*, at the heart of *The Sacrifice*.

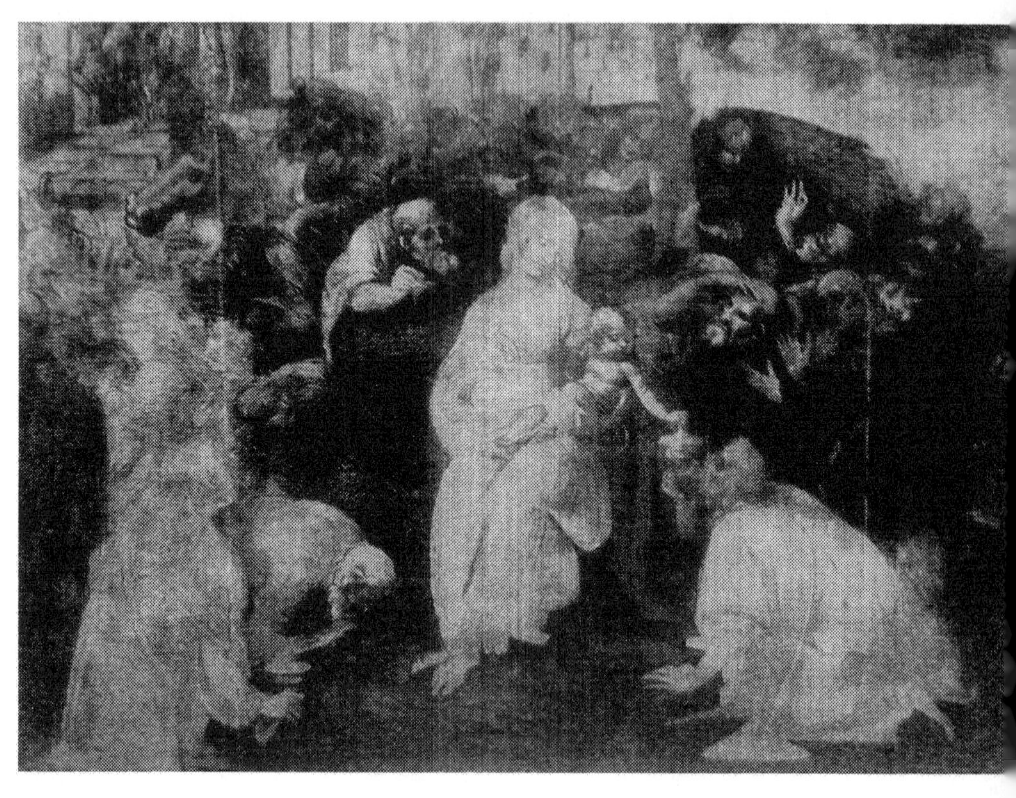

Leonardo da Vinci, *Adoration of the Magi*, detail

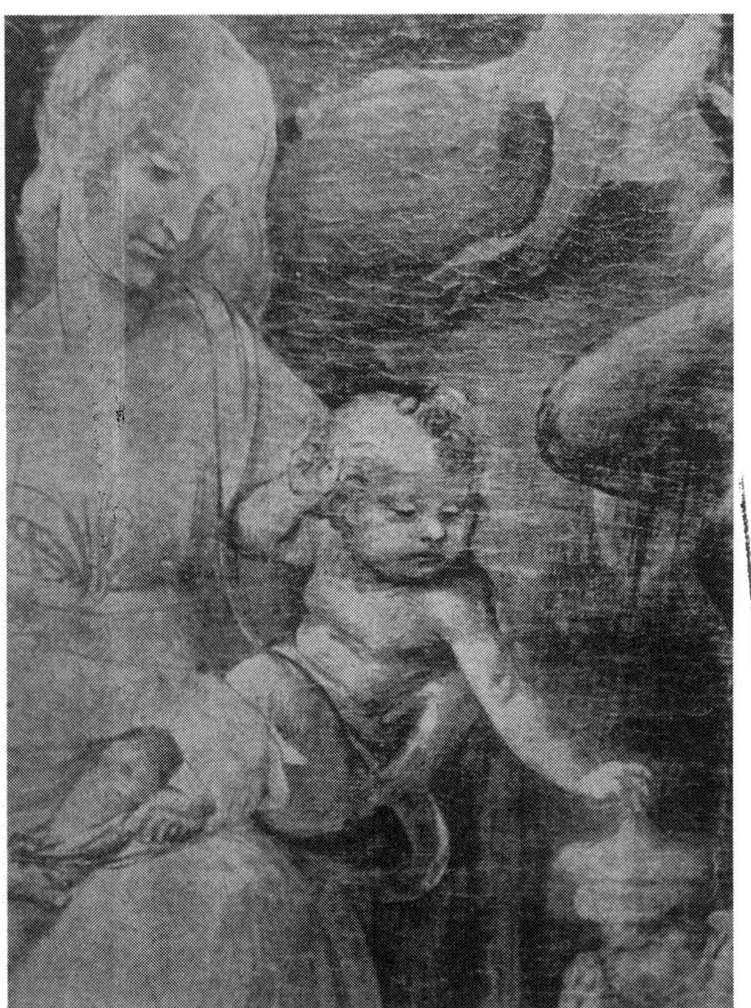

Leonardo da Vinci, *Adoration of the Magi*, detail.
This was the portion of the painting that Tarkovsky chose to
show in the main titles of *The Sacrifice*, before tilting up to
reveal the tree above.

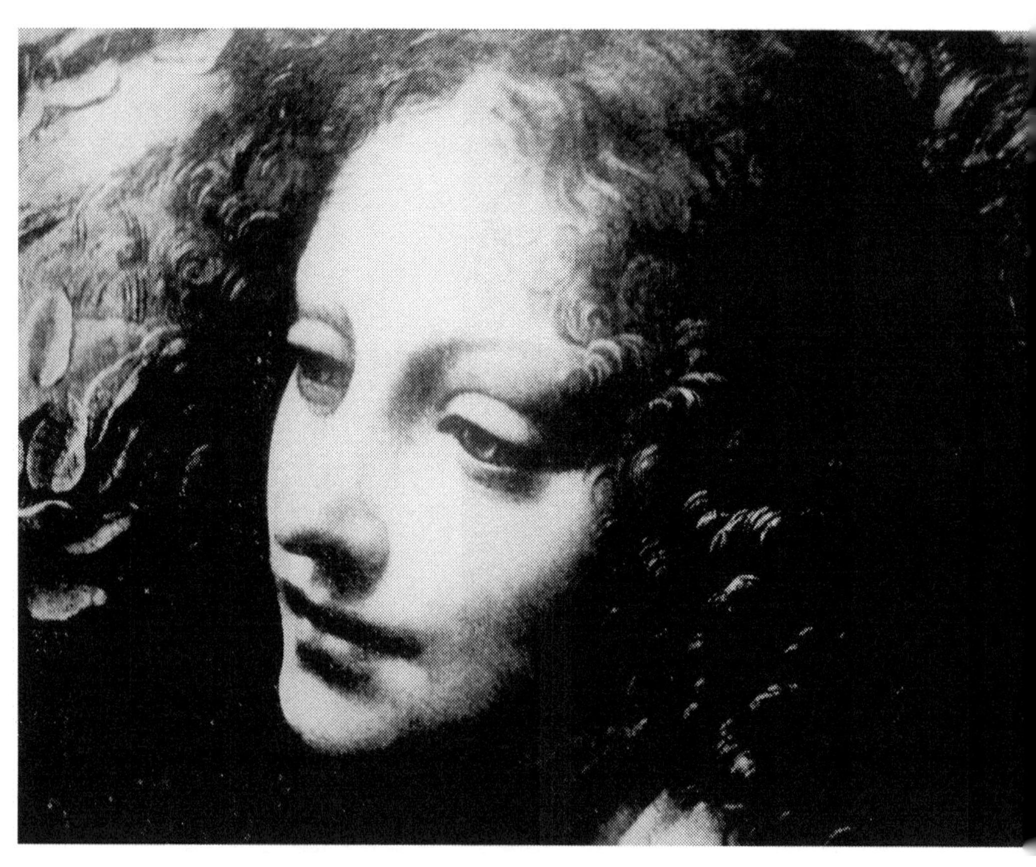

Leonardo's immortal faces: from *The Virgin of the Rocks*.

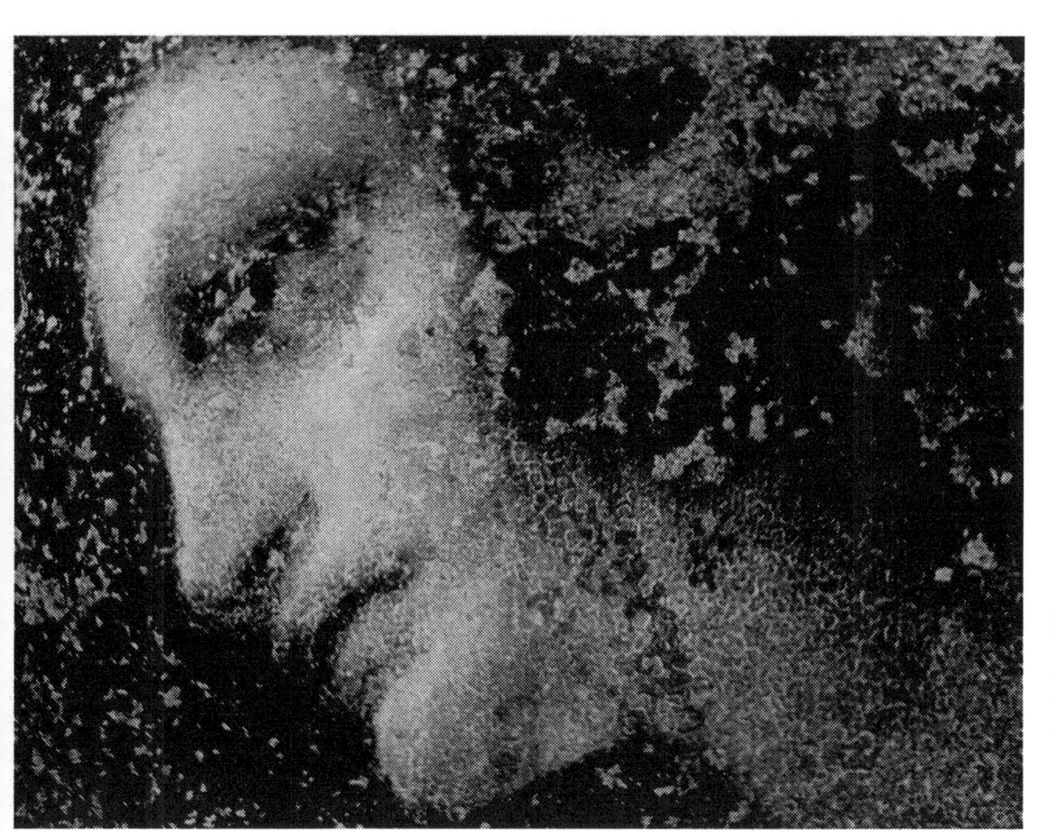

Leonardo's immortal faces: from *The Last Supper,* of course.

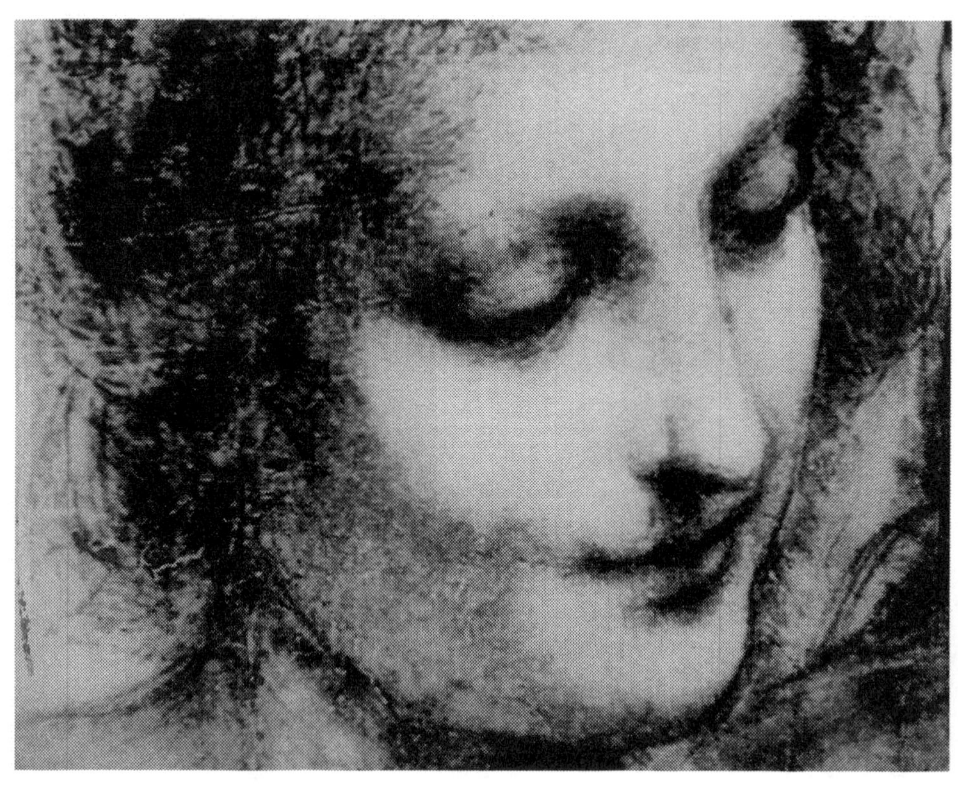

Leonardo's immortal faces: the Madonna from *The Virgin and Child With St Anne*

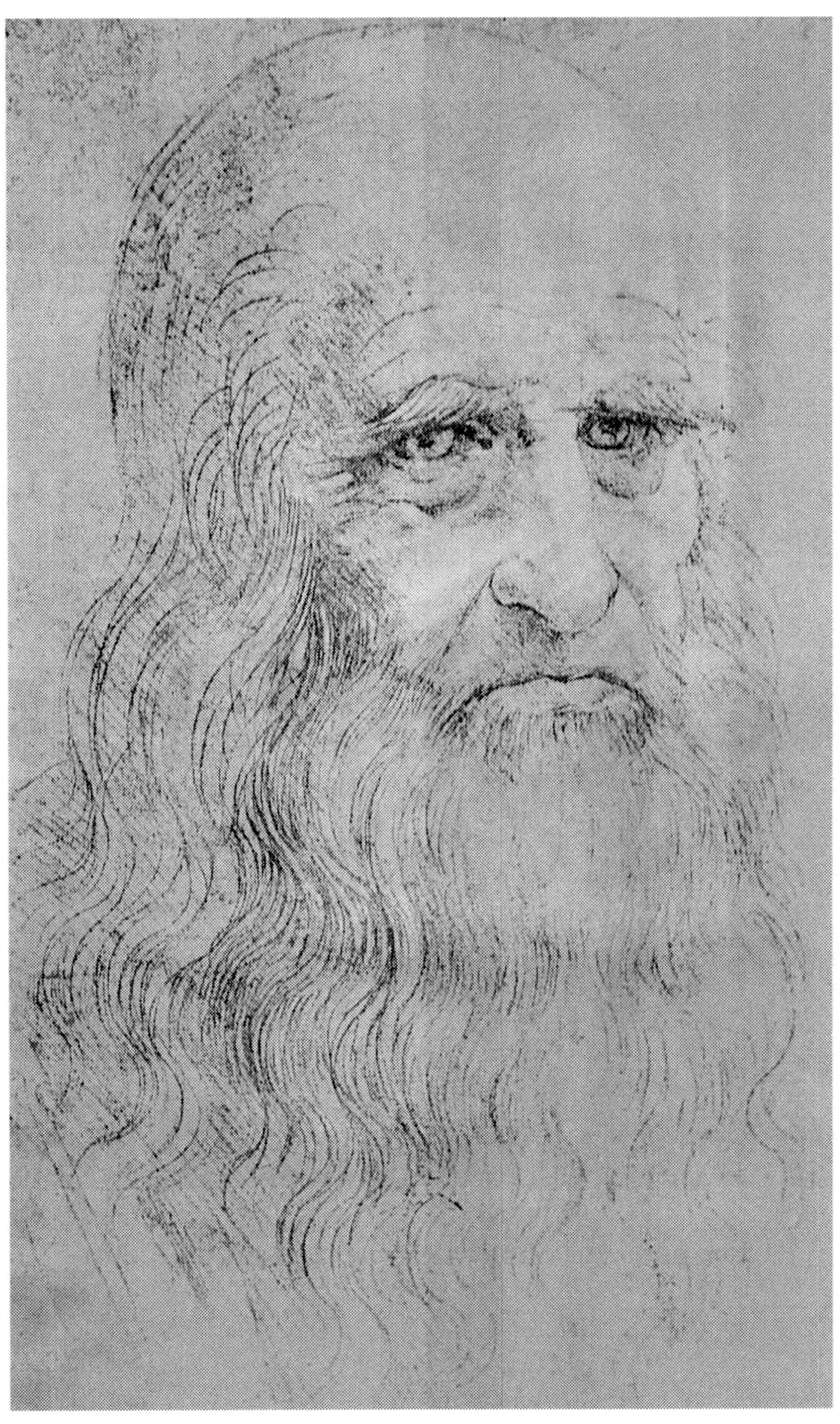

Leonardo's immortal faces: the self-portrait used in *Mirror*.

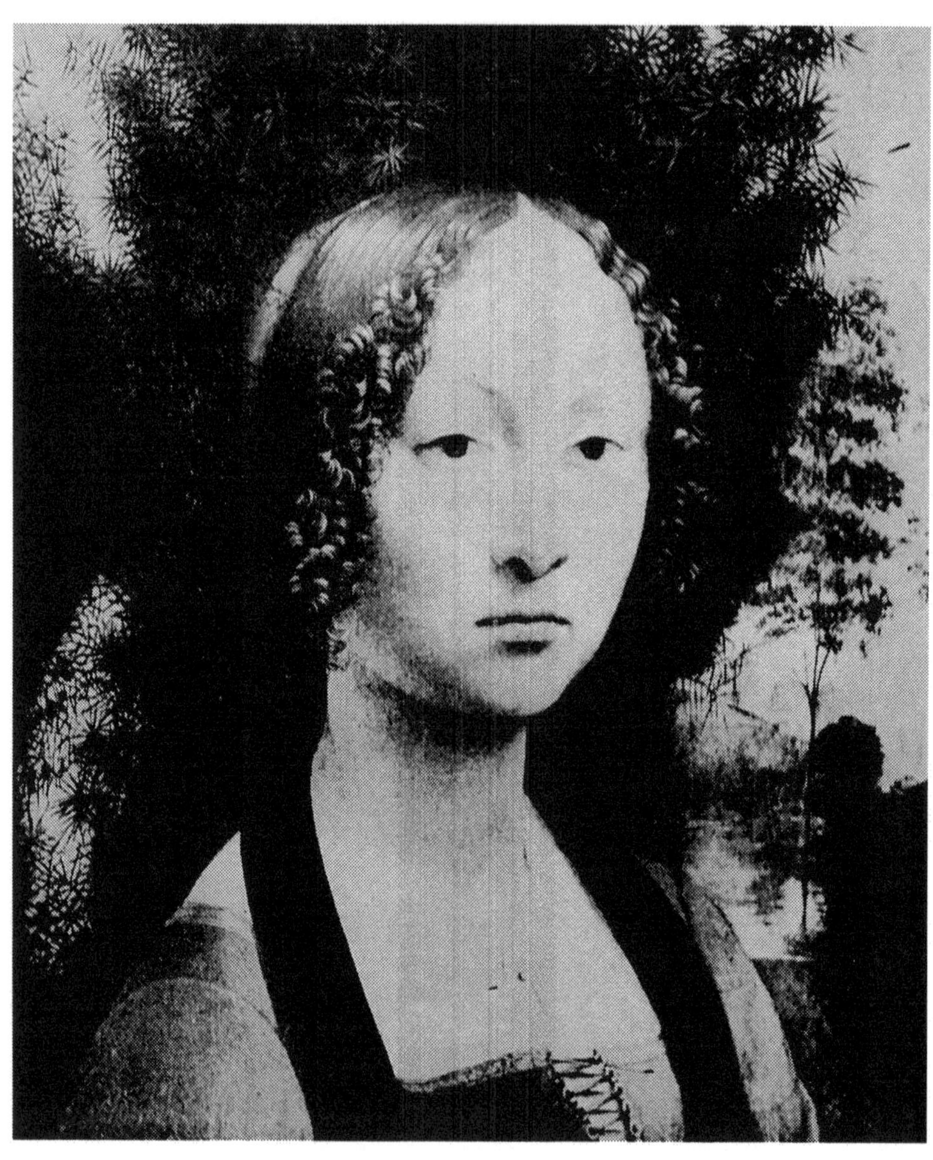

Leonardo's immortal faces: the portrait of Ginevra Benci, used in *Mirror*.

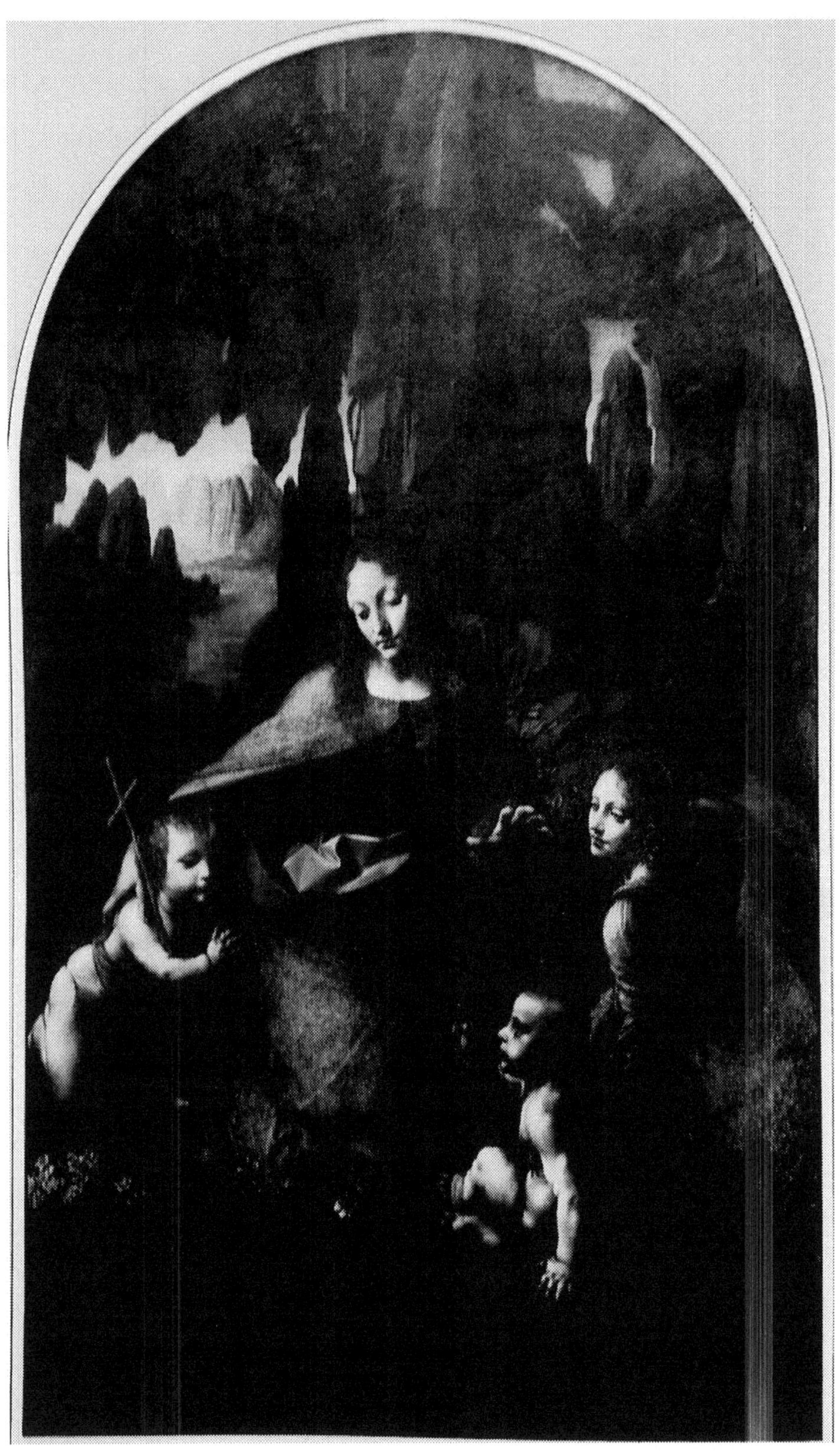

Leonardo da Vinci, *The Virgin of the Rocks*, National Gallery, London

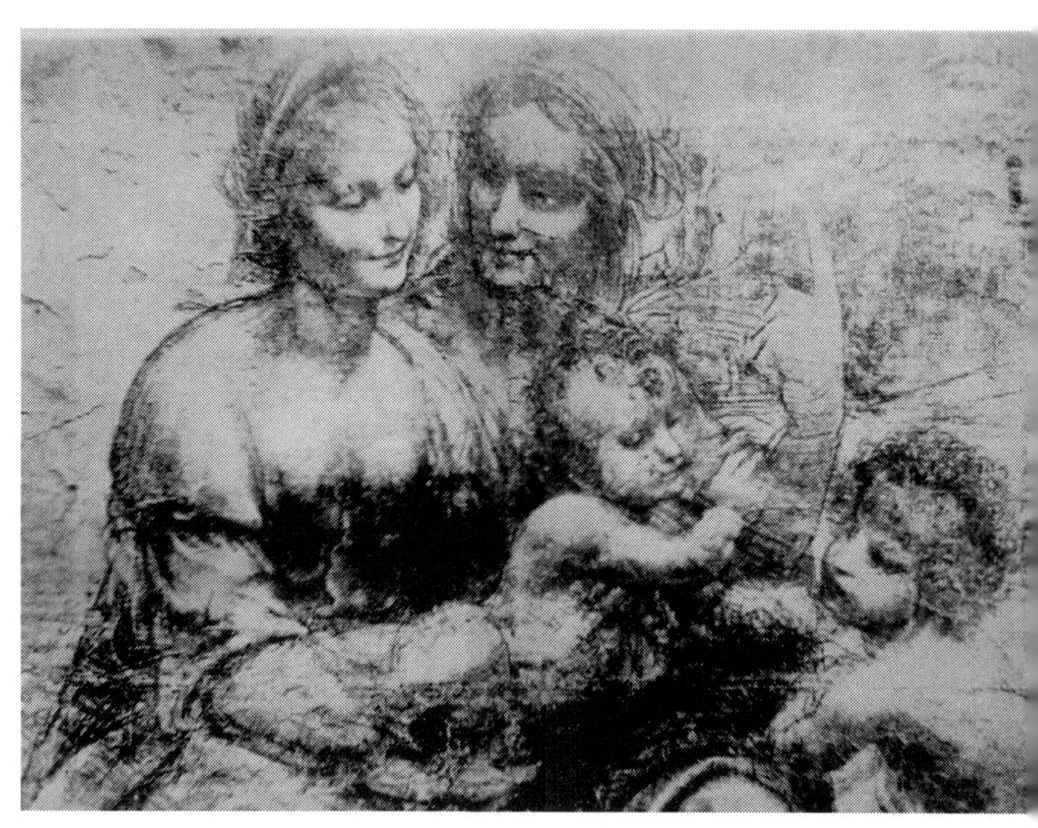

Leonardo da Vinci, *The Virgin and Child With St Anne*, National Gallery, London

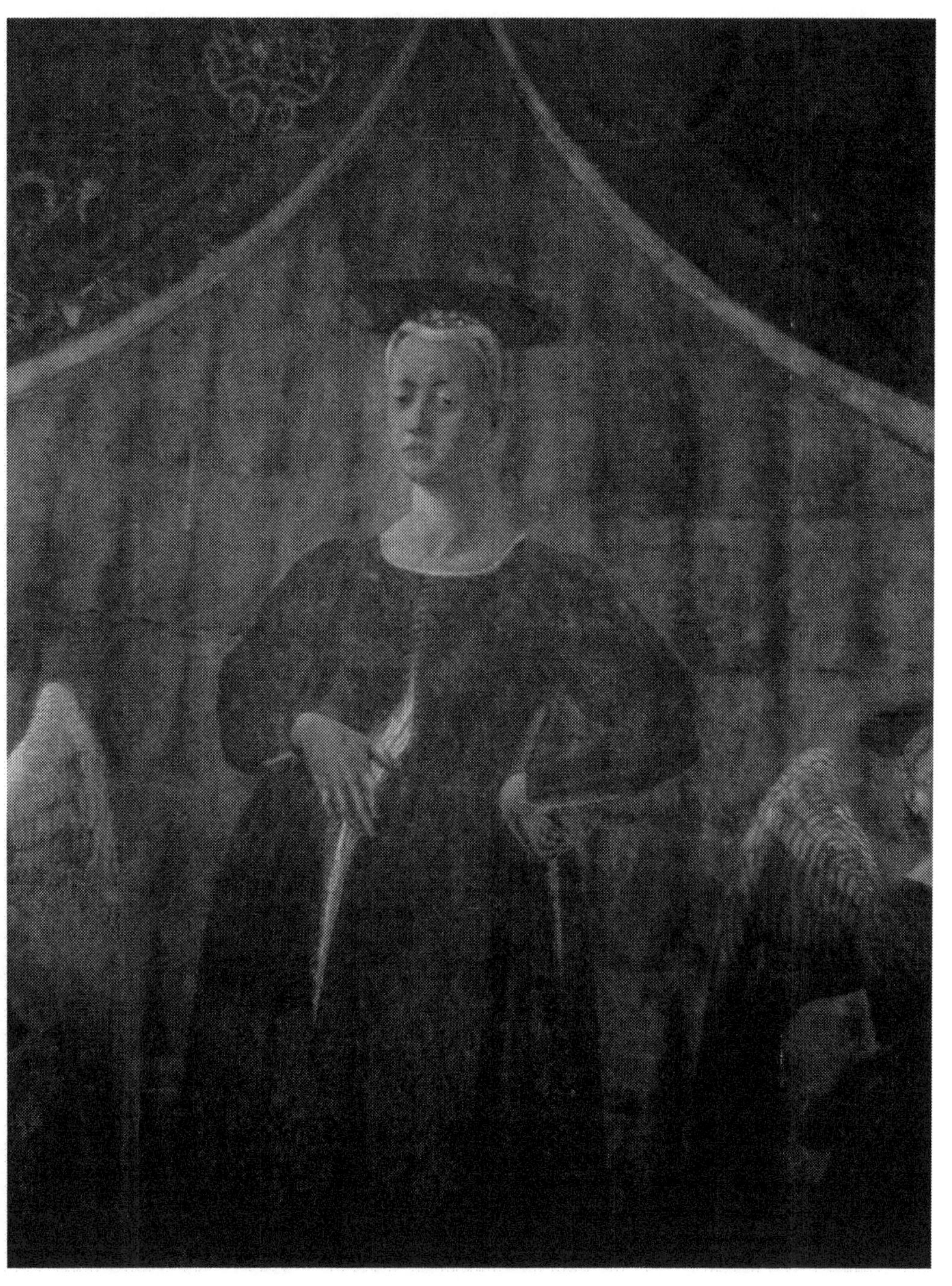

Piero della Francesca's *Madonna del Parto*, centrepiece of
Nostalghia

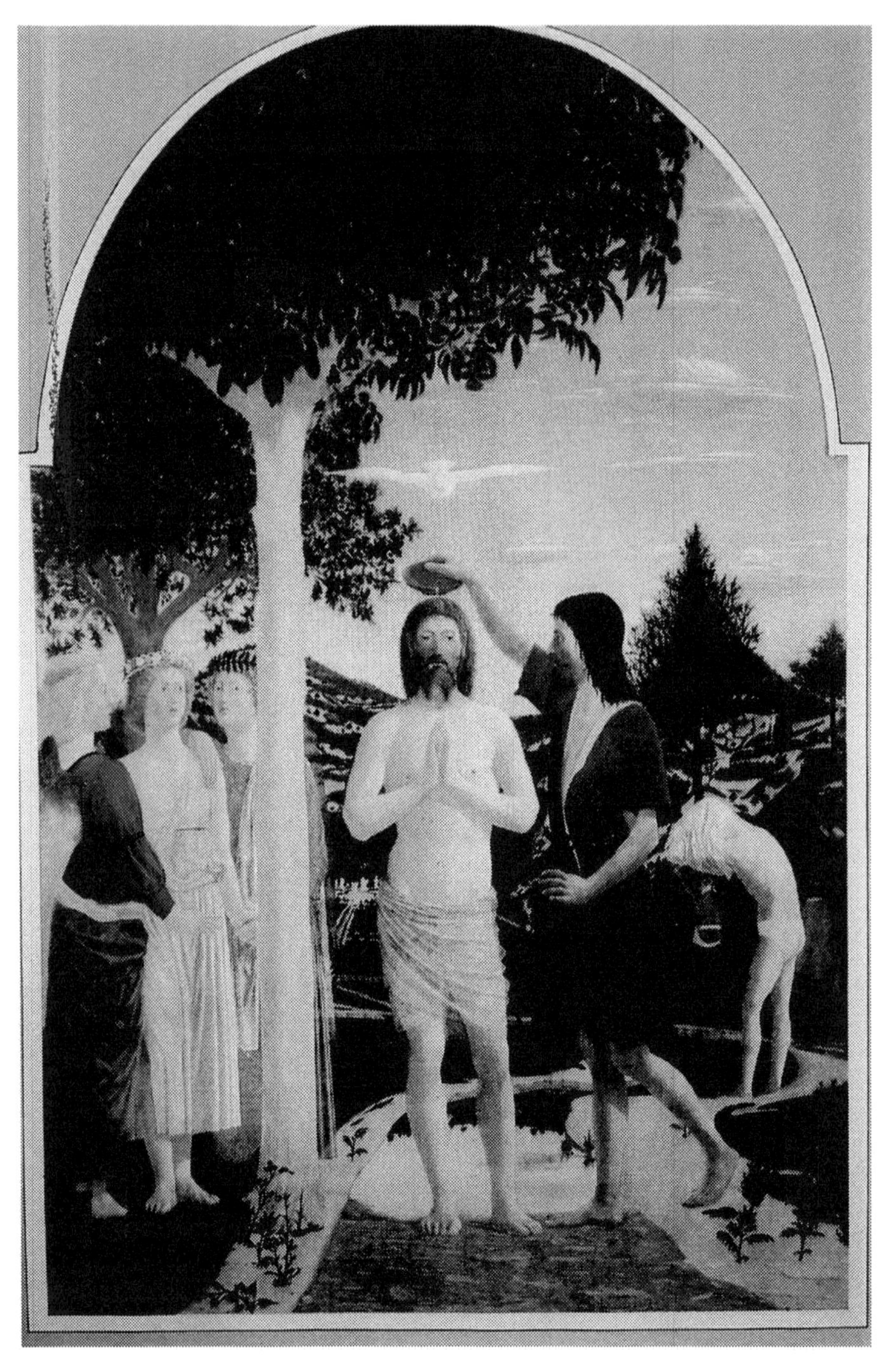

Piero della Francesca, *The Baptism of Christ*, National Gallery, London

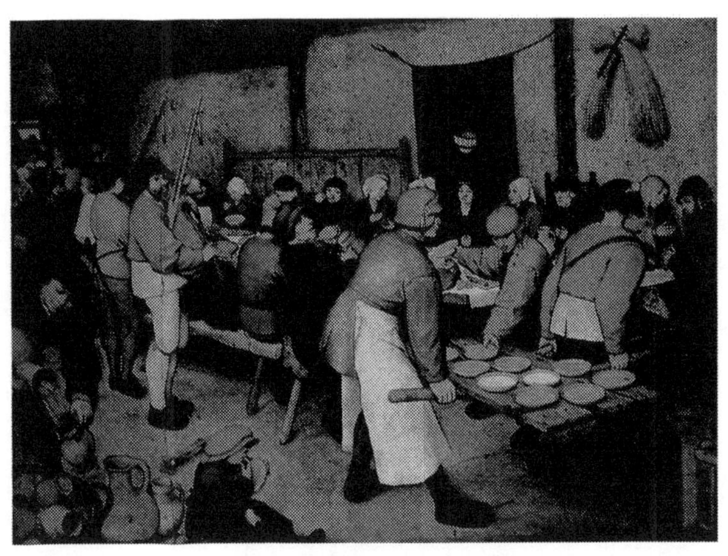

Pieter Brueghel

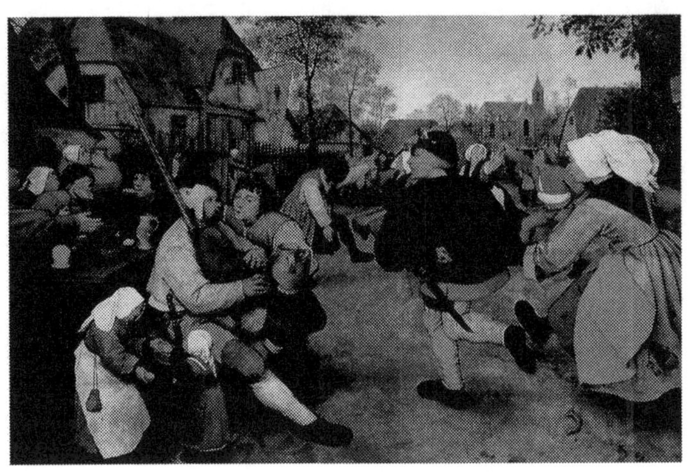

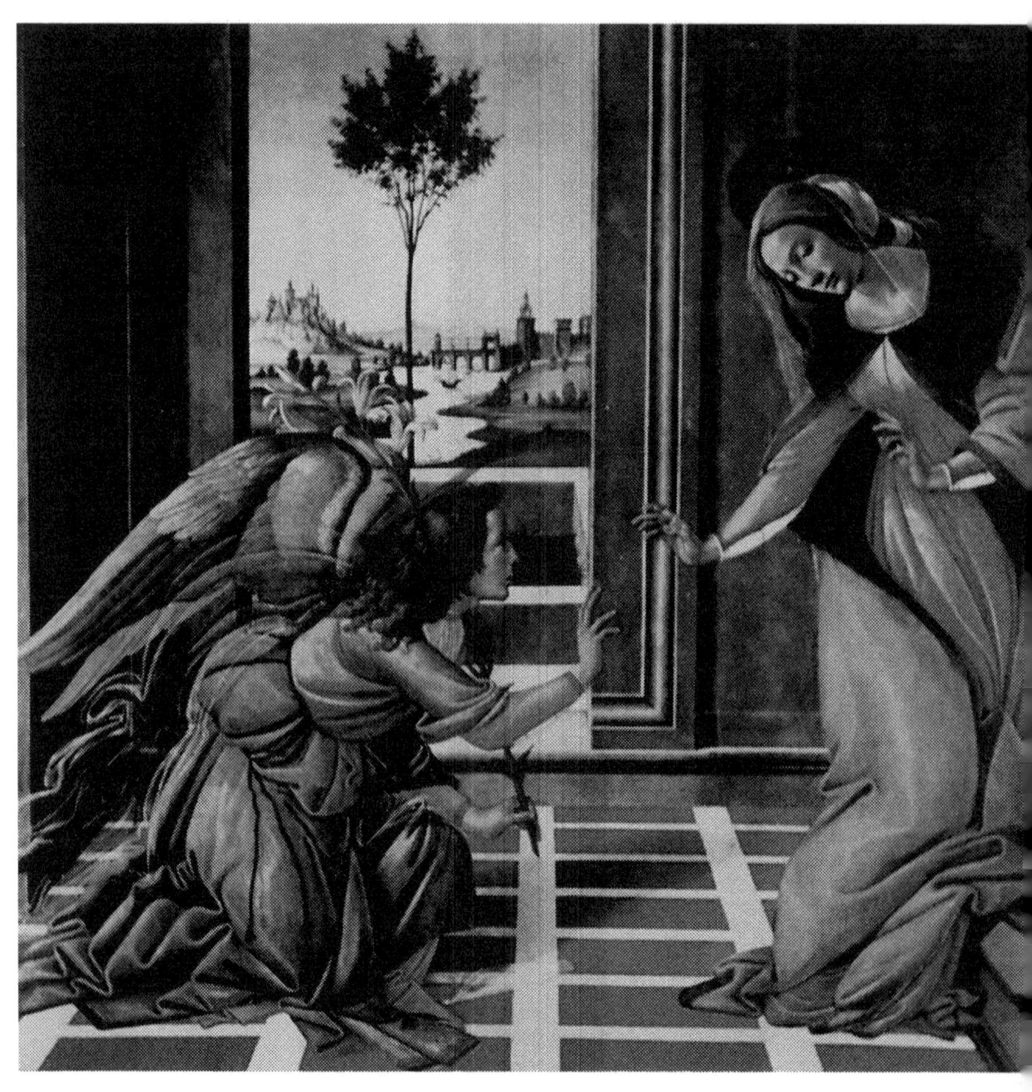

Sandro Botticelli, *The Annunciation*, Uffizi Gallery, Florence

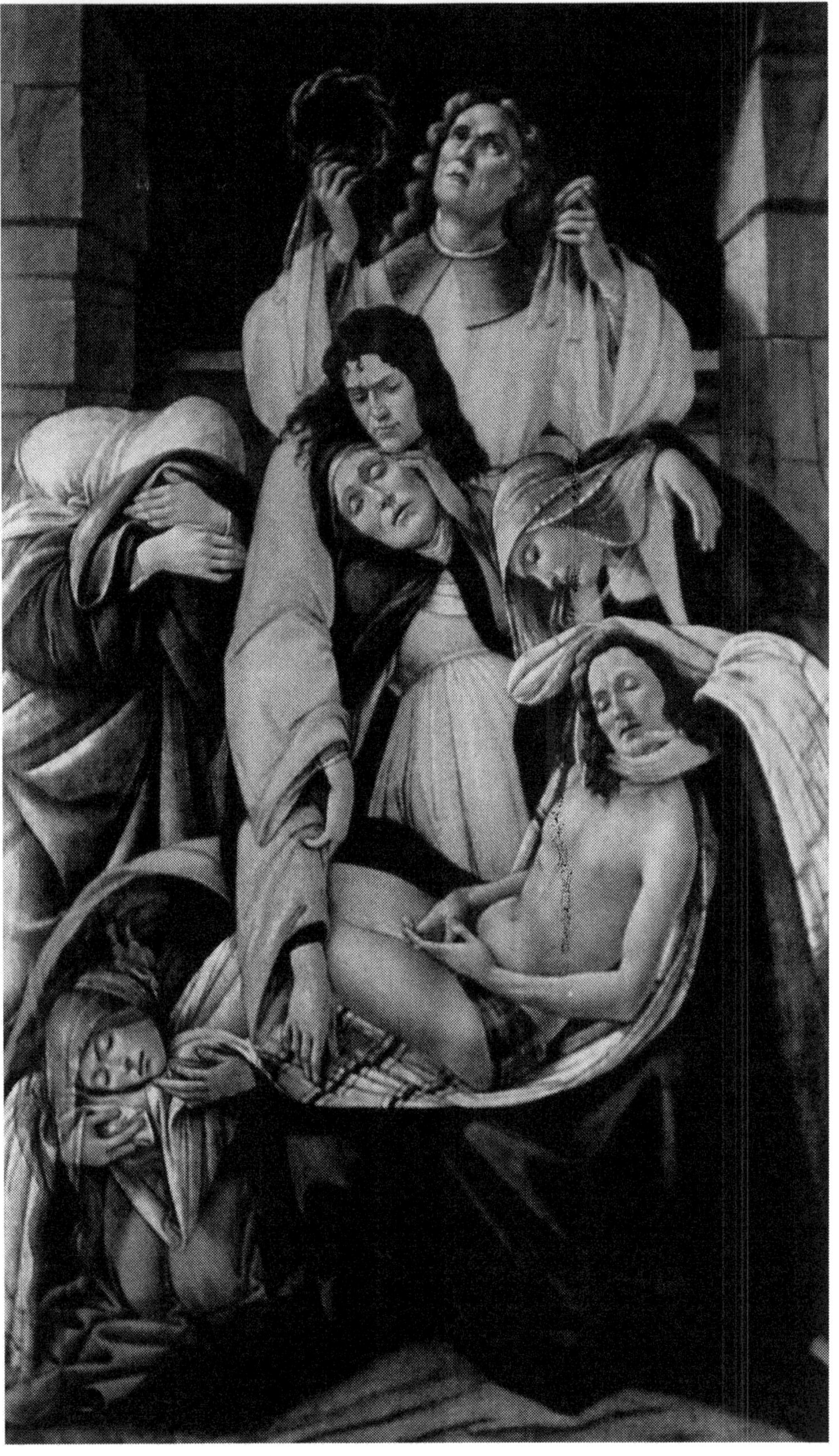

Sandro Botticelli, *Pietà*, Museo Poldi Pezzoli, Milan

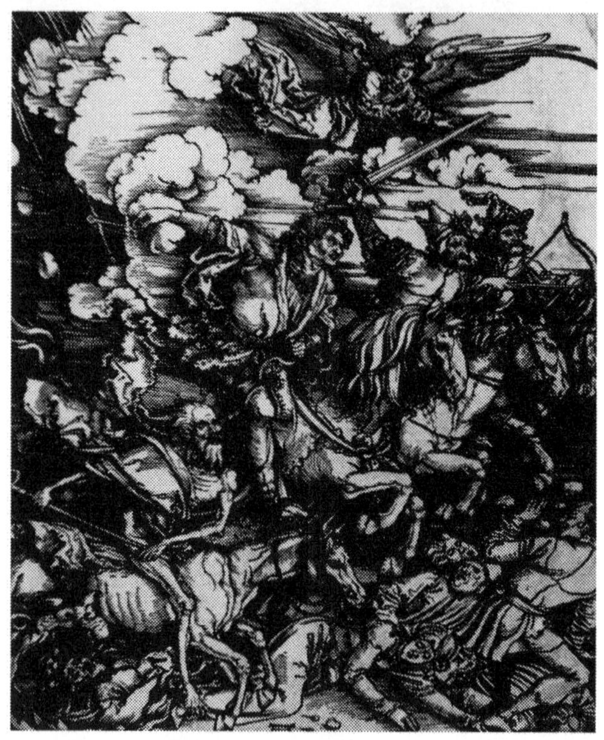

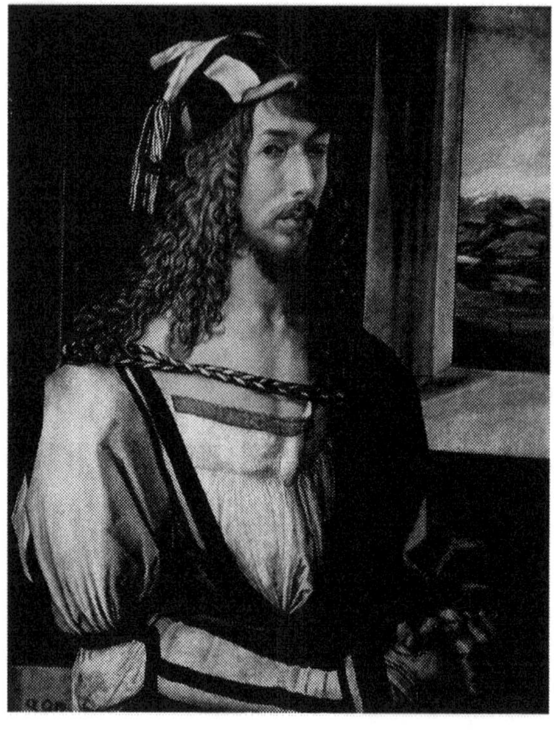

The incomparable Albrecht Dürer. The *Apocalypse* woodcuts appeared in *Ivan's Childhood*.

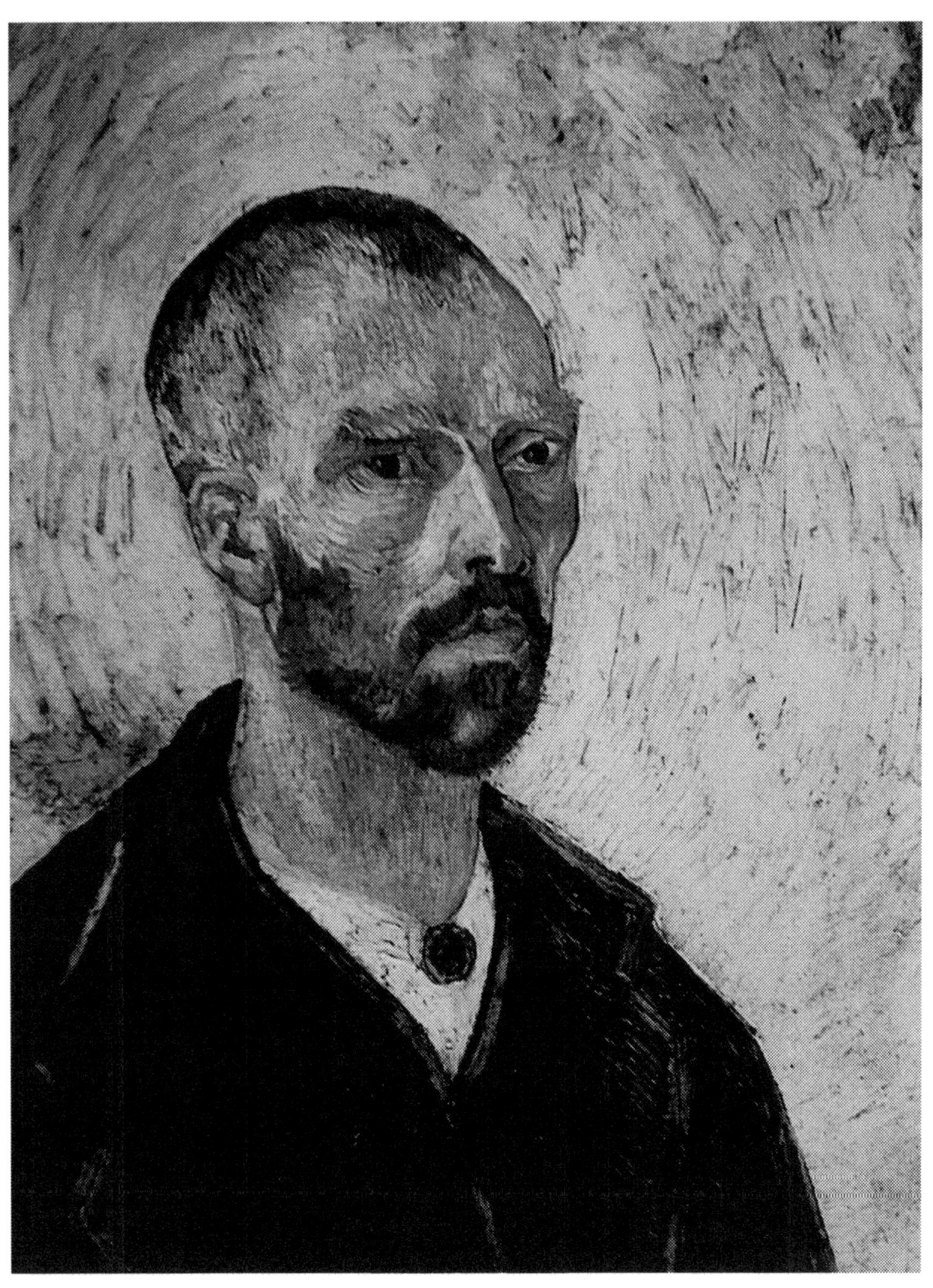

Vincent van Gogh

Some of Andrei Tarkovsky's
favourite filmmakers

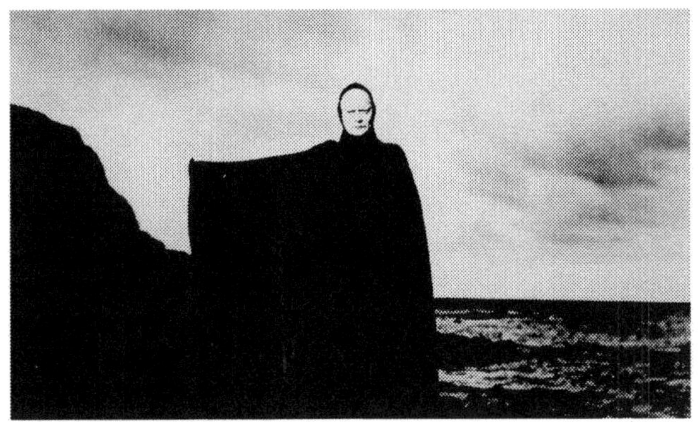

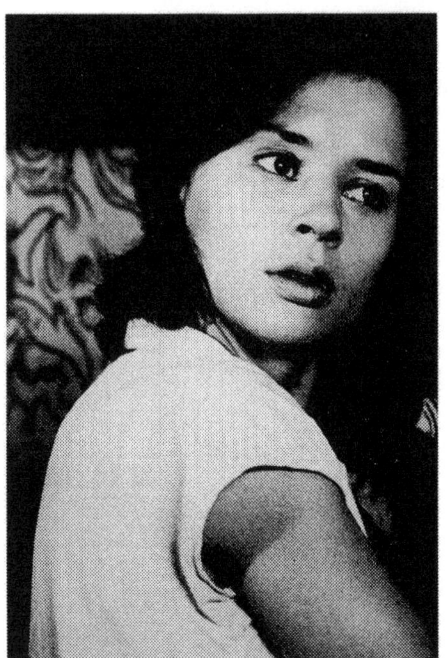

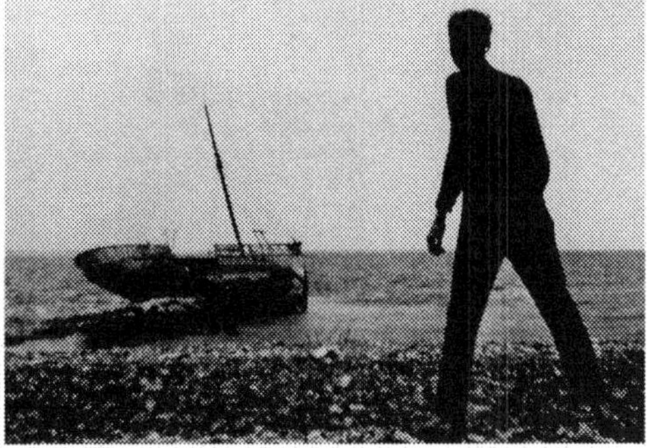

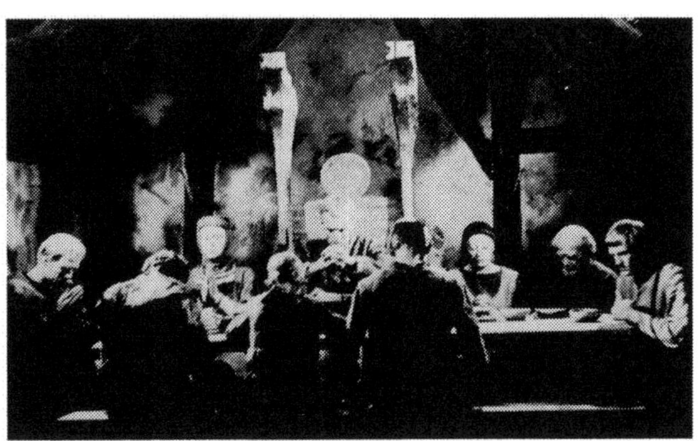

Some of Andrei Tarkovsky's favourite filmmakers:
Ingmar Bergman

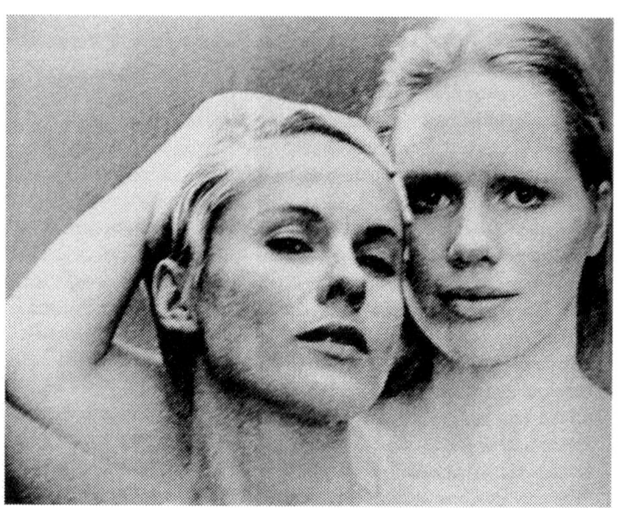

An influential image from Ingmar Bergman's *Persona*, later taken up by Tarkovsky and Fassbinder, among others.

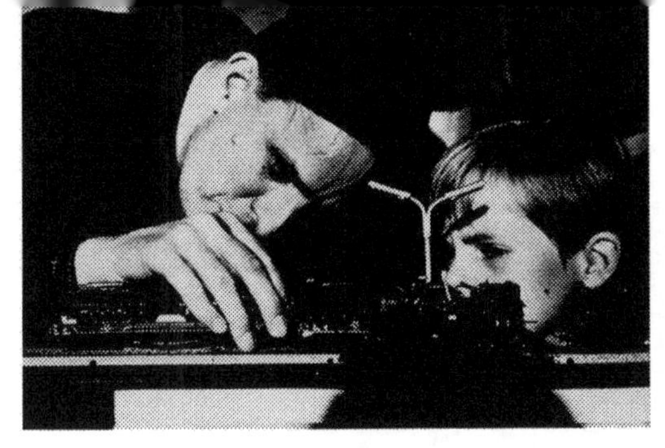
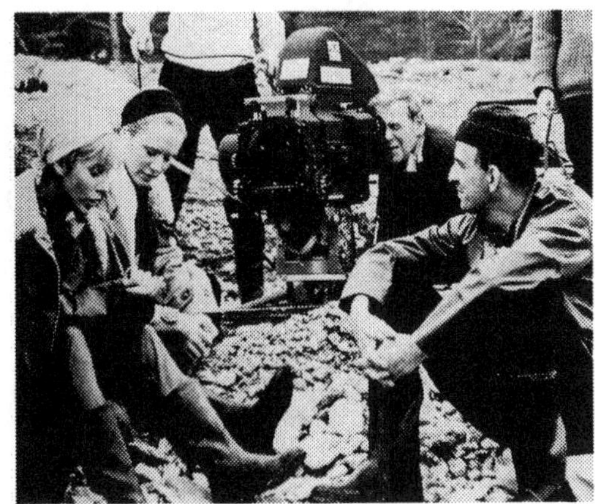
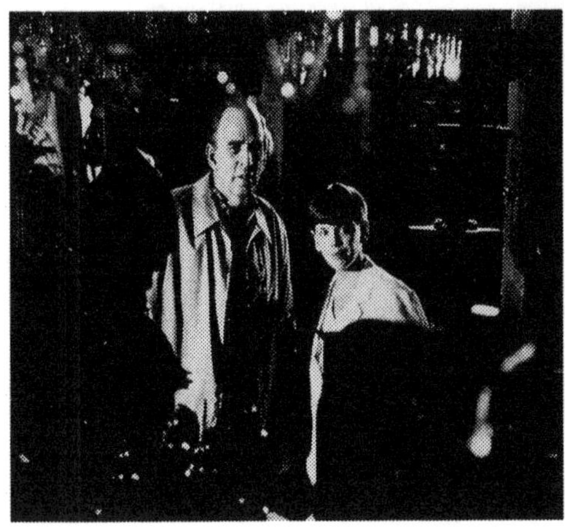
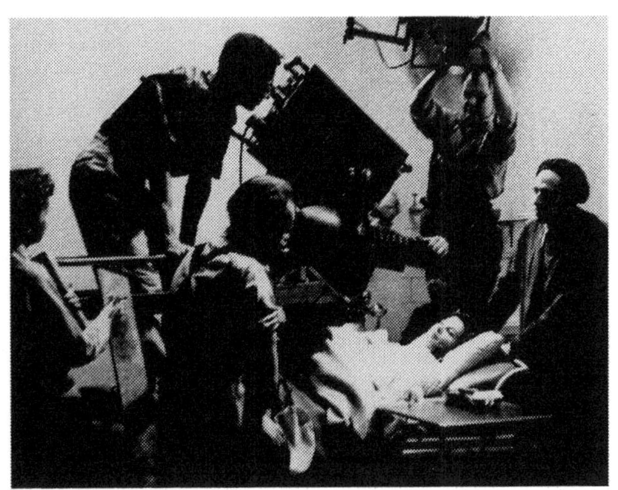

Ingmar Bergman at work.

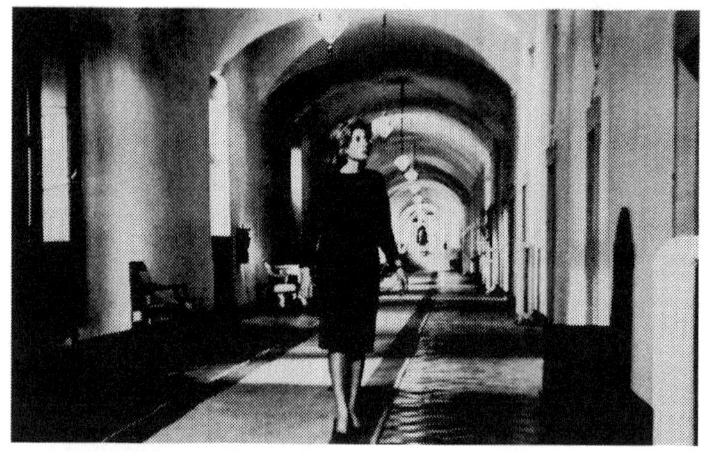

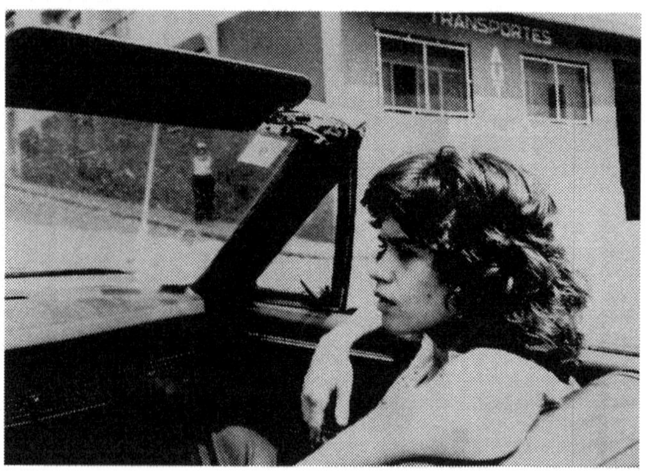

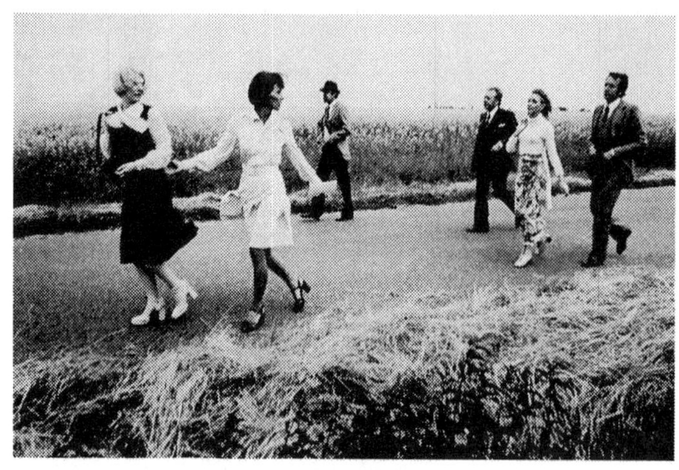

Michelangelo Antonioni

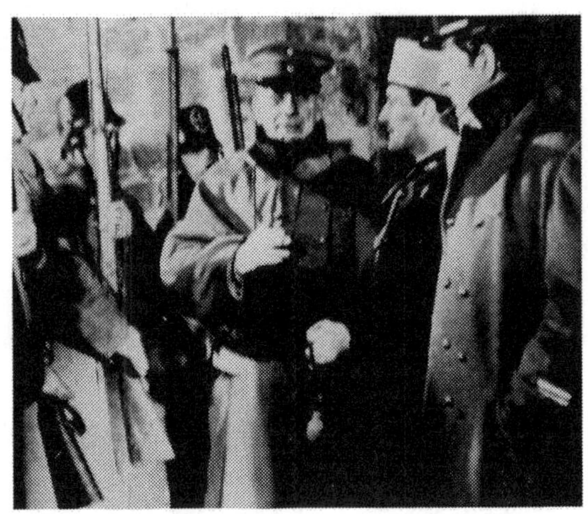

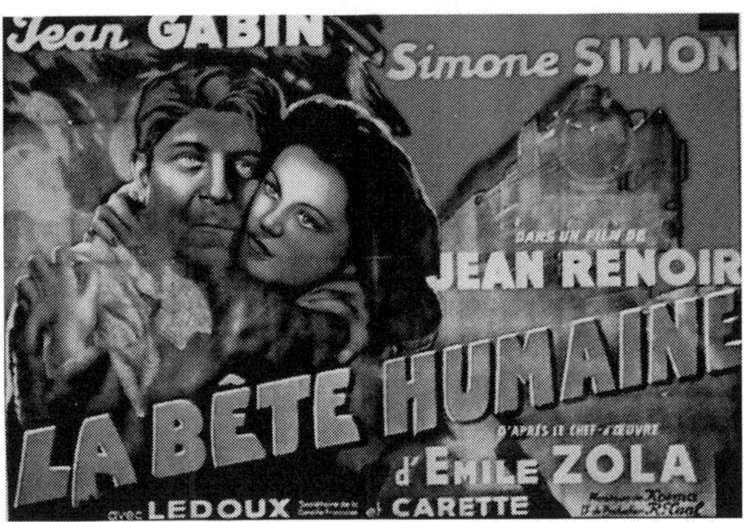

Jean GABIN
Simone SIMON
DANS UN FILM DE
JEAN RENOIR
LA BÊTE HUMAINE
D'APRÈS LE CHEF-D'ŒUVRE
d'EMILE ZOLA
avec LEDOUX et CARETTE

Jean Renoir

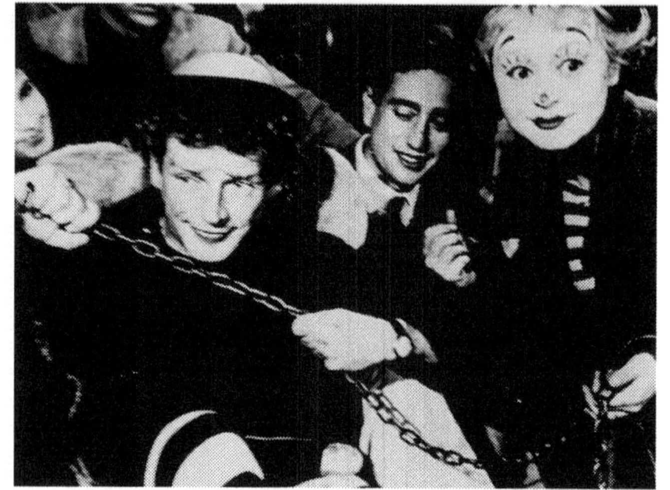

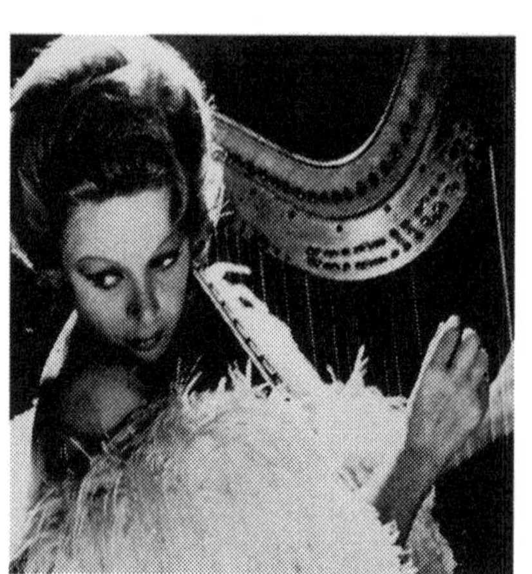

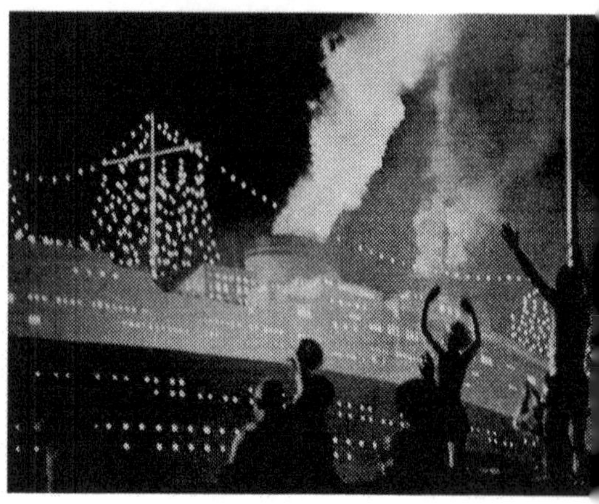

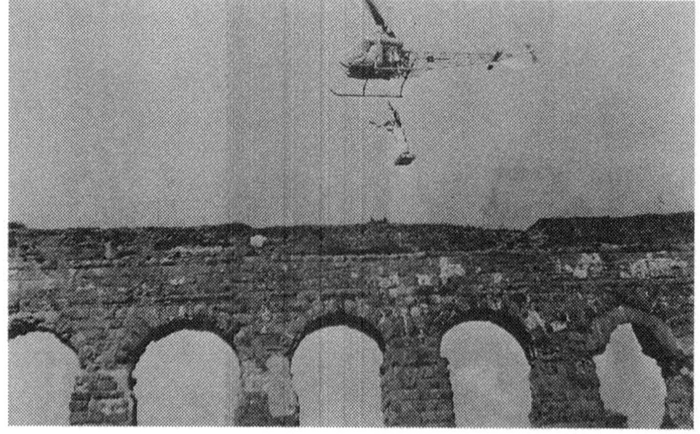

Federico Fellini

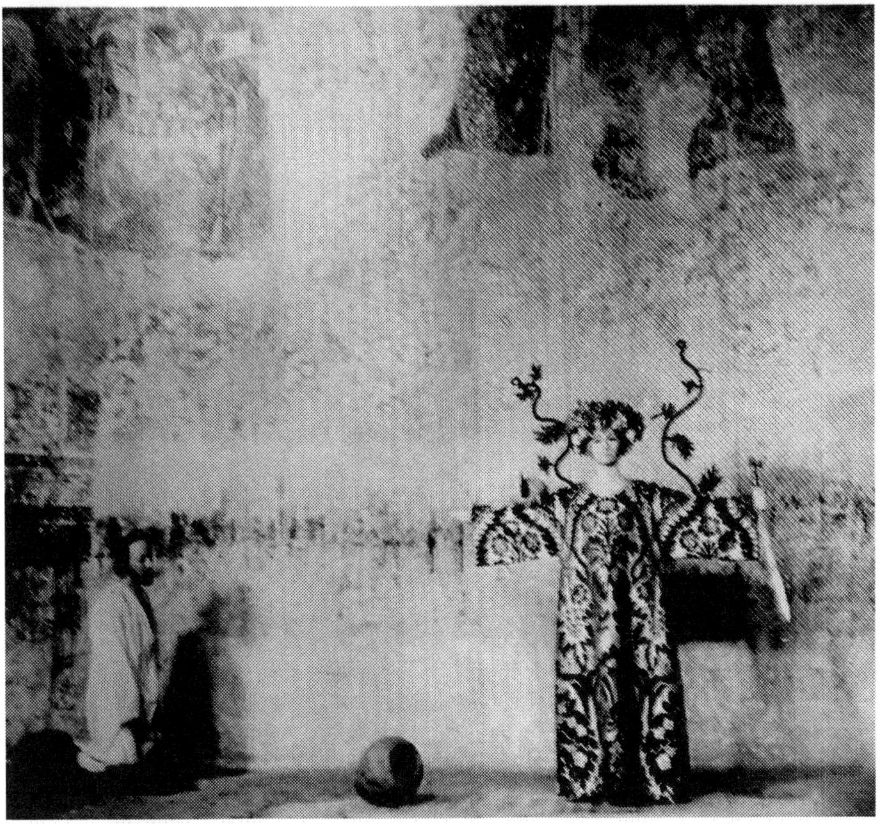

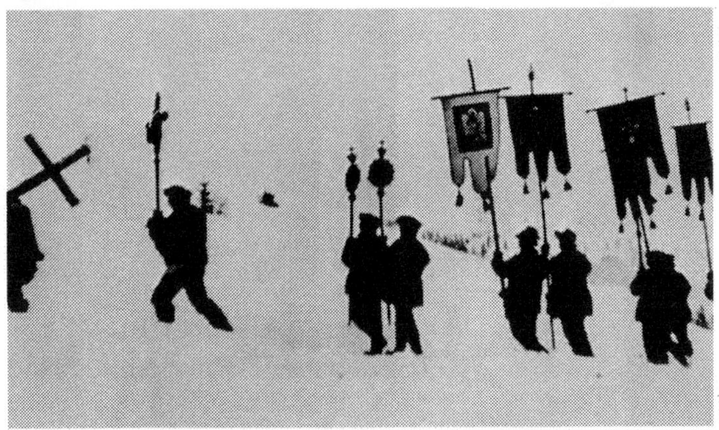

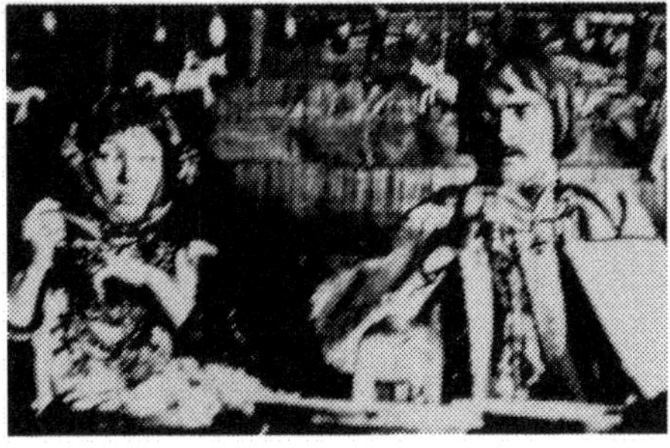

Sergei Paradjanov, one of the most extraordinary filmmakers of
any era.

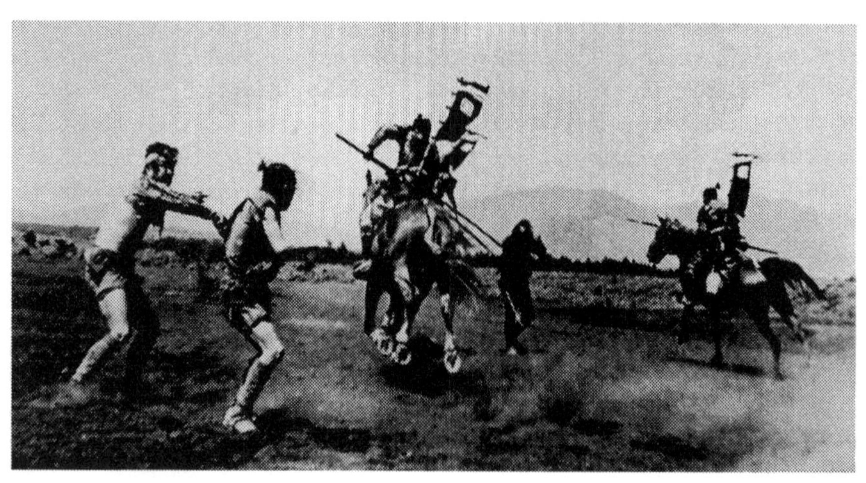

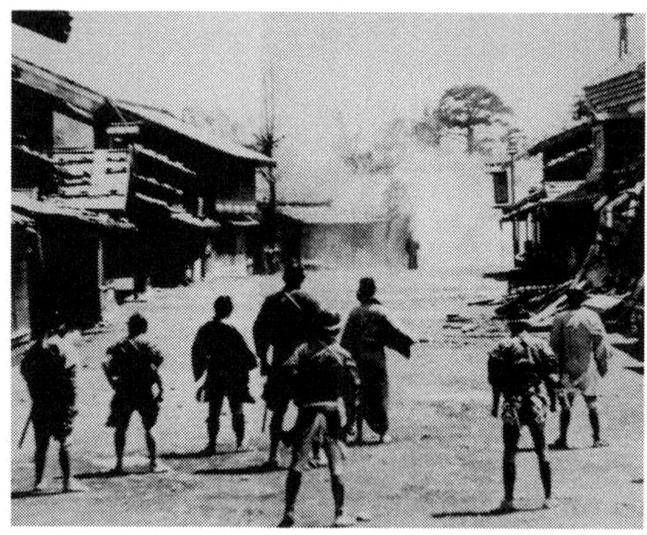

The *sensei*: Akira Kurosawa.
(Examples of Kurosawa's masterful reworkings of John Ford
Westerns).

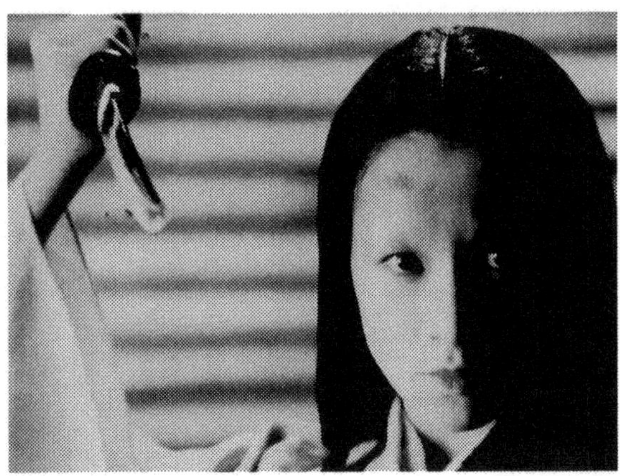

Akira Kurosawa's Shakespeare adaptions.

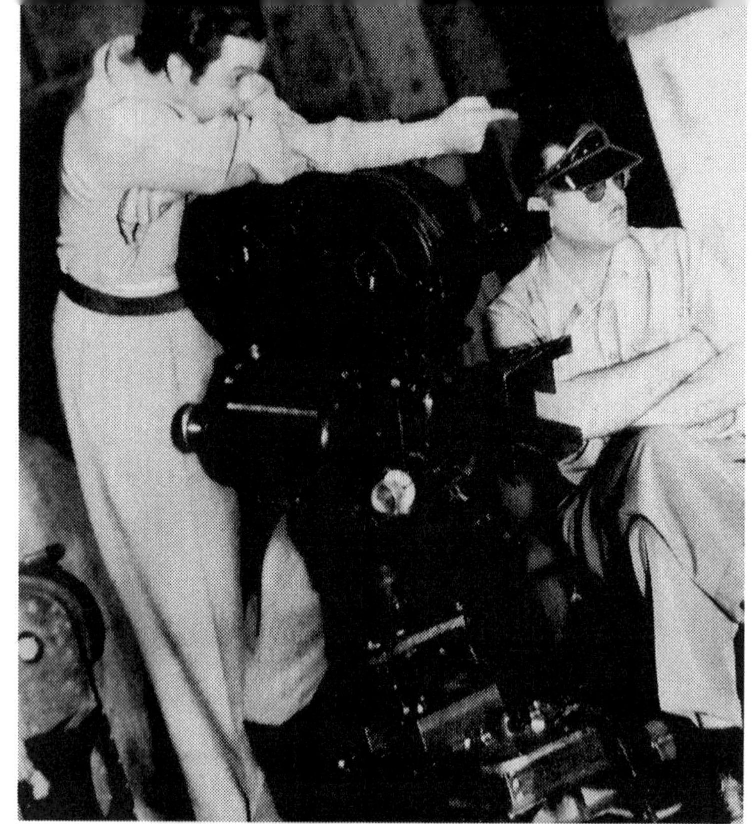

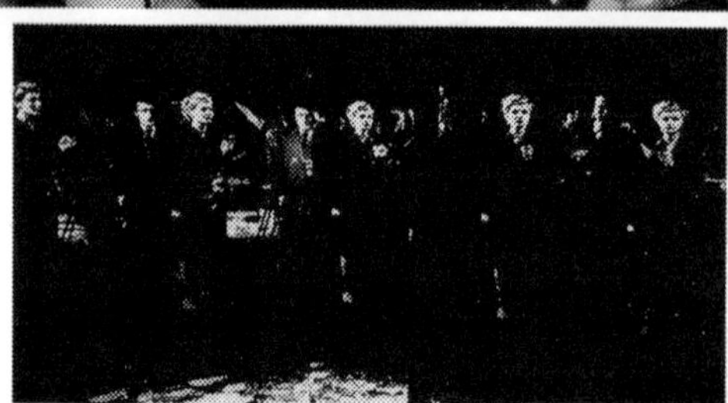

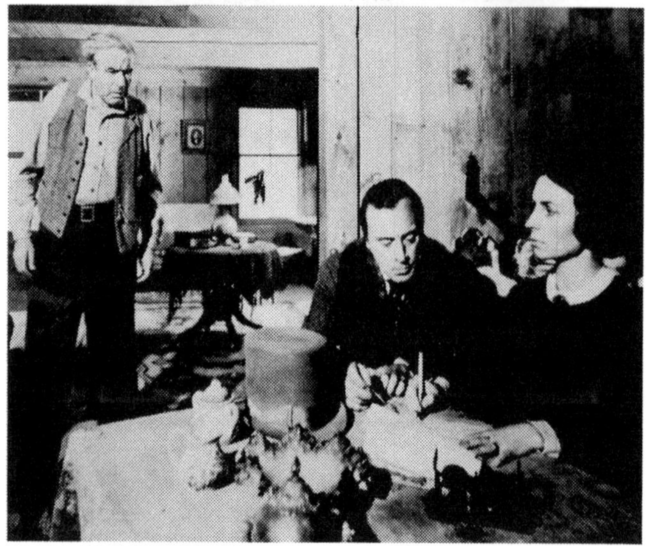

Orson Welles

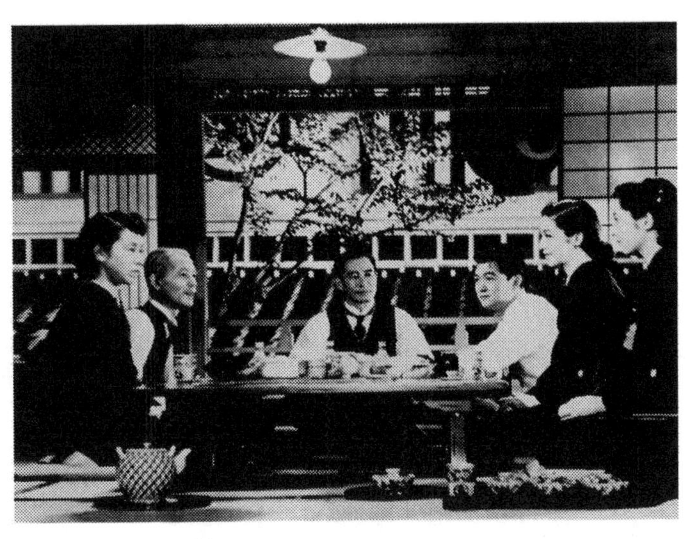

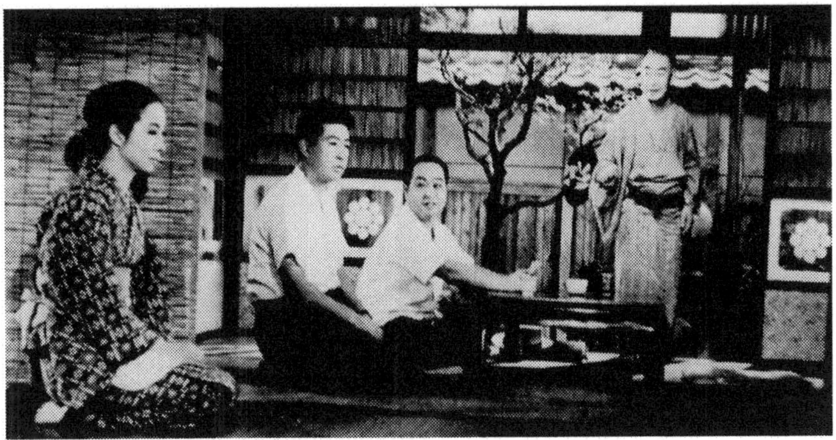

Yasujiro Ozu

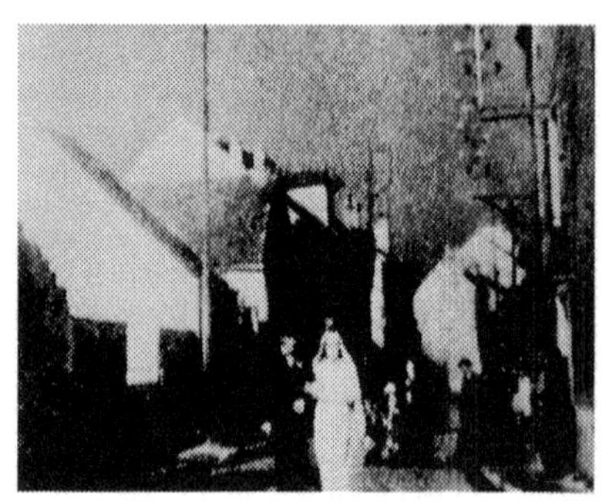 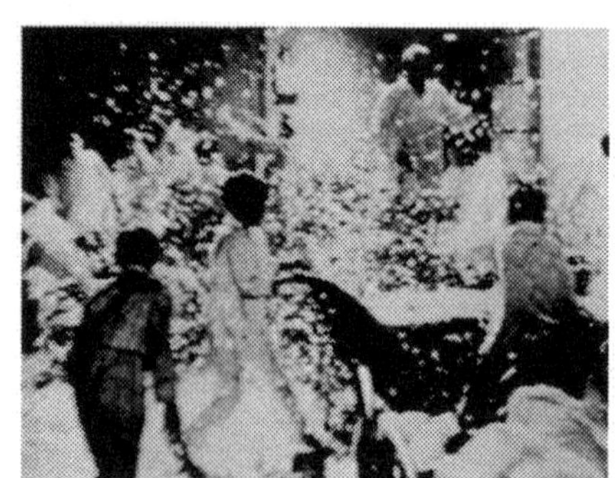

Jean Vigo

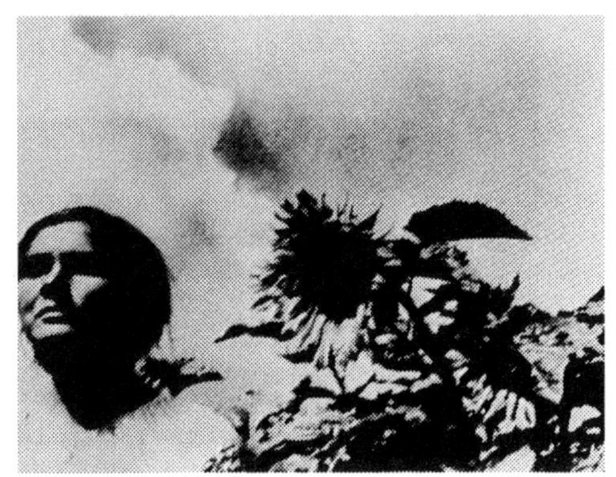

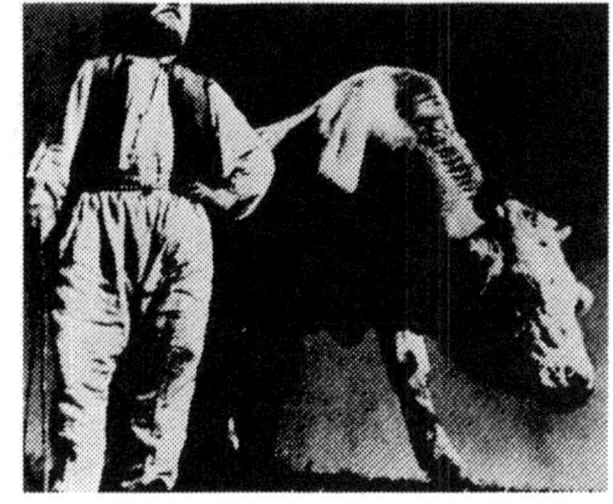

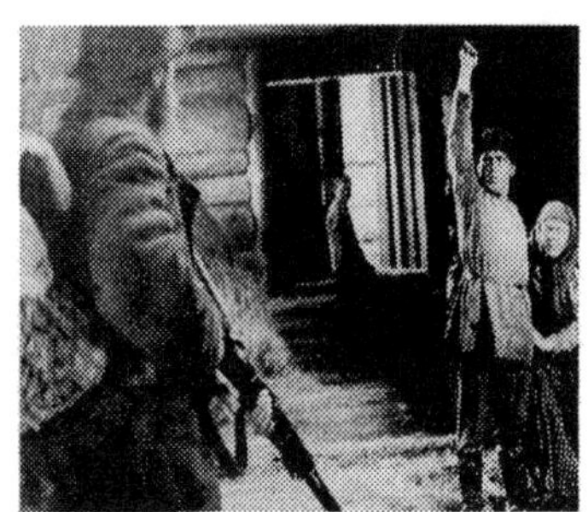

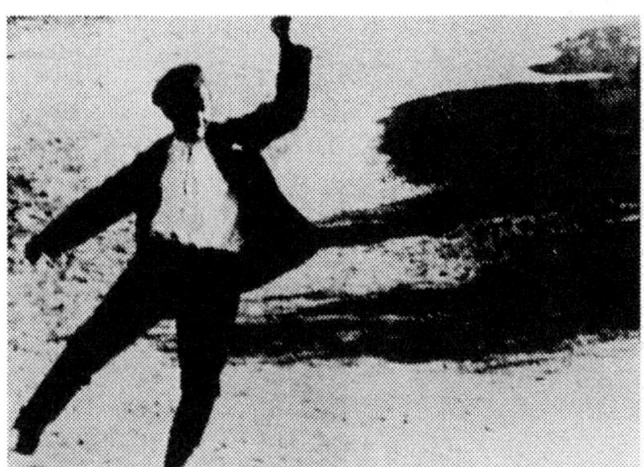

Alexander Dovzhenko

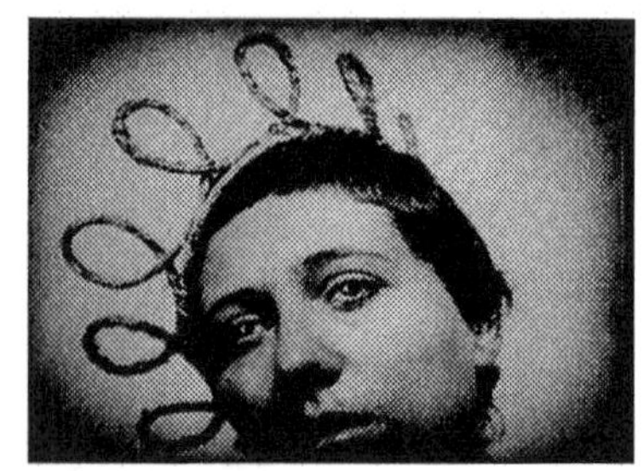

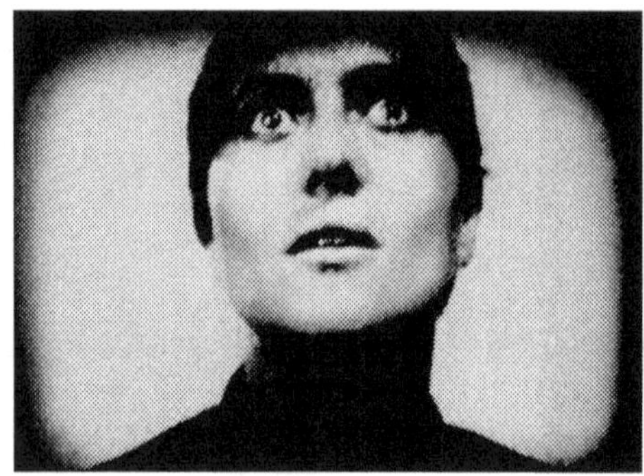

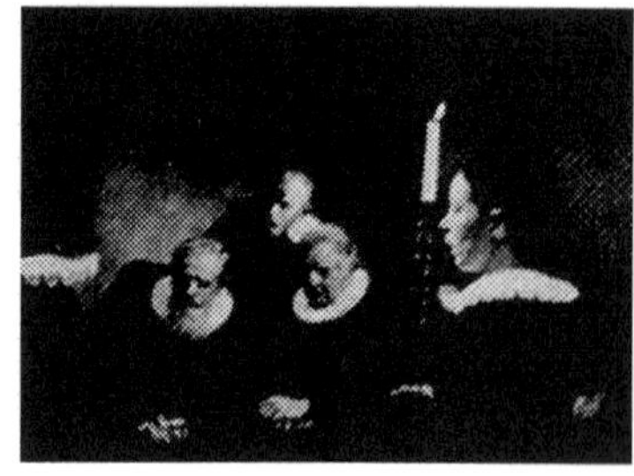

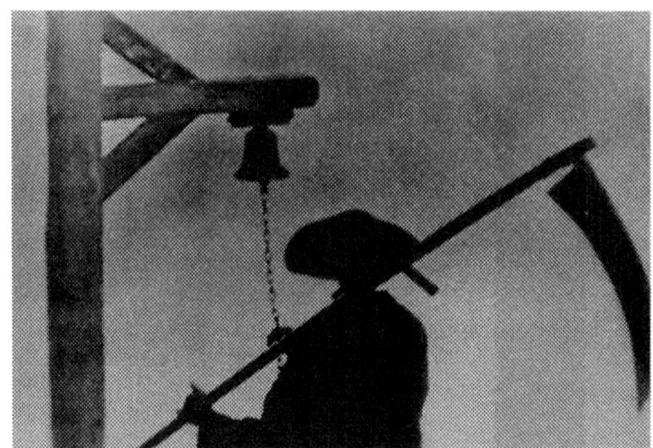

Carl-Theodor Dreyer

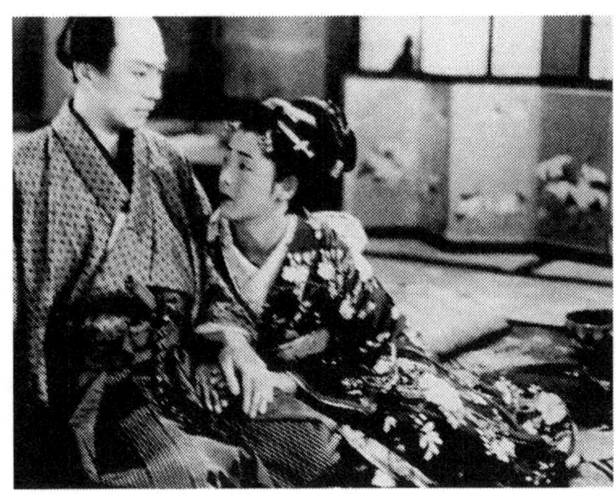

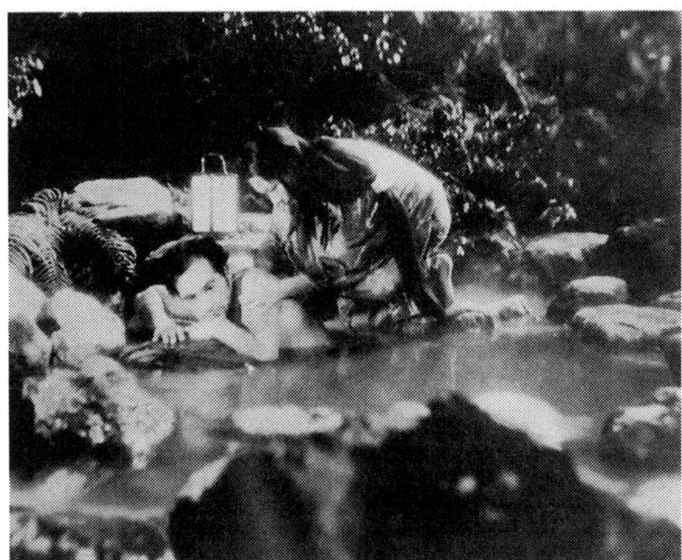

Kenji Mizoguchi.
Mizoguchi wrote that '[i]t is essential that one should reflect for 5 or 6 years before beginning to film. Films produced very quickly are never very good'. If Mizoguchi had practiced what he preached, he would have made seven films in his thirty-four year career. In fact he made *ninety* feature films.

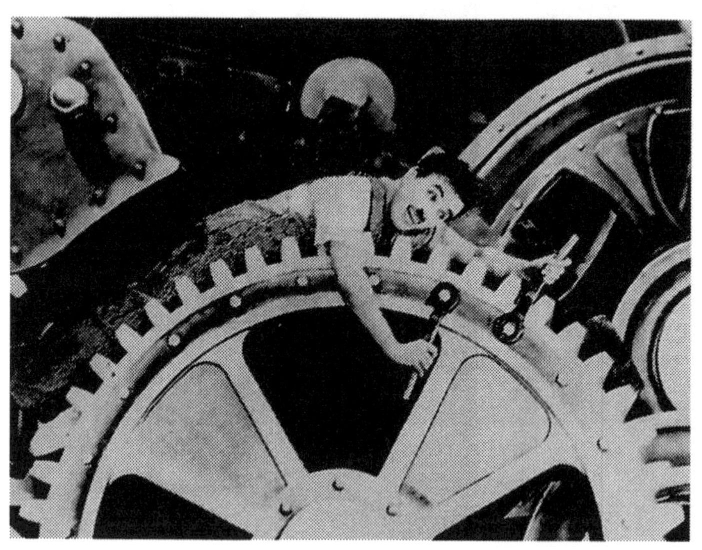

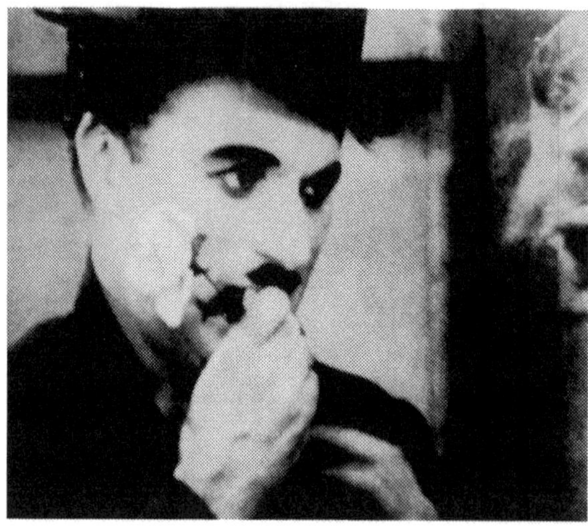

Charlie Chaplin

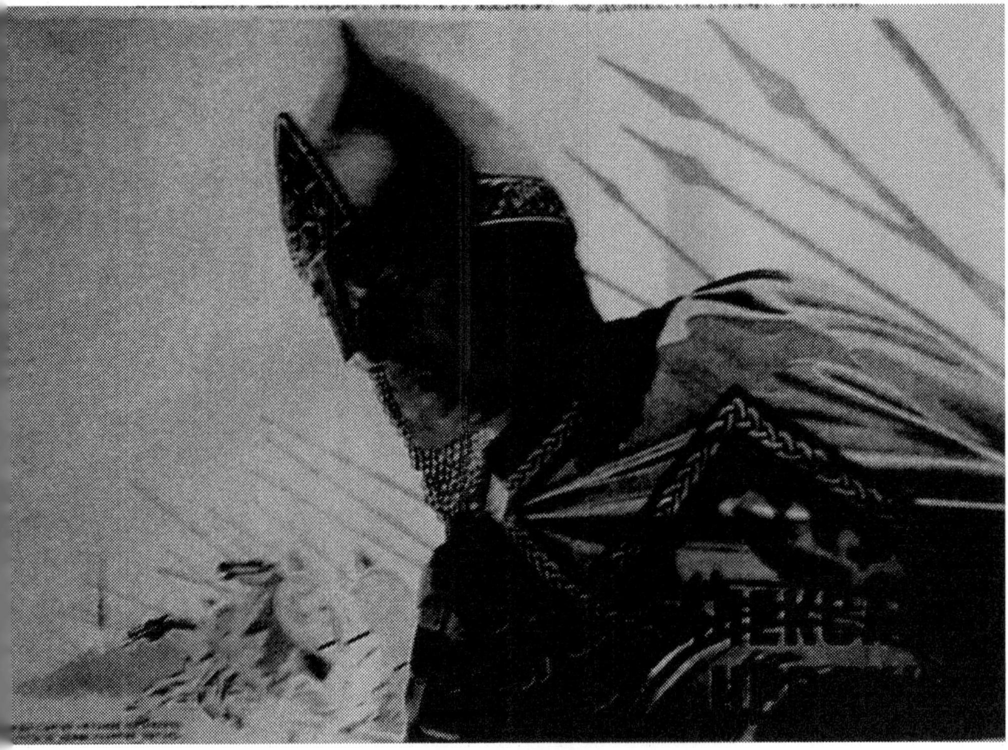

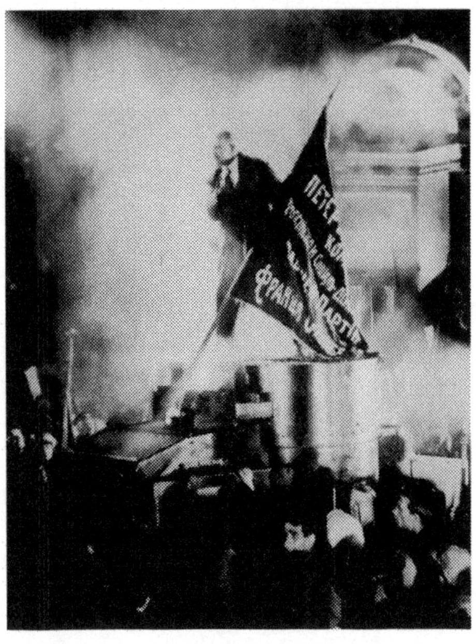

Sergei Eisenstein, a filmmaker Tarkovsky loved to hate (or hated to love).

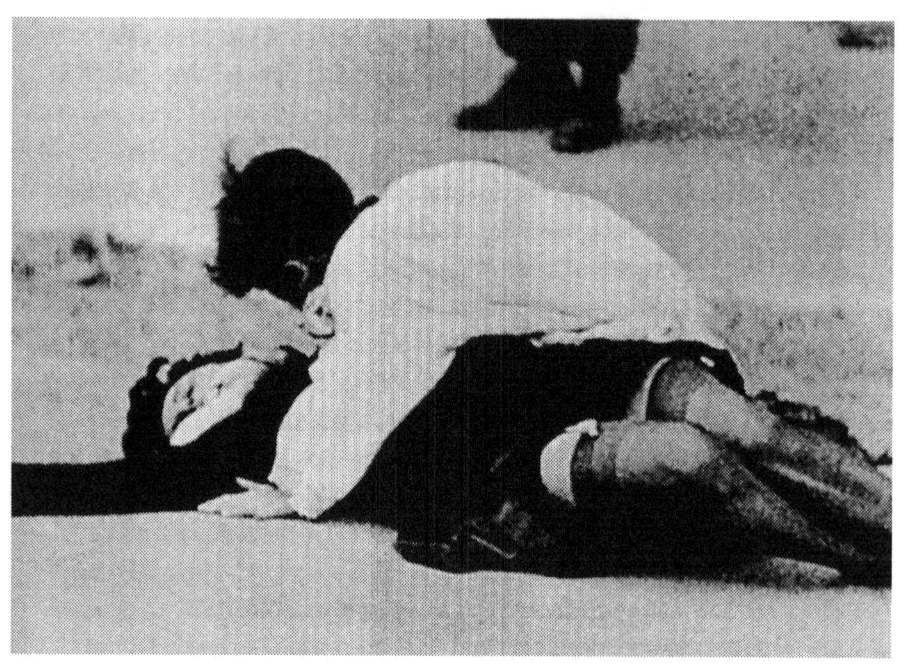

Some more of Andrei Tarkovsky's favourite filmmakers:
Roberto Rossellini, above, and Andrzej Wadja, below

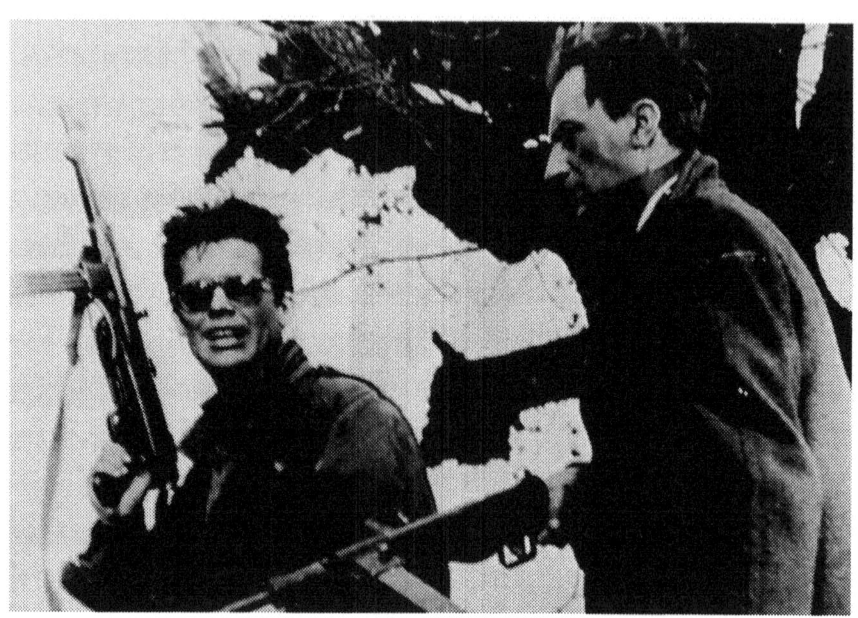

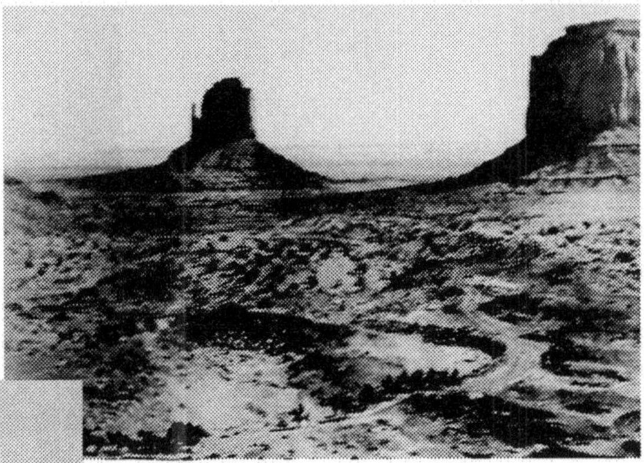

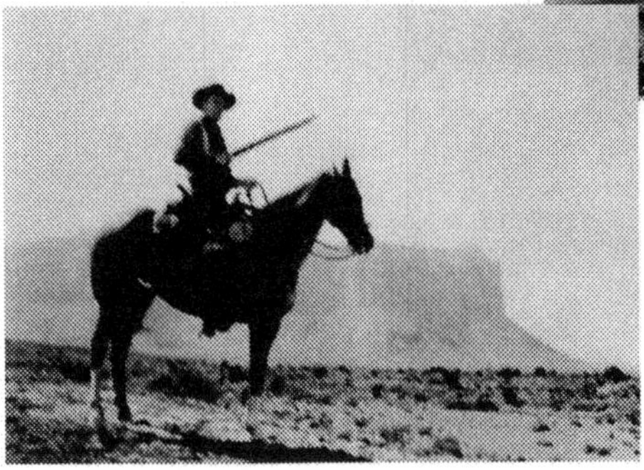

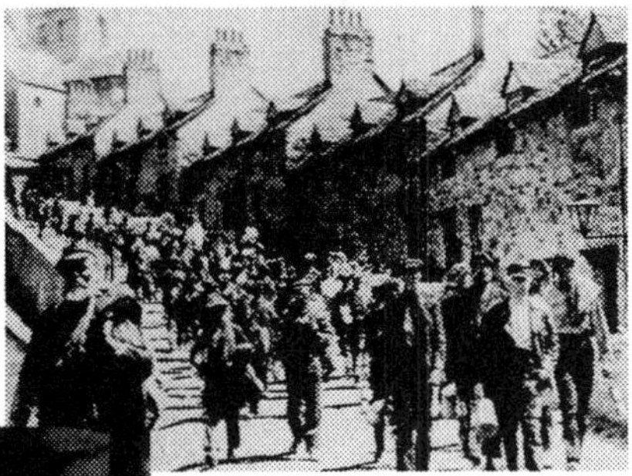

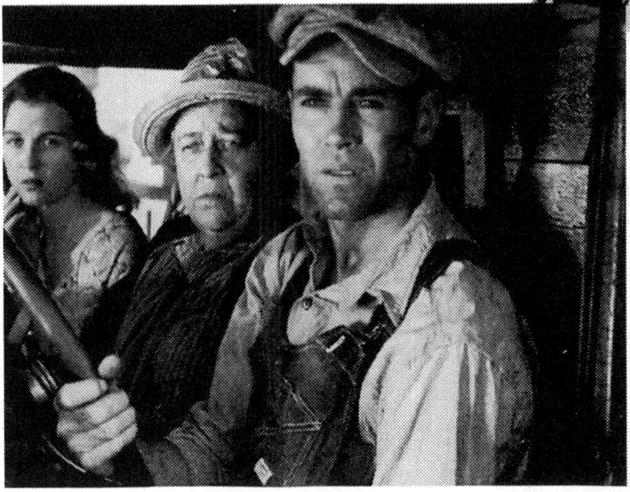

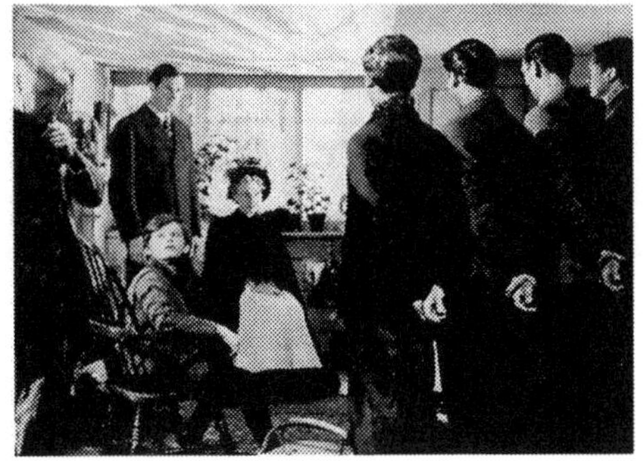

John Ford

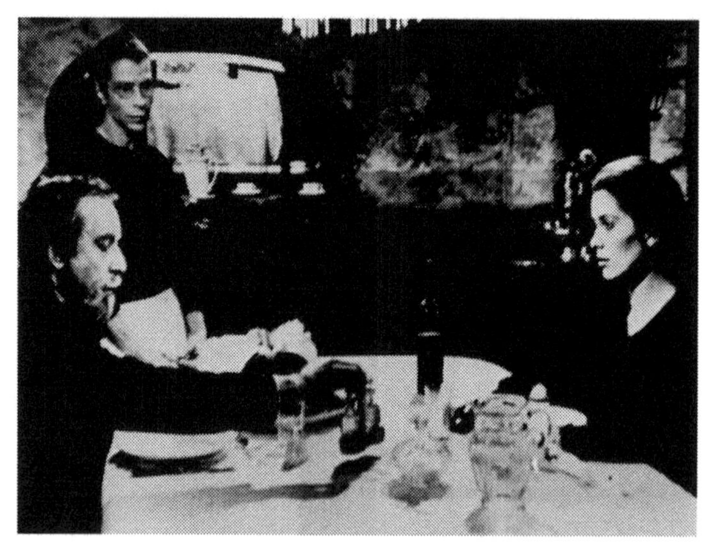

Luis Buñuel

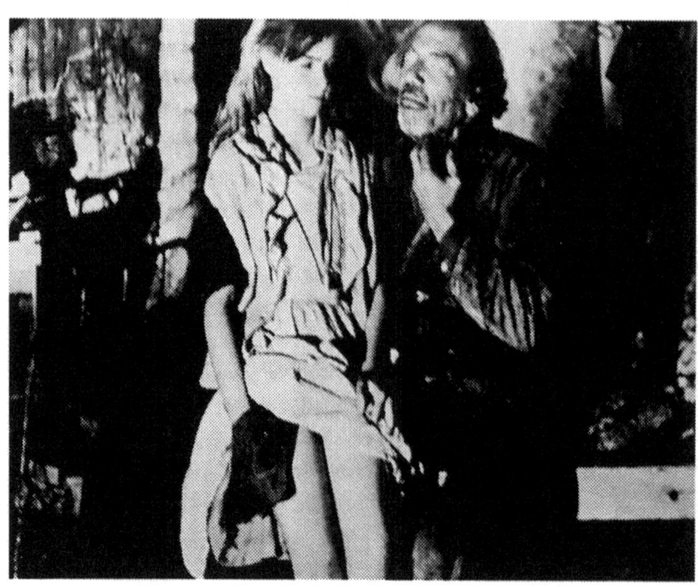

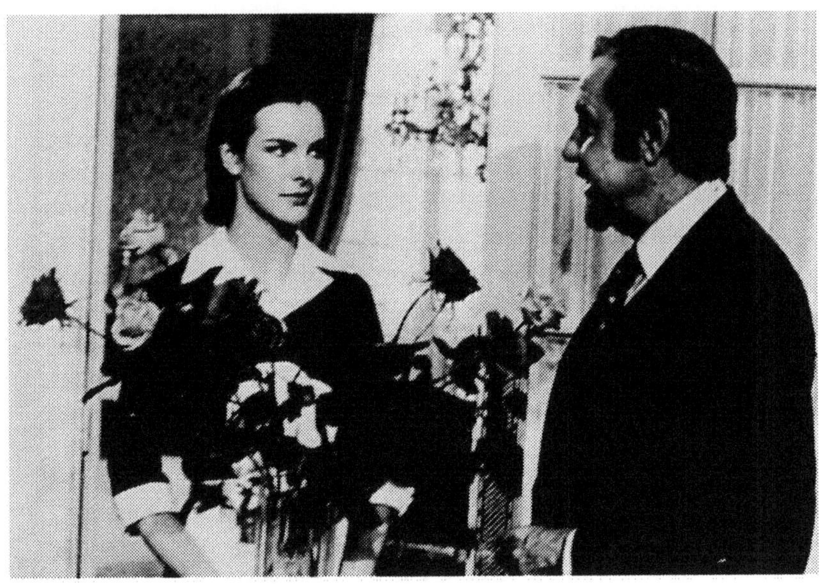

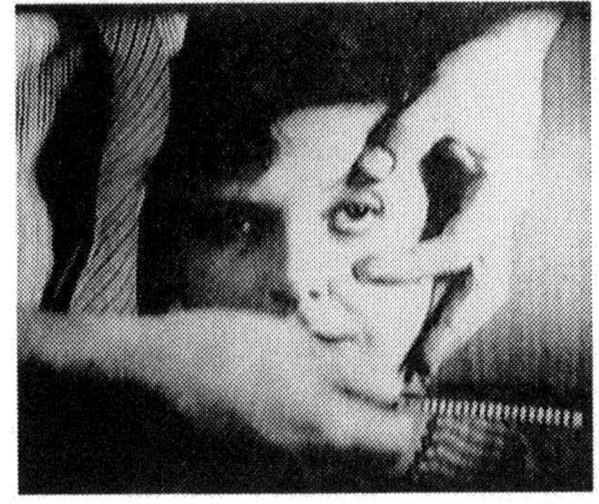

Luis Buñuel

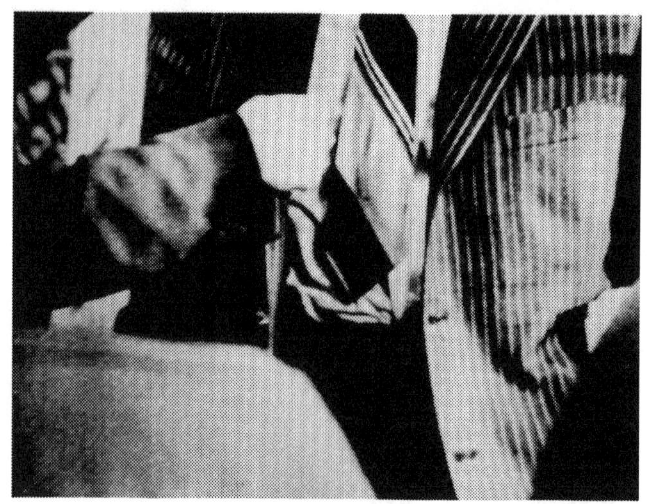

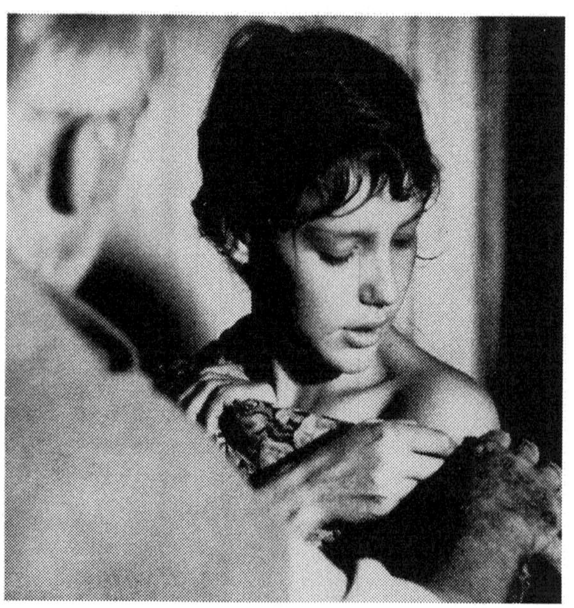

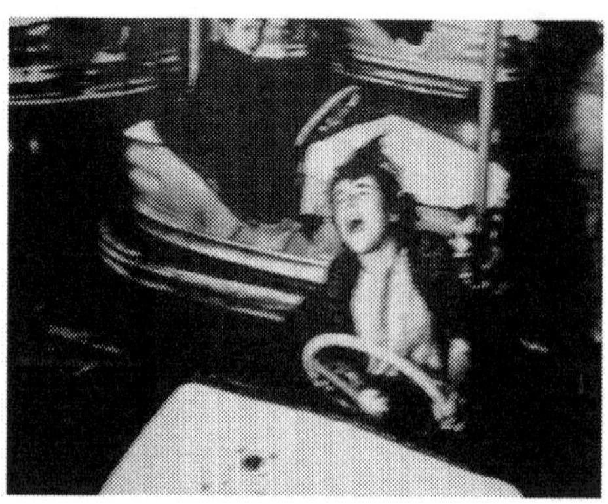

Robert Bresson

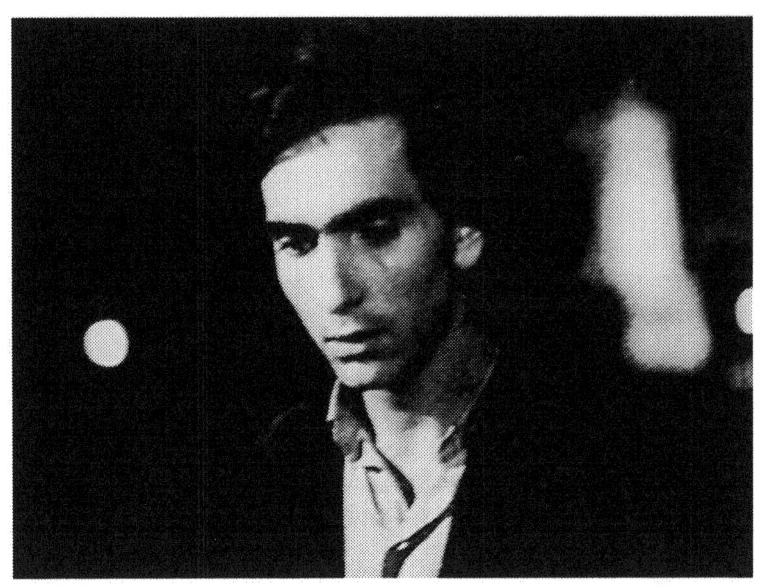

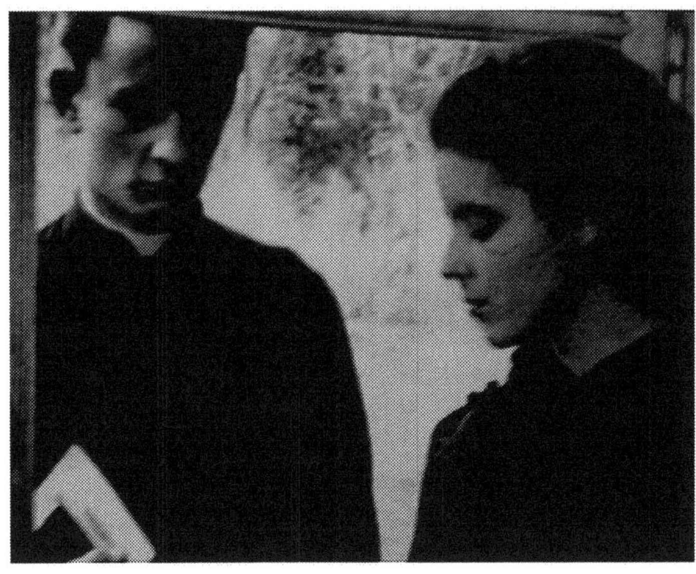

Robert Bresson

Images from
Andrei Tarkovsky's films

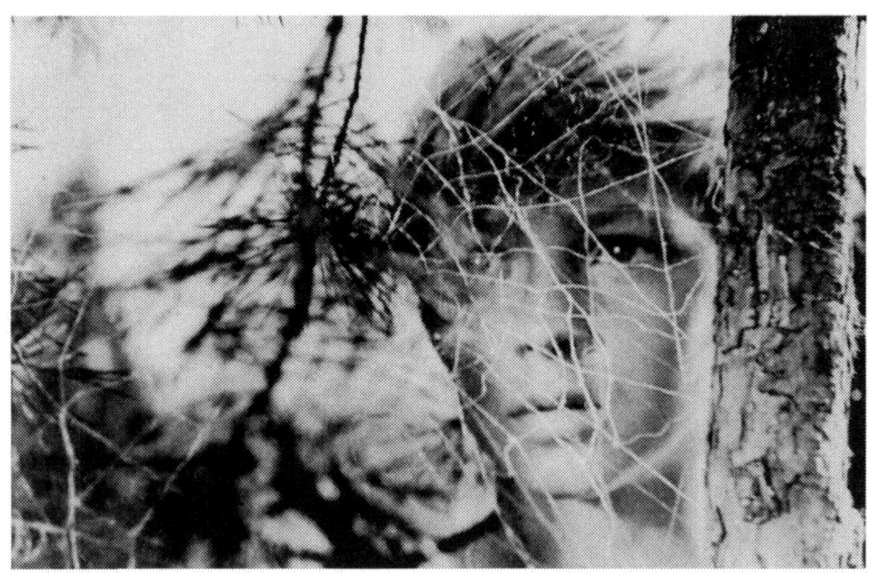

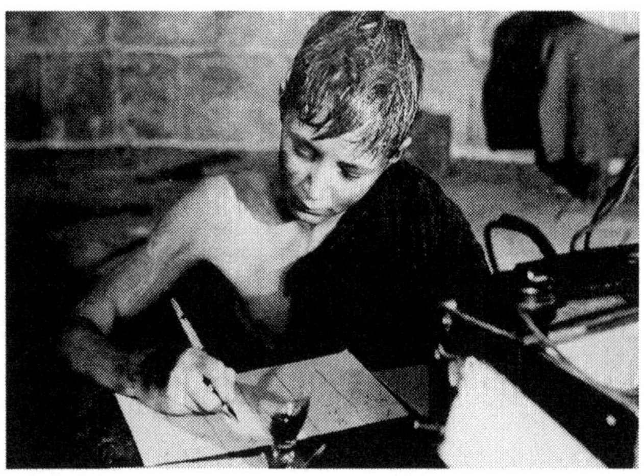

The hero of *Ivan's Childhood*

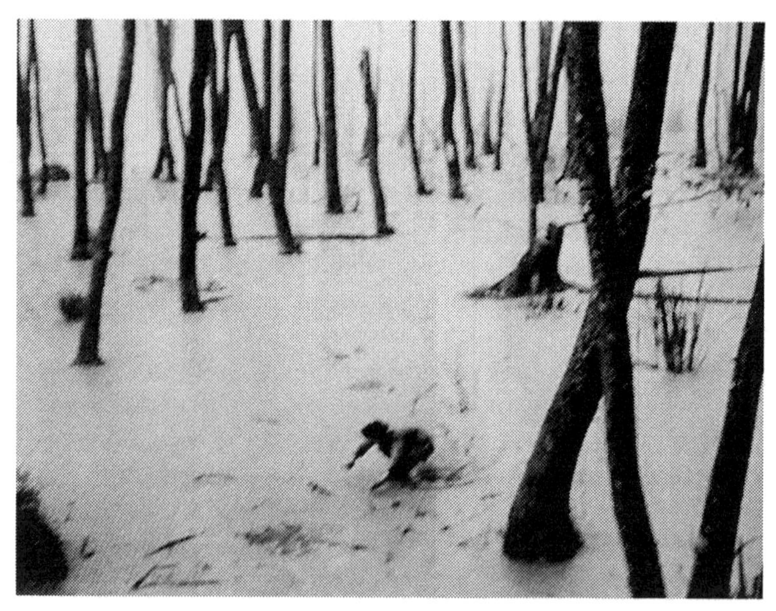

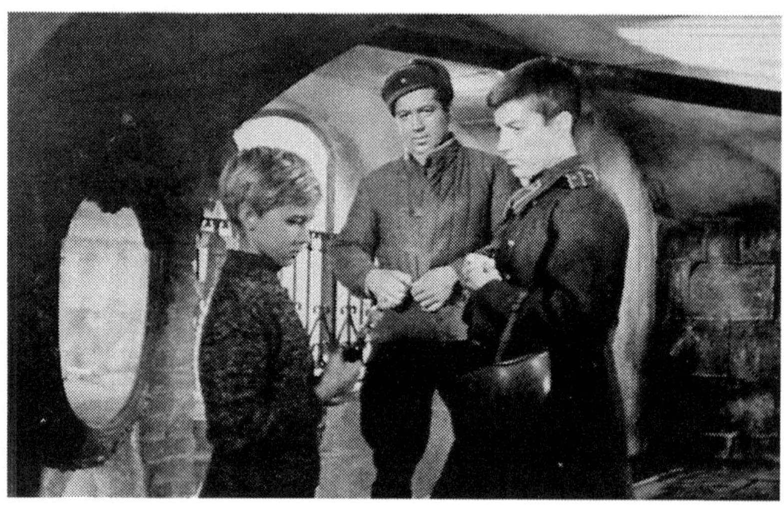

Ivan's Childhod

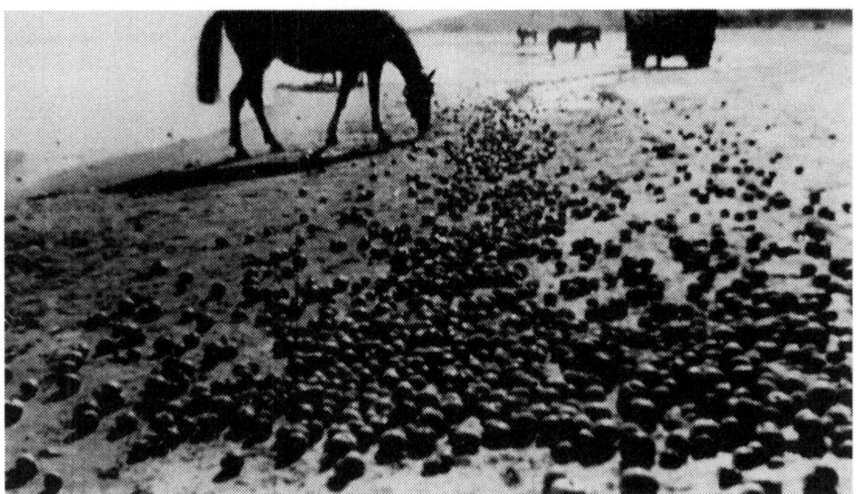

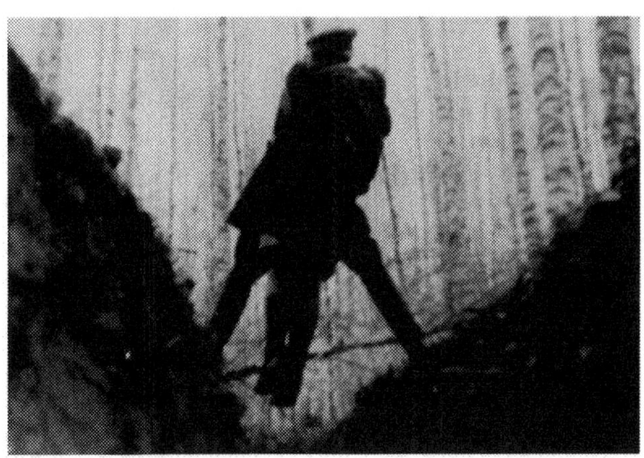

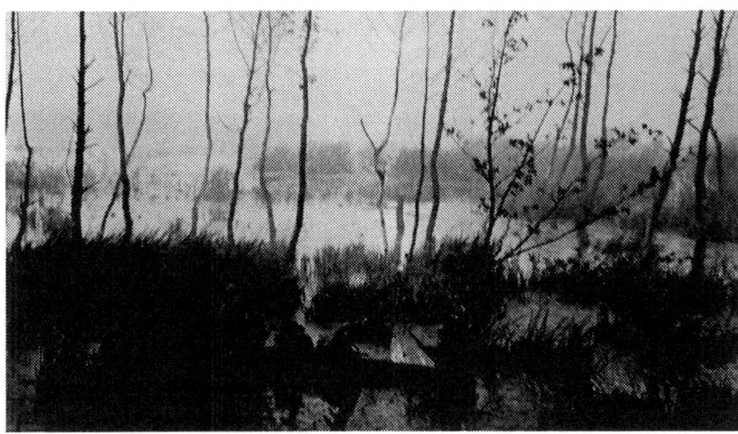

Classic images of Tarkovsky's poetic cinematic style from *Ivan's Childhood*: apples and horses on a beach; love and death in war – a kiss over a trench; and a flooded forest at night.

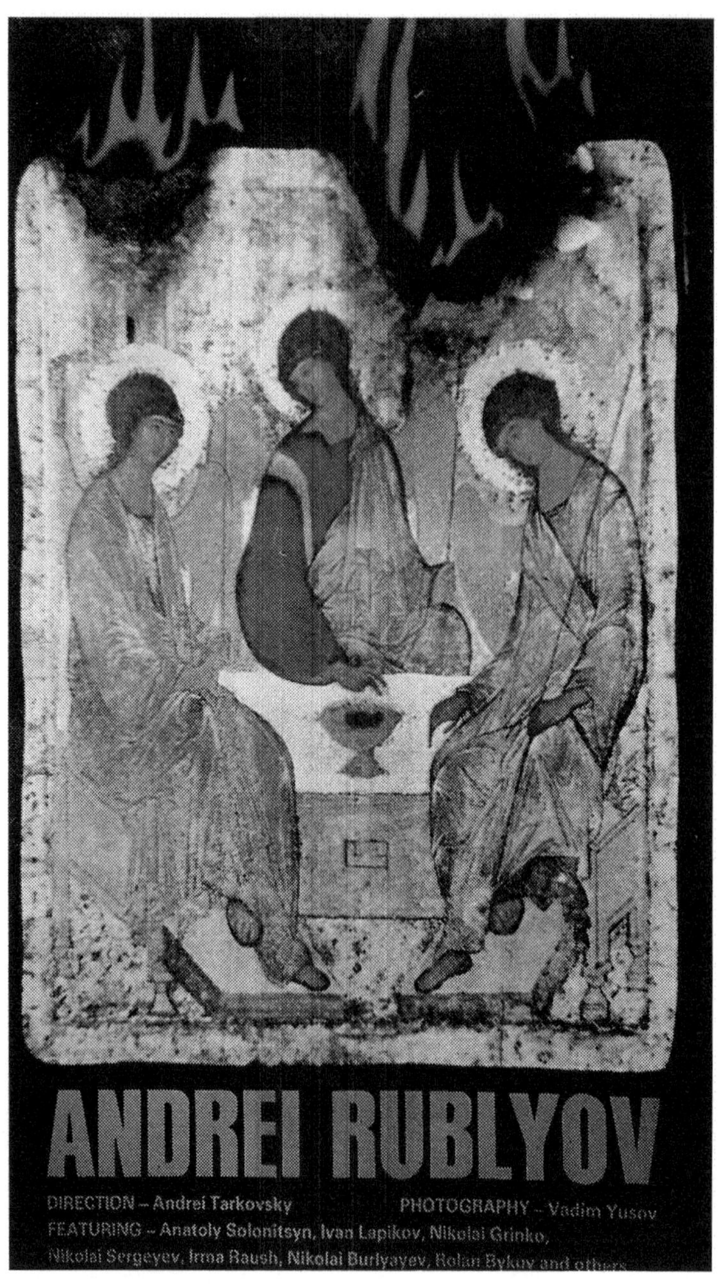

Andrei Roublyov poster

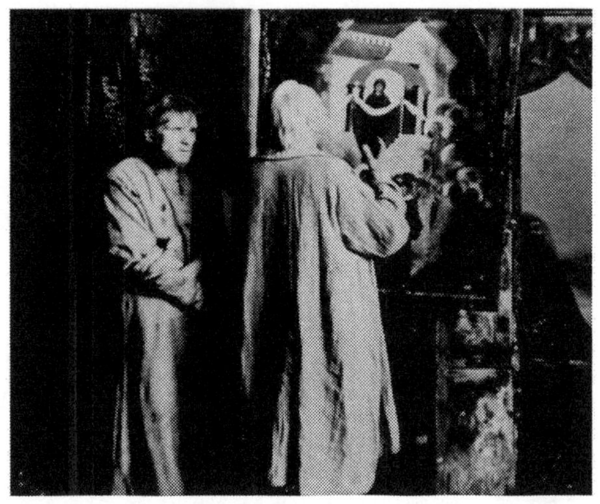

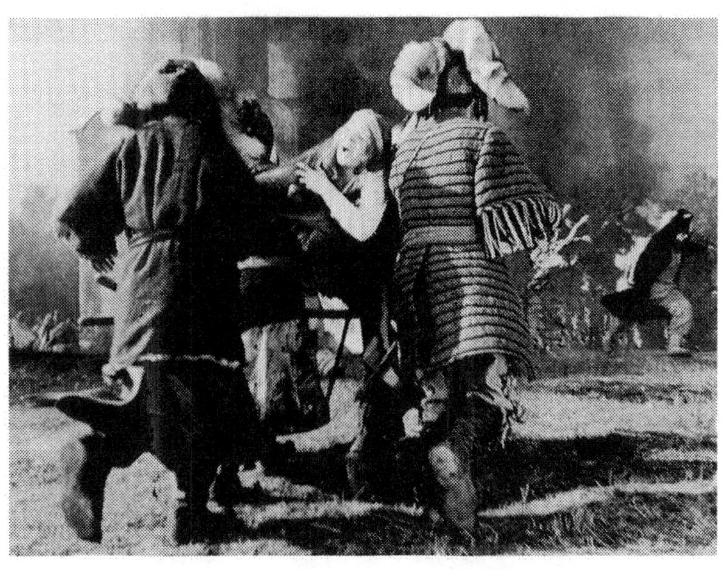

Andrei Roublyov – monks and Tartars, artists and soldiers

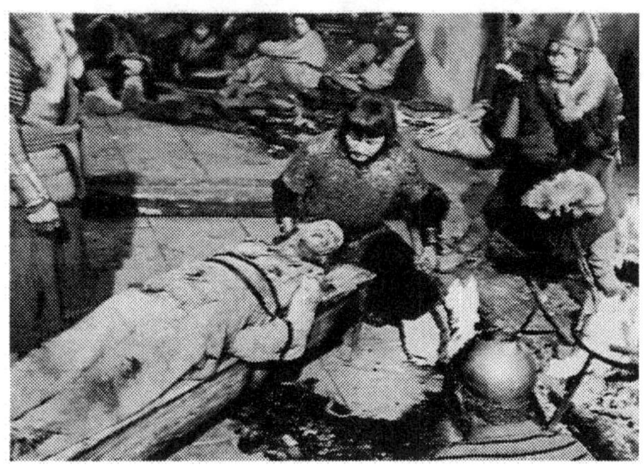

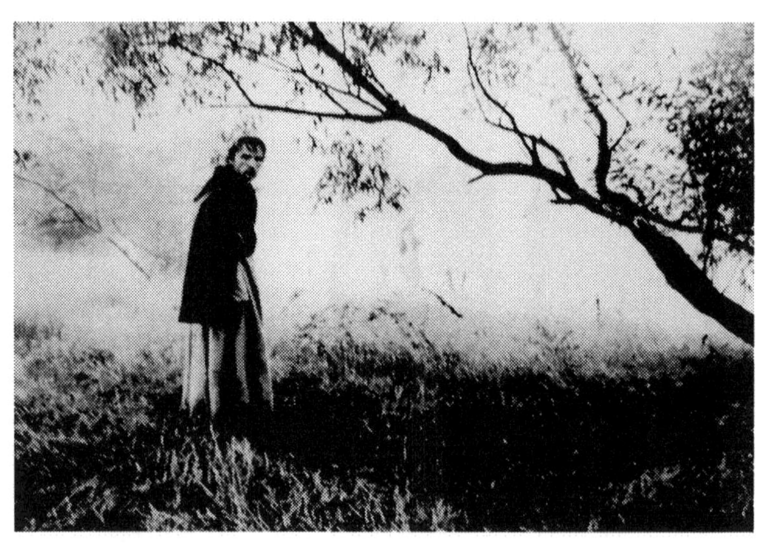

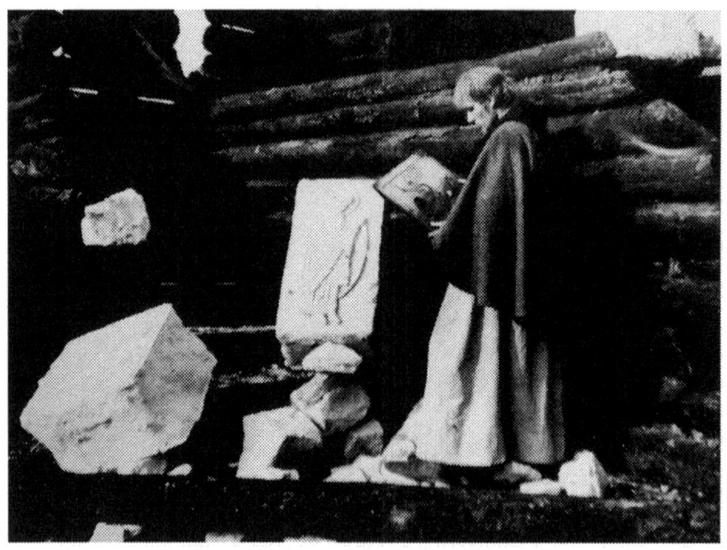

Roublyov alone

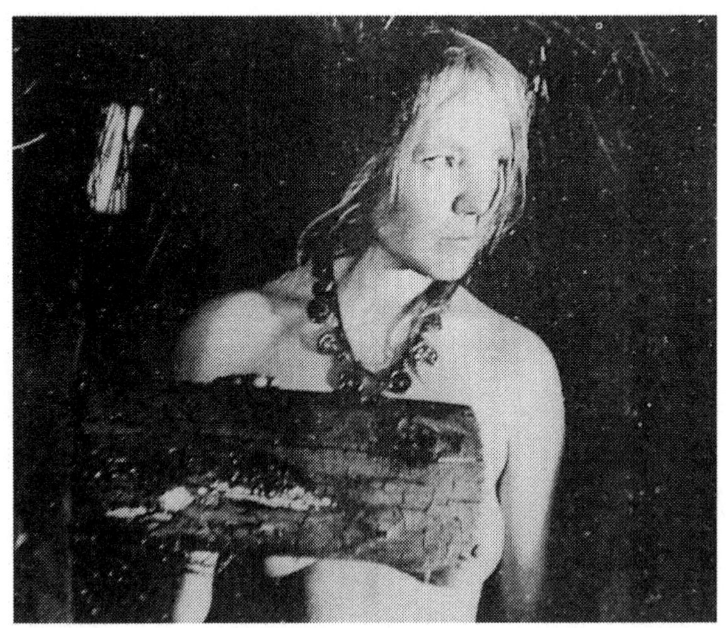

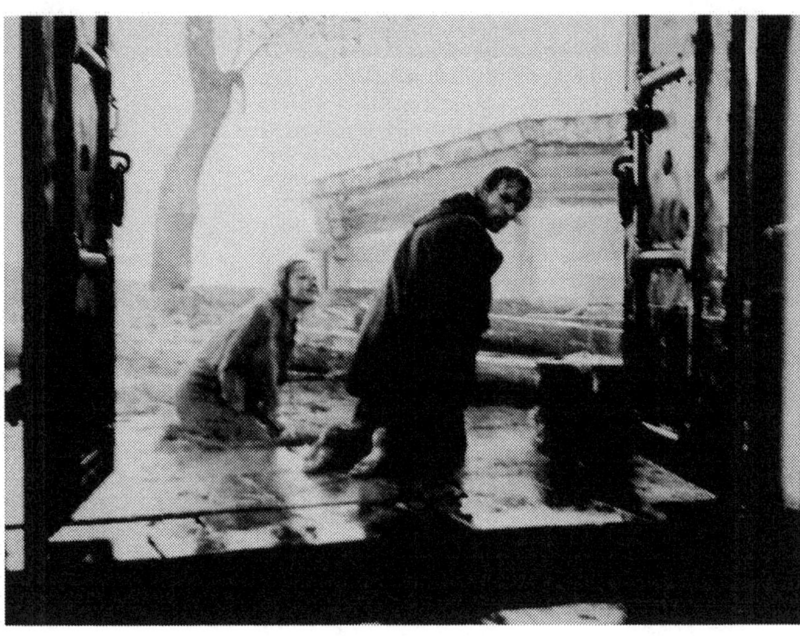

Roublyov and the fool (played by Tarkovsky's wife, Irma Rausch)

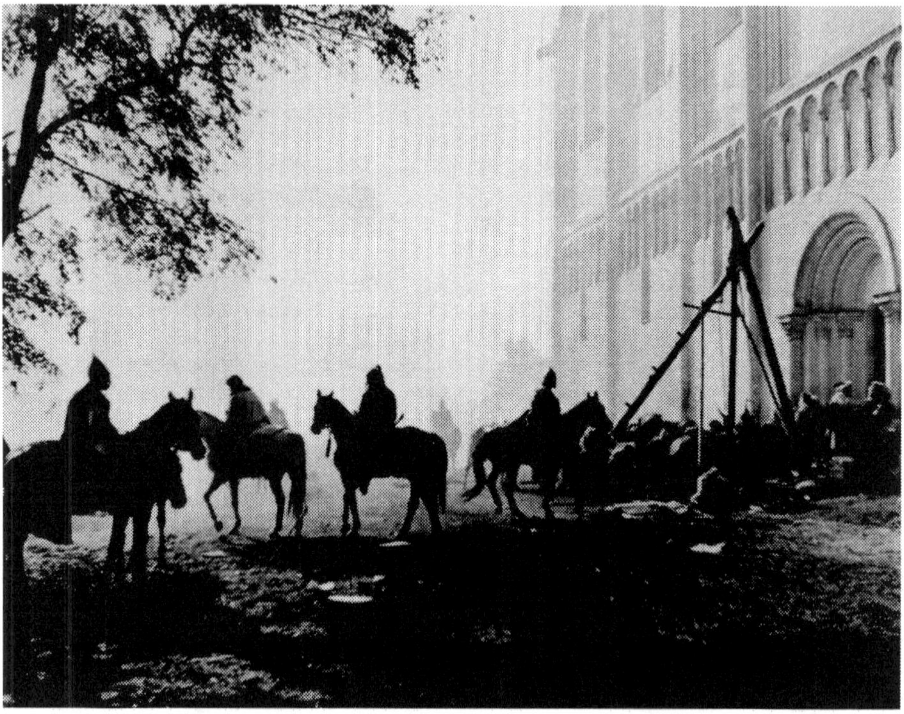

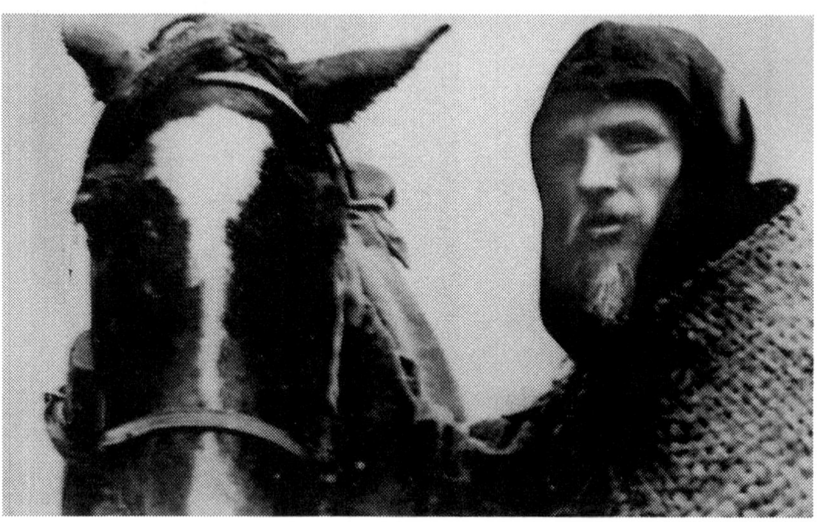

Andrei Roublyov – one of the great horse epics, worthy of John Ford or Akira Kurosawa.

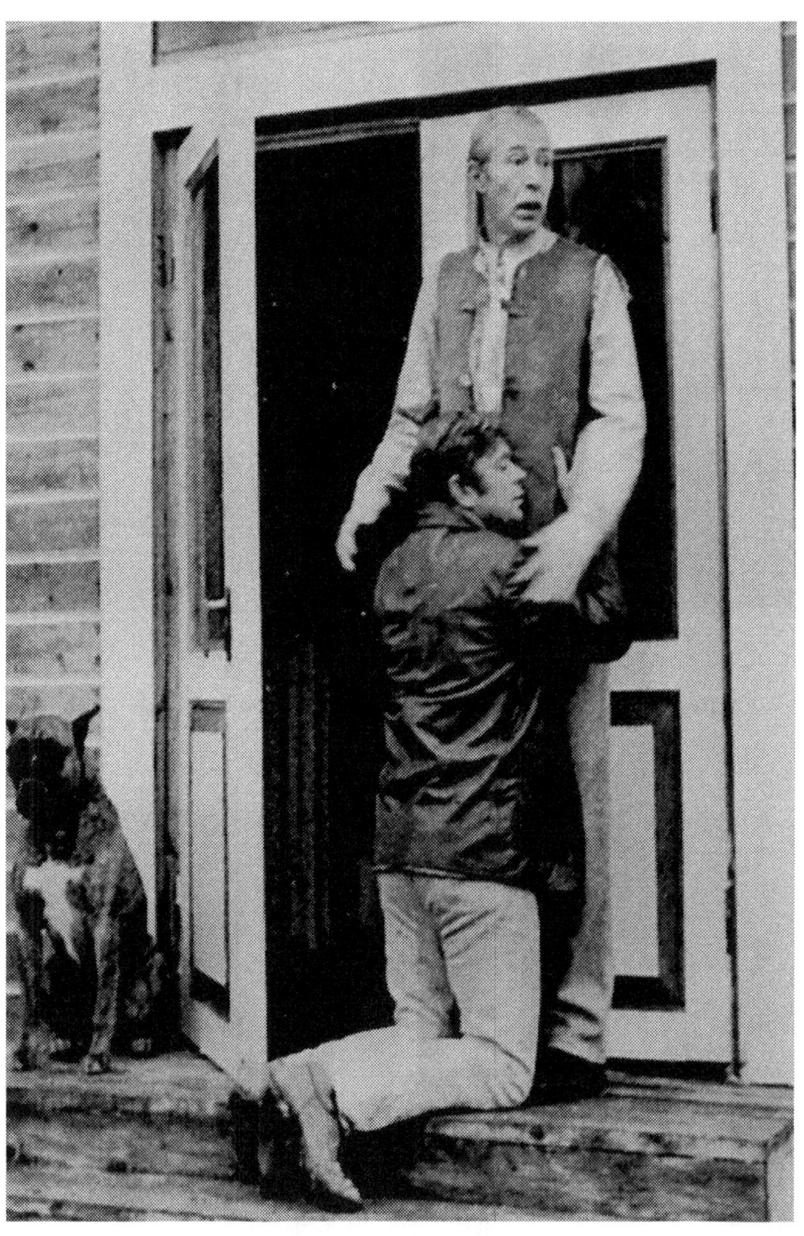

Solaris – the prodigal's return

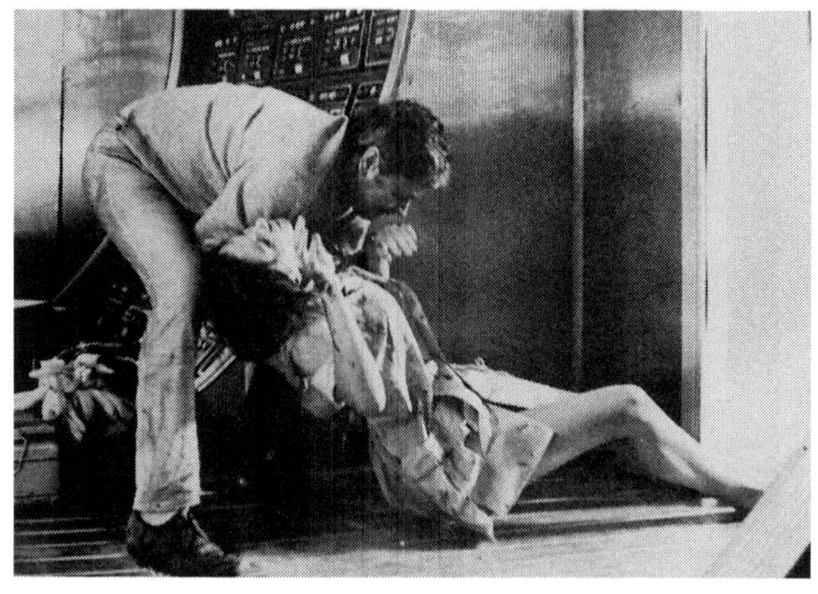

Hari in *Solaris,* played by the wonderful Natalia Bondarchuk

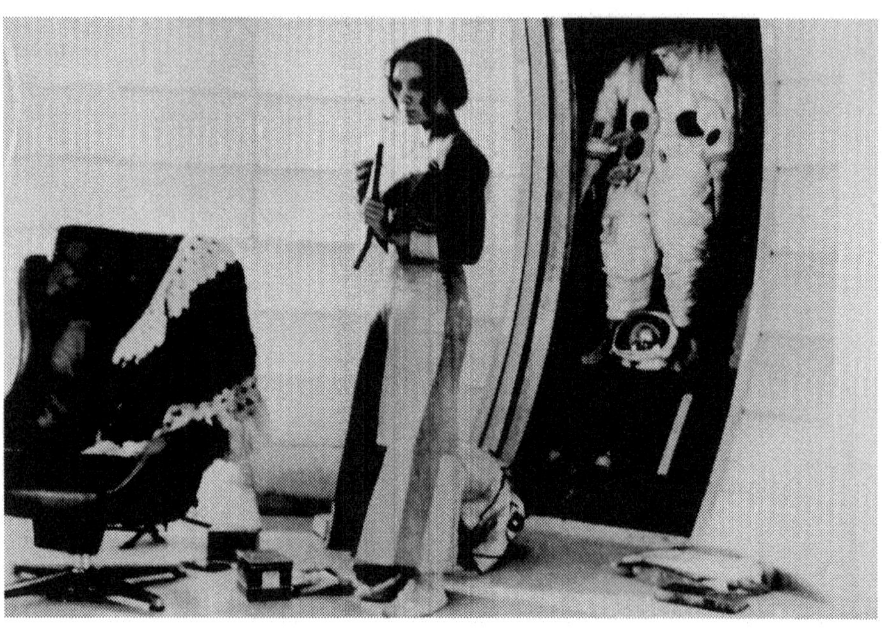

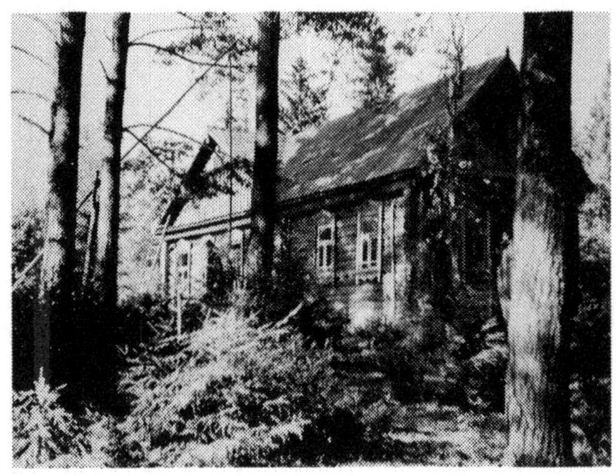

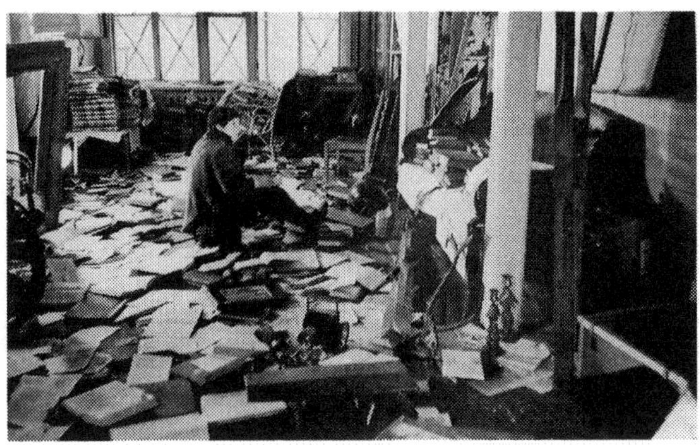

Poetic spaces in *Mirror*. The apartment scene wasn't used in the final cut.

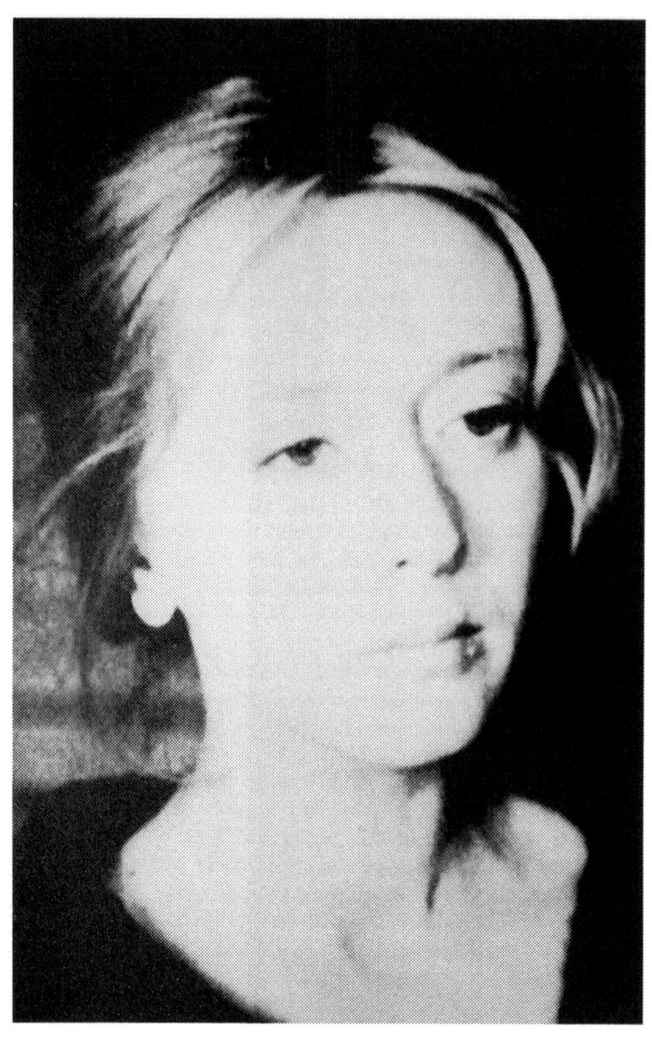

Margarita Terekhova in *Mirror* – one of the great close-ups in cinema

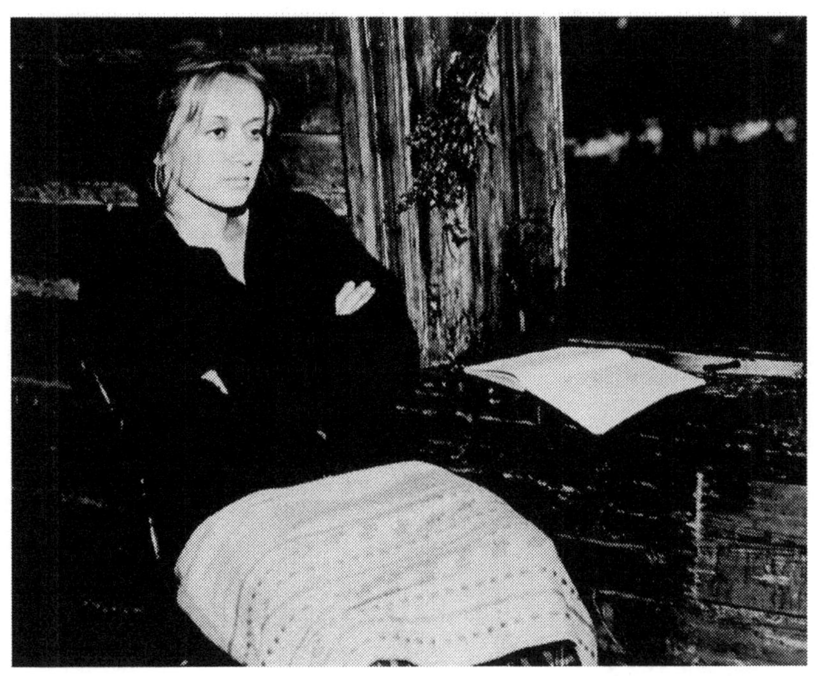

Mirror — Maria — mother

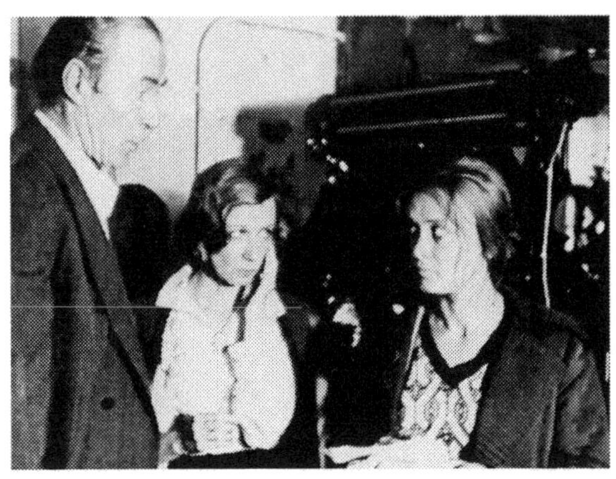

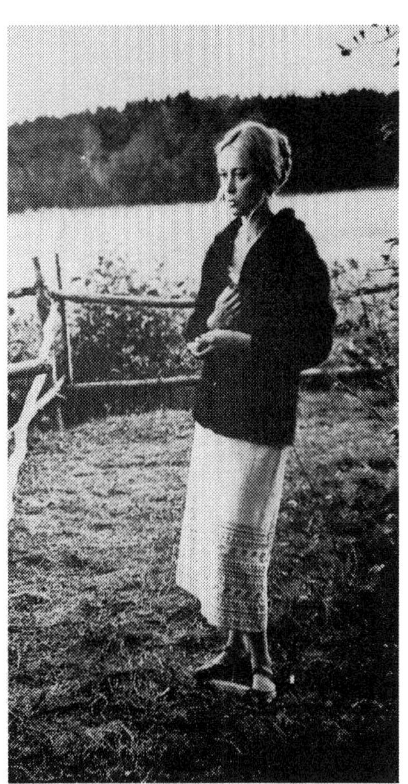

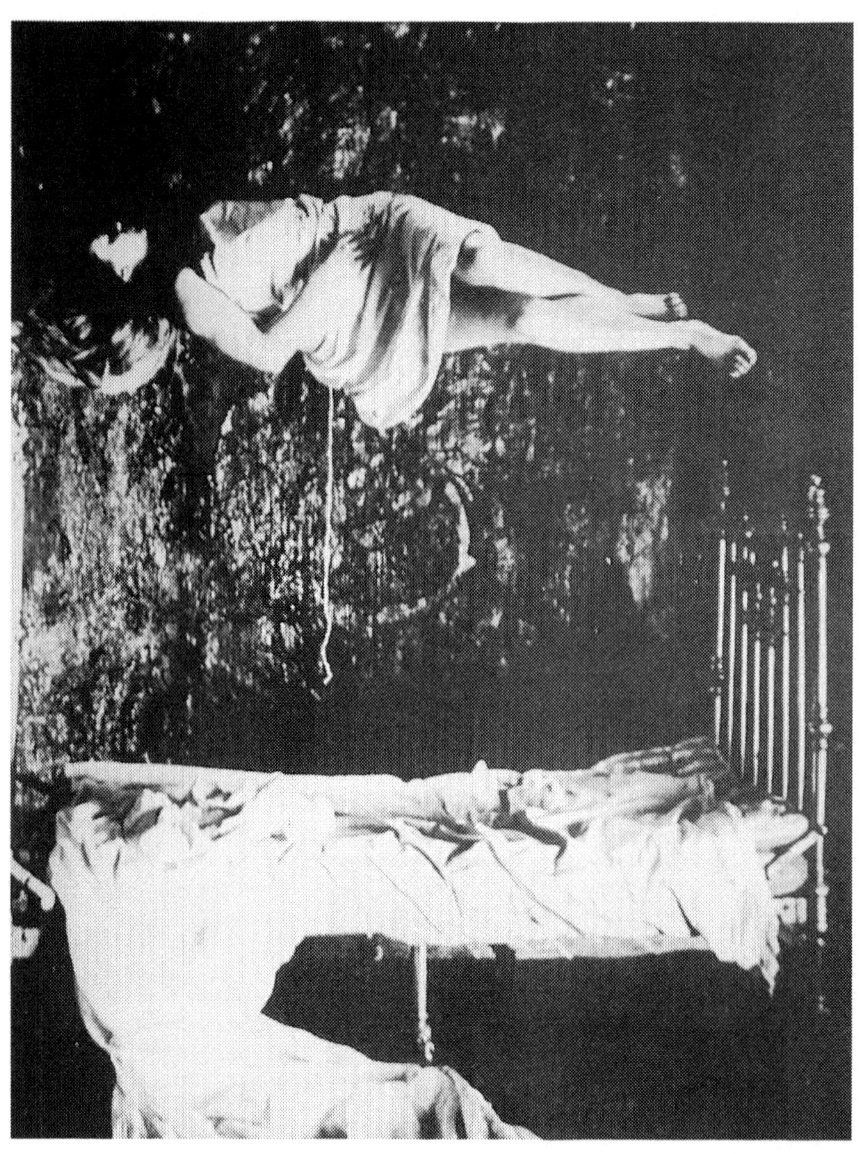

A classic Tarkovsky image: love as flying, a post-orgasmic experience of levitation. Note the metal frame bed, and the highly stylized art direction on the wall.

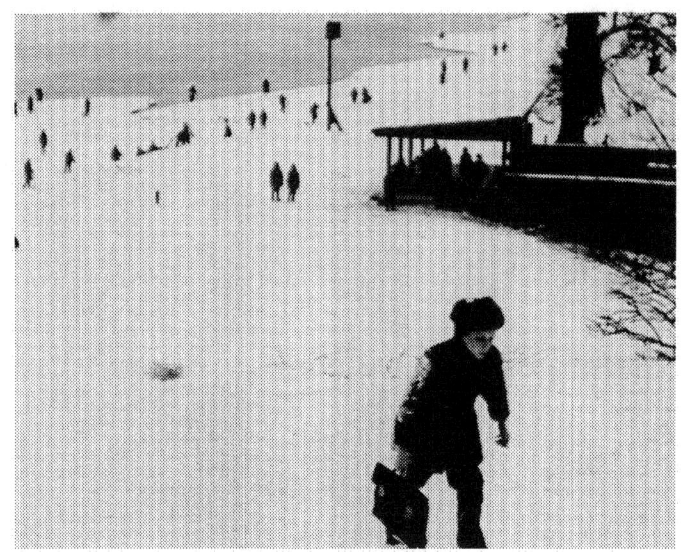

Mirror – a landscape out of Brueghel

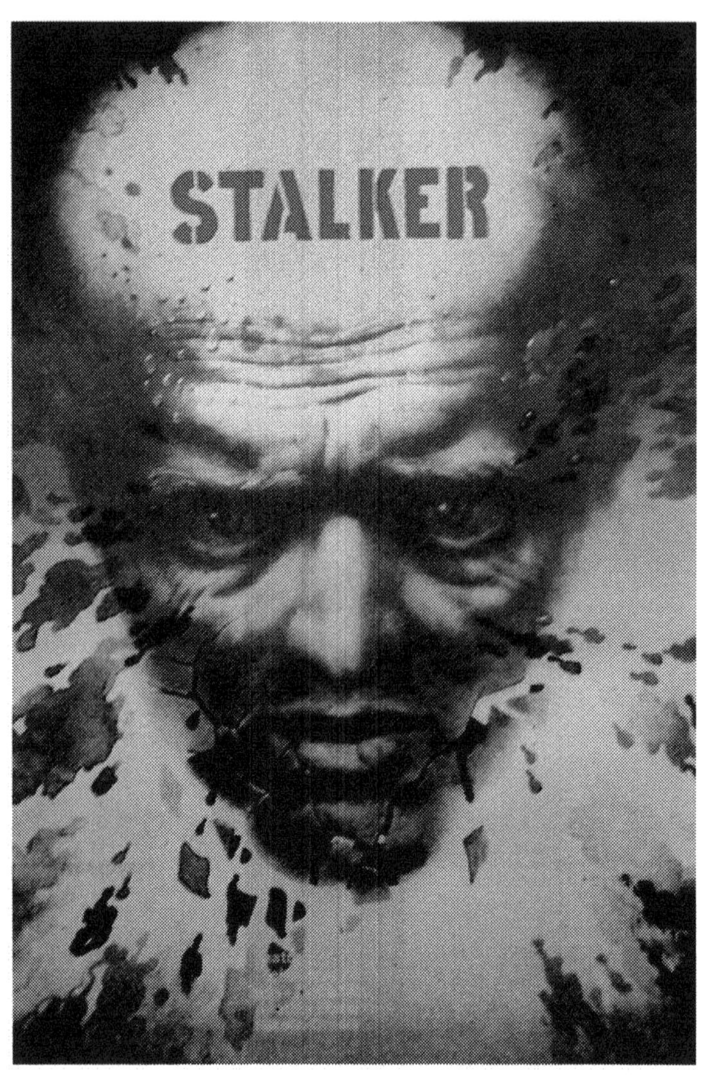

One of the original posters for *Stalker*.

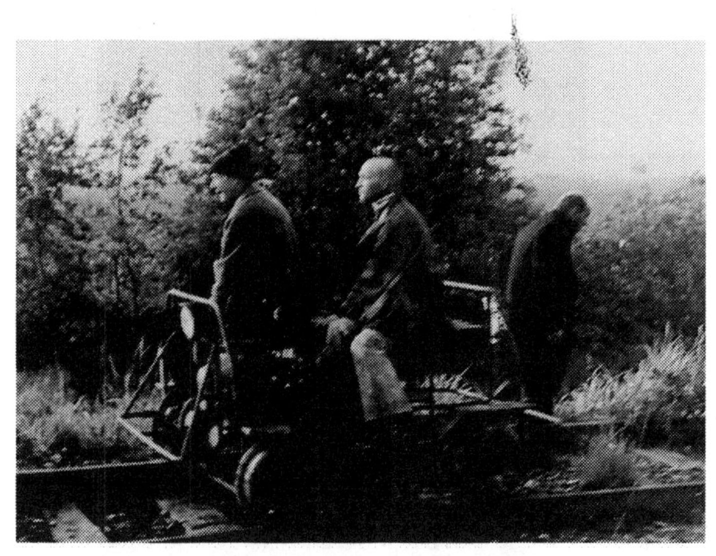

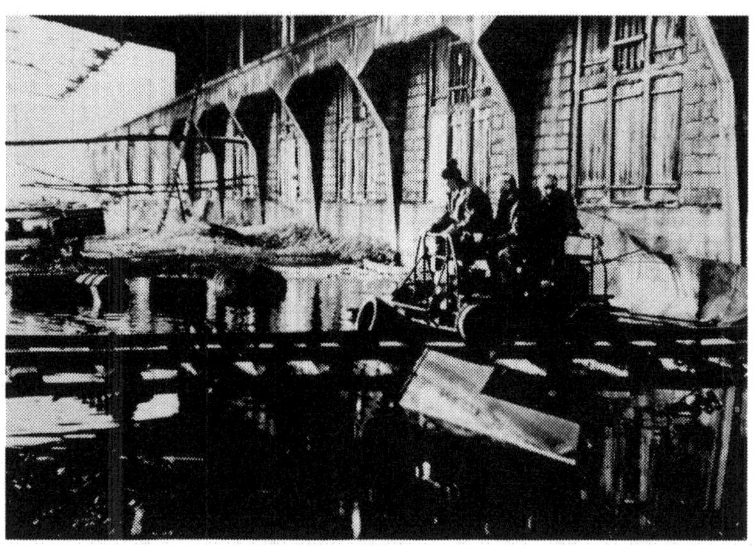

The journey by flatcar to the Zone in *Stalker*

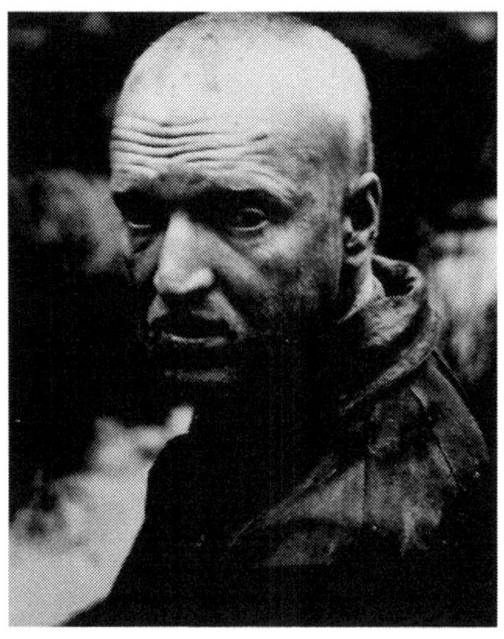

Alexander Kaidanovsky, a brilliant performance as the Stalker.

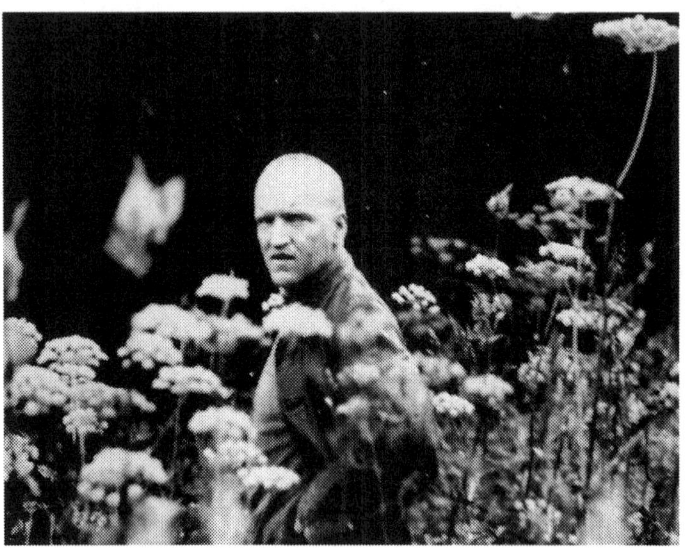

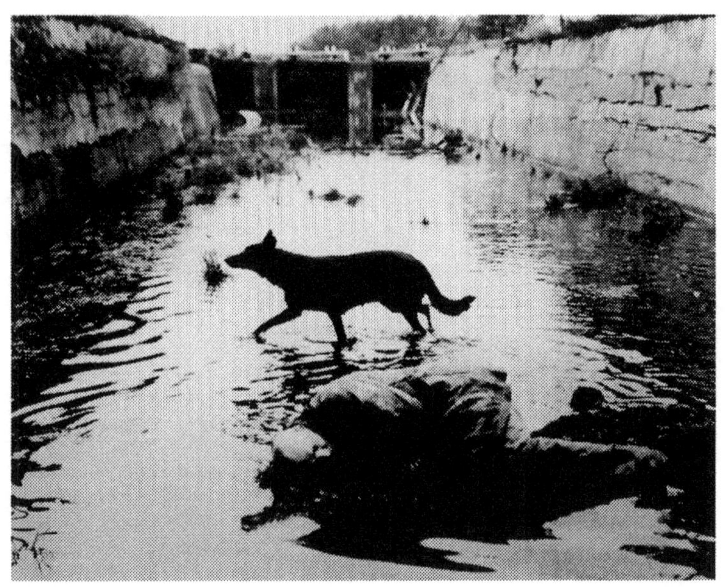

Classic Tarkovsky imagery: a pool, a dog and a dreamer.

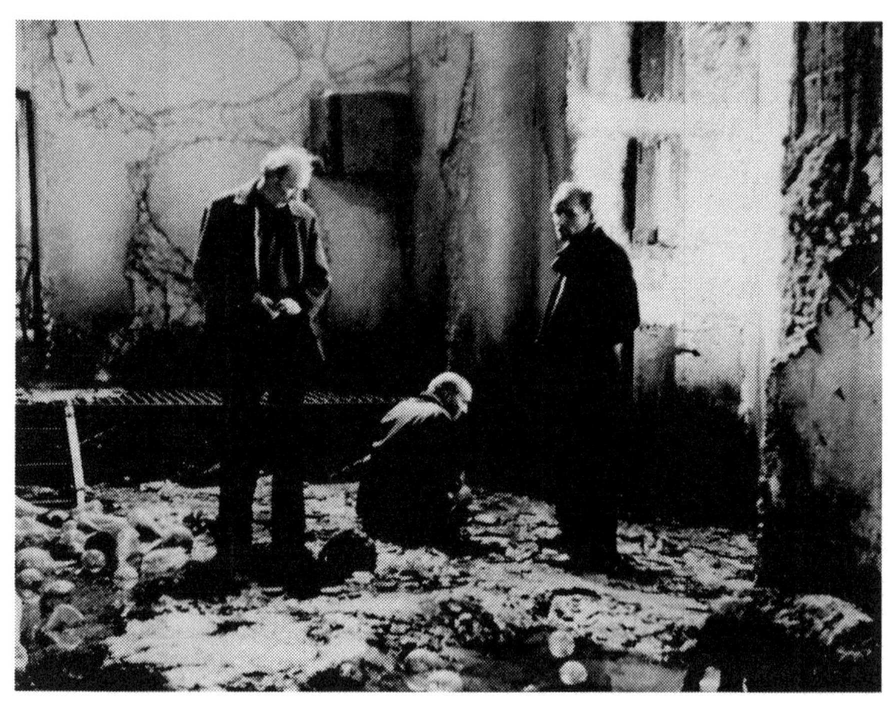

The end of the quest: outside the Room in the Zone in *Stalker*.

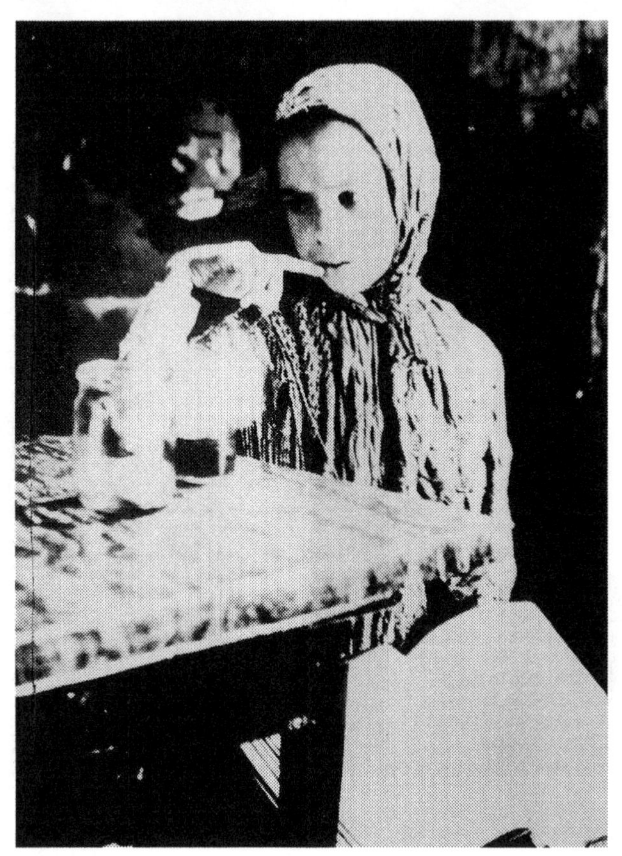

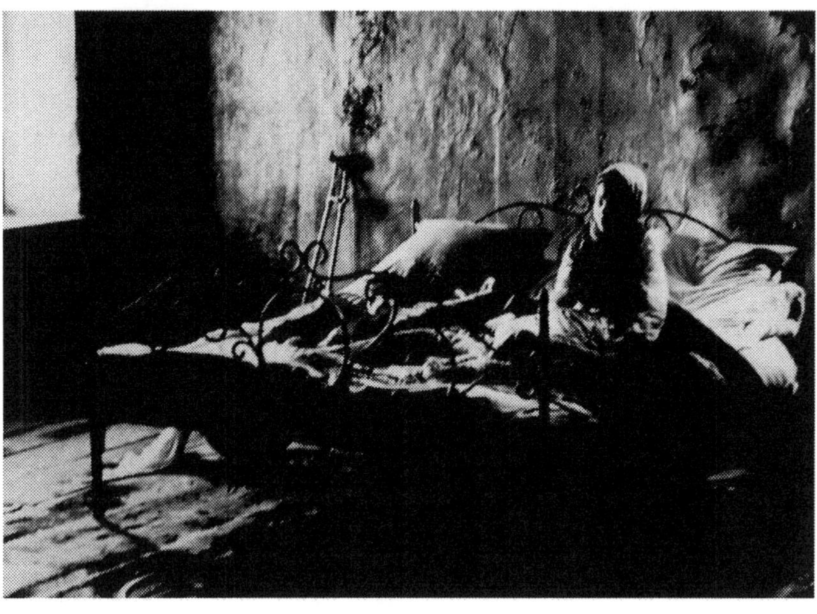

The Stalker's daughter

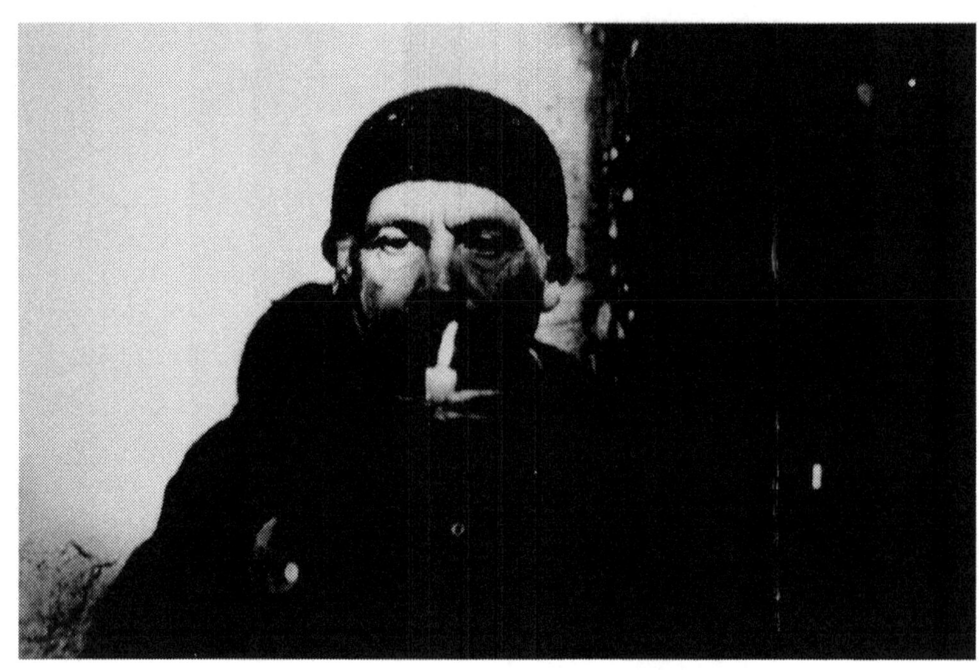

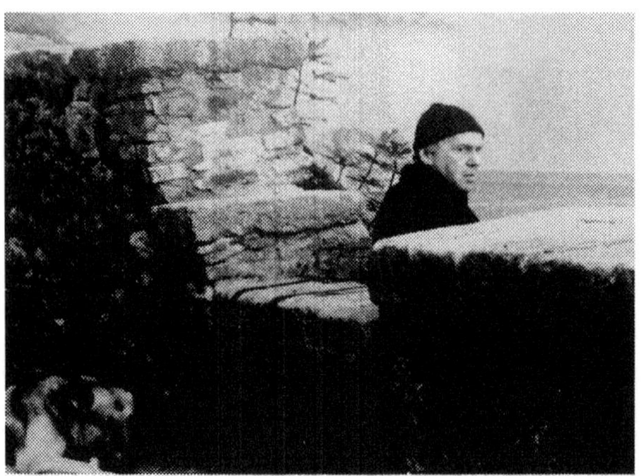

Domenico in *Nostalghia*

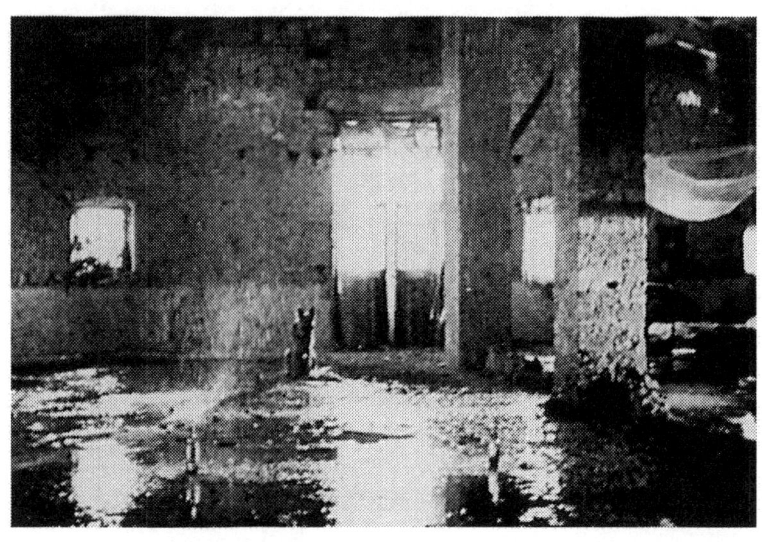

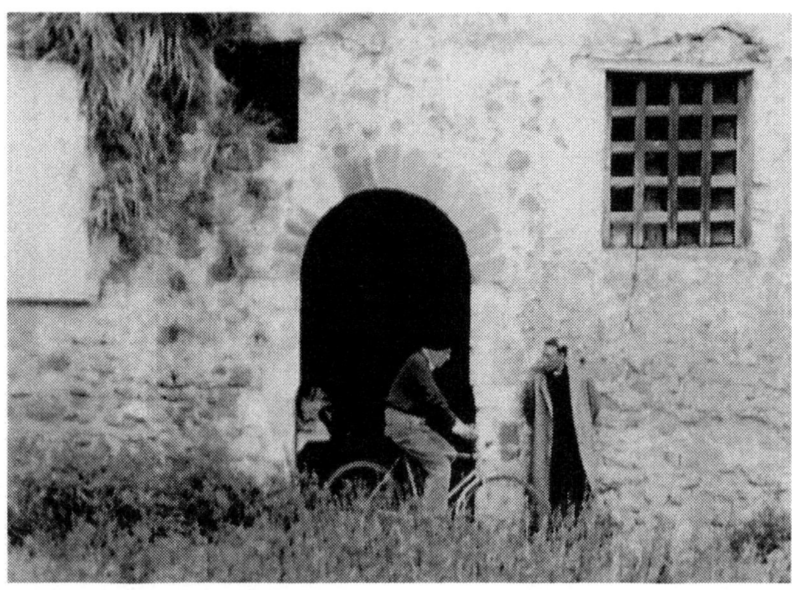

Domenico's realm in *Nostalghia*

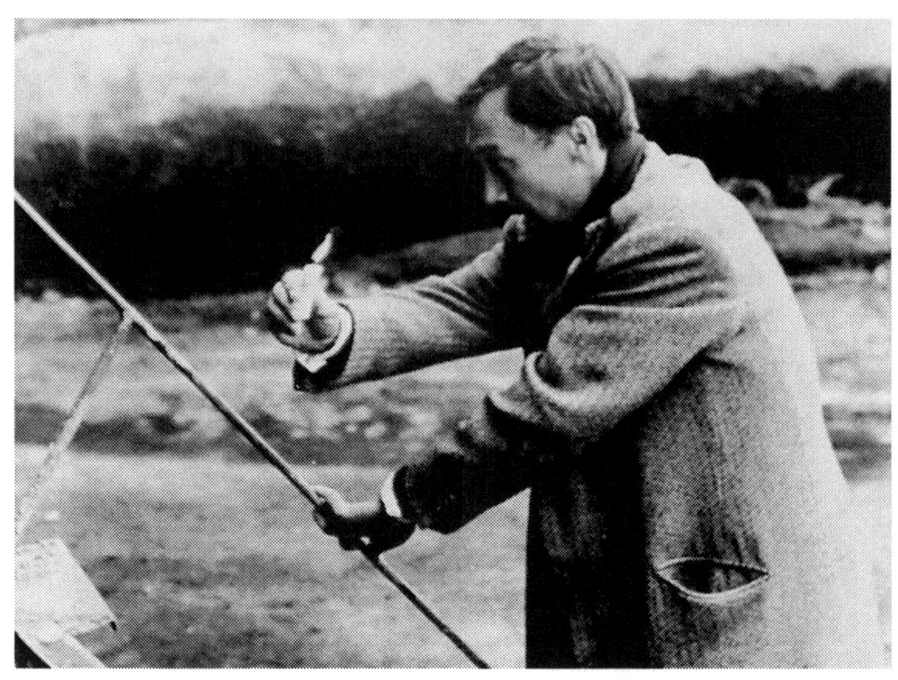

The climax of *Nostalghia* – a nine minute continuous take of a man carrying a candle back and forth, followed by a posthumous dream sequence, below.

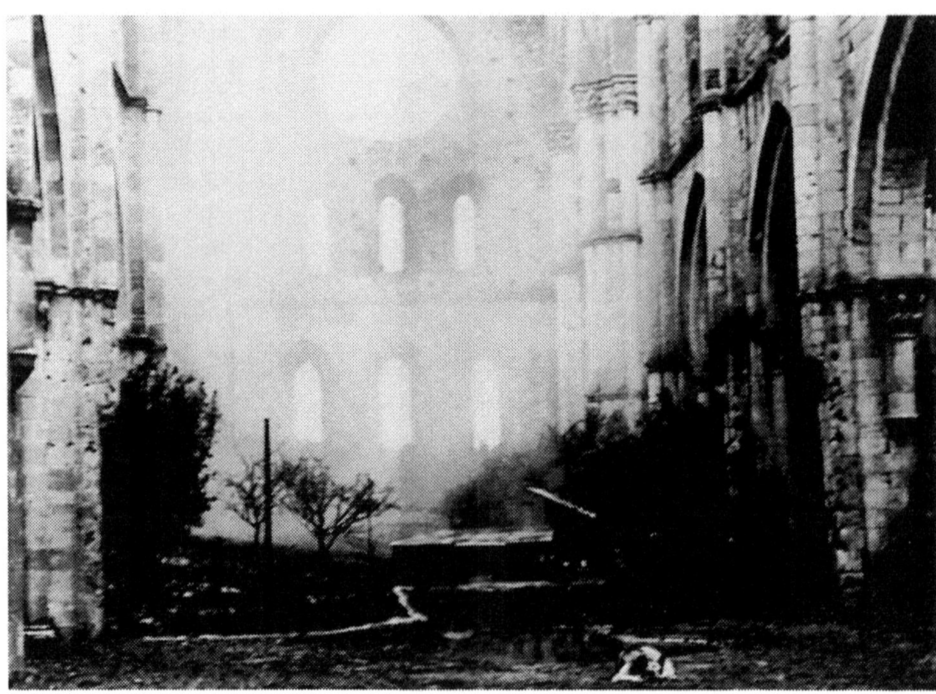

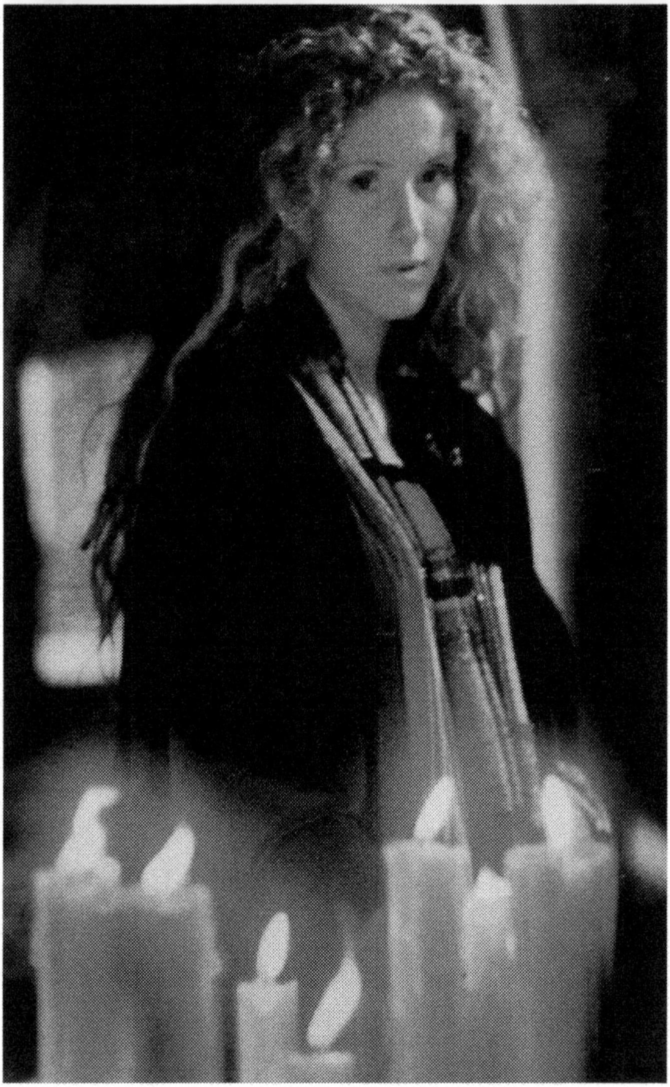

Eugenia in *Nostalghia*, another image of the Tarkovsky woman
— long hair, face of the Madonna (and with an Italian fashion
costume).

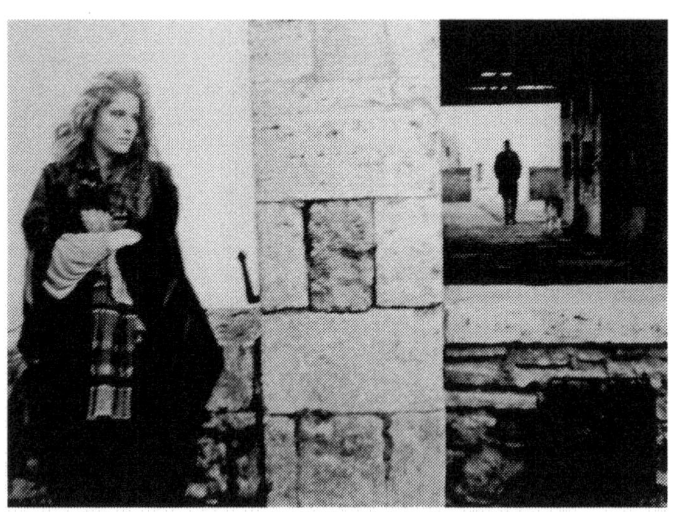

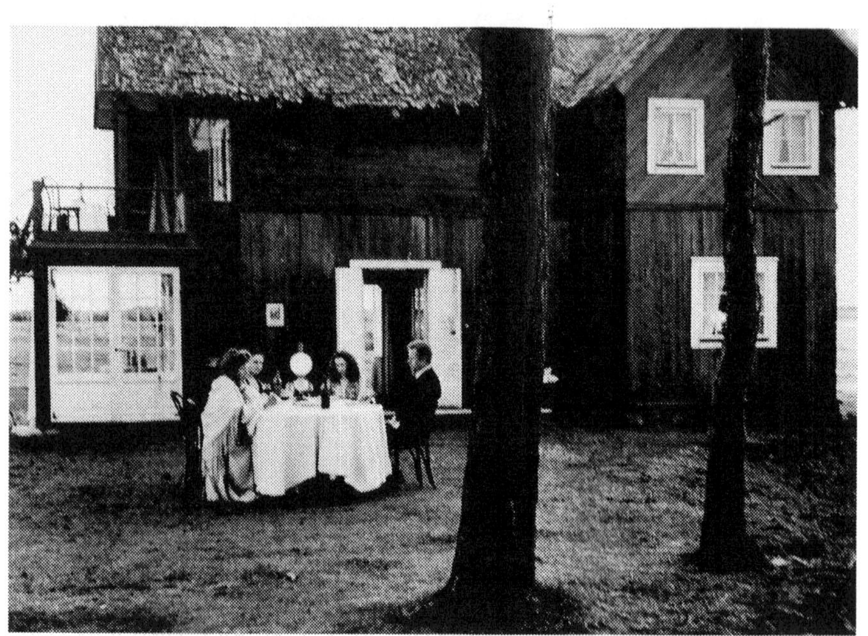

The Sacrifice – Tarkovsky does Bergman, again.

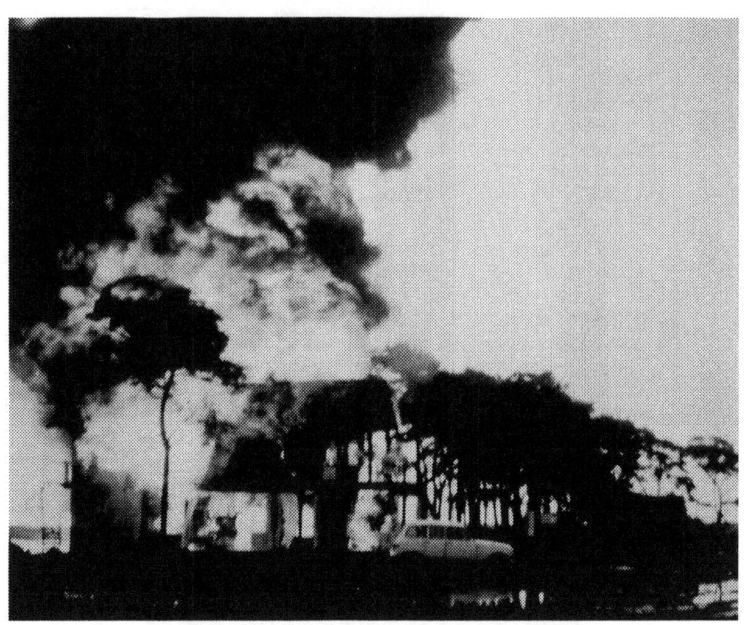

Just before calling action, the sun came out. DP Sven Nykvist advised Tarkovsky to start filming anyway: 'Look, there's nothing you can do…! The sun is coming out, the house is already on fire – and we're on our second house!' But the sunlight worked well with the smoke, and Tarkovsky was 'exceedingly pleased', Nykvist said.

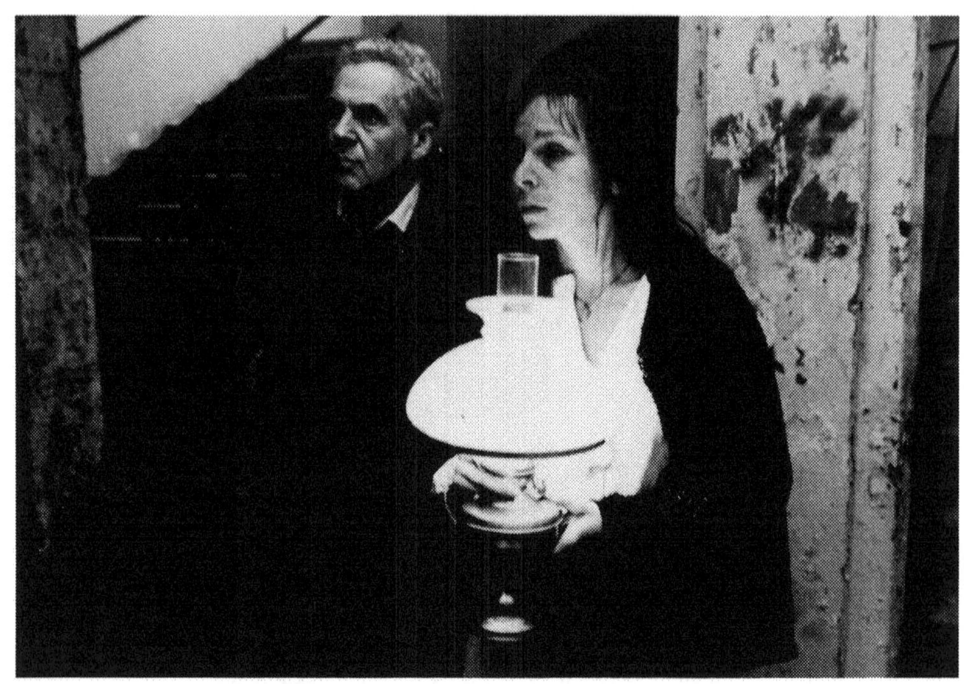

Domenico visits the witch Maria in *The Sacrifice*

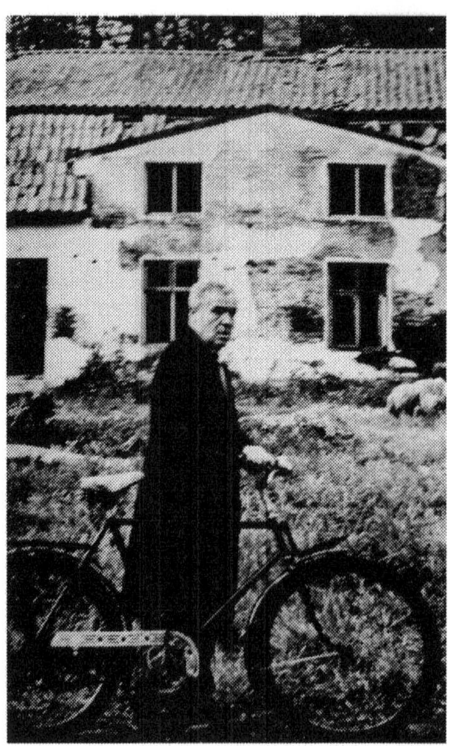

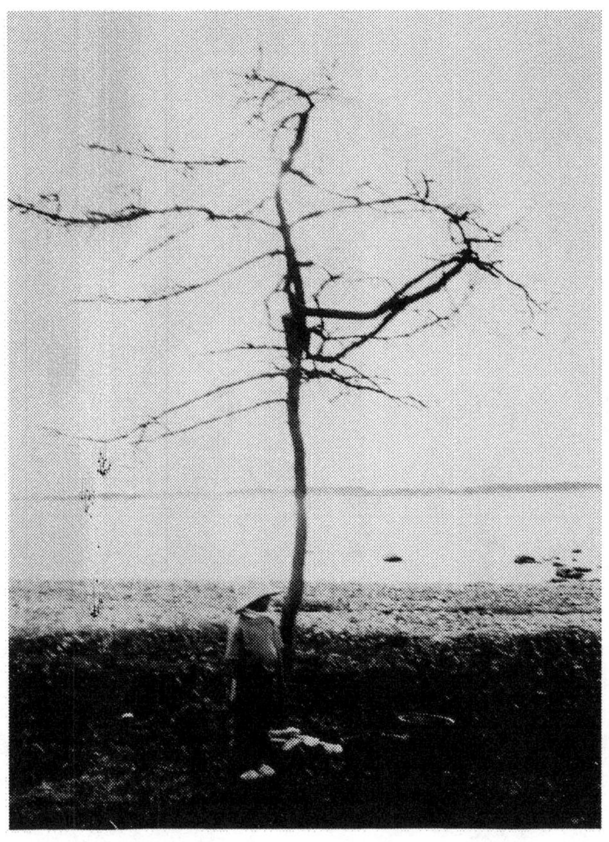

The final, ecstatic sequence that closes *The Sacrifice.*

Little Man asks: 'in the beginning was the Word: why is that, Papa?'
Set against the light, the image of the tree is sublime after such profound darkness throughout the film. An image of brilliance and clarity after such agony and uncertainty.

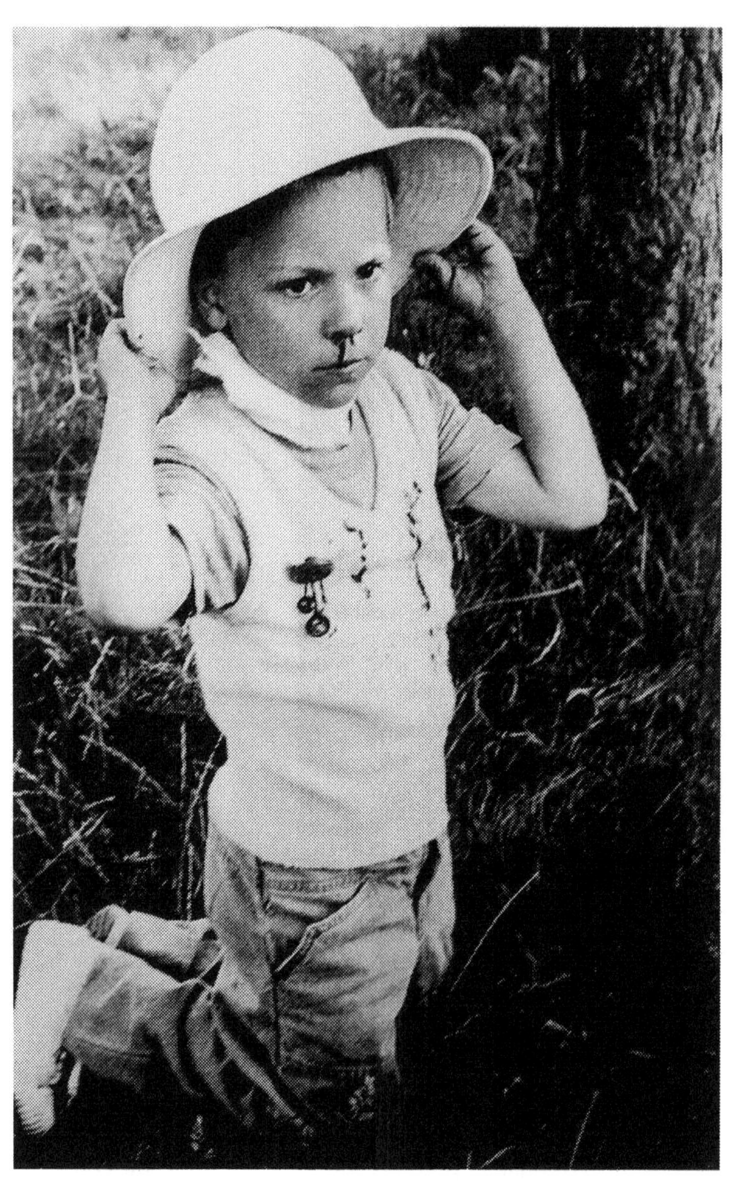

Little Man (Tommy Kjellqvist) in *The Sacrifice*

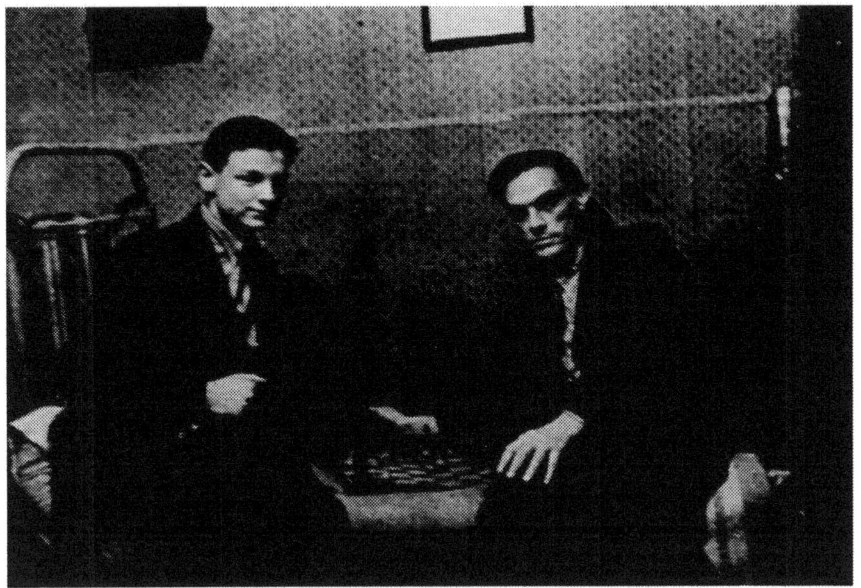

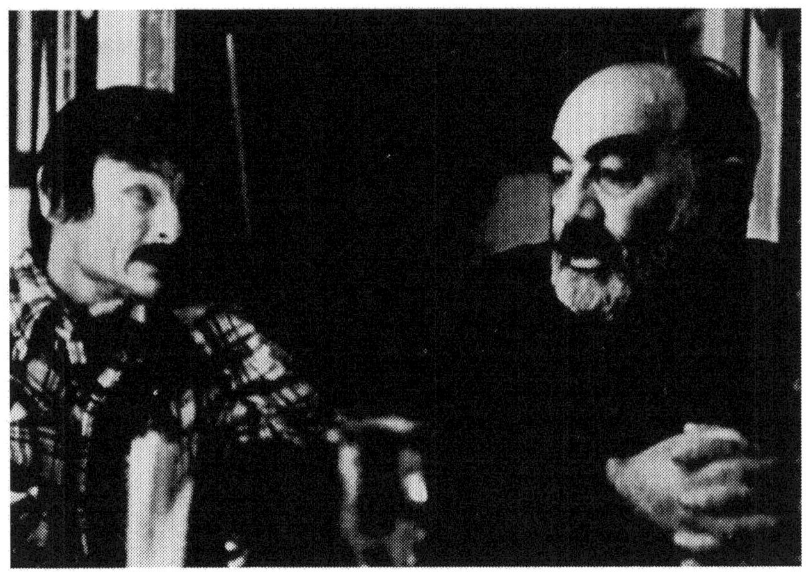

Tarkovsky among the poets: with his father Arseny, and with
Sergei Paradjanov

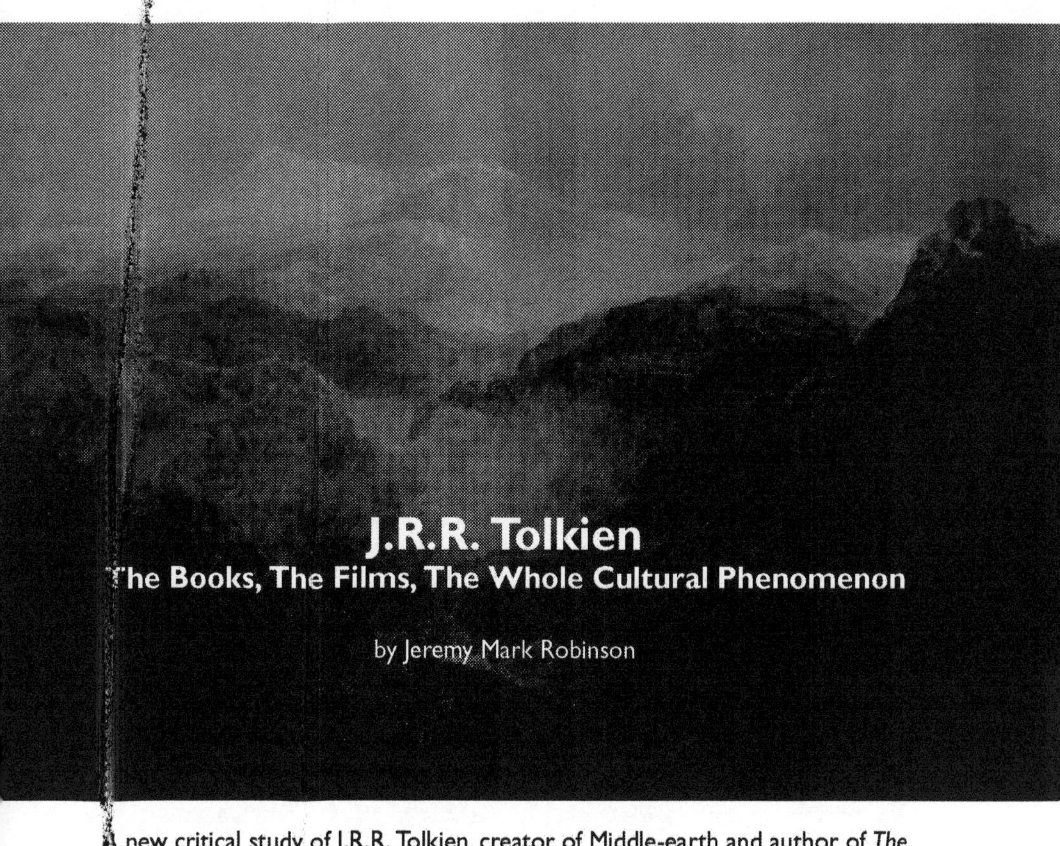

A new critical study of J.R.R. Tolkien, creator of Middle-earth and author of *The Lord of the Rings*, *The Hobbit* and *The Silmarillion*, among other books.
This new critical study explores Tolkien's major writings (*The Lord of the Rings, The Hobbit, Beowulf: The Monster and the Critics, The Letters, The Silmarillion* and *The History of Middle-earth* volumes); Tolkien and fairy tales; the mythological, political and religious aspects of Tolkien's Middle-earth; the critics' response to Tolkien's fiction over the decades; the Tolkien industry (merchandizing, toys, role-playing games, posters, Tolkien societies, conferences and the like); Tolkien in visual and fantasy art; the cultural aspects of The Lord of the Rings (from the 1950s to the present); Tolkien's fiction's relationship with other fantasy fiction, such as C.S. Lewis and *Harry Potter*; and the TV, radio and film versions of Tolkien's books, including the 2001-03 Hollywood interpretations of *The Lord of the Rings*.
This new book draws on contemporary cultural theory and analysis and offers a sympathetic and illuminating (and sceptical) account of the Tolkien phenomenon. This book is designed to appeal to the general reader (and viewer) of Tolkien: it is written in a clear, jargon-free and easily-accessible style.

754pp   ISBN 1-86171-057-7   £25.00 / $37.50

The Best of Peter Redgrove's Poetry
The Book of Wonders

by Peter Redgrove, edited and introduced by Jeremy Robinson

Poems of wet shirts and 'wonder-awakening dresses'; honey, wasps and bees; orchards and apples; rivers, seas and tides; storms, rain, weather and clouds; waterworks; labyrinths; amazing perfumes; the Cornish landscape (Penzance, Perranporth, Falmouth, Boscastle, the Lizard and Scilly Isles); the sixth sense and 'extra-sensuous perception'; witchcraft; alchemical vessels and laboratories; yoga; menstruation; mines, minerals and stones; sand dunes; mud-baths; mythology; dreaming; vulvas; and lots of sex magic. This book gathers together poetry (and prose) from every stage of Redgrove's career, and every book. It includes pieces that have only appeared in small presses and magazines, and in uncollected form.

'Peter Redgrove is really an extraordinary poet' (George Szirtes, *Quarto* magazine) 'Peter Redgrove is one of the few significant poets now writing... His 'means' are indeed brilliant and delightful. Technically he is a poet essentially of brilliant and unexpected images...he never disappoints' (Kathleen Raine, *Temenos* magazine).

240pp   ISBN 1-86171-063-1   2nd edition   £19.99 / $29.50

Sex–Magic–Poetry–Cornwall
A Flood of Poems

by Peter Redgrove. Edited with an essay by Jeremy Robinson

A marvellous collection of poems by one of Britain's best but underrated poets, Peter Redgrove. This book brings together some of Redgrove's wildest and most passionate works, creating a 'flood' of poetry. Philip Hobsbaum called Redgrove 'the great poet of our time', while Angela Carter said: 'Redgrove's language can light up a page.' Redgrove ranks alongside Ted Hughes and Sylvia Plath. He is in every way a 'major poet'. Robinson's essay analyzes all of Redgrove's poetic work, including his use of sex magic, natural science, menstruation, psychology, myth, alchemy and feminism.
A new edition, including a new introduction, new preface and new bibliography.

'Robinson's enthusiasm is winning, and his perceptive readings are supported by a very useful bibliography' (*Acumen* magazine)
'*Sex-Magic-Poetry-Cornwall* is a very rich essay... It is like a brightly-lighted box. (Peter Redgrove)
'This is an excellent selection of poetry and an extensive essay on the themes and theories of this unusual poet by Jeremy Robinson' (*Chapman* magazine)

220pp   New, 3rd edition   ISBN 1-86171-070-4   £14.99 / $23.50

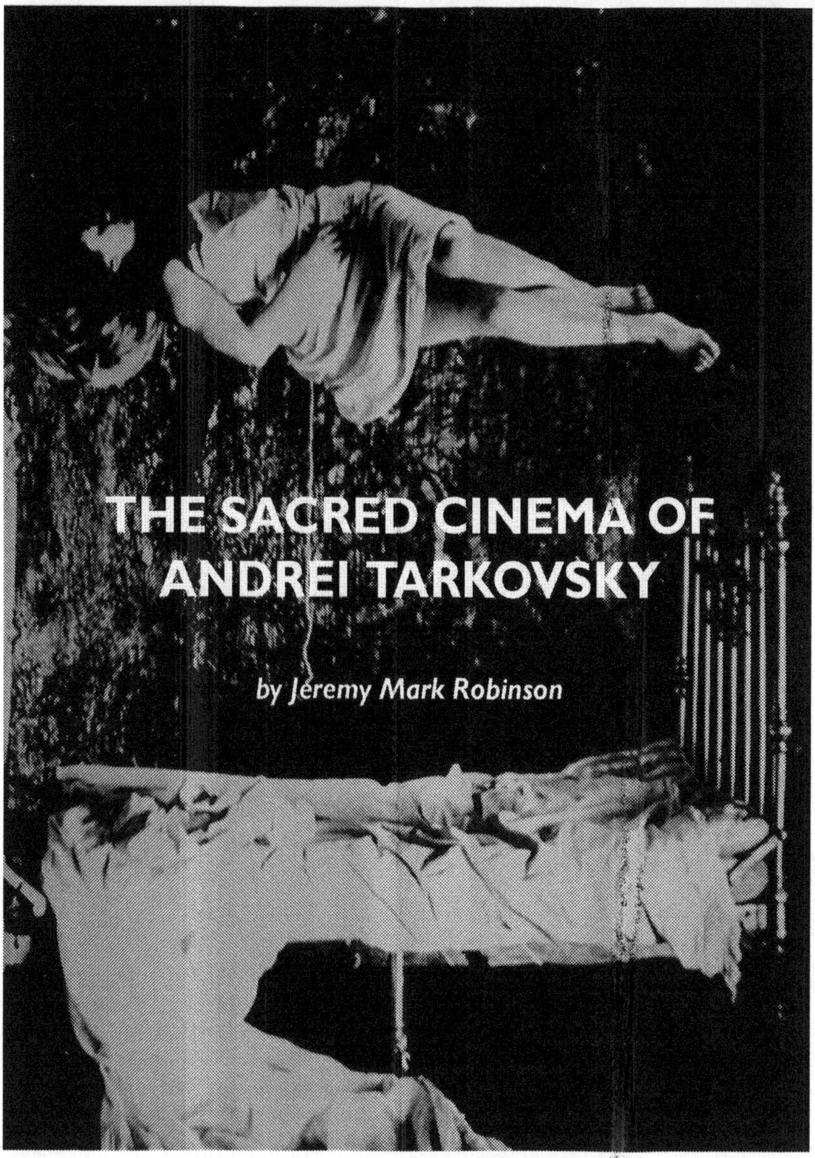

THE SACRED CINEMA OF ANDREI TARKOVSKY

by Jeremy Mark Robinson

A new study of the Russian filmmaker Andrei Tarkovsky (1932-1986), director of seven feature films, including *Andrei Roublyov, Mirror, Solaris, Stalker* and *The Sacrifice*.
This is one of the most comprehensive and detailed studies of Tarkovsky's cinema available. Every film is explored in depth, with scene-by-scene analyses. All aspects of Tarkovsky's output are critiqued, including editing, camera, staging, script, budget, collaborations, production, sound, music, performance and spirituality.
Tarkovsky is placed with a European New Wave tradition of filmmaking, alongside directors like Ingmar Bergman, Carl Theodor Dreyer, Pier Paolo Pasolini and Robert Bresson.
An essential addition to film studies.

Illustrations: 150 b/w, 4 colour. 682 pages. First edition. Hardback.

Publisher: Crescent Moon Publishing. Distributor: Gardners Books.

ISBN 1-86171-096-8 (9781861710963) £60.00 / $105.00

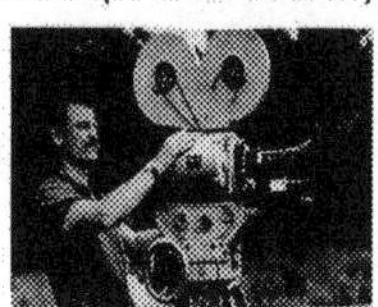

THE ART OF ANDY GOLDSWORTHY

COMPLETE WORKS: SPECIAL EDITION
(PAPERBACK and HARDBACK)

by William Malpas

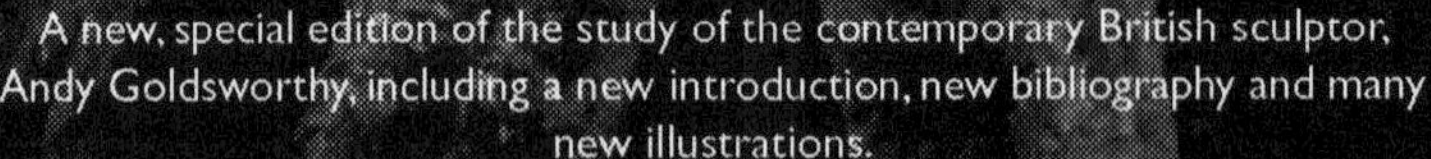

A new, special edition of the study of the contemporary British sculptor, Andy Goldsworthy, including a new introduction, new bibliography and many new illustrations.

This is the most comprehensive, up-to-date, well-researched and in-depth account of Goldsworthy's art available anywhere.

Andy Goldsworthy makes land art. His sculpture is a sensitive, intuitive response to nature, light, time, growth, the seasons and the earth. Goldsworthy's environmental art is becoming ever more popular: 1993's art book *Stone* was a bestseller; the press raved about Goldsworthy taking over a number of London West End art galleries in 1994; during 1995 Goldsworthy designed a set of Royal Mail stamps and had a show at the British Museum. Malpas surveys all of Goldsworthy's art, and analyzes his relation with other land artists such as Robert Smithson, Walter de Maria, Richard Long and David Nash, and his place in the contemporary British art scene.

The Art of Andy Goldsworthy discusses all of Goldsworthy's important and recent exhibitions and books, including the *Sheepfolds* project; the TV documentaries; *Wood* (1996); the New York Holocaust memorial (2003); and Goldsworthy's collaboration on a dance performance.

Illustrations: 70 b/w, 1 colour. 330 pages. New, special, 2nd edition.
Publisher: Crescent Moon Publishing. Distributor: Gardners Books.

ISBN 1-86171-059-3 (9781861710598) (Paperback) £25.00 / $44.00

ISBN 1-86171-080-1 (9781861710802) (Hardback) £60.00 / $105.00

CRESCENT MOON PUBLISHING

ARTS, PAINTING, SCULPTURE

The Art of Andy Goldsworthy: Complete Works(Pbk)
The Art of Andy Goldsworthy: Complete Works (Hbk)
Andy Goldsworthy in Close-Up (Pbk)
Andy Goldsworthy in Close-Up (Hbk)
Land Art: A Complete Guide
Richard Long: The Art of Walking

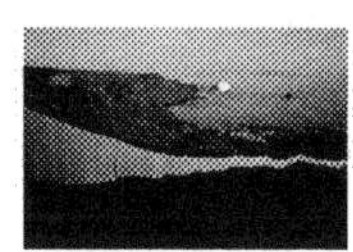

The Art of Richard Long: Complete Works (Pbk)
The Art of Richard Long: Complete Works (Hbk)
Richard Long in Close-Up
Land Art In the UK
Land Art in Close-Up

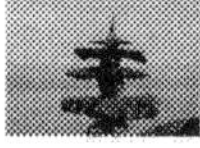

Installation Art in Close-Up
Minimal Art and Artists In the 1960s and After
Colourfield Painting
Land Art DVD, TV documentary
Andy Goldsworthy DVD, TV documentary
The Erotic Object: Sexuality in Sculpture From Prehistory to the Present Day
Sex in Art: Pornography and Pleasure in Painting and Sculpture
Postwar Art
Sacred Gardens: The Garden in Myth, Religion and Art
Glorification: Religious Abstraction in Renaissance and 20th Century Art
Early Netherlandish Painting
Leonardo da Vinci
Piero della Francesca

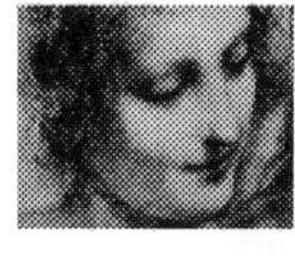

Giovanni Bellini
Fra Angelico: Art and Religion in the Renaissance
Mark Rothko: The Art of Transcendence
Frank Stella: American Abstract Artist
Jasper Johns: Painting By Numbers
Brice Marden

Alison Wilding: The Embrace of Sculpture
Vincent van Gogh: Visionary Landscapes
Eric Gill: Nuptials of God
Constantin Brancusi: Sculpting the Essence of Things
Max Beckmann
Egon Schiele: Sex and Death In Purple Stockings

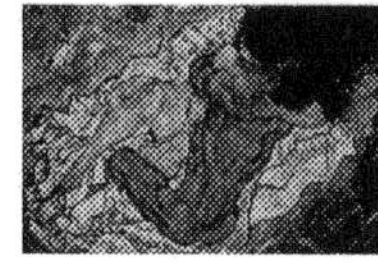

Delizioso Fotografico Fervore: Works In Process I
Sacro Cuore: Works In Process 2
The Light Eternal: J.M.W. Turner
The Madonna Glorified: Karen Arthurs

LITERATURE

J.R.R. Tolkien: The Books, The Films, The Whole Cultural Phenomenon
Harry Potter
Sexing Hardy: Thomas Hardy and Feminism
Thomas Hardy's *Tess of the d'Urbervilles*
Thomas Hardy's *Jude the Obscure*
Thomas Hardy: The Tragic Novels
Love and Tragedy: Thomas Hardy
The Poetry of Landscape in Hardy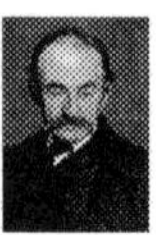
Wessex Revisited: Thomas Hardy and John Cowper Powys
Wolfgang Iser: Essays
Petrarch, Dante and the Troubadours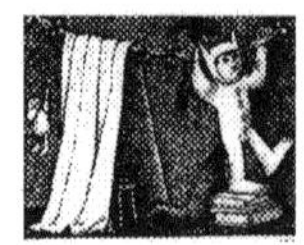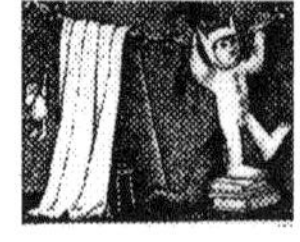
Maurice Sendak and the Art of Children's Book Illustration
Andrea Dworkin
Cixous, Irigaray, Kristeva: The *Jouissance* of French Feminism
Julia Kristeva: Art, Love, Melancholy, Philosophy, Semiotics and Psychoanalysis
Hélène Cixous I Love You: The *Jouissance* of Writing
Luce Irigaray: Lips, Kissing, and the Politics of Sexual Difference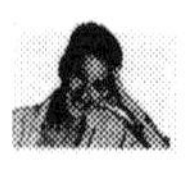
Peter Redgrove: Here Comes the Flood
Peter Redgrove: Sex-Magic-Poetry-Cornwall
Lawrence Durrell: Between Love and Death, East and West
Love, Culture & Poetry: Lawrence Durrell
Cavafy: Anatomy of a Soul
German Romantic Poetry: Goethe, Novalis, Heine, Hölderlin, Schlegel, Schiller
Feminism and Shakespeare
Shakespeare: Selected Sonnets
Shakespeare: Love, Poetry & Magic
The Passion of D.H. Lawrence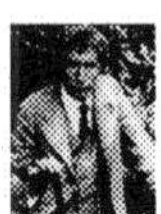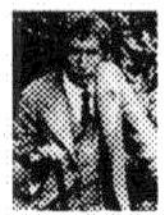
D.H. Lawrence: Symbolic Landscapes
D.H. Lawrence: Infinite Sensual Violence
Rimbaud: Arthur Rimbaud and the Magic of Poetry
The Ecstasies of John Cowper Powys
Sensualism and Mythology: The Wessex Novels of John Cowper Powys
Amorous Life: John Cowper Powys and the Manifestation of Affectivity (H.W. Fawkner)
Postmodern Powys: New Essays on John Cowper Powys (Joe Boulter)
Rethinking Powys: Critical Essays on John Cowper Powys
Paul Bowles & Bernardo Bertolucci
Rainer Maria Rilke
In the Dim Void: Samuel Beckett
Samuel Beckett Goes into the Silence
André Gide: Fiction and Fervour
Jackie Collins and the Blockbuster Novel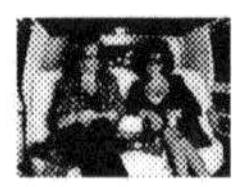
Blinded By Her Light: The Love-Poetry of Robert Graves
The Passion of Colours: Travels In Mediterranean Lands
Poetic Forms
The Dolphin-Boy